Insisting on the Impossible

The Sloan Technology Series

Dark Sun: The Making of the Hydrogen Bomb by Richard Rhodes

Dream Reaper: The Story of an Old-Fashioned Inventor in the High-Stakes World of Modern Agriculture by Craig Canine

Turbulent Skies: The History of Commercial Aviation by Thomas A. Heppenheimer

Tube: The Invention of Television by David E. Fisher and Marshall Jon Fisher

The Invention That Changed the World: How a Small Group of Radar Pioneers Won the Second World War and Launched a Technological Revolution by Robert Buderi

Computer: A History of the Information Machine by Martin Campbell-Kelly and William Aspray

Naked to the Bone: Medical Imaging in the Twentieth Century by Bettyann Kevles

A Commotion in the Blood: A Century of Using the Immune System to Battle Cancer and Other Diseases by Stephen S. Hall

Beyond Engineering: How Society Shapes Technology by Robert Pool

The One Best Way: Frederick Winslow Taylor and the Enigma of Efficiency by Robert Kanigel

Crystal Fire: The Birth of the Information Age by Michael Riordan and Lillian Hoddesen

Insisting on the Impossible: The Life of Edwin Land by Victor K. McElheny

Visions of Technology: A Century of Provocative Readings edited by Richard Rhodes (forthcoming)

City of Light by Jeff Hecht (forthcoming)

The Last Big Cookie by Gary Dorsey (forthcoming)

Insisting on the Impossible

The Life of Edwin Land

Victor K. McElheny

A Merloyd Lawrence Book

PERSEUS BOOKS
Reading, Massachusetts

Library of Congress Card Catalog Number: 98-86713

ISBN 0-7382-0009-3

Figures 1, 2, 3, 5, 6, 7, 8, 9, 10, 11, 12, 13, 14, 15, 16, 17, 19, 21, 22, and 24 are courtesy, Polaroid Corporate Archives. Figure 23 is courtesy, *Life* Magazine, Time, Inc.

Perseus Books is a member of the Perseus Books Group

Jacket design by Suzanne Heiser
Text design by Greta D. Sibley
Set in 11.5-point Adobe Chaparral by Greta D. Sibley & Associates
123456789-DOH-0201009998
First Printing, August 1998

For Ruth

Contents

Preface to the Sloan Technology Series

Technology is the application of science, engineering, and industrial organization to create a human-built world. It has led, in developed nations, to a standard of living inconceivable a hundred years ago. The process, however, is not free of stress; by its very nature, technology brings change in society and undermines convention. It affects virtually every aspect of human endeavor: private and public institutions, economic systems, communications networks, political structures, international affiliations, the organization of societies, and the condition of human lives. The effects are not one-way; just as technology changes society, so too do societal structures, attitudes, and mores affect technology. But perhaps because technology is so rapidly and completely assimilated, the profound interplay of technology and other social endeavors in modern history has not been sufficiently recognized.

The Sloan Foundation has had a long-standing interest in deepening public understanding about modern technology, its origins, and its impact on our lives. The Sloan Technology Series, of which the present volume is a part, seeks to present to the general reader the stories of the development of critical twentieth-century technologies. The aim of the series is to convey both the technical and human dimensions of the subject: the invention and effort entailed in devising the technologies and the comforts and stresses they have introduced into contemporary life. As the century draws to an end, it is hoped that the series will disclose a past that might provide perspective on the present and inform the future.

The Foundation has been guided in its development of the Sloan Technology Series by a distinguished advisory committee. We express deep gratitude to John Armstrong, Simon Michael Bessie, Samuel Y. Gibbon, Thomas P. Hughes, Victor McElheny, Robert K. Merton, Elting E. Morison (deceased), and Richard Rhodes. The Foundation has been represented on the committee by Ralph E. Gomory, Arthur L. Singer, Jr., Hirsh G. Cohen, and Doron Weber.

—Alfred P. Sloan Foundation

Chronology

7 May 1909 Land born, Bridgeport, Connecticut.

1920s

1922 Attends summer camp near Norwich, is shown a polarizer that can take glare off a tabletop. Meets Julius Silver, his lawyer for more than fifty years.

1926 Enters Harvard, leaves.

1927 Begins experiments on polarizers, while reading widely at New York Public Library.

September 1928 Shows his plastic sheet polarizer invention to patent lawyer Donald Brown, whom Silver recommended.

1929 Files for first of 535 patents. Returns to Harvard. Marries Helen (Terre) Maislen.

1930s

1930 Lyman, head of the Harvard physics department, gives him his own laboratory to work on sheet polarizers.

1932 Forms own company with instructor George Wheelwright. Visits General Motors and other leading industrial labs.

1933 Receives first patent, on polarizer material.

1934 Signs first contract, with Eastman Kodak, for polarizing filters for cameras, marketed as Polascreens.

1935 Enters contract with American Optical for polarizing lenses for sunglasses.

1937 Receives Cresson Medal from Franklin Institute. Polaroid Corporation formed.

1938 Buys out rival patent holders with cash and Polaroid shares.

1939-40 At New York World's Fair, millions view 3-D movie through cardboard and plastic viewing glasses supplied by Polaroid.

1940s

January 1940 First publishes work on three-dimensional still photography system, called the Vectograph.

February 1940 National Association of Manufacturers names Land its youngest "Modern Pioneer."

December 1943 On a vacation trip in Santa Fe, conceives basic ideas for instant photography and orders beginning of lab work and patent searches.

1944 First experiments with instant photography. Total synthesis of quinine by Robert Woodward and William Doering, sponsored by Polaroid. Helps produce Vannevar Bush's "Endless Frontier" report on post-war science. At conference in New York, describes small, science-based companies.

1945 With the end of the war, Polaroid suspends work on Navy's Dove heat-seeking bomb project. For post-war reserve, company sells $2 million in new stock.

21 February 1947 In New York, first public demonstration of instant photography.

1948 Receives Rumford Medal, American Academy of Arts and Sciences. First Polaroid Model 95 cameras and rolls of sepia film go on sale. "Rollout" continues city by city.

1950s

1950 Organizes crash effort to solve fading problems with new black-and-white film. Film redesigned and plastic coater developed.

1952 Participates in Beacon Hill study of aerial reconnaissance.

1954 Testifies in Marks patent trial. Heads intelligence project of James Killian's Technological Capabilities Panel, spurs development by CIA of U-2 spy plane.

1955 Begins decades of work on human color vision.

May 1957 After two-week visit to MIT, proposes that all students be given firsthand experience of research.

October 1957 Days after the Russian launch of Sputnik, at meeting of scientists with President Eisenhower, Land urges that the United States foster a spirit of scientific adventure.

1957 Polaroid color film judged "commercial."

1958 Helps start ultrasecret spy satellite program to follow the U-2 and helps design what becomes NASA.

1959 Introduces ASA 3000 black-and-white film. Color vision research published.

1960s

1960 Land and Killian draft report leading to formation of spy satellite procurement agency called National Reconnaissance Office. Land witnesses first demonstration of spy satellite photos in President Eisenhower's office.

1962 Crash effort to develop self-washing system for Polaroid color film.

January 1963 Polacolor, with a negative manufactured by Eastman Kodak, is introduced.

July 1963 Receives Presidential Medal of Freedom.

1967 Carnegie Commission on Public Television, including Land, proposes major U.S. government support for educational broadcasting.

February 1968 Receives National Medal of Science.

June 1968 The Lands' anonymous gift of $12.5 million for Harvard Science Center announced.

1968 Kodak decides to enter the instant-photography field.

1969 Polaroid licenses Kodak to begin marketing its own instant film in 1975.

1970s

March 1970 Basic SX-70 design of an electronically controlled, motor-driven, single-lens reflex camera is decided.

1970 Confronts crises over Polaroid sales in South Africa and labor union attempts to organize Polaroid employees.

Spring 1972 SX-70 is demonstrated for shareholders, financial analysts, press, photo dealers, and employees.

November 1972 Limited marketing begins in south Florida. Kodak switches to its own "integral" film system.

1975 Land gives up position as president of Polaroid, remaining chairman and chief executive. William J. McCune becomes president and chief operating officer.

1976 Kodak introduces instant color system. Polaroid sues Kodak for patent infringement.

February 1977 Induction into the National Inventors' Hall of Fame.

April 1977 As OneStep, a still cheaper SX-70 camera, is introduced, Land demonstrates Polavision instant-movie system. He tells a questioner, "The bottom line is in heaven."

January 1979 The Lands sell stock to fund construction of Rowland Institute for Science.

April 1979 Ground broken for new House of American Academy of Arts and Scientists, donated by the Lands.

September 1979 Polaroid writes off Polavision inventories.

1980s

1980 Resigns as CEO of Polaroid after forty-three years, and McCune succeeds him.

1981 Testifies for thirteen days in the *Polaroid v. Kodak* case. Most SX-70 patents in dispute are eventually upheld.

July 1982 Leaves Polaroid chairmanship and board, begins full-time work at Rowland Institute. Sells large additional block of shares to endow institute. Experiment on human subject fixes color-perception steps in cerebral cortex.

1985 Remaining Polaroid shares sold for philanthropy, including further endowment of Rowland Institute. U.S. District Court upholds SX-70 patents and orders Kodak to leave the field.

1986 Honored as foreign member, Royal Society of London.

1987 Suit against Land in connection with the 1979 stock sale is settled out of court to save legal expenses. Polaroid, also sued, declines to settle and ultimately wins the case.

7 May 1989 Eightieth birthday celebration in archive room of Rowland Institute.

1990s

January 1991 Inducted into Royal Society.

1 March 1991 Land dies.

Overture

> If you dream of something worth doing and then simply go to work on it and don't think anything of personalities, or emotional conflicts, or of money, or of family distractions; if you just think of, detail by detail, what you have to do next, it is a wonderful dream even though the end is a long way off, for there are about five thousand steps to be taken before we realize it; and start taking the first ten, and stay making twenty after, it is amazing how quickly you get through those five thousand steps. Rather, I should say, through the four thousand [nine hundred] and ninety. The last ten steps you never seem to work out. But you keep on coming nearer to giving the world something well worth having.
>
> —Edwin H. Land to Polaroid employees,
> 23 December 1942

Edwin Land's mind was an engine of many cylinders. Much of the time the cylinders appeared to be moving independently. But often, they drove together toward the solution of intellectual and practical problems, for the hours or days or weeks or months required. He was an artist at making the impossible seem possible, and very often he was right. Recounting his life is a meditation on the nature of innovation.

What was the source of his energy and artistic sensibility? He spoke and wrote of research as a search for beauty, an addiction, and a necessity. What was he born to set right? Was he beating back unreason, or seeking the distraction of challenges big enough to claim his attention? Although

Land hinted at answers in conversation and public performances, the truth remained a mystery, perhaps even to him. But he spent little time on such introspection. Oral histories are memoirs, and memoirs are done after all the problems and experiments have ended. He was not prepared to die, or to designate successors, or to put together his reminiscences. For him history was death, the end of striving. People who were genuinely interested in his life, witnesses and helpers, would have to create their own report.

On a large scale, he embodied the innovative character as defined by a group of innovators in 1998: He had "passion, grounded intuition, an ability to listen, and a dash of taste." The passion was expressed in persistence. Although he listened, it was not to conventional wisdom. He took on challenges no one else would undertake and was ready "to run through brick walls." His desire to sell came before his drive to make money. He had "sanity with fierceness."[1] Was Land inimitable and bound to a particular time, or was he the highly theatrical, passionate character who must continue to reappear if anything new is to be achieved? Is he a model for aspiring inventor-entrepreneurs today? This biographical study will explore such enigmas, and the hypotheses that suggest themselves.

∞

Acting in a social structure of his own making, Land was restless and seemingly inexhaustible, wearing out people so that many left Polaroid, the company he founded. The wiser or more tenacious of his assistants knew that they were dispensable, that moments of close contact, even a sense of intimacy, could be succeeded by months or even years of distance, punctuated by intervals of close service when Land needed it. Not every genius can surround himself with selfless people and hold their loyalty, while often not paying them very well and making life all too interesting through staged crises and phone calls at midnight and during vacations.

He attracted an impressive variety of talented people to his enterprises, including several remarkable women researchers, and gave them great responsibility and challenges. His colleagues enjoyed his sense of humor and admired his skill at guessing which of many possible roads to follow and his cleverness in devising shortcuts to get the necessary information without waiting for the best tools and materials. He said he believed in bull's-eye empiricism: "We try everything, but we try the right thing first!"[2] He would go at a problem until it was solved as far as he was concerned and then turn it over to others whose attention had been enlisted, and who sometimes worked on it for the rest of their careers.

Land clearly did not wish to waste his powers on "me-too" innovations. Still, he persisted with problems when they were both vital and not solved, as he did with the polarizer for some fifteen years, and with instant photography, to which he kept returning for thirty years until he got it about right in the SX-70 system of 1972.

In 1972, Land was confident that the SX-70 would work: "If you are able to state a problem—any problem—and if it is important enough, then the problem can be solved." Even before putting the problem into words, the experienced and shrewd scientist has "an inner knowledge of what is feasible." As the scientist and his or her colleagues are deciding that a problem is more important than anything else, "you can't necessarily separate the important from the impossible."[3]

From the vantage point of the fiftieth anniversary of instant photography, one can see Land's life as a story of harnessing a genius to the work of the world. Land arguably "wrote the book" on modern science-based industry. To invent two industries, sheet polarizers and instant photography, he fiercely resisted the normal absorption by the large corporations that admired and encouraged him. He managed to be both famous and an effective secret counselor at the highest levels of the American government.

In founding and leading Polaroid Corporation for almost half a century, Land was the complete opposite of one of the gods of big business, Alfred P. Sloan, who applied cold rationalism and committee work to the organization of General Motors. But even Sloan, the prophet of management as a science, the demon of accounting and forecasting, had to give in to the romance of new devices. He grew almost lyrical in his memoirs as he summarized the evolution of the cars themselves. A key to that evolution was his struggle to find the right role for one of the greatest inventor-entrepreneurs of the auto industry, Charles Kettering.[4]

Land defied the doctrine that marketing is everything. Marketing was based on asking people what they wanted, or had bought already. He held that the business of business was something different: making things that people didn't know they wanted until they were available. His approach to innovation was consistent. Defining a need and the shortest path to a practical answer, he did not think there was a law of nature forbidding what you wanted or specified. Obstacles called for end-runs, or perhaps the reverse of what had been tried first. Imbued with the faith that science would operate most forcefully in small companies, Land was a passionate defender of the patent system he used to armor his enterprise.

∞

Although Land was married to the same woman for more than sixty-one years and was on good terms with his two daughters and sons-in-law and grandchildren, he kept them rigorously out of the public eye. Hence, this book is focused on work. This emphasis is appropriate. Land's life was focused on work that would use his genius. He was in the laboratory at all hours, focusing on a task. He romanticized episodes of complete concentration, for days or weeks, apart from family and daily life. In boyhood, he was already determined to escape from his home in search of greatness.

His work made him powerful and famous and rich—a big deal—and he was swept up in the consequences. In government service, he moved easily up and down all manner of command structures. People couldn't ignore him. They were even a little afraid of him. He could put things so eloquently, and then he could act. He could carry out seemingly impossible projects, from the U-2 photoreconnaissance plane to a technically elegant, though commercially disastrous, instant movie system.

There is evidence that he found convenient excuses to get out of his laboratory and breathe a bit. Even then, he was restless, sleepless, demonic. The idea of instant photography actually came to him on a vacation from exhausting work.

Land's long career included big successes and big disappointments. It had many sides, including iconoclastic research on human color vision; high-level defense assignments; large-scale philanthropy; a cameo appearance in the creation of Public Television; a vain struggle to put his polarizers in every car and movie theater in America; leadership of a company whose sales increased nearly a hundred times in twenty years. Following the iron law of an age of innovation, he unhesitatingly insisted on repeated cycles of new technologies, two of which cost several hundred million dollars each. In old age he was victorious in an epochal fight over patents with his first customer and longtime collaborator, Eastman Kodak Company. His departure from Polaroid, imposed and self-imposed, was by no means smooth.

Edwin Land's lasting importance may be that he embodied, with unusual force, the spirit of innovation that has dominated the last several centuries. He thought and acted on a large stage. He is an example of smart, effective work, work that gives "the world something well worth having."[5]

PART I AN INVENTOR IS BORN

1

Noontime

> If this is preparation for life, where in the world, where in the relationship with our colleagues, where in the industrial domain, where ever again, anywhere in life, is a person given this curious sequence of prepared talks and prepared questions, questions to which the answers are known?
>
> —Edwin H. Land, speaking at MIT about an MIT education, 22 May 1957

In public appearances spanning half a century, Edwin Land spoke an autobiography, disjointed and selective, but revealing. Over and over, he talked about his obsessions: autonomy, learning, education, vision, perception, the mind, and the mining of exhausted veins of knowledge for new gold. His onstage comments, particularly about education, interpreted his own experience. Nowhere did Land make such a gloss on his past more forcefully than in May 1957, at a sunny noontime of achievement, wealth, and influence.

Land was not yet fifty, but his system of instant photography, unveiled ten years before, was finding an ever-expanding market. His shares in Polaroid Corporation, which had developed and completely controlled the new field, were soaring in value toward the hundreds of millions of dollars. His astonishing new observations of human color vision were beginning to attract interest and controversy. The still-secret U-2 spy-plane system that Land had spurred was delivering clear-cut evidence of the real state of Soviet military power.

In the Little Theater of the Massachusetts Institute of Technology (MIT), on Wednesday evening, 22 May, Land joyfully entered into combat about the right form of college experience. He was certain that a cut-and-dried education spent too much time on blackboard problems and on the past. Students did not spend enough time on the urgent problems of the present, where the answers were not known, where experiments were required. By asking questions and performing experiments, the students could strive for the original contributions of effective and fulfilled people. Although MIT was courting Land's patronage, he attacked its system of education. He also attacked the growing view that science was a socially determined, collective enterprise.

The talk at MIT[1] trod the thin line between useful advice and the statement of impossible ideals, between experience that was transferable and experience that was unique. For many years, people wondered if "Din" Land's life and mind were so unusual that they might not be exemplary. Just after Land died in 1991, a former president of MIT, Jerome B. Wiesner, exclaimed to a small group of friends planning a memorial symposium, "Din never had an ordinary reaction to anything!"

It was a springtime of honors for Land. On the afternoon of 13 June, under the trees of Harvard's Tercentenary Theater, Land received an honorary doctorate of science from Harvard University, alongside such dignitaries as the Secretary-General of the United Nations and Robert Woodward, the Harvard chemist who had completed his total synthesis of quinine in 1944 with Land's support. Land was seated a few minutes' walk from the attic laboratory where he had worked as a youth on the sheet polarizer, his first great invention. He was not a speaker at this ceremony.

During his address three weeks earlier at MIT, where Land had been appointed a Visiting Institute Professor the year before, his manner riveted attention on him. A striking profile was set off by thick black hair, parted on the right. Dark eyes projected intensity. The musing quality of his talk indicated an inner conversation, as if he were searching for the right words for the jury of people in front of him, sometimes trying a half sentence and then substituting a complete one. The audience had a sense of watching Land on a high wire, of participating with him in a half-understood personal drama.

For more than two weeks in April and May, Land had acted as a one-man visiting committee to MIT, just a few blocks away from his red-brick rabbit warren of a laboratory, in what had been the old Kaplan Furniture building on Osborn Street in Cambridge, Massachusetts. He had met with groups of faculty and students, talking about an MIT education. What worked? What didn't work? Land's report to MIT's leaders was delivered in an intimate auditorium in the basement of Eero Saarinen's Kresge Auditorium.

The 220-seat room was not quite full, according to one witness. Land's report stung at least some who heard him. Ten years later, this speech, "Generation of Greatness," helped energize the establishment of MIT's Undergraduate Research Opportunities Program, or UROP, a means of giving more than 80 percent of MIT undergraduates a direct experience of research. Forty years later, an MIT President said that UROP, embodying Land's hope of greatness, not just for the few but for the many, was "still one of the strongest features of an MIT education." Even more important than Land's influence on MIT, wrote Charles M. Vest, was "a vision of greatness and boldness of spirit that were embraced by others."[2]

The texts of this and other speeches are valuable because Land kept no diary and left few personal letters. After his death on 1 March 1991, a laboratory associate spent three years shredding his papers, presumably because Land had left instructions to do so. In his speeches Land was showing aspects of his character that he did not mind people knowing. Of course, some references were obscure and went right by his audience. Three years after his MIT speech, he told a meeting of Polaroid employees, "One of the best ways to keep a great secret is to shout it."[3]

On this particular evening, had there been music, it should have been Beethoven. Land displayed an outsized character from a vanished time, at the boundary between rationalism and romanticism, a character who charmed, challenged, exasperated, and controlled many people.

Drawing from his life, Land said that education must produce people who, no matter how tightly they conformed to the innumerable commands of society, would find one domain where they would make a revolution. Students should go as rapidly as possible through all the intellectual accumulations of the past to reach quickly the domain where they would have their own work to do. Lectures must be streamlined. Why not use movies to "can" a professor's best lectures "with the vitamins in"? The professors would be captured "at the moment when they are most excited about a new way of saying something or at the moment when they have just found something new." They would waste less time redoing their lectures. With the movies, students could view the lectures as many times as they needed. The proposal looked visionary in the 1950s, but Land soon launched his colleague Stewart Wilson on interactive lectures using such films. Forty years later, in an era of computer keyboards and screens, interactive instruction became much simpler.

Land showed three examples of such movies. One was a fragment of a lecture on the scattering of light; the second discussed how to minimize certain effects on the transmission of signals; the third was a lecture-demonstration on the pressure that light exerts when it acts as particles. This last film was part of the major effort by the Physical Sciences Study Committee, led by MIT physicist Jerrold Zacharias, to develop a new national high school physics course. In some respects, Land argued, the movies were better than an actual lecture. For one thing, the student could see close-ups of the demonstrations. For another, he said, the movies could reduce the emotional reaction, bad or good, to the lecturer. "Either one is too sensitive to the teacher or one is too insensitive; either one is too wide awake or one is too sleepy."

A second proposal raised hackles. Each arriving student should have an academic "usher," who would promptly set that student on a research project. Land asserted that the ushers would come from the ranks of great scientists who had arrived at the stage in their careers where bringing the young along was as satisfying as making their own scientific contributions.

Nari Malani, a student who heard him, was impressed:

> Land was very excited. He wasn't smooth and clear-cut, but slow, pausing, careful, logical with beautiful tangents and humorous model anecdotes, thus illustrating his ideas in a thoroughly human way. He has found order and organization in a chaotic world. He wants every freshman to have the same chance . . . His vision was clear. He has seen the new horizons.[4]

An MIT education, Land feared, was fundamentally discouraging. A student would get a message that a "secret dream of greatness is a pipe-dream; that it will be a long time before he makes a significant contribution—if ever." This process was a disaster. He asked with passion, "If this is preparation for life, where in the world [will a person ever encounter] this curious sequence of prepared talks and prepared questions, questions to which the answers are known?"

He was talking directly from his own experience. When he had arrived as a freshman at Harvard in the fall of 1926, he had encountered a lot of nice young men who didn't know the connection of anything to anything and who would spend the next ten years reading what he had already read. He wanted to get going on some research that would matter. He wanted to get going on what he thought of as greatness.

To his MIT audience, Land said, "Either you believe that this kind of individual greatness does exist and can be nurtured and developed, that such great individuals can be part of a cooperative community while they continue to be their happy, flourishing, contributing selves—or else you believe that there is some mystical, cyclical, overriding, predetermined cultural law—a historic determinism."

"The great contribution of science," according to Land, was to demonstrate that historic determinism is "nonsense." A scientist thinks, "I do not understand the divine source, but I know, in a way I cannot understand, that out of chaos I can make order, out of loneliness I can make friendship, out of ugliness I can make beauty."

The students he met hoped for greatness. "Everywhere I could sense a deep feeling in the undergraduates . . . [N]one of them dared express it, but every one of them felt, in his head, that if a way could be found of nurturing the timid dream of his own potential greatness which he brought from his family and school . . . Each of these men felt secretly—it was his very special secret and his deepest secret—that he could be great."

Greatness, Land argued, is "a wonderful and special way of solving problems," which allows a worker in a field to "add things that would not have been added, had he not come along." He said this is not the same as genius, which consists of "ideas that shorten the solution of problems by hundreds of years," or of suddenly saying, as Einstein did, "Mass is energy."

> [N]ot many undergraduates come through our present educational system retaining [the hope of greatness]. Our young people, for the most part—unless they are geniuses—after a very short time in college give up any hope of being individually great. They plan, instead, to be good. They plan to be effective. They plan to do their job. They plan to take their healthy place in the community. We might say that today it takes a genius to come out great; and a great man, a merely great man, cannot survive.
>
> It has become our habit, therefore, to think that the age of greatness has passed, that the age of the great man is gone; that this is the day of group research; that this is the day of community progress. Yet the very essence of democracy is the absolute faith that while people must cooperate, the first function of democracy, its peculiar gift, is to develop each individual into everything that he might be. But I submit to you that when in each man the dream of personal greatness dies, democracy loses the real source of its future strength.

When Land spoke, the word "democracy" had domestic and international implications. That year, school desegregation was beginning in response to the U.S. Supreme Court decisions of 1954 and 1955. The American political system also was threatened with a potentially deadly military confrontation with the totalitarian Soviet state. For those in the know, the concern with deterring a Russian attack underlined the urgency of the overhead reconnaissance that involved both Land and MIT's president, James Killian, who was in the audience.

Land did not agree that tutelage should last longer in a civilization as complex as that of the Age of Science. "Does it not mean, perhaps, the opposite; that we must skillfully make them mature sooner; that we must find ways of handling the intricacy of our culture?" As professors in his audience grumbled audibly, he poured scorn on the constant testing and grading. "When the professor says, 'Hand back what I said,' the professor is telling the student that what he, the professor, said is true. Now the role of science is to be systematic, to be accurate, to be orderly; but it certainly is not to imply that the aggregated, successful hypotheses of the past have the kind of truth that goes into a number system."

MIT teachers, doing intensely competitive research at the frontiers of their fields, surely would deny that students were ready to make an original contribution. Land countered with an example drawn from an exciting field of that day. The German zoologist Karl von Frisch had recently discovered that bees navigated with the help of the polarization of light in the sky and that they used this navigational information to instruct other bees—by dances—on the whereabouts of good sources of nectar. Land had contributed some of his polarizing filters to von Frisch's research.[5] Land now suggested that students could be encouraged to ask what the analyzer was for polarized light in the bee's eye, or to study bee "language" in greater detail than von Frisch had yet done: "[T]here are areas where untrained people may work effectively and with limited equipment."

Such use of untrained observers was an old story to Land. At Polaroid, many workers who came from humanistic studies in college or from the factory did useful research in the laboratory. A few years later, Land told an audience at Columbia University, where he had worked secretly at night as a youth, "We have not found anti-intellectualism to be a problem at the Polaroid Corporation, except in the very initial stage of penetration. It only takes a day to change someone from an anti-intellectual to an intellectual by persuading him that he might be one!"[6]

Land's strictures differed greatly from previous Arthur D. Little lectures given by Edward Appleton and Henry Tizard from England, the physicist Robert Oppenheimer, and the psychologist William C. Menninger. The organizing committee had been gunning for Jean Monnet, the French economist who was the architect of what became the European Community, but suspected that he would turn them down, as he evidently did. As a second choice, MIT turned to Land.[7]

One of those invited to hear the lecture but unable to attend was James B. Fisk, executive vice president and later president of Bell Telephone Laboratories. Fisk was much involved in MIT affairs. In April, he had talked with Land about Land's plans for the MIT lecture. Fisk wrote Killian, "As usual, they are very stimulating and I expect the results will be provocative and profitable."[8]

Land knew that his remarks had been provocative. Years later, he recalled with rueful pride that some people wouldn't speak to him for days after the lecture. Three days after his address, he sent a handwritten note to Killian to smooth ruffled sensitivities but also to repeat his insistence on change. Thanking Killian for "the privilege of my association with MIT," he denied that he had found MIT lacking. "In fact, I found leadership which has not only proved itself brilliantly already, but which is searching determinedly for the correct next steps." Although MIT felt "peculiarly responsible" for the knowledge inherited from the past, the administration was "courageous enough to examine tradition, and to take from it what is now required, and to add to it what is now needed." He felt strongly that MIT "has the leaders who can abruptly advance education by a generation." Had he not felt that, "I might have been more light-hearted in my presentation." The letter was signed "Din," the nickname he had acquired in childhood, when the name Edwin was still difficult for his older sister, Helen, to pronounce.[9]

MIT asked Land back. He gave the commencement address in 1960 and spoke at a student-organized Junior Science Symposium in April 1963.[10] On that occasion, he summarized the experiments of Stephen Benton, an MIT student working with him, on the perception of depth and distance. Benton later went to Polaroid and made innovations in holography, which continued after he joined MIT's Media Laboratory. The young man was one of several college students whom Land attracted into his laboratory around this time. The most notable of these was John McCann from Harvard. He collaborated with Land for twenty years on such projects as color-vision research, the development of full-scale photographic replicas of museum paintings, and the organization of increasingly elaborate annual shareholders' meetings.

Introducing Land in 1963, MIT President Julius Stratton, who had succeeded Killian, referred back to Land's "remarkable" lecture of six years before. Stratton summarized it as having urged that "we draw each incoming student, at the earliest possible moment, into a research project of his own to develop, to instill the scientific experience, to make him feel that he is a part of this and to grow with it and to develop these powers of the imagination; and expressed his deep belief [in] what one can do, even at the earliest stages of a career." The 1957 lecture had influenced MIT to set up its Freshman Seminars, in which more than six hundred students took part in 1962–63. The seminars continue in the 1990s.

Land followed up on his comments of 1957. A scientist, he said, does not ask, "Why do I believe what I believe?" but rather, "Why do I *want* to believe what I believe?" He added, "Science, to put it somewhat vulgarly, is a technique to keep yourself from kidding yourself." He told them to get going at once. "The only safe procedure for you, now that you have started, is to make sure that from this day forward until the day you are buried, you do two things each day. First, master a difficult old insight, and, second, add some new piece of knowledge to the world each day. Now does that seem extravagant?"

Back in 1957, Killian had thought over Land's suggestions. He had liked the ideas about starting students immediately on research projects and capturing important lectures on film. On the other hand, he had disagreed with Land's objections to grading and Land's concept of the ushers. Students had been conditioned by previous schooling and would become "restive and impatient" without grades to tell them where they stood. The ushers, Killian thought, would soon become second-class citizens in a research-centered university.

"Dr. Land has an innovating, creative mind," Killian wrote in a memorandum he never published.[11] "The great value of Dr. Land's fresh view of education is its insistence on the importance of a new approach and his great emphasis on a re-awakened concern with the student as an aspiring individual."

"An aspiring individual." Killian's phrase applied perfectly to Land. When and how had Land's aspirations sprung up?

2

Self-Taught Boyhood

> From then on I was totally stubborn about being blocked. Nothing or nobody could stop me from carrying through the execution of an experiment.
>
> —Edwin H. Land, 1976

As he did with so many aspects of himself, Land kept his origins obscure. Brushing off all attempts at a biography while he lived, Land once said, "I'm trying to live down even the honorable part of my past."[1] The religious affiliation of his parents may have embarrassed him. Perhaps he moved so far from his childhood circumstances that they seemed irrelevant. Perhaps it made a better story to keep back almost everything. Later in life he spoke of a determination to escape from his family. Little was left behind except a picture in his high school yearbook, stray newspaper clippings, and fragments of reminiscences, usually offered in public speeches, as if to hide them better.

∞

Edwin Land's grandparents, Avram Solomonovich and his wife, Ella (born Dannenberg), emigrated in the 1880s from the port city of Odessa in what is now independent Ukraine. State-sponsored antisemitism was intensifying under Tsar Alexander III. Traveling most probably in steerage, they brought with them Land's father, Harry, who was born in Russia on 6 April 1880, and a younger son, Sam. At Castle Garden, the immigration center in New York that preceded Ellis Island, the immigrant family had a typical experience. When told that they had "landed," they apparently misunderstood what was meant and were registered as the Lands, and the father's name became Americanized as Abraham.

After a brief stint in New Jersey, Abraham and Ella migrated to New Haven, Connecticut. They had three more sons, Maurice, Benjamin, and Louis, and then three daughters. Abraham started a scrap metal business, removing scrap steel and iron from ports, railroad yards, and factories. A granddaughter of Abraham and Ella, Janessa Stark of New York and Tucson, testified that the family "prized education, initiative, and performance."[2] At a date that is not certain Harry and Sam inherited their father's business.

Also at an uncertain date, possibly at Abraham's death, the Land family's center of gravity moved to Brooklyn. Maurice and Benjamin Land became lawyers. Their younger brother, Louis, went into the secondhand machinery business. The daughters, one of whom married a lawyer, another an architect, and the third a retailer, also lived in Brooklyn. According to Stark, the less successful received help from their more successful siblings. It became customary for about fifty of Abraham and Ella's descendants and their spouses to gather at least once a year at Louis Land's Brooklyn house for Passover seders. In 1948, a newspaper article said that two of Edwin Land's cousins lived in Bridgeport, Connecticut: Oscar H. Dannenberg of 94 Seaview Terrace and Mrs. Nessie Golden of 991 Lindley Street.[3]

In Bridgeport, Harry Land was in partnership with Max Gordon, also in scrap metal. One big contract after World War I was to demolish a U. S. Navy yard in New Haven. Harry Land married Matha or Matie Goldfaden,[4] who had studied physics at Norwich Free Academy in eastern Connecticut. Their first child was a daughter, Helen. Their son, Edwin Herbert Land, was born in Bridgeport on 7 May 1909, when Harry Land was twenty nine. One source gives the address as East Main Street, and another as 254 Stratford Avenue.[5]

After World War I, the Bridgeport scrap-metal business was dissolved and Harry Land moved to the New London, Connecticut area. He set up the H. M. Land Waste Company, occupying warehouses on West Main Street and Washington Square, Norwich, and yard facilities at Falls Avenue, also in Norwich. His main business was to handle all the scrap metal from Electric Boat, the principal builder of submarines in the United States. By 1927, Harry Land had begun to invest his profits in real estate, including two hotels, avoiding the booming stock market. As one of the largest owners of downtown business properties in Norwich, he suffered financially when the Depression-era tenants could not pay the rent. He did not retire until 1961, when he sold his business to the Marcus Company of New Haven. The Land Company's main building was bought and torn down by the Norwich redevelopment authority.[6]

Edwin Land was about ten when the family moved to 1 Crescent Street in Norwich. Attending the Norwich Free Academy, he graduated in 1926. In school, Land "devoured" the physics textbook of his mother, who had been an "A" student in physics.[7] Land's marks were also near perfect. His high school physics teacher, Raymond Case, recalled half a century later that in his senior year, Land "was already working at a level where I couldn't help him." He was also a prize-winning debater and a member of the Norwich Academy track team.[8]

Edwin's sister, Helen Sigal, had two children, Robert and Richard Sigal, and died relatively young.[9] A grandson of hers worked in the 1990s as a lawyer in Israel.[10] Benjamin Land of Brooklyn, New York, one of Harry Land's brothers, was still living when Harry died on 1 April 1965, as was a sister, Mrs. Charles Abramovitz of New Haven. Arthur Land, presumably a nephew, was a bearer at Harry's funeral. Edwin's mother had died late in the 1940s, and the elder Land had remarried. At the time of his death, he had been residing with his second wife at 44 Mott Avenue in Neptune Park, New London. He belonged to numerous civic and fraternal organizations, and to two synagogues, Beth El in New London and Beth Jacob in Norwich. He was buried in the First Hebrew Society Cemetery of Preston, Connecticut.[11]

The Land family's life was stable and conventional. Young Land joined the Boy Scouts. He looked back fondly enough on his experience to make gifts to the Scouts when he became rich. Sixty years after he had joined the Scouts, he was good-naturedly presented with six honorary Merit Badges, for drafting, photography, film chemistry, flash electronics, salesmanship—and dog care. He recalled, "I did get as far as senior patrol leader. Earning badges was something I was too lazy to do. I seem to have gotten there. You shouldn't be too precipitously ambitious."[12]

By the time his father died, Land had not been close to his relatives for many years. Anecdotal evidence suggests that some of these relatives, perhaps including his father, resented how little they shared in Land's ultimate wealth.

Although he was bar mitzvahed, there is little evidence in Land's life of any involvement in Jewish causes, or with Israel. When a Polaroid colleague once had to leave early for a Passover seder many years later, however, Land proceeded to chant the "Four Questions" asked at the seder, in

Hebrew.[13] His Jewish heritage appears to have become as distant for him as it was for his principal Wall Street backer, James P. Warburg.[14] Some consider this remarkable, especially since Land's lifelong business adviser and lawyer, Julius Silver, the nephew of a renowned rabbi, aided Jewish charities in the United States and Israel throughout his life and helped found Brandeis University.[15]

∞

Early in Land's boyhood, his dreams sprang up and whirled him forward. Somewhere in those dreams lay the source of his fanatical persistence, the charm of his public attempts to explain where he was going, the unexpected romanticism of his conversation as he strove for and found a grand problem behind the immediate one.

At the age of five, Land experimented as small children often do, by taking something apart. More than sixty years later, Land remembered experimenting with his family's brand-new phonograph. Dressed in the one-piece pajamas known as Dr. Dentons, with a flap at the back, Land laid out the pieces on the living room rug. Unfortunately, he lacked the time to put them back together before his father came home from work. Furious, his father unbuttoned the flap of the Dr. Dentons and gave his son a spanking. Land was by no means chastened: "From then on I was totally stubborn about being blocked. Nothing or nobody could stop me from carrying through the execution of an experiment."[16]

Somewhere in his boyhood, Land became fascinated with light, an inexhaustible fountain of questions, a treasure for the rational mind. Light is particles. It is waves. As it strikes the surface of the sea, its waves undergo a sorting process called polarization before it dazzles our eyes. Land found out about this as a boy and it held him.

In his boyhood, Land also found out something about business. Business, perhaps even his father's business, was often humdrum and even repellent, but not alien. Although some have speculated that Land wanted to outdo his father as a businessman, he may have just wanted to create something rather than deal in scrap metal and real estate. In Land's mind, business was somehow tied up in the inventions, like the telephone, the electric light, and photography, that changed people's lives and imaginations. He already knew that he wanted to build a life around searching for the causes of things. He also came to know, however, that the searching should result in devices, made by an enterprise that sold them to people who used them.

From his family, Land learned something else: if you intend to be a revolutionary in one domain of life, you must be a conformist in others. In a conference on patent systems in 1964, Land said:

> No person could possibly be original in one area unless he were possessed of the emotional and social stability that comes from fixed attitudes in all areas other than the one in which he is being original . . . [The inventor's] dependency on the fixed attitudes of the society around him is very nearly total, and I doubt whether any person can be happy who rejects this structure of society—intellectual and social.[17]

∞

In a self-taught boyhood, Land may have had few friends besides books. Looking back, Land recalled that he had spent his youth reading novels and other literature. He mentioned two French literary figures, both winners of the Nobel prize in literature, who played their part in the famous Dreyfus case in France. The novelist Anatole France, Land described as "my teacher." From this author, he learned what a cruel place the world was. As a result, Land believed he was shielded from disappointment. A striking work by Anatole France is his novel of revolutionary terror in the France of 1793–94, *The Gods Are Thirsty*. An artist surrenders his work and his love to his role as juror in a tribunal. The Terror gyrates faster and faster, devouring one group of revolutionaries after another. In the end, the artist goes, like the Robespierre he revered, under the bloody knife.[18]

Henri Bergson (1859–1941), the French philosopher, gave much of his optimistic energy to bringing the insights of modern science into philosophy. His *Creative Evolution*, translated in 1911, was on a bookshelf in Land's library-office on Osborn Street in Cambridge. In the book, Bergson asked:

> What is the essential object of science? It is to enlarge our influence over things. Science may be speculative in its form, disinterested in its immediate ends; in other words we may give it as long a credit as it wants. But, however long the day of reckoning may be put off, some time or other the payment must be made. It is always then, in short, practical utility that science has in view.[19]

Land felt the universal, imaginative effect of movies as well. In the 1980s, commenting on a television spy series set in both Tsarist and communist Russia, he said he hadn't seen films so exciting since those of his boyhood. One film he saw as a boy was a version of Dostoyevsky's *The Brothers Karamazov*, which Land recalled as "evocatively Russian."[20]

∞

As a boy, Land became fascinated with toys that fed his curiosity about science. These included kaleidoscopes and stereoscopes. In 1977, he recalled the impact of one of these toys:

> In the midst of one of the most fruitful periods in the history of science 125 years ago, a hint of one great science was treated as a toy. A clue to the solution of a principal metaphysical mystery was passed by unappreciated. In my hometown library the chief delight of the young patrons was not the books but the Brewster stereoscope such as I hold here. Through its lenses the children saw boats and bridges and camels and mountains and of course grottos, the best of all three-dimensional subjects. The stereoscope transported the child through the interplay of stalagmites and stalactites into the distant depths of the caves, having converted the two slightly faded sepia flat dull photographs into a vivid reality in which you could hear the dripping water, smell the dampness, fear the darkness as you sat with your legs crossed under you on the chair in the dear old library.
>
> Where did this new reality exist? In your chest, in your head, in your eyes, or rather did you exist in it? A toy? Or the most powerful metaphysical clue in 3,000 years?[21]

Land had been carried back into the scientific excitement of the first half of the nineteenth century. Then, the theory of the atom took shape, the first organic compound was synthesized, and the phenomenon of magnetism was applied to generating electric current. Discovery after discovery about the polarization of light emphasized the wave nature of light, rather than the particle nature that had dominated Newton's thought. British physicist David Brewster was a widely known student of optics then and also devoted himself to the popularization of science. Brewster's writings conveyed his fascination with the stereoscope and the kaleidoscope.

The library in Norwich held only one book on physics, Adolphe Ganot's *Elementary Treatise on Physics*, published in 1893 by Longmans, Green. Another book that influenced Land far more was *Physical Optics*, by Robert W. Wood, long on the faculty of Johns Hopkins University and a pupil of the great pioneer in optics, Henry Rowland. Macmillan published the first edition in 1905, and the book already was well known enough to be cited as a source for the article "Polarization of Light" in the 1911 edition of the *Encyclopaedia Britannica*. Land used the second edition of Wood's book, issued in 1914. The boy read the book "nightly in the way that our forefathers read the Bible."[22]

In Wood's book, Land found "daring theories and daring adventures and colorful experiments, a feeling for life as seen through science that captivated me from then through the rest of my years." At a conference at Johns Hopkins honoring both Wood and his teacher, Rowland, Land described how he was inspired by the book:

> In *Physical Optics* I read about the Zeeman effect and the Kerr effect, polarized light and mirages, and Wood's own way of doing things, so that as soon as I was old enough to escape from my family at the age of 17, I decided that the world needed a synthetic polarizer, an extensive sheet of polarizing material, in order to be able to carry out on a large scale all the things implied by Wood's stories . . . [23]

The first paragraph of Wood's chapter 9, on the field of polarized light, explains that all the rays of light discussed in the preceding chapters had oscillated symmetrically on all sides of their path through space. Now Wood discussed something new. "Rays of light exist . . . which possess a one-sidedness and behave differently when differently orientated. For example, it is possible to obtain light which a glass or water surface refuses to reflect at a certain angle of incidence. Such light is said to be polarized . . ."[24]

Land remarked, "There is a deceptive simplicity about Wood's style. It is characterized by an elegant choice of appropriate words. Volumes and volumes have been written about polarization for popular magazines and advertisements, and nine tenths of the writing corrupts. Wood's talent was to be clear without corrupting the truth."[25] Land was taken to the edge of fundamental knowledge, and into the thicket of polarization. He was fascinated. The realm of light had a mythic quality for him, as he explained in 1948:

> Since polarization of light is as general a phenomenon as color, it seems curious that it was not discovered until modern times. Had the ancients anticipated Malus in learning [in 1808] that an inclined pile of plates of glass polarizes light, they might, without awaiting our technology or the physics of the last century, have enjoyed and woven into their folklore observations of human ability to control vast and poetic natural phenomena: They could have made the rainbow appear and disappear; they could have deepened the blue of the sky; they could have attached and dismissed from the surface of the sea the long track of the sun's reflection.

Would the ancients have regarded this as a blasphemous appropriation of divine powers? Possibly, Land thought, but they still might have discovered polarization through careful observation of cloth woven of dyed fibers, fibers that most likely polarized light to some degree: "A careful observer could have seen at each point of crossing [of the dyed fibers] a density of the dyeing beyond what he would have expected from holding the yarn of parallel fibers in his hand."[26]

∞

Taking pictures is a branch of the realm of light, and it assumed imaginative importance for the boy. One of the deepest needs for photography, he thought later, comes in early childhood:

> The world around the child is shifting and fleeting and unreliable and hazardous. It cannot be retained; it is constantly slipping away. To a child, a photograph gives a permanent thing that is both outside himself and part of himself. He gets a new kind of security from every picture he takes. I remember the first picture that I developed as a child. It was a picture of our French poodle. The dog really was unavailable to me. He was always running away; there were things he had to do at night as he roamed through the countryside. Then there was a picture I took of him. There I had him. He couldn't get away.[27]

Like most of Land's reminiscences, this one is full of potholes and mysteries. Was the dog his special responsibility? Did Land develop the picture? Did he have a darkroom? Was photography a hobby? Was his family's home in the countryside near Norwich?

∞

In the summer of 1922, Land's interest in the polarization of light grew. He attended a summer camp, Mooween, which had been founded two years earlier on Red Cedar Lake near Norwich, in the Gilman section of Bozrah, Connecticut. Mooween's founder, Barney "Cap" Girden, was a man with great enthusiasm for nature and science and a flair for keeping an enterprise going when times were darkest. What he did in the winters is not recorded. Roderick Gorney, a psychologist who as a boy went to Mooween long after Land, recalled in 1972 that Girden "introduced his charges to an endless array of fascinations, from hypnosis and the polarization of light to the effects on the abdominal wall of man's upright position."[28]

The camp, which Girden left in 1947 and which closed in 1963, had a powerful effect on the boys who attended it, many of them from New York City. At a 1979 reunion, a former camper, seventy-four-year-old Eddie Kessler, reminisced about the camp. He was about four years older than Land but had known him at the camp. Kessler may have been the first camper signed up by Girden: "In 1921 the fee was $350. Cap showed my folks a wonderful brochure with all sorts of terrific pictures, but when we arrived there weren't even roads. We had to walk three miles to get to camp. There was no running water and the shacks had no roofs. When it rained, we had to sleep with our ponchos pulled over our heads. It was the happiest summer of my life . . . I was the first one to take the courage test on Dream Island and the first to become Grand Sachem of the Woodcraft League. For a little guy from the city it was quite an experience."

The 1979 *New York Times* account of the reunion described Girden's determination: "Today, the men see Mr. Girden as part hero and part scamp. During the Depression he kept Mooween afloat by borrowing money from their parents. His debts to them were so great that some boys returned year after year at no cost." One former camper, Danny Winston, who attended Mooween in the early 1930s, recalled: "Cap would pull us out of bed in the middle of the night to watch a thunderstorm. A hundred of us would huddle in the rain while Cap explained why this was the greatest show on earth."[29]

At Girden's camp, Land encountered a striking phenomenon of polarized light. Sixty years later, he brought this up as he argued genially with his friend, the physicist Edward M. Purcell of Harvard, about what is meant by the public understanding of science. They were asking each other what happens in teaching science. Purcell said that "the wonderful thing about science and about teaching" is that all you need is one good example. Land responded, "I'm here with you because when I was a kid some teacher showed me a Nicol prism taking the reflection off a table top."[30] His teacher, Girden, had demonstrated a light-polarizing filter of the type fashioned by the Scot William Nicol (1768–1851) from crystalline calcareous spar.

At Girden's camp, Land also met his lifelong adviser, Julius Silver, who was a counselor there. Land went to Mooween for several summers, except that of 1925, when he made a trip to Europe with his parents. During his last summer, 1926, he was a counselor.

In his first summer at Mooween, thirteen-year-old Land and two or three other boys, including Kessler, the "little guy from the city," were given special instruction in engineering problems. According to a memorandum by Land's patent attorney, Donald Brown, the boys "had the run of what was called the Engineering Building." They learned about and discussed polarizing photometers, which could be used to measure the intensity of a beam of ordinary daylight as compared with a beam of light from a source of predetermined and constant intensity. Both beams were polarized and viewed through an analyzer.

Girden told the boys that people already knew that it would be desirable to have a sheet of some material that would polarize light as it passed through. This polarization happened in crystals of tourmaline. The boys—and presumably Cap Girden—discussed whether synthetic Nicol prisms or tourmaline could be developed, and whether the best thing would be to have a single large tourmaline crystal or many smaller crystals lined up properly. Girden used reflecting polarizers that he had developed in his college work in polarized light. In January 1923, Girden wrote Land "instructing him to read avidly about photometers," and offered to send him all the patents on polarizing photometers. According to Brown, Land did as he was urged. When Land went back to camp that summer, he was "well versed in the photometer art and more especially in the polarizing photometer art."

One evening that summer, Land went driving with Stanley Austin, a counselor. As was typical in the early days of mass-produced automobiles, the headlights were feeble. Land and Austin nearly ran into a team of horses hitched to a farm wagon, which they did not see until the last moment. As usual, this led to a discussion at the camp. Why not boost the intensity of headlights? What about the ill effects of bright headlights at night? Could there be a photoelectric cell to dim the lights when two cars approached from opposite directions? Could the lights be bright and yet free of glare by having polarizers over both the headlights and the windshields? Among the group talking with Cap Girden were Land, Harold Barnhardt (later with American Chicle Company), and Kessler, who later ran a hardware store in Philadelphia, according to Brown's memorandum.

Brown's memorandum also notes that Land was excused from a course at Norwich Academy—it was mechanical drawing, Land recalled—because of his outside research on the polarizing photometer.[31] Land already was showing a taste for doing independent research and an ability to persuade people to bend the rules to allow it.

3

"First Happiest Moment": Polarizer

> The primitive force of his will, the brilliance of his visions, the steely energy of his practical ponderings, must appear queer and incomprehensible to anyone at the standpoint of another Culture, but for us they are in the blood. Our whole culture has a discoverer's soul. To dis-cover that which is not seen, to draw it into the light-world of the inner eye so as to master it—that was the stubborn passion from the first days on. All its great inventions ripened in the deeps, to emerge at last with the necessity of a Destiny.
>
> —Oswald Spengler[1]

In the mid-1990s, the liquid crystal displays in hundreds of millions of pocket calculators and digital watches all over the world made use of simple, inexpensive, plastic sheet polarizers that Land invented in the 1920s with the enthusiasm of youth and that he perfected over the next two decades. These are the same polarizers used in enormous numbers of camera filters, sunglasses, and inexpensive cardboard-and-plastic glasses for watching 3-D movies of the early 1950s. If the major car makers had not hesitated, the polarizers might have been used in every automobile headlight and windshield in the world from the 1950s onward. The prospect enticed some very shrewd investors. Although the polarizers did not find the big market that Land so devoutly sought, they drew him into gritty work from which sprang, by a series of intellectual and emotional accidents, the field of instant photography.

Land's lively interest in the history of polarized light pulled him into the field. For Land, the history went back to the 1670s, soon after Newton began the modern study of light. Newton used prisms to break up beams of light into distinct colors. He thought of light as discrete particles, or corpuscles. Soon afterward, others discovered properties of light that supported a theory of light as waves. The Danish scientist Erasmus Bartholinus placed a rhomb of calcite, or Iceland spar, on some writing, Land explained in an early lecture, "and saw the writing doubled. He did not know it but the twinned line was polarized." In Land's account, Christian Huygens soon "placed another rhomb of calcite on top of Bartholinus', found he could twin the twin, and came to the conclusion that the light passing through the first rhomb had lost a characteristic which it had had before." Huygens had seen one form of polarized light, but could not account for it.

More than a century passed before a series of discoveries in France and England truly opened the field of polarized light and, with it, the study of light as waves rather than particles. Land said that one day in 1808, Etienne Louis Malus, a French military engineer and researcher in optics, "had the enviable experience of looking across the garden through a calcite rhomb to the windows of the Luxembourg Palace glaring in the afternoon sun, and finding that in one of the two images which he saw, the brilliant image of the sun was extinguished. It is proper to regard this experiment as the first use of a polarizer for the elimination of glare."[2]

Land felt that the intellectual and artistic excitement of work on the polarization of light opened a window onto nature—and a source of practical devices. In 1945, he put it this way: "Without the centuries of interest in polarization by scientists who loved science the way musicians loved music, and who had no practical purpose in mind, the modern synthetic polarizers that open up whole industries for us would have been impossible."[3]

Many years of struggle made the sheet polarizer obvious and ubiquitous. Yet it was fitfully noticed. Inexpensive polarizers could be placed almost anywhere they seemed useful.

For the polarizer, as with many other fruitful ideas, the sources, times, and order of crucial steps was somewhat mysterious. Land saw this when he was still young. At the Franklin Institute in Philadelphia in 1936, he said with great assurance: "It is a curious property of research activity that after a problem has been solved the solution usually seems obvious . . . In research, as in the whole civilizing process, why does it take so long to learn so little?" He saw in his own notebooks, or in the slow processes of history, "the same strange interpenetration of methodical, intellectual activity stimulated and interrupted by irrelevant emotional and economic daily problems."[4]

Even in his youth, Land's passion for research on intractable and fascinating problems matched that of other pioneers of science-based industry. An example described by the historian Elting Morison comes from the great General Electric (GE) Laboratory in Schenectady, New York. In 1917, Willis Whitney, its early leader, told people at his alma mater, the Massachusetts Institute of Technology, that they concentrated too much on trade and industry. They must read "the countless uncut pages of science," not only to find new technology but to bring brighter students into the realm of an instinct for innovation, which is "as difficult of analysis as our reasons for developing at all."

Fascinated by the effects of high heat on the filaments of electric light bulbs in his search for more energy-efficient bulbs, Whitney launched William D. Coolidge into his "pretty nearly hopeless" but ultimately successful work in making the metal tungsten in a form where it could be drawn out into a permanent thread. Visiting Coolidge's laboratory frequently, Whitney always asked if Coolidge was having "fun." By this he meant, "Are you still working on that problem no one else has found the answer to?" and further, "Are you still engaged in the most exciting exercise there is in life?" Land expected the same intensity from himself and his co-workers.

Joining the GE laboratory soon after Coolidge, Irving Langmuir, who later was awarded the Nobel prize, identified the new tungsten bulbs as the most exciting topic to begin his work. While exploring electricity and heating, and modeling elementary hydrogen atoms, Langmuir also came to understand and correct many problems with using tungsten in bulbs. Langmuir observed in the 1930s that the tight coupling of science and engineering "enabled us to solve a problem where a few years previously it was not even expected that there was a problem." He asked, "Who knew that we needed the telephone or the victrola?" It was a question Land asked often.[5]

∞

Land's arrival at Harvard in the fall of 1926 may have been a moment of triumph for his family, but he was quickly disillusioned. The often-privileged young men around him did not seem to have either his ambitions or his knowledge. It was time to get started on a program of original activity that would be significant. At the end of the fall, he asked for a leave of absence.

Romantically, he began his quest by briefly exploring the world of authors like Theodore Dreiser. The seventeen-year-old Land took a train to Chicago, eating oranges and talking to Italian workingmen seeking jobs. He took a small room near the stockyards and made a stab at writing the great American novel. The only time Land was ever stopped and frisked by a policeman, he said, was once when he was running back to his room near the stockyards. The policeman thought Land had committed some crime. With a smile brimming with happiness, he recalled later, "I was just happy."[6]

The idea of a writing career seems to have disappeared quickly and he returned to science. Land went to New York City, registering for the spring term at New York University, perhaps as part of an agreement with his father to keep up his studies in return for his father's continuing Land's college allowance. Most of Land's studying, however, was in the vast reading room of the New York Public Library at Forty-second Street and Fifth Avenue. He spent eight to ten hours a day there. He had returned to science, to the field of optics, and in particular to the field of light polarization. There he could approach some of the central problems of physics and, as it turned out, invent useful devices. Free of his family, he felt "a transient need, a violent need" to be just himself, restating, re-creating, and talking in his own terms about what he had learned "from all the cultures." Much later, he described the mood:

> You want to be almost alone, with just a few friends. You want to be undisturbed. You want to be free to think, not for an hour at a time, or three hours at a time, but for two days or two weeks, if possible, without interruption. You don't want to drive the family car or go to parties. You wish people would just go away and leave you alone while you get something straight. Then you get it straight and you embody it, and during that period of embodiment you have a feeling of almost divine guidance. Then it is done, and, suddenly, you are alone and you have to go back to your friends and the world around you and to all history, to be refreshed, to feel alive and human once again.[7]

In a succession of rented rooms in Manhattan, he started doing experiments as he ransacked the library for all it could teach. His stories of that time made no mention of music, movies, the theater, the beach, weekends at home, or friends. It was an adventure of work: work that would be done for as long as it took, even if it took decades, work that would bear him up and pull him along. Later, he kept saying he didn't want to go to bed with a hypothesis untested. A joshing cartoon, made many years later by Maxfield Parrish, Jr., shows Land in his coffin on April Fool's Day 1999, holding up the lid, gesturing commandingly with the other arm, and saying, "Before I go, I want just one more experiment."[8]

Probably during this period in New York—it is not recorded exactly when—Land met the woman he would marry when he was twenty. She was Helen Maislen of Hartford, who soon acquired the nickname of Terre. A 1948 newspaper reported that Helen was the niece of Dr. Samuel Maislen of Hartford.[9]

Meanwhile, Land wanted to do something great. These machine age times were full of technological optimism and anxiety. People were reading Sinclair Lewis's *Arrowsmith* and Paul de Kruif's *Microbe Hunters*. The recent horror of World War I persisted as a symbol of machines grinding and blasting their human masters.

Around 1920, Oswald Spengler had put the final touches on his foreboding story of the twilight of European society, *The Decline of the West*. In a chapter called "The Machine," he wrote of "the Faustian inventor . . . a unique type," a combination scientist and engineer. For little more than a hundred years, such inventors had developed "a drama of such greatness that the men of a future Culture, with other souls and passions, will hardly be able to resist the conviction that 'in those days' nature herself was tottering." The engineer, in Spengler's eyes, was "the priest of the machine, the man who knows it." As long as the world's army of a hundred thousand engineers continued to find recruits, material dangers such as the exhaustion of coalfields will "have no existence." Without engineers, however, "the industry must flicker out in spite of all that managerial energy and the workers can do."[10]

∞

Undoubtedly one of Spengler's recruits, Land needed an energizing principle, an emotional spur. He found it when the idea came to him with new force that a polarizer could cure the glare of automobile headlights. Over many years, and to many people, he told the story of this realization, differing in details and possibly forgetting or considering it trivial exactly when or where it happened. Loving enigmas, he lightly told an enthusiastic woman attending a conference in New York in 1972 that if he were bright enough to have the idea, he was bright enough to have it in the daytime.[11]

As the story goes, sometime after Land arrived in New York and was walking along the street—on Fifth Avenue or Broadway, perhaps alone or with somebody, by day or night?—he got the idea that solving the problem of headlight glare would be a magnificent use for an inexpensive polarizer if he succeeded in making one, as he did. Such polarizers would greatly reduce the hazards of driving at night. The notion lit an idealistic spark in Land's mind, giving him the moral energy to spend twenty years fighting for uses of polarizers beyond sunglasses and filters. More than fifty years after he came up with the headlight idea, in a 1981 interview with a *Business Week* reporter, Land recalled that the field of synthetic polarizers "didn't even exist conceptually. Polarized light itself is a natural phenomenon, but the concept of making polarizer in sheet form didn't exist until I undertook it." Others had tried to make polarizers by growing large single crystals.

The 1920s were not a particularly favorable time for young "spark plugs," as the reporter called them. "I think the world didn't look very vulnerable to sparks when I first started. You need a tremendous amount of literary, political, industrial sophistication when you are young—in order to free yourself of the load of disapproval of your novel undertaking . . . I had met nobody who had ever worked with polarized light. I just didn't want the burden of hearing the reasons why things weren't feasible."

In those days, microscopists were using the well-known, expensive Nicol prisms, named for their nineteenth-century inventor. Inexpensive polarizers were desirable, Land told the reporter. For many purposes, it would "be nice to have that method of controlling light . . . Light has three basic attributes: one is the energy, the amplitude of vibration; the [second] is the frequency of vibration which is involved in the sense of color; and the third one is the direction of vibration. We are always controlling the amplitude whenever you turn a switch on and off, or turn a rheostat. You are always controlling the frequency when you color a piece of paper. But there wasn't any way of controlling in everyday life the third great basic attribute, namely the direction of vibration . . . "

Many, including leading figures in physics, had failed for more than seventy years to make practical polarizers that were cheap, but Land succeeded. Land hadn't been sure that it could be done: "It was gratifying in itself and opened countless fields. Wherever light goes today, polarization is used. In fact the digital watches have our polarizers. I had light valves in mind at that time, but it took from 1927 to, say, 1977—50 years."[12]

Three-dimensional movies also excited him. In a 1976 lecture honoring Wallace Carothers, the inventor of neoprene rubber and nylon, Land said that his own work on polarizers began with his fascination with Brewster's stereoscope:

> [T]he projection of the stereoscopic pair onto a non-depolarizing screen . . . and viewing of the screen with clear, transparent, polarizing spectacles, would be a most rewarding experience . . .
>
> We must remember that at that time the only polarizers were small fragments of dark tourmaline or cumbersome piles of glass plates or extremely expensive large rhombs of calcite split and re-cemented to make what were called Nicol prisms. To the boy the concept of bringing into being a sheet-like material that would resolve incident light into two components, transmit one and absorb the other, was in itself a stimulating dream. But the realization that such a material would open the whole field of three-dimensional projection and viewing provided an irresistible challenge.[13]

However universal a phenomenon it was in physics, polarization had not been harnessed for applied science or industry. Land "could see nothing in 'the laws of nature' prohibiting the existence of a sheet of glass or plastic as large as a window pane that would resolve incoming light into two components and absorb nearly all of one component while transmitting nearly all of the other." He supposed that "such a plate of glass cut in half by a glass cutter could have the two halves superimposed on each other, and the pair would change from black to transparent as one plane was rotated relative to the other."

Science gave Land encouragement. Polarization was important in discovering basic properties of matter. For example, Land had read in R. W. Wood's book about three great discoveries in the study of light interacting with magnetism: the Faraday effect, discovered in the 1840s; the Kerr effect, discovered in the 1870s; and the Zeeman effect, discovered in the 1890s. Faraday had found that magnetism could rotate the plane of polarization of light, an observation that James Clerk Maxwell said was "of the greatest importance to science."[14] Working with electromagnets whose poles had been polished so that they acted like mirrors, Kerr found that the plane of polarization of reflected light was rotated by the magnet. Zeeman's discoveries of doublets and triplets in the spectral lines of an element such as cadmium, according to J. J. Thomson, implied that the electron he had newly discovered was "an ordinary constituent of the molecule."[15] Polarization also could help obtain better views of living tissue, and probe the composition of minerals, metals, and polymers. Early in the twentieth century, astronomers already drew insights from the polarization of light coming from the sun's corona, the nebulae around stars, and the light reflected from the moon.

The science inspired Land to seek a material for glare-free headlights, three-dimensional moving pictures, and color television. It was now time for experiments. He set up his first small laboratory in a rented room on Fifty-fifth Street off Broadway in Manhattan. A few months of experiments drew him away "from approaches using large single crystals." Instead, he moved to the opposite approach. He would make "the optical equivalent of a large crystal by homogeneous orientation of submicroscopic polarizing elements, suspended in low concentration in a clear sheet of glass or plastic."[16]

∞

In later years, Land found it difficult to recall the sequence or timing of his insights. Preparing for a 1954 patent trial when another early worker in the field, Alvin Marks, had brought suit, Land wrote down what he could remember. In a pretrial deposition, he told Marks's attorney, "I was interested in making polarizers for a number of fields, such as laboratory scientific apparatus, Kerr-cell light valves for television, colored displays for advertising, and three-dimensional projection, and somewhere about that time—I am not clear of the exact time at the moment—automobile headlights." He said that early in 1927, he "spent a little time on reflecting polarizers but rather promptly became interested in Herapath's work on large crystals of periodide of quinine sulphate and related compounds."[17]

In the Fifty-fifth Street lab—still living on the small allowance from his father—he worked on a television system, a multichannel system like that of E. F. W. Alexanderson, the General Electric researcher whom Land did not meet until 1932. Land was looking for narrow-band transmission of many channels and ordered quartz plates for this work. After a few months, perhaps in May 1927, Land moved to a little house just off Riverside Drive on 104th Street, which had a basement room he could use as a lab.

There, with the assistance of an ophthalmology student at Columbia, he started exploring a way to use a Kerr cell in television. First, he tried an arrangement of three semi-metallic mirrors, preferably made of an alloy of copper and arsenic, which gave "a whiteish reflection and considerable polarization." In the basement, Land made the alloys and the mirrors. But the lab wasn't appropriate for melting and casting metals. Probably in February 1928, he moved to another basement on 106th Street off Amsterdam Avenue. Land recalled that he placed an ad in the *New York Herald Tribune* or perhaps the New York *World* for a "mechanical dentist." The ad attracted some twenty people, and of these, Ernest Calabro, whom Land referred to as his first employee, was selected to help him.

While Calabro worked to cast metal plates, Land spent the days and evenings in the Public Library. In the physics laboratories of Columbia University, he studied the properties of the metal plates. Marks's attorney asked him whether he was just pursuing a purely scientific interest or aiming at commercial uses. Land replied, "I had very much in mind at that time these large fields, such as three-dimensional projection and television." He repeated that the use of polarizers in cars may have struck him later. Calabro's work on casting the plates for reflecting polarizers "was rather promptly abandoned. I switched to the crystal polarizers." Continuing his library studies of the history of polarized light, Land sought a method of making "large-area transparent polarizers."[18]

∞

While Land strove with his polarizer project, he got a dramatic vicarious taste of inventive success as he read about an event in Rochester. Many years later, he recalled reading in *The New York Times* an account with prophetic overtones. In August 1927, between two safaris to Africa, George Eastman, the seventy-three-year-old photography industrialist, threw a highly publicized garden party at his Rochester mansion to show Thomas Edison a new color movie film, called Kodacolor, and to launch it on the market. It was quite a party. Edison, a pioneer in movies, and his whole family arrived in three sleeping cars from New York. Other guests won the same prizes that Land began winning about ten years later. Eastman and Edison posed together with a movie camera, and *The Times* carried the picture. Adolph Ochs, publisher of *The Times*, said, "This development gives one the impression that nothing is impossible."[19]

The new film proved commercially unsuccessful, and its name was later given to a completely different film. To work properly, the film that Eastman showed off required filters attached both to sixteen-millimeter Ciné-Kodak movie cameras and to the corresponding projectors. Despite a grid of fine lines that resembled early television screens, the process produced bright and colorful pictures. The technology was complex, Land recalled sixty years later. The film had tiny lines, in a form called lenticules, ruled on its surface. The camera lens was covered with a filter with red, green, and blue stripes. "The minuscule lenticules would focus on the film three microscopic stripes behind each lenticule. The color was wonderful, but it took special filters and special lenses and special condensers and so on." Kodacolor, Land remembered, gave him the courage to develop the instant movie system of the late 1970s, which had somewhat analogous features.[20]

∞

In describing the kaleidoscope, Brewster mentioned an English physician, William Bird Herapath, who had discovered in 1852 what Land called "the remarkable polarizing property of the tiny crystals that form upon combining iodine with quinine salt." A student of Herapath's named Phelps found that he could produce small, green crystals by dropping an iodine solution into the urine of a dog that had been fed quinine. Herapath looked at the crystals under the microscope. As Land told the story in 1954, "Herapath was deeply impressed to observe that in some places where the crystals overlapped they were white, and in other places where they overlapped they appeared a deep blue-black. He realized that these were polarized crystals." Herapath had been placing transparent crystals crosswise over one another and observed that they then became opaque.

Over the next ten years, Herapath tried to make the crystals cover larger areas, at least one-eighth of an inch in diameter, large enough to use as filters for his microscope. He dissolved quinine bisulphate and iodine in alcohol and water, heating the solution and cooling it slowly while taking care to avoid vibrating it. In this way he grew ultrathin plates of material slightly heavier than the liquid, which consequently were held to the liquid by surface tension. Herapath gradually mastered the delicate operation of slipping these very thin plates, as much as half an inch wide and three-fourths of an inch long, off the liquid surface where they had formed and onto thin plates of glass. No adhesive layer was used to hold the material to the glass. But the crystals were "so fragile that they would fly apart if barely touched with a piece of blotting paper."[21]

Scientists, particularly Brewster, were tremendously interested in Herapath's plates of crystals, named "herapathite" after their discoverer. They hoped that the plates could be used in microscopes and kaleidoscopes. But the agonizing procedures for making these remained virtually the same for seventy years. A leading British microscopist said wearily, "Promising as they were, these artificial tourmalines of herapathite have not stood the test of time." The story faded. The physics text by Ganot, the only one in Land's town library, referred to Herapath, but more modern physics textbooks did not. Old editions of the *Encyclopaedia Britannica*, but not the latest, mentioned him. The Webster's Unabridged Dictionary of the day mentioned herapathite, though only under "obsolete words."

For Land, the tale of Herapath was not out of date: it was an exciting rediscovery, like reopening an old mine. Land said in the 1940s that the problem struck him as "a kind of Chinese puzzle which dogged him continually, demanding a solution." He also felt a shared sense of proprietorship. Herapath had taken his new polarizer "to his heart" and "felt that it was his very own." His vision and hopes were "a vital stimulus" to Land: "I confess that no one felt [Herapath's] proprietary interest more keenly than I did."[22]

∞

A small step forward was taken in 1926 by the Austrian scientist Adolph Zimmern and a colleague named Coutin. They tried forming the crystals on a vertical glass plate that stood in a solution of herapathite crystals. The scientists hoped that as the crystals formed, they would adhere directly to the glass surface. But this process was perhaps even more glacial than Herapath's. Material was added, extremely slowly, to the bands of crystals forming on vertical glass plates immersed in the solution. The glass plates were withdrawn two inches over forty-five days from the solution as crystals formed. Dirt, shaking, or the wrong temperature spoiled the process. Moreover, the "fantastically slow" rate was impractically slow—no good for making enough material for every headlight and windshield in America.

On the 1930s Alvin Marks found that he could go a little faster, pulling the glass plate out of the herapathite solution at the rate of four inches an hour. The plate would then be coated with incomplete crystals. He would then immerse it in a second solution of the crystals, where crystal growth would be completed. The resulting plates, however, still suffered from "haphazard departures from perfect orientation." Of all these crystals deposited on glass, Land thought, "the crystals prepared by Herapath were far and away the best optically, being single crystals." The latter two processes were not useful "for any precision use or for any large-scale commercial use." Land had repeated all the previous work and was dissatisfied. The Zimmern–Coutin and Marks polarizers were of poor quality and tedious to produce. A few years later, a German researcher named Bernauer developed, and the Zeiss firm had marketed, "perfect crystals" more than an inch across under the name of "Herotar." After Land's plastic polarizing sheets came on the market in the mid-1930s, however, Zeiss abandoned the process.[23]

In 1927, when Land, at the age of eighteen, repeated Herapath's work, he wrote, "It was at once apparent that in Herapath's extraordinary product there resided the clue to the development of satisfactory polarizers and to the utilization of polarized light on a large scale in an industrial way." But for large commercial fields, such as three-dimensional movies or television, "some technique far beyond Herapath's would have to be invented." It was during the next few weeks that Land had his insight about using polarizers against headlight glare. They would have to be "big enough, clear enough, and cheap enough to be used in the windshields and headlights."[24]

What Land did not know was that in confidential "interference" proceedings, several rival inventors were already battling each other and examiners in the U.S. Patent Office over what Land called "the broad idea of using polarized light on automobiles." Later, Land guessed that this ignorance helped him by keeping up the "enormous impetus" of the goal of ending highway glare. The hope of some such system was general enough that Land's childhood mentor-in-print, Robert W. Wood, knew about it. Wood once received a letter from the research laboratory of a large automobile manufacturer with this question: "Can you prepare an extensive area of Herapathite?" Land delighted in recounting Wood's wry answer: "I am extremely sorry to inform you that I do not know how to make a polarizing windshield."[25]

∞

Land shared his idea about headlights with Calabro, the assistant who originally thought he was going to work for a dentist. Calabro was fascinated, Land recalled fifteen years later: "For three months he just stuck around to find out what kind of insane man I was. And for three months I didn't tell him what I was working on, either. At that time I tried to make polarizers by reflecting light from metallic plates, and we made a good deal of progress. Then one day, Ernest and I were walking down Broadway, and I said, 'Wouldn't it be wonderful if we could have a plate of glass and place another over it and rotate it, and go from white to black?' And then he knew I was nuts, but we started."[26]

At this point, Land was taking a momentous step as an inventor. Having been thwarted in one approach, that of growing large crystals, he went in the diametrically opposite direction, making the tiniest crystals possible. Such a turn to the other extreme was what Land called "orthogonal thinking." According to his patent attorney, Donald Brown, "A favorite technique of the inventor [is] to meet failure by a complete reversal of his approach to the problem." But Land was so fertile an inventor that he was not limited to simple reversals of direction. He was also capable, Brown said, of "flashes of genius" and of virtually the opposite, the "deliberate and intellectual" approach he pursued with instant photography many years later.[27]

∞

Excited and enthusiastic, Land went to see his father in 1928. The younger Land had been living on his college allowance. "I was, I suppose, about seventeen then, and I had swiped some of the allowance my father was giving me and [taken] a back room in the basement off the furnace, in an apartment house in New York." Now, convinced he had the solution to the headlight glare problem, he asked for a loan of five thousand dollars. In 1976, Land recalled making the request after taking his father for a drive and saying, "Dad, I think I know how to take the glare out of car headlights. Can I borrow five thousand dollars to get a business going?"[28]

Harry Land thought his son could do it, but wondered if in the competitive industrial world, he would end up with any financial reward. Land recalled his father saying, "All right, if you say it, I believe it. But watch out. Once you develop it, the big companies will take it away from you."[29] Little did Harry Land know that the problem was almost the opposite: that the big companies would work with his son for fifteen years and then refuse the innovation. The younger Land thought little of the risks: "At that time, I had, of course, no obligations, and in the high idealism of adolescence cared not at all about anything except the humanitarian aspects of eliminating glare in night driving."[30]

In reversing his technical approach, he no longer hoped that he could grow enormous crystals of herapathite from which he could cut wafers of large area—much as today's electronic chips are built on wafers of crystalline silicon several inches across, which are sliced like salami from an immense cylindrical crystal. The slices of herapathite would have to be extremely thin. Land concluded, "This was manifestly an impractical program. The program for making polarizers through any process of crystal growth would, in our generation, be a blind alley."[31]

Perhaps in the spring of 1928, Ernest Calabro left Land's employ for a time, and Land hired an organic chemist, Dr. Joseph Friedman, later a principal historian of color photography, to work with him. They would develop ultra-tiny crystals that could be oriented in an electric field or a magnetic field. In a search for lab space, they approached people at Yale but were turned down. So Land and Friedman used the kitchen of Land's parents' summer house on the shore of Long Island Sound near New London. They worked intensely to disperse their tiny crystals in the sort of lacquers used for spray-painting. To grind the crystals small enough for "a fine pigment dispersion in nitrocellulose lacquer," they used a ball mill, which had to be kept going for a month. Land went along the beach at night looking for quartz crystals to go into the ball mill to help with the grinding.

As the fall of 1928 wore on, it became cooler, and Land and Friedman moved to a one-room lab in an office building in Norwich or New London—most likely a building that Land's father owned. Using an electric field, they could orient their microcrystals in the lacquer. The microcrystals, or what Land called "minute platelets," of herapathite took the place of the pigment usually found in the spraying lacquers.

Normally, the lacquer would be a reddish black, Land noted, "but when placed in the electric field in a small cell [it] would rather miraculously become transparent and clear." The electric field was holding the "minute platelets" oriented. The clear solution, "to our delight," proved to be "well polarized." Although the experiment was based on Swedish and German work with colloids in an electric field, it was actually unprecedented. According to Land, it was "the first time that truly polarized particles had been brought to a homogeneous orientation and held there by an electric field."[32]

Working with an electric field was difficult and a little dangerous. An alternative was to expose the suspension of microcrystals to a magnetic field. A Dr. Webb at the physics laboratory at Columbia University allowed Land to use the laboratory's large electromagnet. It worked. "The liquid suspension in a sealed glass cell [changed] from black to white when the magnet was turned on." Many years later Land recalled his excitement:

> Then came the most exciting single event in my life. The suspension of herapathite crystals was placed in a small cell—a cylinder of glass about a half-inch in diameter and a quarter-inch in length. The cell was placed in the gap of a magnet which could produce about 10,000 gauss [a standard measure of magnetic force]. Before the magnet was turned on, the Brownian motion caused the particles to be oriented randomly so that the liquid was opaque and reddish black in color. When the field was turned on—and this was the big moment—slowly and somewhat sluggishly the cell became lighter and quite transparent; when we examined the transmitted light with a Nicol prism, it went from white to black as the prism was turned."[33]

He remembered this event when a reporter asked what was the happiest moment of his life: "Well, there are many, many happiest moments at different stages of your life, but the first happiest moment was when I got suspended polarizing needles to orient in the magnetic field to make the first synthetic polarizer, when I was eighteen or so." Looking back at a dozen exciting moments, Land said that occasionally "there are times when you visualize, you hypothesize, you propose an experiment, and you do it, and it works that first time . . . [It] is a summary of years of hypothesis and analysis and the final visualization. Then it goes from inside you to outside you, in an experiment."[34]

So, in the latter half of 1928, Land had a path to making a synthetic polarizer. With the magnet off, he suspended a test tube of the herapathite-containing lacquer between the poles of the magnet. Then he dipped a strip of celluloid into the tube. After he turned on the magnetic field, all the microcrystals would orient themselves in the same direction. Pulled from the test tube, the strip of celluloid, still wet, was coated with oriented platelets. The magnet remained on and the lacquer dried. The dried celluloid strip had become a polarizer. In the 1950s, Land still had at least one of the original strips made in 1928.

During the 1976 Carothers lecture, Land held up a polarizer for his audience: "You probably have all seen these by now. It seems so plausible now for these to exist. At that time, it was the most exciting fantasy in the domain of physics that an adolescent could have."[35]

∞

As he contemplated large-scale applications, Land the physicist was migrating swiftly into the very different imaginative world of chemistry, where new materials, such as rayon and cellophane, were already making their appearance. In that world, Wallace Carothers's fundamental scientific curiosity, spurred by the leaders of the DuPont research department, would soon energize the development of nylon, the pioneer of a cascade of artificial polymers. Carothers's tense adventure at the boundary of science and manufacturing, which eventually ended in suicide, highlighted the tensions of Land's multi-disciplinary trade.[36] The new materials already were used for photographic film, a realm that Land would explore for the next half century. His inventions used plastic film to filter light and, later, as a base for his special system for recording light in photographs. The functioning of both the polarizer of his youth and the instant photography of his maturity involved arranging elaborate sequences of chemical reactions, some evanescent and others long-lasting. For a physicist, Land would spend a lot of time hiring, conversing with, challenging, and inspiring chemists.

As Land began to think about commercialization, he talked to his former camp leader, Barney Girden, who suggested that he talk to a patent attorney. Julius Silver, Land's former counselor at Girden's camp and by then a lawyer, recommended Donald Brown. It was a fateful juncture in Land's life. What an inventor-entrepreneur needs most are expert helpers on patents and on business matters. For almost forty years, until his death in 1966, Brown helped Land on patents, and for more than fifty years, Silver not only walked Land through a thicket of business deals, but also handled Land's investments. For decades then, Land was attended at the left hand and the right by selfless and wise counselors.

On 19 September 1928, Land went to Brown's office, at the firm of Warfield and Wallace, 247 Park Avenue, with samples of plastic polarizing sheet. Brown's colleague, William W. Fraser, made sketches to start developing an application to the U.S. Patent Office. Brown recalled, "He brought with him . . . several small samples of what appeared to be strips of grayish cellophane mounted between two optical flats. When these strips were crossed, the overlying areas were black; when the strips were superimposed in parallel, the overlying areas transmitted light substantially as did each individual strip." Brown remembered that "this seemed to me to be in the field of 'black magic,' as it frankly still does."[37]

Land was not mesmerized. For one thing, the magnetic-field method did not look promising for continuous production of plastic polarizing sheets. Furthermore, after testing sheets of the material, he concluded that the tiny crystals were not small enough to prevent scattering a lot of light. The needle-like crystals would have to be smaller in one dimension than the wavelength of visible light, that is, smaller than four hundred billionths of a meter, and such tiny needles might not respond well to the magnetic field, in any case.

Land had become convinced that "mechanical flow or extrusion would be more feasible commercially than electrical or magnetic orientation." The task was to make "smaller and smaller colloidal needles of herapathite." He needed to learn how to implant them in plastic solutions and how to orient them "by subjecting the plastic to flow." The need to make needle-like crystals meant going beyond his current ball-mill method, which produced irregularly shaped plates that would orient in the electric or magnetic fields, but not in flowing liquid. By late 1928, he had developed polarizing areas of considerable size by what he considered "a commercially feasible process for large-scale production." The rectangles of polarizer were big enough to run headlight tests.[38]

He laid aside the 3-D application for his polarizing plates. "I believed rather passionately that the greatest service I could perform in my life was to make a polarizer suitable for elimination of automobile headlight glare. It did not occur to me at the age of twenty that if a perfect technical solution of the problem were found, the automobile industry might nevertheless be slow to adopt the program."[39]

∞

Warfield and Wallace filed Land's first patent application on 26 April 1929. Two months later, the attorneys gave him a letter of introduction to Dr. C. E. Kenneth Mees, head of research at the giant Eastman Kodak Company.[40] After another two months, on 14 August 1929, Land wrote from 313 Washington Street in Norwich to Fraser at Warfield and Wallace in New York, thanking him for the letter of introduction and reporting progress with the polarizer. He had succeeded in getting the crystals much smaller.He reminded Fraser that "while the crystals were oriented uniformly, they were still large enough to scatter a great deal of light. Many of them were as long as the wavelength of light." On 11 July 1929, Land reported a success: "I succeeded in obtaining the first really submicroscopic suspension of herapathite, a size reduction of at least 50 times." Specimen polarizers that he viewed under the microscope were "perfectly homogeneous and clear." They scattered no light and seemed to the eye "as clear and brilliant as celluloid." He enclosed a duplicate laboratory record for 11 July.

New problems had arisen, however. Although the needles were perfectly oriented in a ribbon of plastic flowing from a plate, these tiny fibers were "highly susceptible to molecular forces." As the celluloid dried, it was difficult to keep the needles all aiming in the same direction. If Land made the solution gooier, more viscous, the needles held their direction better, but the material would not flow from the plate. Previously, Land had been letting the ribbon fall on a plate coated with a thin layer of fluid celluloid solution. Now he substituted an oily, colorless substance. This was dibutyl phthalate, the ester of phthalic acid, which was often used as a plasticizer. To make the plastic ribbon as viscous as possible without stopping the flow, he vigorously stirred a hot, saturated solution into a jelly of submicroscopic fibers that was incorporated into "a highly viscous and tenacious nitro-cellulose solution." The resulting "smooth ribbons" were free of bubbles, with their needles aligned in perfect uniformity.

This stirring recalled his earliest work, a confident Land wrote to his lawyer. "Vigorous agitation of a saturated solution, to generate rapid cooling due to evaporation, is a rather obvious attack on the problem of precipitating small crystals." To get the needle-containing solution into the viscous plastic, he noted that "printer's ink and some of the finest celluloid lacquers are made by kneading the pigment into a viscous mass." The new method differed from the earlier one in several respects. The saturation of the solution of herapathite was increased by 50 to 75 percent. No longer were the crystals of herapathite dissolved in hot alcohol. Instead, the components of herapathite were added separately. Because Land used "the finest grade highly nitrated cotton in as little solvent as possible," there was more nitrogen in the nitrocellulose, and it formed a "far more tenacious and cohesive mass than the early solutions." Land exuberantly reminded his lawyer, "This method promises to work on any scale and is now being used in making specimens large enough for headlights and windshields for field tests."[41]

That summer, Land thought he had "carried the polarizer program far enough so that I could simply consult and advise a manufacturer." With this hope, he reentered Harvard in the fall, when most of his classmates of 1926 were starting their senior year. It is unlikely that this separation from his fellow members of the class of 1930 bothered Land very much. Soon after the return to Harvard, Land and Terre Maislen were married on 10 November 1929.[42] They set up housekeeping at 40 Linnean Street,[43] a multi-entry apartment building that still stood in the 1990s at the corner of Linnean and Avon Streets in Cambridge. Having heard stories that undergraduates at other colleges were forbidden to marry, Land consulted a dean. The reply was gentle: "Young man, this may be very important to you, but in the long history of Harvard it makes no difference at all."[44] On the Armistice Day weekend when Din and Terre were married, Land lost some ten thousand dollars that he had accumulated in the late 1920s boom in the stock market.[45]

As he worked along as a Harvard physics student, Land kept hoping to end the research and convert his invention into an article of commerce. He was in touch with Irving Weber, director of research at Fiberloid Corporation in Indian Orchard, Massachusetts. Weber had sent Land batches of nitrocellulose solution for his work. In return, Land sent him polarizer samples for testing. On 6 June 1930, Terre typed a letter to Dr. Weber for her husband. Land had improved his process for making the polarizing sheet, so that tests on local roads had gone well. The "product seems near enough perfection now to warrant further work on my part with the object of being able to demonstrate a finished product, requiring no further research."

Weber had demanded a product good enough for road tests. Land replied that "the only specimen that will satisfy the demands of a simple road test is one that is practically perfect." The process was still "makeshift." Scratches, dirt, and optical blemishes had to be eliminated, because they would be "annoying" in the "real test" of one car's headlights shining brightly at the polarizing windshield of another. He had worked out a new process giving "sheets of any desired width and length, and of uniform thickness with good orientation." In road tests the sheets provided "complete glare elimination and high visibility."

The nitrocellulose solution that Weber had sent was "not quite satisfactory" because Land's colloid was slightly soluble in toluene, so that the finished product was darkened a bit. Nonetheless Land was using what Weber had sent. After exams, he expected to resume work on the process "and to be able to give a demonstration soon." He thanked Weber for the nitrocellulose and for his "continued interest."[46] Weber did not reply until 21 June and apologized, saying Land's letter had been held for his personal attention during a period away from the plant. He looked forward to getting more samples from Land and suggested that they meet some weekend during one of his frequent visits to Boston.[47]

∞

Sometime after Land's arrival at Harvard, a physics instructor, Dr. John McCloud, was impressed enough with Land's polarizers that he found for the young inventor what Land once called "a small laboratory" and later "a splendid large laboratory" in the new laboratory building of the Harvard physics department.[48] George Wheelwright III, instructor in the course in electricity and magnetism, may also have played a role in the transaction although Land did not mention Wheelwright's role in later years.[49] Meeting Wheelwright was one of the more significant encounters in Land's life. Born in 1903, Wheelwright was the brash scion of a family that owned a paper mill in western Massachusetts. It had gone bankrupt in the little-remembered but drastic recession of 1921. Wheelwright had gone to Harvard with "no aim," just because everyone did, and had a fine time playing the violin and building a Model T Ford from spare parts. After the bankruptcy, his father telephoned to say, "Son, the company's broke and I can't afford to support you any more." Perhaps with some relief, Wheelwright took a job on a

United Fruit Company boat in the Caribbean and then worked as a globe-hopping assistant to a wealthy artist and photographer for the *National Geographic*. Later, in Santa Barbara, California, Wheelwright tutored and ran a day camp for upper-crust boys. The affluent parents were pleased as well as their offspring, and the operation made money. The profit first went into the stock market and then, luckily, into cash in the summer of 1929. His stash amounted to the best part of one hundred thousand dollars.[50]

Marrying for the first of three times, Wheelwright returned to Harvard College to study physics, mathematics, and astronomy. After he graduated in 1929, he decided to press on for a graduate degree, working with William Duane, a student of X-rays and an expert in the radiation treatment of cancer.

For many years, Harvard's physics department was an empire ruled by a wealthy Boston Brahmin named Theodore Lyman. He pioneered measurements of the spectra of ultraviolet light from the atomic hydrogen of the sun and the stars. The series of spectral lines that he discovered in the ultraviolet range were similar to the series that Balmer discovered in the visible spectrum. Lyman's colleagues considered his discoveries "the experimental cornerstone of the celebrated quantum theory of atomic structure developed by Bohr in 1913."[51]

A wealthy bachelor living in his family's mansion in Brookline, Lyman directed Harvard's physics laboratory and later became the department chairman for a time. In the late 1920s, he raised the money for the new second laboratory building adjoining the Jefferson Laboratory. The new lab was named for him upon his retirement in 1947. As Lyman reminded Harvard's President A. Lawrence Lowell, he contributed six thousand dollars of his own funds each year to help run the department.[52]

Lyman was a globe-trotting hunter in the summertime. He had an exciting assignment in World War I at the front in France, developing a method of aiming artillery. When his active research career ended, Lyman was honored repeatedly with medals and presidencies of scientific societies. Two of the medals, the Rumford Medal of the American Academy of Arts and Sciences and the Ives Medal of the Optical Society of America, would later be awarded to Land. Lyman was acutely conscious of laboratory safety. He had been ill for months after a fire in his own lab back in 1900 and, as laboratory director, had confronted the horror of an explosion in 1922 that killed a graduate student and a carpenter. He knew enough about Land's work at the boundaries of chemistry and physics to fear an accident: Land's work involved volatile materials like nitrocellulose.[53]

As a graduate student, Wheelwright had teaching duties. He was asked to take over the course in electricity and magnetism in which, as an undergraduate, he had earned the modest grade of B+. Just before the course was to open, Wheelwright went to look over the equipment for the standard student experiments. Land was there before him, trying one piece of apparatus after another. Land asked what kind of course Wheelwright would give. Wheelwright replied, "I'm afraid a dull one," because the instruments were rather old. There was no money for new ones, but it was said that the old ones worked. Land told him that none of them worked. "What do you say to that?" he asked the graduate student.Wheelwright replied, "I think it's great." Land smiled and said, "We'll get along."[54]

According to a magazine article in 1938, "Land had a shock of black hair, dark piercing eyes, a jerky manner, and a sophisticated but incurable enthusiasm about almost everything in the world but especially about a light polarizer he had devised in his teens in a rudimentary home laboratory. Mr. Wheelwright, on the other hand, besides a thorough knowledge of physics and a keen sense of judgment regarding human nature, had money. It was a perfect team."[55]

Wheelwright remembered Land as the brightest of the three or four very bright students in a course that involved three long laboratory sessions a week. When any new experiment proved balky, Land would get it running, but he always had trouble writing up the results. This could have been costly for Land's grades, because Harvard's system then was to cut the mark one full grade for each day a paper was late. An A paper four days late earned a failing E. Wheelwright devised a way to minimize the problem. He telephoned Terre Land, who helped in these years with her husband's lab research, and said, "Mrs. Land, can't you do something to get him to finish it?" Terre replied, "Oh, it's the bane of my existence. He does the same on fixing things. He works on it as long as he doesn't understand it, but as soon as he understands it he wants somebody else to do it." Wheelwright asked, "Can't you finish up his experiments for him, write them up?" She said she would. To mark them as soon as possible and save Land's grades, Wheelwright would bike up to Linnean Street to pick up the papers. Wheelwright remembered them as usually "letter perfect."

By the end of the year, which Wheelwright recalled as 1930, he was impressed enough with Land to tell him, "You know, your work is so important that I think you ought to have a lab." Land replied, "I couldn't get a lab." Undergraduates did not have labs. Wheelwright rejoined, "Well, do you mind if I pull some strings?" Land said, "No, if you can do it." Wheelwright intervened, either before or after McCloud did, and Land got his lab.[56]

Land's physics professors came around to see him at work. They claimed to think that Land's work was wonderful, Wheelwright recalled. This did not mean, however, that his physics professors understood their prodigy very well. Unaware that Land worked in his lab most nights and many weekends, they "docked" him when he was late to class like any other undergraduate. In 1971, Land recalled that people like Lyman and Bridgman were "coming by to cheer," but they and the others didn't understand the field he was working in. This was good, in Land's view. Neither then nor later was he awed by the experts, who always knew why something would never work. Even then his rule was that if you're doing something new, you shouldn't work near experts. The onlookers might have had something to contribute, but they also could have come up with a lot of bad ideas—and obstructed things.[57]

Land persisted with his experiments. He had made sheet polarizers and had learned how to make the crystals very small—a trillion of them embedded in each square inch of cellulose. Knowing that the magnetic field would only weakly orient the tiny crystals, which was not practical for large-scale manufacture, he sought an industrial method. A newspaper account in 1936 said that the idea came to Land one day as he played with a sheet of rubber. A short pencil lay athwart the sheet. As Land stretched the rubber, the pencil gradually rotated to a position parallel to the direction of stretch. In 1945, a reporter described Land's next idea: "It seemed reasonable that if the tiny crystals, swimming in a solution, were applied to a thin sheet of transparent plastic, and if the plastic sheet were stretched, the crystals would have to behave like the pencil and align themselves, parallel to one another, in the direction of the stretch. After this, the plastic could be 'frozen' so that it could not snap back, and cemented between protective layers of cellophane-like material."[58]

In retrospect it was easy to state the problem and its solution. In practice, it took years that seemed always to recede before a relentlessly optimistic Land. As he considered "the meaning of stretch and of elongation and considering the type of stretch appropriate for the creation of various kinds of polarizers," the old observations, dignified by time, appeared "casual" and contained little if any insight. In July 1930, Land "investigated mathematically the orientation of needles in the plastic mass as a function of the amount of stretch." To orient the crystals uniformly along parallel lines, Land found, "extremely high elongation" was needed.

For the herapathite needles to line up to within four degrees of the line of stretch, the sheet had to be pulled to fifty times its original length.

Could he get the effect of stretching a sheet by forcing it through the "jaws" of an extrusion press? The answer was a qualified yes. Extrusion was the method for producing his first commercial polarizer, the so-called J sheet. Another way involved sheets of rubber that were stretched before the liquid, needle-bearing plastic was poured on them. Once coated, the stretched rubber was relaxed, and the needles were "oriented around an axis across the sheet," but still not close enough, on the average, to the direction of stretch. Now the sheet could be stretched a second time the other way, that is, at right angles to the direction of the first stretch. The needles were lined up almost perfectly parallel to the direction of the second stretch.[59]

The time came to explain the work more fully to the Harvard physics department. On the afternoon of Monday, 8 February 1932, Land became the first undergraduate to address the department's regular colloquium. First there was tea, then a paper by one of the department's leading professors, Otto Oldenberg, and then Land's talk. It was entitled "A New Polarizer for Light in the Form of an Extensive Synthetic Sheet."[60] He was talking about the J sheet.

He showed his Harvard colleagues the "spectrophotometric properties" of herapathite, demonstrated the new sheets, and gave measurements of their properties. He also demonstrated the "light valve," a device for modulating a light beam to transmit signals for speech and music by passing the beam through a liquid suspension of herapathite crystals across which an electric field was applied. The field was modulated by the microphone output, Land recalled. The colloquium was well attended, and the audience showed "enormous interest in the new polarizer."[61]

Wheelwright had hoped that the colloquium talk would make Land better understood at Harvard. Wheelwright was the helper, the "Dr. Watson" to Land's Holmes. After the session, "the professors piled onto him [Land} to ask questions." Wheelwright went outside to "see what the rest of the class were thinking." Two of his classmates in Bridgman's class walked past Wheelwright without seeing him. Wheelwright considered them "intellectual snobs." One asked, "What do you think of this work of Land?" The other replied, "Oh, I guess it's all right. Didn't impress me. I understood everything he said."

The classmate's blasé attitude riled Wheelwright. Maybe a Harvard physics doctorate wasn't worth the trouble. His professor Duane had died, probably from the effects of the radiation he had worked with, and Wheelwright would have to find a new mentor and a new topic and start all over. Besides, he recalled, "I was much more intrigued working with Land than any degree I might get. I had the strong feeling that if we worked in the lab and it went well, I wouldn't need the degree. And if I had the degree and didn't work in the lab, I'd miss something."

On one of their long evening walks, Wheelwright asked Land, "Din, what about us starting our own lab?" Land was silent for a long time and then said, "An education without a degree." Wheelwright said, "What in hell does that have to do with it? I don't care what you are!" Land said he was almost finished with his work on polarized light. He thought that he could always maintain his contacts at the university, even without the degree that lay only a short distance ahead. The new lab should have some project that each could work on. Wheelwright had the money for this and put Land on a salary of two thousand dollars a year.

In the summer of 1932, the new enterprise rented a room in a garage at the corner of Mount Auburn and Dunster Streets in Cambridge. In the fall, the lab moved to an empty dairy barn on a large estate in Weston that was being sold upon the death of the owner. Wheelwright said that they wanted a place that was cheap and secluded, so that "nobody would know what we were doing." He added, "I forget how I found it . . . I think the place was sold but they weren't going to build on it for a long while." The former milk room became a photographic lab. Land and Wheelwright fixed up a cottage on the estate, where Terre Land could paint. Harry Land came to visit, and so did Otto Wolff, who later designed the first production machinery. Land showed Wolff a piece of polarizer about a quarter of an inch wide and an inch long.[62]

Despite distractions, the main focus for Land and Wheelwright remained polarized light, not only for headlights but also for the viewing of stereoscopic movies. For their projects, the partners found that they needed to be near libraries, specifically the Boston Public Library and the library just across the river at the Massachusetts Institute of Technology. So in 1933, after less than a year in the rural idyll of Weston, they moved the lab to a basement at 168 Dartmouth Street in Boston.

4

Start-up

> Dear Din, I received your precious shipment and turned it over to the laboratory. The material came through in good shape.
>
> —Fordyce Tuttle, Eastman Kodak Company, 3 January 1935

Like other innovators, Land navigated a lot of shoal water when he was young and relatively inexperienced. He had to patent his invention and go right on patenting in the face of rival inventors. He had to learn how to make the polarizer in commercial quantities and enlist the skilled help he needed. Finding customers whose payments would finance future innovation was a challenge, as was learning the arts of publicity. He also had to find financing for his enterprise that would leave him in control of his destiny. In the years between 1932 and 1937, he succeeded so well at these tasks that while still in his twenties, he was regarded as one of the most significant innovators in the United States.

The demands of the enterprise were impossible, yet inevitable. Land and Wheelwright did everything at once. Their little enterprise was based on a great invention, and they wanted to do great things with it. Relentlessly optimistic and relentlessly wary, they used technical cooperation and publicity to persuade people in big industries as different as automobiles, amateur photography, and feature films that polarizers could be useful and profitable. Holding costs to a minimum, they found money to keep going. Throughout they fought off the temptation to sign on with a big company.

Land struggled to perfect the process for commercial-scale manufacture. The headlight glare problem carried Land to General Motors and

General Electric (chapter 6). The work toward three-dimensional movies carried Land and Wheelwright to Eastman Kodak (chapter 7). But these were the larger hopes for the future. What panned out in the short run and gave the company sustaining specks of gold were camera filters and sunglasses. Continually, the young men improvised, often at the last minute, in an atmosphere of crisis. The pressure for innovation did not fade until Land left the enterprise nearly fifty years after it began.

PATENTING

On 13 June 1933, Donald Brown sent Land, in Wellesley Farms, Massachusetts, a telegram: "Congratulations! You are now a patentee!" That morning, Brown had received formal notice that Land's joint application of 26 April 1929, with Joseph S. Friedman of Brookline, Massachusetts, had been successful. Brown urged paying the issuing fee at once.[1]

This was a moment for exuberance. Land had received his first patent. The next day, Land telegraphed Brown at 247 Park Avenue, "Congratulations yourself on wise handling as tough patent and patentee."[2] The patent, which did not cover the broad field of headlight glare but the narrower one of a practical polarizing sheet, was formally issued on 13 July, with the number of 1,918,848, "Polarizing Refracting Bodies." Over the next half century, Land would be granted 534 more patents.

At once cocky and deferential, Land had many more patents in the works to fight off the rivals who claimed to control the entire headlight field. The most important rival, Lewis Warrington Chubb, held the powerful position of director of research at Westinghouse Electric Company in Pittsburgh. Many years earlier, his wife had been killed in a car accident resulting from headlight glare. Chubb applied for a broad patent covering anti-glare polarizers for automobile headlights, but he did not have a practical material. Land had that. In 1933, Chubb's patent application was still pending.[3]

Although artificial polarizers had many potential uses, the heart of the struggle was over headlight glare. Land's patent and his already-pending applications looked strong to experienced eyes. In the spring of 1934, the Eastman Kodak Company reviewed Land's patents, focusing on the continuing conflict with Chubb. Kodak was already studying polarizer samples. One Kodak lawyer judged Land was in "a very formidable patent situation." A second concluded, "We are strongly of the opinion that Chubb is not entitled to claims dominating the polarizing sheet material itself, and accordingly we do not believe that Chubb can become a dominant factor in the field which the Kodak Company contemplates entering." That field was the photographic use of polarizers.[4]

Chubb was not alone. In the 1920s, he had pooled his application with patents of rival inventors, a former U.S. Army officer named Frank Short, who lived for a time in England, and Karl D. Chambers, who died in 1931. Their small outfit in New Jersey, Polarized Lights, Inc., fought "interference" actions with yet other inventors, including Hans Zocher of Germany, whose patent was assigned to General Electric. The Chubb group began talking with automobile companies.

As a leader in industrial research, Chubb knew the research moguls who were courting Land. Chubb and his colleagues, scattered in Pittsburgh, New York, and Newark, New Jersey, had the different outlooks of engineers, businessmen, and lawyers. They expected to control their rival Land completely, but the strength of Land's patents and his successes in manufacturing and marketing eventually forced them to accept a small slice of his enterprise. The letters between them in this struggle illustrate the technological, legal, commercial, and financial maneuvering that surrounded the evolution of Land-Wheelwright Laboratories into Polaroid Corporation.

The rivalry with the youthful Land began soon after Polarized Lights was formed. Land meanwhile kept on filing after his original patent application in 1929, although he and his patent attorney were stunned to find others in the field. Although Land was actually learning how to make an inexpensive plastic polarizer, the rivals were not particularly impressed at first. Having had the idea of using polarizers in automobiles before Land did, they thought this would assure their dominance. But Kodak and others concluded that the actual working material gave Land a transcendent advantage. He was indeed a formidable opponent.

By the mid-1930s, both Land and his rivals were thrashing through a thicket of negotiations up and down a chain of suppliers to the automobile industry. DuPont and Kodak made plastic film base. General Electric (GE) and Westinghouse made bulbs and headlights. Pittsburgh Plate Glass (PPG) and Libby-Owens-Ford (LOF) made glass for windshields. Corcoran-Brown made headlights, and General Motors (GM) and Ford made cars. The rivals talked to them all, and to each other.

Land began working closely with engineers at GM in 1932. The same year, Polarized Lights began talking with engineers and lawyers at PPG. The little company's tone was fairly grandiose: it sought substantial payments for an option on its patents and foresaw much larger down payments and royalties, possibly to be paid for through a merger with PPG, that would reduce tax liability. PPG's president was skeptical, considering the patents sound but scarcely watertight. He asked for enough material for a convincing test.[5]

The partners in Polarized Lights were not long in contacting Donald Brown, and Brown was ready to show them what Land was making. In mid-December 1933, Brown had samples of Land's material, six by eighteen inches, ready to turn over to Edwin J. Prindle, the New York lawyer of Polarized Lights. In New Jersey, Robert A. Smith, the business brain of the enterprise, wrote to Chubb in Pittsburgh: "Our patience seems to be winning out." Prindle cautioned Chubb: Land should not be allowed to give a license on his patents directly to PPG. This would give PPG "a club which they could use, if it proved that we had to use Mr. Land's methods, to get a satisfactory screen for windshield purposes."[6] Early in 1934, Polarized Lights tested polarizer from Land at Mahwah, New Jersey. John J. Serrell, the technical man in Newark, concluded that headlight lenses and full-size goggles made with Land's polarizer were "perfectly practical using 50 candle-power lights." There was enough glare control and illumination of the road "for practical, safe night driving."[7] Land had the material and it worked.

Polarized Lights continued dickering with PPG, which kept asking for a demonstration. Patent disputes with Land continued, but in 1934, Land's relations with Kodak were so close that he was getting ready to make his first shipment of polarizing sheet for Kodak use in camera filters.

Kodak also explored the use of Land's polarizer in automobiles with Libby-Owens-Ford. LOF soon learned of Chubb's long-pending patent application and was interested. LOF "had a reputation of much cleaner dealing than P.P. Glass," wrote Chubb's brother Morris in March 1935. Morris Chubb recommended having the two companies compete for licenses to the Polarized Lights technology. PPG supplied all of Chrysler's needs and part of Ford's. LOF supplied part of Ford's and all of General Motors' requirements. "Between them, they control about 95 per cent of the safety-glass production of the country."[8] Lewis Chubb soon checked with his fellow mogul of industrial research, Kenneth Mees at Kodak, who, of course, had already met Land. Mees said that Kodak's license on three patents only covered the photographic field.[9]

Smith reminded Chubb that Polarized Lights had been in touch with LOF as far back as 1928, "when we didn't have much except some small pieces of Zimmern [material] to show." Now, as discussions between Land and Polarized Lights continued, Land was bringing samples of his material to his patent lawyer's office. Smith urged Chubb to carry out the demonstration for PPG first, and then turn to LOF if PPG did not act fast. Meanwhile, he said, Prindle was checking the U.S. Patent Office records "to see if the title[s] to Land's patents have been assigned."[10] Land was a threat, although they knew little about him.

In April 1935—two years after Land had received his first patent —PPG's engineer R. A. Miller wrote Chubb to say that he had learned about "someone in Boston" who had filed for a patent on similar material and was dickering with Kodak. On 15 May, Land wrote Miller directly, naming four patents in force, and mentioning that many others had been applied for. Miller telephoned and wrote Chubb, urging a meeting with PPG's chief patent attorney.

Smith advised Chubb to tell Miller that he expected victory in a Patent Office interference dispute with Land over the basic material. Chubb already had won an interference action with Zocher, the inventor working with General Electric. Land's technique of orientation by extrusion was, according to Smith, "old, and . . . Land's patents on the broad process will be no good." PPG could be expected to be cautious because it "just recently got stung for a large sum on a patent suit." Prindle, Chubb's lawyer, wrote his colleagues a few days later that Chubb should go over "the limitations and defects" of Land's patents with PPG.[11]

By 4 June 1935, just five months after Land's first delivery under the 1934 contract, Kodak had sent Chubb two samples of its Polascreen filter material for examination. Chubb also had heard that an article about the material would soon appear in the *Journal of the Society of Motion Picture Engineers*.[12] Smith wrote to Chubb the next day to reiterate the idea of an exchange of stock with PPG. He reported the suggestion of his colleague Serrell, that Chubb hang a headlight equipped with Land's polarizer out the window for several months, to expose it to strong sunlight and "all kinds of weather." Chubb's son, Lewis W. Chubb, Jr., was then working in Ithaca, New York, making batches of crystals of iodo-sulphate of quinine and strips of film containing the crystals.[13]

Late that same month, the partners in Polarized Lights felt that they were considerably stronger in their bargaining with PPG. A Patent Office official had rejected Land's move to end Interference 67542 between him and Chubb. On 3 July, Miller of PPG appeared more interested in a deal, but said that the company's president still insisted on a test with full windshields. Chubb asked Miller if this could be done with two glass plates, rather than safety glass, and Miller agreed. Chubb said that they might have to buy wide sheets for the test from Land. He also mentioned that Corning Glass was expressing interest in a system that started out with headlight polarizers and visors.[14]

The same day, the contacts between Land and his rivals intensified. Smith visited Brown's office at 6 East Forty-fifth Street in New York. After the visit, Smith told Chubb and Prindle, "I think that we can get along well with Brown; Silver not so good, but he is not in the picture at the moment." Evidently, Land's counselors were playing a game of "good guy, bad guy."

Although Brown and Smith "joshed" about the Patent Office decision that was favorable to Polarized Lights, Brown mentioned that he would carry the examiner's decision to an appeal board. He had "rather expected" the examiner's ruling. The Short patents, which Smith and Serrell had bought jointly, were "of very great value" in an automobile system, which was the issue between Land and Polarized Lights.

Polarized Lights could combine with Land, Smith said, because Polarized Lights was itself an amalgamation of conflicting patent interests. After the decision on the interference, Smith was in a conciliatory mind-frame: "we would deal fairly, not squeeze him." Brown told Smith that he expected Polarized Lights to have trouble getting Patent Office approval of some broad claims by Chubb, which Brown said "should have been put in the [patent] case 15 years ago." Smith disagreed about the difficulty in winning at the Patent Office. He reported his question to Brown:"Wouldn't it be better for Land to deal amicably rather than risk all?" Brown affably agreed.

Smith was impressed by Brown's friendliness in frankly outlining Land's progress in the last year. "I don't feel it is for the purpose of bluffing or teasing us," he wrote, but rather a statement of facts by way of preparing to get together. Brown described for Smith the arrangement with Eastman Kodak, which Smith in turn reported to his colleagues:

> They sell Eastman the . . . sheets of celluloid polarizer at some fairly high price, as very high quality goods. Land apparently buys the cellulose acetate from Eastman at about $2.00 per pound—they think a very high price—in 25-pound lots. They make a high profit in turn on the material of the sheets they resell to Eastman. I believe Eastman pays not only the sheet cost, but a 10 percent royalty as well. From Eastman, and from [other customers], Land is now getting an income sufficient for his living, and to maintain his laboratory, and I judge to pay his patent attorney.

Smith was told that at Land's laboratory in Cambridge, Land had "some kind of a machine for making sheets 11 inches wide." Smith added, "Land's machine, running all the time, can make 800,000 to 900,000 square feet a year. DuPont tried a 100-pound batch on a 22-inch-wide machine, successfully, but [doesn't] care to talk [about] less than 100,000 square feet on an order." DuPont had been in touch with Land as early as 1932 and was also making polarizer material for Polarized Lights.

Eastman Kodak was not using extruded film, but another licensee was. Smith was told of a contract with an optical company, where polarizer sold for about fifty cents per square foot, to make double-lens goggles allowing adjustment of the degree of light-blocking. The Land enterprise was bargaining with two optical instrument companies to supply the polarizer in microscopes and other instruments, and with Union Carbide for a plastic different from celluloid for safety glass.

Brown told Smith that Land had approached Ford Motor Company about six months earlier with the idea of using polarizers in an advertising display. This tiny opening had broadened to actual demonstrations with cars containing a headlight-glare-control system, which Ford engineers approved. The design used a thin film that transmitted about 60 percent of the light from the lamp and cut off about 85 to 90 percent of the headlight glare for the oncoming driver using a visor. Brown considered this an inferior solution and added that Land had better material that transmitted 40 to 45 percent of the lamp's light and cut off 99 percent of the light to an oncoming driver using a polarizing shield. After a lull, the Ford talks were on again. Land would supply about three square feet per car for headlights, driver's visor, and rear window, for a royalty of twenty-five cents per car and $125,000 down. Ford's counterproposal was just the 25-cent royalty, along with a six-month lead on competitors.

Smith also learned from Brown that Land had told all the auto companies about the Short patents and Chubb's application, so that, in Smith's words, "the auto companies will have to settle or fight us." Brown noted that Eastman Kodak made cellulose acetate, "can control or buy other interests," and was dickering for some kind of combination with Libby-Owens-Ford. Smith joked with Brown about the probable outcome if LOF began using Land's polarizer without recognizing Polarized Lights' patent rights: "We would be tickled to death if they got Ford to use it, as we could then sue and collect, etc."[15]

This exuberant mood lasted only a few days. On the morning of 6 July, Chubb received a chilling letter from Miller of PPG, still asking for samples to test but rejecting any down payment for the "undeveloped" technology. Miller wrote that "the manufacturing difficulties ahead . . . appear to us to be very great and to involve a very considerable expenditure of both time and money before the idea can become commercially useful."[16] Chubb continued to think that Land's patent position was weak and that Polarized Lights should turn to a manufacturer prepared to start with headlights and visors, without waiting for entire windshields.

Chubb and his associates wanted samples from Land, but did not think he was very cooperative. With considerable income from Kodak, Land's adviser Silver didn't think he had to "bother with us." All the initiatives for an agreement had come from Polarized Lights. Perhaps Chubb and his colleagues should send a letter to six major car companies, two glass makers, DuPont, and Kodak to remind them of their group's Patent Office victories to date, including one over Land.[17]

In October, Land's rivals received another rebuff. Chubb and his son Lewis delivered to Miller at PPG the "finished Ford lenses with [polarizing] discs inside and a viewing screen mounted in a brass frame and hinged to the edge of a standard auto sunshade." Miller bluntly told them "that we [Polarized Lights] are wasting our time and that there can definitely be no sale under the present terms unless and until we can get together with the Land interests and come to some kind of three-party agreement." PPG had found that "Land had some claims which seriously hurt our position and that we have some which would likewise hurt his." Miller had seen some of Land's disks. Polarized Lights might control the system for cars, but Land had the actual polarizer.[18]

The publicity following Land's first public demonstration of his polarizer in January 1936 stung Chubb and his associates into sending the letter that they had drafted the previous summer. Deprecating "the recent burst of publicity for the use of polarized light in auto headlights and viewing," the letter warned, "Such work will require authorization under our basic patents, and that has not been given." Polarized Lights received replies only from an assistant patent counsel at Chrysler and from Eastman Kodak.[19]

The partners of Polarized Lights encountered Land's influence at every turn. Meeting with officials of the Corcoran-Brown Lamp Company of Cincinnati, which made all the headlights for Chrysler, they learned that the company had tested samples from Land and found that they worked. People from Corcoran-Brown had witnessed Land's demonstrations in New York and Boston. Apparently, Chubb wrote, "Land is offering licenses to the automobile companies and the headlight manufacturers."

Corcoran-Brown officials told Chubb that "Land was very secretive regarding patents; how the stuff is made; what it is; and would not give any samples for them to work with." For demonstrations, they said, "Land uses goggles . . . in which the upper part only is covered." This confirmed Chubb's "old opinion that this is the best form of viewing screen." Although Corcoran-Brown's experience in state legislation on headlights led its officials to predict that cars would be required to have a fastened-in viewing screen, they were convinced that drivers would prefer goggles.[20]

Meanwhile, Chubb's brother Morris informed him of a possible new way to hurry his patent application along. Patent actions affecting auto safety could be accelerated, in line with a safety campaign then being pushed by Daniel C. Roper, the Secretary of Commerce. The Patent Office was then, and remains sixty years later, a part of the U.S. Department of Commerce. When Morris Chubb spoke to a friend who was secretary to Roper, the secretary was "much interested" and said that he would pass word along to the head of Roper's safety campaign. Chubb thought that these contacts should be followed up: "[I]t would be a good thing to let those in authority know that we have the early rights and thus offset the propaganda which Land is putting out."[21]

Conversations about a deal between Land and Polarized Lights soon became more concrete. On Friday, 14 February 1936, Land, Wheelwright, and Brown met Smith, Short, Serrell, and Prindle in Prindle's office at 40 Wall Street. Smith suggested that they join forces with a manufacturer, which would be given 50 percent of the venture. Of the other half, the shares would be 30 percent to Polarized Lights, 20 percent to Land-Wheelwright. In reply, Brown focused on manufacturing and the payment of fees to Land-Wheelwright Laboratories: sixty-five cents a square foot for the first three million square feet, and fifty cents thereafter. The manufacturer would make a cash down payment, and order one million square feet the first year, two million per year for the next two years, and four million per year after that. Land said that the polarizer machine could make strips fifteen inches wide and seven thousandths of an inch thick. The capacity was one million square feet per year. Equipment for wider strips was being planned.

On Land's behalf, Brown played hard to get. When Smith suggested that the agreement to form a combination should run for only a year, Brown countered that perhaps ninety days would be better. Land, Wheelwright, and Brown went back to Brown's office to think it over and discuss it with Silver. Following standard policy, the Land camp did not reply at once, leaving Polarized Lights, Corcoran-Brown, and even PPG on tenterhooks. Smith wrote Chubb on 24 February, "Waiting on Land, who wants for his option time to expire (we think)." Brooding about Land's publicity, Chubb made plans to deliver a paper at the Illuminating Engineering Society's next meeting late that summer. His patent still had not been issued.[22]

As the string of patents lengthened and the orders came in, the Land-Wheelwright position against their rivals strengthened. While the publicity reverberated, potential investors began to appear. The first negotiation was abortive, but it represented the first sign of interest from the banker James P. Warburg, who later became one of Land's most important—and richly rewarded—backers.

The proposal involving Warburg surfaced barely a month after the direct talks between Land and his rivals. On 19 March 1936, Henry C. Everett, Jr., of Boston met Smith of Polarized Lights in New York to propose a buyout of both companies. Smith was worried about proposition: Land had given Everett an informal option, which had expired. Yet that morning, Everett had talked with Brown and Silver. "A company"—Smith guessed that it was Kodak—"is dickering with Land to go ahead alone," Brown had told Everett. But why didn't Everett preempt this by accepting Land's offer of a month before? As Smith understood the proposed arrangement, Land would get "little or no stock." Given Land's large share in the enterprise that eventually emerged, this plan has an ironic ring. Among the directors whom Everett suggested for the new enterprise was Warburg.

Everett wrote to Polarized Lights on 21 March confirming his buyout offer and requiring acceptance by the twenty-fourth. The offer also was conditioned on securing full rights to Land's patents. Everett's patent attorneys, Fish, Richardson, and Neave of Boston, had reviewed the patents and found them all valid. Brown, however, had not been willing to give Everett any time to secure the agreement of Polarized Lights. Smith reported, "Negotiations . . . have been very rapidly developing with other large interests." Thinking it best, as Smith put it, "to sit tight and not be too anxious [to make a deal]," Polarized Lights turned Everett down.[23]

MANUFACTURING

Soon after Land and Wheelwright formed their laboratory, it became clear that they could not turn the polarizer over to somebody else to make. The step beyond the laboratory into the factory was arduous and called for all of Land's resilience and persistence. When the work seemed complete, there was always just one more problem, one more series of experiments, one more series of challenges in designing and building machines and getting them to run. The inventor-turned-manufacturer gathered and supervised a growing team of researchers, engineers, and marketers.

From 1933 to 1935 Land and Wheelwright worked in their noisy, dusty basement at 168 Dartmouth Street. They then expanded the enterprise to an upper floor of the same building and, in the fall of 1936, moved to larger quarters at 285 Columbus Avenue, on the other side of the Back Bay railway station.

Making the polarizer was by no means as simple as Land later described it. As Wheelwright recalled in 1978, "He thought he had it. . . . The problem with Land and his kind is that when they think they've got something and they can see the end, they discount all the hard work that has to go in between." Land seemed to revel in the hitches, the little failures. He often asserted that an experiment that fails is a better teacher than one that succeeds. Wheelwright recalled a moment of success that disappointed Land:

> We were running that little table that had about 24 little one-inch tapes. One of the hardest things that I've ever seen. But after a couple of months, certainly a very short time, comparatively, we got what we needed. I went out and got some champagne and celebrated. Din was sitting there, you know, looking. . . . I [was] going to crack another [bottle] shortly. I said, "What is the trouble, Din?" "Oh, God" he said, "we shouldn't have gotten this break. Now there are at least 10,000 experiments that we could have run and we'll never run them because we've got so many other things to do. So we'll never know what we missed." I didn't have the wit to see it that way, but I think he was right.

Land cherished total immersion in a problem, and one night Land would not let Wheelwright go home at all. Wheelwright said, "Well, Din, it would be nice to go home." Land replied, "Oh, no. We'll have to go back in the regular world. You see, we've just got our world set so that it's what we want to do, and now we have to go back and listen to what the children didn't do, and the complaints that our wives have." Wheelwright replied, gently, "I realize they will, but they think it's really important stuff."

A marathon effort to produce continuous sheeting began one Christmas Eve and did not end until 11 January. Their machine was working, "making continuous sheeting—not wide, but making it." Meanwhile, according to Wheelwright, "Din was on the floor, sort of crying and working with something—not doing very well." Land asked Wheelwright, "George, what is the matter? My wife has gone home and your wife has gone home. All the help has gone home and we're not getting anywhere." They agreed to go home.[24]

∞

Land's team of helpers grew slowly. Interest widened from rubber-stretching to presses and extrusion as a way to produce large streams of plastic polarizing sheet. The son of an acquaintance of Wheelwright's mother, Robert Blake, was hired to run the machinery. Later on, Blake's car was rigged for tests of polarizers, and still later, he joined the research department of what had become Polaroid Corporation. Present on the day that Blake was interviewed for the job was the consultant Otto Wolff, an MIT graduate working with Allen "Jack" Latham on the first polarizer-making machines. Wolff became an employee in 1937 and rose to be the chief engineer of Polaroid Corporation. In developing the polarizer-making machines, Wolff used equipment that he had first devised for counting returned newspapers. Howard G. Rogers, who became an employee on 3 March 1936, respected Wolff's skill in devising his machine to count returned newspapers: "I think it was quite a complicated thing to design and build."[25]

In 1978 Wolff asked Wheelwright if the people were hired chiefly because they would work for very little money. Wheelwright said no. "We had one criterion Din told me about first, and I think it was a good one. That was, 'I don't care what the people know if they're willing to work hard, and they consider it a pleasure to come here and work.'"[26] That was a principle that Land followed for the rest of his life.

One willing worker was Rogers, who stayed fifty years. Rogers was born in Michigan but was brought up largely in Brookline, Massachusetts. His father was an engineer who worked for the well-known consulting firm Stone and Webster. Graduating from Tabor Academy, the younger Rogers entered Harvard in 1933 and spent a year and a half there. In 1935, Stone and Webster "suddenly had only six months' work for my father," and Rogers felt that he had to drop out: "I wasn't getting enough out of college to want to work my way through. At that time, I decided what I really should have done was to start at MIT instead. So I thought I'd work a while and then save up a little and go to MIT. But I got so busy at Polaroid, that never happened."

Rogers's first job as a dropout was pumping gas at a filling station, where the work soon became monotonous. His brother Nickerson had been hired by Land-Wheelwright Laboratories after he met Wheelwright while skiing. Nick told Howard about the small company, and Rogers went to 168 Dartmouth Street for an interview.

Land took Rogers to the drugstore across the street for ice cream sodas. Rogers had the impression that Land "could see into my head. It was really a kind of interesting sensation of having your head briefly searched for content." But Land had a stronger reason to hire him: he already knew his background. According to Rogers, "His chief need was people whose background he knew, because he was worried about having ideas swiped by big companies."

With Land, Rogers was making ten dollars a week instead of twenty-five at the filling station, but he enjoyed "a job doing something with more variety . . . It looked like I would get a chance to learn some science and solve some problems." Rogers's father thought this was crazy, but he hadn't met Land. Half a century later, Howard Rogers and his wife attended a dinner for his class at Harvard, and he told the story to another couple at the table. The husband said that he, too, had been offered a job by Land. Rogers recalled, "But his father wouldn't let him take it. He said his father told him that Dr. Land didn't have any status—no funds and nothing but prospects."

Enrolled in Land's school of direct experience of science, Rogers soon was "messing with chemicals," which he continued to do for decades to come. "Almost every job I worked on involved chemistry as well as optics." He began by mixing some solids and liquids to make a cement for laminating disks of polarizer. The disks were used in demonstration kits for high school and college courses, which were becoming a small business for Land-Wheelwright Laboratories. As the most recently hired employee, he also swept up the offices. Conditions were not ideal. The basement windows, Rogers recalled, "opened onto the railroad tracks where there were steam trains running with lots of soot. Particularly in the summer it was hard to keep the soot out of the polarizing sheets."[27]

When Rogers started work, the enterprise had about twenty-five employees. Among them was Richard Kriebel. Land had met Kriebel when Land was trying to place a small advertisement for the educational kits in a scientific journal. Land hired him because of his skill with words. Later, Kriebel became secretary of the Polaroid Corporation and pushed many of Land's ideas about a rewarding work life for employees.

As Rogers saw it, Land trained people by asking them to do difficult things. Land wanted to make polarizing sheets with very small crystals of barium carbonate, the smaller the better. So Rogers should look in the chemical texts to see the different ways the compound was made. "I then tried out some of the ways that I had read about and saw what happened. That's the way it worked . . . With any new assignment which I didn't know anything about, I found out how to learn more about [it]. Every project taught me something new." After half a century, Rogers reflected, "There is still a lot I don't know."

Rogers suspected that he had more to learn from Land than from the specialists who also were hired in this period, such as the physicist Martin Grabau. Grabau was an educated naysayer, Wheelwright recalled: "Like all good Ph.D.'s he knew everything that would not work." Once, when visitors came to discuss the headlight program, Wheelwright overheard Grabau tell them, "You know these two boys are under my tutelage. I have to steer them straight and see that they get it right because they're just a couple of kids." Wheelwright was burned up. Grabau didn't last. According to Wheelwright, "He was a great guy. I liked him, but he didn't serve a useful purpose for us for very long."[28]

∞

The temptation to be absorbed by larger enterprises arose frequently at Land-Wheelwright. People both in universities and in industry were more interested in Land's knowledge of polarized light and his brilliance in solving problems than they were in his particular invention. They did not reckon with his determination to remain in control of his destiny.

The dean of Harvard Medical School, impressed by Land when he visited the medical school one day to work on a problem as a consultant, telephoned Wheelwright, assuming that the older man was in charge. The dean insisted that Land be released to work full time at the school: "He belongs here. He's just what we need, and he's wasting his time on all this stuff he describes to us." Land returned to the laboratory after the dean's telephone call. Joking and testing at the same time, Wheelwright said, "Din, I hear you want to go to work at the Medical School." Land shot back, "Jesus, George, don't let me go on a thing like that. Get me out of it."

The same thing happened, Wheelwright said, at General Electric. GE had connections with LOF, which made glass for GE headlights and wide sheeting for windshields. By spending a month at GE, Land got access to the equipment—equipment beyond his means—to make his polarizer in sheets six feet wide. When Land returned with a sheet of his polarizer six feet wide and ten feet long, Wheelwright teased him again: "The research department tells me you want to go there." Land replied, "It's terrible. There were 30 acres involved in what they called a small research program. There were about 15 men working there. We started at 8 o'clock every morning and we work until 4:30. Everything shuts down and turns off and you go home. You start the next day. You don't work Saturdays and Sundays. They keep taking me out and giving me drinks and introduce me to important people and say they need me to work for them."

Pursuing the courtship, William D. Coolidge, the head of GE's laboratories, came to Cambridge and had lunch with Land and Wheelwright in a cafeteria in Harvard Square. Only a few years afterward, Land was standing beside Coolidge in the Waldorf-Astoria Hotel in New York as a "National Modern Pioneer."

Yet another suitor was Kodak. After the contract for camera filters was signed late in 1934, the company proposed that Land and Wheelwright come to Rochester to run a laboratory, in the manner of Leopold Mannes and Leopold Godowsky, inventors of Kodachrome slide film. According to Wheelwright, Silver approved of the idea and came up from New York to Boston to work on the details of the arrangement. "They were going to take us over," Wheelwright recalled in 1978. "We were just about ready to sign. Then one of the vice presidents in charge of production said, 'These young men are too young to know their own mind . . . So we will assign their work for eight hours a day and then in their spare time they can do what they want to.' "[29]

Land never forgot his aversion to circumscribed and supervised industrial research. At the Harvard Business School in the fall of 1977, he told a classroom packed with businessmen holding their twenty-fifth reunion that they were the chief cause of America's difficulties in competing with Japan. This, he told them, was because they locked their laboratories at 4:30 on Friday afternoon.[30]

MARKETING

From their far-from-luxurious quarters, Land and his small band of co-workers sent sample after sample of polarizer to Kodak scientists and engineers. In the spring of 1934, after some months of demonstrations of stereo movies for theaters or homes, Kodak declared its definite interest. Four uses were evident: camera filters, shields at least one foot square for light sources, a means of lighting documents without glare, and viewing spectacles for three-dimensional amateur movies. On 28 April, Brown wrote Silver about a conference between Land and Fordyce Tuttle of Kodak's research department.

The latter two men discussed a contract for Kodak to buy filter material from Land while Kodak served as a general agent for other uses.[31] The first order shipped to Kodak for camera filters at the end of 1934 was for twenty-five thousand dollars' worth of polarizing sheet.

The young enterprise already had begun shipping small batches requested by scientists in industry and universities in the United States. and overseas. In July 1934 a scientist in the radio development department of Bell Telephone Laboratories in New York City bought four unmounted and five mounted sheets of polarizer for $250. The order went out on Friday, 3 August. Wheelwright noted in a letter to Silver on 9 August, "Din wanted the sale as it constituted 'reduction to practice.'" An inventor seeking a patent must not only prove that he was first with the conccept, but also show that he reduced it to practice.[32]

Kodak was also interested in the sunglass field. Tuttle apparently expected to go with Land to see officials of American Optical (AO) in Southbridge, Massachusetts, a leading sunglass company. Kodak discussed strategy. The glasses would be introduced first to the high-price market, and later to a mass market. In July 1934, Silver wrote Tuttle about a five-year contract whereby Kodak would buy no less than 60,000 square feet of sunglass material annually. For the minimum amount, the price would be 75 cents per square foot. The next 10,000 square feet would be sold for 70 cents, the next 10,000 for 65 cents, and amounts beyond that for 60 cents.[33]

Shortly afterward, Land decided not to turn over sunglasses to Kodak and saw AO officials alone. AO decided to use the polarizer in a technical field, ophthalmic instruments, and in the mass market of sunglasses. Land was delighted at the "rather prompt opportunity in the sunglass field to develop a market for many millions of pairs."[34] With the money from this, Land's fledgling enterprise could finance not only its research but also expand production facilities. To supply American Optical under a bigger contract signed in 1935, the polarizers were laminated to glass. Land had to figure out how to do this, first on flat lenses and later on curved ones.

The contact with AO became one of Land's favorite stories. On 27 July 1934, Land telegraphed Silver that he would soon see an "American Optical man" informally through John Toulmin, a friend of Wheelwright's, and asked urgently for advice on strategy, "particularly in light of Eastman letter." He was referring to Kodak's proposal for a relationship broader than one based on camera filters. That day, Silver wrote a letter beginning "Dear Ed," whose crisp tone assumed a more businesslike temperament than usually attributed to inventors.

Land should get AO to sketch out a business plan, Silver suggested. The price should start high and move down. What would be AO's inaugural price? How many pairs did AO expect to sell in the first year? What royalty could Land expect? How long would the glasses stay at a premium price? How many pairs of glasses would AO sell when they moved into the lower-price field? What advantages would flow from a tie-in with Kodak? And finally, what did AO think of a fixed-minimum contract, which Kodak had not said it would reject? Silver told Land that Kodak was talking about separate contracts for each use of the polarizers. Land should not yield the sunglass field to Kodak unless this produced a better deal, perhaps a better royalty in a non-sunglass field.[35]

At the end of July 1934, Land rented a room on the sunny side of the Copley Plaza Hotel, not far from his sooty laboratory. According to journalist Harland Manchester's account about ten years later, Land was "a dark-haired young man of twenty-five who looked as though he might be interested in tennis and dancing." His only luggage was a goldfish bowl with fish in it. He surprised the desk clerk by asking for a room on the sunny side. The account continued:

> After the bellboy had left, he placed the bowl on the window sill where it would catch the sun, stood back, inspected it, then moved it so that the reflected glare became more intense. Then he paced nervously and waited for a knock on the door. As soon as his visitor, an [unnamed] official of the American Optical Company, arrived, he led him to the window and asked him to look into the bowl. "Do you see any fish?" he said. The man squinted and shook his head. The reflection from the water was too dazzling. "Look again," said the young man, holding before the bowl what appeared to be a sheet of smoky cellophane. The glare was gone as if by magic, and every detail of the idling fish could be clearly seen. The visitor was convinced. He was familiar with every kind of sunglass on the market, but he had never seen anything like this.

As had happened hundreds of years before to Icelandic fishermen wielding pieces of calcite, the AO representative could see the fish distinctly and count them. Triumphantly, Land said that this was the material AO would use in its next line of sunglasses, and went off on his first vacation in years.[36]

Wheelwright knew George Wells of AO, who had been "one class ahead of me," and his brother John, who was in his class. On 7 August, Wheelwright had sent test samples, twenty-four pieces four inches square, to George Wells with the proviso that no samples were to leave AO's premises or be shown to outsiders. All samples, regardless of condition, were to be returned in two weeks. Wells wrote back the next day, promising that AO would not sneak a look at the chemical composition. Instead, AO would do its normal tests on "permanency" of the material and how it modified light from various sources. "Let me say again that we appreciate your courtesy and willingness to permit us to study this amazing sheeting."[37]

Reporting to Land-Wheelwright on 21 August, AO also sent back all the samples, including some that had been installed in goggles. AO regarded goggles as a valuable market, for seafarers, professional and amateur fishermen, civilian and military pilots, and drivers. The company concluded that the sunglass field should produce a "respectable volume" and the market in ophthalmic testing instruments would be "valuable." A modest market could also be developed for two-sheet variable-density windows for welding and other uses. The company even had suggestions for the automobile glare problem. "We are most definitely interested in this sheeting," Wells wrote, seeking a further meeting. On 27 August, Land and Toulmin met again, and Wells wrote Wheelwright the next day: "It is safe to say that we are definitely interested in the proposition." More test material went to American Optical on 23 October 1934.[38]

A few months later, in May 1935, AO heard from another enterprise in the polarizer field, that of the inventor Alvin Marks. His company was called Polarized Products. Land-Wheelwright already knew about Marks's enterprise: In March 1935, Nickerson Rogers had sent a telegram from 3 Perrin Road, Brookline, presumably his home, ordering two polarizing plates from Marks, eight millimeters square.

On 10 May, a Mr. Shuman, representing Polarized Products, called on H. R. Moulton, an engineer at American Optical, to demonstrate the Marks process. He had written a week earlier, acknowledging that the Marks material would require much more development before it could be used in spectacles. After the demonstration, Moulton wrote John Wells: "The efficiency of the process is nowhere near as high as the plates made by the Land-Wheelwright method."[39]

On 5 November 1935, AO signed the contract for the manufacture of Polaroid Day Glasses and began selling them in December 1936—just as a splashy polarizer exhibit featuring Land opened in New York. It was the usual Landian high-wire act. When the contract was signed, Land recalled some seven years later, "neither AO nor Polaroid knew how to laminate polarizers, but when we wrote the letters negotiating with AO, we thought we did." The first year, Land said, "we had to take back 75,000 pairs of sunglasses and rush through the building of the laminating machine." It was "the first automatic laminating machine in the world." It cost about $25 then to make a square foot of polarizing material, "put together really well enough to stick." With the new laminating machine, Land-Wheelwright supplied AO glasses with "a reasonably good frame." The inaugural price was $3.75 a pair, later reduced to $1.95. To Land this meant that "millions of people were able to have the security of [multi-layered, laminated] safety glass and the glare protection of polarization."[40]

The name of the synthetic sheet polarizing material had become polaroid. Land's friend and collaborator Clarence Kennedy, a Smith College art historian, coined it. A professor's more erudite suggestion of "epibolopole," Land and Kennedy had thought, "was a little heavy . . . Then Kennedy suddenly said, 'How about polaroid?' and that took immediately."[41]

∞

Kodak continued courting the young inventor in Boston, even while pressing him for delivery of the first sheeting. On 14 December 1934 Kodak's Tuttle wrote "Din" to ask authorization for Kodak to negotiate with a supply house, such as Central Scientific Company, to sell filters to schools and research workers. He reported also that Biggers, the president of Libby-Owens-Ford, had visited Kodak, and that Kodak's president, Frank W. Lovejoy, had directed Tuttle to show him Land's material. "From the conversation that took place after the display," Tuttle wrote, "I gather that both Dr. Lovejoy and Mr. Biggers think that your chances of success in the automobile field are very good."[42]

Land was already looking around for large supplies of plastic base. On 23 November 1934, DuPont Viscoloid Company of Arlington, New Jersey, wrote Land, in care of Silver's office in New York, that they would charge seventeen cents per square foot on an exclusive order for one million square feet of polarizing cellulose acetate sheeting, twenty inches wide and seven thousandths of an inch thick. Viscoloid could start delivery four months after the order.[43]

While negotiating with Kodak and many other companies to sell polarizer, Land-Wheelwright Laboratories was quite ready to discuss the outright sale of patents that might be valuable. In the 28 April letter, Brown told Silver that the Patent Office had approved a second "light valve" patent, and suggested that the light valve patents be offered to Eastman Kodak, General Electric, or "the radio companies."[44]

∞

In 1935, Land felt ready to send samples of his polarizer to Robert W. Wood, the scientist whose textbook had inspired him as a boy. Land recalled that within a year or two of his invention in the late 1920s, "I was able to make a rather respectable material but still not good enough to realize one of my fantasies, namely to send some to R.W. Wood, whom I had never met." He added: "By 1935, however, I did feel ready and I mailed two four-inch squares to him with a short note to explain that I sent the polarizers because of his book. He received them at his summer place in Southampton and wrote back a long letter saying he made himself a Bunsen photometer out there at the seashore and had measured the polarizers, calibrated them, found all their constants, and generally encouraged a continued relationship."

Many focused on Wood as a prankster, Land recalled, or a man caring only about the income from his books, or a distant person. But Land saw him differently. "Here, in our correspondence, I think you see a true test because neither of us knew each other. Ours was a communication through science and about science, and in that medium he was as warm, human, responsive, simple, and direct as a man could be."[45]

∞

Kodak kept testing the filter material from Land-Wheelwright. Each shipment represented a small victory in manufacturing. Wheelwright told Tuttle on 31 August that more sheeting was on the way: a dozen sheets 4 inches square, four sheets 16 inches by 20, and one sheet of 8 by 11 inches "as a sample of what might be done in cloudy material."[46] The tests went well enough that the terms of the first contract could be agreed upon in a meeting with Silver in New York on 10 November 1934. They became final on 30 November. By 5 December, Land was acknowledging Kodak's first check for $2,500. Kodak's research director, Mees, then pointed out that Kodak had many contacts in England through which Land could sell filters for the instrument trade. Mees would have known: George Eastman had bought the Wratten filter company in England in 1912 to procure Mees's services as Kodak's research director.

Land's later memory was that these were jaunty times. Late in 1942, he recalled that first order from Rochester:

> Eastman didn't know what [they] wanted to use them for, but they really thought we were awfully good fun, and we were such nice young fellows, and Eastman was selling $20 million, and what is an order for $10,000? So we got our order. We took the order before we had made anything we could sell to Eastman . . . After all, what was the use of making much if we hadn't sold it yet? So we had the order, and we had to go to work. Oh, we had made little samples, of course, but not something you could really supply Eastman Kodak with. We went to work and went into the laboratory. We had air mattresses on the floor in the lab, and had food sent in, and after working for 20 or 40 hours a man would fall down and we would slip a mattress under him as he fell . . .
>
> We had to build the machines and get the rolls going, and then turn out an awful lot of sheeting, out of which we were able to cut some . . . and send to Eastman. That was Bob Blake and Ernest [Calabro] and I and my wife, and George Wheelwright . . . We packed the whole thing in a small box which we carefully wrapped around in black tape and sent to Eastman Kodak and sent a bill for $5,000.[47]

On 27 December, Land wrote to "Ford" Tuttle that the first shipment—175 sheets of Grade A sheeting of three different densities, including ten one-foot squares—had been shipped by Railway Express. The 195 one-foot square sheets of Grade B material to be sent the next day had "discolored to some extent," and Land said that it was not good material "to standardize with." He suggested that he replace it a few weeks later with better material after a replating job was finished. He anxiously asked to be told the condition of the shipment when it arrived.[48]

On 3 January 1935, Tuttle wrote: "Dear Din, I received your precious shipment and turned it over to the laboratory. The material came through in good shape."[49] It was a triumphant moment. Land recalled, "The company was in business. We delivered in time."[50]

5

Going Public

> I feel badly, I feel I didn't accomplish what I intended to for him. I feel that I lost what I thought was a good relationship, and I don't know what I could have done. You have a short time on the stage. At least I was on the stage and did something.
>
> —George Wheelwright III

Land was ready to tell the world about his invention. Perhaps no publicity that a person or an enterprise gets is as important as the first. In January 1936, Land told the world that he had the material for controlling headlight glare and viewing 3-D movies. Two weeks after his first press release in Boston, he demonstrated the new material at the Waldorf-Astoria Hotel in New York. The event was covered in *The Christian Science Monitor, The New York Times,* and the *New York Herald Tribune* and across the country.[1]

In little more than a year thereafter, Land's fame spread among engineers and scientists. He spoke to a major congress of automotive engineers in White Sulphur Springs, West Virginia, and at the Franklin Institute in Philadelphia. To considerable fanfare, he opened an exhibition on light polarization at the New York Museum of Science and Industry. Land also received a medal from the Franklin Institute, which had been certifying the significance of American inventions for more than a century. It was a signal honor for the twenty-eight-year-old recipient, who was on the brink of being given absolute control of his own company for ten years by a blue-ribbon group of Wall Street investors.

Land, his partner Wheelwright, and his newly hired public relations assistant, Kriebel, played the game of public notice with the same finesse with which Land, his patent lawyer Brown, and his personal lawyer and business counselor Silver, had navigated the shoals of finance and big corporations. They were walking along traditional paths for innovators.

PUBLICIZING

The announcement in Boston may have been precipitated by a statement by an electrical engineer teaching astronomy and mathematics in Hartford Public High School that Land's glare-control material should be used in all cars. Land was in touch with the Hartford *Daily Times* right away. To be sure, he had set out deliberately ten years before to make glare-reducing headlights, but he had developed other applications and already had five patents in force. Kodak was making filters with the polarizer and American Optical was making sunglasses with it. The polarizer could be used in viewing 3-D movies and to provide apartment dwellers with windows that would cut down on neighbors' peeping.[2]

On 16 January 1936, Science Service's story reporting Land's first release gave this popular explanation of light polarizing: "The best way to understand the complicated phenomenon is to regard ordinary light vibrations as a mass of straws tossed up in a wind. They are blown against a picket fence. All straws are stopped except those which parallel the pickets and all straws coming through are lined up in one direction. Polaroid acts as the picket fence."[3]

The company's press release for the demonstration at the Waldorf-Astoria began immodestly: "Polaroid, a light-polarizing glass that solves a problem as old as science, was introduced to the public for the first time today." Reporter Herbert Nichols of *The Christian Science Monitor*, a college acquaintance of Land's, wrote up the demonstration that afternoon. The next morning, *The New York Times* said that glass equipped with the light polarizer "transforms motion pictures into a fairyland of substance and reality." The *Herald Tribune* spoke of a twenty-five-year-old "student" showing off "three rooms full of polarizing glass" with more than eight hundred commercial uses. The Herald Trib reporter spoke with H. I. Day of Electrical Research Products, a subsidiary of American Telephone and Telegraph, who attended the demonstration by invitation. Day was effusive: "We've been working with it in our laboratories for more than a year. It's everything he says it is, and more. There's no doubt that Land has solved a problem that every physicist working with light has struggled with for nearly a century."

Echoing phrases from pages 9 and 13 of the Land-Wheelwright press release, the *Herald Tribune* story succinctly explained that the new material "polarizes light by combing out its waves so that they vibrate in a single plane." It noted that the small, expensive natural polarizing crystals called Nicol prisms were used in only a few laboratories. "By making literally billions of minute synthetic crystals, and orienting them so that they lie in the same direction within the cellulose matrix, [Land] has produced the optical equivalent of a large single crystal," from material that was simple and cheap to make.[4]

The publicity rollout continued. By May, Wheelwright was demonstrating the viewing of 3-D movies to the Society of Motion Picture Engineers in the Hotel Pennsylvania. Although the audience gasped and clapped mildly, the *Herald Tribune* reported, the engineers were wondering how they could "distribute Polaroid spectacles to the 15,000,000 or 20,000,000 persons who go to film theaters every day," and how would the public take to wearing them? The answer would have to wait until the 1950s.[5]

On 2 June 1936, Land went to the semiannual meeting of the Society of Automotive Engineers in the resort and convention center of White Sulphur Springs. As he did so often, he asked his audience to suspend disbelief and imagine an ideal system. How close could one get? Ideally, headlights should be brighter than those in general use and spread their light up to half a mile ahead. And yet they should be barely visible to the driver of a car approaching in the opposite direction. If this could be achieved, Land imagined that "night driving would approach the comfort and safety of day driving." Auto traffic would spread more evenly over the twenty-four hours, and deaths and injuries would decrease.

Land-Wheelwright Laboratories issued two press releases, one focused on headlight glare, and the other on such additional uses of polaroid material as detecting flaws in glassware—including milk bottles for babies. They cited engineers' estimates that up to fifteen thousand American highway deaths were caused each year by nighttime headlight glare. No mention was made of the role of drunkenness. The releases also helpfully listed the numbers of the five patents already issued on the new material, the two licensees (Eastman Kodak and American Optical), and the New York address of the patent attorneys.[6]

Land established his usual practice of a scientific report alongside commercial announcements and demonstrations. At the Franklin Institute in Philadelphia, on 5 November 1936, Land gave the assembled scientists and engineers a homely example, which he called the rope trick. In the example, a jump rope is tied to a tree and run through a succession of picket-fence barriers, the third of which, closest to the tree, had horizontal pickets instead of the vertical ones of the first two. In a simple drawing, a person twirls the rope. The wave motions of the rope before the first picket fence describe a circle. Before the second barrier, the rope waves up and down in a vertical plane. But then the vertical waves in the rope reach the horizontal slats of the third barrier and cannot pass through. The picket fences represented polarizers. He said lightly, "The rope analogy is so simple that it gives a sense of comfort and understanding."

After presenting a charming, short intellectual history of polarizers, Land showed a large piece of polaroid sheeting and demonstrated how it was made. He held up an opaque mass of submicroscopic crystals in an elastic sheet. No light passed through the crowd of randomly oriented crystals. Then the sheet was stretched, which gradually oriented the crystals along the direction of the stretching. Light began to come through. With further stretching, the material became virtually transparent. Then a polarizer made earlier was rotated so that its axis crossed the axis of the newly made polarizer. The light faded as the polarizer turned and finally let no light through.[7] A stylized representation of this phenomenon became Polaroid Corporation's symbol.

The Franklin Institute's Committee on Science and the Arts got to work promptly on Case 3017 concerning the polarizer. It concluded that polaroid was "a contribution of the first order in applied optics." They called it "epoch-making in the field of illumination and color production." Land had contributed to the art and science of optics by his invention and development of polaroid into a commercial product. Consequently, on 14 April 1937, the Franklin Institute awarded him its Elliott Cresson Medal for 1938.[8] Although Land won many other distinctions in the years to come, the Cresson Medal was the first major recognition, and it came at a time when it counted. The formation of Polaroid Corporation was just a few months away.

∞

A member of the Harvard class of 1932, Herbert Nichols had begun reporting for *The Christian Science Monitor* in 1930 to help pay his way through Harvard. Forty years later, he guessed that he gave "Polaroid more publicity, time, and effort than any other reporter." After one of Land's talks, possibly the one in Philadelphia, Nichols had a memorable drive home with

Land. The weather was "miserable, no planes." And so, with Nichols driving, "we set out in an old Cadillac." Hours later, by the time they reached Connecticut, rain was freezing on the windshield. "The roads were slick as glass and I slowed down." But Land was in a hurry. "Dinny gave me a lecture on spinning wheels." Nichols pulled over. "Din, you take over." Land drove the rest of the way.

The next time the two were together was at a scientific meeting in Baltimore, where Land had been introduced by Robert W. Wood. "Din and I went along after breakfast," to see Wood's laboratory and his special machine for drawing extremely fine lines for spectrographic work. Wood's "ability to explain difficult problems in physics, so even I could understand them" impressed Nichols.

Nichols had almost thrown the first press release from Land-Wheelwright in the wastepaper basket. Seeing the reference to "one-way glass," he had harumphed to himself, "That's been known for years." But then he spotted the words "polarized light." He went looking for the little enterprise and found it down on Dartmouth Street. He wasn't much impressed, although the new material "did have possibilities, especially in the auto field." Looking up the patents, Nichols found that Chubb of Westinghouse Electric had the best chance of "maintaining a conflict" with Land. However, Land's rivals were "patenting an idea rather than a process."

At Dartmouth Street, the only one he found was Wheelwright, whom Nichols knew better than Land and who "had a wonderful mode of expression. He did sell me on the future of the materials." Nonetheless, when Nichols later had a chance to buy Polaroid Corporation shares at ten dollars, he passed it up because he expected that Land's company would have difficulty fending off rivals for patents and dealing with the big boys in Detroit.[9]

∞

Land and Wheelwright looked for any high-profile forum they could find. In November 1936, Science Service put on a sound and light show, a "Research Parade" at the National Academy of Sciences in Washington, D.C., to honor the centennial of the U.S. patent law of 1836. That law established the system of having examiners determine the originality of inventions. Among the speakers were Vladimir Zworykin, the inventor of the television tube, and Wood. Chubb and Wheelwright also spoke. Following Chubb, Wheelwright held up two disks of polaroid, "the new tool of science, which makes possible for the first time extensive polarizing areas." He put one in front of his face, and then held up the other. His face was visible.

Then he lined up the two disks so that their "optical slots" were parallel. His face was still visible. Then he rotated one disk until his face disappeared. As the spotlight faded from Wheelwright, the director of Science Service, Watson Davis, intoned from offstage: "You researchers in light, you have us vibrating in all planes. We are tingling with anticipation as to how the future will use the light you bring."[10]

The most glamorous demonstration occurred in December at the New York Museum of Science and Industry, which had opened in February 1936. The museum occupied the Forum Exhibition Hall of the recently constructed RCA Building at Rockefeller Center, in the heart of the communications and financial capital of the United States. The polarizer exhibit was called "Polaroid on Parade" and became semipermanent.

When the museum had opened, Waldemar Kaempffert of *The New York Times* wrote that it was a "real museum" instead of a "mausoleum." Now, "the common people could learn more about the operation of a steam engine or an electric generator from a cut-open specimen in five minutes than they could by poring over the diagrams of a textbook for a week." More than four hundred exhibits at the museum had moving parts or could be set in motion by visitors pressing a button, turning a crank, or pulling a lever. It was called the Museum of Motion.[11] In the same column, Kaempffert described Land's work with polarizers and noted the eightieth birthday of Frederick E. Ives, pioneer of halftone engravings and color printing—and also a winner of the Cresson Medal. Thirty years later, in 1966, Land won a medal named for Ives.

Nichols was at the preview on 10 December 1936. He may have had something to do with the polarizer exhibit. Thinking the museum was a good idea, Nichols talked with Marion Crawford, who was in charge of the museum's exhibits and publicity and was operating on a shoestring. Why go back into history? Nichols asked. Why not try ideas that were "just sprouting"? He suggested an exhibit on polarized light and told Crawford how to contact Land-Wheelwright.

The next thing Nichols knew, polarized light became the centerpiece of the museum, amid the automobiles, the steam engines, the pumps, and a Foucault pendulum. Just before the opening, Land continued his highly successful courtship of the science press with a small party that welcomed, besides Nichols, Kaempffert, and William L. Laurence of *The Times*, John O'Neill of the *Herald Tribune*, Howard Blakeslee of the Associated Press, Gobind Behari Lal of the Hearst newspapers, Thomas Henry of *The Washington Star*, and perhaps David Dietz of Scripps Howard Newspapers. Several of these writers were founders of the National Association of Science Writers and had shared a Pulitzer prize for their coverage of Harvard's 1936 tercentenary celebration, an event that focused on science.[12]

Felix M. Warburg, vice president of the museum, opened the preview. Besides Land, the speakers were Wood; George B. Wells, the president of American Optical; Adolph Stuber, assistant vice president of Kodak; and M. H. Eisenhart, president of Bausch and Lomb Optical Company. The exhibits and demonstrations touted the polarizer in Machine Age style, calling it "the latest tool of science in the conquest of light." The star exhibit was nonglare headlights. Also shown were "selective" sunglasses and what were billed as the "world's first three dimensional movies in full color." Visitors also could see uses of polaroid material in microscopy, highlight control in photography, and color decorations. Tony Sarg moved his "polaroid marionettes" between two strips of polaroid, one at the back of the stage, one in the foreground, so that the puppet characters acted in a constantly changing color setting. Nichols recalled the marionettes dancing in polarized light, "acting and reacting on cellophane all crumpled up."

An accompanying news release quoted Professor Wood: "Polaroid is the most significant invention in the field of optics, certainly within the last generation, probably in the last century."[13] The day after the preview, in a story accompanied by four photographs, Nichols reported that Land was called "the originator of an invention to be ranked with that of the electric light, lens systems, and color dyes." In the ebullience of the moment, Land described how he had done some of his earliest work on polarizers, without saying where. He needed to use some very precise instruments, whose use was restricted to people of recognized skill, and he wasn't on the list: "The solution to this problem lay in the fact that the window of the eighth-story hallway and the window of the physics laboratory were always left unlatched. It was only necessary to pass around the coping from one to the other, and then, since the instruments were kept in a locked cabinet, it sufficed to remove the hinges and get to work on measurements. Then the entire process was carefully reversed."[14] The context in the article suggested that this happened at Harvard. It actually happened earlier, at Columbia University.

Also impressed by the exhibit was a reporter for *The Literary Digest*, a news magazine. Although *The Digest* knew that the affair was elaborately orchestrated, it used two publicity photos by Roy J. Jacoby of Boston, both of which had been used the previous March with an article by Nichols. The article gave this description:

> Stepping into Museum exhibition-rooms in swank Rockefeller Center, the visitor sees a pair of powerful automobile headlights focused down on him from the mezzanine. Blinking from their glare, he steps over to a glass wind-shield, stares through it at the lights. Abruptly the glaring headlights vanish, [and] become twin purple discs, faintly discernible. Suspicious of trickery, the visitor pops his head around the wind-shield frame, [and] discovers the headlights still burning brilliantly, pops back again and tries to figure by what magic a pane of glass can filter the deadliness from so overpowering a dazzle.
>
> The wind-shield is not the simple bit of glass it appears to be. Worker of the optical miracle is a thin, transparent material laminated between two panes of glass. It is called Polaroid and possesses the crystalline property of polarizing light. Polarized light, as lecturers make clear to visitors, is light whose waves move in a single directional plane. Ordinary light is an undisciplined hotchpotch of waves vibrating in all directions.

The new polarizer could be used in movies, sunglasses, stage effects, beauty parlors, laboratories, and photography.[15] This was an attractive range for investors, including Jimmy Warburg, cousin of the museum's vice president, many of whom were preparing to take a flier in high technology with Polaroid.

FINANCING

While Polarized Lights struggled to make batches of its polarizing material, the growing Land-Wheelwright enterprise was being transformed into Polaroid Corporation. The contracts with Kodak and American Optical had helped keep the wolf from the door, but Wheelwright's resources were near their limits. Money was short. In 1936, Land-Wheelwright received an invitation to attend a scientific meeting in England. Since Land was then a hesitant public speaker, Silver and Wheelwright decided that Wheelwright should go over.

During the visit, Wheelwright showed polarizing material to people in the automobile industry, including the Lucas Company, a maker of headlights, and demonstrated the polarizer at test tracks. He impressed a British minister of transport, who, unfortunately, soon took another post. On this or another visit to England in 1936–37, Wheelwright talked to two Norwegians, who invested twenty-five thousand dollars in Land-Wheelwright. Decades later, Wheelwright recalled the two as "watchdogs": "They lifted all the new ideas. And if they thought they were good, they would take it away from you." The Norwegians got the right to sell headlights and lamps and sunglasses.[16]

In 1936, after the first public demonstrations, Wheelwright approached J. P. "Jack" Morgan in New York, who had known his father in college. At an interview in July, attended by a "scared stiff" Land, Morgan was fascinated but claimed that he was too old for such a venture. According to Wheelwright, Morgan put out the word to "people like Kuhn, Loeb, the banking firm that made a specialty of backing Jews with real talent." Morgan asked Land and Wheelwright to do some research on "penetrating fog on ships, because trans-Atlantic crossings made him so nervous."[17]

Perhaps through Morgan's intervention, the banker James P. Warburg was drawn more seriously into what became Polaroid Corporation than he had been with Henry C. Everett's proposal of a buyout of Land-Wheelwright and Polarized Lights in March 1936. Warburg was perhaps the most active intelligence among the investors who bet on Land and the Polaroid Corporation in 1937. Jimmy Warburg was the brilliant and restless son of Paul Warburg, who was not only the German-born architect of the U.S. Federal Reserve System but also its most notable historian. The younger Warburg came from a background infinitely more privileged than Land's, but the two were similar in pushing aside their Jewish heritage, in taking delight in the technical facts of a business, and in fearless dealings with the mighty. In later years, Warburg expressed pride in the success of his Polaroid investment and his ability to rein in some of Land's wilder ideas.[18]

Jimmy Warburg probably became fully engaged with the prospects for Polaroid Corporation at the December 1936 show in Rockefeller Center. Apparently, Silver took advantage of the hoopla in New York to introduce Land to Warburg and Bernard Baruch, one of the best-publicized titans of Wall Street. Warburg in turn introduced Land to his old friend Averell Harriman, the railroad mogul and later ambassador and governor. These valuable introductions compensated for the show's being overshadowed by the news of the abdication of Britain's King Edward VIII in order to marry Mrs. Simpson.[19]

∞

As Wall Street's interest rose, Land and Wheelwright needed to think about their respective shares in the enterprise. Silver told Wheelwright that he should get a lawyer, but the lawyers he retained insisted that Wheelwright should get more than 50 percent. In each interview on the matter, Silver grew more distant. One idea floated earlier was that Wheelwright might take 100 percent of the movie possibilities. Wheelwright had rejected this indignantly: "No. Din and I didn't enter it this way." Neither man had foreseen carving up domains.

Wheelwright asked Silver to represent him as well as Land. Silver said, "George, I can't be your lawyer. I'm Din's lawyer." Wheelwright replied, "Look, you guys get along beautifully; you understand one another; you understand a lot more about things going on than I do. I don't see why we can't come to an amicable settlement and you be the judge of it and you run it." Silver replied, "They never do things this way." Wheelwright remembered his response as, "I don't give a damn." Had he done things the way the money boys do things, he would never have left Harvard and started a lab.

With Silver's help and Wheelwright's almost breathtaking trustfulness, Land and Wheelwright agreed that despite Wheelwright's large original investment, the split of ownership between the two should be 90 percent Land and 10 percent Wheelwright. Forty years later, Otto Wolff told Wheelwright that he remembered the day that Wheelwright said, "Otto, I've been offered 10 percent. What do you think about it?" Wolff thought his answer had been, "If this thing ever amounts to anything at all, 10 percent is going to be a damn good cut." Wheelwright's memory of Silver was "Julie has always been fair with me, has always told me what's going on. Things went quite smoothly."[20]

Warburg joined with Harriman; the two investment firms, Schroder Rockefeller and Kuhn, Loeb; and others in giving Land a remarkable vote of confidence. The financial arrangements for the fifty-employee enterprise, to be known as Polaroid Corporation, called for a total commitment of $750,000, of which $375,000 would be paid right away. This gave the new company a cushion of several years for finding new and larger markets. Moreover, the governance was simple: Land received complete control for ten years. The agreement was embodied in a contract on 10 August 1937.

Land, his wife, and Wheelwright transferred to the new corporation all patents, patent applications, and other interests in the development of the polarizers. The total was valued at $132,627, that is, the estimated total cost of development up to August 1937. Land agreed to sign a ten-year employment contract. The new company had three kinds of stock: common and two classes of preferred. After the completion of arrangements with the backers, the common stock holdings of the Lands and Wheelwright amounted to about 50 percent of the total. The real instrument of control until September 1947, however, was the Voting Trust. By the agreement of the Lands, Wheelwright, and all the investors, 71,500 shares of common stock were placed in the trust, which had three trustees, Land, Wheelwright, and Julius Silver. The greatest of these three was Land. Silver and Wheelwright could not act without his approval, and he could fire either or both of them.

The company took out a $500,000 life insurance policy on Land. His salary for 1938 was $6,000 a year, considerably above the $2,000 that Wheelwright had paid him, but far below the $15,000 specified in his employment contract for the first three years. It rose to $12,875 in 1941; $17,500 in 1943; and $25,000 in 1944. In 1943, after selling some of their shares, the Lands still had 41,265 shares of common, and Wheelwright 4,366 ½.[21]

The next brick in the structure was buying out Polarized Lights. Chubb's little company continued to soldier on while Polaroid Corporation was being established. The Patent Office had finally granted Chubb a patent, number 2,087,795, on his application of 1920. Polaroid promptly sued to overturn Chubb's new patent. Brown's bill of complaint, signed by Wheelwright, bristled with references as far back as the early nineteenth century to prove that Chubb's invention was not original.[22]

The antagonists continued to meet. On Thursday, 7 October 1937, Robert A. Smith of Polarized Lights went to the Kuhn, Loeb office at 52 William Street in New York to see Land, at first by himself and then with one of Land's new investors, Lewis L. Strauss, who had been a partner in Kuhn, Loeb since 1929. Smith was impressed: "Land seems to be the fair haired boy. . . . K. L. have provided several hundreds of thousands of dollars for the new company. Straus[s] says Land is in control without strings. Straus[s] seems to be interested only in the auto end of it and I doubt if he'd be in it if he didn't expect the auto end to go . . . [I] think they both realize the desirability of get[ting] together and the control of the whole when all grouped together. They didn't faint at our [royalty] figures per car."[23]

Strauss was a shrewd, though far less privileged, investor than Warburg. Interested in photography and science, Strauss was involved with the affairs of the Institute for Advanced Study in Princeton. His acquaintance with physicists widened after his parents' deaths from cancer led him to look for cheaper sources of radiation than radium. In his memoirs, he recalled his early enthusiasm for the polarizer: "The worth of this idea and the true genius of Land impressed me at once, a fact of which I am proud."[24] Land was, he wrote later, one of his guests at a dinner late in 1938 for the great Italian physicist Enrico Fermi.[25] Later Strauss went on to become chairman of the Atomic Energy Commission, and the nemesis of J. Robert Oppenheimer. Fond of inventors, he knew R.W. Wood and helped introduce the two musician-chemists, Leopold Mannes and Leopold Godowsky, to George Eastman and Kenneth Mees, Kodak's research director. Strauss lent ten thousand dollars for the early stages of their project.

In such successes, near misses, and failures, Strauss had learned the ins and outs of patenting, including patents with "nuisance value."[26] Chubb's patents and the others held by Polarized Lights had a bit more than "nuisance value" in determining the commercial prospects of Polaroid Corporation. Strauss plunged into the negotiations with Smith. On 15 December, Strauss dropped a bombshell. The patents of Polarized Lights had shrunk to mere nuisance value, he told Smith. Land was inventing his way around the new Chubb patent and others. Chubb's patents were built on light polarized in planes, whereas Land's new system involved circular polarization.

At once, Smith warned his colleague Chubb that compromise was preferable to obstinacy. According to Smith, "Our desires should not outrun common sense calculations."[27] Two days later, meeting Warburg and Land, Smith was impressed with Land's new system. Land had "wonderful results" and gave "very frank and full answers . . . to my questions." The new system for polarizing headlights put much more light on the road than had the previous one. Kodak had tried the system and found it workable and practicable. The material was beyond the laboratory stage and could be made as thin as four thousandths of an inch and as thick as a quarter of an inch. Smith pressed Chubb for a list of questions to ask Land, and warned, "In the meantime, the negotiations are stalled. Perhaps you don't worry about this stalling, but I do. The time to close a sale is when it is ready. . . . I can't imagine you want these negotiations to fail."[28]

Talking again with Smith, Strauss told him that the Patent Office had written to say that issuance of Chubb's patent the previous July had been a mistake. A patent attorney told a shocked Chubb that such a letter was contrary to Patent Office practice. Smith insisted that Chubb provide a list of technical questions about Land's system. Sending them, Chubb observed acidly: "From what you have told us, it sounds as though he has made some very clever advances in the art and I must say I cannot reconcile some of the statements which were made with the customary theory of light." He told his associates that "we are being 'hooked' to go ahead on the present basis."[29] But the next day, Chubb said that his own new tests made "Land's application look very much better."[30] Smith had spent half his time for six years on polarized headlights. He wrote Chubb and Frank Short an exasperated handwritten letter on 5 January:

> I'll admit I'm not quite so free in feeling Land is a liar. It is quite evident that he has in the past been evasive, but he was not evasive with me on 12/17, and I'm quite free and willing to admit he is a very capable inventor, and with a very extensive knowledge of polarizing art. You apparently want to club the disclosure out of him while he still has to consider us enemies. He [Land] still thinks L. W. C. is as much of a crook as L. W. C. thinks E. H. L. to be. I know neither is a crook, and have so told both of you. Given time, you'll both realize it.[31]

It was time for Chubb to accept a buyout. Listing seven different aspects of the system, Smith commented: "Polarized Light[s] did not have a commercial system for any of these until Land's film became known to us. I use commercial in the sense of low-priced, efficient, convenient, and easily adopted on a large scale." In Smith's opinion, Land had not "copied or followed" Polarized Lights on three of the seven systems, that is, those for cars and "multiple oriented dichroic crystals." Land had commercialized dichroic film and colloidal film, as well as uses in sunglasses, cameras, reading lights, movies, microscopes, and other applications, including the new advance in circular polarization. He also possessed a "profitable business, effective laboratory, commercial advertising organization, and ample financing."

Neither side "can proceed without a fight by the other," Smith said. Any step forward by auto companies would be impossible during a patent fight. Strauss wanted a compromise. Land did too, but had to balance the pro-compromise views of Brown, Strauss, and Warburg against those of his senior adviser, Silver. As Smith observed, "E. H. L. controls." A DuPont official had told Smith that Polarized Lights patents largely controlled the system, and Land's company the materials. With this in mind, Smith concluded that the partners in Polarized Lights should get 15 percent, that is, fifteen thousand shares of Polaroid common, and a payment of fifty thousand dollars for rights to the patents.[32] The counteroffer from Polaroid was about half this, in which the principals of Polarized Lights would get cash payments totaling twenty-five thousand dollars and seven thousand shares of Polaroid stock, to be divided among them. Polaroid Lights agreed. The deal closed on 7 March 1938. Lewis Chubb, Jr., went to work for Polaroid, continuing the development of antiglare systems for automobiles.

∞

Settling the ownership did not solve the problem of Wheelwright's role in the new corporation. He was a salaried vice president and a major stockholder—and a fifth wheel. With 3-D movies receding into the future, he gave most of his attention to selling sunglasses. His position was becoming less central, and he began to think that a rival was breaking into his files and underplaying his contributions. His association began to wind down. It wasn't so much fun anymore.

The Wall Street people regarded Land and Wheelwright as babes in the woods, as far as business was concerned: they needed supervision. Near the time of the second payment of $375,000 by the backers, Carlton P. Fuller was dispatched from Schroder Rockefeller to serve as the principal financial officer. Described by one employee as "a charming, sensitive, wise man," Fuller stayed on for many years, managing some technical operations as well as finances. He grew rich on his Polaroid stock. Wheelwright bristled at the idea of a nanny from Wall Street. Forty years after Fuller came aboard, Wheelwright still fumed at the idea: "But we didn't want to do it their way! I mean, after all, why were we where we were?"

Wheelwright's reports did not go straight to Land, as they were supposed to. His scientific interests were in the dim past. He saw very little of Land. Looking back, Wheelwright remembered Land's "guts," his readiness to bet everything on making something work. "I wouldn't have missed the years I had doing that. My life wouldn't have been half as full or interesting." But, Wheelwright added, "I feel badly, I feel that I didn't accomplish what I intended to for him. I feel that I lost what I thought was a good relationship, and I don't know what I could have done. You have a short time on the stage. At least I was on the stage and did something."

One day, Clarence Kennedy, who collaborated with Land and Wheelwright on three-dimensional photography, saw Wheelwright looking unhappy and asked what the trouble was. Wheelwright answered, "I'm not very happy right now. I don't feel close to Din, [able to] be with him and be able to tell him things." Kennedy told him, "Look, George—a man like Land—if you get one act out of a show . . . you've had all you can expect. You've had it and so have I." Land's influence on those around him was beginning to sound monarchical.

Wheelwright was working long hours and losing sleep and weight. Was there anything wrong medically? His brother's judgment was this: "The only thing wrong with you is that you've run way beyond your limit, and you've got to get away from what you're doing." The brother sent him off for six weeks in the California Sierras. During this time, Wheelwright decided that it was time to talk to Land. Wheelwright recalled, "I called him up and we spent, I think it was, two or three days. It was a very emotional scene. He begged me not to leave." But Wheelwright felt emotionally spent and thought his departure would be "for the good of the company."[33] He went off to the Navy for World War II, married again and happily, and made a success of his ranch in Muir Beach on the beautiful Pacific coast north of San Francisco.[34]

∞

The Wall Street investors soon received loud indications that they were betting on a winner. One was the installation of "variable density" windows on the observation rail car "Copper King," of the Union Pacific streamliner *City of Los Angeles*. Polaroid investor Harriman owned Union Pacific. Tourists, business travelers, as well as "Hollywood royalty—the transcontinentals, the smart set, Senators, and tycoons"—could watch the landscape roll by through one of twenty-nine round windows, each twenty-seven inches across. Each had two double panes with polarizers placed between the glass sheets; the outer pane was fixed and the inner rotated by a knob. For maximum light, the polarized panes would be lined up so that the tiny lines within, like the pickets of the picket fence in Land's demonstration, were parallel. Compared to an ordinary train window, the view was already slightly darkened because all polarizers absorbed some light. To change the amount of light coming in, all the "Copper King" passenger had to do was rotate the inner pane at a slight angle to the outer. According to one account, "the overall brightness of the sky is reduced, and details of the scenery, no longer glare-struck, become much clearer." If the polarizer within the inner pane was at right angles to the outer, no light came through at all. It was fun. One account said, "People not only understood but enjoyed it."

Polarizers were not limited to demonstrations for elite travelers. They also played a dramatic role at the New York World's Fair of 1939–40, which was visited by millions and lived on in cultural memory as a climactic expression of technological enthusiasm. Some five million people visited the Chrysler Corporation pavilion at the fair. A centerpiece of Chrysler's exhibit was a twelve-minute film, "In Tune with Tomorrow." Shot by John

A. Norling, the pioneer of commercial 3-D films, the movie combined sequences along an assembly line with a fantasy animation showing parts of a Plymouth car assembling themselves. One account spoke of "fascination and sometimes alarm" in the audience as they saw "wheels and springs and pistons [that] seemed to be moving in thin air, out beyond the screen, somewhere just out of reach of the bespectacled viewers." Major Bowes, the famous host of the "Amateur Hour" radio program, was the narrator, and he appeared in a live-action sequence, the first in 3-D movies. Polaroid Corporation supplied the spectacles that each of the millions of visitors wore to see the movie, in black-and-white in 1939 and in color in 1940.[35]

Also in 1940, Land received one of the most striking of the legitimating honors he later attracted so frequently. He was named a National Modern Pioneer by the National Association of Manufacturers. The association was honoring innovators to observe the 150th anniversary of the first U. S. patent law. The ceremonies had at least two other not-so-incidental purposes: to attack the New Deal tenet that new technology killed jobs, and to build up public sentiment against changing the patent laws, as New Dealers sought to do.

The key to being a Modern Pioneer was putting new knowledge to use. Karl T. Compton, president of the Massachusetts Institute of Technology since 1930, headed the committee to select the winners. Of about 1,000 who were nominated in a national survey, 572 were chosen to be honored in regional dinners in fourteen cities, including Boston. On the snowy evening of 20 February 1940, Land was one of 28 regional winners honored at a huge dinner in the Copley Plaza Hotel.[36] Just over a week later, on 28 February, he was the youngest of 18 individual national winners. For them, there was a banquet for 1,500 people in the Waldorf-Astoria in New York. It was just four years after Land's first polarizer demonstration in that same hotel.

Land's youth and strikingly handsome appearance made him the "star" of next day's stories. In *The New York Times,* Land, in black tie evening dress, appeared in a photo with William D. Coolidge of GE, another winner, in white tie and tails.[37] A group picture used in such newspapers as the Cleveland *Plain Dealer* and the *Buffalo News* showed Land front and center, next to Coolidge. Also in the front row were Willis Carrier, the pioneer in air conditioning; Harry Steenbock of the University of Wisconsin, who developed the process of adding vitamin D to milk by irradiation with light; George Curme of Carbide and Carbon Chemicals, discoverer of such hydrocarbon compounds as vinyl resins and Prestone antifreeze; the Nobel prize winner Irving Langmuir of the GE Laboratory; and Vladimir Zworykin of RCA, inventor of the iconoscope television tube. In the back row, in white tie, stood Edwin Howard Armstrong, inventor and relentless pioneer of frequency-modulated radio. Almost forty years later, Land and Zworykin would be inducted together into the National Inventors' Hall of Fame.[38]

In the pictures, Land appeared delighted to be there and quite comfortable in such company. He and the other winners, all men, were holding large plaques designed by the sculptor René Chambellan. On the plaque, a male inventor in what looks like a laboratory coat holds up a lamp of knowledge whose rays stretch out to airplanes, factories, chemical retorts, and dynamos. On the left, the leaves of time push downward on the long-past tools of pioneering, the ox team and the covered wagon. The slogan reads "Pioneers Build America." A scroll presented to Land honored him for "distinguished achievement in the field of science and invention which has advanced the American standard of living."[39]

Very soon, the anguish and danger and urgency of World War II would provide more immediate justifications for American science and invention.

6

Headlight Glare

> Intelligent men in groups are as a rule stupid, and the very intelligent men in the automobile industry were fantastically and simply stupid. . . . Individually, you will find no brighter people . . . I've sat with them. . . . They are delightful, bright, alert, responsive, share the same ideals that we do. Helpless to do anything decent in the group.
>
> —Edwin H. Land, addressing Polaroid employees, 25 June 1958[1]

From the moment the idea hit him as he walked on a New York street, Land was dedicated to making a polarizer that could allow every car in America to cast a brighter light at night and yet not dazzle the eyes of an oncoming driver. The idea, as Land described it more than thirty years later, was to enable people "to drive at night with great comfort and serenity and without getting tired, without having your pupil contracting and expanding, without that sense of being pushed into the ditch."[2] As we have seen, the well-publicized hope of this was the main spur behind the financing of Polaroid Corporation. The headlight glare problem was the subject of some of Land's very first contacts with the laboratories of major industries. The young man made a deep impression.

At the age of twenty-three, Land made his first visit to the research department of General Motors near Detroit. It was even before he had taken his second leave of absence from Harvard. GM, led by Alfred Sloan, was seizing leadership of the mass production of automobiles, America's leading industry, from Henry Ford. The public was turning away from the pioneer who offered the customer any car he or she wanted as long as it was black. People favored GM's newly evolved concept of many models, with a range of prices and features that changed each year.

Heading GM's research was the legendary Charles Kettering, inventor of the self-starter, which replaced the crank, saved numerous drivers from broken arms, and opened the door wider to women as drivers. Kettering thought big. When, with Land, he was honored at the Modern Pioneers dinner in 1940, he spoke by telephone from his laboratory in Coral Gables, Florida, on the topic "Pioneering Never Ceases": Kettering said,"We have only scratched the surface of invention . . . America is not yet finished."[3]

∞

In 1931, Silver made the first move for Land to the automobile manufacturer by writing J. H. Hunt of the electrical division of GM's research department. The letter did not go to Michigan but rather to a General Motors office at Broadway and Fifty-seventh Street in New York. Silver had seen Hunt's article, "Automobile Headlights," in the April 1925 issue of *Transactions of the American Institute of Electrical Engineers*. The article reviewed efforts to control glare. Now, Silver proposed that Hunt look at the work of "a client who has developed a practical method of solving the problem by means of polarized light."

Hunt was sure to want details about the material Land was making. "Its two absorption coefficients are substantially constant throughout most of the visible spectrum," Silver wrote, "so that the sheets are practically colorless." These thin sheets had an efficiency that compared favorably with Nicol prisms and transcended limits on previous antiglare schemes. Using Land's material, the "analyzing windshield is crossed with the polarizing headlight." Even through the windshield the driver could still see the road because its rough surface partly depolarized the light of the headlights.

The demonstration would require a personal meeting, Silver wrote: "We have only a few samples and we do not care to risk the loss of them by sending them through the mails. The inventor is engaged in research at Harvard University and cannot, at this time, make additional samples other than those in our possession. If you have occasion to come to New York City, in connection with other affairs, we wish you could stop in to see the samples of the product in our possession."[4]

Evidently, Hunt became interested. Silver and he continued to correspond about a meeting. On 11 March 1932, Hunt asked five questions: (1) What were the polarizer's mechanical properties? (2) How much non-polarized light did it let through? (3) How much light overall did it transmit? (4) What happened as it aged? and (5) What did it cost?[5] On 19 March, Silver replied: "The material is mechanically similar to celluloid and has approximately the same weight, and also has the same mechanical strength." The amount of nonpolarized light transmitted varied between 3 and 6 percent "as desired for any particular application." The transmission coefficient was 93 percent of the desired kind of light, and 5 percent of the undesired. The aging was slight and thus similar to that of celluloid. "The original specimens are several years old and are unaltered to date."

Silver acknowledged that the cost was three cents per square foot, more than that of celluloid, but added, "The potential source of supply is extensive." The strong, flexible, and practically colorless sheets could be made in any desired size. Again he asked Hunt to stop by in New York.[5]

Instead, Land and Silver visited Kettering's GM research center in Detroit on Monday, 11 July 1932. It was the bottom of the Depression, little more than a week after Franklin Roosevelt had been nominated for president in Chicago. About two weeks later, President Hoover would suffer a political disaster when soldiers drove the bedraggled Bonus Army from its huts and tents on Anacostia Flats in Washington, D.C.

Land and Silver's visit was a triumph that the young inventor promptly wrote up in a memorandum.[6] He and Silver arrived in Detroit and telephoned a Mr. Richards. As he was out, an assistant, a Mr. Marshall, could see them. At the plant, Marshall took them to see Mr. Folge, head of the Lighting Research Department. Land asked if Folge "was familiar with the general problem of glare elimination by polarization." Folge replied that they had done some work on it. Land then showed him and Marshall some samples of the polarizer. They "were very much impressed and seemed unconcerned about residual imperfections such as dust, striations, and bubbles." Land also demonstrated the use of his polarizer for controlling glare from highways during the daytime.

Land and Silver had their foot in the door. Folge appeared to "grasp all the possibilities immediately" and took Land and Silver further into the sanctum of research. The lighting research room was about sixty yards long, with every surface painted "optical black." At each end were several sets of headlights pointing toward those opposite. Next to one group of headlights was an array of graphic designs and license plates. Three engineers stood behind one group of headlights to test how much the glare of the opposite group "destroyed the details of the background carrying the licenses and designs."

To get maximum glare, the GM engineers had taken out the ordinary glass lens and tilted the headlights' reflectors so that the headlight beams pointed right at the eyes of the observers at the other end of the room. Land recorded, "They then covered one of the glaring headlights with a large sheet of polarizer and observed this headlight through a second polarizer held to their eyes" at the far end of the room. The glare disappeared. Now, as a GM engineer pointed out, the previously invisible background was easily seen. According to Land, this success occurred "in spite of the dust and the striations."

Then Silver and Folge drew apart, perhaps to discuss business, while the engineers tried a second test. They put an additional strip of polarizer over the first on the previously glaring headlight. "The light went out almost entirely, leaving only a faintly purplish glow." Then they tried out a sheet of Land's polarizer on a gauge that happened to be in the room, which tested strains in metals and other materials. Its large black polarizing mirror aimed a beam of polarized light through the samples and into a Nicol prism. They put Land's polarizer sheet directly on a test lens. "The circular strains in the lens appeared vividly."

In the next room, Land and the engineers viewed a polarizer composed of several piles of glass plates. The supplier had specially selected each plate. From a theoretical paper in 1880 by Pickering, the GM engineers had concluded that the plates transmitted 40 percent of the light falling on them. Their twenty-three-year-old visitor said that Pickering's paper was inadequate for these calculations, "because the calculations are based on the assumption of infinitely perfect transmitters." The glass plates did not transmit 100 percent of the light. Land said they should look in Wood's textbook, where Wood described a paper by Stokes "which does take into account the losses by absorption in the glass." The engineers admitted that they hadn't expected the glass plates to be practical for use in cars. They just wanted to keep learning what they could until, someday, they could "obtain such a polarizer as [Land] now presented to them."

Land pointed out a further problem. The stacked glass plates would polarize light, to be sure, but for drivers to see the road ahead, the roads would have to be made of material that would de-polarize enough light from the cars' lamps. This did not happen very well with the common black macadam surface. "With sheets such as I now showed to them, it was plainly possible to have the polarizing axis of both windshield and headlight polarizers parallel to each other, both being 45 degrees to the horizontal. The idea seemed to interest them a great deal; and the engineer to whom I happened to explain it spent a great deal of time explaining it to the rest of them." It was a workable scheme to control glare for drivers and yet allow them to see the road surface.

What about the leftover light from the headlamps in his polarizing system? the engineers asked Land. He replied that it could be bluish or gray. And these colors could be put to use. With the lights labeled with the letters L or R, oncoming motorists could tell a two-headlight car from a one-headlight motorcycle.

Then Hunt arrived. Land knew him as chairman of the General Motors Committee on Investigation of New Devices and the author of the 1925 paper. Hunt "seemed to appreciate the whole situation immediately, and at first seemed to take the new polarizer for granted; but he seemed to be in a great hurry, asked some cursory questions about whether the degree of extinction was proportional simply to the angle or to the square of the angle from ninety (90) degree crossing."

Hunt went with the group for lunch at a large table in the cafeteria. Folge asked Land whether the polarizer could be used in plastics other than celluloid, such as gelatin or Bakelite (the invention of Leo Hendrik Baekeland, a National Modern Pioneer of 1940). Land told him he preferred celluloid, but for patent protection purposes he also had made polarizers with balsam and litho varnish. Water could not be used as the solvent for the plastic. His charts showed them how dyes could remove the residual color in the polarizer without affecting the apparent brilliance.

Leaving the table, Hunt asked them all to meet in his office twenty minutes later. Land and the others continued talking about color and techniques of laminating polarizers to glass. When they reached Hunt's office, Land noticed that Hunt "had become very genial, evidently because of some behind-the-scene discussion with Folge, who seemed quite anxious to obtain the product, if it survived their rigorous experimental period." Folge recognized that the system would require larger headlight bulbs and more powerful generators than before, to make up for the light blocked by the polarizer if not for brighter illumination of the road. Hunt, however, "was not particularly concerned about these details." Apparently, Folge felt that "General Motors could introduce such changes readily."

Late in the afternoon, Land and Silver returned to Folge's office. They were to wait for Kettering himself. The Boss had been alerted. When Kettering arrived, "he was fully familiar with the problem, was satisfied that polarization was an ideal solution, was at first troubled by legislative difficulties; but later, in great good humor, suggested a number of ways around them." Kettering said that years earlier, he had called for help from Wood at Johns Hopkins and on Mees at Eastman Kodak. Mees had sent Kettering "some small polarizing screens of some organic material that could not withstand the heat of the headlight."

Kettering started asking questions. Would celluloid polarizers in windshields discolor and grow hazy with age? He sent for specimens of shatterproof glass that had arrived in India yellow and hazy, even though they had never been taken out of the packing case. The specimens had not even been exposed to the light, which was usually blamed for the deterioration of celluloid. Was the cause long, slow changes of temperature? Land replied that the polarizer need not be placed between the panes of shatterproof glass, whose introduction GM was opposing in any case. The polarizer could be put in a visor in front of the driver, and folded up against the roof except when needed. Folge appeared to agree with Land that this would protect against deterioration.

Could lead glass or glass that was opaque to so-called actinic rays preserve the celluloid? A GM engineer said that special glass was costly and a great deal of glass was wasted in making windshields. There was strong economic pressure to use ordinary window glass.

Kettering then began describing "in broad outline" a "magneto-optic analyzer" he had just heard of. Land told him how the method had first been used by Abraham and Lemoine, next by Beans and Allison, and finally by Allison and his pupils. Using this new instrument, Allison and the students had discovered an element. Land closed his report: "It was by then long after closing time and we adjourned, agreeing to meet Hunt the next morning" for a nontechnical conversation. Armed with a material that worked, Land had gone from a flunky to the top man in a few hours.

∞

The relationship with GM deepened. On 9 October 1932, Land exuberantly telegraphed Silver: "Arrived Detroit Friday evening[.] Saw Folge and John Little and Richardson. Equipping cars for demonstration here Monday night[.] Taking equipment to Anderson for demonstration Tuesday night. Folge say[s] J. L. Hunt very anxious to see demonstration and talk about royalty. I shall wire Monday saying whether they are ready for such discussion. Staying Statler. Probably leaving very early Tuesday."[7]

The same month, Land and Silver were in touch with E. I. duPont de Nemours and Company, America's dominant chemical firm, linked by ownership with GM, the dominant auto company. Officials of DuPont's

Viscaloid division, having heard rumors about Land's polarizer, talked with Hunt at GM—who scrupulously did not disclose what Land had shown him. Soon Viscaloid received a demonstration of Land's polarizer. Land was interested in DuPont as the supplier of the plastic base.[8]

Land did not yet know that the road ahead was twisted and full of potholes. It ended twenty years later in a washout. He did not succeed in putting his polarizer into motor vehicles. Rather than steal his invention, as Land's father had warned, the automobile manufacturers refused to use it, citing a host of difficulties. With great depth and cleverness, Land argued that these difficulties either were smaller than they were said to be or could be surmounted, but he argued in vain. Soon after the rejection in the late 1940s, divided, multilane highways with gentle curves and slopes spread over the United States in the greatest construction program in history. The highways often had trees or glare-reducing fences in the median strip. Drivers increasingly preferred the multilane roads. Headlight glare faded somewhat in importance for those trying to make driving safer. The focus shifted to speed limits and safety belts and better brakes, and the avoidance of drunken driving.

The ultimate lack of interest was a sad result for Land's youthful idealism, which had energized long years of perfecting the design and manufacture of polarizers. In an age that remained optimistic, it was ironic that failure, either rapid or long-delayed, remained the common lot of the inventor. Often, second-best technologies were adopted, or previous technologies hung on by adaptation. To fight the prospect of failure, Land made a string of further inventions; his advocacy became increasingly eloquent. With continued energy and cheerfulness, he turned to other things: inventions in the polarized light field and solutions to a host of military problems in World War II. The invention of instant photography, a sort of wartime hobby, was disclosed to the public just as the car companies were firmly deciding not to embark on polarizing headlights and windshields. By that time, in the late 1940s, Land was a practiced and confident inventor, aided by practiced and competent assistants. The long struggle over glare control for the nighttime driver did not wear down Land and his colleagues; it burnished them.

∞

The nighttime driving experience was already very different in the 1930s from what it had been in the early 1920s, when Land and a camp counselor, skylarking around the countryside, had almost run into a farmer's horse-drawn hay wagon because their headlights cast such a faint beam. The number of cars on American roads was increasing, even in the Depression, and along with it the number of miles driven. Cars were becoming more comfortable and more essential, but more and more riders and pedestrians were being killed, in cars and by them. Then, as now, the victims died chiefly in three types of collisions: when vehicles hit each other, when the vehicles struck some fixed object, or when they hit pedestrians such as those walking along the roadside.

In the 1930s, cars and buses and trucks had supplanted buggies, trams, and trains as the normal way to get around. Electricity was reaching the farm. Moving-picture dramas and comedies, with spoken dialogue and music, vividly showed millions of movie-goers every week the way prosperous people lived. Fueling people's wants, the movies in theaters operated alongside the radios at home, advertising new products, including cars, to vast audiences. As new car models emerged each year, new features were added, including more robust electric systems and brighter, unpolarized headlights. Some 650,000 miles of road had been paved. Will Rogers was wryly telling the Americans of the Depression that they were the first nation to go to the poorhouse in an automobile. As headlights grew brighter, new laws specified that drivers should dim them when they met cars approaching from the opposite direction.

But the driving experience kept changing. In the 1930s, most people drove on two-lane and, even more dangerously, three-lane highways to go out at night for a cooling drive, or an ice cream, or a trip to an air-conditioned movie house. The number of motor vehicles was less than 30 million. Sixty years later and now owning 180 million vehicles, Americans tend to stay home with television broadcasts and video tapes. They travel more than two trillion miles a year in very different conditions. The number of trips to the malls and jobs and children's scheduled activities has grown enormously. For local or long-distance trips in the 1930s, there were only a few divided "parkways," little roadside lighting, and many intersections governed by stop signs instead of traffic lights. After World War II, the multiplying Interstate highways limited the access by pedestrians, horses, and bicycles. Curves, grades, and roadside development also had limits. Intersections were fewer, and more were governed by traffic signals. The jumble of visual clues requiring a driver's alertness was lessened.

As a result, while Land advocated polarized light for nighttime safety on the road, he was trying to sell his invention to an automobile market that kept changing. His enterprise was tiny, and the people he was trying to convince were employees of some of the largest corporations that ever existed. Furthermore, those corporations were organized in a web of professional and technical associations that set standards for the whole industry. The vast automobile industry raised at least as many hurdles for a lone inventor to jump through as did the railroads of the nineteenth century. But Land worked through this system for twenty years.

The experience of the night driver was exasperating, and the exasperation lingered. It was a spur to Land's efforts. In 1947, he described it this way:

> When you meet a car on the highway at night, you play two parts. Because you have to see where you are going, you have to point a beam of light down the road with your headlights. The approaching driver has to do likewise. You are necessarily on the receiving end of his light beam. If you use ordinary natural light, there is only one thing you can do: you must compromise between your need to illuminate the road and your need not to illuminate, and blind, the driver who forms a part of the scene ahead. You can direct the beam a little away from the other car, deliberately avoid lighting up a part of the road that you would like to light up, to reduce somewhat the glare in the other driver's eyes. That compromise has been made in many ways, with great ingenuity. It has never been a comfortable compromise, or a safe one. You always come down to this: for safe night driving, each driver needs to put a powerful beam right where it will blind the other."[9]

A year later, Land sharpened the picture:

> [T]he night driver is faced with a constantly varying, but always substantial, hazard. At every meeting he is called upon to compromise between looking through the oncoming lights, watching the road center for possible sideswipe, or concentrating on the right edge to avoid the road shoulder, or a pedestrian. Guided only by his own instincts, he must decide on the correct moment to depress his lights [the optimum distance would be 1200 feet]. Thus each passing calls for concentration, judgment, and eventually some positive action on his part. The inevitable result is fatigue, annoyance, and discomfort.[10]

In both descriptions, Land referred to a compromise. Now if there was one thing that Edwin Land hated more than anything else, it was compromise. Who said it was impossible to reach an ideal solution?

Year after year, Land worked a treadmill of specifications. What needed to go on the headlamp? What should be the polarizer for the complementary device in front of the driver? Would it be installed in windshields or visors, or in spectacles that the driver would wear? Drivers needed "a highly efficient, highly transparent polarizer with very uniform orientation."

The automobile industry soon sped up the treadmill. The car makers sought a polarizer that could be laminated to the glass on the front of the headlight. Unfortunately, at this spot, wind and water and dust and sun would bombard the polarizer. Withstanding all these elements was a task of "almost unbelievable difficulty," Land commented. "Almost no other part of an automobile is required to have stability for the life of the automobile in the sense that it must remain absolutely unchanged."

The key issue was safety. Automobile paint, for example, did not weather well; after a few years, it grew dull or even faded. But this was not a hazard. With polarizers, the requirements were more stringent. To light up the road properly, the polarizers needed to let through as much light as possible. This was some 40 percent of the light emitted by the filament within the headlamp and bounced off the reflectors at the back. The polarizer must not deteriorate and begin letting through the components of the light that would severely annoy an oncoming driver. The undesired components must be kept below 0.1 percent. Land saw the requirement this way: "A polarizer on automobile headlights must start out on its career as a perfect optical device—and remain perfect for perhaps ten or fifteen years."

Perfect? The polarizer would have to stay perfect in Florida sunlight. The dyes in the polarizer would have to be much better than those used in clothing, such as "your necktie."[11] Later, Land wondered if the car companies weren't deliberately setting up a Herculean task. At the same time, the car companies wondered if Land, with his usual insistent optimism, wasn't sweeping difficulties under the rug.

With the 1940 models, the car companies again sped up the treadmill by introducing much brighter sealed-beam headlights. But Land kept up, as he later recalled:

> We set to work all over again—against the assurance of our friends in the plastics industry that there were no plastics capable of standing that range of temperature, and against our own certainty that there were no polarizing crystals that

> would stand that abuse, even if we found a plastic to embed them in. It took many months to arrive at a solution: a polarizer containing no crystals, made up of a plastic of a new kind. With this new polarizer perfected, we proceeded with the materials and devices for using it; the development of an adhesive for bonding it to the front of the lamp, the development of a coverglass that would protect the film without depolarizing the light; the design and testing of dozens of different viewers; and the combining of these developments into a matched system, adjusted for the slope of the windshields, and the use of safety glass. We had a great number of inventions to make and a new mass production process to perfect.[12]

To combat weathering, Land and Howard Rogers had invented the K sheet. The K sheet consisted largely of polyvinyl alcohol (PVA). Selective dehydration formed a special compound from some of the PVA, called polyvinylene. The new sheet radically restated the invention that had launched Land's career by moving completely away from the domain of iodine-containing crystals that to be oriented. The new plastics could absorb light selectively. A wide range of plastics, including cellulose, nylon, polyvinylidine chloride, and polyethylene, had "long-chain molecules that can be oriented." The molecular orientation could be accomplished by extension, that is, by Polaroid's now-classical technique of stretching.

The most valuable plastic was PVA, Land explained in 1948, "because it lends itself to high extension and because its simple and unique bond structure causes it to absorb dyes vigorously." Then the PVA could be treated specially. "[T]he most efficient and most stable of polarizers is made by forming, within the polyvinyl alcohol sheet, one of the simplest absorbing structures, polyvinylene." The polyvinylene was formed by what Land called catalytic dehydration. For the sheet to act as a wear-resistant polarizer, only about 1 percent of the PVA had to be converted into polyvinylene, a straight-chain polymer in which carbon-to-carbon double bonds gave "intense directional light absorption."[13]

As before, the main elements of Land's system were a polarizing layer that conformed to the curvature of the headlight lens and a viewer for the driver to look through to see the road ahead. The driver could choose from several viewers: a pair of spectacles, a visor, or the windshield. On each car, the transmission axes on both the headlights and the viewer would be parallel and set at an angle of about forty-five degrees to the road. Thus, for an oncoming car, its transmission axes would cross those of the first car at an angle of ninety degrees.

Land used National Safety Council data to determine that this system would work better than the standard clear-glass system. The safety council data calculated the safe stopping distance at the legally required headlight power. The safe stopping distance corresponded to how far the light would reach, the reaction speed of the driver, and the capacity of the brakes to stop the car without skidding. A 1935 car with "the old reflectors," putting out 10,000 units of what was called beam candlepower, could not stop safely above 35 miles per hour. The 1939 car's headlights would put out four times as much light and would have a maximum safe stopping speed of 48 miles per hour. In the 1940 cars, the new sealed-beam headlights would have six times the output of the 1935 car, and the safe stopping speed would be 50 miles per hour.

By December 1939, Land was sure that Polaroid had developed the "perfect" material to go with the new headlights. Together, the polarizers and headlights could "fully solve the problem of comfortable and safe seeing with headlights at night." Polarization was now "practical, technically and economically." The industrial committees and state regulators—the "bodies collaborating in headlight standardization"—could introduce the polarizer-based glare-reduction system.[14]

∞

In his enthusiasm for a radical solution to nighttime glare, Land envisioned a future when drivers would be "freed from the terror of blinding lights" and spread their driving more evenly over the twenty-four hours. Speaking to an audience of automotive engineers in 1936, Land foresaw "a greater number of safe and comfortable driving hours," and a saving of "perhaps as many" as 15,000 lives a year. "Night driving will become practically as safe and comfortable as daytime driving."[15]

He clearly exaggerated the importance of headlight glare in highway safety. The press release accompanying his talk to auto engineers also attributed 15,000 annual highway deaths to nighttime glare. To be sure, night driving was more perilous than daytime driving. In 1935, 14,620 people were killed in auto accidents between the hours of 6 A.M. and 6 P.M. During the twelve dark hours starting at 6 P.M., 21,480, almost 50 percent more, died. Of these, more than 5,000, or an average of 14 a night, died after midnight, when only 3 percent of the nation's cars were on the road. In the 1990s, with six times as many cars driving more miles per car per year, annual highway deaths were only slightly more than 20 percent above the levels of the mid-1930s.

A *New York Times* editorial in November 1936 was almost certainly spurred by Land's publicity campaign, which already had produced several stories in the paper. The piece said that figures were "too general" to conclude how many deaths must be attributed to "mere darkness" or to headlight glare. The editorial made a guess of 5,000 a year, only a third of Land's figure. Cars' electrical systems were delivering more power for brighter and brighter headlights. Each driver's safety thus depended even more on the courtesy of other drivers and on good inspections to maintain the headlights' aim that had been set at the factory. To be sure, *The Times* wrote, the beams could be polarized so that they could be still brighter, but this would call for "special lenses, windshields, or spectacles."[16]

As GM's interaction with DuPont showed, car companies were not the only parties to the vast transaction that Land was proposing. Lamp makers such as General Electric were potential allies. After all, Land was urging a whole new system of lighting, involving more bulbs, brighter bulbs, and higher power use. The potential for GE's alliance appeared in June 1936, at the very first professional society session Land addressed. Also speaking was Val J. Roper of the Nela Park engineering department of GE in Cleveland. Roper specialized in studying drivers' perceptions and reactions and how much light they needed to stop safely at various speeds. At first he found problems with Land's system, but gradually over the years, he saw ways around them.

Roper took the problem of nighttime glare seriously. His research with drivers told him that a car traveling at legal speeds at night, with the standard headlights and with the driver's vision affected by the glare from an oncoming car's headlights, could not stop safely in time to avoid hitting a dark object, say, a person in dark clothes walking along, or across, a country road. It took drivers "time to see," especially if they weren't expecting the obstacle. A particular problem was a person beyond the oncoming car.[17] Over the next few years, Roper refined his measurements, using the brighter, twenty-five-watt headlights being installed in cars of the late 1930s and the even brighter sealed-beam lights that became standard with the 1940 models.

Initially, Roper worried that the polarizer system gave back only a fraction of the original light reflected from the road ahead. The polarized lights would have to be much brighter, perhaps twenty times brighter, just to do as well as the twenty-five-watt lamps in general use. With the current brighter lamps giving drivers a longer view of obstacles and more time to stop safely, the lights proposed by Land-Wheelwright Laboratories might have to be sixty times brighter, using fifteen hundred watts of power. That would push up the electricity demand dramatically. Highway accidents and deaths at night, the period during which the death toll was rising, were much more frequent than in daylight, when the toll was falling. Roper feared that the states might rush to adopt the polarizer scheme as a "panacea." This fear was ironic, indeed, given the ultimate failure of Land's proposal.

Roper approved of Land's goal of making highways safer through reducing glare: "Mr. Land's paper deals, and not improperly, with the ideal. That is the way progress is made. But before we embark on a program of such vast proportions, we would be indeed imprudent if we do not carefully weigh all alternatives."

In Roper's opinion, the headlight systems of the late 1930s weren't bright enough for safety. But what could be done? One-way roads? He discounted these as "not practicable of general attainment in our generation." But what about two-beam headlights? Their aiming could be better controlled: oncoming drivers would not be blinded and each would see better down the right side of the road. The lamps could be maintained better, and safety organizations could educate drivers to use low beams in meeting approaching cars. Roper knew what he was talking about. Such improvements went into effect in 1940 with sealed-beam headlights.

Could Land's system be used anywhere but in the country? "Beams of a form and power meeting the requirements of the country highway would be too uncomfortable and hazardous for pedestrians in town and city." Furthermore, the high-powered lamps would be brighter than drivers needed to see their way in lighted cities. Because of many stops and starts and periods of slow driving, car batteries would experience "excessive drain."[18]

Despite the skepticism, Land's vision of glare-free roads at night was reaching the public as well as road-travel experts. The state highway regulators already were endorsing moves toward much brighter headlights. They put on pressure through their organization, the American Association of Motor Vehicle Administrators. To look into Land's ideas, the Automobile Manufacturers Association formed a committee whose members included such leaders as J. H. Hunt of GM. In an aggressive stance, the committee told the headlight makers, such as Westinghouse and GE: "We (the auto industry) have given you 80-mile-an-hour cars and you (the lighting industry) have not improved the lighting beyond that of 10 years ago, which is good for only 40 miles an hour or less—Let's see you get busy, and also make it simple."

∞

By September 1941, Polaroid's K sheet had made Val Roper of GE less of a skeptic. He told a meeting of lighting engineers about his many experiments at the GM Proving Grounds in Warren, Michigan: "The recent development of an entirely new polarizing material [the K sheet from Polaroid], which appears to be stable under conditions of use and can be readily applied to the outer surface of the headlamp lens, suggests a complete reappraisal of the problems and potentialities of polarized headlighting."

Roper's tests showed that the polarizers did not cut down on the driver's margin of safety. Admittedly, polarized lights had to be brighter and draw more power (probably 125 watts) than did the unpolarized. But in 1941 and afterward, Roper saw a reasonable way out. New cars should carry four lamps, two providing unpolarized low beams for use in town and along lighted roads, and the other two for a polarized high beam that could be used all the time in the country. There would be no need for dimming. Over the years of converting to the new system, drivers of cars with the polarized lights would need to switch to lower beams when they confronted older cars. Old-car drivers could buy polarized spectacles for protection, or even install auxiliary polarized lamps that could be run with their existing power supply.

Could such a conversion have any priority as America slid into World War II? Roper spoke three months before Pearl Harbor, but nine months after President Roosevelt had called for the United States to become "the arsenal of democracy" to sustain Britain's resistance to Hitler. Roper answered his question with another: "Would it not be in the interest of 'National Defense' to do everything which will facilitate 24-hour traffic movement and maximum safety?"[19]

Land's drumfire of publicity in the late 1930s kept up the pressure for work like Roper's. The arcane field of polarized light had to be made comprehensible to the public, the driving public. For this purpose, Land found a good platform in a highly favorable *Fortune* magazine article about Polaroid in September 1938. The article described polarizers at their best: "Instead of being blinded by glare, your eyes see only two luminous purple disks, flat as a couple of plates and not projecting any beams. And behind these you can actually make out the detail of the car's hood and fenders and even see the people in the front seat and the license plate. Glare has vanished."

Such a system worked perfectly on a flat road. To meet the greater difficulties of roads where the sides curved down from the middle, so-called high-crown roads, Polaroid had devised a second sheet to be laminated onto the first polarizer. The second sheet would increase the cost from three dollars per car to four dollars. *Fortune* was worried that the use of Polaroid filters would have to "be legislated at one swoop into headlights and windshields of every car on the U.S. highways, down to the lowliest jalopy." The obvious interim solution was to equip every car with a visor or sell glasses to every driver.[20]

Such publicity plainly eased Land's task in inducing car manufacturers to cooperate with lamp makers and state officials to study his antiglare system. The journalist Harland Manchester, an admirer of the polarization scheme, wrote in 1948 of Land's arrangement with the big companies:

> [Land's system] attracted such wide attention among automobile and traffic experts and informed motorists that manufacturers could not ignore it, but they wanted time to work out details before committing themselves. It was obvious that if the system were to be effective, it would have to be adopted simultaneously by the entire industry. So in 1939 the Automobile Manufacturers Association struck a bargain with Land. He would refrain from publicizing the glare-free lights, and they would cooperate in a thorough engineering job and come to a decision. This work was conducted jointly by the Association, the General Electric Company, and the Polaroid Corporation."[21]

As it turned out, all research on the antiglare project stopped for World War II, as did civilian car manufacturing. Arrangements for the future continued nevertheless. On 1 March 1944, Polaroid and the Automobile Manufacturers Association signed an agreement that covered what would happen if continued cooperation achieved a commercial antiglare system for motor-vehicle headlights. The agreement set forth schedules of prices and royalties. Interestingly, the agreement mentions rear-window polarizers, a sign that Polaroid and the car makers were looking at the problem of glare from behind as well as in front. If the licensed car companies made inventions that improved on one or more of the licensed patents, Polaroid would get a license to make it until three years after polarized headlight equipment appeared on more than 50 percent of American-made passenger cars. The patent licenses could be canceled if not used within eighteen months.[22]

Perhaps because the automobile manufacturers knew the power of Land's eloquence, publicity was very much on their minds as they were deciding to drop the polarizer anti-glare system. GM staged a demonstration in 1947 for the press at its Warren, Michigan, proving grounds. Two reporters, Herbert Nichols of *The Christian Science Monitor* and Manchester, recalled the demonstration indignantly.

Manchester considered the demonstration biased: "In a thirteen-hour program of lectures and demonstrations at Detroit, experts studied not only the dramatic advantages but every disadvantage in the proposed anti-glare system." Manchester endorsed the solutions that Roper and others had worked out long before. These included two polarizers-equipped high-beam lamps for open road driving in the country, and two lower-beam "city" lamps, that could also be used as fog and parking lights. Hence, drivers in both country and city would have to learn only a few new tricks, and country pedestrians could wear inexpensive polarizing glasses. To meet a GM objection that the polarized lamps gave no warning to cars approaching corners or the opposite sides of hills, Land had devised a simple solution: leaving a small opening at the top of the polarizer to emit two warning pencil beams of light. Manchester rejected GM objections that drivers of new and old cars would have to follow special rules in a five-year changeover period. Whenever new-car drivers met old cars, they would switch to the "city beam" just as they did in dimming their lights. For protection against glare, old-car drivers could buy two inexpensive polarizing visors. The price of the new equipment, thirty to eighty dollars per car, was the same as a good heater or radio.

Manchester ridiculed the car makers' assertion that the public was not demanding polarized headlights. "The lack of demand is hardly surprising, since the invention has been kept out of sight for nearly a decade, and then put back under wraps after being shown to only a handful of people." He suggested that the thrity-six polarizer-equipped cars, owned by automobile manufacturers, GE, and Polaroid, be sent around the country for public demonstrations.[23]

In 1972, Nichols recalled that he had ignored the invitation to Warren until Manchester called him to say that the auto makers were "about to do a snow job on it," inviting auto editors who mostly knew little about technology. Nichols did not remember any Polaroid representatives at the demonstration, which—despite much cold water thrown by the GM officials—struck him. "For two hours we rode around in various cars. We saw how the lights reacted coming uphill and downhill. We could see the driver in the other car. We could see people making [roadside] repairs even with headlights full on. The oncoming headlights had a purple glow, even though they had a higher candlepower." Nichols "listened to the spiel. They just sold it down the river. . . . The principal argument by GM against [the polarizer system] was that there was no proof whatever that glare was a problem on the highways." Most journalists there focused on this point, Nichols said. "This was the big play: the headlight problem was very much overrated." He and Manchester were the only reporters to "write praising the system and advising the state safety directors to take notice and bring it about."

GM's attitude was simple, Nichols felt. "They just didn't need anything to sell automobiles. They realized they could sell all the automobiles they could make" after the five-year hiatus of the war.[24]

∞

After the war, despite the gathering clouds of disapproval in Detroit, Roper kept working. He focused on what the car makers said was the big problem: the years of transition when polarized headlights and viewers would be installed on all new cars but most older cars would lack the equipment. What would happen when the driver of a polarized-headlight car approached a car that still used unpolarized sealed-beam lamps? Roper said that "with proper usage, the driver of the polarized car on the average will be able to see somewhat further during the transition period—as compared to present conditions—and the driver of the sealed beam car on the average will be about as well off as at present."

In 1947, a third of the cars on the road still used headlights from the era before sealed beam. Comparing the nighttime seeing for sealed-beam and pre-sealed-beam cars, Roper estimated that "the range of seeing distances encountered during the period of transition to polarized headlighting would be no greater" than the range of seeing distances many drivers of old and new cars were experiencing just after the war. On 10 November 1947, Roper gave his opinion to the state motor vehicle regulators, and less than a month after that, before the twenty-seventh annual meeting of the Highway Research Board of the National Research Council. Both meetings were the subject of brief articles in *The New York Times*. The Highway Research Board also heard from Land and Hunt. Land was optimistic, Hunt the opposite.[25]

By then, the car companies had definitely decided to turn down the polarizer idea once and for all. To do this, they referred the matter to the state motor vehicle regulators, recommending "against the adoption of polarized headlighting at this time." The presentations to the board were not quite an appeal to a higher court, because the car companies already had made their decision. But the board included professors of highway engineering and representatives of drivers, road builders, and state highway commissions.

Hunt said, in effect, "You can't get there from here." The full benefits of the system would come only when all cars were equipped with the polarizers. Unfortunately, there was no quick way to convert some thirty million old cars for "universal rural use." The period of "mixed use" would be long. This would disappoint those who had paid for the new system. "Careless or discourteous" drivers of older cars could not only buy visors to protect themselves against the bright new polarized lights, but also use their high beams when they encountered the new polarizer-equipped cars. There would be as many careless or discourteous users of the new polarizer system as there had been since 1940 with the drivers of sealed-beam cars, "and just as hard to control through police power as at present." Glare would continue to be a problem, and some states might repeal permissive legislation for the polarizer system, thus causing problems not only for interstate driving but also for selling mass-produced cars. The problem with warning drivers as they approached corners or hilltops was not solved.[26]

Land was indignant at this catalog of potential difficulties. He agreed with the car makers that glare reduction could not be complete without every car using the proposed polarizer system. But he turned one of the car makers' arguments on its head. Most roads were not perfectly level and straight. In situations with curves in a road and a slight three-degree slope, a sealed-beam car using low beams could blind an oncoming car with a 20,000-candlepower beam. On a straight road with only one degree of pitch, one sealed-beam car could throw 40,000 candlepower into the eyes of an oncoming driver.

The polarizer-system headlights generally provided drivers a clearer picture of distant objects than did the sealed-beam system, Land said. Polaroid headlights, which appeared to polarizer-equipped oncoming drivers about 1/250 the brightness of a sealed-beam upper and 1/7 that of the lower beam, provided a "visibility distance" in Roper's definition of 400 feet when two approaching cars were 200 feet apart. With sealed-beam uppers, the figure was 175 feet, and with lowers it was around 200.

The polarizer system also abolished what Land called the "blind driving zone." When two sealed-beam cars approached each other, each driver had a zone to the right of the approaching headlights where dark obstacles could not be seen. "All of us, as we drive at night, habitually drive into this zone on faith, hoping there is no obstacle in the road, but with a sense of hazard and insecurity." In such a situation, "you cannot see a dark obstacle at sufficient distance to permit you to make an emergency stop." Pedestrians would obviously be safer with the polarizer system.

The transition problem was overblown, in Land's opinion. Headlight strength had been rising since the invention of the automobile, as the technology changed from oil to acetylene, acetylene to early incandescent lamps in increasing variety, and then from the bulb-and-reflector lamps to the sealed-beam. Each period had been one in which "the driver of the old car has been placed at somewhat of a disadvantage facing the lights of a new car." Introducing the new system would "bring about approximately the same step-up in maximum beam candlepower that we have experienced since 1940 when the sealed beam was introduced." It was easy to learn to use the new system, and the hazards from misuse or discourtesy were no greater than with sealed-beam headlights. As for the cost of introducing more powerful generators, the car companies had managed it without trouble in 1934, when power increased 50 percent, and in 1940, when the power demand went up another 25 percent. The polarizers in the new system would probably cost two dollars by themselves and, by the 1944 licensing agreement, would be available from several competing manufacturers.

In the period of transition, minor disadvantages would probably be canceled out by minor advantages. Among the advantages Land saw were these: "[T]he viewer appears to clear up a dirty windshield. When it rains, the viewer removes the scintillation from the drops on the windshield. On wet pavements, the system eliminates most of the glaring reflections from the oncoming car's lights." He repeated his old idea that in a glare-free world, many drivers would choose the less congested traffic of nighttime and thus make traffic flows more even.

Land was confronting the eternal dilemma of the innovator:

> If you will look back over the history of important new improvements that we now take for granted in our day-to-day life, you will find, I believe, that each was introduced for obvious and overwhelming reasons, but that at the same time each of these improvements presented a number of minor disadvantages which may have seemed significant at the time but which we have now come to disregard. You will also find that the minor disadvantages have been balanced by a number of minor advantages to which little attention was given when the improvement was introduced. If pressed, I am sure we could all point out a

> number of disadvantages of such overwhelming improvements as the telephone, the electric light, or even the automobile. All of us could at the same time point out a great many advantages of these improvements beyond the obvious ones.

To Land, "the most feasible method of introduction is to build the equipment into all new cars on a certain date, and make universally available viewers for removing the glare from the new headlights." He was confident that the system was ready. In 1951, he told colleagues in the Optical Society of America, "We have available for the system polarizers of such stability and high efficiency that little would be gained by making them better." The polarizing headlamps GE had developed, three times as powerful as current headlights, would deliver 50 percent more light.[27]

He objected to the car companies' top-down delaying strategy. They had asked the state regulators' help in resolving "nationwide problems of introduction" and indicated to them "their readiness to consider proceeding if the public shows sufficient interest in glare elimination." Land told the board, "Not Polaroid, not the automotive industry, not the vehicle administrators, not even your group alone should presume to arrange this program; but all of us working together can arouse the public to an awareness of the remarkable fact that a practical means for eliminating glare is now available."

In this tangle, Land detected an ironic obstacle to the introduction of the glare-reduction system: a lack of incentive. He thought this lack of a profit motive was what killed the project. Normally, a company like Polaroid would develop an improvement such as safety glass or the automatic transmission and then sell it to one car company that was searching for competitive advantage and profit under the free-enterprise system. Most improvements in American cars had come because the profit motive had "brought them from the laboratory, through the troubles and expenses of introduction to final use by the public." With the antiglare system, however, this typical advantage would only arise when two cars from the same company encountered each other on the road at night. Land had to acknowledge one part of Detroit's assertions: "To be fully effective, it should be built into new cars of all makes at the same time. But if this is done the competitive advantage is again removed."[28] After all the cooperation among private companies, highway glare reduction turned out to be a job for agencies representing the public.

Land's words were eloquent, but had no effect. He was distressed that the car industry would not apply the "full power and experience" that would have "readily solved" the problems of full-scale adoption. Many years later, in 1981, Land came to a simpler explanation of why the automobile companies rejected the "perfect" polarizers that had "passed all the tests." He believed that the car industry was "cautious then about doing anything that was interesting and exciting."[29]

In 1974, he spelled out other reasons behind the car manufacturers' caution: "When the idea came to maturity, the automobile companies were not economically motivated, because they could sell all the cars they wanted. It was a complete solution to a technological problem, but the changeover would have involved a large undertaking. Some features of our proposed system that were then called objectionable, like the use of four front lamps, are now common practice—and interest in the idea, by the way, is far from dead."[30]

Perhaps Land had been unwise to agree to cool off his publicity offensive in return for industry cooperation. The silence may have resulted in apathy, which the polarized-light expert William A. Shurcliff, writing in the 1960s, thought was the "main cause" of the failure.[31] One could argue that Land could have made almost as vivid a case for polarized headlights in the late 1930s as he did in 1947 and, through the impact of publicity, forced the car companies to adopt his system. But in the late 1930s, Land had barely formed his company. Although its capital was augmented in 1937 after it had acquired powerful friends on Wall Street, Polaroid was a tiny new-technology start-up. Land and Polaroid had learned a lot in the intervening years of war service and the invention of one-step photography.

Perhaps the greatest lesson was this: Sell to the public, not to a small coterie of big-company engineers. Drawing the lesson in 1974, he remarked, "I knew then that I would never go into a commercial field that put a barrier between us and the customer. I didn't set out to make money but to get the polarizer used. It would have saved 400 lives a night."[32] Twenty years of hopes were disappointed. But inventor and company were ready to move on.

7

Three Dimensions

> The shooting of the two images is being done today with hair-splitting precision, and there are now available lenses that interlock to perfection. One big studio has done a Technicolor 3-D movie of "Kiss Me, Kate," which is painless, rounded, and has the effect of whisking the audience into the most privileged seat of a live theatre. Judging from the couple of reels I saw, I should say that the test of 3-D will be the public reception of this film.
>
> —Alistair Cooke, August 1953

For Edwin Land's eightieth birthday tea on 7 May 1989, in the archive room of the Rowland Institute for Science, menus on thick gray paper with ragged edges listed several Italian dishes prepared by a nearby restaurant. The cover photo also had an Italian theme. It showed a fanciful ascension of urns and columns into which the fifteenth-century sculptor Desiderio da Settignano had set a bowl, brimming over with fruits and leaves. The photo had been taken in 1929 by Land's friend, art historian Clarence Kennedy, using his low-contrast time-exposure methods. The scene was in the Tabernacle of the Sacrament of the sober, gray church of San Lorenzo in Florence. Though lacking deep shadows, the image still had an unusual three-dimensional quality.[1]

The prints from Kennedy's negative, specially made sixty years later at the Rowland Institute for Science, recalled some of Land's oldest preoccupations. One was the viewing of three-dimensional images, still or moving. Another was photography as an intersection of science and art. A third was converting scientific insights into businesses that would affect many people.

The idea of showing people two images instead of one, to give the impression of depth in a three-dimensional world, went into practice soon after the invention of photography swept across the world in the 1840s. It was then that Sir David Brewster invented the type of stereoscope viewer that had enchanted Land as a boy. The stereoscope, like all its successor devices, was based on the fact that human beings, like many other creatures, use two eyes a few inches apart to perceive shape and distance. To achieve a stereo effect with two-dimensional film, one took two photographic images of the same object or scene from different vantage points, usually about as far apart as two human eyes. For stereo movies, two cameras would be lashed together, with their lenses a few inches apart. Their film would be exposed and projected in synchrony.

But how could one see the films? Would customers peep into a box as they had for the earliest movies, or could they wear spectacles and sit back to watch a big screen? The cheap plastic polarizer that Land invented opened the door to inexpensive glasses that customers all over a large theater could use. The filtering action of the polarizers assured that each eye would see only the picture shot by one of the two movie cameras. Each of the two projectors would have a polarizing filter, one for the right eye, the other for the left.

Three-dimensional movies, like television, were a technological possibility in the air when the youthful Land was struggling to make an important invention in the field of light. Just then sound movies were coming in and the first television images were being sent over telephone lines. He soon became more excited about using polarizers to conquer headlight glare, but the idea of movies with a sense of depth never left him.

By the late 1920s, viewing objects stereoscopically had become an obsession with Kennedy, a teacher at Smith College since 1916. Kennedy became important to Land as a scout for some of the very capable young women who joined Land's laboratory, as a collaborator on three-dimensional images, and, more deeply, as a fellow spirit who understood the importance of art in science and science in art. Kennedy spent years in museums and chilly, ill-lit Italian churches, building his huge collection of photographs of Renaissance sculpture, which he donated to Din and Terre Land when he retired from Smith in 1960.[2] The collection was for teaching. He wanted a method to project the images in stereo, to give students the impression of depth.

Born in Philadelphia in 1892, Kennedy received degrees in both architecture and art history from the University of Pennsylvania. He joined the art department at Smith while working on his doctoral degree at Harvard. As a Harvard Fellow at the American School for Classical Studies in Athens, he became interested in photographing works of art. In the 1920s, he went on to make photographs for the catalogs of the Boston Museum of Fine Arts and the Frick and Widener collections, and to start his work in Italy.[3]

Kennedy knew that teachers of art history lacked good photographs of sculpture. Many pre-Kennedy photographs, a cataloger wrote in 1965, "were not faithful to the original. They were either so poor technically that they were of little value, or they distorted the form with harsh or incorrect lighting." Many lesser-known works had not been photographed at all.

In Florence, many monuments had never been cleaned or photographed in detail. Somehow Kennedy got permission to clean them, and he did so painstakingly. He had an eye for what the sculptor wanted to achieve with location, lighting, and color, and this governed his selection of backgrounds, lighting, camera angles, and juxtaposition of forms. The cataloger of Kennedy's collection described some of the challenges: "He was not just a technician on assignment. He worked under extremely adverse conditions, which included skeptical curators, slow film emulsions, cumbersome equipment, and poor facilities. Most of the sculpture was photographed on location, so he had to devise all his own backgrounds and reflectors. Exposures were extremely long, even 24 hours, and during this time he would constantly rearrange his lighting to bring out forms hidden in shadow."[4]

Kennedy's knowledge of Italian sculpture was highly respected. In 1939, the Italian government allowed masterpieces by Michelangelo, Donatello, Della Robbia, and others to be brought temporarily to the United States for exhibition. The Museum of Modern Art in New York was the last stop on the tour. As he had been at the Palace of Fine Arts in San Francisco, Kennedy was the consultant to the New York museum when it showed the collection to 250,000 visitors over two months. His particular concern was "modeling with light." An admiring co-worker said that Kennedy wanted objects lighted "so that their universally acknowledged beauty and power would be evident even to the casual observer. Such lighting results had not been achieved previously."[5]

Early in March 1934, Kennedy wrote from Smith to the Carnegie Corporation of New York that "something very important has happened." He had run into Land and his partner, George Wheelwright. After learning of their existence from someone named Ives, presumably Herbert, son of the photographic pioneer Frederick Ives, Kennedy obtained their address from Kodak's research department. On 22 March 1934, the "two young inventors, who have their laboratory in Boston, gave me, on my own machines here at the College, a convincing demonstration of the practicality of studying from stereo-projections on a screen."

Kennedy asked to use their method and materials in a lecture to fellow art historians a few days later. This would be the first demonstration of polarizers as viewers of twin images. Land and Wheelwright worried about how well it would go, Kennedy reported. Nevertheless the men agreed: "For the moment they are disposed to permit it and to assist me in setting up the apparatus on the basis that it would be a more or less informal try-out that would not have embarrassing reverberations in the commercial world."

The commercial possibilities were very much on Land's and Wheelwright's minds. Kennedy noted that "by good fortune, the material which has enabled them to cut the knot is not, I take it, inherently expensive, and I broke into their midst just as they were engaged in a carefully planned campaign to sell the idea, in so far as it could be applied to moving pictures, to some cinema director, with, very properly, visions of gold in their eyes."

Wheelwright and Land told Kennedy that he had been "far more critical and demanding in what I asked them to achieve than the movie czars, who asked to be impressed, with pomp and ceremony, rather than persuaded." Kennedy was exhilarated. "My instinct tells me that after doing a lot of tacking in uncharted waters I have at last headed the ship in the right direction."

Kennedy's Carnegie-sponsored project would take a new direction.[6] With "innocent and simple" polarizing glasses, a few students could study the images together "on a small and perfect screen" and discuss them. They could take notes and refer to them. Later that year, Kennedy discussed the idea of hiring Land as a consultant on the project for an annual fee of three thousand dollars and soon did so. In January 1935, the art historian reported that "I have been in almost continuous consultation with Mr. Land, and as a result a great many things are moving rapidly."[7]

Kennedy described the work in what Wheelwright called the "big talk" at a meeting in Boston. He wore ill-fitting, rented "full dress" as he introduced Land to the audience. Wheelwright recalled, "I don't know which one was more nervous."[8]

∞

Probably also in 1934, Wheelwright and Land went to see Kenneth Mees, Kodak's research director, about 3-D movies, which were then more Wheelwright's department than Land's. The inventors brought about fifteen minutes of footage. Mees reassured them that Kodak never saw inventors without being sure they had patents, as Land and Wheelwright did, so there could be no question that Kodak was trying to steal the invention: "We will see anybody who has an idea. We just ask them, please, to have patents before they come."

Mees told his visitors, "I don't want to see the movies because I understand the principle: what I want to see is the material you're doing it with." When Wheelwright took out "those little disks" of polarizing plastic and showed them to Mees, the latter said, "That's all I need to know." He summoned leading Kodak men from around the world who happened to be in Rochester attending a meeting on the deep, worldwide Depression. He told Wheelwright that he could have two men and any cameras or projectors he needed. For the next three mornings and afternoons, Wheelwright recalled, he showed the movies to a stream of Kodak people. When one or both projectors gave out, Wheelwright would "rush out" to a Kodak technician, "and we'd clamp two new ones together." Noting that he had exhibited the invention to people from all over the world, Wheelwright was "absolutely overwhelmed with the enormity of this thing."

Kodak was interested in several uses for Land's polarizer, including the photographic filters the company began buying later in 1934. But movies also interested Kodak. They wanted Land and Wheelwright, together or alone, to come to Rochester to run their own lab, the way Mannes and Godowsky had done with Kodachrome. The two young men said no.

Because Wheelwright refused to work separately from Land, the Kodak people made a proposal. If Wheelwright would put his test films on the train at Back Bay Station in Boston at 4:30 P.M., the Kodak laboratories in Rochester would develop them and get them back to Boston about twenty-four hours later. Wheelwright said that he would need a lot of film, five thousand feet, which meant ten thousand feet for the two cameras. Kodak supplied film and developed it, without charge, over the next two years. But Kodak never got into 3-D movies. "They never used them," Wheelwright said. "They didn't know what to do with them."[9] Presumably Kodak did not see an early market for 3-D home movies. For Kodak, it was just another of hundreds of might-have-beens.

∞

The contact with Kennedy continued. In June 1935, a representative of the Carnegie Corporation traveled to Smith College and reported, "The slides so far made indicate a real use. Mr. Kennedy and Mr. Land are experimenting with the best way to show them. One way would be to set them up in boxes in a dark room in a museum for individual inspection." It was still difficult to avoid distortion when projecting 3-D slides for a large classroom of students. But the method clearly could be adapted to color slides. Polarized light would also be good for reducing glare from paintings in galleries.[10]

Kennedy, like many of Land's associates in the decades ahead, found various ways to make himself useful as a consultant to Land's company and remained a lifelong friend of Land and his wife. He was the co-designer of the first model of Polaroid's polarizing, glare-reducing desk lamp, which bore a strong resemblance to the classical lamp with green glass on countless library tables. Kennedy's design soon was supplanted in the market by a modernistic Art Deco concept from Walter Dorwin Teague, designer of such artifacts as the Bluebird Radio, shown at the Brooklyn Museum's exhibit "The Machine Age" in 1986.[11]

Kennedy gave his primary attention at Smith College to studying and teaching about Italian Renaissance sculpture. Kennedy produced *Studies in the History and Criticism of Sculpture*, in eight volumes, and the college published them over many years. Kennedy died in 1972. The collection he had given to the Lands included photographic equipment, slides, transparencies, notes on photographing sculpture and stereo vision, five thousand negatives, and twenty thousand prints. In the 1990s, the collection was stored and displayed in the Rowland Institute for Science.

Work on the movies continued. Kodak began supplying Wheelwright with its new Kodachrome film. Wheelwright took it with him on a succession of annual vacations in Bermuda. When Land first publicly demonstrated his polarizer in January 1936, Kennedy showed the application in sculpture classes, and one newspaper noted Carnegie Corporation support, the showing of 3-D movies, and the Kodak involvement.[12] Another account noted that the double camera lenses were as far apart as human eyes, that the polarizers on each projector were at right angles to each other, and that the viewer's spectacles had corresponding polarized lenses, one for each eye.[13] A third account referred to the 3-D movies simply as "life-like,"[14] but a fourth was more enthusiastic: "Observers were ushered into a seemingly living fairyland of forms and colors." The pictures put out by a pair of projectors and seen through special spectacles "took on all the semblance of real life. Flesh color became realistic. The human form became rounded."[15]

In May 1936, Wheelwright gave the pitch to the Society of Motion Picture Engineers in the Hotel Pennsylvania in New York, which, eleven years later, was the site of Land's first public demonstration of instant photography. A reel of miscellaneous short subjects was shown in a small room off the hotel's ballroom on a screen about fifteen feet in front of a newspaper reporter. In one scene, "[a] fishing boat moved slowly up to [a] Boston wharf while in the foreground the ropes and rigging of another boat appeared so close and real one could almost seize them . . . The most lifelike scene was a children's garden party, in which four youngsters seated about a table scrambled for a basket of favors wrapped in pink tissue paper. A small boy nearest the camera turned and leaned back in his chair at one juncture, creating the impression that he was about to tumble out of the screen 'window' into the laps of the spectators."

The assembled film technicians were skeptical. They couldn't see a practical way to put 3-D films before the public. [16]

In the Berlin Olympics of 1936, the African-American runner Jesse Owens upset his German hosts by winning the 100 meter, the 200 meter, and the long jump. There, too, twin cameras using a proprietary Zeiss-Ikon polarizing filter called Herotar were aimed at the finish lines of the running races. The cameras simultaneously recorded the time that the first runner crossed the finish line and 3-D views of the runners.[17]

Later that summer, Wheelwright went to England in a search for cash to keep Land-Wheelwright Laboratories going. Demonstrating the use of polarizers to control headlight glare and to view 3-D movies, he showed two movies shot in Kodachrome. The British magazine *Engineering* praised the "particularly pleasing results."[18] At the December 1936 "Polaroid on Parade" exhibit, a 3-D movie using Kodachrome became a regular feature of the New York Museum of Science and Industry and ran at the museum for many years.[19]

∞

As early as 1933, the Land-Wheelwright enterprise had high hopes of a solid connection with Hollywood. Warner Brothers, which had hit it big with its pioneering of sound in *The Jazz Singer,* was contemplating a similar triumph with 3-D. A letter from Julius Silver recorded four demonstrations for representatives of Warner Brothers, including "Major" Warner, one of the brothers. The demonstrations occurred on 29 and 31 August and 1 and 29 September 1933. At that point, Warner Brothers wanted to set up its own equipment with Land's assistance.[20] In later years, the favorite story at Polaroid was that Major Warner had sight in only one eye, which would render an appreciation of 3-D movies impossible. Whatever the truth, Warner Brothers apparently conveyed its doubts to other movie companies. But its interest in the field continued. It is not clear why one of the powerful Wall Street backers of the Polaroid Corporation in 1937 could not reopen the path to Hollywood, but these were the fat years for Hollywood's big studios and for movie theaters, big and small.

In 1935, the major film studio Metro-Goldwyn-Mayer put a toe in the water with different technology, releasing short 3-D films with sound, called *Audioscopics,* with a humorous commentary by the well-known Pete Smith. Large audiences saw the film produced by J. F. Leventhal and John A. Norling of Loucks and Norling Studios in New York.[21] Norling also made the twelve-minute stereo movie shown in the Chrysler pavilion at the New York World's Fair of 1939–40 (see chapter 5). Norling's setup used polarized spectacles from Polaroid and established the commercial pattern for many years into the future. Simply doubling up existing systems, Norling did not need the costly development of techniques for putting both images on a single strip of film. Two thirty-five-millimeter Bell and Howell cameras were mounted "upside down" with respect to each other, so that their lenses would be only 3.25 inches apart. Norling's team shot the 1939 movie over thirty-six days. More than thirteen thousand frames, with each part of a Plymouth moved a predetermined distance, were needed for the animated "stop-motion" sequences. In 1939, up to seventeen thousand people a day saw the film. According to Norling, the movie depicted "actual operations in the half-mile-long Plymouth plant at Detroit, and a trick-assembly picture that shows the Plymouth car magically coming into being without the apparent aid of human hands. The various parts of the car, numbering many thousand, come waltzing in together or separately, each to take its proper place in engine, chassis, or body—all in carefully synchronized step to the beat of the music."[22]

Despite these tantalizing successes in the late 1930s, Land began to think that Wheelwright had run out of ideas in the stereo field. The strain contributed to Wheelwright's departure from Polaroid in 1940.

∞

Meanwhile, with Clarence Kennedy as one of his collaborators, Land developed a still-picture technology that he called the Vectograph. With this technology a stereo image was created by putting the two images, one for the left eye and one for the right, on a single strip of film. Now, only a single projector would be needed. The technique appeared suitable not only for lantern slides but also for movies. The user didn't need a stereoscope, just Polaroid spectacles, to look at Vectographs in the form of paper-backed prints, transparencies lighted from behind, or slides or movies projected on a screen. Land's publicist Richard Kriebel described it in 1943 as "fundamentally a new kind of pictorial representation. At its most spectacular, it is a three-dimensional picture in the form of a single print."[23]

The spark to ignite the Vectograph work came to Polaroid with a Czech inventor named Joseph Mahler, who was hired in 1938 just as the German dismantling of Czechoslovakia got under way. As Stephen Benton, who worked with Land in the 1960s and 1970s on the three-dimensional technology known as holography, put it, "Land quickly recognized the elegance of the polarization anaglyph" that Mahler had shown him. Land worked with Mahler along with such other trusted technical people as Cutler D. West, Howard G. Rogers, William F. Ryan, and Frederick J. Binda.

In the 1990s, Benton, by this time at MIT's well-known Media Lab, wrote that "Vectographs still represent the highest technical development of polarized 3-D print and projection technology." Later, Land's ideas on three dimensions blended with his color-vision research (see chapter 13).[24] Land was very proud of this further step in the field of inexpensive polarizers and described it several times over the next four decades. During his Carothers lecture in Wilmington, Delaware, in 1976, he recalled with amusement his first demonstration to the Optical Society in 1940:"It was the time of the Roosevelt–Willkie election and I had the glasses arranged so that if you closed one eye you saw the Democrat and if you closed the other one, you saw the Republican. I asked all the Democrats to close the left eye and the Republicans to close the right eye, and of course they all applauded."

The key to the invention, he said, was the hitherto unrecognized fact that "three dimensional pictures could be obtained if the two images of the stereoscopic pair were made in terms of percent polarization." In a Vectograph, Land said, the shadows are regions of high-percentage polarization and the highlights are regions of low-percentage polarization. "Two pictures so made, one for the left eye, one for the right, with their axes crossed, can be superimposed and yet viewed independently with analyzers. Such pictures can be made by printing with iodine on sheets of oriented polyvinyl alcohol."

Printed in layers on opposite sides of a single film support, the two images produced an effect analogous to that of the "anaglyphs" that Louis Ducos du Hauron invented around 1860. Du Hauron began using the anaglyphs in 1891 for stereoscopic projections of black-and-white images. The anaglyph system called for images printed with red and green inks to be viewed through corresponding red and green filters. Seeking to make "polarization anaglyphs," Land and his colleagues came up with a process that was similar to the making of color separations by dye transfer, with iodine as the substance transferred instead of dyes.

Mahler had seen, according to Land, "the analogy between a pair of such images with orthogonal orientation of their polarization and the anaglyph using red and green inks for printing with red and green lenses for viewing." Land said that "vigorous program[s] to produce first black-and-white stereoscopic Vectographs, and later full-color Vectographs . . . were successful in the laboratory, and the black-and-white Vectograph was released for extensive use during the war." Polaroid supplied two million dollars' worth of still Vectographs to the U.S. military.[25]

Mahler and Land received their first Vectograph patent on 11 June 1940, just as Land published an article naming Mahler as "the most active worker" in the group. "His early conception of the effectiveness of this kind of three-dimensional print, and his intuitive skill in using new processes, are responsible to a large degree for the progress of this development." The iodine/polyvinyl alcohol images resembled Polaroid's H sheet.[26]

Three weeks later, a small item in *The New York Times* reported the invention of the Vectograph and in October, Land demonstrated the process to the Optical Society in Rochester. He mentioned the movie-film application, although the necessary special film supplies were not yet available. The Associated Press reported that less than four minutes were needed to make reliefs from the original negatives, dip them in a chemical solution, and press them onto a film base. The process permitted "two complete and distinct pictures to occupy the same place at the same time without distortion of tone, loss of detail, or other interference."[27]

Substituting dyes for iodine in the polarizers, by methods that the Polaroid researchers already had explored, would allow the creation of color Vectographs. With color Vectographs, filters were not needed on either lantern-slide or motion-picture projectors and the full light of the projector's bulb was available to throw the images onto the screen.

The Vectograph invention recalled inventive leaps such as Land's switch from macroscopic crystals to submicroscopic crystals in the late 1920s. In the late 1930s, he dropped crystals altogether for special types of polymers, such as polyvinylene. In all that work, however, the light coming out of Land's polarizers, over a wide range of frequencies, was arranged in vectors that were as parallel as possible. But now, Land and his colleagues were exploiting what Land called "a controlledly non-uniform vectorial field created with or in polarizing surfaces." The vectorial inequality they were using could involve differences in either the length or direction of the vector.

By the time of the Rochester demonstration in October 1940, Land had been contacted for war work (see chapter 8). Less than two months later, Land committed his company completely to military projects for the duration. Militarized, the Vectograph provided stereo images of the Normandy invasion coast and many other battlefields.[28]

∞

After World War II, American prosperity exploded, and surprisingly, 3-D movies got a new chance in a booming market where many new industries flourished. One of these was Polaroid's instant photography; another was television (a medium ideally suited to demonstrating in "live" ads the development of a sixty-second print). Television not only swiftly absorbed many "stars" of radio but also annexed a large share of the audiences that had crowded the movie theaters in the 1930s. Movies, of course, had sound and color and a big screen, not to mention the sense of occasion and the stimulation of a large audience in one darkened hall of fantasy. The little screen, however, offered entertainment at home, without the cost of theater tickets. It began eroding the audiences for Hollywood films, particularly the bread-and-butter "B" movies that often formed a double bill with more ambitious pictures. Daytime attendance fell by half from 1946 to 1952, and many small theaters closed. Hollywood had to do something to get its audiences back, or at least to stem the exodus. The sense of "being there" in the movie theater had to be intensified.

In the early 1950s, several candidate technologies competed to go beyond the normal movie screen, which was just one and one-third times as wide as it was high. To project the audiences into the scene, the screen would have to be widened. The expensive, three-camera, three-screen process called Cinerama was similar to the one used by the filmmaker Abel Gance in his Polyvision epic of 1927, *Napoleon*. Opening in New York in September 1952, *This Is Cinerama* drew large crowds. A second process, Wide Screen, projected films onto screens one and two-thirds times as wide as they were high. The third process, which proved enduring, was known as CinemaScope. It used screens two and two-thirds times as wide as they were high, usually about sixty feet across. The only novelty that did not require widening the screen was 3-D.

The way was paved for all these experiments by the introduction of new color movie films from Ansco and Kodak. Up until then, movie producers relied on huge Technicolor machines with three cameras built into each. Now, smaller cameras could be located much more freely than before, for 3-D as well as the multiscreen and wide-screen processes.[29]

Although Hollywood had forgotten about 3-D until the emergence of television, Polaroid had not. Land and Mahler kept patenting refinements of the system. In 1945, as the war was ending, Land said on the radio, "In the peacetime world, perhaps, we shall have three-dimensional motion pictures—even three-dimensional television."[30]

Using the Vectograph method, movie makers no longer would need to synchronize two projectors or face the loss of light in filtered projectors. Polaroid tested it. According to William Ryan, who received a patent in the 3-D field in 1957, Polaroid had rented the Los Angeles plant of Cinecolor, a company producing images in two colors, red and green. Polaroid planned to test the concept by preparing several reels of black-and-white Vectograph motion pictures for such wartime uses as training films for naval gunners. The work was a challenge. Stero film enthusiast Lenny Lipton explained that to make color Vectograph prints, stills or movies, in a manner resembling "the old Technicolor process or the Eastman dye-transfer process, would have taken a facility capable of printing color matrices (actually two pairs of cyan, magenta, and yellow matrices)."[31] The work went further than Lipton thought. Polaroid and Technicolor worked together in printing color Vectograph movies and in developing the process, as Vivian Walworth recalled many years later. Ryan of Polaroid was the liaison with Bill Schmid and others at Technicolor. To achieve sharper images for wide screens, Schmid collaborated on improving dye-uptake "mordants" for Vectograph film.[32]

Searching fiercely for new business after the war, Polaroid did not limit itself to 3-D movies. As an outgrowth of their work on color Vectographs, Ryan and two Polaroid colleagues, Samuel Kitrosser and Walworth, developed Polacolor, a cheap color-film process used for Paramount cartoons. Ryan and his co-workers set up a small factory in Cambridge to make it.[33] The factory was closed after manufacturing several million feet of film; the company cited labor difficulties in the film industry and the great distance between Cambridge and Hollywood.[34]

Before Vectographic movies could be perfected, the fad for 3-D movies broke like a hurricane. On 26 November 1952, a mediocre action film called *Bwana Devil,* made by the independent producer Arch Obler, had its premiere in New York and drew huge audiences. The audience used Polaroid spectacles to view the film. The "Natural Vision" process used for

Bwana Devil had been developed by film-script writer Milton Gunzberg and his brother, Julian Gunzberg, an eye physician. Milton had visited Polaroid in May 1952.[35] Although the ideal solution of 3-D Vectographs on a single film strip was outrun by events, Polaroid still prospered. Production of plastic polarizing spectacles reached six million a week by May 1953, and Polaroid had orders for seventy million more.[36] The situation was almost exactly opposite to Polaroid's failure with the automobile industry. The company was flooded with orders for spectacles just as its major business, instant photography, was taking off.

Despite the boom, people at Polaroid were skeptical about the long-term prospects. An internal memorandum detailed the concerns: "We now have all the elements of a satisfactory black-and-white stereo motion-picture process. Putting these elements together, in several thousand theatres, with no technical stereo experience, on short notice—90 days from now—looks like a most formidable project." There were large and small problems with viewers, filters, screens, light intensity, installation, and economics. Theaters running films for three days to a week would have difficulty buying enough pairs of polarizing glasses or getting resupplied in time. They would hesitate to buy the best screens. How would minimum standards of installation be maintained?

The memorandum asked, "How can a theatre, especially the small theatre, justify the expense (from $100 to $3,000 or more) on an average run—three days to a week, when they don't even know if there ever will be a second picture?" Long-run houses could risk more on big orders for viewers, and might get their money back over about ten weeks, "if the stereo did bring in more business."[37] The overriding need was to minimize the risk of being a one-shot novelty.

The same issue worried the Polaroid board of directors, which asked Land for a special report in which Land was less pessimistic than others. Praising the movie industry's past advances, he said that 3-D could be the next. The four previous major advances heightening the sense of reality in movies were "the use of distant haze to enhance the illusion of depth, the use of exaggerated perspective in set design, the use of traveling camera to accentuate change in perspective, and the movement of foreground objects with respect to the background." The wide and curved screens of Cinerama and CinemaScope, however, still produced flat images, "in the sense that it presents the scene as a one-eyed man would view it." A stereoscopic picture, he wrote, could "convey a conviction of realism that can be presented in no other way."

A true sensation of depth required two images and a viewing mechanism to allow the brain to combine the two. Other approaches, such as the "parallax stereogram," on which Frederick and Herbert Ives had spent much of their lives, had failed. Ducos du Hauron's anaglyphs, although they used color filters, could not be used for color pictures. A mechanical shutter, displaying the left-eye and the right-eye images in rapid succession, presented "obvious" technical and commercial problems. One was thus left with the Polaroid viewer, "the third and only practical type." Nothing better had come forward in the twenty years since the company first demonstrated it.

The early success of the 3-D movie technique reminded the movie industry of the burst of customers when sound was introduced in the 1920s, and color in the 1930s. Quick exploitation, however, might lead to a quick crash. What would follow? "Leaders in the industry are apparently making every effort to see that their first stereoscopic pictures are good entertainment as well as good examples of the stereoscopic technique." Land hoped that the movie moguls would not forget that "there is no substitute for a good show."

From the beginning, movie makers had been forced to learn that a new technique must be "easy on the eyes." Three-dimensional pictures would have to be shot correctly and projected correctly so that the films could be seen comfortably by those wearing Polaroid's spectacles. To help the industry, Polaroid was providing technical advice and pushing the development of the one-film, one-projector Vectograph technique. For two-projector films like *Bwana Devil,* theater owners had to go to the expense of buying new equipment. To keep the two projectors in synchrony with each other, "the picture must be interrupted occasionally for the insertion of new reels."

As he had with the automobile makers, Land spoke of "the great challenge and the great opportunity" and appealed for the cooperation of the film industry:

> Over the years, the motion-picture industry has given the world a succession of spectacular demonstrations of the power of realism in entertainment; first, with the motion itself; then with sound; then color. Now the talents of this same industry have, quite literally, a new dimension to exploit; all the space in the world (again, quite literally) to work in. This space can be thrown away, as a passing novelty. Or the industry can determine to use the space, the solid realism of the new

> dimension, as a true addition to the medium they have created. This would be our best assurance that people will be wearing glasses after the novelty has worn off; they will be enjoying themselves, carried away by the realism of the art.[38]

Land based his hopes on such films as the musical *Kiss Me, Kate* which was shot in three as well as two dimensions. It surely met Land's definition of a "good show."

One of those who liked *Kiss Me, Kate* was the English-born journalist Alistair Cooke, who summarized Hollywood's fight for more realism. Television, he wrote in the *Manchester Guardian* in August 1953, was technically "still at the stage of the Keystone cops," held back "by a complacency more ferocious than Hollywood's." Still, television allowed people at home to watch Hollywood's bad movies "in listless comfort at their elbow." Now 3-D could give embattled movie-theater operators a cheap alternative to Cinerama. "The exhibitor needed only the matching lenses and bigger rewind reels; he could pass on the cost of Polaroid glasses, at ten cents a pair, to the customer. The result has been several small fortunes and healthy-looking queues winding round the corner." Although 3-D was "a poor substitute for the rounded dimension of live players," reproducing faithfully the cardboard cutout effect of stereoscopic slides, "the relief is in motion." Early defects of synchronization that caused headaches were being cured. "The shooting of the two images is being done today with hair-splitting precision, and there are now available lenses that interlock to perfection. One big studio has done a Technicolor 3-D movie of 'Kiss Me, Kate,' which is painless, rounded, and has the effect of whisking the audience into the most privileged seat of a live theatre. Judging from the couple of reels I saw, I should say that the test of 3-D will be the public reception of this film."[39]

Cooke and Land were too optimistic. Bad movies overwhelmed the good, and many reviews were unfriendly. Early in 1953, the five short subjects that had been exhibited at the 1951 Festival of Britain were shown in New York: two animations, a trip down the Thames, a visit to a zoo, and a visit to a ballet company. According to Bosley Crowther of *The New York Times*, "the stereo process here unlimbered is either much over-rated or under-done." He added, "It is amusing to see abstract doo-dads rhythmically dancing over the audience's heads, as they do in the cartoon films in this program, but when a person seems to emerge from the screen—or, worse, a part of the person, cut off at the waist or down one side—the illusion is wholly distortive and makes no artistic sense."[40]

As long as the movie industry maintained a flicker of interest, Polaroid kept trying. In 1952, Polaroid's Walworth took part in a demonstration for Jack Warner of Warner Brothers at the Astor Theater in New York, using color slides to show the quality of good 3-D. Ryan served as a Warner consultant in the filming of the 3-D thriller *The House of Wax*, starring Vincent Price.[41] To reduce synchronization problems and expense, the twin images were squeezed onto a single strip of film.

The *New Yorker* review of *House of Wax* was scathing: "For some reason that will probably turn out to be an optical impossibility, this picture looked better to me without the glasses than it did with them—a bit fuzzy, perhaps, but not so insistently demanding on the eyes." The producers, "having invested nervously in a system they don't know much about . . . have hedged their bets by applying the new technique to something they know *all* about—stories whose powers of stupefaction are equaled only by their age." The reviewer left the theater early.[42]

Audiences complained that the colors appeared washed out, probably because of the polarizing filters on each projector, and there still were the headaches from the slight asynchrony of the two film strips. In the spring of 1953, a round table of leading projectionists in Britain concluded that "the presentation of 3-D demands much higher standards of knowledge and skill in the projectionist . . . [and] calls for the employment of at least four senior skilled projectionists in the box." The chief projectionist of the National Film Theatre in London said, "We have had some weird and wonderful complaints here. Some people never get any three-dimensional effect at all. It can reveal eye defects that people never realised they had."[43]

In October 1953, Land's colleague Lewis Chubb, Jr., took the heat at the annual convention of movie engineers. He noted that the polarizing filters for the projectors used the heat-stable K polarizers invented for sealed-beam headlights. The movie engineers must use brighter projector lamps and projector lenses with low focal lengths, taking "every dodge we can to get light on the screen." The screens themselves must be highly reflective for the polarized light thrown on them from the projectors. To save money, theater operators would try screens with a sprayed surface rather than an aluminized one. Chubb urged that "the very most be made out of the art of polarizer manufacture so that light on the screen will not be compromised nor colors distorted or softened."[44] He was setting a high standard.

Spurred by the hope of big sales, Polaroid engineers and scientists wrestled with the technical problems. The physicists Robert Clark Jones and William A. Shurcliff worked on methods to measure and cure problems with both projectors and screens. They published their results in the journal of the motion-picture and television engineers' association. Polaroid experts visited a hundred movie theaters showing 3-D films and found twenty-five with images enough out of synchrony to be disturbing. The demands on the projectionists were severe. They had to adjust the focal lengths of each projector to within 0.5 percent of the other. Additionally, each projector's lightbulb had to receive the same amount of power, or amperage, to give equal illumination. The shutters of each projector needed to open and close at exactly the same times. Even if the projectionists achieved all this, there was a further complication. About 5 to 10 percent of people lack altogether the ability to construct a 3-D sensation from two pictures. Perhaps another 10 percent put together a stereo picture imperfectly. Consequently, projectionists might adjust conditions to their own vision and give eyestrain to most others in the theater.

Polaroid pushed the development of devices to sense which of the two projectors was ahead by, say, a fraction of a frame out of the twenty-four per second and to use a manually operated differential gear to get them back together. Shurcliff and his colleagues designed a cheap, small, handheld stroboscopic detector, which many movie theaters bought. But what if one projector led the other by exactly one frame or two frames? Much brainstorming produced no answer. Then Shurcliff noticed that at each change of scene in the film, the brightness changed noticeably. An instrument could detect the changes of brightness on each film strip and tell which projector was ahead, by how many fractions of a second, that is, by how many frames. Polaroid made and distributed the instrument to hundreds of movie theaters. Shurcliff himself was sent to the big New York Loew's theater to show the projectionists how it worked.

Movie makers and projectionists were not granted enough time to learn the rules for good stereo. When stereo-film perforations were damaged, inexperienced projectionists cut out sections without regard to synchronization. Movie makers, inexperienced in stereoscopic filmmaking, only gradually learned the correct separation of camera lenses or how to avoid eyestrain. The left-eye and right-eye prints required processing so that each had the same ratio of lightness and darkness. Time was running short, however. The coup de grâce came from rival manufacturers of polarizing spectacles trying to beat Polaroid on price. Shurcliff recalled that these were "so badly made that the polarization was incomplete [and] image separation was incomplete."[45]

Hollywood turned to other systems. The first CinemaScope picture, *The Robe,* opened on Wednesday, 16 September 1953, at the Roxy Theater in New York. Short 3-D films resurfaced at Disney theme parks later. Land's interest in Vectographs continued, and he demonstrated color Vectograph slides at the Optical Society of America. Even in the 1990s, Walworth was collaborating with the Vectograph research of Jay Scarpetti at the Rowland Institute.[46]

8

"The Best Damn Goggles in the World"

> Most military research is foreign to real science. . . . What you do in wartime for patriotic purposes is to give up flexibility and freedom to get some specific things done. In war, you beat the plowshare into a sword.
>
> —Edwin H. Land

Around Christmas 1940, German bombs fell most nights on English cities while Americans listened on the radio. Hitler's attack on Russia, which created a war on two fronts and made his ultimate defeat much more likely, was six months in the future. Land met his employees as usual, for his annual view of the young company's present and future. But what he said was unusual. He may not have had the polish of his later public performances, but he spoke with the confidence gained in many years of invention, technical problem-solving, publicity, and industrial organization. It was a somber moment in the world, and for the company. The world was at war, and the company wasn't making much money.

The war situation, even though America had not entered it, was frightening. A few days before Land's talk, the recently reelected President Franklin Roosevelt, refreshed from an outwardly relaxed but reflective Caribbean voyage, gave a press conference. He unveiled his unique concept of Lend Lease as a means of sending immediate assistance to Great Britain. His analogy for the plan was lending a length of garden hose to a neighbor whose house was on fire. The aid was sorely needed, because Britain, standing alone against Nazi Germany since the previous June, was about to run out of money to pay America for supplies. Days after Land spoke to his employees, Roosevelt, in one of his radio "fireside chats," would propose that America become the "arsenal of democracy."

With characteristic prescience and impatience, Land launched Polaroid onto a new course, which he later called a "big change." He told the employees that one year from then, the United States would be in the war. So, starting at once, Polaroid's only purpose would be "to win this war." Anyone who disagreed with this goal was free to leave. He told the employees that he didn't expect to make much profit. He repeated the gist of his talk two years later: "We didn't exist for any profit, nor singly for the welfare of our employees, or to provide the consumer market with sunglasses; that had been our start. We now existed for one purpose: to win this war."[1]

Land spoke of "the disease that is spreading over the world," a disease that "goes on for generations" and that "does not stop when war stops." He did not make clear whether he thought the disease was intolerance or totalitarianism. He may have been thinking of the antisemitism that drove his grandparents from Russia and now, decades later, was fueling Hitler's "final solution."

He was determined to enlist Polaroid early for the desperate, explosive American mobilization of engineering and science. This effort would be an equalizer in the inevitable world war with the Axis dictatorships of Germany, Italy, and Japan. Some of the time lost in the 1930s would be regained.

This new age of scientific endeavor had begun only six months before in a brief conversation between President Roosevelt and Vannevar Bush, a veteran inventor, teacher, and leader of academic institutions. In 1939, Bush had become president of the Carnegie Institution of Washington. He soon took over as chairman of the board of the twenty-five-year-old federal aviation research organization, the ancestor of the National Aeronautics and Space Administration (NASA). He started learning his way around Washington with the help of an experienced civil servant. A testy and shrewd New Englander with a strong instinct for acquiring and using power, Bush had spent much of his professional life at MIT, where he had led the development of a mechanical computer called the differential analyzer, and served as vice president and dean of engineering.

From severe disappointments in World War I, Bush, like other leading scientists, knew intimately the balkiness of the military mind at having scientists around to give advice. The military was slow in adopting new technology, even if it was desperately needed to catch up to the enemy.

Bush and such colleagues as James Conant and Karl Compton, the presidents of Harvard and MIT, were determined that the scientific mobilization be done better and faster this time. They saw that scientists would somehow have to obtain an independent source of money to develop new weapons quickly, while devising strategies to persuade the military to use them. A key feature of their plan for harnessing scientists to problems of urgent military importance was the abandonment of the central lab concept of World War I in favor of creating labs right where the scientists already worked, at the universities and companies.

Bush devised a scheme and presented it to Roosevelt in a ten-minute White House meeting on 12 June 1940. The meeting was arranged by Harry Hopkins, Roosevelt's closest counselor in the early war years. Roosevelt approved the scheme with speed that alarmed Bush. The National Defense Research Committee (NDRC) and its enlarged successor, the Office of Scientific Research and Development (OSRD), created in 1941, set up vast programs of work on radar, the proximity fuse for artillery and antiaircraft shells, jet propulsion, and the atomic bomb.[2] Through these intense experiences, American engineers and scientists learned a thousand lessons about how to get the resultant weapons built and used in the current war—lessons that reverberated for decades ahead. Thousands of scientists plunged into war more completely than ever before and learned large-scale lessons in the integration of large technical systems. They acquired not only a grudging respect for the military men who were just beginning to understand these researchers, but also a sense of responsibility for their inventions that the scientists could never escape thereafter.

Almost certainly with encouragement from Bush and Compton, emissaries from Bush's organization began calling on Land. When Samuel Caldwell of the NDRC's fire-control division met Land on 1 November 1940, they discussed a rangefinder. A $140,000 contract for this project was written a year later, on 1 December 1941, to run until 31 August 1944. As often happened with NDRC projects, work may have begun long before the official contract.[3] This contract eventually developed into Polaroid's plastic optics department. By the time of the bombing of Pearl Harbor, Polaroid had made special filters for various Navy instruments and developed a machine-gun trainer that simulated tracer bullets for the first time. To the accompaniment of realistic noises, the operator turned a life-size twenty-millimeter gun against a three-dimensional picture of an attacking plane. Polaroid made 110 of these trainers.[4]

∞

Polaroid's war work was based solidly on Land's and his company's preoccupation with polarizers and on the knowledge of plastics that Land's group had been forced to acquire to make the polarizers practical. The polarizers could be used, as in peacetime, to control glare, and for 3-D reconnaissance photos for both training and damage assessment. It turned out that plastics could be molded into accurate but inexpensive lenses, which could take over many tasks that had been reserved for expensive glasses that required meticulous grinding. Polaroid also had the know-how to make many types of nonpolarizing filters and different types of gun sights.

Many years later, Howard Rogers recalled the request from Bush's organization to develop plastic optics. The NDRC feared that the supply of precision lenses and prisms, largely from Germany, would be cut off, and that there would be a shortage of trained U.S. optics workers. Could the lenses be made of molded plastic? In the end, Rogers said, Polaroid's efforts were not "terribly important" for turning out "large quantities of precision optics." The pressure of war led to shortcuts, Rogers said. "People became very inventive in being able to make up for the lack of people that were good at the grinding and polishing part of it." The emergency optical work forces did well at turning out spherical surfaces, those that "you get if you rub two surfaces together with grit between." Where Polaroid plastic optics came into their own was in making lenses whose surfaces were not spherical, "which couldn't be turned out easily with even a skilled optician."[5] Molds could turn out aspheric lenses and mirrors much faster than they could be made of glass. Polaroid would return to this technology with a vengeance in developing the folding SX-70 camera of the 1970s.

As Land emphasized to his war workers, the underlying theme was accurate aiming to hit targets located by such means as sound or radar echoes. Polaroid's job was "to deliver fire-control equipment in a hurry." The guns whose fire was to be controlled were mounted on tanks that were rushing forward in unfamiliar, often ill-mapped territory. Antiaircraft guns on land and sea, and thousands of fighters and bombers, needed better fire control, too. The ultimate in controlled aiming occurred over the English Channel during the summer of 1944, as German V-1 pilotless bombers flew toward the immense target of London to spread terror and war-weariness. On the English coast, radar from MIT came together with a fire-control system from Bell Labs, and shells mounting proximity fuses from Johns Hopkins, to shoot the V-1s down.[6]

∞

Everywhere, gunners had a common problem: glare. To aim at their targets, such as tanks or planes, they often had to look into or near the sun. They needed goggles, polarizing and nonpolarizing goggles, and Polaroid gave them goggles by the millions. Land called them "the best damn goggles in the world."[7] The goggles were so ubiquitous that people took them for granted. It caused little stir, but great pride at Polaroid when U.S. Army General George Patton, commander of U.S. forces in the invasion of Sicily in July 1943, wore the goggles of a tank-man—and his famous pistols—for a photograph that appeared on the cover of *Newsweek* shortly after the invasion.[8]

Variable-density goggles helped antiaircraft gunners, machine gunners, and gunners aboard fighters and bombers. These goggles contained a pair of polarizers for each eye, a miniature version of the round windows of the "Copper King" observation car of peacetime. As the gunner turned the knob on each lens, he could darken the scene as much as he needed to see clearly.

Vision problems at night were the mirror image of those during the day. On many Navy and Merchant Marine vessels, the commander faced the contradictory need to be in his lighted bridge, glancing at charts and controls, and outside in the dark, trying to get a glimpse of enemy ships and planes and submarines. Pilots getting ready for night bombing missions had a similar conflict. They were summoned on short notice to lighted briefing rooms to scan the maps and get their orders, and then they had to go out into the dark to planes whose engine propellers were already turning. The problem was that human eyes take about half an hour to adjust from bright illumination to the darkness of night. Here, too, goggles could help soldiers and sailors and airmen remain dark-adapted.

The dark-adaptation glasses, Land told his employees, were designed in cooperation with the Navy, on a principle "suggested by a number of physiologists." Wearing them, he said, one could go into "an ordinarily lighted room . . . read your charts and then go outside." Taking off the glasses, "in two minutes, you are dark-adapted so you can relieve the watch immediately . . . This is a trick that didn't exist before our work."[9]

As the fighting men aimed their guns, they were usually in a topsy-turvy environment. Men in tanks needed equipment more forgiving than an eyepiece they had to bring right against an eye. Patton urgently pointed out this problem during the North African campaign of 1942 and 1943, America's first ground attack against the Axis in the Atlantic war. For this campaign, Polaroid worked on special telescopes and sights.

Land served as a consultant to Division Five of the NDRC (National

Defense Research Committee), which was concerned with guided missiles, and to Division Two, concerned with the effects of weapons. Besides filters for goggles, the company made periscopes, lightweight stereoscopic rangefinders, aerial cameras, the Norden bombsight, and a mechanism that antiaircraft gunners could use in training their tracer fire.

Polaroid was one of six companies the Navy asked to bid on a device, for one or two men, to find the elevation of aircraft above the horizon. Before the other five companies had even acknowledged the Navy's request, Polaroid sent in a working model of the Position Angle Finder, which could be held in one hand.[10]

∞

When Land met his employees on 23 December 1942, they were so numerous that he had to assemble them in the University movie theater in Harvard Square. A photograph taken on the occasion shows him standing straight, crooner-like behind a tall microphone. At his right on a small table stood one of Teague's polarizing desk lamps, a reminder of company tradition. He noted that "five-sevenths of you weren't with us last year," just after Pearl Harbor. Many people didn't know much of Polaroid's history. Many did know that if you crossed two disks of polarizing plastic and rotated them, you could gradually change the view from transparent to black. But the company's secret was the same:

> If you dream of something worth doing and then simply go to work on it and don't think anything of personalities, or emotional conflicts, or of money, or of family distractions; if you just think of, detail by detail, what you have to do next, it is a wonderful dream even though the end is a long way off, for there are about five thousand steps to be taken before we realize it; and start taking the first ten, and stay making twenty after, it is amazing how quickly you get through those five thousand steps. Rather, I should say, through the four thousand [nine hundred] and ninety. The last ten steps you never seem to work out. But you keep on coming nearer to giving the world something well worth having.[11]

Each employee, Land asserted, had the capacity for creative work. The picture of "great men in attics" was "baloney." Such myths led to photographs in newspapers of scientists with their microscopes (he had been so depicted himself). The myths left out all the work by "a little guy with no scientific training" that was necessary "before the scientist could look through that microscope." He hoped that each employee would experience the kind of work "that is just about the greatest thrill there is in the world, that feeling of living in a little universe in which all you have is your eyes and your head and an idea which, if solved, will give the world something new."

Polaroid, Land insisted, wasn't "big business" profiting from the war. In the year since Pearl Harbor, the company's sales had more than quintupled, to five million dollars, but the dollar amount of profit remained the same. He wanted the company's sales to quadruple again in 1943. Actually, they merely doubled but almost reached his twenty-million-dollar target the year after. "We have no purpose now except to win."

Land had something new to show the employees, about which he was intensely excited, "a new kind of sight," the Optical Ring Sight. "Here is the essential part of it, a glass disk. It takes the place of old-fashioned sights with the old big lenses in them, [and] does the job more accurately. It really puts the spot on the enemy when you look through it. . . . Any dumb bunny can be a good gunner with this. You don't have to do anything except turn the gun." With satisfaction, Land said, "It really is a revolution in sights." The military need for such a small, convenient, and inexpensive sight was acute. It was 1.5 inches in diameter and used plates of calcite and circular polarizers.[12] The sight was widely used in antiaircraft guns and anti-tank bazookas. In 1991, Howard Rogers would show it in a videotape made for Polaroid's commemoration of Land's life.[13]

Land turned to wartime uses of the 3-D Vectograph, which was in use late in 1942 in stereoscopic reconnaissance of the Guadalcanal battlefields and would be used in mapping all the Normandy beaches for the 1944 landings.[14] It was a new way of seeing. Normally, "if you look from an airplane you are very far away and your eyes are too close together. Now that the Vectograph is available, the pictures are taken a quarter of a mile apart. . . . When you look at the picture you see the houses and trees standing right up in the picture." That meant a lot to the tank corps. It had "to know ahead what kind of terrain it is going to cover or what kind of mud hole it will get stuck in." Looking forward to peace, Land predicted that the Vectograph department could be "as large as the company today." It would be "just the new kind of photography that they have been looking for since the beginning of it—you might say, since the beginning of painting or drawing."[15] He had begun to think more deeply about some new kind of photography—just a year before he thought of one-step picture-taking.

∞

Polaroid's heavy involvement in aerial reconnaissance underlined a need for color filters. The Metrogon reconnaissance cameras demanded yellow or red filters about six inches in diameter to cover a field of ninety-three degrees at an opening of f/6.3. The filters could not vary more than a few wavelengths of light from perfect flatness. Grinding such lenses from glass would not be cheap. Land saw an opportunity and a challenge. Why not use colored plastic between sheets of glass? Although the quarter-inch-thick plates of glass he had in mind often contained defects, the lamination of the plastic would fill in tiny imperfections on one side of each sheet. He needed only one good side, and if the two sheets were chosen carefully, he could combine them to cancel out the errors. To reduce optical problems further, the filter disks each had a tapered spot of metal in the center. Although testing for the good side and for errors was a formidable task, as much organizational as technical, thousands were made.[16]

∞

Japan quickly felt the backlash from its desperate gamble in attacking the U. S. fleet in Pearl Harbor. Only six months later, Japan's strategic "edge" was blunted at Midway, when planes from a smaller American fleet, placed nearby with the help of recently cracked codes, sank four of Japan's big carriers. But although the Pearl Harbor attack had thrust America into the war and united its people, the "Germany first" policy that had been agreed on with Britain limited the Pacific theaters to only a third of the nation's exploding war effort. Nonetheless, by the autumn of 1944, American forces in the Pacific had surged far forward toward Japan, seizing a beachhead in the Philippines and acquiring bases in the Marianas for long-range bombing of Japan itself. General Hideki Tojo's cabinet resigned.

At this juncture, having lost hundreds of hard-to-replace planes and trained pilots in battle, Japan turned to a practice that could use pilots with little training: sending them in planes designed as suicide missiles against American vessels. The so-called Kamikaze, or "divine wind," pilots began taking a heavy toll on ships and men.

The Kamikaze threat created special dangers for aircraft carriers whose planes were returning from missions after dark. Electric lights at visible wavelengths, which would help the pilots flying back over a vast ocean, would also help the Kamikaze pilots see their targets. It took courage for an admiral with many planes out chasing the Japanese fleet, as happened west of the Marianas in June 1944, to keep the lights on to help his pilots get back.

A partial answer to this new danger had already been devised to defeat an earlier danger at sea: submarines lurking near Atlantic and Mediterranean fighting ships and convoys of transports. Mercury-vapor spotlights aiming upward could be seen by the pilots above but not by the submarines below. The spotlights could be filtered to cut down on the visible light emitted outside the zone of final approach.

The concept looked promising for the new danger in the Pacific. Ultraviolet light, also given off by the mercury-vapor lamp, would cause the brightly colored strips on the sleeves of the Landing Signal Officer (LSO) to glow with fluorescent light. American pilots descending to the carrier deck could see the movements of the torches in each of the LSO's hands, which would specify how fast they should be flying, and how steeply they should descend. In the last ten to fifteen seconds before landing, the pilots also would catch sight of the recessed blue lights outlining the landing area.

But there was a new problem for the LSO. The ultraviolet light from the special spotlights would blind him. In the ultraviolet, the lenses of the LSO's eyes would fluoresce—so intensely that he couldn't see the descending plane and give it the standard arm signals to tell the pilot to keep coming down to the heaving carrier deck or to go around and try again. The LSO needed special glasses or goggles. In the words of Louis Rosenblum, who worked on the problem for Polaroid, the lenses would "absorb all of the ultraviolet light emitted by [the] mercury vapor spotlight, would not fluoresce, would transmit as much visible light as possible, and would be stable under the heat, brilliant sunlight, humidity, salt air, and other harsh conditions of the tropical regions of the western Pacific."

Polaroid responded with characteristic speed when, on Monday morning, 25 September 1944, Lieutenant Commander Robert Peckham of the Navy arrived in Cambridge to enlist Polaroid's familiar help in both the invention and the manufacturing of special goggles for LSOs and then returned quickly to Washington. The contract, production, and shipping would happen later. Polaroid had developed appropriate material, a new, thin, non-polarizing plastic film with a new dye, which could be laminated between two sheets of clear plastic for strength and protection and cut into the right shape for aviators' molded rubber goggles. Polaroid was making the goggles by the thousands each week.

Peckham asked for fifty sets for the most critical nighttime carrier operations. But Land suggested providing the 200 sets that would supply all Navy carriers operating at night near the enemy. He also suggested that Peckham save travel, time, and paperwork by staying a week and taking the entire order back with him.

Land asked the twenty-three-year-old Rosenblum if he could make the necessary contacts with production, purchasing, and quality control. When Rosenblum said he could, Land stood and said, with a touch of bravado, "O.K. Do it. But be sure not to neglect your other quality-control duties." Rosenblum guessed that the total value of this rush order agreed to in half an hour was no more than two thousand dollars. As Rosenblum and Peckham got up to leave Land's office, Land said, "If you run into any technical organizational problems, just leave word with Mrs. Billings," his secretary. As they reached the top of the staircase, Land came out of his office, his eyes twinkling, and gave the cocky young Rosenblum further advice: "Try not to ruffle too many feathers." Nine days later, Peckham and a string of porters carried the 200 sets of goggles aboard the overnight express to Washington. The special goggles were on their way to the Pacific, in time to bring nighttime pilots safely onto carrier decks off the Philippines, Iwo Jima, Okinawa, and Japan itself.[17]

∞

The Navy missile project, code-named DR-5 or Dove, was so secret that Land didn't discuss it in general meetings with his employees. It was a separate compartment of the company that eventually grew large and focused on the particular problem of hitting the enemy's ships at sea.

Like most other problems of fire control, hitting the target at sea had preoccupied military men and their suppliers for decades. Immense arrays of talent had worked with great ingenuity on accuracy. The problem was bad enough for the crews of moving tanks, but it was especially bad at sea, where the ship that fired its guns usually was plunging through the waves, as was the target, the enemy ship. Knowing exactly where you were when the gun went off and exactly where the enemy would be when the shell arrived near its target was a mathematical problem of great complexity, about as complex as the management of great networks of telephone switching machines or power generators. In the United States, contractors like Sperry Gyroscope and Ford Instrument worked for decades on fire control for the Army and Navy, while Bell Labs worked on the telephone network, and Vannevar Bush used his differential analyzer to solve equations describing the operation of electric generators. These three engineering traditions came together in the crucible of World War II.[18]

The search for a better way of hitting targets with shells drove many minds toward rockets that could be aimed, through some sort of on-board guidance, at their targets. This was the sort of problem that Bush felt was ideal for civilian scientists, operating with their own money from the government and free from the toils of military "expertise."[19] The Navy asked Polaroid to work on a plane-launched, guided anti-ship bomb that might be more accurate and put fewer pilots at risk than either dive-bombers or torpedo planes.

Land and the physicist David Grey, for many years a leading optics expert on Land's team, pondered Land's question: Why did bombs dropped from an airplane—flying level but high to reduce danger from fighters or anti-aircraft guns—almost always miss their target, even though it was relatively big, such as a battleship or an aircraft carrier? To ward off problems that had stymied attempts to guide missiles, the group focused on a missile that would home in on its target by sensing the infrared light from a source of heat, such as the funnels exhausting fumes and vapor from the steam turbines of a warship.

Land told Grey to study the problem of steering a falling bomb by line-of-sight toward an aircraft carrier moving at full speed. How could one keep the bomb turned toward the moving target? The bomb would not always point straight along its downward path. Grey figured a way to compensate for this, using a gyroscope that would always be pointed toward its target. The torque needed for aiming the gyroscope would measure the force required for steering the bomb. "Immediately Din understood the principle," Grey recalled. Land caught the basic idea for a steering package that would go onto a normal-size bomb dropped as usual from as high as possible, with no special action by the bomber crew.

In the apartment that Land maintained in war-crowded Washington, Grey and a few others spent about a week drafting a proposal for the steering package. They spelled out the components and how they would be assembled into a cube-shaped control unit less than a foot on each side. Two components already existed: the heat-sensing thermistor from Bell Labs and the rugged, sub-miniature vacuum tubes developed for the highly secret proximity fuse.[20] Hitherto, the detonators of artillery shells set the explosives off at a certain time after firing. The proximity fuse was different. It placed what amounted to a tiny radar in the nose of the shell, so that the explosive would go off at a predetermined distance from the target. Starting in the Solomons in 1943, the first targets of the proximity fuse were airplanes at sea. Only in the Battle of the Bulge in December 1944 did the proximity fuse begin operating over land, devastating concentrations of German soldiers and weapons.[21]

For the thousand-pound guided bomb, the Navy awarded a contract that paid a total of seven million dollars to Polaroid over several years. The contract represented a substantial fraction of the company's wartime business. For the tests, the Navy provided bombers and support crews.

To better steer the Dove rocket, Land's team dispensed with a rear-tail rudder and instead used four vanes down front, looking somewhat like the visors of a cap, which would be aligned with the bomb's longitudinal axis and operate immediately. To study the relationship between the extension of the vanes and lateral forces on the bomb, the team installed an eight-millimeter movie camera in the nose of a dummy bomb. To obtain a very compact, pre-war Keystone home-movie camera, Land sent a letter to a list of customers provided by Keystone, offering a war-bond to anyone who would contribute a camera to the war effort. Hundreds were sent in.[22]

After the first test at the Monomoy bombing range off Chatham on Cape Cod in Massachusetts, the team had difficulty retrieving the film. The bomb's tail fins stuck out from a watery hole about twenty feet wide and three feet deep. On what Grey called "just a sandbar dropped by ocean currents," pumping was next to impossible, although the team members kept trying until they were ordered off to make room for the next bomb test. To save time, Land wanted to stay at the site anyhow, maintaining that the safest place in a bombing range was in the center of the target area. Land's associates nonetheless hustled him to safety.[23]

Bombing practice began. Land, Grey, and William McCune took an "enforced siesta," during which Land discovered "an ugly black bug that, when placed in sunlight, became beautifully iridescent. Study of the polarization of the colors helped pass the idle time." When bombing practice ended, they returned to their crater and its fins: they found the missile intact after the bombing, but not its surroundings. The grass was burnt, the water pump's gasoline tank had exploded, and all the hoses were "scorched and useless." The center of the target area hadn't been safe, after all. Only a shovel remained, and it wasn't enough to retrieve the film.[24]

After tests at a site on northern Cape Cod, a complete Dove missile was tested just before atomic bombs ended the war suddenly.

McCune had worked little with Land in his first five years at Polaroid, but the Dove missile project drew them together. McCune was called Land's executive assistant, but in effect, he served as project manager and Land was technical director. Many years later, McCune recalled a visit to Monomoy that showed the same unrelenting intensity in Land that Grey had recalled. One spring, after a Polaroid "evening at the Pops" in Boston,

Land and McCune drove down to Chatham. It was so late when the two got there, that all the inns were closed. The lights were on in the lobby of one, however, and Land and McCune decided to wait there until the proprietor appeared. As hours passed, they did not doze in their chairs, because the room was well-equipped with puzzles. Land never relaxed much. Although McCune proudly recalled success in once getting Land to go on an overnight bicycle trip with a sleeping bag, and once to go skiing at Pinkham Notch in New Hampshire, McCune could hardly remember a time when Land wasn't involved with "some form of mental gymnastics." The puzzles occupied him until morning.[25]

∞

The work on the heat-homing bomb was frenetic and fit Land's style of restless energy and speed. On 28 May 1945, Polaroid employee W. Lewis Hyde wrote to his parents about a "hectic week because Mr. Land . . . decided all of a sudden that the things we were doing in our lab were pretty important, and has been in all week helping us do them. The man is a whirlwind. . . . He has about three ideas a minute and about two of them manage to get tried and tested."

The group was examining materials as different as beeswax and brass. Land asked, "Why haven't you tried vitreous enamel?" This involved melting the enamel onto brass. Hyde hemmed and hawed, citing temperature-control problems in ovens. Land ordered some enamel by special messenger. Avoiding ovens, the researchers just "heat[ed] the brass up with an oxygen torch until the stuff fuse[d]." Land wanted to spray the enamel, but they lacked special equipment. A glass tube served. Through it, the enamel was sprayed on lab windows until the researchers achieved "a good even coat." Land then taped the brass to the window so that it, too, could be coated. People ran "in and out with the working models of one of the old ideas dating from an hour or more ago." To write it all up, Hyde wrote, would take a year, "but we will never get to do the work—we'll just go on to something else unless it seems to justify a patent."[26]

When the war ended, Land decided to to leave the heat-homing bomb project. There are several explanations: a sense that the main technical problems were solved, doubts that the Dove would be ready in time to be used in the war, or his growing preoccupation with instant photography. There may have been a more general consideration. More than thirty years later, Land said that he didn't like doing military research in peacetime:

> One of the problems with government contracts is that one must define a finished undertaking before doing the research in order to get the contract. That's necessary in wartime, but in real life your research has its own impetus. You follow it where it takes you and, if you tell it where it's going, you've stopped it before you've started. Most military research is foreign to real science. . . . What you do in wartime for patriotic purposes is to give up flexibility and freedom to get some specific things done. In war, you beat the plowshare into a sword."[27]

The day after Japan laid down its arms on 14 August 1945, Land went to see McCune while the latter was listening to a radio broadcast of the celebrations. With his mind already focused completely on postwar survival, Land wanted to get rid of Dove immediately and commit McCune, Grey, Wolff, and other talented people to instant photography. The struggle to develop the new technology, as Polaroid marketing executive Peter Wensberg wrote, was in Land's eyes "a race to finish the camera before we run out of money." To halt Polaroid's participation in Dove, Land would call the Navy. To start turning Dove over to Eastman Kodak, McCune should call Rochester at once! Kodak had done brilliant work on the proximity fuse.[28]

By Christmas of 1946, Land could look back at the still-secret project as something "completely successful" that was now being "continued by other companies that are specializing during the peacetime in that kind of work." He praised "the extreme competence of the group of scientists, machine-makers, tool-makers, designers, engineers, and management people, who, involved in that project, carried it through in two years from a wild dream." People able to revolutionize a weapons field in two years, he added, "can also revolutionize any particular commercial field that we choose to enter." It was Polaroid's "duty to use those people as effectively as the Navy did in the war."[29]

9

"Who Can Object to Such Monopolies?"

> Most large industrial concerns are limited by policy to special directions of expansion within the well-established field of the company. On the other hand, most small companies do not have the resources or the facilities to support "scientific prospecting." Thus the young man leaving the university with a proposal for a new kind of activity is frequently not able to find a matrix for the development of his ideas in any established industrial organization.
>
> —Edwin H. Land, 1945[1]

During World War II, Land sought passionately to be useful, and he used every contact to that end. His definition of usefulness was broad, for his intellectual interests ranged widely. Despite his youth and the small size of his company, Land was noticed and listened to on such topics as the individual and collective aspects of invention, including the proper kind of industrial organization to foster invention and to put the results to work. One reason for this receptivity to Land's ideas was a widespread and continuing anxiety that individual inventors were being squeezed out by a society of large enterprises with big laboratories and batteries of patent lawyers.

The special form of intellectual property represented by patents was near the center of the anxiety. Land believed in patents as a protection for the small fish among the big fish. Like copyrights, patents recognized intellectual property and granted it protection in the courts. This arrangement roused a host of paradoxes. An inherent tension lay between inventions and their adoption, the process known as innovation. In return for disclosure of an invention, the inventor was granted a short-term monopoly on its exploitation. This monopoly, however, might slow down the diffusion of an invention through innovation and postpone any benefit it might bring. Other innovators might be inhibited from entering the new market, thus delaying expansion of production, reduction of price, and adoption by large numbers of customers. These classical disputes remained lively fifty years after the war.

Under a patent, the inventor would either set up a business to make and sell the invention or turn it over to an organization that could. But was the inventor an individual—a person highly valued in American and Western culture—or just a cog in a wheel? Instead of being a yeoman pioneer on a new frontier, a place of special value in American history, the inventor might be one of many employees in a large industrial lab, assigning patents to the company. Alternatively, the inventor might be an individual granting licenses to large companies, often on condition that they put the invention to use within a certain time. By creating intellectual property, patents often provided a basis for people to invest in using a new device or system. Yet many wondered whether the invention would bring more good to more people, and sooner, if it were put in the public domain. Such conflicting feelings heightened the distaste that many in the academic world felt for patenting inventions in a field like human health. These feelings intensified when an invention arose from research supported by tax-sheltered philanthropies or by governments.

Debates about the nature of inventions as property sharpened during the near-catastrophe of the Depression. Many regarded the collapse after 1929 as proof that the commercial and industrial system did not know its own best interest and was working against the interests of the majority. It was thus no accident that patents were a central subject of an unusual federal executive-legislative commission at work from 1938 to 1941: the Temporary National Economic Committee, or Monopoly Committee. Among the 552 witnesses who testified in 193 days of public hearings published in thirty-one volumes were research leaders well known to Land: Vannevar Bush of the Carnegie Institution of Washington, William Coolidge of General Electric, Charles Kettering of General Motors, and Frank Jewett of Bell Telephone Laboratories. None of the research leaders bought the idea that in the era of the big corporation, the individual inventor was dead.

The committee's special counsel wanted to know if the patent system was losing its democratic character. Bush replied that even though much useful work was done in large groups in large corporations, individual inventors still counted and had a democratically equal status in the eyes of the Patent Office. Corporate research, Bush said, was "a very new and beneficent phase, a group phase, but the individual phase has not disappeared." While conceding that individual inventors were not protected sufficiently, Bush said, "the day of the individual inventor is not past, for as fine as these cooperative groups may be and necessary to our general progress in this country, they do not cover the entire field."

Bush and those who questioned him shared a common enthusiasm for the frontier and the individual, but they differed on how to keep them alive. According to Bush, the patent system did not need radical change but adjustments to support individual inventors. Among these were streamlining both the applications and the "interferences," the often-lengthy disputes between inventors, which had tied Land up for years. Bush did not favor plans for compulsory, nonexclusive licensing of patents, because this would reduce incentives for investors and actually favor large companies that did not depend on a single patent. Nor did he favor a blanket prohibition of cross-licensing or "pools," because that was often the only way to get a practical system on the market.

Bush and those who thought like him prevailed. The Monopoly Committee made its report shortly before Pearl Harbor, but the war put off action. Before the war ended, President Roosevelt named a new National Patent Planning Commission, which included Kettering. The new commission rejected the Justice Department's proposal of compulsory licensing, an idea that the Monopoly Committee favored. In the eventual legislation, the focus was on adjustments to the patent system, as Bush had recommended.[2]

∞

The war did not suppress Land's eagerness to carry mundane enterprises to a higher plane. An intriguing example of this drive lay at the frontier of invention and science. Under Land's wartime sponsorship, the first total synthesis of quinine, a scarce material of great medical importance, was devised. Proposing the synthesis and carrying it out was Robert Woodward, a young chemist at Harvard and later winner of the Nobel prize, who became a part-time Polaroid consultant on 1 June 1942.

Land knew a lot about quinine. Because the herapathite crystals he worked with as a youth were made of iodo-sulfate of quinine, quinine was a crucial component of all the early polarizers developed by Land-Wheelwright

Laboratories and Polaroid Corporation. When Japan occupied Indonesia, choking off most of the world's quinine supplies, finding a substitute became an urgent matter for Polaroid. Land made a two-pronged attack: completely redesigning the polarizer to eliminate the need for quinine, and the total synthesis of quinine. Both quests were successful, one commercially, the other technically.

The search for a quinine-free polarizer began in the late 1930s, because of the need to find materials able to stand high heat from automobile headlights and weathering by wind, rain, dust, and sunlight. The substitutes were made of polymers such as polyvinylene and were stained with iodine. The stained H sheet replaced the J sheet as Polaroid's basic commercial synthetic light polarizer.[3] According to Donald Brown, the key to this success lay in Land's work on "non-crystalline polarizers, polarizers made by staining or dyeing molecular oriented sheets or films of synthetic organic plastics." Highly efficient light-polarizing sheets, Land had discovered, could be made of transparent plastics, consisting of long-chain polymers such as polyvinyl butyral or polyvinyl alcohol, brought to a rubbery-elastic state, stretched to the limit, and then stained with a polarizing dye.[4]

In World War II, quinine gained enormous new importance because malaria was rife in regions where Allied armies would have to strike at the Axis. Quinine was the traditional substance for treating or preventing malaria. This debilitating, often fatal disease, still not conquered in the 1990s, is accompanied by recurring episodes of chills and fever, induced when *Plasmodium* parasites, injected by the bite of *Anopheles* mosquitoes, destroy red blood cells. In the early days of modern treatment, episodes of the disease went on for weeks or months, with up to twenty relapses of slowly diminishing severity. One type of the disease occasionally caused the blood vessels of the brain to be choked by the microbe *Plasmodium falciparum,* sending the patient into a coma or paralysis. The main military worry was that malaria could knock soldiers out of combat, unpredictably and for long periods, after they had been transported great distances at vast expense.

In the 1940s, it was estimated that three hundred million of the world's more than two billion people suffered from malaria, and that three million died from it annually. Malaria was rampant in the Pacific islands, where America first checked Japanese expansion in 1942 and then began rolling it back. The disease was rampant in India, where American forces rushed supplies over the Himalayas to China and prepared for invasions of Burma, and in Africa, including North Africa. Constant prevention measures were not always feasible.Field armies could not spray every forest, drain every nearby stagnant expanse of water, or coat the water with a film of oil. Soldiers could not constantly live and fight behind mosquito nets, or keep their sleeves rolled down and their trousers tucked inside their socks at night. Unchecked, malaria could decimate Allied armies.

The cinchona bark plantations on Japanese-occupied Java and Sumatra had provided 97 percent of the world's quinine in 1920. In 1941, as the United States confronted Japan over its drives into China and southeast Asia, the Americans foresaw danger to the chinchona supply. The United States then bought enough bark to make six million ounces of refined quinine sulfate, and held it for use by the armed forces. Frantic efforts were launched to increase production in Latin America, the original principal source of cinchona bark and the place where its curative effect had been discovered. American druggists, hearing of lives lost to malaria on Guadalcanal, donated to the Red Cross millions of quinine capsules that they had in stock.[5] The Americans estimated that three million soldiers might go to malarial regions. If each received 0.3 grams a day, the Army would have used thirty tons of quinine a month and run out in only four months.

As soon as Woodward began consulting at Polaroid, Land wanted his thoughts on quinine-free polarizers. Not long before, Polaroid had been so short of quinine that it had asked government permission to keep using its limited stock for one more month, while it completed arrangements to use substitutes. Woodward told Land that in his graduate work, he had looked into the possibility of synthesizing quinine. He had worked out a plan and always regretted not carrying it out. To Land, it was clear that Woodward's synthetic quinine would be too expensive for polarizers, though it could be an important military contribution.

On 1 September 1942, a month after American forces had gone ashore on Guadalcanal, Woodward submitted to Land a memorandum spelling out his ideas for the synthesis.[6] The next day, Land telephoned a very busy Bush in Washington and, the same day, followed up with a letter. To be sure, Land wrote, Polaroid was switching its production away from quinine but up to then, he had not seen any practical method for synthesizing it. Now, Woodward's plan "seems very promising and we would be very pleased to do this work here."

Land said that the main substitute, atabrine, was toxic and that the British forbade its use for aviators and generally regarded it as "undesirable in the field." Since atabrine had only been found after testing twelve thousand compounds, Land wrote, it was unlikely that another substitute for quinine would be ready "in time."[7] Atabrine was indeed given at the

Figure 1. Normal headlight glare blinds oncoming driver.

Figure 2. Polarizing filter invented by Land removes glare, reveals oncoming driver and pedestrian beyond.

Figure 3. Physicist George Wheelwright III, co-founder of Land's first enterprise, rotates pair of polarizers to show light blocking.

Figure 4. 1938. Wall Street investors have just given Land, 28, complete control of Polaroid Corporation for 10 years.

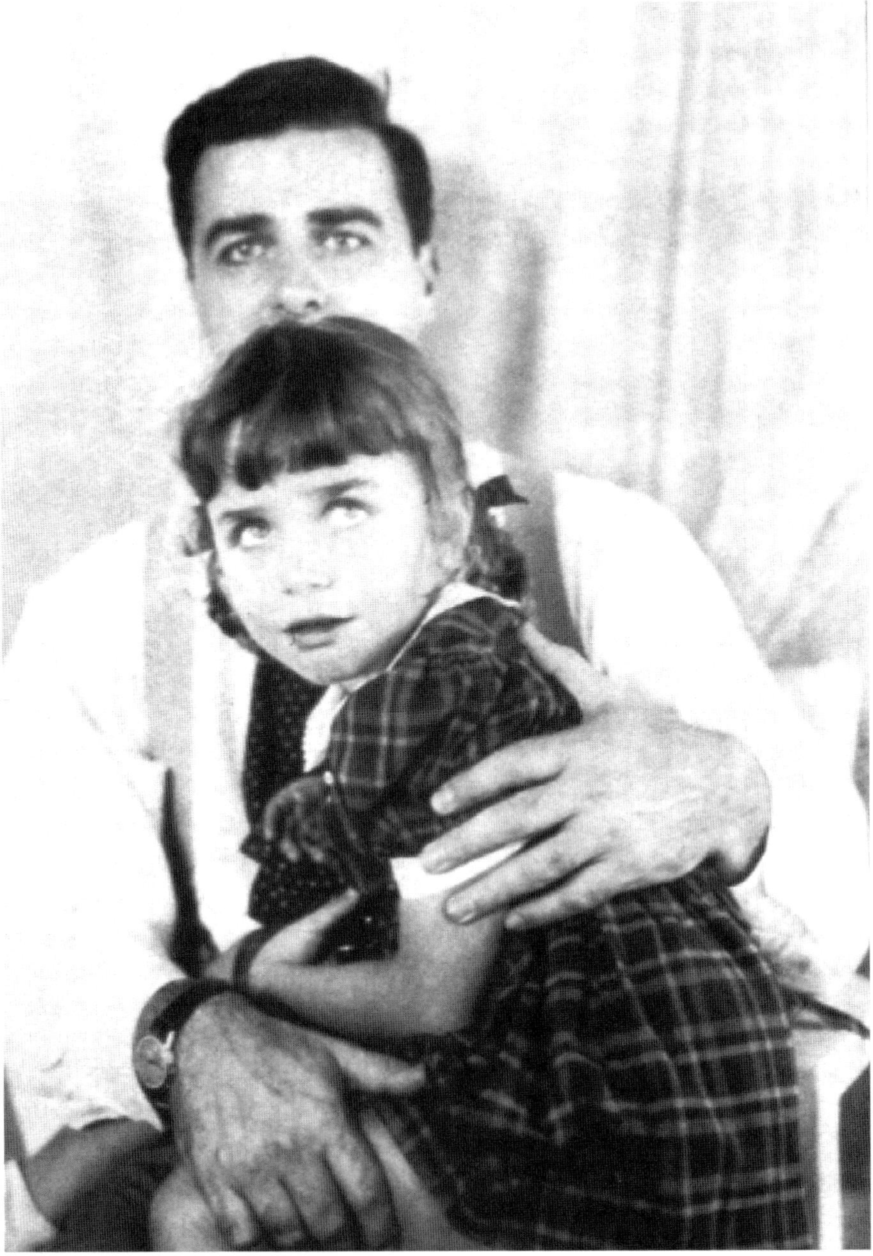

Figure 5. 1940s. Land holds daughter Jennifer, who, on family vacation in Santa Fe in December 1943, asked why she couldn't see the picture right away.

Figure 6. 30 January 1947. Land is preparing to demonstrate instant photography for the first time. Already committed to pipe smoking.

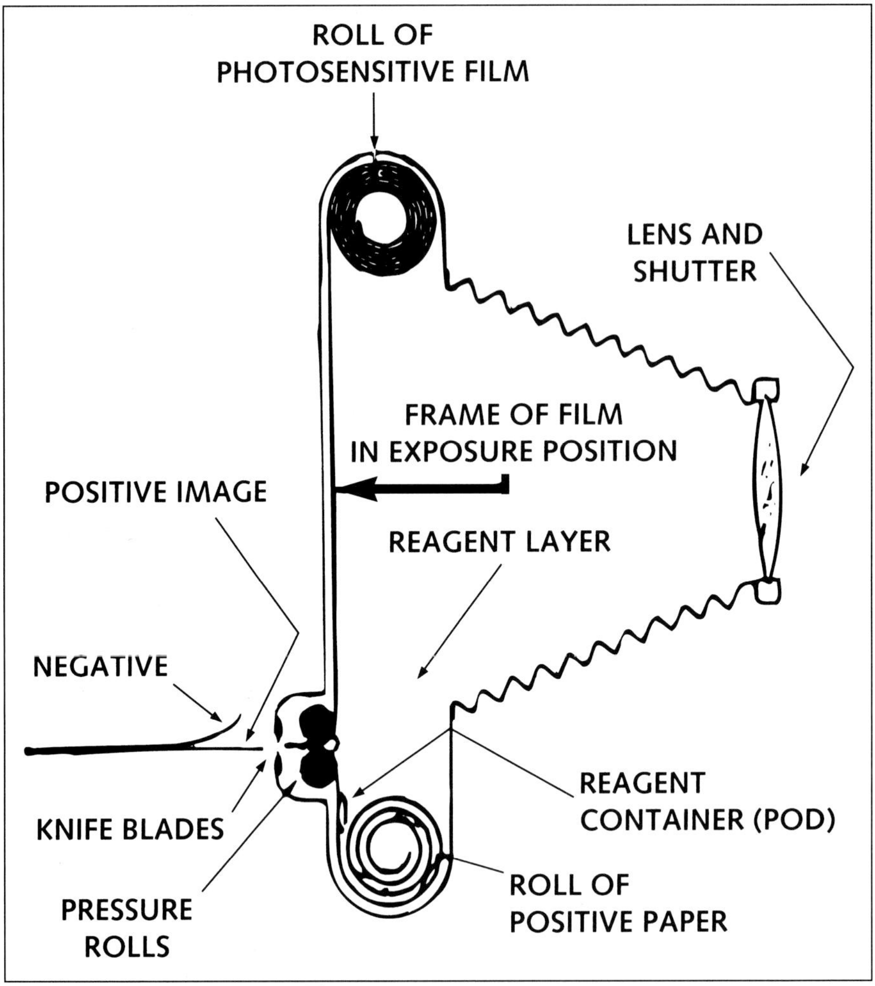

Figure 7. Idealized diagram of instant camera, used in newspapers, showing prints developing outside camera. For many years, film backing was not reliably opaque, and so development occurred in the camera's dark chamber.

Figure 8. Beaming Land at press briefing, surrounded by photographers, one of whom looks skeptical.

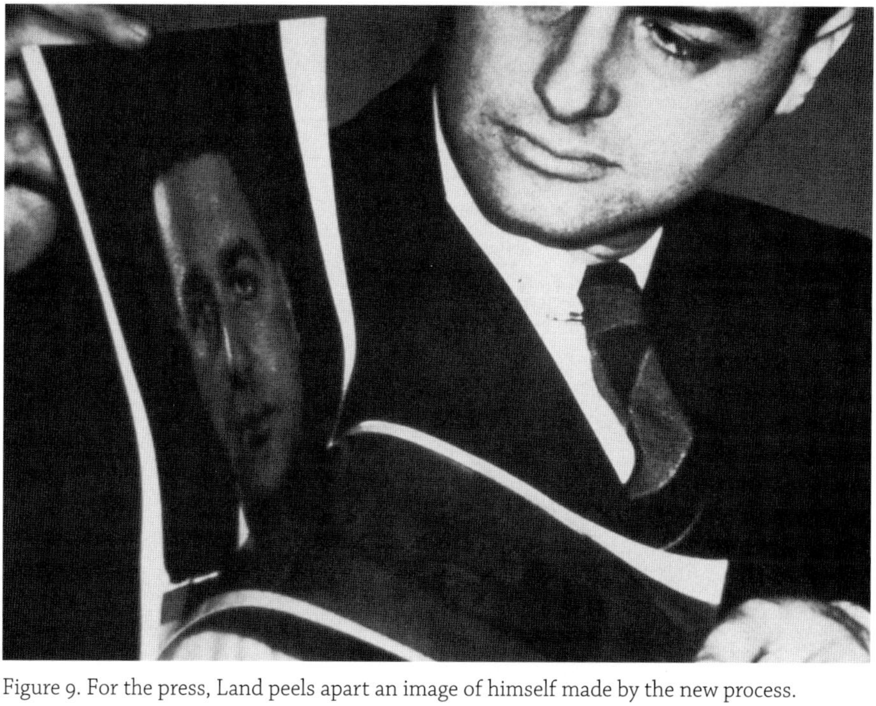

Figure 9. For the press, Land peels apart an image of himself made by the new process.

Figure 10. With one of the first instant cameras, Land peels apart a finished print, sixty seconds after the picture was taken.

Figure 11. 23 May 1946. Howard Rogers, Harvard dropout, after a decade working on Land's polarizer inventions, soon will start the fifteen-year trek to instant color.

wrong rates and over too short a time. It was known that quinine could control acute attacks of malaria and could also be used, at a dose of 0.3 grams a day, as a preventive. Prolonged use of quinine, however, led to "ringing in the ears, blurring of vision, nausea—symptoms that are a source of discomfort to any one, and of danger to aviators." Even so, it would have been used, if supplies had not been short.

I. G. Farben, the vast German chemical cartel, began looking for quinine substitutes during and after World War I, investigating thousands of compounds. In 1924, the company found one substitute, called plasmochin. It was most effective against the life stage of the malaria parasite that a mosquito would take up as it sucked in blood for a meal. It was toxic to humans and not very effective against the forms of *Plasmodium* that attacked human blood cells.

The yellow dye called atabrine, found in 1932 by I. G. Farben during the search that came up with plasmochin, appeared to be the only alternative. Unfortunately, the first ten years' experience with atabrine in the tropics indicated that it would be less effective against acute attacks than quinine and too toxic for use as a long-term suppressive drug. The skin of some people who took it turned yellow, hinting at damage to the liver and other organs from prolonged use, and soldiers heard rumors that the drug would affect their virility. In some patients two tablets of atabrine induced severe pain, nausea, vomiting, and prostration. Still, supplies of quinine were critically short. To stretch the supply, afflicted soldiers were put in the hospital for a minimum of two weeks and given two days of quinine, five days of atabrine, two days of no medication, and then five days of plasmochin to prevent relapses. To protect soldiers from becoming ill, atabrine could be given as a suppressive two days a week.[8]

In 1941, to forestall control by other organizations, Bush had organized the Committee on Medical Research (CMR) as part of his scientific empire. The committee pushed hard to cast more light on the treatment of malaria. By June 1942, it had more than seventy studies under way at universities and companies throughout the United States, using additional species of the parasite from Mexico and India and testing infected monkeys, chickens, canaries, ducks, and turkeys. These studies showed that the malaria parasites underwent many changes of form within the host cells. The drugs could affect the life stage that occurs during the two weeks between the insect bite and the parasite's reappearance in the bloodstream.

The committee's studies also reevaluated the presumed dangers of using atabrine as a suppressive or preventive. They found that American-made atabrine was identical with the German formulation. The dye's yellow color was found to indicate only an affinity for tissue proteins. When one tablet of atabrine, instead of two, was taken daily, with food, there was little stomach trouble. Six or seven tablets a week were enough to maintain the suppressive level of fifteen micrograms per liter of blood. But the benefit diminished as soldiers continued to take atabrine. Fortunately, a related skin disease and a form of psychosis linked to the drug affected less than one in a thousand.

In a study the CMR started in November 1942, researchers found that the old pattern of using atabrine against acute infections did not work well. The doctors had been giving three tablets of atabrine a day to get the effective antimalarial dose of thirty micrograms per liter in the blood, but it took three days to build up that dose, longer than quinine. When the doctors stepped up the atabrine dose in the first twenty-four hours, however, they found it just as effective as quinine. They also found that atabrine prevented any relapses with *Plasmodium falciparum*, something quinine could not do. Consequently, the sequence of quinine, atabrine, and plasmochin was stopped in August 1943.

The armed forces had plenty of atabrine because a chemist for Winthrop Chemical Company in Rensselaer, New York, which had been licensed by the Germans in the 1930s with a partial formula, had reconstructed the whole process. With the help of the pharmaceutical giant Merck, atabrine production soared from five million to five hundred million pills a year. The price dropped to $4.50 per thousand pills, a small fraction of the $66 that I. G. Farben had charged in 1933. In December 1942, Winthrop was honored by an Army-Navy "E" banner for excellence in production.

Meanwhile, the CMR continued to seek alternative drugs for malaria. The effects of more than fourteen thousand compounds were studied in animals. More than eighty compounds were tested in human guinea pigs, including prisoners in penitentiaries in Joliet, Illinois, and Atlanta, and residents in a reformatory at Rahway, New Jersey. When these tests did not come up with effective substitutes, efforts turned toward modifications of plasmochin. By the end of the war, this route looked promising for the future.[9]

Land's letter to Bush on 2 September 1942 dropped into the middle of this tremendous effort. Bush was alert to the stick-in-the-mud tendencies among doctors. As an assured and experienced inventor, Land wrote, "I have great faith in Dr. Woodward's ability and believe that although the quinine problem is classical, it can really be solved promptly now that he has described an inherently feasible synthesis."[10] Land evidently had struck the right combination of skepticism and urgency and captured Bush's interest.

Following his usual practice of turning ideas over to the experts, Bush wrote Land back two days later to say he had already brought the subject up with the chairman of the CMR and found "a great deal of interest indeed." Bush thought it would be easy for Land and the chairman to meet, "as you are both frequently in Washington."[11]

The following day, the chairman, A. N. Richards of the University of Pennsylvania, wrote Land directly, saying that substitutes for quinine already were being tested on "experimental infections," presumably in prison volunteers. He would put Land in touch with William Mansfield Clark, chairman of the NDRC's chemistry and chemical technology division. Clark was Richards's chief adviser on the chemical aspects of the quinine problem.[12] Three days later, on 8 September, Clark wrote Land asking for an outline of Woodward's plan. He inquired, cordially, "Is the Dr. Woodward whom you mention Dr. Paul Bartlett's assistant at Harvard?"[13] Woodward was, and he sent Clark a draft plan on 14 September.

Woodward, who had earned a Ph.D. from MIT at the age of twenty and studied for three years as a Junior Fellow at Harvard, did not minimize the difficulties. "It seems to me obvious that quinine could be produced synthetically only at a cost many times that of the natural product. For example, I should be pleasantly surprised if the enclosed synthesis, which I believe is about as short as could be devised, would proceed in over-all yield exceeding .1% to .2%." Still it might be undertaken in the present "trying times."[14] Marines were hanging on grimly at their air base on Guadalcanal, and soldiers were massing for the assault in North Africa. A week later, Clark wrote Woodward to say that his plan had been sent "confidentially to referees having no commercial connections."[15] A week later, he forwarded Woodward a letter from a leading expert on antimalarial drugs at Johns Hopkins University,[16] and then in October wrote to ask him to submit his plan to a "conference" to advise on the policy for quinine synthesis.[17]

Land could detect signs of a tangle, a delay, and even a probable refusal. He raised the stakes. Writing Clark on 2 November to offer cooperation with the conference, he added, bluntly, "We feel that we should proceed at once on our own responsibility with the suggested synthesis. In this way we may have something more concrete to contribute when the committee is ready to function."[18] Two days later, Clark sent Land the list of committee members who would "review the situation in the large." Even though Woodward was going ahead before applying for government support, he might like to submit his plan for comparison with others already submitted.[19] On 9 November, Land sent along six photostats of Woodward's plan, and three days later Clark wrote back, sending congratulations on "the excellent manner in which this proposal has been prepared."[20]

Would it be judged practical for use in the present war? Clark wrote to Land on 14 December that Woodward's proposal was "one of the two better schemes proposed."[21] The same day Clark wrote Woodward that his committee "took into consideration the known antimalarial activities of some of the isomers of quinine, the limitations in the supplies of certain raw materials, the time necessary to carry the synthesis from the laboratory scale through the pilot plant, and a good many other matters, and concluded that it would advise the CMR not to invest in the financial support of any program for the synthesis of quinine." He thanked Woodward and Polaroid for "splendid cooperation."[22]

Land wrote promptly, asking for more details,[23] and Clark replied rapidly and cordially with some specific comments on Woodward's ideas and suggested that Woodward talk further with a specific committee member.[24] Land replied that he would keep Clark informed about progress on Woodward's synthesis,[25] which was completed in Woodward's lab at Harvard. A year and a half later, on 11 April 1944, there was more than progress to report: Woodward had done it.

∞

Woodward's principal collaborator, William E. Doering, started with him on the project at Harvard and continued working on it after he landed a job as an instructor in organic chemistry at Columbia University. He continued the collaboration by telephone, and was able to travel up to Cambridge for the vacations at Christmas 1943 and Easter in 1944. A month after the achievement, he described to *The New Yorker* how it felt:

> Pasteur got an alkaloid from natural quinine, quinotoxine, in 1853, and in 1918 Rabe turned quinotoxine back into quinine. If we could make synthetic quinotoxine, it would be just one tiny step back to synthetic quinine. Well, one half of the quinotoxine molecule had already been duplicated, so we went after the other half, figuring that everything would be rosy—we'd have made another step in the great tradition. Everything was not rosy. Woodward had a blueprint for this thing, and I helped with the mixing. Chemistry is the world's most discouraging business, I guess, with one hour of thrill for three hundred of sweat, and it's always the *last* experiment

> that works. I get sick thinking of the details, but we worked fourteen months—February first, 1943, to April 11th, 1944, at eleven A.M. *sharp*. Boy, what a moment!

The New Yorker said that the project was "a public service endeavor" that got under way after Polaroid had bypassed its original dependence on quinine. The first month went smoothly, and Woodward and Doering had put together "the skeleton of the molecule's unduplicated half." But then came trouble. Doering's account continued:

> The next move was heartbreaking. Matter of opening atomic rings and knocking out a hydrogen atom. It took eight weeks. Twelve weeks for the third step, because we kept losing a key oxygen atom. Lord knows where it went but it wasn't there. You have no idea how depressed we got. We took to mumbling to each other. By September we were speaking in clear tones again: we had found the atom, each move was taking only five weeks, and the lab was filled with bottles of crystals, beautiful crystals. Organic chemists love crystals.

On Easter Sunday, Woodward and Doering were ready to combine the two halves of the molecule. From 9:30 one morning to 4:30 the next, they mixed and stirred and heated, but all they got was a dirty brown oil. They tried some natural crystals as "seeds." Nothing happened. On 10 April, they obtained crystals, but these would not purify completely. So they "had an ice-cream soda and went home at three A.M.," Doering recalled. "It was Woodward's birthday and I've never been so blue."

The next day, things went better, and Woodward and Doering had a fraction of a gram of "fluffy, faintly yellow, needle-like crystals." Tests followed, including a complex one in the darkroom, which succeeded. Doering came out of the darkroom and told Woodward, "This is it!" Woodward checked, and emerged smiling. He shook hands with Doering, and they called Land. Although Land seemed stunned, he recovered quickly and invited them to lunch at the Copley Plaza. Woodward had two scotch-and-sodas and Doering two daiquiris. Doering almost forgot the formula in a black cardboard folder under his chair.[26]

Despite his initial surprise, Land had been expecting the news. He had begun drafting a letter to Clark of the CMR malaria project on 30 March.[27] Now, on 14 April 1944, Land telephoned the news straight to Bush.

Land summarized the conversation for his files: "He said that I was a gentleman and a scholar to have called him and what did I want?" Polaroid, Land said, "did not now want to take the military responsibility for deciding just how the project would be handled from here on." Land suggested a small advisory committee, consisting of Bush, one officer each from the Army and Navy, and perhaps himself, to study whether both Merck and American Cyanamid should be brought in. Bush's first reaction was that this was a purchasing problem to be handled by the Quartermaster Corps. This was not what Land wanted to hear. Thinking quickly, he reminded Bush of the complexities of the whole field of antimalarial drugs. Bush reconsidered. The CMR should have a direct role in synthesizing compounds that might be more valuable than quinine. He wanted to think over the question of immediate publication. Bush thought that A. Baird Hastings of Harvard, a member of the CMR, should talk to Land.[28]

Soon after, Clark wrote Land that Polaroid was free to approach any company.[29] On 1 May, Land wrote out a memo of what he would say in another phone call to Bush. Did Clark's letter represent Bush's opinions? He still wanted Bush's "personal slant" on which manufacturers were the best. E. R. Squibb company had also shown interest in the Woodward-Doering process. And the government censor had cleared the story for publication. Land was prepared to hear that Bush could do nothing more. If so, Land wouldn't bother him further.[30]

Bush said that he hadn't seen Clark's letter and that he realized Polaroid needed government guidance on licensing Woodward's synthesis. He would follow up and call Land back. Bush believed that biological tests of the synthetic quinine would be needed.[31] The next day, Bush cordially telegraphed Land that he was "taking some of your questions up definitely with the Committee on Medical Research." He hoped to get back to Land, "shortly . . . [but] not as immediately as I had hoped."[32] Two days later, Bush again telegraphed Land that the CMR, meeting that day, probably would decide what advice to give Polaroid. "Of course production problems will be important."[33]

On 9 May, Bush suggested that Land's men talk with Donald Keyes of the War Production Board, which would decide what to do next about production.[34] The next day, Woodward, Doering, and three Polaroid officials met with Keyes and a large group, including Roger Adams, a member of the NDRC in Bush's organization; four men from the Chemicals Bureau of the War Production Board; and one representative each of the War and Navy Departments.

They agreed that the cost of quinine made by Woodward and Doering's synthesis was three thousand dollars a pound, almost two hundred times the sixteen-dollar price for the natural product. Cheaper reagents should be found for at least two steps in the synthesis. But they saw "very little chance, even after several years of research and development," of getting the price of the Woodward-Doering process down to sixteen dollar a pound. They agreed that some new work should be done with different forms of natural quinine, to produce enough for clinical tests. This work, however, which would not be done at Polaroid, would require pilot plants that would be difficult to start up in the face of acute wartime shortages of the qualified people.[35]

While the government was increasingly skeptical about the possibility of, or need for, proceeding with Woodward and Doering's synthesis, a barrage of favorable news stories, such as the interview with Doering, followed Polaroid's announcement of the quinine synthesis.

∞

The Polaroid announcement said that it was uncertain if "the rather intricate process involved in this synthesis can be made commercially practicable." The main interest of Land's company was "in the scientific and military contribution involved in this project."

Polaroid set an "embargo" on publishing the story before Sunday, 7 May 1944, the date that the Woodward-Doering scientific paper appeared in the *Journal of the American Chemical Society*.[36] The date had been agreed on with the journal's editor. Nevertheless, as so often happens when a science story is defined as "hot," a writer for the North American Newspaper Alliance found a way to break the story early. The story in *The New York Times*, by the paper's leading science reporter, William L. Laurence, was datelined Cambridge and ran on page 1, on Thursday, 4 May.[37] A month later, *Life* magazine ran a multipage spread on the achievement, for which the science photographer Fritz Goro documented each stage in the synthesis with model chemical structures, the laboratory apparatus, and closeups of the crystals.[38]

It was the beginning of important journalistic collaborations for Land. Less than three years later, Laurence would prominently cover Land's announcement of instant photography. In 1972, Goro would take a widely reprinted sideways view of Land's SX-70 camera, using laser beams and smoke to show the intricate pathway of light from the lens to the photographer's eye. At *Life*, the men in charge of science coverage were Gerard Piel and Dennis Flanagan, who in 1948 refounded *Scientific American*. In 1959 and 1977, the magazine ran articles by Land about his work on color vision. For many years, Polaroid bought a two-page color advertising spread at the center of the magazine to describe the company's work in science. In 1991, Piel, long retired from the magazine, wrote a Century Club memorial tribute to "Edwin H. Land, autodidact."[39]

The publicity about the quinine synthesis drew attention from many quarters, including private individuals, companies, and representatives of interests overseas, including the Soviet government and the wartime Office of Price Administration (OPA). The Anti-Trust Division of the Justice Department requested copies of any licensing agreements.[40] Unfavorable coverage came from the journalist I. F. Stone, then reporting for Marshall Field III's New Deal newspaper, *PM*. Stone charged that Polaroid's monopolistic control of the invention would restrict its use in war or peace.[41] Polaroid and Bush were annoyed, but soon Bush became philosophical. He reflected that "if one were attacked by a sheet like *PM*, one should just relax and enjoy it. For no one would believe it and no one would copy it. The real benefit of absurd attacks is often overlooked."[42]

By Wednesday, 10 May, Stone had dug further and uncovered and reported a significant fact: the military was not interested in synthetic quinine. Bush's staff had bounced Stone over to the War Department, where an official who refused to be named told him, "I can tell you this much. Since our supplies of atabrine are adequate, we're not worried about antimalarial drugs and we're convinced that atabrine is just as good as quinine."[43]

The truth of Stone's report was confirmed in a letter from the War Production Board to Polaroid on 1 August: "The supply situation of quinine is not considered sufficiently acute to warrant Government sponsorship of an obviously long-term program on synthetic quinine." Bush wrote Land on 24 August. The Committee on Medical Research had decided against testing either the manufacture or the biological effects of the Woodward-Doering compound. The next day, the War Production Board followed up with a draft letter to more than twenty companies that had told Polaroid of their interest in making quinine by the Woodward-Doering method. The letter said that military and civilian production of antimalarials was sufficient, and that "quinine is not critically needed." While acknowledging that the synthesis was "a brilliant research accomplishment," they were convinced that it needed testing in a pilot plant, a long-term proposition.[44]

Stone also found that Harvard was uncomfortable with Woodward and Doering's research, because the university's policies forbade patenting medically significant inventions.[45] So Land had to telephone James Conant, not as the wartime czar of atomic energy but as the president of Harvard. Soon, Conant met Carlton Fuller, executive vice president of Polaroid. Polaroid's board of directors quickly resolved to issue nonexclusive licenses "on a reasonable royalty basis." Conant assured Land that Woodward had not known of Harvard's policy because Harvard hadn't notified him. He congratulated Land on Polaroid's part in "a discovery which I think will stand as one of the landmarks of pure science in the history of American organic chemistry."

Woodward promptly went to work on developing a practical method for converting quinine to quinidine, a by-product of the Woodward-Doering synthesis that showed promise as a heart drug.[46] Woodward's synthesis was lastingly famous among scientists. In 1957, he received an honorary doctorate from Harvard on the same day that Land did. In 1965, his pioneering in chemical syntheses brought Woodward the Nobel prize.[47]

∞

The war was making a revolution in American science, and many asked how the revolution could be carried over into peacetime. Late in the war, with relatively few people thinking about the postwar risk from Soviet expansion into Europe and Asia, the main concern was to hold onto the wartime prosperity and not sink back into the oppressive, long stagnation of the Depression. The connection between science and prosperity seemed stronger than before the war, just as the connection between science and military effectiveness was clearer.

There were many issues. The war seemed to scientists like an intensive drawing down of a well, the pool of fundamental knowledge. The well needed to be replenished, as did the supply of trained talent in science and engineering. In America and Britain, the war had drawn thousands of young scientists and engineers into new problems, teaching invaluable lessons in the translation of science to engineering and vice versa. The war had interrupted the training of the still-younger talent that would be needed soon.[48]

The war demonstrated the strength of established scientific and technological institutions such as Johns Hopkins University, California Institute of Technology, Massachusetts Institute of Technology, and Bell Telephone Laboratories. These institutions drew on their existing competence and provided platforms for vast new research enterprises. The Applied Physics Laboratory at Johns Hopkins worked on the proximity fuse; the Jet Propulsion Laboratory at Caltech worked on rockets; and the Radiation Laboratory at MIT worked on radar. The struggle to develop new weapons and to deploy them in time to help win the war also highlighted the usefulness of smaller enterprises like Polaroid in moving nimbly and rapidly to innovate. Polaroid's performance foreshadowed the vital role of small firms that became obvious during the electronic and biotechnological revolutions that gained momentum in the 1970s.

Vannevar Bush had been schooled through increasing responsibility as a teacher, a project manager, and an administrator at MIT. He had no exaggerated reverence for the labs of the big companies and a good deal of concern about the proper use of patents to energize, not stifle, new enterprise. In the 1920s, he had helped Raytheon get started in the radio business, against the fierce rivalry of four major manufacturers. Raytheon and several other ventures gave Bush firsthand experience on the choppy waters that these start-up companies in advanced technology had to navigate. Small firms had a place in Bush's thinking about the future of science in America, and he already knew and respected Land and Polaroid.[49]

While Land worked on technologies that could guarantee Polaroid's future in a peacetime economy, he too was thinking more broadly about the fate of science-based companies such as his. People were impressed by his use of polarized light in antiglare systems and 3-D movies, which led to his Cresson Medal and Modern Pioneer award. During World War II, Polaroid grew explosively as a fast-turn-around military problem-solver and pushed into quinine synthesis despite discouragement. Land was established as someone whose views about postwar science would be of great interest.

A sign of the respect that Land commanded was the invitation to address the Standard Oil Development Company Forum at the Waldorf-Astoria hotel in New York on 5 October 1944. The forum's title was "The Future of Industrial Research." Speakers included Under Secretary of War Robert Patterson; Frank Jewett, the founding president of Bell Labs; and Harry Darby, president of American Cyanamid. Land told the conference that "the small company of the future will be as much a research organization as it is a manufacturing company" and that "this new company is the frontier for the next generation." In the "next and best phase of the Industrial Revolution," Land expected businesses to be "scientific, social, and economic" units, on the periphery of big cities and in the countryside, which will be "vigorously creative in pure science" with contributions comparable to those of universities. He thought that "the career of the pure scientist will be as much in the corporation laboratory as in the university." He had acted on this idea already by hiring chemists like Elkan Blout and Saul Cohen, and physicists like David Grey and Robert Clark Jones, promising them the chance to work on their own problems as well as those of Polaroid.

In this new type of social unit, Land expected a different boundary between management and labor. "All will regard themselves as labor in the sense of having as their common purpose learning new things and applying that knowledge for public welfare," Land said. "The machinist will be proud of and informed about the company's scientific advances; the scientist will enjoy the reduction to practice of his basic perceptions." For many years into the future, technicians and scientists in Land's own laboratory and elsewhere at Polaroid would continue to have this experience.

He thought of an industrial group of about fifty scientists studying intensely the recent advances in "newly available polyamide molecules, the cyclotron, radar technics," color photography, and enzymology. If they were "inspired by curiosity" about such fields and determined "to make something new and useful," they could "invent and develop an important new field in about two years." As he said this, he had begun the effort to develop the new field of instant photography in about that much time.

The scientists would patent the inventions based on "know-how deliberately acquired by the group." The patents would give the new type of science-based company a "justifiable" monopoly. Land asserted that he was ready to join Bush's challenge to the antimonopoly feeling that had intensified in both the Progressive era around 1910 and the New Deal in the 1930s:

> Who can object to such monopolies? Who can object to a monopoly when there are several thousands of them? Who can object to a monopoly when every few years the company enjoying the monopoly revises, alters, perhaps even discards its product, in order to supply a superior one to the public? Who can object to a monopoly when any new company, if it is built around a scientific nucleus, can create a new monopoly of its own by creating a wholly new field?

The new research-based enterprises would create jobs, not by multiplying the number of workers in one activity but by multiplying the workers' activities and economizing on the labor needed for each product. These activities themselves would use equipment that was "light-weight and automatic, requiring relatively small capital investment and relatively few operators." Land was advocating an increase in the size of the pie, not the redistribution of its pieces. Thus, a company spending more than usual on research, and pushing harder than usual on developing its manufacturing processes, would build machines, costing a few hundred thousand dollars. The machines would not only turn out many millions' worth of goods but also be easy to modify or discard as customers' needs changed.

In his 1944 Waldorf-Astoria talk, which he repeated in 1946 in Toronto, Land was stating a kind of charter for his business career. He thought such new companies would be an antidote to totalitarianism:

> Year by year, our national scene would change in the way, I think, all Americans dream of. Each individual will be a member of a group small enough so that he feels participant in the purpose and activity of the group. His voice will be heard and his individuality recognized. He will not feel the bitter need, now felt by countless thousands, for becoming a member of a great mystic mass movement that will protect him and give him a sense of importance.

Land wanted the profits of such a nimble company to enable it to experiment with new markets. He expressed an already-formed conviction that would create many tussles with his marketing people:

> I believe it is pretty well established now that neither the intuition of the sales manager nor even the first reaction of the public is a reliable measure of the value of a product to the consumer. Very often the best way to find out whether something is worth making is to make it, distribute it, and then to see, after the product has been around a few years, whether it was worth the trouble.

For the next thirty years, the enterprise he planned to build himself would prove able to take such risks—but not, as shown in the 1980s, forever.

The longer that companies like Land's kept their investment on research heavy and their investment in machinery as light as possible, the more they would gain intangible, even unpublishable, knowledge of production that they could draw on constantly. Research-based companies would become steadily richer and thus more able to make "an investigation of public taste by actual marketing." Such a company, in other words, could afford to make mistakes. In such a company, Land said, "A research program is never a failure. . . . Almost inevitably the research program which appeared to have failed several years ago results in new knowledge that some clever individual finally adapts to his company's needs."

A few weeks before Land's talk, Conant expressed fear that industry would lure too many scientists away with fat salaries. Land replied by suggesting that industries share basic researchers with universities, as he was already doing. Industries would gain deeper appreciation of the professional ethics of pure scientists, and university scientists would gain new aptitudes. They also would escape from "fads and trends" in pure science into wider fields and "greater human stimulus."

Land then enunciated an important doctrine that he himself did not follow over the next thirty-five years of his own industrial career. The ultimate danger for the successful, small, research-based company was to become large. Land suggested a cure:

> Perhaps some of the younger—and the older—men should take one of the numerous products which the laboratories will have developed, and base a new and similar company on this product. Ideally the parent company should control the new company for only a few years, setting it free for a life of its own as soon as it has the necessary strength. . . . Such a program seems to approximate an attractive industrial counterpart of Jefferson's concept of an American agricultural democracy.[50]

The model was adopted many years later by George Hatsopoulos of Thermo-Electron, a multi-faceted company in Massachusetts. In the 1970s and later, many large companies took Land's advice of 1944, as when DuPont turned over the invention of the water-resistant, yet "breathing," fabric called Gore-Tex to its inventor.

∞

Late in 1944, as many new weapons went into use and victory drew nearer, Bush induced President Roosevelt to write him another letter like the one of June 1940 setting up the National Defense Research Committee. This time, on 17 November 1944, FDR asked Bush to give him a report on post-war organization of American science. The result, entitled *Science: The Endless Frontier,* was published in July 1945, three months after Roosevelt's death. One of the people who helped draft the report was Land.

The report advocated an independent science-funding agency, directed by a nongovernment board of scientists. President Truman, some of his advisers, and influential members of Congress objected, and the project of a National Science Foundation (NSF) was delayed five years. The argument was fundamental: Should science be controlled by scientists or by a national policy external to science? The debate was still going on in the 1990s. Land was a soldier in this war in which each side claimed victories.

Bush's report strongly defended the patent system, which surely was highly agreeable to Land. To help with the report, Bush named four committees, one to address each of four topics Bush doubtless drafted at Roosevelt's request: declassifying secret knowledge, helping "the war against disease," organizing federal aid to government and private research, and "discovering and developing scientific talent in American youth."

The seventeen-member committee on the third topic focused on what became the NSF. It was headed by Isaiah Bowman, president of Johns Hopkins University, and included Oliver Buckley, president of Bell Telephone Laboratories; Oscar Cox, associate of FDR's leading counselor, Harry Hopkins; physicist I. I. Rabi of Columbia University; and Land. According to the Bowman committee, the proposed National Research Foundation would guarantee that the United States did plenty of basic research, in addition to the highly focused applied research of government laboratories, industry, and the military services. In a section on aid to industrial research, the Bowman committee also defended the patent system: "Patents are the life of research."[51]

Of course, industrial research and patenting were highly concentrated: in 1938, when thirteen companies employed a third of all industrial researchers, application did "not work equally effectively in all industries." Oil companies did a lot of research, while the coal industry lagged. The committee urged that universities, engineering schools, and nonprofit research institutes hold "clinics" to help small businesses get started doing research.[52]

Then a tangle arose, and Land was in the middle of it. He wanted the proposed foundation to take steps to encourage the establishment of small scientific enterprises like Polaroid. Others on the committee, however, didn't see how a government agency could do this. Land and some others on the committee were particularly concerned about encouraging those researchers who were driven to apply the most recent basic findings. He argued this so forcefully that the committee, perhaps out of weariness, simply reproduced his remarks in its report. In seeking new types of industry, Land wrote:

> We should not be satisfied with the cycle of displacement of one good technical product made of metal by the same product made of plastic, and so on, in a rather unimaginative utilization of fundamental developments. What is required is rapid invention and evolution of the peacetime analogues of jet-propelled vehicles, bazookas, and the multiplicity of secret, bold developments of the war.[53]

As he did at MIT in 1957, Land urged that students should be aimed at original research. "New types of industrial activity could be aided if students of engineering and science were strongly encouraged at the undergraduate stage to study unsolved technical problems and to invent solutions for them." When they graduated, they should be encouraged to "strike out for themselves" and make their inventions practical "in an actual enterprise." Most bright young scientists and engineers would go to large companies, where they would have a struggle:

> There is a long path of duty which the young scientist must pursue before he can become very effective in original contribution. Furthermore, most large industrial concerns are limited by policy to special directions of expansion within the well-established field of the company. On the other hand, most small companies do not have the resources or the facilities to support "scientific prospecting." Thus the young man leaving the university with a proposal for a new kind of activity is frequently not able to find a matrix for the development of his ideas in any established industrial organization.

For such a "potential scientific entrepreneur," university work could make him a good scholar "but may dampen his early leanings in the direction of the commercial development of his ideas."[54] Land had dropped a brief autobiography into Bush's grand design for science after 1945. The Bowman committee members knew they had to pay attention, but probably did not know what to make of Land or what he was saying.

Later in 1945 Land was called to testify to Congress on the report. He used the moment to inveigh against the idea of collective, secret invention, even in the newly revealed domain of atomic energy. The atomic bomb cast a "terrible shadow," Land said. Americans and the rest of the world did not understand the nucleus, and Americans did not understand the Russians. In the next ten years, America would have to "negotiate, argue, trade, bargain, and finally get to understand" not only the British and French, but also the Russians. Land could not have foreseen how, in the 1950s, he would help acquire some of that understanding and create a basis for more.

Land favored government research, but he did not want it to be a substitute for research by the thousands of science-based small businesses he hoped that America would create. He insisted that "the small business grows strong by having its own scientists and by building itself around their efforts." Small businesses certainly would be useful to the government in both war and peace, but they could not take government contracts if the government "automatically" could license rival firms under any resultant patents. The Senators must understand that "the very existence of the small companies in competition with large companies depends on the maintenance of their patent structure."[55]

10

Sepia in a Minute

> If you sense a deep human need, then you go back to all the basic science. If there is some missing, then you try to do more basic science and applied science until you get it. So you make the system to fulfill that need, rather than starting the other way around, where you have something and wonder what to do with it.
>
> —Edwin H. Land[1]

"Atavistic," for a tendency to hark back to ancient ideas and experiences, was one of Land's favorite words. This is a clue to his problem-solving mind and to his persuasiveness in enticing colleagues into his adventures. Even as a youth, he began revisiting very old problems, mostly concerned in some way with light, for the new insights they yielded. Memory, strong memory, without a great deal of embellishment or rewriting, became an important ingredient of his charisma. It was a charm of total comprehension laced with humor. Those who talked with him had a sense of immense untapped reserves, things he remembered and brought into unexpected associations and observations. Among his memories were the thousands of steps taken to work out the details of systems with the properties he wanted. Though the difficulties might have challenged his optimism, he was fond of referring to them. He brought the remembered facts and processes together again and again in intense marathons of experimentation. This was his way of cracking the nut.

The ability to make discoveries, Land thought, was an ancient, and poorly understood, human characteristic. Intense, undivided attention was essential: "I find it is important to work intensively for long hours when I am beginning to see solutions to a problem. At such times, atavistic competences seem to come welling up. You are handling so many variables at a barely conscious level that you can't afford to be interrupted. If you are, it may take a year to cover the same ground you could cover otherwise in 60 hours."[2]

Such an atavistic approach infused his first great adventure in photography. He would go back, in his own experience and also in the history of photography, to invent a startling new method of taking pictures. His invention would allow virtually instant comparison of a photograph and its subject. As with the polarizer, there would be magic in it, but now it was not a magic for small groups of highly trained technical specialists. It would turn out to be magic in daily life.

∞

As the stupendous American war effort built up, and Polaroid's with it, Land occasionally slipped away for some rest and a chance to think about the future. By late 1943, in Santa Fe with his family, the future was beginning to look ominously close. The concerns of 1940 were crowding back. What would Polaroid do after the war? What would happen when Land's unique ten-year grant of control expired in 1947? Would the company rely again on the dream of polarized headlights in every car? To that end, a blizzard of challenges to these headlights had been robustly met, but would the car companies really embrace such a complex system? If the dream vanished, what would the experienced innovators of Polaroid do?

In 1960, Donald Brown, Land's patent attorney, looked back on those days. He said that Polaroid's commitment to military problem-solving had given the company "a greatly expanded research and engineering division with very little, if any, civilian commercial business, and with a considerably expanded plant." To keep its employees and to continue developing and growing, Polaroid would need "some new product . . . some enlarged field of commercial activity."

By late 1943, it was clear that the Western democracies and Russia would win the war. The price in lives was mounting rapidly, but victory seemed certain. Experience had tempered Land's immense optimism: some mountains could take too long to climb. He couldn't wait for something to turn up. At least as insurance, Land's enterprise would need an initiative, an invention on demand. Under such pressure, Land's spirit was likely to aim at something grand and unexpected. But as Brown noted, his approach to the new opportunity would also be "deliberate and intellectual," systematic and thorough.[3]

At thirty-four, Land had already decided that "the photographic field was ready for a major invention." What would the invention be? The answer came in a casual question to a prepared mind. In the "charming town" of Santa Fe, Land took a photograph of his young daughter Jennifer, who asked why she couldn't see the picture right away. Something about the question hit Land. Jennifer was sent to her mother. It was time to go for a walk, alone, immediately, and think about the question. The simple answer seemed to be, Why not?

Thirty years later, in San Francisco, where the audience included his wife and many photographic engineers and scientists, Land recalled:

> It was a lovely day in Santa Fe. I was visiting my family, commuting across the country. There was about an inch of snow and wonderful sunshine and you could walk with no coat. And so, I went for a walk, haunted by my daughter's question, stimulated by the dangerously invigorating plateau air of Santa Fe. And during the course of that walk, the question kept coming, "Why not? Why not make a camera that gave a picture right away?"
>
> I think we all solve problems in one way only, namely in terms of our own personality, experience, and background. Prior to that day, I had been working with my colleagues on a number of photographic processes—in particular one called the Vectograph, which makes images in terms of vectorial inequality, three-dimensional images. We had been making those for military purposes, and in the course of doing that had learned a great deal about image-making by transfer from wash-off relief—transfer of iodine solutions—then passing them through a pair of rollers [from] a donor sheet [to] a receptor sheet.
>
> Strangely, by the end of that walk, the solution to the problem had been pretty well formulated. I would say that everything had been, except those few details that took from 1943 to 1973.

The audience laughed appreciatively.[4]

Land's little daughter had given him a task. He was happy that there was an answer. He told an interviewer in 1976, "'There was an inch of snow on the ground, the sun was bright and there was a marvelous smell from the pine woods. . . . I went for a walk and found, to my delight, that I knew enough about the camera process to put it together in my mind."[5] He recalled, "Within the hour, the camera, the film, and the physical chemistry became so clear to me that with a great sense of excitement I hurried over to the place where Donald Brown, our patent attorney (in Santa Fe by coincidence) was staying, to describe to him in great detail a dry camera that would give a picture immediately after exposure."[6] One-step photography, instant phtogrphy, had been born.

∞

Clarence Kennedy had helped bring Land into photography. First, there was Kennedy's project of displaying sculpture three-dimensionally to art students. Then Kennedy collaborated with him on the Vectograph, which Land described as "a basic invention that lets you put both pictures on one sheet at the same time." In the war, "an enormous undertaking" brought the Vectograph to skies above the battlefield. "So I was deeply immersed in photography, constantly."[7]

The passage through a pair of rollers that deposited an image on each side of the thick film base was vital to the Vectograph process. Could the mere pressure of rollers convert exposed film into a photographic positive? As usual, Land was in the realm of unconventional notions. He never thought of entering the regular business of photography. "I guess because I didn't believe in it. . . . I didn't believe that conventional cameras would survive." Looking back in the 1980s, he said, "I couldn't see what they were for, and I don't now."[8]

Soon after inventing one-step photography, Land began defining a new kind of experience. Just a few years later, after instant photography went on the market, he observed that standard amateur photography deprived the public of the artist's ability to compare "the original subject and partly finished work." It was an activity of "limited and sporadic interest." A gulf had arisen "between the majority who make snapshots as a record and a gamble, and the minority who can reveal beauty in this medium." Instant photography could give millions of users an artistic interaction with the subject.[9]

With the exception of medical images, Land was less interested in the interaction of such an emotional experience with commercial applications, however useful. Despite Land's tepid interest, an immense variety of uses for one-step photography arose. Its applications in business, engineering, and science, by increasing the overall market for instant photography, accelerated the cumulation of manufacturing experience and improvements that drove down costs, enhancing company profits. Land's great predecessor, George Eastman, understood that great insights and thousands of tiny improvements not only opened the photographic experience to yet more users but also paid for both the incremental improvements and the major innovations.[10] The numerous offshoots of mass-market photography would energize the manyfold growth of Polaroid Corporation in the 1950s and 1960s.

In 1981, Land denied that he had been much of an amateur, "conventional" photographer in 1943: "We never did anything conventional!" In the 1940s and thirty years later, he found "still photography techniques slow and clumsy and unrewarding." Still, he had a Rolleiflex and he took his daughter's picture, and she asked her question.

In Land's view, the consequences of his daughter's fateful question were felt very rapidly. "It was the fastest development in a whole new field that there ever has been industrially." Slightly more than three years elapsed from conception to the first public demonstration early in 1947. A maze of features was invented, tested, and put together, during and after the war. "Every concept in it is new," Land recalled, "the kind of photography, the kind of image making, the kind of photographic system, the way of developing, the way of taking it."[11]

∞

Back in 1943, not only was the idea new, but the process was difficult. Developing the photographs was a problem, as was transferring the image from the photographic negative to the positive. Stabilizing the images was an equal challenge. Land knew that "the whole image photo technique would have to be conceived of," and factories built to make the new systems. It wasn't "a question of taking some old system of photography and somehow pulling it out of the camera." At least not in the way he worked.

"If you sense a deep human need, then you go back to all the basic science." The need and the basic ingredients of meeting that need had been worked out in one walk. How else could the impossible become possible? "Unless you can imagine the undertaking as carried out, as I did that day, you completely inhibit the prospect. It becomes an absurdity." It would seem too hard to put together something that would "become part of everyday life." But once the basic idea had been reduced to practice, he could begin in 1948 by selling film that delivered prints with the sepia tones of the newspaper rotogravure sections, and go on in 1950 to black-and-white, and in 1963 to color. Land had something that "had to be made." Each system was an advance upon the known concepts of traditional photography, Land asserted in 1981. "As it has been said of many great processes, they certainly stand on the shoulders of processes that preceded them," but, Land added, "I had to do what no one else had done." He was "employing some old processes as the basis of generating new ones." At no stage in the sequence of inventions was it ever "a question of appropriating any photographic process that ever existed."[12]

Nonetheless, Land stuck to tradition when it would be unnecessary and disadvantageous to depart from it. As it turned out, the pictures could not be produced solely by the pressure of rollers, although rollers would be crucial in getting the process going. A basic fact was the enormous amplifying power of silver halide grains that photographers had been exploiting since 1840.

Deep into the future electronic age, in the 1980s, Land still praised photographic film as a "magnificent, absolutely unparalleled" recording device that rose from the pure intuition of intelligent, hardworking people:

> That wonderful material, the first solid-state recorder, [was] done intuitively by the [human] race in the 1850s to 1870s in a way much more impressive than any scientific achievement as we know it today could be . . . It records the whole image at once, just as your eye and brain record the whole image at once. It records it in graduated detail. It records it with just a few photons of light. Twenty photons on a grain. And then it is converted with the snap of a finger from being a recording medium to being the final image. Nevertheless the grains are put on at random. They look grainy because they're not in an orderly arrangement as electronic things are. It makes one wonder—and we're not the first to wonder—how much, how far you could go, if you knew how to put them down in orderly arrays.[13]

The molecules in these light-sensitive grains consist of silver atoms bound chemically to atoms in the halogen series of elements, including chlorine, bromine, and iodine. These elements have all but one of the permitted number of electrons in their outer shells. Another, complementary series of elements, such as silver, have just one electron in the outermost shell of electrons. Silver binds easily to the halogens. Grains of silver halide are formed and dispersed in gelatin, to create what is called, not strictly accurately, a photographic emulsion.

Controlled mixtures of halide grains, mostly silver bromide and silver iodide, with the help of inorganic chemical sensitizers, usually sulfur and gold compounds, can imprint in themselves a memory of the impact of a tiny amount of light. The imprinted memory, or "latent image," is amplified a hundred thousand times or more by "development" in a solution of photographic developer, which converts exposed grains into particles of metallic silver to form a visible image, the negative.

Before a judge many years later, Land said that the exact events of exposure had been studied from the beginning of photography and remained controversial. But he could give "a typical example of what the theory is." As soon as the shutter opens for a fraction of a second, individual quanta of light, photons, hit the grains and form photoelectrons that migrate to one or another imperfection in the crystal lattice of the grain. As the brief exposure continues, further charge accumulates, and the silver is converted atom by atom to silver sulfide within the grain. If the collection, the invisible speck of silver-sulfide molecules, is large enough, say, two hundred atoms of silver, the photographic developer will donate more electrons so that "the grain will actually squirt out microscopic fibers of silver." This forms "the elementary particle in the negative that you get from the drugstore."

Exposure "modifies the silver-halide grains in a way that is invisible to the eye, but which is nevertheless a real image . . . [an] invisible image, often called the latent image. [This] becomes the controlling and determining factor for all the subsequent processes leading to the final print." Such processes became practical, he said, only after the photographic industry "learned how to make that latent image stay there until you're ready to use it, so if you take pictures in Europe on black-and-white film, and come home, the latent image will still be there."[14]

∞

Land may have wanted no part of conventional photography, but his new field was a natural extension of his passion—light, which had led him into polarization and three-dimensional images. Capturing images on film was congenial intellectual territory at the intersection of rationalism and romanticism. Restudying and restating the "old, old knowledge" of photography took him back to the same time in the nineteenth century when the science of light polarization was expanding and the stereopticon and the kaleidoscope were invented. It thrust Land into direct, decades-long contact with the mass psychology of amateur photography.

Almost synonymous with the modern age, photography was born just as the railroad and the telegraph together began to speed the movement of goods and people. Photography rapidly became a domain of art and science and amusement, suffused not only with complex technologies but also with such emotions as the love of children and pride in social position.[15] Now, a century later, Land would compress a whole photographic darkroom into the space between two thin layers of specially coated material. He would go beyond a century of complex technological evolution that made photography available to ever more customers. Instant processing harked back to the early days of photography, when images could be seen forming, or even to painting, where the image sits before the artist as it takes shape. Some of the very earliest photography had been far more immediate than the systems created late in the nineteenth century. In those later years, the film, or even the whole camera, went off to the factory for processing. Roll film supplanted the variety of plates of glass and metal used during the first sixty years of photography. Millions could take pictures instead of a few thousand. Photography had evolved into a remote, "black box" sort of magic.

The roll film, which George Eastman exploited most notably, built on the technology that had begun with Louis Daguerre and Henry Fox Talbot. Lenses evolved alongside negative and positive materials to sharpen the images and drastically shorten the exposures. In the early development of photography up to 1875, the silver halides were coated onto both metal and glass plates, or impregnated into paper. There were both wet and dry processes. Some processes led to the development of a positive image on the original exposed surface; others to the printing of a complementary positive from a negative on a separate sheet. Until the 1880s, however, the apparatus was so elaborate and cumbersome that it was difficult to transport. Photography was limited to professionals and valiant amateurs.

Gelatin was not limited to glass plates, which were the first products of Eastman's company in Rochester. It had the great merit of being applicable to a flexible backing like cellulose nitrate (or today's cellulose triacetate or polyester) film. With the perfection of systems for producing rolls of gelatin-emulsion film, the door to amateur photography opened for millions. Photography became an increasingly powerful and widespread tool for the artist, the journalist, and the scientist.

Eastman, the chief organizer of the fantastic expansion of photography, started out as a bank clerk. He invented a plate-coating machine in his spare time and built a company around it. He started producing roll film on flexible supports. His cameras rapidly became smaller and cheaper, and consumption of roll film soared. Then a new source of demand appeared: movies. People soon were consuming more film as movie-theater customers than they were as picture-snappers. At each stage of the rapid expansion from the late 1880s to around 1910, Eastman had to convert himself into a new type of businessman, institutionalizing his previous work. He moved from problems of engineering and production to problems of marketing. From marketing, he moved to finance and a constantly shifting pattern of industrial alliances, including cartels.[16] This evolution quickly carried Eastman into realms of management that were of less interest to Land.

∞

In choosing "one-step photography" as the name of the process, Land "wanted to describe . . . the whole system that would do the operation, presenting a picture directly from a dry camera, without darkroom."[17] Normally the whole darkroom sequence took many minutes: development and stop baths and washing and drying to prepare the negative; and a corresponding, equally elaborate process for making prints. Land claimed that these darkroom steps, requiring careful timing and temperature control, "represent opportunities for someone who wants to work at length in the darkroom, but for the average amateur they represent hazards." Now, somehow, all this would be compressed into a minute.

One-step photography would also compress the stages in space—into a microscopically thin region between a strip of film and a strip of print paper. No silver could be washed away, as in the normal darkroom. Instead, the exposed silver would be trapped in the negative, while the unexposed silver traveled to the opposite sheet to form a positive almost simultaneously. The system had to distinguish between exposed and unexposed grains of silver halide. The silver had to concentrate as needed on the positive. When the print was ready, the highly reactive conditions of one minute had to settle down into a permanent calm. For all this, Land needed a whole team of chemicals, some embedded in the positive, and others released by the rollers. "A large part of the art is . . . getting [the silver] to aggregate not as colored deposits of brown or yellow, but as a rich, deep black."

With instant photography, Land sought to escape the "quite uncontrollable system" of the darkroom. The instant positive was "the symmetrical partner of the negative" and each would form at virtually the same time. The exactly timed process would use only enough chemicals to create one picture. Stored until the moment of use, that quantity of processor chemical could be much more alkaline and active than what was safe to put into a darkroom tray.[18]

Patent attorney Brown thought of Land's approach as methodical:

> In 1944, before commencing any research, before making any tests, he devised some six or seven methods of accomplishing the desired result and he determined which of these were most likely to succeed. Moreover, he [established] a set of specifications for the camera which was to be used in the process—its weight, the size of the print, the maximum time allowed for development of the negative and formation of the positive, the general type of camera to be used, and so on. He then set up a small private laboratory and with the help of two laboratory assistants conducted, in his spare time, experiments establishing the operability of the process.

According to Brown, the first patent application was made in the spring of 1945. "The revolutionary nature of the process may be indicated by the fact that of the first 200 applications in this field which we filed, only one case was rejected on prior art," that is, was deemed by the patent examiners to duplicate a feature already known or patented. By the time Brown spoke in 1960, Polaroid had obtained about 300 U.S. patents in instant photography, including about 120 in Land's name. Outside the United States, instant photography patents totaled more than 700 in twenty-five countries.[19]

Brown could look at the multitude of patents in 1960 with satisfaction bordering on wonder, but in 1944, he was impatient to start applying for patents. He wrote to another of Land's patent attorneys, Charles Mikulka, to complain that the patent work was "slow." Mikulka's reply reminded Brown that Land had definite and detailed ideas of how to protect his new field. In a memorandum approved by Land, Mikulka wrote that "Land felt it important to spend time on a few well-drawn, basic patent applications, which then would be followed by a series of narrower applications." The memo also noted that "Land was constantly inventing, describing new embodiments of an invention just when Mikulka thought he had finished an application."

Land wanted to work directly with a patent attorney, whom he expected to have "a sound knowledge of past photographic history." Land

and his patent attorneys began charting the various approaches and embodiments, so that he could pick topics for experiments. Mikulka, in tuen, could make sure the applications had appropriate scope, and could prepare for the follow-up applications. It became standard practice for the responsible patent lawyer to "attend regular research project meetings."[20]

∞

The work apparently began earlier than Brown said it did. In the musty files of Polaroid Corporation, removed in 1996 to bulk storage near Land's old laboratory at 2 Osborn Street, lie the almost-daily laboratory reports of the project code-named SX-70. The entries were either handwritten or typed on ditto masters, now-obsolete forms producing copies in blue ink. The first entry, dated 31 December 1943 and witnessed by Land's Vectograph colleague, Joseph Mahler, is by Eudoxia Muller, later Robert Woodward's wife. On 18 December 1943, "according to Mr. Land's instructions," she tried the first experiments in transferring an image from a negative to a positive when they were in direct contact. She made two prints with a wash-off relief film like that used in Vectograph work. One print was successful, the other not.

Using the light of a six-volt headlight, Muller exposed the wash-off film for thirty 30 minutes and then bonded it with developer to a sheet of Kodabromide photographic paper. Previously, she had soaked the paper in a solution of the classic fixative hypo (sodium thiosulfate) for about three minutes and then washed it in water for about five minutes. By fixing and washing the Kodabromide, she removed the silver halide, leaving a plain gelatin receiving layer on a paper base. She dipped the emulsion-coated print paper in developer for about a minute and then placed it against the gelatin side of the wash-off film. After pressing the film and paper together several times with a small rubber roller called a squeegee, she left the film and paper in contact for about two minutes. Muller reported: "An image appeared almost immediately on the wash-off. Not until the paper was taken into the light did it show an image."

She described the print: "The whole surface is bright yellow, the dye from the wash-off relief. The image is pale, showing the [optical properties] of the statue in the original negative. The lines and clear exposed areas come out clearly."[21] It was one of those tiny beams of encouragement at the beginning of the "four thousand, nine hundred, and ninety" steps.

∞

On 12 January 1944, Maxfield Parrish, Jr., son of the artist and a collaborator in Land's research shop, filed a blue-ink report on his work with a "device for applying great pressure with narrow rolls." He was already working on means of spreading reagents between two sheets of photographic paper. His report carried a sketch of an array of eight rolls of varying diameters.[22]

On 30 January, Howard Rogers's daily report said that he had conducted experiments on "developer matrix, the developer to be released with the film still in the camera."[23] The next day, in a report witnessed by Land, Muller described work on removing developed but unexposed gelatin from wash-off film without disturbing the desired properties. In February, she reported success in getting a positive image.[24]

Soon, work began on a tiny packet that would hold just enough of the processing chemicals for one picture. The packet, or the "pod," was crucial to the one-step photograph. In early September 1944, in a note witnessed by Muller, Fred Binda said that the pod was "to be placed and affixed between the negative and the receiving sheet so that after the negative is exposed, the film is wound between rolls causing the 'pod' to break open along one edge, allowing the developer to flow out and develop the negative." The language in the report is a little stiff, as if the writer were already thinking of a patent application. Binda's first pods were made out of brown Scotch masking tape lined with paraffin. The tape was folded over, and then the developer, in a viscous solution of sodium carboxymethyl cellulose, was put in. Binda sealed the pods with paraffin along three sides, with reported success: "These pods were tried out and they worked very well, the pod breaking open quite uniformly."[25] Another beam of encouragement shone on the entire process.

In 1947, before Polaroid had learned how to make a commercial film, Land showed the fledgling instant photography system to Kenneth Mees and others from Eastman Kodak. Land recalled giving the pod less emphasis in his demonstration than other aspects of the process: "I showed Dr. Mees some of our early work using the pod. I was so excited and proud of the image-making systems we had made. I regarded the pod as a nice piece of plumbing. Then Dr. Mees gathered everybody around—Kodak people and the Polaroid people—and I got set for all the wonderful phrases about what great chemistry—and he held up the pod and said, 'Gentlemen, this is the transcendent invention.'"[26]

Land's respect for the pod went up. By the time of the demonstration to Mees, the rectangular, flat pods that were so crucial were made of paper covered with lead foil, which in turn was clad with a plastic called polyvinyl butyral and sealed at the edges. The seal for the front edge, designed to break under the high pressure of the rollers, was made of ethyl cellulose. Land recalled proudly forty years later that the little packet could hold highly alkaline reagents "for ten years or more."[27]

The pod was vital because Land had specified that the one-step process be outwardly dry. The tiny reservoir of chemicals worked better than dispersing them in tiny droplets, which Land called "minute frangible cells," of the sort used in the "no carbon" copy sets used with credit cards. For his process to be virtually dry, he could not use fountain-pen sacs, damp sponges and sprays, or wet rolls. According to Land, it "took some courage because it implied that what the camera was to do to the film must be done with extraordinary simplicity [for the user], and that what the film was to do itself was to be unusual."[28]

How could the instant film contain the means of processing itself? Land enumerated the questions: "Since the most popular component for processing a film is liquid, water, a number of questions arise: Can a liquid be released by rolls? How small an amount of liquid can be released to develop a given area? Can this liquid be confined within the film during storage? How can the liquid be distributed with adequate uniformity as the film passes through the camera rolls? How can the camera be kept dry and how can the film be kept apparently dry?"

Land had not yet chosen the chemicals, but it seemed logical that the amount needed for developing the negative would be sufficient to form the positive as well. This thought cheered Land. In contrast to the chemicals in a darkroom tray, the one-step liquid and its contents would be used only once. The amount of developer needed for one picture amounted to one-twentieth of a cubic centimeter, which, when spread out over the picture, would form a layer just a few thousandths of an inch thick. The rectangular, flat pod, stretching along the leading edge of the film, would work admirably to contain this fluid.

The fluid was highly alkaline sodium hydroxide. Once the rollers pushed it from the pod, the fluid had to spread uniformly between the two sheets of the film sandwich. Land compared the fluid, which was thickened with carboxymethyl cellulose, to cold cream. He was charmed that the thickener turned out to be suitable for many jobs. It was always fun to dazzle listeners with the number of promising experiments surrounding the final choices, and the possibilities—often opposite possibilities—that flowed from tackling a seemingly impossible task.[29]

∞

Land started his own SX-70 experiments as early as March 1944, a bootleg enterprise amid the pressures of war work. In spare moments, he struggled with many problems with the sideline project. He was already thinking of how to spread the pod chemicals evenly and make the negative and positive develop almost simultaneously. He knew that, for a sharp image, unexposed silver in the negative must not wander. It must travel as short a distance as possible to the layer where it formed a positive image. The mountain looked high, but Land, like his colleagues, found encouragement early. "One of the startling experiences," he recalled later, "was to find out, once you have in mind a final purpose, how rapidly initial results can be obtained."[30]

After he succeeded in getting dyes to transfer, he then moved to silver transfer. Exploring the relationship between the structure of silver deposited into an image and its color, he experimented with Kodak Contrast Ortho film. He added some hypo to a developer called D-8. To receive the image, he used either filter paper or blotter paper, which he wetted with developer. "Next we put this wet sheet of filter paper down on a Plexiglas sheet, took the film, which had been exposed in the camera, rolled it against the filter paper, and left it there for about a minute. At the end of the minute we peeled it off, and what we had was a negative and a black-and-white positive image on the filter paper."

In thick gelatin receiving layers, the color was brown, and Land guessed that this was because the silver was in small particles spread far apart. Forty years later, at a conference in Rochester on the history of photography, Land simulated that early experiment: "This image formation takes place without any other chemistry at all, and so you can see the spectacular simplicity of the transfer process itself. And it is also a comment on human obtuseness, I suppose. As far as I know, no one had done that before. You expect it to be hard, you can't imagine it being true, but there is just nothing to it."

The "next simple step," Land recalled, was "to have the blotting paper be damp and, without needing the tray of developer, to run the two sheets together through rollers and peel them apart—and that's the whole process." In this manner, he took a picture of Donald Brown that survived decades later, to be copied and shown at the Rochester conference in 1986.

A portrait of Eudoxia Muller, also copied and shown in Rochester, was taken in a different way. The image was transferred not to blotting paper, but to a thick, impure gelatin emulsion from commercial film that had been "fixed out" with hypo. This removed exposed grains of silver halide and left residues that could "nucleate" the silver of the positive. The silver in the image was deposited in "very fine particles."

In 1945, Land used yet another process to take a picture of a Polaroid board member, the banker James Warburg. Not only did a thickening agent make the reagent more viscous to assure an even spread, a high concentration of lead acetate lay in the positive paper "receiving sheet." The lead interacted with a complex of silver and hypo so that the silver was deposited in the reagent fluid, in a thin layer of particles right next to the negative, and thus formed the image. Of this image, Land said, "These are rather large particles, which give a good dark neutral image, and it is an extremely sharp image, because the silver migrates only a minuscule distance between the surface of the negative and the surface of the reagent."

The next experiments foreshadowed the film demonstrated in 1947. The positive paper was dried with lead acetate in it. Its surface was coated with a mixture of colloidal silica with lead, zinc, or cadmium sulfide. Since a paper like this could be mass-produced, one could begin to think of the camera to use with it. Ideally, the camera would use negative and positive papers, each with one side completely opaque. The film sandwich, after passing through the pod-crushing and reagent-spreading rollers, could thus avoid further exposure to light when it came outside the camera to finish its development.[31]

∞

Afterward, Land always insisted that he had to see the system whole from the beginning. Otherwise, the system would have been impossible. The ideal specifications in his mind led to ways to achieve them. His memory of this sequence of thought and experiment changed little, although, with repetition, he sharpened his view of what he and his colleagues had achieved.

The aim he described in 1947 was to devise "a camera and a photographic process that would produce a finished positive print, directly from the camera, immediately after exposure. From the point of view of the user, the camera was to look essentially like an ordinary camera, the process was to be dry, the film was to be loaded in one of the usual ways, the positive print was to look essentially like a conventional paper print, and this print was to be completed within a minute or two after the picture was taken."[32]

Two years later, Land amplified the specifications:

> The picture must be available promptly after it is taken, and must be large enough for evaluation. The [characteristics]

> of the overall process must be so chosen as to lend [themselves] to recording scenes in haze, sunshine, and shadow, as well as by flash-light. The resolving power of the total system must be beyond the demands of the eye for the chosen size of picture. The final image must be stable. The camera should be as small and as light as is consistent with the picture size chosen, and should be dry and easy to load. The process must be reliable, safe, dry, or apparently dry, and behave well over a wide range of ambient temperatures and relative humidities.[33]

Land followed the innovator's classic pattern of introducing a change in a setting as conventional as possible. Instant cameras of the 1940s were to fit into photography as the electric lightbulbs of the 1880s had taken their place alongside gas lamps. Each innovation was imagined as a system. Related experiments opened up scores of alternate forms and applications that could be followed up later. Land wanted to start a whole field, a whole industry—and control it.

Camera design involved tradeoffs. The film must be inexpensive and the picture area big enough to satisfy the customer. On the other hand, these elements must not be too large or the camera would be too bulky. In practice, that meant a folding camera using roll film for pictures between 2 ¼ by 3 ¼ and 3 ¼ by 4 ¼ inches.

To compress darkroom processes right into the film, Land and his coworkers were plunging into chemical choreography. The classic hydroquinone developing agent reacted with an alkaline substance like sodium hydroxide to form a water-soluble sodium salt in a watery environment. Now, two ionized oxygen atoms were tied to the ends of the hydroquinone's benzene ring. Each oxygen atom could donate its extra electron to the silver ions bound in silver-halide crystals.

In highly alkaline and active conditions, the hydroquinone finished its work very fast, in the first seconds of processing. Then other processes took over, to complete the first-generation prints, those put on the market in 1948, in sixty seconds. By 1960, the time was down to ten seconds in some black-and-white films, as fast as the marketing people thought advisable. Land later liked to say that he had gotten it down to five seconds in the laboratory. Hydroquinone traveled in a sort of advancing wave, into the gelatin emulsion on the surface of the water-impermeable backing of the negative, and sought out grains of exposed silver halide. In the classic manner, the developer created its thickest network of reduced silver grains where the most light fell. The developer also partially neutralized the alkali compound, which slowed the process to a halt.

The positive image was less classic, and there were many possible ways to create it. Land tabulated ten types of images, many of them invisible, that could exist in the film: exposed and unexposed grains of silver, developed and undeveloped silver, oxidized developer and unoxidized developer, neutralized and un-neutralized alkali, and hardened and unhardened gelatin.

Perhaps one could convert the silver of the negative into a mirror, as in nineteenth-century tintypes. Or one could pull the unexposed silver out of the negative, get it over to the positive, and develop it there. Some of the ten images or combinations of them, including an image in hardened gelatin, looked promising. But Land had to choose. "There is, of course, a vast difference between producing some sort of image from some sort of emulsion and forming (over a wide range of ambient temperatures) a stable positive of good quality from an emulsion of high speed." He focused on exploiting the undeveloped silver, the unoxidized developer, and the unneutralized alkali.

Characteristically trying extremes and opposites, Land experimented with keeping developer to a minimum, and then with keeping the alkali to a minimum. Each experiment produced on unexposed photographic paper a positive that was not very sharp, "but one with good contrast and one that can be fixed, washed, and kept."

A third class of experiments involved adding the silver-halide solvent, hypo, to the reagent team. Hypo (sodium thiosulfate) had been used since the 1830s to fix countless negatives after their development. Fixing removed the unexposed silver halide grains. The hope was that hypo, which Muller had used in her very first experiment, could be used and reused, acting as a "messenger" to transfer the silver of the unexposed grains across to the positive to develop.

A happy feature was that the messenger's trip was typically very short. Soon after the liquid reagents were spread, they would be sopped up by the negative and positive layers. Little was left in the middle except the carboxymethyl cellulose thickening and spreading agent. Thus, the layer between the positive and negative shrank, while the negative swelled enormously. The original distance shortened, from about the thickness of a piece of paper, about twenty-thousandths of an inch, to a distance fifteen times smaller. The grains of unexposed silver that had dissolved out of the negative would travel a short and straight path to the nucleating centers on the surface of the print. That helped make the picture sharp, matching almost exactly the scene captured in the negative.

The unexposed grains that were dissolved and carried by the hypo were just the ones that would be thrown away in a normal darkroom. Penetrating the negative alongside the developer, the hypo solvent sought out grains of unexposed silver halide, forming a soluble complex with the silver halide of these grains. On the positive, the other shore, the hypo would release the complexed silver. Because the complexed silver was reduced to insoluble metallic silver and trapped, the hypo was freed for further ferrying. This fast and short journey was a one-way chemical gate for the silver–hypo complexes. Using hypo again and again required relatively few hypo molecules.

Insuring that the complexes ended up in the positive and stayed there called for additional steps. To study the details of forming the complexes, Land's team added different amounts of hypo. Working with both slow and fast negatives, they explored whether the complexes would break down spontaneously to form metallic silver, and whether they would do that in the negative, the reagent layer, or the opposite surface of the positive. In slow negatives that happened, but not in fast ones. Land was determined to work with speedy film that would be forgiving if the customer moved the camera. This called for releasing the unexposed silver from its hypo complex at the desired time.

The first step toward this was to place some kind of sulfide in the reagent fluid. Land could envision a "chain of circumstances." The hypo would dissolve the silver-halide grains and momentarily protect the silver from the reducing action of development, as it carried the complexed silver from the original sites. But the silver in the silver halide would actually prefer to associate with the sulfide, forming silver sulfide. Now, the silver would be open to reduction to metallic silver. And if that reduction occurred where it was wanted, a good positive print would result.

In this process, however, the sulfide ions had not been tamed. Moving rapidly, the ions would start too many silver sulfide grains growing. If these got too large, the positive picture would be too dense. If they remained too small, the picture would be bright yellow. Moreover, grains from the shadows of the negative, where a lot of silver would be available, would grow larger than those from lighter tones. The result was "an unpleasant combination of blue shadows and yellow highlights." Furthermore, some sulfide ions would get into the negative and "fog" it and correspondingly drop the silver concentration in the positive. Silver particles of uniform size were needed "so that highlight and shadow are the same hue."

The hypo complexing and releasing system would do little good unless there were enough "ferry slips" on the far shore to unload the cargo. To build the ferry slips, Land's group tried another sulfide, this time fine particles of a heavy-metal compound that was insoluble in the developer. These particles were arranged in hollow clusters or "galaxies" on the surface of the positive. Within the galaxies, "active sites," collecting centers, would form so that the silver built up properly. The galaxies were about the size of the eventual silver cluster that formed.

To hold the metal sulfide particles firmly in place, they were embedded in a suspension of very fine silica particles that were not soluble in the reagent liquid. The result was a "goo," as the laboratory people called it, which did not take up liquid or swell. The galaxies and the eventual particles of metallic silver were thus confined in a narrow layer.

This was not the end of the problems. The sulfide ion, having bound the silver and made it susceptible to reduction by the developer, might wander off and become a rogue again. The cure was to form the galaxies at "a relatively high concentration" of heavy-metal salts on the positive. When the goo was spread, the heavy-metal salts dissolved slowly and released metal ions. These ions would capture wandering sulfide ions, convert them to insoluble metal sulfides, and redeposit them very near their point of origin.

By these steps, Land recalled, his team was achieving "a type of intensification" that fascinated him, a "gain in speed, and a gain in sharpness both in exposing and printing." The silver in the positive was arranged in particles about one-millionth of a meter (one micrometer) across, and they had much greater "covering power" than did the silver in the negative. Most silver in the positive came from near the surface of the negative. To Land's delight, the possibilities were numerous. Indeed, silver particles could even be formed right next to the negative within the plastic thickening agent, a fact he later exploited in perfecting instant transparencies.

The timing of all these processes had to be precise because each controlled the other. The amounts of such chemicals as the reactive hypo and the sulfide ions had to be adjusted carefully. For example, both the hypo and the sulfide had to be present in very small quantities. With too much of either, the process left tiny amounts of silver thiosulfate and silver sulfide in the highlights of the positive. Later, these could turn into metallic silver and darken the image.[34]

In all this work, it was vital to control the exact shape and size of the particles of silver in the thin image layer, but in those days before electron microscopy, Land was largely guessing. "Thirty years later," according to Mary McCann, who joined Polaroid in 1960, "many of the original experimental images were examined by electron microscopy, and his predictions of the form and size of the silver particles proved quite accurate."[35]

∞

Land and his group had worked out a diffusion transfer process yielding sepia prints that did not have to be coated, many of which have lasted without degradation for more than fifty years. Such stability was not achieved easily. It was the third great step in the process, after exposure created the latent image and after development and transfer created the negative and positive. The key to a picture that "would survive over the generations," Land said, was "stopping all those processes, preventing new processes from occurring," so as to hold things where they were. Researchers had a "romantic tendency" to concentrate on getting the latent image and the visible image "and hope that you won't have to face the third step." In practice, however, they had to find a different stabilization method for each successive stage of one-step photography: sepia in 1948, black-and-white in 1950, peel-apart color in 1963, and non-peel-apart or "integral" color in 1972.

In sepia pictures, stabilization was achieved with soluble lead salts and water-soluble esters. These compounds were embedded during manufacturing in the clay-like baryta, or barium sulfate, coated on the print paper. When the alkaline processing fluid was pressed between the positive and negative, the esters and salts began reacting to bring the alkalinity down, but they could not be allowed to do this too fast. There had to be enough time for the silver image to build up, in a jungle-gym-like matrix, within a very thin layer in the positive. The salts and esters could then break up into alcohol and neutralizing acid, but they could not be allowed to go too far. If the environment became too acid, sulfur compounds would be produced that would attack the silver in the image and destroy the picture.

Once the sixty seconds of sepia processing was complete, the positive and negative could be peeled apart. In contrast to later processes, the layer of reagent was not stripped away, but left on top of the positive, "as a kind of protective layer."[36]

These feats continued to excite admiration for decades. In 1988, the physicist and science writer Jeremy Bernstein said that having "the negative and the positive made at essentially the same instant" required genius. "How much of this process Land envisaged that night in 1943 I do not know, but Nobel prizes have been given for less." He cited the Nobel prizes in physics that had been given in 1908 to Gabriel Lippman for a method of reproducing colors photographically and in 1912 to Nils Gustaf Dalén for a device that automatically regulated the lights of buoys and lighthouses.[37]

Stabilization was the vital chemical problem that brought Land's long-time friend, the chemist Saul Cohen, into the mainstream of Land's concerns. Land was "like a brother," Cohen reflected after Land's death, although they differed profoundly in their attitude toward their Jewish heritage. Cohen's ancestors left Russia well before Land's did. After graduating from Boston Latin School and summa cum laude from Harvard, Cohen found his career hampered by his obviously Jewish name. After twelve universities turned him down without an interview for a graduate teaching post, the Harvard chemistry department voted to offer him a scholarship so that he could go on to earn his Ph.D. degree, which he did in 1943.

Robert Woodward, who had become a consultant to Polaroid in 1942, proposed that Cohen meet Land to discuss a chemistry research position that was opening up at the rapidly expanding Polaroid Corporation. Cohen rejected this idea, because he wanted to continue "playing," that is, working on the chemistry problems that interested him. Elkan Blout took the job at Polaroid. Cohen went off on a National Research Council fellowship to the University of California at Los Angeles. He then took a job at the Pittsburgh Plate Glass Company, working on such things as the polymers needed to coat the window panes of bomber gun turrets.

In the summer of 1945, just as the war against Japan was ending, Cohen could no longer keep "playing." He spoke with Woodward again about Polaroid. When Cohen went to see Land, he was kept waiting. Cohen fumed. When admitted to Land's office, Cohen had to wait some more while Land thought very hard, silently, about something else. Land broke the silence by saying that it was all right for Cohen to come to work at Polaroid. Cohen replied by asking if there were anything in particular that Land wanted him to work on. Land said that if Cohen didn't know what he wanted to work on, then he shouldn't come to Polaroid. Cohen asked if this meant he could work on what interested him. Land said yes. Can you afford this? Cohen asked. Land replied, "Don't ask me what I can afford."

Cohen had asked a prescient question. Three months later, Land held the customary Christmas meeting with employees in the University Theater in Harvard Square, Cambridge. Cohen was sitting so far back that Land appeared very small, alone on the stage beneath a big proscenium. Cohen remembered that Land held a small piece of paper "in agony." Land announced that most of the more than 1,000 Polaroid employees, busy for years with war work, would have to be laid off. Because Land couldn't afford Cohen, the chemist found an expedient to stay at Polaroid, by arranging a research contract with the Army Signal Corps laboratory at Fort Monmouth, New Jersey. He was to work on the problems of initiating and terminating the chemical chain-building called polymerization.

One day early in 1947, just weeks before Land was to address the Optical Society of America in New York and reveal his instant system, Blout asked Cohen to go across the street from his lab at 730 Main Street to Land's laboratory at 2 Osborn Street. There, in a large, white room, Land took a picture. After a minute, Land pulled the positive print away from the negative. This was the first time Cohen had seen this system for instant photography and he was impressed. Land, by contrast, was gloomy. In an hour, said the inventor, the photograph would be a "black mess." The image was not stable. At the New York meeting, Land would take many pictures of people who would be impressed. When they got home, however, and looked at their image again, it would be obliterated.

Cohen asked Land to describe the chemistry of the process. Land did, and asked, "Would you do it that way?" Cohen asked how long Land had worked on this approach. Three months, came the reply. Then, Cohen said, Land shouldn't do it that way because it wasn't working. In a few minutes, the chemist suggested dipping the print in a compound that would stop the degradation of the image. Cohen referred to this as compound A of a class of chemicals.

Soon thereafter, Cohen was summoned again. Land held up a stable print. It looked like a success until Land took the print and snapped it in half. "What have you done to me?" Land asked. The chemical had made the paper base of the print brittle. Cohen calmly suggested compound B. That worked.

Sometime afterward, Cohen had a conversation, probably with Donald Brown, in which he was asked, in effect, to agree that his contribution was not fundamental. Admittedly, Cohen had provided the solution, but Land had posed the problem and worked on many other means of stabilization. For many years, Cohen repressed the memory of the conversation because he cherished his friendship with Land. When he checked decades later, Cohen learned that his name was indeed not on the patent.

Whether or not his contribution was fundamental, Cohen was consulted again and again about the chemical architecture of the sepia and then the black-and-white films. Chemical by chemical, Cohen participated in radical reformulations of the films. It wasn't play: it was work. In 1950, he accepted a teaching position at the new Brandeis University in Waltham,

Massachusetts. Cohen went to tell Land that he would be leaving in three months. Land asked why. Cohen reminded Land of his promise that he could work on what interested him, that is, that Cohen could play. Instead, Cohen was working. Land replied that Cohen's submission to all the requests for him to "work" was a sign of a defect in his character. From Julius Silver, who was involved in the founding of Brandeis, Land probably knew more about the origin of the new university than Cohen did. He was almost certainly relieved that Cohen was not taking his skills to a rival company. Remaining a Polaroid consultant into the 1980s and a friend of Land's for life, Cohen was certain that Land respected him for preserving his autonomy by working on his own problems, not somebody else's.[38] After all, Land insisted on this all his life.

∞

By 1946, it was time to let the rest of Polaroid in on the secret of SX-70. On Christmas Eve, at the movie theater in Harvard Square, the employees gathered. The proceedings began with what one person present recalled as "a stirring rendition of the famous [Purcell] Trumpet Voluntary by a Boston Symphony musician." Some employees were a little late because, as Land put it, "a happy busload of people started their Christmas party a little early." The bus got lost and had to be reclaimed by co-workers he called scouts. The mood was joyful, although the microphone was balky. Land said, "In general that sort of thing and the microphone not working are indications of the war being over. I think we'd just as soon not have the microphone going and have the war over." He added, "In the previous four or five years when we were busy killing people, in however good a cause, we all felt we had to fill ourselves with force and violent enthusiasm for Christmas. This year, we sort of take Christmas in our stride."

After a show by a magician and Land's review of company performance and goals, Land told the employees to be good detectives as they watched a clip from a silly Warner Brothers movie called *The Horn Blows at Midnight*. An angel, played by Jack Benny, is bound on a mission to Earth. A passport photo is needed by the heavenly administration. Using an eight-by-ten studio camera, another angel takes a portrait of the first. Effortlessly, as in all heavenly events, the finished print comes forth at once from the camera. An onlooker recalled, "Just then, the screen went black, the house lights went on, and Land, who had been standing there, said, 'That's SX-70!'"

"Most of the people who walked out of the meeting were still puzzled," but not the small laboratory "harem" of high school and Smith

College graduates who had labored "in a large old industrial loft-type building with no ceiling and a variety of exposed beams, pipes, and conduits . . . disguised by paint and lighting."[39]

Land had introduced the film "about a subject I cannot talk to you about . . . I'm not free, in other words, to tell you anything about SX-70 for a couple of months, but what happens in this movie happens in heaven, and I can't see why I am responsible for anything you learned from heaven. If you keep your wits about you, and if you're good detectives in the way our magician taught us to be, you will see near the end of this movie something that may probably suggest to you what SX-70 is." Detectable in the 78 rpm records made on the occasion is a tone of euphoria in Land's voice.[40]

∞

Early in 1947, Land used the new sepia film to make portraits of people who had been and still were important to him. Among them were Clarence Kennedy, Fordyce Tuttle of Kodak, William Coolidge of General Eletric, the Polaroid physicist David Grey (then working on lenses for the first instant camera), the polymer chemist Herman Mark, and the Army photoreconnaissance pioneer George Goddard. Another subject was Joachim Lehmkuhl, the founder of U.S. Time, who was preparing the way for his company to manufacture Polaroid cameras and components over several decades.[41]

Another portrait was of Vannevar Bush, who had wryly forecast one-step photography in his 1945 article, "As We May Think,"[42] and was now corresponding with Land about a lightweight, small microfilm reader that would handle like a book. Bush was deeply interested in easing the retrieval of the vast and swelling stores of information in the books and periodicals of libraries. A pioneer in analog computing, Bush lamented "a growing mountain of research" in a time when specialization was required for progress and yet was catching researchers in a bog. He foresaw "cheap complex devices of great reliability" to organize information, and make it easy to find and display. Fascinating generations of computer scientists, his proposed "memex" foreshadowed the personal computers of the 1970s and later.

Bush wrote to Land about his idea, even though he knew of Land's all-consuming preoccupation with one-step photography: "I would be rather fearful of relying on great established organizations in this general field in connection with an innovation that is as unorthodox as this particular one."[43] The two met to discuss the Fresnel lens of the proposed microfilm reader and its applications, and corresponded about it for at least two years, but a commercial system did not result.

At one point in his 1945 article, Bush coyly asked, "Will there be dry photography? It is already here in two forms. When Brady made his Civil War pictures, the plate had to be wet at the time of exposure. Now it has to be wet during development instead. In the future perhaps it need not be wetted at all." In the published version of his first paper on one-step photography, in February 1947, Land referred to Bush's question of a year and a half earlier.[44] By the time Land's paper appeared, as the portrait attests, Bush had visited Land and seen a version of his dry photography.

∞

Shortly before his talk at the winter meeting of the Optical Society of America, Land demonstrated the one-step process to members of the press in a small room of the Hotel Pennsylvania in New York. The watchwords were "on the spot" and "right away."

Friday, 21 February 1947, was such a snowy day that many events from Maine to North Carolina were canceled. President Truman even skipped his usual morning walk in Washington. In New York, the snow began falling around 4:30 P.M. the day before and kept right on until 3:15 in that afternoon.

At his demonstrations, Land told the reporters that a camera that used the new film was being designed for mass production. Only several months later, he said, would the marketing date and price be announced. He used a motorized camera taking eight-by-ten-inch pictures. A roll of negative sheet was at the top, and a roll of positive sheet, with long pods stretching from one side of the paper to the other, at the bottom. Right after a frame of negative was exposed, the motor drove the leading edge of each roll together and into a dark chamber. After a minute, the positive could be peeled away.

By the new method, according to the front-page story in *The New York Herald Tribune*, the photographer would take the picture, "develop it in full daylight on the scene by simply pulling it out of the camera," and then "see his finished work 50 seconds later." The photographer would need "no bulky tanks, injection devices, or special equipment," nor would he use special lenses or filters. "There is nothing difficult for the operator to learn." There would be "no waiting for processing."[45]

The "revolutionary new camera," William Laurence wrote in *The New York Times*, "accomplishes in a single step all the processing operations of ordinary photography." He quoted Land as saying that the new camera "will make it possible for anyone to take pictures anywhere, without special equipment for developing and printing and without waiting for his films to be processed." The story ran on the paper's "second front" page, with a small diagram provided by Polaroid Corporation and the paper's own photo showing Land holding up an eight-by-ten portrait of his own face, with the negative peeled back from it.[46] A similar photograph was published in *Life* magazine.

Land told the reporters that with this system, a photographer could take a trial portrait of someone and tell the person to stay in position while he checked the lighting and the pose. A report in *Time* magazine put it this way: "If a picture does not suit him, he can snap another immediately and hope for better results within the minute." Land took pictures of the reporters.[47]

The process did not leave the photographer with a negative that could be copied, although Land said that later developments would include a film type that yielded a usable negative. For Land, photo-processing firms could balance the business they lost from this lack of the standard negative. They wouldn't make the original print, but they could copy it at the customer's request. This argument impressed a trade magazine, *National Photo Dealer*: "Most likely the new processes will greatly increase the use of photography, so that the reprint business will be a substantial one." This would include enlargements and the negatives of copies.[48]

Although the pictures made in the demonstration were "of excellent quality," the *Herald Trib* reported that most of them bore "small parallel streaks like film scratches" running in the direction along which the film had been drawn from the camera. Some pictures "showed minute blemishes and pin-hole spots," and none of them was made available for "full-scale newspaper reproduction."[49] The magazine *Minicam Photography* described a photograph of the scene taken by Herbert Nichols of *The Christian Science Monitor*. Land was smiling broadly at a ring of unsmiling reporters and press photographers. The caption read: "Skeptical 'Show Me' expressions of newsmen contrasted with the inventor's jovial 'know how.'"[50]

Both Laurence and Nichols noted that the chemical-bearing pods next to each frame of film carried just enough processing fluid for one picture. The unexposed silver of the negative, normally discarded in processing, now was used to make the positive.

A *New York Times* editorial the same day as Laurence's story called attention to Vannevar Bush's hope of "a way of snapping pictures and looking at them immediately" and said that the call had been answered. Land's process was more sophisticated than the speedy darkroom techniques used for processing motion pictures, blueprints, or amusement park photos. "He simply presses the exposed film and a strip of paper into a sandwich. The 'ham' in the sandwich is a sticky yet almost dry mixture of developer and fixer which is squeezed out of a capsule. A turn of a knob and out comes the picture—a permanent positive." The method was not simple, but it was new, the editorial said. "All this seems so simple that, as usual, we wonder why it was not done before."[51]

On Wednesday, 5 March, Land repeated the demonstration for reporters in Boston, in the rooftop ballroom of the Parker House hotel, using an eight-by-ten-inch studio portrait camera and a four-by-five-inch Speed Graphic news camera with flashbulbs. He was both self-deprecatory and self-congratulatory about his accomplishment: "I don't know much about photography. But as an amateur hobbyist I have read most of the histories on it, particularly those dealing with the Fox Talbot experiments. What I've been able to develop here has been inherent in the photographic process for a hundred years."

Land said that Polaroid wasn't sure yet whether it would make its own camera or sell a special adapter for other cameras. Eventually, Polaroid did both. A reporter for *The Boston Herald*, Rudolph Elie, Jr., was admiring: "The finished picture is as good as anything you'd ever get back if you left a roll of film at your own corner drug store." One professional photographer or commercial film processor who attended was more dramatic: "Well, that finishes us. Me, I'm going back to the farm."

Despite being carefully "briefed on what to say and what not to say," Elie reported, Land was candid about details, indicating that "he and his associates have the situation pretty well in hand: clearly, nobody is going to muscle in on it at this stage of the game. They've got it sewn up in every seam."[52]

Although many of the details "escaped me entirely," Elie was impressed, as was the representative of *American Photography* magazine, by Land's remark that "it's easier to solve a whole bunch of problems all at once, as he did in this case, than to solve them one at a time. What he did, he said, was to draw up a list of all the things he wanted to do with his new process: develop, wash, fix, print, dry, and finish photographs all at once in the shortest possible time." The writer from *American Photography* put Land's argument this way: "Inasmuch as all the factors in a given chain of results are mutually interactive and simultaneously potent, they must all be attacked at once, as the final result is dependent on all the mutual inter-relations."

In the opinion of *American Photography*, the impact on the total business was likely to be modest: "For almost all commercial business the production of a multitude of identical prints is much more important than the quick production of a single print, which is desired by press photographers, many professional portrait workers, and the amateur in general . . . The process as at present announced requires more expensive cameras, a precise exposure and a fairly constant light source, a film obviously more expensive to produce, and a contemplated negative for every print."[53]

But these sage observations did not dominate Land's conversation with Elie of *The Herald*. Now that the system was a reality, Land said, forty seconds seemed too long. "I get impatient waiting for them to come out myself."

Elie wrote that Land "looks a little as you'd expect Cary Grant's younger brother to look, which is to say, dark, handsome, and tall enough to look anybody in the eye." Riding down in the elevator with Land after the demonstration, Elie asked him, "What next?" Land replied, in a soft-spoken but slightly reproachful tone, "Well, that's the modern mind for you. Never satisfied. Always looking for something new."[54]

11

"A Whole New Industry"

> We live in a world changing so rapidly that what we mean frequently by common sense is doing the thing that would have been right last year.
>
> —Edwin H. Land to Polaroid employees, 25 June 1958

In 1947 and 1948, to reach the market, the experimental one-step sepia film had to become Type 40 film. The company had to design and build automatic machinery to assemble its innovative positive with the more conventional negative supplied by Kodak. A practical camera for the fast films needed by amateur photographers had to be designed. At first, the Model 95 camera was made by a company called Samson United in Rochester, New York. But in the crisis year of 1950, Polaroid had to change suppliers, and the changeover to U.S. Time of Middlebury, Connecticut, took months.[1] The marketing department had to learn how to sell cameras and film directly to the public.

Characteristically, Land's first public demonstration on that snowy day in 1947 had differed from the standard new-product introduction. The press was invited, to be sure, but the radically new type of picture-taking was unveiled at a scientific meeting. Science reporters had learned to trust Land. In their hands, his ideas went forth before the system went commercial. The diagram he gave out to the press as well as scientists and engineers depicted "an idealized camera and film."

At the demonstration, he had used a standard, if outsize, camera. The negative, the positive, and the pod of processing chemicals ran through rollers, albeit motorized, and the final image indeed was peeled apart from the negative in about sixty seconds. But before a commercially produced camera could reach customers, twenty-one months of work lay ahead. Only then could Polaroid sell cameras and film of sufficient speed and accuracy to please customers by minimizing mistakes. People liked the new system—even if the first film produced sepia prints—and purchased it as fast as Polaroid and its suppliers could make it, but it fell short of the ideal.

A key feature in the idealized diagram was a film with exterior surfaces opaque to light on each side, so that the photographer could pull the film sandwich through the rollers and outside the camera for its one minute of processing. But such a film was not ready in 1947 or 1948. It became practical only in the 1960s. Looking back in 1981, Land said, "We didn't know how—for a long time after that—to make . . . opaque backs that were free from pinholes, that would be able to keep out the sunlight, which, of course, was millions of times brighter than the light used for taking the picture." In the early Polaroid systems, the film remained inside the camera as it was processed, and the customer opened a door in the back to peel the print apart from its negative.

The problem was both technical and economic. The available light-blocking material was either too thick or too expensive. If the backing on each side were too thick, it would be too stiff to go around the rollers to bring the negative and positive together and squeeze the processing liquid between them reliably. Because the negative was larger than the usual thirty-five-millimeter or two-inch films in standard use, the materials in this negative would inevitably cost more. "If that black backing was as expensive as implied by all these difficulties, then it was not economically feasible." Land recalled that consequently, "we were not able to proceed to develop a camera of this type at that time, nor indeed did we for a long time after that."[2] In the midst of partial successes and compromises, Land was looking forward to an ideal system, no matter how long it took.

∞

Land's leap into the new field had several now-familiar features of high technology. One was the pre-announcement of a new product. This practice is often criticized as overpromising so as to preempt rivals. Decades later, the electronic industry used the term "vaporware" to describe the early announcement of an unperfected innovation to "beat" other rivals to the punch. An innovator, however, must not be too late in preparing customers' minds.

The plunge into one-step photography implied a reinvention of Polaroid Corporation, which had already been reinvented several times. The small band of engineers and scientists had first evolved into a maker of sunglass lenses for American Optical and camera filters for Kodak in the 1930s. Then, in the 1940s, the researchers and factory workers mobilized to make a plethora of optical devices for the American military.

Such bold reinventions were certainly no more drastic than those in the steel industry in the last quarter of the nineteenth century. As manager, bond salesman, and builder, dealing in iron for bridges and steel for rails, the insistent Andrew Carnegie drove on. After his first success with steel rails, he knew that he must quickly and continually seek economies of scale. He had to find new markets to absorb the rapidly expanding output, such as buildings and naval armor. All the while, he fought for control of coke and iron ore supplies, and whittled away at the costs of transportation.[3]

As befitted a twentieth-century entrepreneur, Land built his career around science and invention, although he was less of a businessman than Carnegie. Land nevertheless reveled in the repeated reinventions. Both men were in a hurry, knowing that the demand for innovation would never let up. They did not just exploit new technologies and new materials, as personal computers did later. At short intervals, they had to rethink their decisions about making or buying a component, and about the channels for selling a product. In the late 1940s, in its new field of instant photography, Polaroid was no longer selling through another company. It was moving one vital step closer to ultimate consumers.

At first, sales were just a few million dollars a year, and Polaroid could not tie up scarce resources in real estate or big factories. The long prewar struggle to make even a little money had taught Land and his advisers to be cautious, even old-fashioned, in most aspects of business. The sale of additional equity on Wall Street in 1945 prepared for the choppy seas of postwar reconversion, but Land and his advisers refused to take on debt. The company's buildings were still mostly rented. Polaroid remained primarily an innovation shop, only making what was particularly challenging—and secret.

The clever and complicated positive of the new film was a prime example of this type of innovation. The company made this but "outsourced" other components, such as cameras from U.S. Time and huge rolls of negative film from Eastman Kodak. Negotiating with these giant suppliers, principally through Bill McCune, whose engineering responsibilities kept growing, was a stiff challenge. What Polaroid wanted had to be manufacturable. Over many years, McCune had to force the compromises of engineering on an impatient Land.

No matter how confident Land may have been that the new convenience and immediacy of one-step picture-taking would sell itself, the scientist-innovator had to start talking to sales and marketing executives and the leaders, designers, and copywriters of advertising agencies. To keep the marketers on their toes, he and his little laboratory family had to show real interest in what these people from a different culture were doing.

At first, the company was too poor to put much pizazz into its marketing. In 1948, the highly experienced J. Harold Booth came in from Bell and Howell, a leading maker and marketer of home-movie systems, as executive vice president. Booth had almost no money for splashy ads. Instead, instant photography rolled out, city by city, and sold itself at first by word of mouth and demonstration. When the first Model 95 cameras and Type 40 film were sold at the Jordan Marsh department store in Boston, the day after Thanksgiving 1948, they were snapped up in minutes. The scene was so hectic, as people at Polaroid liked to remember, that one customer was sold a nonworking model.[4]

The campaign leaped to sunny winter vacation spots in Florida. People on holiday bought the new system, tried it, liked it, and took it home with them. As more cameras and films became available, the photo shops of more and more cities carried them. Soon, the company had some cash for advertising on live, black-and-white television. Sixty-second photos were ideal for TV. The well-known singer Perry Como and popular TV hosts such as Dave Garroway, Steve Allen, and Jack Paar could show off the Polaroid camera, take a picture, let it develop for sixty seconds, peel it apart, and hold it up for the viewers.[5]

The reverberations of this new photographic experience transcended the cleverness of the inventor, the quality control of the engineer, and the talent of the advertising agency. People liked instant photography more than anyone could have predicted. On New Year's Eve 1956, the one millionth camera was sold at a dealer's shop in New Jersey.[6] The second million followed soon after. It was a novelty at a time very receptive to novelties. The end of the war had released the biggest avalanche of pent-up mass consumption in history. After a decade of depression and half a decade of war, customers wanted houses and cars and refrigerators and television sets, and they had saved the money to buy them. Waves of children, long-delayed children, made their appearance. It was a time of prosperity and hope, with many happy events to record. Land had provided people an impulsive and forgiving way to do that.

∞

Photography as it was dissatisfied Land. In November 1948, he told the Photographic Society of America in Cincinnati that photographers comprised two classes: "those who take themselves seriously as photographers, and those who don't." The first group, seeking an artistic effect, was ready to make judgments and choices throughout the many, often highly technical, steps of making a finished print. The second group, far larger, was the snap-shooters. They "have made a quick decision about the brightness of the day and the arrangement of the subject matter, [and] snap the trigger and pray that when the pictures come back from the photo-finishers, two or three of the prints will be worthwhile." Snap-shooters were not interested in the details of lenses, shutters, and the varying sensitivities of films. But if they could see their prints right away, many could learn quickly how to improve their pictures for a more pleasing aesthetic effect.

For this vast second group, Polaroid devised a camera that stood halfway between the "elementary" types sold at low prices and the intricate ones sold to serious amateurs and professionals. About the same size as the ordinary cameras for making 3 ¼ by 4 ¼ inch prints, the Polaroid instant camera would often be used to take portraits. So the focal length, or distance between the lens and the film plane, was 135 millimeters. A bellows protected the light path. The photographer opened the front of the camera and moved the lens forward on rails until it locked in place. Except for the small door at the back for peeling out the prints, the body was of die-cast aluminum with a brushed-chrome finish. David Grey designed the three-element lens, with all its surfaces coated, and Eastman Kodak made it.

The film speed was equivalent to 100 on the ASA scale, fast enough to allow lens openings between an 11th and a 45th of the focal length, f/11 to f/45. The largest aperture was a bit more than 12 millimeters and the smallest was 3. Snap-shooters did not have to fiddle with f-numbers. Instead they used a simple "exposure value" dial with settings from 1 to 8, each admitting half as much light as the one before. A setting of 1, the widest, would be used for subjects in dark shade. For average subjects in bright sunshine, a setting of 5 was suggested. The narrowest setting of 8 was for bright snow scenes.

The exposure value dial simultaneously controlled the lens aperture and the timing of the shutter, whose key component was a blade—Land called it a vane—that flashed across the lens opening under the control of springs and cams. Mounted on clock bearings, the blade was held in place by a tiny magnet. When the photographer pushed the shutter button, the blade was released, kicked off by a spring, and traveled through a circular arc only as far as the dial setting permitted. Striking a bounce spring, the blade flashed back to the starting position and was recaptured by the magnet. The design by Land's lab colleague Murray N. Fairbank was accurate to plus or minus 10 percent, as thousands of test exposures showed.

Land's little company could not order a shutter off the shelf. Land found, "almost to our horror," that "shutters with the best names in the world on them were useless for our purpose, because the apertures were not accurate. We had to design our own precision shutter."

The need for accuracy, Land said, was "more than philosophical." The photographer had no "chance to correct any error in exposure of the negative by the way you develop it or by the way you print it." In conventional systems, the exposure of the positive could be adjusted in the darkroom to compensate for overexposed or underexposed negatives. Users of ordinary cameras got their prints back from the photo-finisher days or weeks later and so had little idea of what exposure they had used: the amount of processing in the lab varied considerably. A one-step photographer could see results on the spot, but the film lacked the compensatory steps of the laboratory. Land said that the user of an instant camera "is testing the reliability of the shutter each time he takes two pictures in succession."

Polaroid film was more convenient than the regular roll films of the day, which needed to be threaded onto spools. To load it, the photographer just opened the camera back and dropped in the roll of the negative at one side and the roll of the positive, with the pods attached for each print, at the other. The positive and negative rolls were connected to the same strip of paper, or leader. Closing the camera back, the photographer pulled the leader to a pair of stop holes, which held the film in the correct position to take the first picture. It was the first drop-in loading for a roll-film camera.

The underlying task, Land said, had been "the careful balancing of the simultaneous growth of the negative and positive."[7] Achieving that balance—alongside the details of silver halide, film speed, developer, and physical chemistry in the positive—involved the vexed question of what type of chemical stabilization was best to make the picture permanent.

∞

In June 1947, soon after the unveiling of his new photography, Land was faced with a public questioning of its novelty. The challenge was issued by a close student of the world literature of photography patents, Lloyd E. Varden, technical director of Pavelle Color Company in New York and a Fellow of the Photographic Society of America (PSA). In the journal of the

Optical Society of America, Varden wrote that features of Land's inventions might have been anticipated and that Land did not sufficiently acknowledge the wartime "diffusion transfer" patents of André Rott in Belgium. Nor had Land referred explicitly to contemporary work by Edith Weyde in Germany. Their inventions were used by the photography firms Gevaert and Agfa to make document copiers after the war.[8] In September of that year, Varden described Rott's and Weyde's work in detail in the PSA's journal.[9]

Land was unyielding in his reply. He had focused on a system of photography. Its camera, resembling ordinary cameras, performed an apparently dry process to yield a finished print. This print, resembling a conventional paper print, was removed from the camera almost immediately after exposure. He had claimed, "In photographic literature there appear to be no references to such a system of photography, even as an ideal," and he repeated this. While the statement was "accurate as it stands," Land said he had not meant "to imply that the system I was describing was unrelated to principles already known in photography." From the beginning, he said, he had used "as far as possible, established and proved principles and materials." The patents that Varden had mentioned "are related no more closely to my own procedures than the work of many other previous investigators, certainly fifty and possibly as many as one hundred, a list far too long to be made a part of my article." None of the prior work had described a pod that was capable of preserving reagents from air, which could be ruptured to spread the chemicals for instant and simultaneous development of the negative and the positive. Nor had they described a system for stabilizing the print without washing, or methods for making the process work over a wide temperature range.[10]

This did not close the exchange, however, because Varden was assigned to cover "diffusion-transfer reversal materials," for the successive 1952 and 1962 editions of the major photographic handbook, edited by C. B. Neblette.[11] In 1950, Polaroid patent attorney Charles Mikulka prepared to talk with Varden. The attorney wrote in a memorandum that before Land ever heard of Rott and Weyde, he had already progressed beyond making positives with slow emulsions: "Land was [the] first to successfully work with fast emulsions; first to directly produce stable prints, i.e., prints requiring no washing, toning or other after treatment for their permanency; first to produce a diffusion transfer process which directly gives positive prints having adequate density, homogeneous hue in highlight and shadow, and full tone gradations; and first to develop a process operative over a wide range of ambient temperature."[12]

Mikulka was not entirely comfortable with his assertions, however. In his early search for prior patents, right after Land's idea of December 1943, he had missed Rott's because it had been cataloged as an invention in the decorative field, not photography. Rott's invention was limited to high-contrast materials. Mikulka had found no patents for a system, or any invention that would lead obviously to a system.

In 1972, Mikulka said that Land had damaged his scientific reputation by "cavalier" treatment of Rott and Weyde in his 1947 paper for the Optical Society's journal. By the late spring of 1949, when Land described his system in a lecture at the Science Museum in London, he cited Rott's and Weyde's work—along with that of R. D. Liesegang and Captain Colson in 1898, Erich Stenger and Alfred Herz in 1922, and the Schering-Kahlbaum company in 1931. Of Rott and Weyde, he said they had "reported interesting progress in silver transfer processes."

Mikulka recalled Edith Weyde, whom he had met many times by the early 1970s, as "a very sharing and brilliant scientist" who had established herself at a higher level than Rott. At one point in her work, she was already farther along than either Rott or Land. Eventually Polaroid negotiated a settlement with both Gevaert and Agfa, leaving Polaroid with picture-taking worldwide and the other companies with document copying.[13] Varden soon became a consultant to Polaroid.

∞

In the years of commercializing instant photography, Land's scientific reputation remained important to him. His early work on polarizers won him a Rumford Medal from the American Academy of Arts and Sciences in 1948.[14] The following year, he and such colleagues as Elkan Blout, David Grey, and Robert Clark Jones published their work on the development of an ultraviolet microscope that could translate its colors into the wavelengths visible to the human eye. Sponsored by the U.S. Office of Naval Research and the American Cancer Society, the new microscope differed from electron microscopes by allowing observations of living tissues.[15] In June 1949, Land lectured on the new microscope at the Physical Society in London. It was his third lecture in as many days. On the prior evenings, he had described one-step photography to the Royal Photographic Society and his work on polarizers at the Royal Institution.[16]

Scientists thought of Land as one of them. In 1951, he became president of the American Academy of Arts and Sciences, and he gave the first comprehensive review of his work on polarizers at a symposium of the

Optical Society. In October of that year, Land was one of six lecturers at the celebration in Chicago of the twentieth anniversary of the American Institute of Physics. The six speakers included Enrico Fermi, the Italian Nobel laureate who had achieved the first sustained nuclear chain reaction just nine years earlier. Land's topic was optics.

The unending procession of Land's inventions and devices, the introducer at Land's Chicago lecture said, was not only useful to the world but also stimulating to young scientists. In "supposedly old and worked-out diggings," Land had bent the laws of nature to his will. He added that Land's camera already had received the ultimate accolade: influence peddlers in Washington, then known as "five percenters," gave the cameras as presents along with mink coats and deep freezers.

Optics, Land said, is a "mother science," giving birth to ideas used in many parts of physics. Optics was making progress in many fields. Its techniques not only helped survey the heavens but allowed the viewing of ever-tinier objects, including both normal and diseased living tissues. He speculated jovially that "the engineers who designed the eye were perhaps more clever than those who designed the ear." Of human color vision, a topic that later obsessed him, Land declared that it was the "very beginning of vision in the human." He exclaimed, "How nebulous, how preliminary, our knowledge of the mechanism of vision is!" Physicists often claimed that their passion for optics was a search for truth, Land said. But the real reason that people choose optics was "because they love it."[17]

∞

Once instant photography hit its stride, Polaroid could afford to pay off arrears of dividends on preferred stock, which had been issued at the company's founding, and to retire the stock itself. Many acres were purchased in Waltham, Massachusetts, where factory after factory went up. The stock split, one share for two, in 1954 and again in 1956. In 1957, the stock split again, three for one, and Polaroid shares were listed on the New York Stock Exchange. Between 1954 and 1958, the price of a share, corrected for the splits, rose sevenfold. An analyst at the Wall Street firm Dreyfus and Company, however, did not see a problem. Ninety-four percent of Polaroid's business, he said, was in fields protected by patents. A high ratio of price to earnings was justified.[18]

In 1954, Polaroid introduced a lower-priced camera, called Highlander, to be sold alongside the original Model 95 and the high-end Pathfinder. The company showed its eagerness in marketing and how much it had learned about reaching customers. To push the Highlander, eight teams, from vice presidents to engineers to secretaries, a total of 120 employees, swung from city to city over two days to visit stores, give out kits to dealers, and take orders. The cities they visited represented almost 70 percent of Polaroid's camera business.

The company was already spending $100,000 a year on customer service. Two of three camera purchasers, each given a free roll of film, registered with Polaroid and soon received a personal letter of welcome from Land. Six weeks after their purchase, customers received a detailed questionnaire about any problems they encountered and which features they liked best. Eight times a year, Polaroid sent the registered owners a booklet of picture-taking tips, entitled *Minute Man*.[19]

The growth amazed employees and investors alike, and perhaps even Land. In 1950, sales were $6.4 million, after-tax profits $700,000. The company's hoard of cash and marketable securities, the war chest for a company that intended to grow from within, was $500,000. There were 429 employees at the end of the year. In 1960, the sales were $99.4 million, after-tax profits $8.8 million, and the war chest $11.9 million. The total number of employees reached 2,873. Polaroid continued its phenomenal growth throughout the 1960s. The totals for 1970 were $508 million in worldwide sales, $61.1 million in after-tax profits, $201.5 million in the war chest, and 10,528 employees.[20]

In the mid-1950s, the growth was so great that business journalists began asking how a scientist could keep track of such an enterprise. Land replied: "To be a scientist and manager is one integrated activity. What the scientist can provide is an insight into the future. He doesn't have to ask experts or wait for a vote on some research idea."[21]

∞

In the late 1950s, Land could still meet the entire Polaroid staff, although it was twice as large as during World War II. He continued to talk to his employees as no other chief executive officer in business ever has. He was a co-worker, and the employees knew that he spoke his own stuff.

What explained the astonishing growth? "Now partly that was work," Land said in 1958, "and partly that was brains, but very largely it was having the guts, the guts to be immodest in the right way."[22] In 1960, he told his employees, "In a few wretched buildings, we created a whole new industry of massive international significance." Once instant color film went on the market, "it's very unlikely that there will be many families in the country without at least one Polaroid camera."[23]

The employees were building "one of those few companies in the country . . . [that] can be proud of what it is making . . . Whatever else is happening in the country today, people enjoy what you are making for them." He added that the customers "don't want to give up . . . the fun of taking pictures with the products you are making." Polaroid was so competent that someday, "when we get a moment," it might tackle movies, which he called "this archaic approach for the reproduction of motion." His audience laughed delightedly when he said, "If you have wondered why Polaroid is not yet in the movie business, it is because we haven't made up our minds about the way to re-build that from the ground up."[24]

Reviewing the company's ever-expanding package of benefits for sickness, retirement, and schooling, he laid particular stress on schooling, because progressive mechanization was sure to abolish most people's jobs. A quarter of the employees were taking courses at the company and outside. These courses involved at least an hour and a half of lectures and homework per week and ranged from injection molding of plastic to the basics of chemistry and mathematics.[25] He told the employees, "We live in a world changing so rapidly that what we mean frequently by common sense is doing the thing that would have been right last year . . . The world is a scene changing so rapidly that it takes every bit of intuitive ability you have, every brain cell each one of you has, to make the sensible decision about what to do next. You cannot rely on what you have been taught. All you have learned from history is old ways of making mistakes. There is nothing that history can tell you about what we must do tomorrow. Only what we must not do."

Wages for their labor accounted for only 20 percent of the company's costs, and soon would be 10. "Your children will face an utterly different world . . . The present is catching up with us."[26]

∞

As the company grew, Land hoped to manage with as few extra people as possible. "Let's keep small. Let's keep intimate." That meant harder or more efficient work, but also a larger share in future returns.[27] Ten years earlier, the instant camera had been "an extreme and unbelievable dream," and the dream of "a worthwhile, satisfying job for every man" looked equally distant. Land said, "I like to get into situations in which no one believes me." Among the doubters in "powerful industries all over" were Kodak, Exacta, Agfa, and Gevaert, who "watched us grow right up and take over their field. And they didn't believe a word of it until it was too late."[28]

A team of "six top Russian economists," visiting America in 1959, during a thaw in the Cold War, had gone home impressed by Polaroid. "They had a wonderful time. They intended to stay only half an hour but came in the early afternoon and did not leave until late at night," Land said, and "when they left the country after having toured the whole United States, they left word that the place which impressed most of all was Polaroid."[29] To Land, America seemed like "a country without a conscience," where people were adjuncts to machines. In a world where people were "just adding and dividing," Land said, "the result is more automobiles than you want."[30]

A year later, he returned to the theme: "All of our confidence has to come from making things. . . . Let us not make more of something there is too much of. Let us find out what is desperately needed, although people may not know it. Let us find out what will beautify the world, although people may not know it. Then let's learn and learn and teach ourselves, and support each other in doing that until we lose ourselves in those tasks."[31]

In the right kind of company, Land said, people were not afraid of experimenting, either technically or socially, because they knew that failures were the "very essence" of progress. "You must expect failure after failure after failure before you succeed."[32]

Outsiders as well as insiders were impressed by a company that grew 30 percent a year. In 1961, *Time* magazine said of Land: "Few men have merged the worlds of business and science with greater success." Land was described as presiding over his fast-developing company "like a physics professor engaged with his students on a great adventure." He disdained market research. Instead, industry "must have an insight into what are the deep needs of people that they don't know they have."

Land told the magazine that discoveries were made "by some individual who has freed himself from a way of thinking that is held by friends and associates who may be more intelligent, better educated, better disciplined—but who have not mastered the art of the fresh, clean look at the old, old knowledge." At Polaroid, where employees could take many courses and switch back and forth between production and research, where scientists were encouraged to work at least part of the time on fundamental research, Land thought he was creating "the ideal company."[33]

To a remarkable extent, he succeeded. There were moments, however, when things went sour. Around 1970, there were protests about opportunities for African-Americans, the apartheid regime in South Africa, ending the Vietnam war, and civilian scientists' work on weapons systems. Polaroid was not immune to these protests.

In 1968, workers angry at Land's call for hiring more black workers had forced him to backtrack.[34] Early in 1971, demonstrators protesting Polaroid's involvement in South Africa and Land's key role in defense nearly prevented Land from speaking about his color-vision research at the American Physical Society in New York. A few weeks later, Land's color vision demonstration apparatus was all set up for the Harvard physics colloquium, but demonstrators thronged to the classroom. Land did not show up.[35]

In 1970, a union tried to organize workers at the company. Land regarded the attempt as an intrusion, and in August 1970, he sent photocopies of a handwritten letter to each of Polaroid's ten thousand employees:

> To those of you who have worked with me, and grown up with me, and created an industry with me, I need not recall that our proudest product is not our film, not our cameras, but is rather a kind of company in which you are not "workers" but men and women. Our determined purpose is to carry Polaroid through the rest of the way to the full realization of the dream: ten thousand individuals, every one different from every other, every one bringing his special talent and his special wisdom to our tasks. Polaroid is on its way to lead the world—perhaps even to save it—by this interplay between science, technology and real people. I have waited many years for this next great step in our growth toward the perfect scientific-human company. I cannot imagine that many of you could turn away now. This may be a moment in which the thousands of you who know should teach the few who have not been here long enough to understand. With warm regards, Edwin Land.

The union organizing effort faded.[36]

In 1970 and 1971, employees and outsiders demanded that Polaroid cease selling its products in South Africa, including its photo-identification equipment, even though the company contended that its ID-2 was not used in the passbook system of apartheid. Some critics even took out large advertisements urging a boycott of Polaroid products. To meet the criticism, Polaroid sent a committee of two executives and two workers, including two African-Americans, to South Africa. The committee, including Vice President Thomas H. Wyman, recommended continuing sales through Polaroid's South African dealer, which amounted to about $1.5

million a year, but said that the dealer should upgrade the status of its black workers. Polaroid took the advice.

The furor led Land to go beyond his usual formula of demonstrating new products at the annual shareholders' meeting and to hold his first press conference since 1947. He told reporters that the amount of sales in South Africa was so small that the outcry surprised him. The decision to stay in South Africa and press for reform, he said, was more expensive than getting out would have been.[37]

12

Black-and-White: Meroë Morse

A day is all too short. It always seems to me that we just really get warmed up to our problems and then it's time to quit.
—Meroë Morse

Even before sepia went on the market in 1948, Land already had his eye fixed on the next goal: moving instant photography swiftly on to black-and-white prints, the medium of the mass of photographers. Kodak's research director, Kenneth Mees, "sent word down from Rochester, in a kindly way, that Land would kill himself if he tried to make the process black-and-white." Land reflected later, "That was a good warning. He taught me not to kill myself." But the pursuit of how to do it was "rather thrilling."[1]

Black-and-white film presented new problems in making the image permanent. Stabilization, as it had been for sepia, was a painful challenge, forcing Land once again to reinvention. He found that he could not use the same complex arrangements by which sepia prints became stable without washing.

Working alongside him on these problems was Meroë Marston Morse, a cheerful, intelligent, energetic young woman who had come to his laboratory in 1944, straight from Smith College. There she had majored in art history, the field of Clarence Kennedy, who was then more than halfway through his many years of teaching. Although she took not a single course in physics, chemistry—or business administration—she, like others from Smith, showed aptitude in Land's laboratory, stimulated by Land's insistent mind.[2]

Morse's role at Polaroid grew steadily over the years. The laboratory she oversaw grew in the push for faster and faster films, for transparencies, and for films yielding a negative as well as a positive. Dealing with Landian overstretch on many levels at once, she had to be a diplomat and encompass a widening range of tasks. One typical day in August 1959, she was not just planning an extension of her black-and-white laboratory in Polaroid's Building IV in Waltham. She was also reviewing the space, budget, and equipment needs of her expanding laboratory in Cambridge, and arranging direct telephone lines from Cambridge to the pilot plant in Waltham for a colleague (Frank Martin), herself, and Land. Martin, originally at Osborn Street, had moved to Waltham to start the pilot work. He assigned codes for all photographic chemicals and oversaw who had access to the identity of a particular chemical.[3]

On the same August day, she wrote to Land at the Hotel Sacher in Vienna, reporting on work in her laboratory, as she usually did wherever Land was.[4] She also sent a jovial, almost familial, letter to the photographer Ansel Adams in San Francisco:

> Dear Bishop Adamopopulis: Received your postcard—was quite distressed to see how worn out and beat you are!!! You have been working too hard. . . . The only way I could tell it was "you" was by the shoes. Seriously, this was just what I needed to buoy my spirits (notice I said "boy" and not "girl") on arriving back to find a mountain of the usual work.
>
> Spain and Majorca were indeed beautiful. Have you been to Spain? It is very like California, and in some regards, more so. I understand now why the Spaniards settled California and why they brought with them the names they did. You would enjoy the rolling and mountainous countryside, clothed in all shades of burnt sienna, raw umber, yellow ochre, and here and there a patch of brilliant green; and nestled into the dip of the hills occasionally, like a handful of dice . . . a cluster of gleaming white houses."[5]

Adams, who first met Land in 1948, was an important consultant on both technical and aesthetic issues for Land and the company. As an artist, Adams surmounted "the challenge of making a nonsentimental statement about a grand insight into the abstract," Land recalled admiringly in 1974. This challenge, Land thought, "is multiplied a thousandfold when the components of the subject have names and reminiscences to characterize them—tree and twig, brook and boulder—components assembled furthermore not as accidents, but in their natural habitats, as ordinary, 'beautiful' arrangements."[6] Land enjoyed Adams's tough business sense, self-promotional ability, and sense of fun, but the photographer's commitment as an artist probably counted more. Preparing for an exhibit at the Metropolitan Museum of Art that was to include more than twenty Polaroid prints, Adams wrote that one-step silver diffusion photography had become "a most important branch of the great tree of photography. My interest in the Polaroid Land process is primarily esthetic."[7] By then, he had been testing and criticizing one-step cameras and films for a quarter century. Morse worked with him constantly.

In April 1960, Adams gave a ninety-minute course entitled "Expressive Photography" at three Polaroid sites. Fifteen people in Morse's laboratory signed up, two of them for a session for advanced photographers. Stanley Mervis, for decades one of the principal patent lawyers at Polaroid, recalled, "His classes were great. I took several of them." Adams used a picture that Mervis had taken to illustrate an article in *Popular Photography*.[8] In June, Morse was planning a trip to California to see Adams and his family, but she didn't know if she could "escape": "We are under extreme pressure—more than we have been under since 1950," the year of crisis for black-and-white.[9] As she wrote, Polaroid was preparing to show an ultrafast amateur film with an ASA speed of 3000 at the international photographic exposition, Photokina, in Cologne. It was a leap far beyond the ASA 200 and 400 films introduced in the mid-1950s. As part of Land's drive toward ever-faster films, Morse and her laboratory staff had worked on it for years.

In September 1960, the California visit abandoned, she wrote Adams about his next visit east. "Everyone is looking forward to your visit, to the inspiration and excitement. People very frequently talk glowingly to me about the classes and what they learned. I feel you are accomplishing something very important from a cultural and humanitarian point of view, as well as photographic."

She encouraged one of Adams's assistants, Gerry Sharpe, to come along to help him during the Cambridge visit. Sharpe evidently was apprehensive about working with the technical people at Polaroid. Morse was sympathetic, and her reply shows a great deal about the culture at Polaroid: "I am confronted continually with talking to my peers on technical matters and it is frightening." Morse was working with such formidable chemists as Milton Green and Saul Cohen. "Perhaps you could tell her sometime, if it would reassure her, that 50 percent of the people in the Lab have not had more than a high school education, and, of our technically trained people, only a few are specifically trained for their jobs."[10]

∞

Black-and-white instant photography proved to be no simple, incremental step beyond sepia. Beyond the crises of stabilization, there were crises of production and quality to surmount. Many of these lay ahead when, on 1 May 1950, black-and-white film emerged from Morse's laboratory and the engineering and production departments and went on the market as Type 41. As planned, the new film used the same cameras as those for sepia film. As with sepia, an eight-picture roll cost $1.75. The ASA speed of 100 was the same as that of the sepia film and the widely used Kodak Super XX panchromatic film.[11]

As usual at Polaroid, the black-and-white introduction was a high-wire act. The film was not ready until the last moment, which Land admitted a decade later at a meeting of employees. Proudly, laboratory workers posted the *Life* magazine advertisement for black-and-white film. The workers felt a thrill that Land called "a peculiarly poignant kind of thrill, a very special Polaroid kind of thrill, because . . . when that ad went up . . . we didn't have the black-and-white film ready to sell." The film soon became available, however, because, as Land boasted, "We have never failed to deliver what we promised."[12]

A photography writer for *The New York Times*, Jacob Deschin, reported that black-and-white film had advantages over sepia: "The prints appear to be somewhat sharper, tone values are better graduated, and the images more brilliant and detailed. The over-all image color tends to vary from black to brown-black, or 'warm' black. On the whole, the results are more pleasing than the sepia and will have wider acceptance."

And when would instant photography produce negatives? It could be done, Land said, but market research showed that the time and effort needed wouldn't pay off at that time. Meanwhile, people could obtain negatives from Polaroid's copy service, as well as sepia or black-and-white copies of their prints.[13]

By July 1950, black-and-white pictures were coming into the copy service. The service constituted an important feature of Polaroid's support for its customers from the beginning of instant photography. While Morse found the prints better than sepia, they were showing some of the problems that she and her co-workers had been struggling with in the laboratory. Defects included fingerprints, streaking, browning, yellowing, and a tendency for silver to pack, mirrorlike, in certain high-density areas. Sent in by twos and threes, the pictures had been made on production sheets numbered from 382 to 498. Visiting the copy service, Morse found the pictures on the whole encouraging. They gave "a far better impression than the adjacent sepia prints for clearness, brilliance, and sparkle." Only a few were scratched, and a few more had bits of developer clinging to their edges. But there was bad news: almost all "showed finger prints marring the picture area."[14]

While Polaroid waited for further hints of customer problems, demand surged for sepia and black-and-white, and the company struggled to make enough. Almost daily, Land received handwritten production reports from David W. Skinner (who would be named vice president of manufacturing and a director in 1951, and general manager in 1956) and handwritten laboratory reports from Morse, with whom Skinner was collaborating daily.

On 12 July 1950, Skinner wrote to Land on Cape Cod: "Just a brief report of where we stand as Meroë's mother is waiting for her. We are going along reasonably well. Positive assemblies yesterday 9400 and also 9200 rolls assembled. Only about 4,000 black-and-white because Number Two machine is scratching the sheet and we will have to shut down to retune the machine." He reported extensive troubleshooting by Arthur Barnes, Otto Wolff, and Bill McCune on a film layer called the A coat, and a decision not to shut down production, as was customary in the summer, for two weeks in August. Production was falling behind orders, and Executive Vice President J. Harold Booth wanted to produce at a top rate. A key problem on the production machines was wear on the Teflon-coated rollers.[15]

The next day, the machines turned out 10,000 rolls, about 6,000 sepia and 4,000 black-and-white. Orders for rolls that month were averaging 10,000 a day so far, but they were building up. The total production the day before had been 6,000 sepia and 7,250 black-and-white.[16] Skinner reported orders for 13,000 rolls of black-and-white on 27 July. So far in July, Polaroid had shipped out 115,000 rolls of black-and-white, but hadn't "made a real dent in the back-order situation."[17] On 10 August, Skinner reported a backlog of 70,000 rolls of sepia film.

That same day, Skinner told of plans to protect pictures that already appeared vulnerable. "The Sales Department is considering furnishing some plastic [cellulose acetate] covers, to protect the pictures immediately after they are taken from the camera. They might put four pieces in each six pack box and plan on using one for each two pictures on an individual roll." But Harold Booth had agreed to await the outcome of tests in a hot room.[18]

Morse's lab and the production people worked closely together. The lab researchers systematically varied the amounts of particular materials in each layer of the film. Daily, the lab and the factory compared laboratory and production techniques. Laboratory results suggested adjustments on the production machines, and production samples came back constantly to the lab for testing. The collaborators focused on the heating of the layers of chemicals as they were coated on the film base. The primary questions were, How much, and for how long? On 14 July, Arthur Barnes visited the lab to see how Morse and her assistants coated their film. In the lab, he noticed that the coats smoothed out as they dried. It was different in the factory on Ames Street. There the coats dried so rapidly that ridges of polyvinyl alcohol remained set. The same day, Skinner reported that the number two machine was producing about twice as much positive as it had two weeks earlier.[19]

Along with the notes to Land, Morse sent samples of photos, usually with indications of the conditions used for taking them. One batch consisted of "some lovely pictures . . . from Gretchen [Baum] who is on vacation." Of a photograph by Bill McCune, she wrote, "I sent the cat by Bill, not because it's a good picture, but it's a good black-and-white subject."[20]

The August issue of *U.S. Camera* displayed a sample of black-and-white photographs from Land's laboratory family. Morse's shot of Land caught him in a sports jacket and tie, smoking a pipe. Land's photo of Morse showed her standing in a suit, every inch the research executive, looking down at a report. Land also took a photograph of the strobe-light pioneer Harold Edgerton and Edgerton's daughter.[21]

On 10 August, Morse reported that "a beautiful black-and-white picture" came in from Ansel Adams, who had just become a Polaroid consultant. "It was a picture of a dead tree against some woodland background—a flat lighting but in the best Adams tradition." Adams had written that "the material is beautiful in quality." Because Polaroid had not yet shipped him any film to test, Morse speculated that he had obtained the Polaroid film from his wife's studio. Richard Kriebel, Polaroid's chief of publicity, told Morse that he would seek Adams's permission to use the picture in the *U.S. Camera* annual.[22]

The tone of Skinner's and Morse's notes to Land was jovial, even familial. One day, Skinner advised him to "take it easy and let us do the worrying for a while."[23] The next day he wrote: "I hope you're feeling much better and the cooler weather will make it a little more pleasant for the weekend."[24] One of Morse's notes ended, "Everyone wanted to join me in greetings and well wishes." A few days later, she wrote Land: "A day is all too short. It always seems to me that we just really get warmed up to our problems and then it's time to quit."[25]

∞

Sepia had been stabilized by hydrolyzable esters and soluble lead salts, implanted under the image layer of the positive. As the buildup of silver in the image layer neared completion, the esters and salts neutralized the alkaline developer that had energized the process. When neutralized, the developer lost its ability to reduce silver and undergo oxidation to form quinones. Meanwhile, the lead salts went to work on the polymer in the processing fluid, hardening the plastic into a thin protective layer.But in black-and-white film, Land and Morse were forced to use a different scheme of stabilization. Now, the image would form in a thin silica receiving layer coated on a thin waterproof layer. Stabilizing compounds could not diffuse from lower layers into the receiving layer.[26]

A problem more serious than finger marks on the print arose about six months after black-and-white film went onto the market. A fraction of the black-and-white pictures faded seriously. Frantic workers at Polaroid struggled to find the source of the problem. Land's conclusion was that humidity and contaminants in the air were attacking the image from above and below. He formed two teams. One, led by himself and Morse, concentrated on redesigning the film for greater stability. The second, led by Elkan Blout, developed a simple coater that the photographer could swab across the picture within two hours of taking it, and a cylindrical applicator. The coater accomplished the washing step that the sepia positive did for itself. After synthesizing more than two hundred new polymers, Blout and his chemists found a plastic that would form a hard, dry, flexible, insoluble, transparent shield for the image so that it would not yellow with age. Although the customers might have been expected to find this step clumsy, they accepted it. It was, according to *Fortune,* "the first and only real crisis in sixty-second photography."[27]

Through the crisis and after, black-and-white film sales spread over the world. Carlton Fuller wrote to Land from Sweden in August 1956: "It would do us all good to get away into countries where Polaroid is practically unknown. The expressions of amazement when you take a beautiful picture right out of the camera would exhilarate any individual in our whole organization, including you."[28]

By 1957, ten years after one-step pictures were first shown, *The New York Times* reported "remarkable improvements" in the quality of Polaroid prints. "Once just acceptable, later adequate, it is now equal in tonal range and brilliance to some of the finest prints made by the usual darkroom routines. The projection film, especially, due in part, of course to the fact that a transparency will reveal more values than a print, is beyond criticism."[29] The *Times* was writing about the results of torrents of experiments in Morse's laboratory, day after day, year after year.

∞

In a time when few businesses accepted women in positions of responsibility, Land welcomed and brought along the work of ambitious and creative women—single women and working mothers alike. They participated vigorously in Land's "sun and satellite" system of research management, where people, including Land, freely lent a hand as satellites on each other's projects. Who the sun was depended on the project. A participant in this system recalled emphatically half a century later, "It was fostered."

In this view, "Land's confidence that bright people could perform valuable research, given the opportunity, extended to women at a time when it was difficult in many companies (Kodak, for example) to obtain a laboratory job at all, even with excellent [scientific] credentials." Land's team included "bright women who were highly artistic and bright women with strong backgrounds in chemistry." Land valued an artistic background and interest, which was strong with Meroë Morse, "because he considered visual perception as necessary as the knowledge of chemistry in judging lab results visually."[30]

Where others worked intensively on problems and then left the laboratory to marry, Morse stayed on and on. Her responsibilities grew, as both a staff and a line officer, as a planet and a sun. She took on more and more problems at many levels of subtlety. With a warmth and diplomatic finesse that built trust among many who had to work on difficult problems with Land, she provided Land with an invaluable buffer.

Although Morse was clearly awed by Land, she was not frightened of him. She had the secret of telling Land, in a light yet earnest tone, about the day's progress and frustrations in her clean, calm laboratory on the second floor at Osborn Street. Her notes to Land, when he was getting some rest at his weekend house near Hyannis on Cape Cod and later in southwestern New Hampshire, were cheerful and highly detailed. She wrote in a clear, bold longhand. Sometimes she would write these notes while on the train from Boston south to her mother's house on Buzzard's Bay. She told Land what progress had been made on experiments that they had discussed, and she outlined the next steps. Although she was completely focused on the laboratory, her notes expressed an affection and a confidence that had grown over the years. Land returned the original notes to

Morse, and she put them in loose-leaf notebooks that she carefully preserved and deposited in the Polaroid Corporation archives.[31]

In those archives, she also deposited many items showing a life of her own. Posters advertised her services as an artist who made chalk sketches for the audiences at folk music concerts. The programs showed that she performed several times at these concerts. Occasional letters came from people who had enjoyed her sketches. Morse preserved the syllabus and her notes for an extension course in chemistry. Women who had worked in her laboratory, after they married and moved away, would send baby pictures and affectionate notes, to which she would reply warmly. One year, after one of her foreign trips, she used a picture she had taken of a church portico in Spain as the illustration for her Christmas card.

Living in the Back Bay section of Boston, she played the harp and served as a director of the Cambridge Settlement House, where she taught courses in art and photography for children. She also was a volunteer counselor of a jobs clearing house.[32]

The range of her responsibilities continually widened. On Land's behalf, she managed the details of Polaroid's relationship with Ansel Adams. Her files contained many letters and memoranda that reported complex interactions with the U.S. Army Signal Corps and the U.S. Air Force about searches for better electronic and photographic reconnaissance for the military. Other correspondence chronicled Polaroid's many collaborations with Eastman Kodak and with the rapidly expanding photographic division of DuPont.[33]

People working in many parts of Polaroid saw to it that she, as well as Land, received copies of memoranda on a wide range of subjects. They wanted another judgment, another pair of eyes, in Land's immediate circle. She was trusted to use her influence judiciously in the context of utter loyalty to Land, out of a desire to help him, shield him, and shoulder burdens for him.

At first, Morse addresssed her reports to "Mr. Land," but in 1949, after Land received an honorary doctorate from Tufts University, she began her notes, "Dear Dr. Land." By 1955, the salutation was less formal, "Dear Boss." She also used the term "the Boss" in conversing with others, and "Boss" when talking with Land in the laboratory.

On 28 March 1955, Land was again out with a cold, but Morse continued her daily reports: "Today has been a most successful day tarnished by the news of your continued illness." She and her associates were cutting down on bubbles marring the pictures. They would send to Land that night a model film pack, a filter and filter holder, a "darkish" slide of flowers, and a bright but defective picture taken with a sample film from DuPont.

She sent demonstration pictures taken with a new high-speed processing fluid, which had been tested for three days at 120 degrees Fahrenheit. She closed, "I'm sure I've forgotten something important but lots more tomorrow. Best of everything to you from all of us here."[34]

Two days later, she reported receiving a small sample from the Gevaert Company: "Started George Fernald on his new project today. He's a good lad."[35] On 4 April, she wrote that an idea that she should have had years earlier led her to use gold and another substance to produce a much improved transparency. "Am I stupid—Don't answer that!—I still haven't quite seen the light."[36] Three days later, after reporting that she had conveyed Land's greetings to Henry C. Yutzy, Kodak's director of research and Land's intimate partner in spy-plane work, she wrote, "I hope you do forgive the informality and occasionally poor style of this letter. By writing them myself, sometimes in the midst of confusion, I am surer of getting them off."[37]

The next day, after reporting "good news on the transparent front," Morse mentioned a difficult problem of supplying material to the military. "Wish you were here to handle this on your level."[38] Morse and Land were then experimenting with filters on projectors as part of an exploration of color photography. A tiny accident and a perception of Morse's opened up Land's many years of studying human color perception (chapter 13).

∞

Morse preserved correspondence surrounding the Franklin Institute's award of the Howard Potts Medal to Land for instant photography in October 1956 The medal matched the Institute's Cresson Medal twenty years earlier for the polarizer. As with the earlier medal, Land had distinguished predecessors and successors as winners, including Coolidge of GE (1926) and the television tube inventor Zworykin (1947), both Modern Pionieers with Land in 1940.[39] Receiving the medal, Land demonstrated the new Polaroid transparency film from Morse's laboratory, with an ASA speed of 1000. He showed slides taken that day in Philadelphia, and of the audience. The demonstration opened with a huge blowup of an open eye and concluded with a slide of the eye closed in sleep.[40]

Morse was there. At the dinner after the lecture, she was seated at the same table with Mrs. Land and Crawford Greenewalt of DuPont and his wife. Greenewalt not only was head of DuPont but was famous for his high-speed photographs of hummingbirds. As Mrs. Milton Harvey of the Franklin Institute had coached her, Morse talked with Greenewalt about the hummingbirds and was fascinated. She reported later to Mrs. Harvey:

> May I tell you again how much I appreciated your courtesy and assistance in making our way easy. I certainly enjoyed meeting you. Sitting next to Mr. Greenewalt was an interesting experience. There was quite a bit of general conversation at the table, but when I had the opportunity I discussed photography and especially photography of hummingbirds, as you suggested. He and his wife are extremely charming people.[41]

∞

In Land's laboratory, where he insisted on the impossible, researchers had to work intensely and long and overcome feelings of personal inadequacy. No one experienced these pressures more sharply than did Howard Rogers, Polaroid's most noted inventor in the color film field, which was the next mountain beyond black-and-white. Rogers had come to Land's enterprise almost a decade before Morse did, but he was very impressed with her. In 1969, Rogers recalled:

> I know the difficulty of the problems she solved, and the scientific and artistic skill she brought to bear in solving them. Like many people of great effectiveness, she seemed to have more strength and energy than most people, and could work longer on more problems at once. She somehow could keep her charm and cheerfulness when there was a deadline to meet. The magic produced in her laboratory often seemed to go beyond what could reasonably be expected from the starting materials.

When Morse arrived, Rogers recalled, she quickly adopted the Polaroid style in the laboratory: "to propose the hypothesis, to test the hypothesis, to modify the hypothesis, to test with another experiment—a sequential train moving at high speed, several hypotheses and experiments per hour." When her laboratory ran at full tilt, alternating between hypothesis and experiment, three shifts of technicians worked around the clock. "And yet the environment was calm. The results seemed more like the magical growing of a plant in time-lapse pictures."

During and after his often-desperate fifteen-year quest for instant color pictures, Rogers found Morse very warm, thoughtful, and helpful, on technical and personal problems alike. "Her sincere compliments and careful attention to my question, almost seeming to make my words increase in importance, always made the problem seem easier, quite aside from the technical suggestions she made."[42]

Land and Morse were unquestionably fond of each other, although to all appearances they saw little of each other outside the laboratory. Among people outside the laboratory there were rumors that they were lovers. Decades later, a laboratory colleague scoffed at this: "I was there and I knew of no widespread rumors." The gossip doubtless arose from the fact that she and Land worked closely for more than twenty years, that she seemed to know his mind well, and that she never married. The colleague responded to this speculation: "Meroë was dedicated to the work, and the fact that she never married is irrelevant. She was one of a growing number of women who have chosen careers over matrimony."[43] Another colleague said, "Every nice thing said about her was deserved. I don't believe there was an affair . . . nor does anyone else I know that worked closely with Meroë. I can understand how someone could start such a rumor, either in spite because Land trusted Meroë instead of them or . . . to explain why a non-technical person could have such responsibility and weight."[44]

Land's charisma and romanticism may have contributed to the gossip. It may also have been a way of humanizing Land, whom many found daunting. Many in corporate life assume that power is an aphrodisiac, and find infidelity more interesting than the opposite. But no substance has emerged for these rumors. Land and Morse clearly focused intensely on their work and maintained, undiminished, their authority as director of research and head of the black-and-white laboratory.

By tact and good sense, Morse gradually acquired much influence on questions great and small. She maintained good relations with the marketing and engineering people who struggled to restrain Land's wilder ideas and convey to him both the psychology of customers and the realities of production. With all these groups, Morse was increasingly important as an intermediary. People came to trust her as a sensitive, discreet, objective person who focused on the job and not on power. She worked well with both men and women, subordinates and nonsubordinates alike. Many who worked with Land spoke with excitement of being under his eye in a crisis. Morse and Land agreed that all the brilliance was for a larger purpose, well beyond power, manipulation, or the staging of human dramas to stave off boredom. Morse's attitudes and behavior evidently reinforced the sublimation of ego and softened the edges of Land's energy.

In all his speeches and writings, Land stuck rigorously to male nouns and adjectives in speaking of people in general. Nonetheless, he enjoyed working in partnership with women, long before the change in the status of women at work accelerated in the 1970s and later. He encouraged and challenged their creativity and gave them responsibility to a degree exceptional in business or laboratory life. The spirited and intelligent women he recruited, often from Smith College, found wide scope in experiments, writing periodic summaries of research in instant photography, performing delicate and secret work with government and industry, and dealing with multiple layers of diplomacy, administration, and public relations. He frequently mentioned his delight that people could move from other pursuits, including art history, into the laboratory and flourish there.[45]

In Maxfield Parrish's joshing cartoon, showing Land in his coffin on April Fool's Day 1999, demanding just one more experiment before he went, he is surrounded by a bevy of identical women associates, each with long, curly, blond tresses. All are weeping. All wear black armbands. One of them wears two.[46] Land's son-in-law Philip DuBois showed the cartoon to a 1993 meeting of the Society for Imaging Science in Cambridge, Massachusetts.

∞

Land was close to his family and shielded them from the usual publicity surrounding a famous person. They cared for him in his old age. Din and Terre's marriage lasted more than sixty years, from near the beginning of Land's adventures until his death, well after he left Polaroid Corporation. After his death, Mrs. Land undertook such memorial enterprises as a special exhibit at Norwich Free Academy and the publication of all of Land's essays.

On occasion, during a laboratory marathon, Terre would brusquely summon him home to 163 Brattle Street to fulfill a social or family engagement. They shared vacation homes on Cape Cod and then in New Hampshire and took vacations together in London and the American Southwest. They each owned massive blocks of Polaroid stock, most of which they held until late in Land's life. Terre Land took the lead in their numerous charities, but almost never appeared in public.

In the winter, she frequently went to Tucson, Arizona, alone. More than likely, she missed their early comradeship in the laboratory, before their daughters were born and when the enterprise consisted of just a few people. Her daughters, Jennifer and Valerie, and their families compensated for the loss of camaraderie. In the decoration of their homes, Terre's taste ruled, and Land spoke of them as her territory.[47] Near the end of her husband's life, she decorated his new office on the Charles River in the style of the Southwest. A print of Ansel Adams's famous photograph of moonrise at Hernandez, New Mexico, hung over the fireplace. Frequently, the Lands vacationed with Ansel and Virginia Adams and shared friendships with other couples.

In 1960, the Lands gave a rare interview together. It happened that Marilyn Adams, the daughter-in-law of the newspaper columnist Cedric Adams (no relation to Ansel), had worked at Polaroid. She was with her in-laws when they were guests at a friend's beach cottage. The Lands were staying next door. Marilyn recognized Land, and her parents-in-law invited them over. Land talked with Cedric about his inventions and his project of making workers' lives more interesting. Mrs. Land made it clear that her husband's absorption in his projects could be exasperating. "There are occasions when I'll be talking to him directly and I know that he is not listening to me. His mind is miles away. But all I have to say to him is, 'Polaroid,' and immediately I have his full and complete attention."[48]

∞

Morse's laboratory constantly refined the black-and-white films. Their sensitivity increased dramatically. Transparencies were highly successful. A version that produced both a positive and a negative went on the market, as did high-contrast films for commercial art. In 1958, Land said that the new ASA 3000 film from Morse's laboratory was "about 20 times as sensitive as our present film." This meant that "you can take pictures in your living room at night without a flash bulb." Cameras to use it could have "lenses so tiny you can hardly see them. . . . Because they are so tiny, they are always in focus." In addition, the shutter for such a lens could be controlled by a photocell. Now, "the speed of the shutter depends on how much light there is. . . . No matter how fast something is moving, how far away it is, no matter whether it is morning, noon, or night, no matter whether the cloud goes over the sun . . . the picture comes out meticulously sharp, perfectly focused, and perfectly exposed."

For best results, the new film called for "fill-flash," which produces light that just fills in the shadows while leaving the sense of a normally lighted room, with little points of light on the subject's faces where highlights ought to be.

Polaroid had designed a device good for about a thousand flashes. Robert Casselman, the head of sales, had recognized the need, and Dexter Cooper designed the device. In a backhanded complement to the sales force, Land asked, "Isn't it nice, by the way, to have a sales manager who can have a brilliant realization?" This "Wink Light" used an ordinary tungsten filament through which an extremely short electric pulse was sent to get the filament very hot, bright, and white before the filament melted. For the pulse, a condenser was charged by the battery.[49]

Even after the splash of Polaroid's entry into color pictures, black-and-white films played an important role in expanding the company's customer base. In 1965 a new small-size black-and-white film was used in a small, light, white plastic camera called the Swinger. With a list price of $19.95, it had a photometer that displayed the word "Yes" when the light conditions were right. Television ads showed a starlet in a skimpy bathing suit, strolling with the camera down a beach, and helped make the new camera a hit. The ad campaign was a long step further into mass marketing. A Big Swinger, taking larger pictures, went on the market in 1967. Polaroid was reaching many new customers and encouraging them to upgrade as they got the hang of instant photography. The stream of new models was an answer to a fundamental problem: the cameras were novelties, used briskly for a while, and then relegated to the closet. Fresh features and fresh excitement were needed.[50]

In March 1967, Polaroid announced coaterless film, another achievement of Morse's laboratory. This black-and-white film did not need to be swabbed with a coater and produced a finished image in thirty seconds. It was a long-delayed answer to the humiliation of 1950, when black-and-white had been forced to become a two-step process. The coaterless film was to go on sale in 1968.[51] To demonstrate the new film at the 1968 annual shareholders' meeting, Land called on "two rogues of distinction," Ansel Adams, and the famous portrait photographer Yousuf Karsh. Using the big-format camera that Land had used in New York in 1947, Karsh took a portrait of Adams. "In terms of scientific improvement," Land said, coaterless film "ranks with our basic contributions in the technology of photography." The same meeting was also notable for the projection of subtractive color transparencies, and a live demonstration of additive color film.[52]

Morse was coauthor, with Land and Leonard Farney, of a paper presented in June 1968 at the annual meeting of the Society of Photographic Scientists and Engineers. Land spoke for two hours on the complex topic of solubilization by incipient development, on which he and Morse and Farney had worked for fifteen years. In some instant images, along with the normal positive that used silver transferred from the negative, there was a weak negative as well, presumably formed because very slightly exposed grains became soluble very early in development, hence the name *incipient development*. The work opened a path toward negatives of a sensitivity up to ASA 2000. Although the new phenomenon might be universal in all silver-halide photography, Land said, it probably would not have come to light without the unceasing effort to perfect black-and-white instant films. "The investigation has been a luxury for us," Land said, " because we have been able to bring to bear all the resources of our laboratories on a problem which may have no use at all. To do this, you have to be a very prosperous company, and you have to be a research man who can push around that prosperous company."[53]

∞

Meroë Morse's career was cut short by cancer. By the late 1960s, recognition of her achievements was growing. In October 1968, Morse went to Northampton to receive the Smith College Medal, given each year to a person whose life and service exemplified "the true purpose of liberal arts education." President Thomas C. Mendenhall noted that she had majored in art, but for more than twenty years, she had concentrated on science. She had contributed to every major development in black-and-white film at Polaroid. He estimated that black-and-white still accounted for half of Polaroid's business. But she had done more: "You join your own warmth, imagination, and curiosity with a sympathetic appreciation of others and a keen eye for their different talents, to help bring purpose and direction into the lives of all you have touched."[54]

In May 1969, the Society of Photographic Scientists and Engineers named her a Fellow. She was the first woman to receive this honor. The society cited her fourteen patents and her many achievements in developing one black-and-white film after another.[55]

In June 1969, as Morse's illness progressed, another link to the past was broken. James P. Warburg, one of Polaroid's original backers and a company director ever since, died of cancer. Land praised Warburg for approaching life and politics as a scientist does, with a faith in reason, determined to mobilize minds to solve problems. But Land's mood was grim: "In spite of his cheerfulness, Jim was not an optimist. He believed that things left to their own devices would go from bad to worse."[56]

Meroë kept working until the last few days of her life. She died on 29 July 1969 at the age of forty-five. Two weeks later, people gathered to honor her memory in the Memorial Church at Harvard. Land evidently did not trust himself to speak. Instead, he prevailed on Howard Rogers, a most reluctant speaker, to express what Land and her other colleagues felt:

> Everyone who came in contact with her felt uplifted by her presence and attention. . . . Hard problems were made easier, and impossible problems possible. She was . . . capable of making strangers feel at home instantly, yet she herself was self-effacing. . . . Her humanity was so great that she loved everyone, and wanted to make sure that as many people as possible had the opportunity to develop the full use of their talents. Admiration and love for Meroë are built into the deepest core of us, and she has lastingly improved the quality of all our lives.[57]

Land remembered her fondly. At times, after her death, he assigned her little office on the second floor of the Osborn Street building to visitors. In his sixties, he bounded up the metal-edged stairs two at a time to accompany the guest there. If the visitor worked late, he would come up to chat, his eyes shining. The room had only two mementos of Meroë. One was a color photograph by Marie Cosindas, showing Morse in a flowered dress, slightly plumper than in earlier days, her arms relaxed in front of her. Her expression was warm. The other memento was a rotating pipe stand, holding several pipes that Land and Morse had enjoyed smoking together.[58]

When Meroë died, Land lost a soul mate, a work mate, and a protector. His most severe quarrels with the technical and non-technical sides of his company sprang up after she was gone.

13

Instant Color: Howard Rogers

As soon as Howie described his molecule, we knew it would exist. It was an ideal molecule, and we therefore took it for granted we could bring it into being.

—Edwin H. Land, January 1963

As usual, late January 1963 was bright and mild in Florida. For the long-awaited instant color film, it was a good time and place to start selling. As with sepia in 1949, relaxed vacationers could record good times in mild weather and bring the pictures back up north. The film was called Polacolor. Like so much else in Land's life, its introduction had seemed impossible almost until the day it happened. The struggle was even more arduous than for the earlier films: a much larger team took three times as long and spent fifteen million dollars.[1] To be sure, through these fifteen years, Polaroid was gaining the economic strength to sustain such an effort. At times, however, the struggle was almost maddening.

For Land, the effort and the result were foreordained. "I had color in the back of my mind from the beginning," he said later, "as one naturally would, since photography in general was starting to go from black-and-white to color." Color was a required natural evolution. "Just as we wanted the sepia to become black-and-white, we wanted the black-and-white to become color."[2]

The challenge of color forced Land to take long steps forward as an inventor and a manager of inventors. When he began on the polarizer in the 1920s, he worked virtually alone. But once his company started up in the 1930s, he began collaborating with other inventors, such as Howard Gardner Rogers. Becoming one of Land's most practiced and trusted problem solvers,

Rogers worked not only on the radical re-statement of the sheet-polarizer invention, but also on plastic optics during World War II. As he had hoped when he joined Land in 1936, he certainly learned some science and solved some problems.

When sepia was introduced in 1947–48, Rogers began the long leap forward to color. Day by day, week by week, problem by problem, he told Land where he was on his journey, and Land reacted and suggested things to try. Suggestions came from other people, notably Elkan Blout, who supervised a small army of chemists synthesizing and testing thousands of compounds. Blout helped invent a crucial improvement to Rogers's basic invention.

At first Rogers worked across a desk from Land in the old red brick building on Osborn Street. Later he had his own laboratory on the second floor. Later still, additional labs, annexing more and more space, tackled the details of the swelling color enterprise. And at the very end of the color research process, Land staged an inventive marathon to solve a major remaining problem.

A wiry, almost elfin man with a wry sense of humor and spiky crew-cut hair, Rogers was self-effacing. Although he disliked public speeches, he was confident, admiring Land and yet not overawed by him. Fascinated by science and not insensible to its romantic side, he and his wife had a decades-long hobby of traveling to view eclipses of the sun. Rogers's modesty, always selling himself short, contrasted with Land's "gentle arrogance," according to Charles Mikulka, long a leading patent attorney for Polaroid Corporation. Mikulka said in 1972 that Rogers's contributions, although less voluminous than Land's, were equal in quality.[3] In 1993, the Society for Imaging Science and Technology presented the first Edwin H. Land Medal, endowed by Polaroid Corporation, to Rogers.

Like other great inventors, Rogers had his own views about creativity. Considering the subconscious important, he didn't always agree with Land's insistence, when an obstacle was reached, on focusing harder and harder on the latest obsession:

> I found . . . that sometimes working on more than one project, or thinking a little about other projects while working on a particular one . . . helped in overcoming a stoppage in the thinking or progress on the main project. Thinking along another line or two might open up a new approach. . . . Then I became more and more impressed at the power of the subconscious. . . . If you put good input into your subconscious,

> that is, carefully observed results and carefully thought-out analyses, and let some good hard facts into your subconsciousness, along with the need to know the answers to some problems or the need to invent the way out of some difficulties, then sometimes further focusing and work wasn't as helpful as just a little time, or a change of scene, or a stimulus of another sort [which] would sometimes bring the answer.

Despite Rogers' occasional preference for indirection, he valued Land's approach. "The chief difference was that I had some difficulty focusing. . . . Dr. Land's main effect on me was to focus me, which was a great help in getting faster advances in the color project."[4]

The color assignment came to Rogers almost casually. He had eased into the instant photography project in the 1940s, trying "to carry out some of the approaches to instant photography that Dr. Land had thought of but hadn't had a chance to really work on. So I worked out some of the methods of making alternative kinds of pictures to the main ones he was working on." This was part of Land's pattern of patenting alternative or opposite ways to reach a particular goal. With those tasks behind him, Rogers moved from the periphery to the center of Land's photographic work. Land had a custom of putting a list of things to do on a blackboard. "One day down at the bottom of the list, it just said, 'color,'" Rogers recalled. "So I pointed to that and said, 'Can I do that?' and he said, 'Sure.'"[5]

Land's memory of Rogers' request was more ebullient:

> I had a laboratory in which I was doing the black-and-white work with a group of people around me, and on the blackboard was a daily list of things to give attention to, to see if you can make the images darker, extend the [temperature] range, check for grain and mottle, and so on, all sorts of experiments going on. At the bottom of this list of five things one day was a phrase, "Get going on color." Howard Rogers. . . . came in, saw the list on the board, and said, "I'd like to tackle number 5."
>
> I said, "Well, that's fine. Take a chair and you sit down on the opposite side of my desk. When you are ready, when you have watched the way we are doing this, and it has gone along long enough and you really have the feel of how we develop the negative, how we hold back the development of the negative, how we use the viscous reagent to time the relationship between

> the forming of the negative and positive, when it's all sunk in, when, after that, you seem to have a family of ideas for processes analogous to this that might lead to color, let me know." So he sat down in that chair and after a while, he got up and said, "I think I'm ready." But the "after a while" was about a year and a half later."[6]

Land was working with half a dozen assistants, darting in and out of "darkrooms all the way around the edges to carry out experiments," Rogers recalled. There was a lot going on.

Rogers' memory of the assignment was simpler than Land's. "Just sit there for a year or so and take it all in, and then think how to do it." So Land's tale was a slight exaggeration, "because [Land] already [had] invented a few approaches to color," and some of the first experiments in 1944 produced intended blue dye or unintended bright yellow silver images. "My first assignment was to just try some things and see if we could get something that worked. So the job became one of finding the best approach and then developing it to see if it would do what we wanted." As for sitting full-time at a desk, Rogers said, "It wasn't quite like he said. I did have a desk. I did sit there some of the time, but I also did some experiments."[7]

As in all Land's projects, the work went forward under the twin adages of "Never go to sleep with a hypothesis untested" and "Every problem can be solved with the things in the room at the time." Rogers felt that each precept "had so much truth in it that it was worth saying." They were Land's way of saying, Damn the difficulties. According to Rogers, "It's often true that research seems difficult and dangerous, but only because something that you might try might not work. . . . Of course that's a big risk; and in fact. . . . lots of even very good researchers treasure the difficulty of the thing they are about to attempt. So they're not about to make it look easy." If they just went ahead and did it, the task might not seem so impressive. Land's approach was almost the opposite, in Rogers' eyes:

> Rather than being impressed by the difficulty, he tended to look at it as something really simple. That changed your attitude about how difficult things were to tackle. He had great skepticism about what the experts said, which was a very healthy skepticism. Often, if you come to where the end of the knowledge is, in any field, what the books say may be all

> wrong . . . They may be due to the author having talked to an expert, and the expert coloring what he says by what he thinks, which may not have a lot to do with the actual situation. Because, unless you have done the final experiment yourself, how do you know for sure where the truth lies?"

Here again, Land's atavistic impulses came into play—in search of novelty, not precedent. Rogers said that Land "always believed in taking another look, a new, fresh look, at the old knowledge. Of course, the older the knowledge was, the more likely it is . . . that things are more different than you might think."[8]

Rogers recalled that Land "had a technique for doing sort of an evolutionary type of research under speeded-up conditions." Land would describe "the theory and what was supposed to happen" to lab colleagues or to consultants like Robert Woodward or Saul Cohen. Waring blenders mixed the viscous reagent in small batches and a small machine made a few pods for containing the test reagent. One could "make a really professional-looking experiment, all in a few minutes."

In such work, Land jumped to opposites and took big leaps instead of baby steps. Rogers explained that much of Land's "day-to-day methods were intriguing": "I guess you could say exaggeration was a tool for helping to move things faster. That is, if something worked, or if it didn't work, you might want to try twice as much, just to see, to find out . . . the limits of what the situation called for. So, rather than working initially in small increments, he would try to work in the big changes. He also thought it was important to try, when you got stuck, the opposite of what you thought might work."

These principles emerged in the whitewater of experiments, not in a seminar. "I wouldn't really say it was a dialogue. Dr. Land liked to come out with insights and sayings and so on in the course of conversation. It wasn't something that was the subject of discussion really. It was just his descriptions of how he operated or how he thought things worked." Usually, when Rogers met Land, at least once a week, they were alone. When Rogers "had an improvement, I would go show him. I usually had an experiment in my back pocket when I went to see him." Rogers recalled, "He really trained me. I think the way he trained me was by letting me see the way he operated and then leaving me free to proceed."[9]

∞

What did Rogers, Land, and their collaborators come up with after fifteen years? An instant color film that worked in existing Polaroid cameras. But now, dyes, not silver, moved across from a multi-layered negative to the positive, forming a print that did not need to be coated. As Land put it in 1981, color performed "the task of taking three separate pictures of the world, with all in perfect registry."[10] The dyes of Polacolor were hooked into the "dye developer," a unique type of molecule invented by Rogers. As its name implied, the molecules had one portion that acted as photographic developers, and another portion that acted as image dyes. The molecules were equipped with an insulating bridge of atoms that prevented unwanted reactions between the dye and developer. Blout had foreseen the need for this atomic bridge and had worked on it. Instant color was not quite a one-step process. To prevent the gradual curling and subsequent cracking that bedeviled photography, the photographers had to mount the pictures immediately on rectangles of adhesive cardboard furnished with each package of film.

The structure of the Polacolor negative was more complex than sepia or black-and-white negatives. It was an eight-layered cake of light-sensitive and dye-containing coatings, and spacer layers that by their depth and makeup slowed some of the chemical reactions. The dyes in their layers served first as light filters during the brief exposure to take the picture, and then had one of two fates. Either they were trapped, or made insoluble, in the exposed regions of the negative, or they remained soluble and free to migrate in the unexposed regions. Their destination was an ultra-thin lattice, in the positive, of dye-grabbing chemicals called the "mordant," analogous to the fibers of a cloth. There the print image built up.

When the picture was snapped, blue and green and red light from the scene flashed through the lens into the multi-layered negative. Blue light hit a layer of silver-halide crystals in a gelatin emulsion that had been made sensitive to blue light by tiny amounts of sensitizing dyes. The blue light went no farther because, just beneath, a layer of dye developer of yellow color—the complementary color for blue—acted as a filter protecting the lower emulsion layers from exposure to blue light. Green and red light kept going. The green light hit an emulsion layer of green-sensitive silver halide. Just beneath, the layer of magenta dye developer blocked green light from going farther. The red light kept going and hit a red-sensitive layer just above a layer of cyan dye developer.

The spacer layers were transparent, but they separated the color regions from each other in the crucial early seconds of development. The spacers were sufficiently thick and impermeable to hold each dye developer close to the silver-halide emulsions of complementary sensitivity, so that the dye developers would not interact with the wrong emulsions. Cooperating with a nimble little auxiliary developer, the dye developers helped develop exposed grains, which were consequently made insoluble and held in the negative. The tiny amount of highly mobile auxiliary developer was constantly regenerated by interactions with the exposed grains and the dye developers. In Rogers's description, the auxiliary developer acted as a "messenger." Where grains had not been exposed, the dye developers would not be captured, but were released to migrate over to the ultra-thin dye-uptake layer in the positive, the mordant. Where blue light had fallen, yellow dye developers reduced grains of the blue-sensitive emulsion and were trapped in the negative, but the magenta and cyan dye developers beneath that particular spot on the film were free to move into the positive image layer. Captured there, they added together to form blue.[11]

The new domain, once again, presented the old challenge: providing a stable image in the positive image-receiving sheet after the positive was peeled apart from the negative. For color, Land invented a two-layer substructure beneath the mordant layer. Alkali metal ions were captured, in effect returning water to the surface layer and thus making the positive self-washing. In this way, formation of unwanted salt deposits on the surface was prevented.

∞

The fifteen-year story was one of hard work and puzzlement, Land said in Atlantic City on 1 May 1963. He was introducing the report on Polacolor to the Society of Photographic Scientists and Engineers. Referring to seemingly endless obstacles, Land remarked, "I was going to say failure, but the beauty of science, of course, is that one never fails, one only moves on to the next experiment." The talks he and his colleagues, including Rogers, gave in Atlantic City were perhaps the most elaborate presentation that Polaroid scientists ever gave.[12]

Polacolor built on earlier technologies: "What the black-and-white process taught us, was first . . . all the mechanics of spreading developer between the negative and positive," Land recalled. "[It] taught us the sequence of overlapping delays that had to exist between the time when the negative first started to develop, and then the positive would start to form and the negative would continue to develop, and the positive would continue to form." In this survival school, the Polaroid team was being trained how to "match the lightness distribution in the world with a satisfying lightness distribution in the print" and to be able to do this over a wide range of temperatures.

"As has been said of many great processes," Land recalled at a 1981 patent trial, instant photography processes "certainly stand on the shoulders of processes that preceded them." To begin, Land said, "I was employing some old processes as the basis of generating new ones." But so-called diffusion transfer images, with their "symmetry, the unified production of negative and positive . . . [were] a whole new domain in photography."[13]

Dyes were not wholly unfamiliar: some of the first one-step images had involved dyes. A dye-forming process, a "tried" mechanism, helped Rogers and Land enter the domain of color. The mechanism involved molecules called couplers, a staple of color photography since Rudolf Fischer discovered them in 1912. Fischer had trouble forming satisfactory images with the developer. When Rogers began attacking the color problem intensively, he put couplers and color developers in the standard pod, or in the negative. The result was that dyes were formed in exposed areas as the silver halide was developed to silver. In unexposed areas, couplers migrated to the positive, encountered oxidizing agents there, and formed dyes. The dyes were less mobile than either the developers or the couplers. Excellent images with a single dye could be made this way, but how on earth could the method lead on to pictures with three dyes? "We were young and perhaps this was foolish," Land said, "but what we would like to take credit for is starting and continuing our work in color during all the troubled, turbulent, and exciting years."[14]

In the "primitive first dye image" of the Polaroid executive Carlton Fuller, made in 1944, the negative hardened during development. Indeed, the hardness of the developed area was the dye-controlling mechanism. When dye was applied from the front, it passed through the negative to a support sheet and formed the image. The negative was peeled away. "This is not itself a useful process," Land noted, "but it suggests, at least, that one can make a picture in an instant with a dye."[15]

In 1951, after sustained work on color was under way, "another, more serious" stage was reached, still using a standard color developer and a coupler. An oxidizer lay in the positive. In the classic manner, where light had fallen on the negative and exposed silver-halide grains, the developer molecules converted the exposed silver halide to metallic silver, becoming oxidized and interacting with couplers to form dyes. The dyes and silver were "anchored" in the negative.

But in order to dispense with some ninety minutes of darkroom processing, the instant color system introduced a new twist. Where there had been no exposure, developer and coupler molecules sped from the negative through the gooey reagent to the positive. There, the oxidizing agent converted the developer into its oxidized form, and the developer and coupler reacted to form the dye of a monochrome positive. Couplers held promise. As Vivian Walworth, a Polaroid researcher for many years, put it: "Other [non-instant] processes were using color development with couplers very effectively during the 1950s. The problem . . . for instant . . . color development was matching rates of processes forming the three color images."[16]

Land recalled that couplers were "the way we probably would have proceeded, as would any sensible person experienced in color photography; but this looked so promising that it was rather dull." In 1953, Howard Rogers had his exciting new idea, "which was to hitch each of three preformed dyes, one for the minus blue [yellow], one for the minus green [magenta], and one for the minus red [cyan], to a developer . . . and then to hope that the gods, who had so far been very kind, would continue to favor us."[17] Rogers hoped that the new, larger dye developers would be caught in the negative where exposure had happened, and released where it hadn't. Late in 1957, three-color prints were emerging in the laboratory and were shown excitedly to Kodak.

∞

Rogers already knew that he liked instant photography. Forty years later, he said, "I remember the awful experiences of getting a roll of film back from ordinary processing and finding that I hadn't noticed the telephone line, or the power line, that was running through the corner of the picture. . . . I would notice also that the picture could have been better composed or timed, or could have been further—or closer." With instant photography, a person had a chance to "correct the problems" on the spot.

In the black-and-white lab, according to Rogers, Land "felt unprotected about alternative processes that other people might get patents on . . . so he had me working on some alternatives." Helping out around the edges gave Rogers good experience for his color work. An early task was "a positive image in terms of dye" where a layer of polymer was hardened into a barrier, stopping the dye in places where development took place, but letting the dye through where it hadn't. It worked, but each of these alternates to Land's primary system "had its own difficulties." Still, the effort was not wasted. The "un-obvious advantages and disadvantages" of different types of instant photography built up in Rogers' memory, in what he called "the library," from which he could draw in the long years ahead.

Working and observing in the black-and-white laboratory, Rogers was imbued with the doctrine that the color system must fit in with the basic characteristics of its predecessor: "The customer wasn't supposed to know that it was a wet process." The mechanical setup, with pods carrying the processing fluids between the negative and the positive, was to be the same. Color film was to be used in the same cameras used for black-and-white.

Land's early success with getting dyes to transfer from a negative to a positive was a two-step process. The couplers would move over to the positive, which then was dunked in an oxidizing chemical to reveal an image. Rogers's first task, using one desk and one darkroom in Land's second-floor lab, was to get monochromes in one step. The dye called cyan, a blue-green that is complementary to red, worked fastest. Yellow, complementary to blue, and the red-blue dye called magenta, complementary to green, were more sluggish. Rogers spent a year or more getting good one-step monochrome positive prints with all three dyes.[18]

∞

Fischer's trouble with couplers after 1912 took more than twenty years to overcome. Kodachrome only went on the market in 1935. The successful inventors were Leopold Mannes and Leopold Godowsky, scientists and musicians. They worked at first in a basement in New York and later at Eastman Kodak in Rochester. Their invention was first used for slides and then movies. Its multilayered negative was developed by a "reversal" process into a color positive. In Kodachrome, couplers rested in special layers; but in most color-film processes they were added to the developing fluid in the laboratory. All these processes involved bleaching out the exposed silver, and then the unexposed silver.

In 1972, Rogers recalled that he carried over one comforting, basic principle from the first generation of one-step photography: solubility. The components of the ultimate color film would be soluble, if not in water, then in organic solvents. Solubility implied that one could move things around—and to the chosen destinations—if one were clever and persistent enough. Solubility seemed inherently applicable to color.

Fischer's initial success had added to Rogers' confidence about solubility. If you could move the chemical, you could get it to end up where you wanted it and make what Rogers called Fischer's "beautiful monochromes." But the next step, three-color images, was blocked. When

Fischer sought chemicals that would produce multicolored images, they wandered, and the results were "all messed up." To tackle Fischer's problems, Kodak and the German firm Agfa took different paths. Agfa found a way to anchor the couplers until the color developers reached them. Kodachrome solved the wandering problem a different way, by developing the three layers one at a time. For an instant color film, of course, neither the Agfa nor the Kodak method would work.[19]

∞

Having succeeded in making coupler-developed images for each color, but only one at a time, Rogers needed to move on to stacking them. He would adhere to the classic system of "subtracting" color from the negative into the positive. To get around Fischer's troubles, Rogers started simply enough, by putting conventional color developers into the Polaroid pod and ran at once into seven or eight standard problems. One of the worst was temperature. Couplers for different colors reacted at different rates, depending on temperature. According to Rogers, "Kodak deals with the problem by finding one ideal temperature for all the layers and then eliminating the temperature variation. The laboratory temperature is controlled to a gnat's eyebrow [no more than four degrees either way]." But instant color, like instant black-and-white, would not be processed in the laboratory. It would be processed on the spot, over a wide range of ambient temperatures.

Another problem Rogers encountered was the toxicity of the chemicals: "The original color-developer compound acted like poison ivy on your skin. Kodak coped with it by keeping the process in the lab. Later, when they made kits for home processing, they changed the chemicals that gave people dermatitis. . . . [At Polaroid] we tried to deal with the toxicity issue by taking the color developer out of the pod and putting it in layers on the film. But we were unable to keep all the moisture out. The developer tended to oxidize on the film and change the film-speed [sensitivity to light] of the layers."

At the outset, layered films looked like a big problem for instant color because there was a major threat of "cross talk" among the dyes. "It didn't seem reasonable to think you could have three colors layered on top of each other and expect the dyes to transfer through other layers where other dyes were also transferring. I thought it would be a mess." Furthermore, the dye at the bottom of the stack would have much further to travel during processing than the dye at the top. To make things worse, the dyes might "self-group," or clump.

To address these problems, Rogers put the oxidizing agent in the positive sheet. The requirements were stringent. The oxidizer must not move or form dyes even if unused; it must be stable in storage and not affect the dyes of the final positive image. And where should the developer be placed? Putting it in the negative, in or behind the layers of silver halide that were sensitive to blue, green, and red light, would prevent developer from reaching the positive except where Rogers wanted a particular dye to be formed. Pre-placed developers, however, proved difficult to stabilize.

Rogers needed three good colors, which must not interfere with each other. Could he avoid the headaches of layering by putting everything in a single layer, as Land suggested? Land envisaged a single layer of side-by-side elements. Also, Rogers looked briefly at one of the alternatives considered for sepia and black-and-white films. Perhaps little bubbles on the film, like those in carbonless copies, could encapsulate light-sensitive materials along with other chemicals for development and dye formation. But difficulties quickly warned Rogers away from that approach.[20]

It was preferable to use something reminiscent of the Kodak movie film of 1927, which used structures called lenticules and which was projected through a striped color filter. Some of these techniques surfaced again with the dye bands that were the basis of Land's instant movie system of 1977. With stripes instead of a stack of layers, the materials for producing all three colors would lie in what amounted to a single plane. To start making the single layer of stripes, Rogers tried a two-color arrangement. For this, spots of silver halide, with its appropriate coupler, were imprinted on top of a continuous layer of another color with its coupler. Between the spots, the upper layer consisted of an impermeable plastic. In 1963, Rogers said, "This was an exciting moment, even though the amount of color difference was limited."

Rogers clung to the single-layer concept. He painstakingly developed an elaborate, complete, and reliable stripe system. Developer was no longer stored in the pod, but in the film. "I coated an acetate base with the first color and then made grooves in it with a toothed drum. The drum pushed down through the coated layer and depressed the acetate below it. Then we put an insulating layer at the bottom of the groove and put the second layer over it." A tiny yellow filter capped the layers in the groove. A razor-thin metal blade "doctored," or scraped off, any spillover. The stripes for the third color were embossed at right angles to the grooves containing the other two.

Stripes of material to form red dyes alternated with rows of alternate squares of material to form green and blue dyes. The layout was somewhat like the clusters of glowing red, green, and blue dots of the "additive" color system on a television screen. Although there was "some interference" between the colors, Rogers claimed that "the pictures obtained seemed impressive for this stage of the program."[21]

The most important apparatus for Rogers was a film-coating machine with rollers about four feet apart, on which "you could build up many coats quite easily." For his work with stripes, he had a machine for embossing and for doctoring. To expose pictures, Rogers simply used a strobe light in a box with stripes of filter to separate the colors. Motorized steel rollers spread reagent that he was testing.

The striped single layer had one insuperable problem. The materials for each color covered only one third of the picture area. To be sure, the color-forming materials diffused a bit to the right and left as they crossed over to the positive, bringing the colors of the print a little closer to those of the scene. The colors remained pale, however. No matter how hard Rogers tried, he couldn't get enough of the different dyes transferred over enough of the picture. To put the tiny squares and stripes of color even closer together, he tried 166 lines per inch, and then a finer grid of 225 lines.

Another fundamental problem was the variable rates of dye formation by the couplers. Rogers "realized that we needed to use a chemistry [in] which there was little or no difference in rate between the different reactions." He pre-formed dyes in conjunction with couplers. The couplers could be split to release the dye from a ballast group that had anchored it in the negative. Couplers made the dyes insoluble, which helped even out their rates of movement. The new system didn't need an oxidizer in the positive and so was simpler.

Could there be an even simpler chemical system, without using couplers at all? If so, this would cut down on the number of reagent chemicals required and would bring the reaction rates for the colors in line with each other. Rogers had the insight in 1953. One could link a preformed dye directly with a developer in the same molecule. Now, development of the silver halide would have just one function, controlling the transfer of dyes. Rogers realized that "we really wouldn't have to use a coupling process at all if a developing group was put on a dye." Of his greatest invention, Rogers said, "That turned out to be a happy thought."[22]

Ten years after Rogers, on a spring morning, first had the idea of linking the dye and the developer, he described his happy thought to *Life* magazine reporter Alix Kerr. "The fast [couplers] interfered with the slow ones," Kerr wrote. The pictures they produced took five minutes to process themselves, and then came out a muddy muddle. Rogers set the firm's chemists to changing the chemicals so that they would all work at similar speeds. They still produced stained and murky pictures."

Rogers had been thinking over all the problems. He asked himself, Why not stop tinkering with the classical chemicals of color photography? Why not combine preformed dyes and developer groups in a single molecule? Rogers went to tell Land, who was enthusiastic. As Land recalled ten years later, Rogers told him, "Gee, instead of generating a dye, which is rather a tedious operation, why don't we . . . take a good stable dye, hitch it to a developing molecule with some kind of link?" The hydroquinone developer group would be insoluble in water, but it could make a salt in alkali. Dissolved, the dye developer molecule, when it contacted an exposed silver-halide grain, would "deliver its electron" and become the quinone. No longer able to make a salt, the quinone would be in "a state of low solubility" and hence immobilized in the negative. But, "where the silver halide is not exposed, it can't deliver the electron; it stays as the salt and comes over to make the positive."

Rogers never forgot the feeling of that morning in 1953: "When an idea like this comes, that you're sure is good, it spreads throughout your body. I felt intoxicated, but more 'all there' than usual—almost as if I were a giant. Then I went to draw my new molecule for Dr. Land."[23]

Land regarded Rogers' advance as "spectacular." It meant that "you didn't have to have the delay involved in waiting for the dye to be manufactured [by coupling in the film] for the reactions to occur." In 1963, Land recalled: "As soon as Howie described his molecule, we knew it would exist. It was an ideal molecule, and we therefore took it for granted we could bring it into being. We work by exorcising incessant superstition that there are mysterious tribal gods against you. Nature has neither rewards nor punishments, only consequences. You can use science to make it work for you. There's only nothingness and chaos out there until the human mind organizes it."

Land added: "This is the most exciting part of being human. It is using our brains in the highest way. Otherwise we are just healthy animals." He also asserted that "every creative act is a sudden cessation of stupidity."[24] In a few weeks, forms of Rogers' molecules could be made, and made to work. Ahead, however, lay years of testing to make sure they could work together.

∞

In the stripe system, Rogers's new dye developers, with their preformed dyes, did a little better than couplers, yet the result still was pale—and muddy. In the single layer of the stripe system, only one-third of the picture area was occupied by each color. Further, the chemicals "were all conjugated together, so that anything that happened to the developer changed the color of the dye." The yellow was dark blue in the highly alkaline environment at the start of processing and only went yellow when balance was achieved between alkalinity and acidity. Dye developer with its insulating bridge had produced better dyeing and better developing, Rogers recalled, but "we never did get enough density."[25]

Nonetheless, Rogers looked on the bright side: "Even though they were pale, you could tell the colors apart, which is a great advance." Instead of being discouraged, Rogers and Land were emboldened to return to a layered arrangement in which dyes for each color would be drawn from the entire picture area.

With layers, Land and Rogers found further encouragement. They found that "there wasn't any limit on the density of each dye that we could get transferred." And they could use other layers to help control things. They could push the dye layers farther apart by inserting polymer spacers between them. The isolation of the colors was better than in the stripes.

Land looked back on the return to layers as more "startling" than making the dyes stable and placing them "under control of the developer." Although it seemed unlikely, "you could indeed control . . . three layers of photosensitive emulsion and three layers of dyes. So, even though the dyes were passing through each other and passing through all the emulsions, you nevertheless could have each layer do its job in the way it ought to be done."

Each layer of dye developer needed to be separate from its associated light-sensitive emulsion. It might have been attractive to shorten the molecules' journey to the positive by putting them right in with the emulsions. The grains in each emulsion layer had been sensitized to a particular color band, and the light-absorbing dye developers were complementary to these colors. Unifying dyes and emulsions "would enormously reduce the quantity of light available of the very wavelengths with which you were trying to expose. So you'd have a great drop in what's called film speed or sensitivity."[26]

In the layered system, the reactive chemicals burst from the pod, pushing first into the blue-sensitive layer and its adjacent layer of yellow dye developer. The alkaline liquid raced even faster, causing the layers to swell. For a second or two this increased the distance that the reagents would have to travel to reach the layers of green-sensitive silver halide and magenta dye developer. Space bought short, but crucial bits of time. The alkaline liquid did yet another service. It altered the spacers, the upper and then the lower, to make each in turn permeable to the relatively slow-moving dye developers.

Rogers knew that "we would have to make sure that dyes set free in their own layer didn't get trapped while transferring through exposed silver halide in other layers." Land called the idea "hold-release." In such an ideal system, "dyes would be held close to their own emulsions until development was over, and then be allowed to transfer."[27] This called for dye developers that developed fast and moved at a moderate pace. Polaroid researchers found them.

The yellow, magenta, and cyan dyes were released from the negative so that they arrived in the positive at the same time and formed the complementary colors of blue, green, and red. This simultaneous arrival was progress, but the dyes had different distances to travel and would start at different times. In two-tenths of a second, yellow dye developers would go to work on the blue-sensitive layer. At the half-second mark, the magenta dye developers would get going in the green-sensitive layer. The cyan only began working in the red-sensitive layer two and one-half seconds after the alkaline fluid had been let loose from the pod. At five seconds, most development work was over, and at ten seconds, dye developers began appearing in the positive. There, the developer group did a new job. The developer was crucial for binding to the jungle-gym lattice of the dye-grabbing polymer, the "mordant" in which the image formed.[28]

Rogers had to choose the best type of developer group for each color molecule. His first candidate was the familiar hydroquinone, which has "a very low activity when it's neutral . . . so you can coat it in a layer and put it in a negative and not have to do anything until you make it alkaline at the time of processing." It was not quite that simple, however. The developer groups went through a lot of evolution in the chemistry labs.

∞

Another key idea of the time, though not much discussed in public, was the auxiliary developer. It was invented to serve a need. To make a practical color process, "you are in a hurry to get the discrimination between the more exposed and the less exposed" silver-halide grains. Land called it "a very soluble reducing agent in small quantities." Speeding to the exposed grains, the small band of auxiliary developers quickly reacted with the grains, donating electrons and becoming oxidized. Moving almost as fast as the alkali, the auxiliaries rushed a short distance to nearby dye developer molecules, in the layer just beneath, and oxidized the dye developer. That step converted the dye developer into a form "of very little solubility so it stays there." The other dye developers could migrate to the positive. It was, Land said, "as if that small molecule carries the image right along with it."

By oxidizing and immobilizing big, slow-moving dye developers that corresponded to an exposed grain, the auxiliary itself had been reduced and thus freed to do more work. Oxidizing and being reduced again and again, the auxiliary developer was recycled as the hypo had been in the sepia and black-and-white processes. Land didn't like the term "auxiliary developer," preferring "operative developer" or "primary developer." Whatever its name, without it, the color process would not be useful. Land was proud of the primary developer: "We use a very small amount of it." But the dye developers also played their part in development. They re-reduced the mobile developer so that it could do its job. "The dye developer is a vigorous and vital and major participant in the development process."[29]

∞

The work of getting rates of movement in line was not limited to the developers. There were years of work on hundreds of dyes. Syntheses of new compounds mounted into the thousands. Myron Simon, who had been making color developers and couplers, made the first cyan dye developer that really worked, Rogers recalled. Simon went through many steps in chemically tuning the cyan dye developer to improve gradually its absoption spectrum. Even "quite a bit of tinkering" only achieved a cyan that made for "reddish-blue skies and dullish greens." He kept adding or shifting chlorines, hydroxyl groups, and alkyl groups to create "a versatile class of dyes" with better absorption properties.

As the chemistry team grew larger and kept expanding down Osborn Street, Milton Green's laboratory hunted for a more stable yellow, or a "juicier" developer group. Green also worked on magenta and yellow dyes. The dyes had to be soluble. How different were their solubilities when they were oxidized or reduced (de-oxidized)? The chemistry team could not always count on obtaining the desired chemicals to start off the syntheses. To be practical, syntheses could not have too many steps. Manufacturing the chemicals on an industrial scale required compromises.

After synthesis, the compounds went to the physical chemists, who measured speeds: how fast did the alkali push down into the negative, or the polymers swell, or "fogging" occur, or dyes push through the spacers? Howard Haas, George R. Bird, Lloyd Taylor, and others measured the dry thickness of all the layers, the amounts of dye and silver halide in the negative, the solubilities of dye developers, the propensity of the polymers in the negative to pick up dyes, and the effects of temperature, alkalinity, and concentrations of the chemicals.

The scientists were impressed by the system they worked on. Analytical chemist Richard S. Corley tested several hundred dye developers. He used both combustion and many wavelengths of light to determine makeup, molecular weight, and exact functions. He spoke of "the wonderful intricacy of the Polaroid color photographic process."[30]

The chemical components were only part of the problem. The color processes had to work together in the right way, with the right timing. Development of the silver halide by the auxiliaries took a second or two. Other processes lasted up to the sixty-second mark, when the positive was peeled apart, and beyond. The system that had been designed to remain stable for months on the shelf was suddenly put in motion after a picture was taken. All the components had to go where they were supposed to, in step with each other. The dyes had to build up in the "mordant" image layer designed by Haas and such colleagues as Taylor. The reagents had to become harmless in the positive or safely imprisoned in the negative.

By 12 December 1957, the Polaroid scientists were ready to take their first official picture with the material that would eventually be named Polacolor. The event was announced in the annual report.[31] The initial pictures were so pale and blotchy, Rogers said, that "only a mother could love them." For brighter colors, Polaroid added what Rogers called a quaternary salt, such as phenol ethyl picolinium bromide, to the processing fluid. The salt reacted with the quinone group and made the molecule larger. This cut down on the danger of re-reducing the dye developers, which would release them from bondage to exposed grains. Once trapped, molecules would stay trapped. For Rogers, "That was one of the main things that made the colors better." Another trick was to coat an anti-fogging compound in the positive, from which it could diffuse over to the negative to regulate development of the unexposed silver halide. This kept more dye available for going over to the positive.[32]

Two and a half years later, in 1960, Land demonstrated the Polacolor system in a standard Polaroid camera at the company's annual shareholders' meeting.[33] By then, Polaroid was deep in the effort to get instant color film out of the laboratory and into the commercial market. The first question that had to be tackled was, Who could make it? Although Polaroid was growing by leaps and bounds, and new film-assembly factories were going up in Waltham, it was still only a modest-size company. The potential market for instant color looked large—as it proved to be—but the capital necessary to enter the color domain would also be large. Because Land hated debt, Polaroid made a special stock offering in 1958 that raised eleven million dollars. The size of the challenge convinced Land to farm out the manufacturing of the color negative, as he did many times with whole systems or parts of them. Polaroid would focus on the positive it had designed. The company would face enough challenges in designing factories for the positive and film assembly.

In December 1957, Land turned to his old friends at Kodak. At a meeting of Air Force science advisers, when he showed the color print to Henry Yutzy of Kodak, Yutzy said, "That's commercial." It was, Land thought, a "benign reassurance about the status of our ten-year-old drive." The two companies still shared enthusiasms, and so Kodak would "study production techniques and develop methods for the manufacture for us of materials for the new color process." Billed first as an alternate supplier, Kodak became the only supplier by 1962. Polaroid started a parallel program to make its own negative someday. Meanwhile, Land's company remained solely responsible for its reagent chemicals and color positive. Kodak's production machines, Land said, brought instant color to the market "five to ten years sooner than it could have become available without the cooperation."[34]

The laboratory negatives of 1957 and the public test photos of 1960 involved coating layers of the negative with organic solvents. "But then Eastman Kodak couldn't handle those non-aqueous solutions," said Rogers.[35] For Kodak factories to make the color negative, Polaroid had to switch to water-soluble gelatin. This required "quite a few drastic changes to the process" and four years of work. In some ways, Land said later, the processes of 1957 had "a higher degree of technological elegance than the process finally adopted, jointly." According to Rogers, the color isolation was not as good as in Polaroid's method, where the spacers were laid down from organic solvents rather than water.[36]

Polaroid had to develop and teach Kodak chemical engineers the deposition of the spacers and dye-developer layers in water and "how to make good dispersions of the dye developers in water." Kodak insisted on making its own dye developers and had to be taught how. The massive transfer of technology from the little firm to the big one was often irksome. Indeed, it may have worn away interest in further technical collaboration between the two companies. The design of the negative was frozen. In 1960, for example, a suggestion by a Kodak senior scientist was rejected as impractical. Frequent meetings between Polaroid and Kodak people trailed off. There was no cooperation on what might come next.[37] A flame had gone out.

Manufacturing, not marketing, was the key question, according to Rogers. Once the product could be made, it would go on the market "with just the volume to fill the pipelines" and production would grow from there. Rogers looked back philosophically on the complexity and delay: "Three years actually isn't bad time for going from a lab coater to a coater that coats material three or five feet wide, and by the mile."[38]

∞

By 1962, Polaroid had overcome many obstacles to instant color photography: the agony of couplers and bubbles and dots and stripes, of tuning the dye developers with each other and everything else, of allying with Kodak for negative production, and of restating the film's architecture to mesh with Kodak's manufacturing practices. But there was still one big problem. Within seconds after Polacolor positives were peeled back from the negative, they required vigorous, almost instant wiping with a protective coating. Otherwise, oxidation darkened the picture. The protection step would convert Polaroid's much-heralded instant color film from one-step to a clumsy, hurried two-step. It was a far more drastic situation than for black-and-white, where coating could be done hours after peeling the picture out of the camera. For color, Polaroid ordered the materials for the coaters, which required "some gums we had to get from strange places." Boxes were designed to hold the vials of coater, and production began. The instructions read, "Coating must be done within five seconds after removing the print from the camera. This will give you truer, brighter colors and add much to the life of your picture." Land was gloomy. He recalled twenty years later, "It's almost impossible to get a customer to coat in five seconds." The customer had to open the camera, pull the film, tear out the print, put it on cardboard to prevent curling, and then apply the protective coat. "So the five seconds is almost gone before you start."

It was galling. It was a compromise. Land complained that "the picture we wanted was the one inside the camera, before you peeled it out." He didn't like "terminating an elegant process with a clumsy afterstep." The time for marketing was approaching. Finally, Land couldn't stand it any longer. On Labor Day 1962, he told his staff that he would free the Polacolor experience from that second step of coating—and do it before the film was due to go on the market the following January. To work more efficiently with colleagues, Land moved upstairs to a special part of Rogers's lab. "I dropped everything else I was doing," Land recalled. Although "we were all ready to produce" the Polacolor positive, production was held up. For the next four months, he averaged four hours' sleep a night. By Christmas, Land and a small team, working in the small white laboratory, had completely redesigned the Polacolor positive to eliminate the coater.

Along the way, they cut the "imbibing" time before peeling apart the print from ninety seconds to sixty. Progress with the ideas was so rapid that on 15 October, Land, knowing that Yutzy would not attend a defense advisers' meeting in Cambridge that week, telephoned him. He recalled speaking "enthusiastically with Yutzy about the possibility of its success."[39]

In January 1963, Land said that the crash effort of late 1962 was "no more eccentric than saying you don't go to bed when you're halfway up a mountain."[40] In those months, Land felt, the pressure made him and his associates work more effectively than if they had all the time they needed. "Almost every day last fall we took on things which people might think would take a year or two. They weren't particularly hard. What was hard was *believing* they weren't hard."[41]

A few months later, Land told fellow photographic researchers that he had always dreamed of "an honest-to-God one-step process." There was no question that after coating, the black-and-white print was "one of the most stable one can make." But color was the main event. It seemed to Land "a shame, with color about to come out, not to take advantage of the years of wishing and thinking, decades of wishing and thinking, not to eliminate that whole operation from this process."

The crash effort was "an exciting adventure" for Land. "I was concentrating on this undertaking of vital importance to the company and to the future of all instant photography. I was working day and night. I was being effective, and the group around me were being effective." The commercial pressure was great. "Everybody was standing by. We were supposed to start shipping the film in a few months." With Kodak making the negative, the positive was the only domain in which Land could solve the problem. "We couldn't touch the negative. Indeed most of it was made." He added, "The only place where I could do anything immediately practical would be in the receiver layer. And so that's what I concentrated on. . . . My task at that moment was to make something that would work with that negative."[42]

The mobilizing chemical was a crucial factor. Released with the other agents when the pod burst, this "relatively enormous mass of sodium hydroxide molecules" spread swiftly between the positive and negative, dissolving the dye developers and setting them in motion. In this highly alkaline environment, the dye developers either migrated to the adjacent light-sensing layer to be trapped by exposed silver halide grains or moved out of the negative into the thinnest of dye-capturing layers in the positive. But how could the alkaline molecules be discarded when they were no longer needed and were actually a threat to the stability of the final image?

"They're there when you get through with the picture," Land knew. "They go right along with the dyes and fill the positive sheet." Hence, the sodium hydroxide molecules were dangerous in several ways. They prevented the image layer from coalescing into a hard, shiny surface, and they were available for oxidation. Unless the prints were coated with acid, the prints changed so fast that they lost "the virginal beauty of the picture contained within the camera." Stabilization was vital. As before, achieving it would be like choreographing a ballet. Land's team had to figure out a great deal. He defined the challenges: "How to maintain the system alkaline long enough for the negative silver halide grains to be developed, for the dye to be controlled in the emulsion, for the dye to migrate to the positive layer, for the three dyes to dye the positive layer, and then and only then to have the alkalinity dry rapidly to stop, to slow up the process to a point where it was safe, and the image will not be damaged or altered by further dye transfer or by decomposition of the dyes or by the return of the dyes from the positive back to the negative."[43]

For stabilization, massive amounts of alkali had to be neutralized "in the right way at the right time, and neutralized in such a way that the image is left clear and brilliant." Pushing at a feverish pace, Land's team tried a simple technique when they opened the back of the camera to peel the color positive away from the negative. They used a medicine dropper to put tiny quantities of boric acid onto the picture. The beauty lasted.

For the next experiment, they thought of duplicating a technique from the original sepia process of 1947. There, acidic molecules came "up from underneath the picture after it was made." In color, however, the mass of alkaline hydroxide molecules would have to be matched by "great masses of acid molecules." The acid would stay near the picture and make it muddy and a little sticky. The problems would be in neutralizing too quickly or without control, and keeping the acid molecules where they belonged.

"And so, we decided to do it the other way," Land said. A "high polymer" layer with big, immobile acid molecules was placed in the positive sheet, "way down under the picture," next to the paper base and isolated from it by a spacer layer that slowed things down appropriately. The acid groups would be right in the polymers, which were a type of plastic that could be dissolved and coated in the film factory. The acid polymers would stay where they were put, unable to migrate, waiting "as a receptacle and receiver."

Now, the alkaline hydroxides would carry the dyes into the image layer and gradually penetrate through the timing layer to the immobilized acids of the polymer layer. The hydroxides would react with the acids and release a tiny amount of water. In a sense, Land said, this "purges the system of alkaline by sequestering it outside of the system."[44]

The polymer of the timing layer, Rogers recalled in 1972, had to be designed with a low permeability, so that the alkaline molecules would not get to their destination too quickly, reducing solubility and stopping the dye transfer prematurely. After the dyes had built up in the positive, more and more of the hydroxides, the sodium ions, would reach the acid layer and react with the acids, releasing pure water into the film. The alkaline sodium ions, having done their work, would be pulled out of the image layer where they were no longer needed and be trapped in the acid polymer layer. In the ultrathin world of the film, the water would move the balance between acid and alkali to neutral. Chemical reactions would stop, and the dyes would be frozen in place.[45]

In sixty seconds after the print was peeled apart, the alkalinity would already have dropped a thousandfold. In the five minutes afterward, the pH, a measure of the alkalinity, would sink another ten thousandfold. The polymeric image layer would undergo bonding among many of its hydrogen atoms and become tough, shiny, and resistant to fingerprints. Land said exuberantly, "It washes itself out."[46] Land's memory of the achievement remained vivid many years later: "We were able to meet . . . our original plan for delivery with this entirely new product. . . . Henceforth . . . we've never needed a coater in color."[47]

When the self-washing Polacolor went on sale, news coverage was lavish. *Life* ran Fritz Goro's photo of Rogers and colleagues, including Elkan Blout. In the photo, which spread over more than a full page, the Polaroid researchers were gathered around a table with five thousand vials, representing the five thousand compounds they had tested over fifteen years. Rogers recalled, "The vials were being set up on one of those rickety portable tables. When they had gotten them almost all set up, somebody bumped into the table and knocked them all over—5,000 vials! They had to be set up again. But the second time, to make sure they were stable, they put a double stick tape on the bottom of every one. It took a while, but the picture turned out okay."[48]

As the first supplies of film moved in trucks to Florida, Land and his laboratory co-workers pressed on. Further inventions eventually produced a blizzard of patents. "In our work, we have to keep in practice like musicians," Land said. " Besides, there are still vast potentialities to be realized in color film. To us, it's just like bringing up a child. You don't stop after you've had it."[49]

By 1963, color had become the experience of choice for the amateur photographer. The same year, Kodak introduced an extremely simple color camera for the mass market, the Instamatic, which sold in the millions. Mass manufacture of easily taken color images was a scientific and industrial response to a demand of the imagination, converted at great cost into technological reality. The demand for color had at least as much impact on instant photography as on any other photography. Worldwide, popular desire for pictures in color multiplied inexorably. Color had been preferred in the age of paint, and so it was in the era of chemical and electronic image recording. Less than a hundred years after the first black-and-white daguerreotypes, color was thrusting forward, first in lantern slides, movies, and glossy magazines, and then in snapshots processed in laboratories, in television broadcasts, in sections of newspapers, and in millions of camcorders. In 1963, instant color snapshots were made and viewed at the very graduations, weddings, and beach parties where the pictures were taken.

Polaroid Corporation's already explosive growth accelerated. Sales multiplied sixfold in ten years. For a long time, Land's factory for invention became the archetypal high-technology darling of thousands of investors. It also became a center of creativity and excitement in marketing. Polaroid created a friendly mental picture of a complicated battery of technologies that produced something the public wanted more and more. In less than a decade, Polaroid rocketed toward near-equality in amateur picture-taking with its giant supplier, Kodak.[50] Edwin and Terre Land became worth hundreds of millions of dollars in Polaroid stock, and began to make major philanthropic gifts.

∞

Both Rogers and Land lived many years after their drive to color. Land praised Rogers highly in 1973: "In my life I've known few people who are saints or seem like saints." Rogers believed that "anger is wasted emotion." He remained a "continuous and reliable contributor. You have to be awfully good in research for people to tolerate you, because a lot of the time you seem nuts. This kind of madness keeps you perennially young."[51]

What did Rogers end up thinking about his great patron? After Land's death in 1991, his strongest memory of Land was "not so much of features as of presence. Dr. Land's presence was such that this is outside of people's ordinary experience. I think that you could tell that this was a power. [This] sometimes made it difficult to talk to him. It took me years to be able to tell him something straight off and say what I meant."

Rogers spoke about Land's influence on his own work: "He got me much more skeptical, I guess. He taught me the importance of an experiment as distinct from somebody's opinion. I learned to be careful [about] thinking what I read was gospel. I learned to think and observe for myself and question anything that really didn't feel quite right . . . He really gave me the incentive to learn. The problems he gave me to work on were the problems that gave me the incentive to find out a lot more than I knew."

Land, he thought, was not wholly happy when the struggle to realize innovations pulled him beyond the laboratory: "He would have liked to build a research company. I think he was discouraged a little when he found that nobody else could really nurture your new baby the way you could. He found that you really had to go into production on items in order to make them successful. . . . When he finally did undertake to go into manufacture, he did it very well but I think he'd rather not have had to." Nonetheless, Land applied the same intensity to manufacturing as to research: "I think to him it was all the same. [He] was focused on getting a particular thing going."

What did he think of Land's dictum that every problem can be solved with the things in the room at the time? "Obviously it isn't always true. But I think it made a point that people are not likely to marshal all the tools unless they're really forced to." Working with Land, Rogers discussed possibilities, went away and did the experiments, and came back with the results. Experiment and analysis, experiment and analysis. "The process of research is continuing to compare the way things are, that you determine by experiment, with the way you think they work. You usually find that the things are not exactly the way you think they are."

In 1991, Rogers was asked what he missed most with Land gone. "The exciting conversation," he answered. "Dr. Land didn't have any small talk. His talk was always of larger issues."[52]

14

Color Vision

> It is my own experience that a premature attempt to explain something that thrills you will destroy your perceptivity rather than increase it, because your tendency will be to explain away rather than seek out. Postpone disillusionment, if it must come, to the last possible moment. Fly with your mind without assuming that nature has set a very special trap for you.
>
> —Edwin H. Land, West Point, New York, 19 May 1955

Early in 1955 a small accident in the laboratory plunged Land into the mystery of color vision. It became a passion, and for thirty years, it was his most intense effort in basic research. The work thrust him forward to the view, increasingly prevalent in the 1990s, of the brain as a physical entity, shaping and shaped by a physical world.

The unexpected turn did not arise from Land's usual approach of seeing a need and rustling up the basic science to meet it. After helping start work on the U-2 spy plane (chapter 15), he was back thinking about black-and-white film, including transparencies. But the long slog to color pictures was getting longer (chapter 13).

He thought he should know more about color. It was not just a demanding branch of photography. Physicists had been fascinated by color ever since Newton, and so had physiologists and psychologists. Their basic assumptions had gone unquestioned for nearly three hundred years. Human color perception resulted either from the energies of light reflected from objects in the world, or from adaptation by the eye and illusions arising in the brain.

Newton discovered a spectrum of light that included the primary colors of red, green, and blue, and such other colors as violet, yellow, and orange. He had a beam of light enter a darkened room through a small opening and shine through a glass prism that spread out some seven bands of light on the opposite wall. He exploited his great discovery, Land said, by studying "the color properties of objects around him in the world. . . . If he took a red book or a red apple and moved that up and back in the spectrum, it was brightest in the part of the spectrum that looked red and darkest in the part of the spectrum that looked blue." In other words, an apple appeared red because a preponderance of "red-making" rays reached the eye from that apple.

But why did the apple still appear red at noontime, when it was bathed in bright blue-sky light, and red when the sun was low in the sky at dawn and sunset? The perception of colors was nearly universal in any kind of light. What explained this "color constancy"? Preoccupied with the idea of light as particles, Newton left this question aside.

To be sure, Land said, "an object that looks red will be *most efficient* in reflecting red rays. That is, if you have blue rays fall on it, it will reflect, say, only five percent of them. If you have red rays fall on it, it will reflect 95 percent of them." Paradoxically, Newton went on to an incorrect idea, that, "*because* more red light was reflected from the apple that is red, that we see it as red. Now that turns out not be true." Newton had discovered only half a fundamental law.[1]

The fascination with color continued. One of the great minds of the eighteenth and nineteenth centuries was Goethe, a scientist as well as a poet, novelist, and philosopher. For ten years, he studied the puzzle of the colored shadows that painters had long noticed. At nearly the same time, Benjamin Thompson, Count Rumford, also experimented with colored shadows. He concluded that they were a deception, an illusion.

The ideas that Newton spelled out in his *Opticks* (1704) were refined but not changed fundamentally. At the beginning of the nineteenth century, the physicist and physiologist Thomas Young (1773–1829) postulated the existence in the eyes of receptors for each of the three primary colors: red, green, and blue. These colors are the long, middle, and short light waves within the narrow range that the human eye can detect.

Half a century later, in 1855, the great mathematician and physicist James Clerk Maxwell (1831–78) went further. Primarily a physicist exploring light, not a physiologist probing the machinery of vision, Maxwell enlisted the new techniques of photography to help determine whether red, green, and blue were sufficient to create a full range of color. He had three identical black-and-white photographs taken through little flasks of fluid colored red, green, and blue. The filter pictures were converted into transparencies. Then he projected each of the images, the "red" image though the red filter and so on, onto a screen so that the images were in register. The result was the world's first color photograph.

At almost the same time, the great German physicist and physiologist Hermann Helmholtz (1821–94) also revived the theories of Young. Studying color blindness, Helmholtz developed his ideas that colors at a point are determined by the ratio of the three energies at that point. This notion resembles the principle of a modern color television set, with triplets of red, green, and blue dots, at each of hundreds of spots along each of the hundreds of lines on the screen, lighting up according to the relative flow of electrons from the three color "guns" at the base of the tube.

Helmholtz engaged in a fundamental controversy with another German student of vision, Ewald Hering (1834–1918). Such capacities as perceiving the arrangement of objects in space, Hering held, were part of a human being's natural endowment, as if they were "innate ideas" of the sort postulated by Descartes. Signs for height, right–left position, and depth were built into each point of the retina. Helmholtz, according to the Harvard psychologist and historian Edwin Boring, followed the opposite, empirical tradition of Locke. He believed that the local signs had to be learned. According to Land, Helmholtz believed that color was a matter of becoming "accustomed and trained."[2]

∞

Pursuing a practical one-step color photography, Land decided that it would be interesting to repeat Maxwell's work with modern, far more sensitive films and instruments. He rang the changes on the classic experiment and confirmed what others had observed since 1897, "that one could skip the blue and still achieve a wide gamut of colors." The lack of a blue filter represented the blue-poor light of sunrise. So two projectors were set up, one with the red filter, the other with the green, each to project pictures that had been taken through the same grade of filter. On this and many later occasions, the pictures showed a tabletop display of fruits and other groceries. What would happen if one or more of the filters were taken off?[3]

One day early in 1955, he and Meroë Morse spent some time with the projectors. When the red and green filters were on, a range of colors appeared on the screen. Then, either the green filter cap fell off or Land took it off. Now the light from the green projector was white, and it flooded the screen. In this situation, Land would have expected to see mostly pink.

Just a few weeks later, at West Point, New York, Land reported his experiments publicly: "I was casually playing with the green filter to produce this effect when Meroë Morse said, 'Why is there any color now?' My casual answer was, 'Oh, that's just the color fatigue effect.'" In other words, it was adaptation, a matter of becoming accustomed and trained. The explanation sounded a bit glib. "As the day went on, my scientific conscience began to bother me." Pondering Morse's question, he went home and slept for a time. But "that night at two o'clock I awoke with the feeling that this phenomenon was a remarkable one."[4]

As longtime co-workers John and Mary McCann put it in 1994, "About 2 A.M., Land sat up in bed saying, 'Color adaptation! What color adaptation?'" and went back to the lab. He began searching for "evidence of color adaptation as the explanation for what he saw and he never found any."[5] Back at the laboratory he thought that "if the brightness of the white projector was reduced to match the brightness of the red light (the intensity of light going through the red projector), the white might become a useful primary color." He turned on the red and white projectors again. This time, however, he avoided simply flooding the screen with white light. He turned down the intensity of the white light, so as not to mask the light from the red projector, and got the surprise of his life: the screen was filled with "a remarkably extensive palette of colors," lifelike and persistent.[6]

These discoveries came about well before the time when a scientist as founder and chief executive of an advanced-technology company would become commonplace. Land nevertheless had his "scientific conscience" and was convinced that everything he did came from the attitude and methods of a scientist. Others accepted him as one; they knew that certain scientific experiments would interest him, and that he could be helpful.[7]

Land made his West Point report in May 1955, soon after the first accidental "red-and-white" discovery, as he accepted a medal from the Society of Photographic Scientists and Engineers. Long before any formal scientific publication, he demonstrated the effects that he and Morse had seen. Chastened by his first snap judgment, he said, "What I like to do is relax and enjoy it for a while rather than try to explain it all away . . . I believe in encouraging the romanticization of a wonderful phenomenon . . . Fly with your mind without assuming that nature has set a very special trap for you."[8]

The small band in Land's laboratory had already searched the scientific and patent literature. Of the persistence of color with only red and white light, they urgently asked, "How well is it known? Who knows about it? What can we do with it? What can we learn about it?" They rushed "to our standard color-photography texts and to our psychology books and to our psychologist friends—but no good leads." After a month, Howard Rogers found references in a textbook on color photography. In 1914, William F. Fox and William H. Hickey of Kinemacolor in America took out a British patent on using red-and-white as a movie process. It called for taking frames alternately through a red filter and no filter. In 1929, Anthony Bernardi began obtaining a series of British patents on a process that used red and green filters for taking movie pictures and red and white for projection.

Apparently, however, none of the scientific students of color, in psychology or colorimetry, had published a study in this field. The work was ignored and forgotten. Hence, Land entitled his West Point lecture "The Case of the Sleeping Beauty."

The lecture was not the usual scientific communication, refined over months or years and intensively reviewed. As leader of a thriving industry and solver of impossible problems, he felt confident enough to risk bringing his hearers virtually into the laboratory where, a short time before, he had found out new things, which he did not yet understand. He felt that the results should be shown "while the details are fresh in my mind . . . without the benefit of hindsight." In the nineteenth century, he said, scientists did this all the time, conveying a "sense of delight and adventure." In the twentieth century, however, "cold formalism" had taken over, masking the "real working world" of scientists. He claimed that "the world outside of science has only the vaguest idea of how we go about our business of scientific exploration."

More people should know about "the way we feel and the way we act and the way we worry and the way we wonder and the way we dream while we are doing our work." He preferred "to investigate by setting up classical experiments, watching them, and ruminating about them. Accordingly I asked Gretchen Baum [a laboratory assistant] to arrange such typical subjects as bowls of fruit, to photograph them separately through red, green, and blue filters onto our black-and-white transparency material, and to project them superimposed."

With two of the three filters covered, the range of colors disappeared. But when a second color was added, the color sensation "became vivid." It was more than random playing around: "I am convinced that this kind of naive and direct relationship to nature by an experimenter is a vital part of this sort of scientific development. Only by looking with your own eyes can you know the feeling that red is not red and green is not green and blue is not blue unless some other color is in the field of view . . . I submit that it is the visual experiences at a time like this that lead to convictions which lead to hypotheses which lead to science."[9]

∞

Already he knew that the new hobby was more than a charming sideline. The colors were "no laboratory curiosity, but rather an extreme demonstration of color constancy, a visual faculty we make use of every day." A lemon seen at noon would be yellow to a person's eyes, and it still would be yellow in the reddish light of sunset.[10]

The color vision research attracted great public interest and a corresponding level of skepticism, even hostility. Land was not just attacking previous notions of how color is perceived. He began proposing alternative explanations of color perception, suggesting systems in the retina of the eye or the cortex of the brain, or both, systems he called "retinexes" that made computations, that is, comparisons of lightness in each of the three major bands of visible light. He apparently used the term "retinex" for the first time in 1963.[11] Not until nearly twenty years had passed did he begin to attract neurophysiologists to the search for mechanisms that might behave as he postulated.

In the 1950s, neurophysiologists had already begun to map the vast tangle of the architecture of human vision. Using microelectrodes inserted into the brains of cats and monkeys, they started probing the organizations of brain cells to see how they respond to shape and motion in the world. Mapping territory barely penetrated before, the new biophysics of the brain was bound to attract intense interest, and prejudice. The topics were universal: perception and all other aspects of consciousness such as color, taste, smell, touch, dreams, intellectual capacity, and athletic ability. Perception, however, was also a most arcane science. Until late in the twentieth century, the workings of the brain, responding to stimuli from outside, were assumed to be so complex as to defy measurement. Exploring the brain and its functions was widely thought to be an excursion into the unknowable, as genetics once was.

Some even found these excursions into the architecture of consciousness either blasphemous or a final assault of scientism on humane values. The brain was an ultimate sanctuary for those drawing their self-respect from the existence of a domain beyond the rational, free from the numerical calculations of scientists and business people alike. Now, even here, the "reductionist" division of things into pieces small enough to measure, describe, and analyze, was breaking in on the ineffable. The explorers replied that they had touched just one shore of a vast ocean. Still, they were finding actual structures in the cortex of the brain that were responsible for aspects of vision.

During this momentous growth in knowledge of the chemistry, physics, and physiology of the brain, Land approached human color vision from the outside. Although he used the report of human subjects on what they saw, his work gradually resonated with the rest of brain science. At the end of the 1980s, his work appeared less removed from the mainstream of science than when he started. Doubtless Land aroused sharp distaste by denying that color was an illusion. The effects he uncovered were stripped of the influence of surroundings, memory, or adaptation, he said. They were irrefutable, not a repetition of prior work, and required explanation.[12]

Often in science, a researcher will open a door and then not go through. Land was not this unlucky; he eventually stimulated and worked with other investigators. It also often happens that a scientist fails to get above a critical level of attention from other scientists. By contrast Land won immediate and wide attention, and became a magnet for controversy.

The physicist-businessman made bold to enter this domain of few data and much emotion because he sought distinction as a scientist working on fundamental problems as well as making inventions that millions of people used. He was self-taught and thought in his own way, but he suffered from a tendency to overcomplicate both his demonstrations and his conclusions. Working always with a small group, Land shielded himself from discouragement. Some visitors, such as the biologist James Dewey Watson, who ran a laboratory bursting with conferences, visitors, and gossip, came away with a sense of stifling insulation from criticism.[13] Others, like the physicist Richard Feynman, who enjoyed arguing with Land, found it hard to understand where Land was going.

Land liked the sense of doing battle against the odds, against mainstream thought. Perhaps he enjoyed this a little too well for the normal functioning of the business called Polaroid Corporation. Still, the controversy over color vision stung him to refute critics by refining his experiments for decades, while sharpening his proposals of how the sensation of color comes about. His focus was mostly that of a physicist challenging notions brought forward by other physicists. Evidently, the criticisms of psychologists struck him as a bit thin. They did not seem to come up with powerful experiments of their own.

The public, ignoring the academic debate, was fascinated for thirty years. Although audiences may have been puzzled, they were still excited by a sense of watching a drama in which Land seemed to discover things as he talked. The presentations were not suave. Land was impatient to get to the demonstrations, which he clearly regarded as the heart of the argument. Over and over, Land insisted that people could not learn much about science without doing experiments. Reading, that is, catching up on the accumulated knowledge of the past, should not blind them.

Each demonstration involved experiments with the audience members as participants thrust into an arcane world in a darkened room. As if at a magic show, they were enthralled as well as persuaded. At the same time, he understood the perils of lecturing in darkness. In 1975, he asked his audience to close their eyes briefly for a demonstration that color was not a matter of adaptation. When he asked, "Please remember to open them when I tell you," the audience laughed. Once describing how he kept his hearers awake, he said he took a lesson from George Wald of Harvard, who recently had told an audience, "The point I want to make will come in the last few minutes of the lecture." Land spoke with a New England accent, referring to "faw" for four, "theyah" for there, "fah" for far, and "culla" for color.

Land seemed to half expect some new insight to occur at each step. Sometimes hesitating, at other times rushing through passages, he not only used vocal italics, raising his voice slightly, but often repeated phrases, such as "color is independent of energy." At the 1975 lecture, he pronounced each syllable of the word "light-ness-es."[14] Audiences knew they were characters in a drama. The complex details and the half-understood asides were dazzling and mystifying.

Although Land wanted to be understood, he persisted in his unusual exposition. He spent little time on the cultural background of perception and the brain structures that achieve it. There were no words about the general problem of vision or of vision as a window into the brain. Perhaps he thought it too obvious to explain that color was a passionately engrossing problem for physicists, biologists, and psychologists alike, or to mention that he was wrestling with the basic disagreement over the nature of color: Was it actual or an illusion?

It took him almost twenty years to articulate the idea that he was exploring the long-held tenet of "separation" between mind and the physical world outside. To Land and a growing group of biologists, the brain was a physical entity. Electricity and chemistry were essential for it to function. This physical structure reacted to, and processed events in, the world outside it. Thought, perception, learning, memory, consciousness were fundamentally physical. There was what Land called a "polar partnership" between mind and the rest of reality.[15]

∞

Among those who saw Land's demonstrations in the early 1960s were two students of the visual cortex, David H. Hubel, an American raised in Canada, and Torsten N. Wiesel from Sweden. They shared in a Nobel prize in 1981. As an undergraduate physics student at McGill University in Montreal, Hubel had been inspired by Wilder Penfield's mapping of brain functions in humans during brain surgery. Hubel and Wiesel had begun their twenty years of collaboration in the laboratory of Stephen Kuffler at Johns Hopkins University, and they moved with him to Harvard in 1959.

Kuffler had pioneered studies beyond the cells of the retina, into the retinal ganglion cells of cats. This was just the beginning of what scientists already knew was a multistep path of the biological processing of information from the more than one million visual receptors—rods and cones—in the retina, but it was as far as he could go with the technology of the day. In 1953, he found a difference in the way the ganglial cells handled light from the center of a visual field compared with that from its concentric surroundings. Certain cells would not react much to diffuse light, but would fire "like crazy" if they detected a dark spot in a light field. They had been excited. If the spot were white and its surrounding dark, the cells wouldn't fire at all. They had been inhibited. Other cells had the opposite preference.

Hubel and Wiesel asked themselves if they could find this "center-surround" effect further up in the visual system of the cat, in its visual cortex. They tried passing light through holes of varying sizes in rectangles of brass or glass, but to little effect. One day in 1958 in the basement of the Wilmer Ophthalmological Clinic at Johns Hopkins, one of the men pulled a glass slide out of the ophthalmoscope, and the cells in the cat's visual cortex "went crazy." The cells were responding to the edge of the slide, not to the halos of light through the holes. Hubel and Wiesel then tried many different orientations of the edges. They found that columns of cells specialized in reacting to particular orientations of the edges. The more the researchers looked, the more specialization they found.

Later they went on to the visual cortex of monkeys. Within a few years, Hubel was able to describe "a rich assortment of functions" in the visual cortex. The cells there organized signals that passed from the eye through layers of intermediate cells, in what Hubel called "the first step in perceptual generalization." One class of these cells recognized lines and contours, and another recognized motion and direction.[16]

Color was more complicated and eluded them for many years. Before moving to Harvard, Hubel and Wiesel had encountered some cells that responded to color in the optic nerve of a spider monkey. "We found a cell that we didn't seem to be able to drive at all with white light," Hubel recalled many years later. "In sort of desperation we started grabbing objects around the room. We found that a film box . . . [a] yellow film box—just waving that in front of the animal in just the bright part of its visual world, made the cell 'fire' like crazy."[17]

The complexity of what they were exploring impressed the two scientists, although they were relieved at how much of their work involved relatively simple concepts, such as excitation and inhibition. In a lecture at Harvard in 1975, Hubel explained that "the eye immediately begins a very sophisticated processing of the stimuli falling upon it, and that process continues to increase in complexity as one traces the signal further and further along."[18] In 1963, he wrote that a single set of cells at precortical and cortical stages of visual processing was not enough to explain vision, "any more than one could understand a wood-pulp mill from an examination of the machine that cuts logs into chips."[19]

Hubel recalled Land's demonstration many years later. Starting with two slide projectors, say, one red and one green, and overlapping a spot in each image, "you get what is indistinguishable, practically, from spectral yellow. It's an absolutely counter-intuitive thing. You're used to mixing red and green and getting purple or brown or something like that. It's an enormous surprise to see it generate yellow. [It's] the same with blue and yellow, to add those and get white rather than green is counter-intuitive and strikes everybody as very surprising."

It was also clear that one couldn't "predict the color of an object just knowing the spectral content of the light reaching you from that object. You've got to . . . analyze that over the entire scene before you can arrive at a conclusion as to what the color is." But what would Land's results suggest then to a neurophysiologist? Hubel said, "There was no question about his results. But we just couldn't see how the cells we were finding at the time went along with his stuff."[20] It was many years before they found cells that might participate in "obeying" Land's proposed rules.

∞

The accidental discoveries, Land was certain, demanded a new theory. He gave a popular description to the radio reporter Robert Zalisk in 1985:

> The great question is: How do we know the apple is red? Why does it look red? If, in particular at noon, there might be more blue light coming to the apple than there is red light? Some people thought that maybe, we got *used* to the change, or the pigments in our eye bleached and changed and then you got used to it. But, you can take a camera shutter—look out at the world through a camera shutter—and see the world in a tenth or a hundredth or a thousandth of a second, and you find the eye works in just the same way, that it does not need time to get used to it. There's no getting used to it, or adapting, involved.

How could this happen? Land invoked his retinex theory. "There must be some way in which some kind of process, some arithmetic process, is being carried out which tells us that the red apple is red, that the green leaf is green, no matter what wavelengths are coming to our eye from the apple or from the leaf." This arithmetic process was different from the comparison that Newton had postulated. Land proposed that for different objects in a scene, the eye assessed the reflectivity separately for each of the three primary wavebands of blue, green, and red.

The red-sensitive cells would all work together. "They look at the apple and then they compare how much light is coming from the apple—how much *red* light is coming from the apple—as compared with the amount of red light coming, with a special kind of average, from all the rest of the scene." The red apple looks bright against the rest of the scene. In the blue-light comparison, it looks dark. A similar comparison is made in green light. Each comparison produces a numerical value, and those numerical values are then compared to produce a final color estimate.

The numbers do not change as the amount of red light in the world changes, or as the amount of green or blue light changes. If a double amount of red light fell on the whole scene, the apple would also receive double. The ratio would remain the same. "By comparing *those* numbers," Land said, "I have something that stays constant. They'll be the same three numbers no matter whether it's sunlight or early morning light. . . . That will give you constant color."[21]

The full-blown retinex theory took time to evolve. For two years after 1955, Land could not spend much time following up the first insights.

Other problems absorbed his attention. But collaborators in color phenomena, such as Sara Hollis Perry, Elizabeth Hill, Myra Herbert, Nigel Daw, and, starting in 1961, John McCann, succeeded Meroë Morse, who was increasingly absorbed in the challenges of the black-and-white laboratory that she headed.[22] Land was working with Morse on the black-and-white film that could stop motion in ordinary light and develop in ten seconds (chapter 12). The struggle to turn Rogers's invention into a workable color film began to succeed, and in 1957, Henry C. Yutzy of Kodak saw the Polaroid picture that he thought would be commercial (chapter 13). This was not long after Land's stint as a one-man visiting committee at MIT, in which he demanded a bigger place in education for original experiments (chapter 1). At almost the same moment, Land declared to President Eisenhower that young Americans could like science as much as football (chapter 16).

A theme linking all these activities was the human need for direct experience. And in 1957 he resumed carrying the direct experience of the color phenomena to scientific audiences. Disillusionment had not come. On 24 October 1957, just over a week after the fateful meeting with Eisenhower, he described his "scientific detour" in another invited lecture, at the Rochester Institute of Technology. The colors he demonstrated were far more vivid than they had been back in 1955. "This phenomenon known since about 1914," Land said, "is either starting to draw us into a state of magical confusion, or else it is something that has to be taken, from a psychological point of view, rather seriously."

A question remained from the red-and-white work of 1955. Could the white light, the sum of all wavelengths, somehow have supplied all the colors besides red? At the end of his lecture, Land settled that point. He projected the red, or long-wave, image through a red filter as before. On the projector for the shorter wavelength he installed an orange filter. On the screen, even without white light, the audience saw a wide range of colors, including yellows, greens, and even some blues.

The lesson seemed to be that physicists and physiologists had not looked at whole images, in which objects in the natural world were spread across a scene. According to the journalist Francis Bello, Land was arguing that "the eye was made for looking at natural objects. . . . The subtlety of its operation was entirely lost when it was subjected to rigorously analytic experiments, based on spectroscopes and the matching of spots of color in which no images are involved." An animal that evolved the ability to sense "a full range of hues running from red, orange, yellow, green, down into blue . . . could see the leopard in the leaves, in a way that his competitors couldn't. He would survive the leopard . . . and go on to build the world we live in."[23]

∞

With *Sputnik* in orbit, the fall of 1957 was a time for making science more accessible to the American public. Late in November, Land spoke at an autumn meeting of the National Academy of Sciences at the Rockefeller Institute in New York, later Rockefeller University. A Polaroid Corporation press release described Land's "scientific detour" and put forth the idea of "an atavistic binary-receptor system as a stage in the evolutionary process."[24]

Land told him the audience, which included Harold Schmeck, a reporter for *The New York Times*, that a mixture of red and white light would normally be expected to yield shades of red, white, pink, and reddish brown. But instead, "The combination of photographs and lights produced startlingly realistic color pictures that included shades of blue, green, and yellow." Land found no close association between the wavelength bouncing off objects into the eye and the color the eye sensed.[25] With these statements Land had "astounded an audience of scientists."[26]

A few months later, in April 1958, the National Academy of Sciences staged a symposium on "new developments in color vision" in Washington. For this and for later publication in the academy's journal, Land presented a battery of twenty-two experiments designed to answer criticisms. In one, Land had the room lights turned on fully, flooding the screen with light. Then the lights snapped off, and the audience saw the gamut of colors instantly, without time for adaptation. In others, Land explored "achromatic" situations in which the audience unexpectedly saw the scene in one color. Again, Land turned up the rhetorical volume:

> We have come to the conclusion that the classical laws of color mixing conceal great basic laws of color vision. There is a discrepancy between conclusions that one would reach on the basis of the standard theory of color mixing and the results we obtain in studying total images. . . . Our experiments show that in images neither the wavelength of the stimulus nor the energy at each wavelength determines the color. . . . Thus it may be necessary to build a new hypothetical structure to explain the mechanism for seeing color.

Such a system, he suggested, would involve "a new coordinate system" for predicting the color of objects, "a ratio of ratios." Land asserted that "the departure from what we expect from colorimetry is not a small effect but is complete." When he wrote up his lecture for publication, Land was already working hard to disarm critics:

> The colors in our experiments appear immediately, and do not alter appreciably with time, and we do not seek to explain them as effects of adaptation. To the best of our knowledge, the gamut of color is much larger than that noticed by Hess [in 1890] or predicted by any theory concerning chromatic adaptation; our newly discovered achromatic situations are not predicted by any previous theories; nor is there any basis in those theories for our dimensionless coordinate system. . . . Furthermore it seems that none of the previous work in any kind of color matching or system of complementary colored shadows (Goethe) can be the basis for the observed fact that the colors in our images, arising from unorthodox stimuli, correspond in hierarchical order to the colors that the observer would have seen had he been at the original site.[27]

Soon after the April 1958 symposium, Land began using an instrument, a dual monochromator designed for him by his longtime optics expert David Grey and another associate. They built it to give Land more flexibility in conducting experiments than when he was constantly changing filters. In October 1958, Land gave an invited fifty-minute lecture to the Optical Society of America in Detroit. Chairing the session where he demonstrated the new equipment was one of the most distinguished students of color perception, Deane B. Judd of the National Bureau of Standards.[28]

Land was already attracting attention from journalists that few scientists ever achieve. According to the respected science reporter Jean Pearson of the *Detroit Free Press*, Land used the usual red and white filters in his Detroit talk, as well as blue and white, and in each case, full color appeared on the screen. Land spoke of the eye's using light reflected from the scene to form at least two "identical but separate records of the scene," one with longer wavelengths and the other with shorter. Pearson was impressed: "The advance in the science of color should lead to a revolution in photography, television, and color reproduction in printing. And physics textbooks will be revised to junk the centuries-old concept of how color is transmitted to the eye."[29]

Scientists also were enthusiastic. One who was present recalled, "This came like the dénouement of a clever mystery. Most of the audience seemed truly taken aback and the applause was vigorous . . . I can only say that it was truly a show to remember."[30]

On 18 November 1958, Land returned to the Harvard physics colloquium, to which he had presented his first work with polarizers twenty-six years before. The next day, the leading psychologist B. F. Skinner enclosed an old paper of his on a color illusion and wrote, "Dear Dinny: It was an almost unbelievable demonstration, but I think you are on the right track in explaining it and the more I think of it the more plausible it becomes."[31]

Also writing that day was George Wald, who later received the Nobel prize in 1967 for isolating the actual pigments in the color-sensing cones of the eye. He told "Din" that he had heard the lecture and seen the demonstrations. "You have made a lovely and wonderful thing, and I think it is fundamentally important. I think I see what it means and that it is telling us something clear, direct, and simple." Instead of absolutes, Wald wrote, Land had introduced "a complete relativism." Even in 1704, Newton knew that color was made inside us. But, "he still thought and we did that the red- or blue-making rays lie in specific places in the spectrum. You have now shown that they lie anywhere in the spectrum and that all we are concerned with is the ratios of short to long wavelengths, and the ratios of differential sensory response that they evoke."[32]

Both letters were preserved in Meroë Morse's papers.

∞

Clearly, Land was pursuing his research into a mysterious and contentious field because it fascinated him and put him in touch with polymathic geniuses of the past. But the resultant attention brought him secondary gains. To be working on one of the most interesting scientific subjects doubtless added something to his prestige as a scientific statesman. More generally, the startling results brightened his image as a wizard, the man equally at home running a company, inventing new products, advising the government, urging changes in education, and probing a vexed question of science. Reinforcing this image was the new, somewhat feverish prestige of post-*Sputnik* science. Land had more freedom to choose which business or research problem to work on. It was exciting for people at Polaroid that "the boss" was beating back a frontier of knowledge, while the company grew explosively. Polaroid was truly a science-based company.

The work also reinforced his excuses for limiting people's access to him. In March 1959, Morse wrote diplomatically but bluntly to her lab colleagues, asking each to make a check mark that they had read her memo. They should channel their requests to see Land through Morse's assistant, just as other requests went through Land's assistant, Natalie Fultz. "I think all of us at one time or another have been perplexed," Morse wrote, "as to what procedure to follow when we wanted to see Dr. Land, or urgently wanted to have a letter, message, or experimental result delivered immediately. It is difficult to judge whether or not our interruption is well timed, and we hate to barge in at an inopportune moment."[33]

Land's prestige was very high. In April 1959, Francis Bello of *Fortune* wrote glowingly of the man and the company:

> If a man of the Renaissance were alive today, he might find running an American corporation the most rewarding outlet for his prodigious and manifold talents. In it he could be scientist, artist, inventor, builder, and statesman, and, through it he might gain the ear of the princes of the state. It would be an exciting company. It might not be the world's largest, for size alone would mean nothing to him. But it would probably be the fastest-growing company that a man still in the prime of life could have created from scratch. (He would, of course, disdain buying up the work of other men.) It would be a company created in a man's image, molded by him in every significant detail, building a product—the embodiment of his genius—that would be unique in all the world. He would gather around him extraordinary associates, selected with meticulous care, who would share his passions and his enthusiasms, who would create and build with him. Such a man, as it happens, does exist.[34]

A month later, *Fortune* published the story "An Astonishing New Theory of Color." Echoing a theme detected by Pearson in Detroit, the article claimed that "every textbook dealing with color will have to be rewritten." With the help of spreads of diagrams and pictures, the magazine explained how Land had shown "that the eye does not need 'red' wave lengths of light to see red, does not need orange to see orange, yellow to see yellow, brown to see brown, green to see green, blue to see blue, or purple to see purple." Using black-and-white pictures and various combinations of filters and light sources, Land could produce a wide range of colors where only one or two colors, according to classical theory, were "really" there.

The language was strong. With scientific frontiers moving "deep inside the atom, to the edge of the universe, inside the cell, or outside the atmosphere, the day seemed long past when someone could make a starkly simple discovery that would overturn a common belief about our every-day relations to our everyday world. But Land has done just that. Once again, it turns out, we have been fooled by nature's deep subtlety into accepting a half-truth for a larger truth." The report concluded, "In demolishing the presumed reality of colors, Land has revealed the eye to be an instrument of unsuspected and awe-inspiring subtlety."[35]

Lay interest increased. A few days after a *Scientific American* article by Land in April 1959, *The New York Times* reported, "The results run counter to virtually all current theory."[36]

In his *Scientific American* article, Land focused on the effects with red and white. Hundreds of readers wrote in, asking how to make the pictures. They received instructions from Polaroid about the "correct balance" of five factors needed for good results: the film, lighting, filters, exposures, and suitable scenes. Two reasons for care were that the brightness of yellows is close to that of whites, and the brightness of blues is close to that of blacks. The yellows could not be overexposed, nor the blues underexposed.[37]

∞

The excursion into basic science influenced Land's views about science in industry. He told the Boston Patent Law Association in April 1959 that the barriers between applied and basic science in industry were breaking down, so that "the application of a great new scientific principle occurs to the scientist at the same instant that the principle occurs to him." Doubtless thinking of the color vision research, Land told the patent lawyers, "We have moved to the point where a need in applied science may be the precise stimulus for a discovery in pure science. The human mind is able to become integrated again—as it must have been before the Victorian era when purity became associated with lack of utility."[38]

Although he said that the color vision work would not be applied in Polaroid color film, he was interested in the possible use of the two-color system to make color television sets simpler. Such work went on at Polaroid for some time.

When a recruiting firm sent researcher Lawrence K. M. Ting from Los Angeles for an interview at Polaroid in 1964, John McCann showed him "astonishing demonstrations" of the retinex theory, and "a dim but exciting demonstration of a two-color cathode-ray tube displaying a multicolored still scene." Meeting Land in the maze of hallways around the Vision Research Laboratory at Osborn Street, Ting was asked to describe what his eyes had just seen. "What colors were there?" Ting recalled Land asking him. "How could that be possible? Already he was using my senses in an experiment, piquing my curiosity, creating the beginning of a need to satisfy a scientific question in me, and probably enjoying my confusion in what I saw and could not understand."

Ting soon joined the group of fewer than ten scientists, engineers, and technicians, led by Dexter Cooper, in the basement of 730 Main Street, to work on the project called Cyclops. Almost ten years after Land had made his first patent disclosures on two-color television, Cooper's group had learned a lot about color cathode-ray tubes, including the settling and layering of phosphor plates. The group needed people with Ting's skills, however, to move from research into development. The basement near the Red Line subway running under Main Street was a rattly environment for the phosphor-plate operation. As Land committed money, the group prepared to grow beyond thirty people. They moved to 38 Henry Street, where they found "lots of space, high ceilings, and expansive windows with lots of light," and the sort of model shop that Land found indispensable.

In August 1964, Polaroid and Texas Instruments signed an agreement to share information leading to a two-color prototype television set. Ting recalled it as "a typically Land-type concept of not hindering research and development, yet hopefully being able to benefit in any fashion on the outcome." Land came over, usually on the way home in the evening, or called two or three times a day. "He could hardly wait for results before outlining the next experiment," Ting recalled. "He would pace back and forth, challenging us with questions, thinking out loud, hypothesizing." Working many late nights after take-out dinners, and exhausted by Land's energy and enthusiasm, the two-color group relished intervals when Land's attention went elsewhere. But even when he could not visit, Land wanted to see the daily results. To this end, Land, Cooper, and Ting rigged a two-way video service between Henry Street, Osborn Street, and Polaroid's headquarters building.

The project expanded to contacts with Bell Telephone Laboratories, which had developed a Picturephone for the 1964–65 World's Fair in New York. Bell Labs used its computers to generate one of the displays of randomly colored rectangles that Land and his associates called Mondrians, after the

Dutch abstract painter Piet Mondrian. Land, McCann, Ting, and another associate flew down to Murray Hill in New Jersey for a demonstration. On the plane back to Boston, Land said he found the presentation a "cold, unfeeling hardware representation of human nature and man's wondrous senses. . . . Sometimes it is better and more exciting to let each little experiment lead you to hypothesize and direct you to the next experiment or step."

After a year's intense work with Texas Instruments and many visits between Cambridge and Dallas, the engineers concluded, according to Ting, that "perhaps we had an industrial, rather than a consumer product and both companies' interest lessened." In 1967, Polaroid patented a design of a color television set, using only one electron gun instead of three. Unfortunately, the new design was chasing a moving target of manufacturing cost. As so often in the history of technology, the price of older, admittedly clumsy, processes was descending too rapidly.[39]

∞

Although Land was riding high, the incandescent press coverage soon heated up a storm of criticism by scientists. The color vision experiments were said to be trivial or anticipated, so that claims of a fundamental contribution were absurdly inflated. Critics accused Land of failing to give nearly enough credit to his predecessors. The effects he was demonstrating could be explained by adaptation. The idea of color as an illusion, as a product of learning—not the result of mechanisms built into the eye and brain—was vigorously alive.

Many years later, Hubel said that the world of color science contained "many rather colorful characters, hot-tempered and mostly in disagreement with each other. . . . The world was not eager to accept these original demonstrations and subdivided itself into two camps. One of [them] said that we had known it all along, and it's been thoroughly investigated. The second [contained] people like Horace Barlow and William Rushton who didn't believe it at all." Hubel chuckled. "Even though they saw it, they thought that this was some sort of magical set of tricks."[40]

The questions came thick and fast after the article in *Scientific American*. In September 1959, Land replied with an omnibus letter in the magazine. He continued to hold that classical theory, based on Maxwell's three primary colors, was inadequate. That theory focused on tiny points in a field of view. The color at each point was based on a ratio of the three wavelengths of light. As Young had recognized, Land said, a wider area had to be considered: "Extended areas of the retina are significant in determining the sensation for each point in the image."

Land disagreed with using adaptation or a local and momentary adaptation defined as "induction" to explain such phenomena as the colored shadows. The critics said these adaptations, in combination with the ideas of Young, Helmholtz, and Maxwell, explained the color at a particular point, but Land rejoined that such effects required time. The idea of induction was that "the induced color was not real." Because the array of colors appeared instantly, adaptation was ruled out. The induction idea made sense, he said, insofar as it held that "all of the retina which is exposed is involved in the sensation at each point in the image. Indeed, that is the heart of our position."

Most work on induction involved "unquantitative speculation," according to Land. He cited only two exceptions, a paper in 1894 by C. Hess and H. Pretori, and another in 1938 by Deane B. Judd and Harry Helson. He said that Judd and Helson had brought "surface colors out of the world of mystery." Judd's work might eventually explain the color effects that Land was seeing, but it did not explain the achromatic effects that he also had found. Calling for "a new science of color images," Land showed his awareness of the widespread questioning and rejection of his ideas: "It would be a sad thing . . . if it were thought that our interest in this field . . . implied any trace of lack of appreciation for the solid values of other fields of vision, but we would find it equally sad if those who have done so well in these other fields cannot see their way clear to join us in this new adventure."[41]

∞

In a journal article soon after Land's omnibus letter, Judd weighed in with a verdict on the two-color work: nothing new. To be sure, the work on achromatic effects was new and deserved attention. Land had demonstrated that projecting many different pairs of primary colors could give a full-color sensation, but Judd held that "no new theory is required." He believed that Land's conclusion that color sensation could not be explained in terms of wavelengths was wrong. Land's finding of long-wavelength (approximately red) and middle-wavelength (approximately green) dominance in color perception resulted in "less general or detailed predictions" than did his own work with Helson back in 1938.

"It is nevertheless remarkable," Judd wrote somewhat patronizingly, "that in a few years of intensive study Land, and his associates, should have been able to rediscover independently so large a fraction of the known phenomena of object-color perception, and it is not too surprising that he should have been led by them to the false hypothesis that color in images cannot be described in terms of wavelength."

Land deserved credit

> for pointing out how much can be learned about object-color perception simply from two-color projections of middle-wave and long-wave records. We are indebted to him even more for presenting the phenomena so clearly and dramatically . . . By these demonstrations thousands of people have been introduced to the fascinating facts of object-color perception previously hidden from all but a few-score students of this specialized subject. . . . His oral and written presentations are to be criticized chiefly because of lack of any serious attempt to relate the results of his experiments to previous studies of the same phenomena.[42]

Just below Judd's paper, the journal published a brief and unyielding reply from Land:

> We feel these experimental results require the kind of coordinate system we have used in order to correlate, predict, and understand. They are results which classical laws of color mixing do not predict, and they lead to rules which, we must regretfully insist, cannot readily be related to Dr. Judd's formulas. His formulas are wavelength-rich and time-dependent; our experiments demand formulas which are nearly independent of wavelength and fully independent of time.[43]

In a letter he drafted in 1985, Land said that Judd eventually apologized:

> Although Judd had carried out his experiments with Helson many years before I reported and demonstrated my experiments, he still was not able to make the formulas they had developed for those experiments apply to my experiments five years after I first showed them nor have the computations ever been published. Judd was decent and distinguished; he was sincere, he was a friend, and before he died he did apologize to me for having written the article. Unfortunately, the net effect of the Judd article was obfuscatory, and for a whole generation of students, it delayed the understanding of the early basis of retinex theory.[44]

∞

For many years, the epicenter of color vision research was a large, black-walled room in the bowels of the former industrial building at the corner of Main and Osborn Streets. From the early 1960s to the late 1970s, Land's principal collaborator was John J. McCann, who joined Polaroid full-time after graduating from Harvard in 1964. His wife, Mary, a microscopist, was a fellow researcher at Polaroid; they settled in Belmont, Massachusetts. John McCann took part in many public demonstrations of Land's findings and published scientific papers with Land and independently. Increasingly, he became interested in using computers to test a wide variety of theories. Like many in Land's laboratory "family," McCann acquired many secondary duties, including a central role in creating full-size Polacolor replicas of paintings and conveying Land's wishes about details of the elaborate annual Polaroid shareholders' meetings. Others who assisted Land in color vision work were Julius "Jay" Scarpetti, Jeanne L. Benton, and Marie Watson. At the Rowland Institute in the 1980s, Sara Hollis Perry, Michael Burns, Robert Savoy, and David J. Ingle all worked on different aspects of the subject.[45]

The praise and criticism, and possibly Land's growing fortune, won him many invitations to speak about color vision, at scientific societies and university commencements, in the United States and abroad. He spoke twice at the Royal Institution in London, in 1961 and 1973. In the mid-1960s, the Ciba Foundation in London organized a symposium, "Color Vision: Physiology and Experimental Psychology," at which Land could face his critics. Some of his speaking invitations were accompanied by honors. He spoke twice in Cleveland, in 1963 and 1966, and in Detroit in 1967. In 1966–67, he gave the William James lectures at Harvard. In 1974, he again lectured at the Physics Colloquium in the new Science Center, which he and his wife had given anonymously to Harvard. This time he spoke about the "ratio-making sense."[46]

In the 1960s he went beyond red-and-white to experiments with the Mondrians. He also used a board with randomly arranged, overlapping, colored-paper cutouts, where well-known shapes had unexpected colors. He used matte paper that reflected light equally in all directions. The experiments explored the comparisons of "lightness" that he suggested must occur on each of the three primary wave bands. In such a random layout, especially if light were thrown on the boards in a strobe flash, the eye and brain could not be expected to learn and adapt. The eyes did not need to move to cover a wide area in a single flash. The shades of color the eyes saw would be unexpected. Using projectors with rheostats to change the light intensity, and installing filters and wedges, he could illuminate areas of widely different shades with exactly the same amounts of light of particular wavelengths, and measure this precisely with photometers. Yet, human subjects reported that the cutouts and rectangles kept their colors.

Land continued to explore the effects of pairs of wavelengths. To reproduce the array of colors in the scene, Land said, one picture needed to be taken with the shorter wavelength and superimposed on a second, identical picture projected through a filter of the longer wavelength. If the process were reversed, "cool colors become warm, and warm colors become cool." How far apart did the wavelengths need to be? Not very far, was the answer. His "long record" in one experiment was sodium yellow, with a wavelength of 589 nanometers, only eleven nanometers longer than the "short record," mercury yellow, at 578 nanometers. Yet, he told an evening audience at the Royal Institution in 1961, "one still sees a substantial amount of color."[47]

The work called for a readiness to leave the well-trodden path and to travel at right angles to it. He told graduating seniors at Stanford University in 1962, "You turn to your unconscious; you pray to your God; and somehow out of all that, you see a new way, and then you act quietly, without argument."[48]

He began to refer to the new work in neurophysiology. In Cleveland late in 1963, just after Hubel's popular article about the visual cortex, Land said, "Naturally, we hope that the contemporary vital and brilliant programs in visual neural physiology will bring support to our heuristic mechanism."[49] At the Ciba Foundation symposium, he referred to "the miracle of the eye," in which memory has a small influence. "Color constancy, far from being a mere illusion, is the basic phenomenon of vision. . . . The miracle of the eye is its ability to hold objects in their position in the lightness scale, independent of the fluctuations in the illumination—and to do that, in our opinion, independently for each retinex."[50]

At Harvard in October 1966, he talked about "the wonderful world of the lightness scale," and the ability of the separate retinexes to calculate "a reliable scale of blacks, whites, and grays." This was a "genetic miracle." Evolution must have favored animals able to deal with "a universe that is everywhere fluctuating in quality and quantity of illumination—from clouds, from leaves, from shadows cast by objects on themselves."[51]

In Cleveland two weeks earlier, he had made his simplest and perhaps most charming demonstration of the difference between lightness and brightness in the perception of color. He showed a characteristically high-contrast black-and-white photograph by Ansel Adams of the Mission San Xavier in Tucson. It was taken at a bright noonday. Except for an iron gate and a pair of decorative lines on gateposts, the surfaces in sunlight and shadow were all of white stucco. Land was delighted with it. "The illumination varies from place to place, partly because of the direction of the sunlight, partly because of the shadows cast by sections of the building on other sections. We are looking at it from the side of the portico that the sun does not reach, but only the sky light . . . The brightness of the illumination is changing unpredictably and very beautifully."

The photographer's light meter, Land said, cannot distinguish between a black cat in the sunlight and a white cat in shadow, but humans can. "We tend to take for granted our ability to know that the shadowed portion is also white and not gray."[52]

At the Cleveland talk, a reporter asked Land how color vision fit into the rest of a life in which he already had no time to spare. Land replied, "Certainly, I am first of all a scientist, but life is an integrated whole. No man is just a businessman or just a scientist. We are each many things." He was fifty-seven then, and the reporter asked about retirement. "If you're a research scientist what you want is not retirement but another 500 years."[53]

∞

Over the years, Land continued to feel misunderstood. Some people claimed too much for his results, while others were dismissive. Reacting to a review of a book about color vision, he wrote in 1972: "What usually happens is that someone studies the red-and-white experiments and describes the work with the excitement he feels. This then triggers a response from a second commentator that is as skeptical as the first was exuberant. It is my experience that if both of them sat in the same room and looked at the same experiments, they would probably agree with each other on the colors they saw."

He asked people who wanted to understand the evolution of his findings and theories to look at each of a series of papers, usually based on a lecture-demonstration. "I know of no short cuts."[54]

This assertion drew a suave rejoinder from Arthur Karp of the Stanford Research Institute. While Land had never claimed it, many people whom Karp met believed that mixtures of two colors would produce all color phenomena, and that Polacolor film used only two colors. "Perhaps . . . they paid more attention to popular journalists than to the original author."

While critics certainly were not "exuberant," they were not "skeptical" either, Karp wrote. A better phrase was "seeking for perspective." Looking back to the two-color experiments of the 1950s, with the blue projector off, he thought people's eyes adjusted at sunset and sunrise to the absence of blue light. The later three-color experiments, Karp acknowledged, involve conclusions that "are clearly unique and incontestable." He urged that people read Land's papers "in reverse chronological order."[55]

∞

The criticism drove Land toward more general questions of the philosophy of science and the nature of consciousness. In a Phi Beta Kappa oration at Harvard in 1977, he protested the idea of humans as the most advanced product of evolution, "as if a separate product had been packaged, wrapped up, and delivered from a production line." He preferred looking at human consciousness as "a mechanism more and more interlocked with the totality of the exterior . . . being in a thousand ways united with, and continuously interlacing with the whole exterior domain."

He rejected the idea of a human spirit afflicted by "tragic separation and isolation" from the world. "Of what meaning is the world without mind? The question cannot exist." In a symphony, "the opening theme asks a question and the closing theme states that the question is itself the answer." Through science, the mind seemed to have been schooling itself in "reverence, insight, and appreciation of itself," so that it could pursue understanding "with all the techniques of thoughtfulness that the mind has used for investigations away from itself."[56]

In 1978, Land visited one of his favorite places, the Royal Institution in London, where Rumford, Young, and Faraday had worked. Twice, Land had spoken there on his color vision studies. It was the bicentennial of the birth of Sir Humphry Davy, the great electrochemist and the inventor of a safety lamp for miners. Later that year, in a speech at the Franklin Institute, he recalled that "whenever I am back near Faraday's laboratory I feel the kind of inspiration that might come at a shrine. I am always impressed by the homespun simplicity of his experiments, the earthy sequentiality whereby they follow each other so simply and sensibly to arrive at conclusions of vast and romantic scientific significance."

Despite Land's affection for the Royal Institution, at lunch after the celebration, Sir George Porter had stung Land with questions that had to be answered. Porter, a student of fast chemical reactions, was director of the institution. According to Land, Porter told him that "science in general deals with the objective world outside ourselves. . . . Science seeks by observation, by theory, and by experiment an increased understanding of this objective world. . . . Investigations of a field like color vision lead us into a subjective world." Porter asked if "the subjective world could be investigated by scientists." The observations involved inner consciousness. Can these phenomena be measured scientifically?

Land gave his response at the Franklin Institute in the form of a letter to Porter. Back in the early nineteenth century, Land said, "there was nothing less occult and remote in physics and chemistry than there was in the array of sensory processes." And yet, scientists of the level of Davy, Faraday, and Maxwell chose to devote themselves to chemistry and physics. Scientists of equal genius were not caught by "those sensory domains which we now call subjective." Land wondered, a shade bitterly, if a lack of rigor in one branch of science does not, somehow, "affect the ultimate rigor of the rest of science."

The physical scientist's task of making objective such phenomena as work, force, energy, even atomism, did not call for more talent than that needed to illuminate an internal world. That world, Land said, "is being built and rebuilt, moment by moment, in the course of retaining our relationship with our external environment." The mechanisms in this world are

> insensitive both to voluntary and involuntary influence . . . [and] carry out their task of reconstructing the world with such extraordinary skill that we scarce credit their existence. . . . I am convinced that our inner world, its structure and rationality and plan and organization, will, when it is penetrated, be the basis of sciences with the same grandeur as electricity and magnetism, although this wonderful eventuation may well take another miracle like the coexistence of a Faraday and a Maxwell.[57]

So what? Land was asked in 1985, when the Rowland Institute announced David J. Ingle's finding that goldfish, whose brains are far less elaborate than those of primates and humans, also behaved as "a retinex animal." Land replied:

> A scientist has to believe that all truths are interlocked. If you hold a major fallacy in your mind in the field of color, then that major fallacy will be a disease that will permeate all of neurophysiology, and, indeed, all of science. So that you might say that a scientific program is a continuous sort of

> medical program for curing the disease of ignorance and misinformation, making the whole body of science a healthier body. . . . I feel that between the skin and the soul there's a layer of magnificent mechanisms. Understanding those mechanisms will inspire us with a greater faith in the significance of life, and a greater faith in our own importance because we carry those evolved mechanisms in us.[58]

Land had begun talking to the neurophysiologists. In the early 1970s, he invited David Hubel over from Harvard Medical School to Osborn Street for a demonstration of the SX-70 camera and film (chapter 18) before they went on the market. Mixing martinis, Land ebulliently plunged a self-contained SX-70 film unit into a drink, to show off how impermeable to water the film was. Hubel recalled twenty years later how impressed he had been with Land's willingness to sacrifice a good martini.[59]

This genial interaction went along with scientific discussions. In 1975, Land was chairman of a session on visual perception at the Optical Society of America, with Hubel as the speaker. Hubel noted that a subsurface layer of macaque monkey cortex, one millimeter square, contained enough "apparatus" to analyze a particular region of the visual field. Beneath any square millimeter of the cortex lay one hundred thousand cells.[60]

At Harvard the same year, Hubel referred to the "center-surround" phenomenon that Stephen Kuffler had found in 1953 in the retinal ganglia, involving opposite effects in the core of a visual field from effects in the concentric surrounding area. When an electrical impulse from the eye reaches one or a whole group of neurons, according to Hubel, "it can do two things: it can either make [the neurons] fire in turn, or it can act in just the opposite direction, an inhibition, and stop them firing at all." The receptors telling a particular neuron to shut down tend to be grouped around those telling the neuron to fire. Hubel used the analogies of "bull's eye" or "fried egg." As light passed over the field, the surrounding region sends shutdown signals, but when it reaches the core, neurons fire rapidly.

The opposing actions made sense to Hubel. "This is a very efficient way to extract the biologically useful information from the environment. Animals are not interested in the total amount of light diffused through a scene. What we, or an animal want to know about are variations in intensity, and contrasts." Diffuse light does not set the cells popping, but a sharp contrast along a line, a boundary, will cause the cells to fire rapidly. "As a consequence, the animal will see it very clearly."[61]

Like Land, Hubel and Torsten Wiesel were not free from controversy. They gained over many years much evidence that the system they were exploring was innate, fully formed at birth. Other scientists, however, came up with evidence of large and permanent modifications in cortical cells through early experience. Hubel said in his Nobel lecture in 1981 that after birth it was uncertain whether established connections withered, or failed to develop.[62]

∞

In the early 1970s, the neurophysiologist Semir Zeki of University College, London, was pushing microelectrodes into an area of rhesus-monkey cortex known as V 4. He began finding clusters of cells with particular color preferences. In one oblique-angle penetration, the electrode found three cells that fired more actively than normal when the monkey saw blue light and less vigorously when it saw red. The next five cells were excited by green and inhibited by purple. The next cell responded to white light only. The last two cells were excited by red and inhibited by blue. When he plotted the cells' peak sensitivities to different wavelengths, Zeki found a degree of order that impressed him. It looked as if "colours may be mapped in an orderly way in the cerebral cortex."[63]

In July 1978, Land had just begun planning his place of retirement from Polaroid: the Rowland Institute. The same month, he first visited Zeki's laboratory. Land had considered the visit for some time, he told Zeki. "I've known about your work for some years, but I've waited for it to mature before I could approach you." Zeki reflected later that "however spontaneous his remarks may seem, there was behind them a good deal of thought and caution."

Would the responses of color-coded cells that Zeki was studying "correspond to, and obey, the rules of color perception?" Perhaps the monkeys could be shown Mondrians with their "rectangles of arbitrary shape, size, surround, and color," with matte papers reflecting light of any wavelength the same in all directions. The Mondrians could be lighted variably in the way Land had done for human subjects whose brains could not be probed with electrodes. It seemed to Zeki that Land's "perceptual experiments were so readily adaptable to electrophysiological ones" that he should try.

Zeki and his co-workers were excited that "a man of such a high position in the world of learning and of science and of technology could take the plane, time and again, to witness an experiment in London." Land would "just come and sit in on the experiment and ask questions and try to learn."

The first afternoon, Land said, "This sounds all very interesting. Why don't we go and do some shopping? Let's go to Paper Chase and buy some paper to put together . . . a Mondrian." What they put together was not up to Land's standards. To do the experiment "in a proper way," he would fly back to Cambridge, collect what was needed, and return to London. Zeki was delighted but terrified. "I was afraid that the experiment would fail." Land put them all at ease by saying, "I'm a scientist. Experiments fail. Don't worry about it. Let's do it." Soon Land was back. He "was forever asking questions. Indeed, he became, to all intents and purposes, an electrophysiologist."

Late one evening, he wanted to make Polaroid pictures to record the monkey cells' responses as they flashed on an oscilloscope. Zeki didn't keep Polaroid film but offered to check whether his colleagues had any. Seeing the potential for amusement, Land went himself "to cadge some film." He found a scientist who had a pack, and startled him by promising fifty packs in return the next day. The fifty packs arrived.[64]

Zeki's results were submitted to the weekly journal *Nature* in November 1979 and were published the following April. The work was supported by the Science Research Council, the British equivalent of the U.S. National Science Foundation. The journal took a rare and widely noted step with the article. So that readers could understand the results better, a set of three filters—red, green, and blue—was bound into each copy. One cell that Zeki's group found would respond only to light that human observers saw as red. But it would do this only when all three projectors were turned on with the long-wave, middle-wave, and short-wave filters installed. It would not respond to the red projector alone. If any two projectors were turned off for this and many other cells, the firing rate fell off sharply.

Zeki's group was finding some color-coded cells, but by no means all, that responded to light reflected from the Mondrian display, but the need for all three projectors did not fit neatly with Land's idea of a comparison of lightnesses in each wave band of light. If the monkey's cells were making such a comparison, it would have to happen before the processed signals from the eye reached those particular cells. Zeki still thought the Landian processing might be found somewhere within the V 4 region of the cortex, which contains repetitive representations of each region of the retina—lying far back in the visual system. Still, they could try Land's experiments with setting his projectors so that identical triplets of light energy reached the monkey's eyes from each rectangle of the colored Mondrian. As Land's theory predicted, the absolute flux of light did not affect the cells' firing.[65]

Land's sense of humor delighted Zeki. At a scientific meeting they both attended, Land was asked "a rather aggressive question" after a talk he had given. He responded, "That is a fair question which has been unfairly asked." As Land answered the question, the questioner whispered to his neighbor. Land stopped and looked at the questioner. "The penalty for asking a question is that you have to listen to the answer!"

Land was concerned that the people in Zeki's laboratory ate well. He would bring along sandwiches prepared by Caroline Pearl, his English-born executive chef, or order "a big basket of nice things" to be delivered from Fortnum and Mason. Once, when "the experiment was going especially nicely," Land decreed a celebration at "a rather nice restaurant." When Land ordered a fine wine, the waiter looked surprised, then obsequious. "This waiter," Land told his fellow diners, "like some of my colleagues, thinks I hit upon that wine by chance."

To bring some of Zeki's experiments closer to the computer equipment and programs of John McCann, the manager of Land's vision research lab, Land flew Zeki's team across the Atlantic to Children's Hospital in Boston. Electrical impulses from the single cells in the monkey's brain were beamed via rooftop microwave dishes to McCann's setup across the Charles River. Clearly, Land was captivated by "the huge technological fun of having a physiological experiment conducted in one place and the results analyzed elsewhere."

In Zeki's laboratory, Land spent many hours with the technicians, going over how they prepared electrodes and explaining "the importance of his view of color vision." He was usually considerate, but once, during an experiment, his passion for results came through: "Silence, nature is speaking."[66]

∞

Wiesel and Hubel had gone their separate ways in the 1970s. At the beginning of the 1980s, Hubel and his new colleague, Margaret Livingstone, found cells in a different part of the visual cortex that also responded to color. Many were cells that were more complicated than "opponent" cells responding one way to light from the center of a scene and another way to light reflected from the immediate surrounding. In these "double opponent" cells, a small red spot at the center of the field would excite; a small green spot would inhibit. In the surround, the colors would have the opposite effect: red would inhibit and green excite. The cells would not respond to white light or to any wavelength of diffuse light. They would be inhibited by a wide expanse of red or green.

Land's former colleague, Nigel Daw, who later moved to Washington University in St. Louis, had found double-opponent color-responsive cells in goldfish retinas in the late 1960s when he presented wired-up fish with spots of various colors. The finding was exciting because it appeared to open the way to understanding the brain's processing of color signals. Daw and his colleague Alan Perlman then tried and failed to find double-opponent cells in the brains of monkeys. Some were found later, but they appeared to be few and scattered.

Gradually, the neurophysiologists focused on a layer of the monkey cortex where most signals come in from lateral geniculate bodies, peanut-size organs in the brain. In 1980, Charles Michael of Yale found double-opponent cells in the lateral geniculate. Hubel and Livingstone already had a hint of what to do next. Margaret T. T. Wong-Riley of the Medical College of Wisconsin had sent them photographs of orderly regions that she detected in the cortex when she cut through it vertically. She had used a new method of staining sections of the tissue to localize energy-producing parts of cells. The same year, Hubel and Jonathan Horton at Harvard and Anita Hendrickson at the University of Washington independently tried slicing the cortex horizontally. Groups of stained cells formed a polka-dot array, scattered across tissue with a quite different appearance. To annoy their competition, Hubel and Livingstone called the polka dots "blobs." The cells within the blobs, concentrated in layers 2 and 3 of the visual cortex, appeared connected to the lateral geniculate bodies, just as layer 4 had been shown to be. Half or more of the cells in the blobs were double-opponent cells of the sort that would be needed for Land's model of color perception. But these cells detected only small areas of the visual field. Hubel told a journalist, "They are not the answer to your prayers as far as explaining Land's work goes but they may be an intermediate."[67]

The exact biological mechanism for the effects that Land had found was still elusive. But one question could be answered: where the computations were carried out. Land and many others long had guessed that it was in the visual cortex, but they were not sure. In 1982, Land and two associates, Mike Burns and Sara Hollis Perry, collaborated with Hubel and Livingstone on a decisive experiment—with a human subject.

He was J. W., a man of less than thirty then. Two years earlier, neurosurgeons had operated on him twice to relieve severe epileptic seizures. They had cut the organ known as the corpus callosum, which links the visual cortexes on the left and right sides of the brain. After the surgery, J. W.'s seizures moderated in number and severity. His intellectual and physical capacity appeared unimpaired, and he was not color blind.

The separation of the two halves of the visual cortex opened the way to an experiment: would J. W. report colors in the same way on each side of his field of vision? The question could be asked because, as with most people, the language center of J. W.'s brain was on one side, the left. Land's theory predicted that colors were computed by comparisons over a relatively broad area. If the computations involved took place in the retina, there should be no difference in what J. W. would say about colors in the right and left portions of a test scene.

In a darkened, dark-walled room, J. W. sat in front of a display in which a brightly colored Mondrian display occupied half the visible field slightly to the left of the center line. The information about the Mondrian would be detected by his right visual cortex. From the right edge of the display over to the edge of the Mondrian was a large rectangle of black velvet, with a nearly rectangular "test spot" carved out of it. In the center of the spot was a small "fixation" point, in which a sequence of letters would appear about three times a second and J. W. would call them out. This would keep J. W. focused on the test spot. When Land barked the word "color," J. W. had been instructed to respond with the color he saw on the display.

Land and his collaborators had tried the experiments on other subjects who had not had J. W.'s operation. The researchers had tried alternating filters on three projectors that caused the color of the test spot to change from white to purple and back again. When J. W. looked at the display, Land would bark, "Color," and J. W. would say, "White." He always saw white, even when the other subjects saw purple. The right half of his brain was silent.

But what if a mirror threw the display onto the other side of his field of view? Now, the side of his brain linked to his speech center was seeing the Mondrian. And J. W. called out, "White, purple, white." Evidently, the site of the computations was in the visual cortex, not the retina.[68]

The findings from the blobs and from the work with J. W. elated Land and his associates. On 21 September 1982, people from the Rowland Institute of Science and Hubel's laboratory met in a hot, crowded room at Harvard Medical School. Both Hubel and Land were preparing talks at major scientific meetings. Each man rehearsed the findings in front of an audience of students and others, including Torsten Wiesel, who had moved to Rockefeller University.

Hubel introduced Land, who repeated Max Planck's remark that a scientist often has to wait for those disagreeing to die off. Reviewing his work over almost thirty years, Land said jubilantly that he was "reporting on old work, much of which was done last week." Hubel and Livingstone would be reporting "recent work, which was done yesterday." He showed a photograph of J. W., smiling, with Hubel and himself. He said that after the experiment, "Holly and I and David and Margaret went to a cocktail bar that afternoon and wrote the most beautiful abstract you ever saw."

Hubel mentioned an evening meeting a year before on the subject of the blobs in the visual cortex. Among those debating whether color computations could be done in the retina were Hubel, Livingstone, Donald Glaser, and Francis Crick. They noted that the columns of cells in the visual cortex had to take care of the slightly different perspective of the two eyes, as well as motion, orientation, and color. He showed slides of experiments leading to the discoveries of the blobs, and of the members of his research group. Livingstone took up the story with a discussion of the antagonism between the center and the surround.

After a break, to give a personal demonstration of the importance of context in perceiving colors, Hubel had put on a loud blue shirt and a red tie. He displayed a red paper with a blue square in the middle. The colors of the shirt and tie changed dramatically when colored lights were manipulated. It was an illustration of how a double-opponent cell worked in a Landian world. A pressing question was the degree of connection between the blobs and the color-sensitive cells that Zeki had found in V 4. Zeki's cells apparently covered a wider field of vision than did the cells in the blobs.[69]

A couple of days later, Hubel presented the blob work at the first McDonnell Conference on Higher Brain Function at the Washington University School of Medicine in St. Louis. The talk was extensively reported in *Science* and *Nature*. The latter publication called Hubel's talk the "showpiece" of the conference. Each journal mentioned the connection to Land's findings.[70]

Early in November, Land presented the work with J. W. at two conferences in Minneapolis. It was a triumphant moment. The connection between the color effects that Land had explored so long and the biological structures in the visual system had grown much closer.

A basic question about Land's work was whether his proposed mathematical calculations of color "match the way the eye and the brain do it," Hubel said at a conference in memory of Land in 1991. "This may or may not be relevant. Probably any kind of algorithm you can come up with will be equivalent in a mathematical sense to the way the brain does it." But the brain has other problems. "Vision isn't just color. It involves form, movement, stereoscopic depth, the ability to dark-adapt. All of those have to be handled at the same time. So you couldn't necessarily expect the brain to do it the way that a physicist might predict from a knowledge of color."[71]

15

U-2 Spy Plane

> We told you that this seems to us the kind of action and technique that is right for the contemporary version of the CIA: a modern and scientific way for an agency that is always supposed to be looking, to do its looking.
>
> —Edwin H. Land to Allen Dulles, November 1954

At the age of forty-five, in the year of his twenty-fifth wedding anniversary, Land was pulled into one of the most secret, most significant activities of the Cold War, the development of reliable reconnaissance of Soviet strategic weapons. The work, consultancy on a grand scale, led in a few months to the design of the famous U-2 spy plane, which exploded myths about huge Soviet bomber and missile forces soon after it began flying in 1956.

The commitment to electronic and photographic flights over the Soviet Union itself, not just around the borders, was not determined by public debate. The decision was taken inside the administration of Dwight David Eisenhower, one of the most genuinely conservative of presidents and the first to confront the prospect of thermonuclear war. Although he occasionally threatened thermonuclear war, he feared and abhorred it and did far more than is understood, even forty years later, to stave it off.

In 1954, Eisenhower faced a conundrum more easily presented than solved. He thought that the main danger from the potential enemy was an act of madness, a surprise attack, a nuclear Pearl Harbor. Averting this went far beyond the prompt warning of an attack, or an inventory of targets to strike in retaliation. America's military mission was not a sprint but a marathon, not preemption or conquest but deterrence. Endless crash efforts like that of World War II would bankrupt the nation. A sufficiency of weapons must be ready, in a timely, rapid sequence, but the nation must find ways to pay for it at a steady rate that would not arouse major opposition. To know what a sufficiency was, America must obtain accurate, complete, analyzed information about numbers and placements of Soviet strategic weapons. This information must include images of the Soviet Union from overhead. America could not base its weapons effort on fevered imaginings. Although the Soviet Union was obviously not infinitely rich or determined, and its leaders certainly had no wish to incinerate themselves, physical intelligence of their weapons was vitally needed. To take the trick, that is, to deter nuclear war, Eisenhower knew that the American president must be able to look at the opponent's cards. Military strength and accurate information were inseparable. But how could he get the information, and soon? The regular military and intelligence structures seemed unable to devise the means, so he turned to scientists, including Land. Surrounded by powerful and conflicting interests, Eisenhower had to proceed indirectly, even stealthily. His experience as supreme commander in Europe and long experience with the ways of Washington gave him unusually strong preparation for his task.[1]

The effort to get hard evidence and a reasonable deterrent went into high gear on Saturday, 27 March 1954. That morning, Eisenhower met with his Science Advisory Committee and asked them for a root-and-branch study. How could he avoid a sudden, overwhelming attack? What weapons would the Unisted States need, and how soon? Land was named a member of the steering committee of the study that Eisenhower requested, and head of its intelligence project, focused on surveillance. Headed by James R. Killian, president of MIT, the Technological Capabilities Panel (TCP) study quickly gave Eisenhower the intelligence-gathering apparatus he needed—and an overall blueprint and timetable for strategic weapons. Partly because of Land's urgent energy and penchant for shortcuts and quick answers, the U-2 pilots gave the president his "postcards" of Russia much more quickly than had looked feasible. For years into the future, Eisenhower would have additional confidence in restraining the nuclear arms race.[2]

In helping significantly with this, Land accomplished something secretly that may have been more important for more people for a longer time than anything else he ever did. Land's secret career as military adviser leaped up to a new level and enabled him and his fellow scientists to demonstrate the power of rational inquiry to brake the most dire consequences of the scientific revolution. He moved toward the center of a domain of excellence not of his own making —American defense in the age of total war—and showed that he could thrive as well there as in environments he controlled more completely.

Eisenhower enlisted the scientists just as the nuclear arms race was reaching a new and vastly more frightening intensity. America had just committed itself publicly to a policy of nuclear retaliation and secretly decided to build intercontinental missiles as fast as possible. Hydrogen bombs made of convenient, "dry" material were shrinking to the size that bombers and missiles could carry. On 1 March 1954, the United States exploded the biggest H-bomb it ever set off. The test in the Castle series was called Bravo. Instead of the expected force of five million tons of TNT, it developed fifteen million, showering fallout over American test personnel, Marshall Islanders, and a crew of Japanese tuna fishermen. The world became fallout conscious and knew that an H-bomb could destroy a city. Just then, the U.S. government was struggling with the threat from Senator Joseph R. McCarthy and the disgrace of a vendetta against J. Robert Oppenheimer, the leader of those who designed the first atomic bombs. Air Force intelligence officers on the rooftop of the American embassy in Moscow saw and photographed a new, swept-wing intercontinental jet bomber, the M-4, as it rehearsed its flight for the May Day parade through Red Square. An American intelligence flight, using an RB-47 bomber, flew provocatively deep into the Soviet Union.[3]

March 1954 seems to be when world leaders ultimately realized that nuclear war had become unthinkable. The multimegaton hydrogen bomb had been born as a munition of war, and at that moment, died as a weapon in the minds of world leaders. It was clear to Eisenhower, to Prime Minister Winston Churchill of Great Britain, and perhaps to the Soviet leader Georgi Malenkov that the hydrogen bomb, indeed any nuclear weapon, could never be used.

But it was not clear to the agency on which the United States relied to deliver a crushing blow to the Soviet Union, if that nation ever tried a nuclear Pearl Harbor. On 15 March, leaders of the U.S. Strategic Air Command (SAC) gave a briefing to a representative of the Navy. Similar in detail to one given the previous summer to the Joint Chiefs of Staff, the briefing envisaged an all-out attack on the Soviet Union by 150 B-36 and 585 B-47 bombers. Just what would be the signal for such an attack was not quite clear, as General Curtis LeMay, SAC's commander, explained it. The Navy observer reported, as if he were shaking his head: "The final impression was that virtually all of Russia would be nothing but a smoking, radiating ruin at the end of two hours."[4]

∞

Many years of largely secret government service had prepared Land for the work leading to U-2 and beyond. He had said in 1945 that the key postwar challenge was to understand the Russians.[5] Although Polaroid got out of intensive military work after the World War II, it did not do so entirely. Land gained further experience with Project Charles, whose final report was presented to the chiefs of the armed services on 1 August 1951. This first of a series of "Summer Studies" focused on air defense in a time of growing anxiety. The topic was uncomfortable for the U.S. Air Force. The very concept of a distinct air service, established only in 1947, rested on the idea of a strategic attack force, designed to win a war by itself. Defense was secondary. For the Air Force, the best defense was an overwhelming offense; a corollary principle was that in air warfare, defenses were particularly leaky.[6]

Yet in World War II and after, the political leaders of both democracies and dictatorships alike insisted on talking about and building air defenses, and taking at least some money away from the bomber men to do it. The soul of the defense was radar, an invention of the 1930s in which physicists played a central role. Radar, pushed most notably at MIT's Radiation Laboratory in World War II, became an increasingly efficient way to detect the size and location of an attacking force. With radar, the attacking force could be struck hard on its way to targets and would do less damage. This had proven as true over Germany as it had over England. To many, the need for air defense in the early 1950s was even greater than in the late 1930s, when scientists had mobilized against the impending threat from Nazi Germany. The bomber forces that SAC was amassing in Europe, the Pacific, and the United States in the fifties were looking vulnerable.

For the work on Project Charles, Land assigned one of his leading optical scientists, David Grey, to participate with him.[7] Many connected with Project Charles were veterans of the World War II radar effort, and well-known economists advised on the details of dispersing American industry. Among the consultants to the study were Jerome B. Wiesner of MIT, later President Kennedy's science adviser and president of MIT, and the computer pioneer John von Neumann. The Project Charles report pushed for better North American air defense, including a new, large research organization that became the MIT Lincoln Laboratory in Bedford, Massachusetts. The report underlined the problem of dispersing American industry to spread out targets. It argued for a radically new, centralized air defense system built around the emerging high-speed digital computers of the sort being pioneered by MIT's Jay Forrester.

In one passage, the Project Charles report recommended use of one-step Land-type photography to record images off radar scopes. This would deal with a prime Air Force worry, which crystallized after the Chinese invasion of Korea in November 1950, that the service's "verbal and manual methods of communicating and displaying position plots obtained by radar were too slow." Land proposed, and the study backed, a system to help automate, two or three times a minute, the display of information about moving targets for military ground-controllers. In such a system, the report said, "the processing problems are dealt with in a photographic manufacturing plant rather than at a radar station."[8]

To the scientists studying how to achieve effective air defense, the longest possible warning of an attack was vital. For this, information about a hostile force soaring over the Arctic was not enough. America must have direct, accurate information about the forces in the Soviet Union. What were they, and where were they? These facts could not be determined just by sniffing around the edges. Devices for taking pictures and for scooping up information about radar sets and missile tests would have to fly over the Soviet Union and bring their information back. The issue of strategic intelligence was squarely before the engineers and scientists of Project Charles. Their final report opened with a statement of the inequality of information between the United States, an open society, and the Soviet Union:

> The problem of defense of the United States against air attack is characterized above all by lack of knowledge of what we have to defend against. The enemy has the initiative. Our intelligence tells us essentially nothing about his plans; informs us only partially about his present capabilities; and, as to his future capabilities, leaves us essentially dependent on assumptions that he can, if he chooses, do about as well in any aspect as we expect to do ourselves. Moreover, we have to assume that he is informed in detail about our present air defense and its weak points, and has considerable information about our plans for the future.[9]

The need for further study was obvious. Soon after Project Charles, SAC sponsored the follow-up study, Project Beacon Hill, in the early months of 1952. Land, who had been working on reconnaissance during and since World War II, was a member of the follow-up study. During the war, Land had come to know the Army photo-reconnaissance expert George Goddard and the astronomer and lens designer James G. Baker. Land, Baker, and the Harvard physicist Edward Purcell, who had worked on radar in World War II, worked together on Project Beacon Hill.[10] There also, Land and James Killian deepened their mutual trust. Killian was already sharpening his knack for the more political side of science.

In probing the need for better reconnaissance and analysis, the scientist-expert consultants were enmeshed in the endlessly tangled quarrel over air defense. What was the point of reconnaissance for precise knowledge of Soviet forces—the identification of targets, or fixing a ceiling on how many of which type of weapons the United States should buy? Military attitudes, often stressing the offensive, diverged from those of civilian politicians, always subject to public pressure for some kind of damage-limiting shield. The dispute in Britain in the 1930s over fighters and bombers was being fought again. Where should the most money go, for attack or defense? Was the prime purpose of air defense the protection of civilians and cities, or was it the protection of strategic bombers and missiles? In devising air-defense systems, which should get emphasis and dollars, the tweaking of existing set-ups or a bold attempt at integrated systems built around emerging electronic digital computers? The discussion heightened the rivalry between the Air Force, Army, and Navy. Within the Air Force itself, the discussion caused rivalries, such as those between established agencies and new groups, between those who wanted missiles soon and those less eager, and between air defense and strategic bomber commands.

The arguments thrust Killian and many others into heavy flak. Under faculty pressure in 1951 to cut down on classified research at MIT, Killian rejected a proposal from the Navy to do antisubmarine work, but acquiesced in the Air Force demand to get into air defense with what became Lincoln Laboratory. According to Ivan Getting, a supervisor of Project Charles, the argument was that "the dangers to the nation from an attack by airplanes carrying A-bombs was a different order of magnitude [from] . . . the need of protecting shipping."[11]

Killian was still skeptical and wanted to take things one step at a time. He had insisted on Project Charles to review the need and the potentially available solutions. Once Lincoln Laboratory started up, he fiercely defended it against rivalry from other programs and from Air Force anger over a 1952 Summer Study that accused the bomber enthusiasts of a "Maginot Line psychology." Killian also wrestled with a more general military dislike of dealing with freewheeling scientists. Early in 1953, Killian threatened to pull MIT out of air-defense work. In consequence, a rival project at the University of Michigan was eliminated, and the Air Force began instilling a more cooperative attitude and cutting down on interference with the way Lincoln Laboratory operated.[12] This harsh school tested Killian's suavity, but it prepared him for the 1954 project into which he drew Land from the start.

Land, too, was receiving much training in skepticism about the military mind. During Beacon Hill, Land heard James H. Doolittle, the famous leader of the carrier-based 1942 raid on Tokyo, lecture on the difficulties of getting electronic detectors and cameras over the Soviet Union. The Air Force position was that planes that could accomplish this could not be developed in less than ten years. Land, on the other hand, always insisted that there was no law of nature decreeing that you absolutely couldn't do what you wanted. He guessed that Doolittle and the Air Force were wrong and took a small mental step toward the U-2.[13]

Work on advanced reconnaissance was already under way at several places, such as Boston University, Wright-Patterson Air Force Base, and the RAND Corporation, which General LeMay, of all people, had started as a "think tank." The RAND studies included work on reconnaissance satellites that could not be shot down and that could repeatedly survey not only weather conditions but also the places where bombs had hit. Veterans of the World War II scientific mobilization such as Vannevar Bush forcefully grasped the need for intelligence. Bush's dyspeptic book *Modern Arms and Free Men*, published in 1949, breathed a deep irritation at military commanders who refused to face the demands of a scientific age. Surprise attack preoccupied him. The intelligence system could be quite cheap, but would have to go beyond "Mata Hari methods . . . and agents who know no science": "One thing is certain: if another great war is started by a dictator, it will be opened by a smashing, great surprise offensive calculated to paralyze us before we are aroused . . . We could not open a war in this manner, but our potential enemies could . . . We live in a goldfish bowl in this country . . . A great democracy cannot be ordered into war . . . [T]he preparations in a democracy would be obvious.[14]

Another milestone on the road to the U-2 was Land's experience as a member of the Scientific Advisory Board of the Air Force, which he joined sometime before January 1952. The board was headed by the famous aerodynamics pioneer Theodore von Kármán of the California Institute of Technology. Inevitably, the board learned much about translating new scientific findings into advanced military systems. The military had enduring propensities to study problems to death, to retard acceptance of new systems by loading them down with unwieldy specifications, and to buy new systems that were only a half-step ahead of the previous ones.

In January 1952, Land attended a meeting of the board in Florida, near the Cape Canaveral missile-launching site. In von Kármán's absence, Doolittle, now of Shell Oil in New York, took the chair. Leading Air Force officers and civilian scientists attended, including General Nathan Twining, later Air Force chief of staff and chairman of the Joint Chiefs, and Mervin J. Kelly, president of Bell Telephone Laboratories.[15] Land was getting used to such company.

The Beacon Hill study began the same month under the leadership of Carl F. J. Overhage of Kodak, who later directed Lincoln Laboratory. For Land and the others, the focus was detection and surveillance. Several topics were barred: intelligence by secret agents, the decoding of radio messages, and the special methods of detecting atomic explosions. They also left aside the tactical battlefield issues considered by a project called Vista, one of several studies that involved Oppenheimer and irritated the military.[16] In the Beacon Hill report, which was in draft by the end of April, Purcell wrote a chapter on radar and other electronic means of detection. Baker covered photographic surveillance with standard and specialized equipment, and Land wrote "A New Approach to Photo Reconnaissance."

The opening "context essay" defined Land's topic this way:

> In the post-war world, intelligence and reconnaissance are more important to the United States, by several orders of magnitude, than in the pre-1945 world. The age of scientific warfare has already produced the intercontinental striking force with atomic weapons. It is now producing intelligence instruments of comparable efficiency and extreme speed. Since they exist, or will soon be developed, they must be used to the maximum; otherwise an enemy could use them better.[17]

As American and Soviet forces built up year by year, "the question then becomes: which is smarter?" The United States seemed to be stumbling over its own feet in intelligence, trying to collect all the information about everything, paralyzing the analysis of such key topics as "basic weapons and basic combat units." With information on forces hard to get, the Air Force emphasized instead the industry and economy of the

Soviet Union. Yet the importance of the enemy's forces was inescapable: "Our problem is to ward off knockout in round one, in order to come out for round two."

To get a true census of Soviet forces and weapons, the Beacon Hill group saw two basic opportunities, electronic and photographic. Massive detection of radio and radar signals from military units would be valuable, not so much for their messages, as for identifying units and capturing indications of size and movement. Photoreconnaissance would go beyond simple cameras to very powerful, specialized instruments. Standardization should be carried "to its greatest practical limits and utility." But specialization should be carried "right out the window." The cameras would become less bulky and complex and could fly on missiles and rocket planes. On such platforms, however, stability was vital: "Image-motion compensation and anti-vibration mounts are now musts, and, as the Vista report stated, should be pushed with greatest vigor. Lack of them is now an intolerable limitation on quality."

In a premonition of what became the U-2, the Beacon Hill team urged the development of an airplane that would fly at seventy thousand feet, an altitude of thirteen miles, from which instruments could look far into the Soviet Union from a point some forty miles away from the frontier. They also favored the X-2 rocket plane, which might reach forty-five miles up, and a rocket able to go up two hundred miles. "Applying the astronomer's technique to observing Planet Earth," such vehicles would aim their cameras down through an atmospheric haze that lies mostly below ten thousand feet. This is the same haze through which astronomers must look outward to photograph objects billions of light-years away. A camera with a sufficiently long focal length, looking obliquely at Russia from two thousand miles in space, would capture as much detail as would a camera in an airplane only seven miles high.

Such indirect methods were of limited use, however. "Reluctantly," the scientists turned to the more radical idea of sending planes and rockets directly over Russia:

> We don't wish merely to state the obvious need for up-to-date pictures and scope photos inside the Soviet Union, from a strictly intelligence standpoint, leaving the matter there. We as citizens realize there are very grave questions of national policy involved in any peacetime invasion of enemy airspace and, speaking as citizens, we should want these given the most

> exhaustive attention. We presume that a decision on this question of high policy would not be made without knowing what the various vehicles could accomplish: How well could they evade detection? How well could they avoid interception? How useful is the information they could bring back?[18]

These were the questions that Eisenhower would be asking Land and others two and a half years later. In defining the importance of intelligence from overhead, Beacon Hill anticipated the tight flight-planning of the U-2 project. The group did not like a camera-equipped balloon, such as those of Project Gopher, drifting across Russia: "It can be directed only in the general sense that wind currents over the Soviet Union can be anticipated. Locating its photographs on the map would be uncertain and difficult. . . . Controlled search of the Soviet Union, in our opinion, would serve a much better purpose than random, uncontrolled search. Vehicles capable of precision search can be produced, with effort, in the time period immediately ahead."

Speed was the key to survival of a spy plane, whether it operated very high or just over the treetops. Too many existing planes were vulnerable to fighters and anti-aircraft guns. Speed must be put "above all else." Unlike the usual status of reconnaissance as an afterthought, the special needs of the spy plane needed to be in the design from the beginning, even if the craft were a converted fighter. Only the highest-performance aircraft of a given moment should be considered. Again anticipating the U-2, the Beacon Hill report held that it was vital to keep weight down by "an integrated, balanced designing of the package as a whole," so that the maximum of intelligence-gathering equipment could be carried. This would include "interchangeable noses or pods" for photo, radar, infrared, and electromagnetic detection. The vehicles could include the very-high-altitude Canberra bomber, unmanned aircraft such as the Snark, X-2 rockets for border surveillance, high-altitude balloons, other rockets, fighters, and modified subsonic and supersonic bombers. Although simple equipment could be mounted in combat planes, in addition, specialized military intelligence units should "go all out for the highest quality of reconnaissance."[19]

Collecting data was not enough, Land and the others held. From a vast river of facts, it was imperative to fish out those data most vital for top commanders and civilian officials. Consequently, data recording and handling must be streamlined and automated to the maximum. Then, only the most important information would flow up the chain of command, and lateral distribution to people who didn't need it would be inhibited. The work should be done by valued and rewarded professionals, "keen analysts" able to comb with unflagging interest through "vast quantities of material in search of nuggets . . . qualities not unlike those of a good police detective or newspaper reporter." They would need a "sharp, investigatory type of mind." Officers for intelligence analysis needed qualities very different from pilots, engineers, or supply officers, and should be chosen carefully, instead of by "rotation or casual choice." Furthermore, the Air Force lacked a master list of its research projects concerning intelligence, and scientists and industrial producers at one end were not talking directly to military planners and end-users of intelligence at the other. The Air Force needed a simple system in which "one group asks, in effect, 'What do you need?' and the other asks, 'What can you produce?'"[20] All these prescriptions implied inherent problems in military practice that seemed difficult to cure. It was a stiff indictment.

∞

The members of the Beacon Hill study were not finished with the conversation on reconnaissance and intelligence. Gathering at Lincoln Laboratory in January 1953, they bluntly asked Air Force people whether their findings were being used. The Air Force officers waffled. As James Baker recalled in a memorandum, they spoke at length of "the difficulties and conflicts encountered in implementing study reports." This was not reassuring. The scientists concluded with wry understatement that "there exists a continuing need for contact between the USAF and civilian scientists in the intelligence area." They found the way by convincing von Kármán, Doolittle, and an Air Force general that the Scientific Advisory Board should set up a panel on intelligence, to succeed the one on physical sciences being dissolved. The first members were Overhage, Land, and Jim Baker. Added soon after were Allen F. Donovan of the Cornell Aeronautical Laboratory, Stewart Miller of Bell Telephone Laboratories, Duncan Macdonald of Boston University, and Philip G. Strong of the Office of Scientific Intelligence of the Central Intelligence Agency (CIA).

On 3 August 1953 the new Intelligence Systems Panel first met in Boston and heard briefings from three Air Force research groups and the aircraft manufacturer Convair about the work on a reconnaissance version of the B-58 supersonic bomber. Originally only fifteen people had been invited, but attendance swelled to thirty. The panel obviously occupied a "strategic position," in Baker's view, and so drew increasing attention from the CIA and the Air Force Division of Intelligence. The panel's scope included "all overt means of data collection, data handling, evaluation and dissemination." It was expected to think of the special needs of the Air Force's strategic, tactical, and air defense commands and to give full weight to "electronic, photographic, thermal, passive, and other means of surveillance." Baker said that the panel would move on from the insights of Projects Charles, Vista, and Beacon Hill and try to keep up with "rapid changes in intelligence needs, vehicles, techniques, timing problems, and countermeasures."[21]

On 24 and 25 September, Baker's panel met again in Washington, starting off with briefings by Edward R. Allen, chief of economics research at the CIA, and Strong, on "a priority listing of intelligence needs on a national basis." After discussing the Air Force's role in intelligence, the panel heard a formal briefing by the Air Force Directorate of Intelligence. Baker thought that these sessions would keep his panel "from wandering away on attractive but relatively unimportant tangents." He also reflected that although the panel was designed to support the mission of the Air Force, "we know also that anything we can do to further national objectives will be desirable."[22] Baker could see a potential for divergence.

On 21 October, Baker reported on his panel's work to the full Air Force Scientific Advisory Board in Colorado Springs. He then spent two weeks visiting places where he could see development and manufacturing work on pilotless planes, rockets, and missiles. The speed and height of reconnaissance platforms would obviously rise very soon, requiring "almost a new order of magnitude in our thinking." Spy satellites seemed possible by 1962.[23] They actually began operating in 1960.

∞

Meanwhile, early in 1953, the infrastructure for interpreting intelligence photographs grew more sturdy. Strong and his boss, Robert Amory, shared the wish that the CIA would set up its own analysis of science-based intelligence, rather than rely on the military. The CIA already was expanding its Office of Scientific Intelligence. Arthur Lundahl, a veteran of photo-interpretation in World War II who later taught a course in aerial reconnaissance in Chicago, was recruited to form the CIA's Photographic Intelligence Division. This later became the National Photographic Interpretation Center, established in a dingy building at Fifth and K Streets, N.W., in Washington. Lundahl gave the center the code name Automat because it reminded him of the New York City chain of low-priced restaurants where customers put coins in slots and extracted prepared dishes. Lundahl's customers could come in and pick up whatever interpreted pictures they needed. Gradually Lundahl's center grew and became extremely effective at briefing officials, from the president on down, about what the pictures showed.[24]

In January 1953, the Air Force Scientific Advisory Board met again in Florida, only two months after the giant "Mike" superbomb explosion in the Pacific. The board heard Edward Teller and John von Neumann predict that thermonuclear warheads weighing only 1,500 pounds would create explosions with the force of one million tons of TNT. This meant that the hugely destructive warheads could be launched on rockets as well as bombers.[25] Now the question was, Who would have the most rockets, and when?

In New York, as he prepared for his inauguration on 20 January, Eisenhower went over his proposed inaugural address with his designated cabinet officers. Harold Stassen, who would be head of foreign aid, thought a particular sentence on science was a slap at scientists. Vividly recalling his recent briefing on the Mike explosion, Eisenhower replied: "I said they gave us, as our final gift, the power to kill ourselves. That is what they have done, too. Just listen to the stories of the hydrogen bomb. And it doesn't do any good to run. Some day we will have to get these boys up to tell us some of the facts of those things. They are terrifying."[26]

In March 1953, apparently heeding the Beacon Hill recommendation, the Air Force issued a "design requirement" for a one-man reconnaissance plane, to fly at seventy thousand feet. It would be armed. Because the number of planes to be ordered was expected to be small, the Air Force bypassed the large aircraft firms—including Lockheed—and went to Fairchild and to Bell, while also asking the Glenn L. Martin Company, as a stopgap, to modify the high-flying Canberra bomber that it was manufacturing under license.[27]

A reason behind the new Air Force interest in reconnaissance, according to English aviation writer Chris Pocock, was SAC's hunger for definite targets in the Soviet Union. Writing in 1989, Pocock asserted that "the team at SAC intelligence was tearing its hair out just trying to assemble a target list long enough to justify the 1,000 B-47s [medium-range, four-jet bombers] that were on order! Apart from Soviet cities and the perimeter radar and anti-aircraft defenses that had been identified by the probing flights, they really didn't know where to send the bombers."[28]

∞

Almost simultaneously with the preceding events, a new figure at the Air Force plunged into moves that culminated in Land's intelligence study of 1954 and its by-product, the U-2. Not yet forty, Trevor Gardner, a native of

Cardiff, Wales, had moved fast in his career. After working at California Institute of Technology in World War II, he moved on to General Tire and Rubber as a thirty-year-old vice president. Not long afterward, he founded Hycon, a reconnaissance camera research and manufacturing company in Pasadena, California. Joining the new administration in 1953 at Eisenhower's personal invitation, the "blunt, decisive, impatient and profane" Gardner became special assistant to the new Air Force secretary, Harold Talbott, and promptly ordered a review of all missile programs. Three years of rattling the blue-suited professional Air Force officers had begun.

Gardner soon learned that the Air Force was not a monolith on missiles. There were two schools of thought: go slow, and hurry up. Most of the weight of the Air Force, including SAC, the Tactical Air Command, and the Air Staff, was in favor of moving slowly on the intercontinental ballistic missile (ICBM), called Atlas. A good way to delay Atlas was to set its requirements very high. The Air Research and Development Command led the hurry-up school. In ARDC's view, the Russians might be ahead in missiles. Therefore, the specifications should be relaxed so that the Americans could catch up quickly. Agreeing with this view, Gardner pushed for von Neumann's highly influential committee to study ICBMs and demanded immediate action. Gardner contemplated new organizations, possibly outside the Air Force, to get the ICBMs developed, built, tested, and deployed in time to blunt the Russian threat.[29]

The Air Research and Development Command had limited funds to pursue the go-fast strategy. Nonetheless it soon submitted a memorandum ranking the intercontinental Atlas missile project more highly than less ambitious missiles and pilotless planes. In July, the Joint Chiefs of Staff, under pressure from Eisenhower to cut duplication while freeing up money for new technologies, recommended review of the missile programs of all three services. Gardner picked up the ball by calling in the Atlas project engineers for a major briefing. He ordered special committees to do urgent studies of both strategic and nonstrategic missile programs. The Air Staff had recommended that von Kármán's Scientific Advisory Board do the studies.

Von Neumann's Strategic Missiles Evaluation Committee, almost forgotten forty years later, was one of the most influential bodies of the Cold War. On 9 November 1953, it met for the first time. Just two months later, it recommended an all-out effort. The committee membership showed a typical pattern of people from leading institutions, such as Hendrik Bode of Bell Telephone Laboratories, George B. Kistiakowsky of Harvard, and Clark Millikan of Caltech. A year earlier, they all had served on a panel that espoused the hurry-up thesis, though less vigorously.[30]

∞

The drive for better reconnaissance moved in parallel with the speedup in rockets. In January 1954, three companies, Bell, Fairchild, and Martin, submitted designs for a high-flying reconnaissance plane to Bill Lamar and Major John Seaberg of the Office of Bombardment Aircraft Branch at Wright-Patterson Air Force Base. Lamar and Seaberg had written the design requirement issued the previous March. But another player had entered the game: Clarence "Kelly" Johnson of Lockheed Aircraft, a rough-spoken, ferociously competent aircraft engineer who ran a streamlined, fast-moving, isolated, secret, and independent development branch of his company. Soon after it was set up in World War II, this unit in Burbank, California, came to be known as the "Skunk Works," because of evil-smelling chemicals from a plastics factory nearby and an apparent analogy to Injun Joe's whiskey still in the comic strip "L'il Abner."

In 1953, Johnson was brought in by Strong of the CIA. Strong and his boss, Amory, had spent much of the year trying, with only partial success, to gather information about Soviet missile testing at a site in the Ukraine known as Kapustin Yar. Amory had told his colleagues, "We just can't ignore it. This is going to be a major new thing, this whole missile development, and we've got to get on top of it in the beginning and judge it." Predictably, Air Force Chief of Staff Twining said that the site could not be photographed. Strong riposted by persuading the British to send a Canberra over Kapustin Yar to Iran, where it arrived full of bullet holes. Amory recalled much later: "The whole of Russia had been alerted to this thing and it damn near created a major international incident, but it never made the papers." The British said, "Never, never, never again," and came to think that Kim Philby, when he was later identified as a mole, had tipped the Russians off.

Strong went out to California to get Johnson going on a design. In April 1954, as the officials at Wright-Patterson continued studying the three proposals that had reached them in January, Kelly Johnson went to the top. He informally exhibited a design called CL-282 at Air Force headquarters in Washington. The CL-282 combined the fuselage and tail of the F-104 fighter that Johnson's people had designed with a new seventy-foot wing. Trevor Gardner told him to submit the proposal formally, which he did in May.[31]

At the same time, Gardner was helping to organize the surprise-attack study to be headed by Killian. At a cocktail party, Gardner had told Lee DuBridge, chairman of Eisenhower's science advisers, that his group's efforts were worthless. DuBridge's group should go into the subject of surprise attack in search of the true story. A month or so later, the scientists, including DuBridge, heard the president repeat the same request.[32]

∞

In May 1954, Seaberg at Wright-Patterson reached what he thought were final decisions about high-flying reconnaissance planes. Johnson's proposal was turned down almost at once, on the ground that the proposed engine was not powerful enough. The Fairchild M-195 proposal also was turned down, and Bell Aircraft was instructed to go ahead with its twin-engine X-16. This was powered by an adaptation of the J-57 Pratt and Whitney engine being used for hundreds of fighters and bombers, including the B-52. The contract with Bell was signed in September. In June, Martin in Baltimore was told to build the first six of an eventual twenty twin-engine RB-57 Canberras with big wings for SAC.[33]

On the same day in June, Air Force headquarters, probably thinking of Gardner's threats of an independent agency, ruled that the Atlas intercontinental missile would have the highest priority in the Air Force. Complete responsibility for it went to Bernard A. Schriever, now a lieutenant general, and his office on the West Coast. The von Neumann committee was enlarged and continued in business. Soon it held hearings with the Air Force and its contractors to hammer out the project's organization for its fast track.[34]

Back at the original Skunk Works, Lockheed's Johnson and his designers scrapped their idea of adapting the F-104 fighter, except for the cockpit. They tried a new design, involving pressurization of the cockpit and the payload bay, a new undercarriage for takeoffs and landings, and a more conventional tail. Johnson fixed on the goal of having the plane in the air eight months after getting the green light, and Gardner continued to espouse Johnson's design.[35]

∞

At almost the same time, long before the formal letter came from Eisenhower, Killian began pulling together the Technological Capabilities Panel. He immediately convened his steering committee at MIT, including Land, to review whether the scientists could fulfill Eisenhower's request of 27 March. They thought that they could and told the White House so. Full-scale work began in August. The panel divided its work into three major projects: offense, defense, and intelligence. Offense (Project 1) was headed by Marshall G. Holloway of Los Alamos, who had led the design and testing of the Mike device in 1951–52; defense (Project 2) by Leland J. Haworth of Brookhaven National Laboratory, a later director of the National Science Foundation; and intelligence (Project 3) by Land, who was not the first choice for this responsibility. Killian had first approached Bruce S. Old, formerly of Naval intelligence, who worked at Arthur D. Little, the Cambridge-based consulting company. When Killian told him to seek a leave of absence as he had the other project leaders, Old had difficulty arranging this. The job then went to Land.[36]

Land had to change some of his plans. He was already on leave from Polaroid, living in Hollywood and advising Alfred Hitchcock on 3-D movies. He nevertheless came east and formed his project group. It was small: Land liked the idea of committees that would "fit into a taxicab." He chose Baker and Purcell from Harvard; Joseph Kennedy of Washington University in St. Louis, who had helped isolate the artificial element plutonium used in nuclear bombs; the statistician John W. Tukey of Princeton University and Bell Telephone Laboratories; and Allan "Jack" Latham, Jr., Land's old colleague from the early days of Polaroid.[37]

In a 1984 interview, Land recalled that he and his colleagues quickly became convinced that U.S. intelligence was in a poor state. "We would go in and interview generals and admirals in charge of intelligence and come away worried. Here we were, five or six young men, asking questions that these high-ranking officers couldn't answer." Nor were the young men all that impressed with the CIA. But one early CIA contact did impress Land, Purcell, and his colleagues: Arthur Lundahl, the head of CIA's photointerpretation group. With such competent people to interpret photographs, Land's enthusiasm increased for flying directly over Russia to get pictures.[38]

In mid-August 1954, when Land was in Washington, Strong of the CIA showed him a drawing of Kelly Johnson's proposed high-flying spy plane. Here was something that would carry Land's Project 3 far beyond paper studies and admonitions. Gardner of the Air Force had given Strong of the CIA the drawing at a meeting on 12 May. This move was ironic because it had been Strong who had urged Johnson to begin his independent effort the previous fall. The Air Force had no official interest in Johnson's design, Gardner told Strong, but perhaps the CIA might have a use for it. The same day, Strong wrote a memorandum to his colleague Richard M. Bissell, Jr., special assistant to Allen Dulles, head of the CIA, but received no reply.[39]

∞

Land was stunned that the Air Force was not interested. He immediately telephoned Baker, who then had an apartment in Washington to work more efficiently on projects for the Air Force and Killian's Technological Capabilities Panel. He told Baker, "Jim, I think I have the plane you are after." Although Baker was chairman of the intelligence systems panel of the Air Force Scientific Advisory Board, he had not been told about Johnson's CL-282, the Martin RB-57, or the Bell X-16.[40] Nor had his fellow panel member Allen Donovan of the Cornell Aeronautical Laboratory, who had already been thinking for Baker's panel about what a plane for reconnaissance at seventy thousand feet would need. For one thing, it must have only one engine: single-engine planes were simpler and had better safety records. This would have eliminated the Bell X-16 and the Martin RB-57. Second, it must have the wings of a sailplane. Third, to be light enough to get to seventy thousand feet, the plane needed exemption from an Air Force requirement that all aircraft be able to withstand a gust of wind of fifty feet per second when traveling at full speed at sea level. Both the Bell and Martin planes were designed to meet this standard. Now, with the backing of Trevor Gardner, Donovan went out to the Skunk Works in Burbank and reported back favorably to Land and Baker.[41]

The next problem for Land was to get into direct contact with Johnson, with due regard for the minefield he was stepping through. It did not seem a simple matter of picking up the telephone. Land wanted the approval of Air Force Secretary Talbott and made an appointment with him in September.

Land went back to Cambridge fired up. He set up a center for bringing together all the elements of the reconnaissance plane. The small room was at 2 Osborn Street, the modest red brick building that contained his office and laboratory. He invited an engineer from Pratt and Whitney to describe for the Project 3 committee the J-57 engine they were adapting for high-flying reconnaissance. Land wanted to discuss what it might do for the Skunk Works design. To explore the latest developments in film and cameras, he brought in Henry Yutzy, director of research at Eastman Kodak, and Richard S. Perkin, president of Perkin-Elmer Company. Garrison Norton of Gardner's staff in the office of the secretary of the Air Force was often the only federal employee to attend these exploratory sessions.[42]

Yutzy told the Project 3 group about a new film that Kodak was developing, with a base formed of a plastic called Mylar. This could be made as thin as one-thousandth of an inch and yet keep its strength between 40 degrees below zero and 120 above. Along with others, Fordyce Tuttle of Kodak, Land's old friend of the 1930s, was working on it. Specifications of this new film were important because the length of film determined how many images could be recorded on a given sortie. Photointerpreter Dino Brugioni later said that the so-called Estar film allowed "enormous quantities" of film to be spooled onto a single roll or stored in a single magazine, thus extending the useful time of a reconnaissance plane's flight and hence enabling coverage of more territory and sites of interest.[43] At bottom, as Purcell recalled in 1992, it was a matter of bits of information per pound of film.[44] Yutzy also mentioned the disturbing fact that Kodak could see little commercial future for its ultrathin film. Land replied with one of his lectures about national duty, in this case to advance the techniques of aerial reconnaissance. America needed to know how many Bison bombers the Russians were building. Kodak agreed to keep working on the new film.

Another key innovation for this project was Baker's pioneering use of computers to design lens after lens for aerial reconnaissance. He could vary three major elements of the design—the light-bending properties of the lens glass, the air space between lenses, and their curvature—on Boston University's card-programmable computer, without having to actually grind glass and put the lenses together on the bench. His old leader, George Goddard, recalled admiringly that Baker invented cameras with focal lengths of 40, 60, 100, and finally 240 inches, with lenses that compensated automatically for changes in the air's temperature and pressure. The automatic compensation cut down on the distortion that could come as a pilot flew higher, where it was safer, but where the thin atmosphere's temperature and pressure changed unexpectedly. Baker's inventions, in Goddard's view, opened the era of "truly exotic photographic systems." The new systems greatly increased the camera's ability to capture detail on the ground. In World War II, resolution never exceeded 25 lines per millimeter, but Baker carried this to 60 and then 100 lines.

For Gardner's Hycon company in California, Baker already had worked out specifications for three different cameras, called simply A, B, and C. The first, A, consisted of three cameras with 24-inch focal lengths. C was a single camera with a 66-inch focal length. The B camera, weighing about 450 pounds and incorporating a Baker lens, looked particularly promising to Land. It was a panoramic camera with a focal length of 36 inches, which swept from horizon to horizon in a succession of seven shots. The idea promised great economy of film. The system had a further refinement. There could be two such cameras, each with a reel of film rotating synchronously but in the opposite direction from the other, providing stereoscopic views and happily assuring equal weight distribution in the airplane.[45]

Baker liked the arrangements in Kelly Johnson's plane for installing up to 750 pounds of observing equipment in what was called the Q-bay, just forward of the engine and just behind the pilot, where the wings joined the fuselage. Normal airworthiness standards would have run a big spar from one wingtip to the other right through the Q-bay. However, Johnson joined each wing to reinforced sections of the body with six bolts of high-tensile-strength steel. Now there was room for bulky cameras or other detection equipment.[46]

In mid-September 1954, Land kept his appointment with Air Force Secretary Talbott. Accompanying him was James B. Fisk of Bell Telephone Laboratories, the deputy director of Killian's Technological Capabilities Panel. When Land asked permission to speak to Kelly Johnson at the Skunk Works, Talbott said he would think it over. Land recalled almost exactly thirty years later that no answer meant no action. He wanted an answer on the spot. Not knowing the secretary and exhibiting a taste for the dramatic, Land raised his voice and tried a shot in the dark, "All right, Mr. Secretary, I guess we'll have to tell the American people all about you." It worked. Talbott immediately picked up the phone and called Johnson to set up an interview with Land, who wondered if Talbott "may have had a guilty conscience."[47] What that guilt was about, was difficult to tell forty years later. Was it Air Force nervousness at a weapons review ordered by the president, or astonishment that a rejected project had been picked up by that study? The incident is puzzling, because Gardner was working hand in glove with Talbott.

∞

Johnson kept in close touch with his CIA contacts, who, a year earlier, had tipped him off about the Air Force's spy plane requirement. Soon, in October, Johnson needed to come east to talk with the Pratt and Whitney people near Hartford, Connecticut, about adapting their J-57 engine for his CL-282. Even with heavy modifications, on which the Pratt and Whitney engineers were working feverishly, the engine would deliver only 7 percent of its sea-level thrust at seventy thousand feet. It needed a special freeze-resistant fuel with a composition like that of the popular bug-spray Flit. Jimmy Doolittle arranged for his company, Shell Oil, to provide the fuel.

Land invited Johnson to meet him and Killian at his Brattle Street home in Cambridge. Land had suggestions from his panel for Johnson, to adapt the CL-282 even more completely to the system for photography of the Soviet Union. Land and Killian were about to present the plans to top people in Washington, including the head of the CIA and the president. They had become convinced that using uniformed Air Force pilots in armed planes to overfly Russia in peacetime increased the risk of war. Presumably they knew at least something about the long history of incursions by British and SAC pilots. They wanted unmarked, unarmed planes flown by civilians—the sort of operation for which the CIA would be the best organization.[48]

Meanwhile the other subgroups of Killian's study were working hard on their recommendations. These included endorsing full speed ahead on intercontinental missiles. But the Technological Capabilities Panel advocated similarly urgent development of intermediate-range missiles, or IRBMs, that could be ready sooner. These would provide insurance—a counter to Soviet IRBMs—during the period before the ICBMs could be deployed.[49] Land's panel also was preparing its recommendation that the United States move fast to launch satellites to spy on the Soviet ICBMs. The panel believed that getting an airplane to collect crucial information much sooner was so urgent that they would have to put a system together and get it going, as fast as possible. They feared that if the project were assigned to the Air Force, Johnson's light plane would get squeezed out by the heavier, larger, and less valuable RB-57 or X-16.

The CIA needed convincing. Its chief, Dulles, belonged to the tradition of covert operations and information dug up by human spies. Land met Dulles and Trevor Gardner, and Dulles was reluctant to take on so technical a project, especially one that seemed to him so military despite the Air Force rejection of it. Land was worried. Early in November 1954, he sent off three documents: a two-page summary of plans for getting the CL-282 ready in twenty months (that is, by 1 July 1956), a three-page memorandum entitled "A Unique Opportunity for Comprehensive Intelligence," and a 135-word cover letter. Land asserted: "A single mission in clear weather can photograph in revealing detail a strip of Russia two hundred miles wide and twenty-five hundred miles long and produce four thousand sharp pictures."

In the cover letter, Land wrote in a categorical tone:

> Here is the brief report from our panel telling why we think overflight is urgent and presently feasible. I am not sure that we have made it clear that we feel there are many reasons why this activity is appropriate for CIA, always with Air Force assistance.

> We told you that this seems to us the kind of action and technique that is right for the contemporary version of the CIA: a modern and scientific way for an agency that is always supposed to be looking, to do its looking. Quite strongly, we feel that you must always assert your first right in pioneering in scientific techniques for collecting intelligence—and choosing such partners to assist you as may be needed. This present opportunity for aerial photography seems to us a fine place to start.[50]

The language is not suave; it borders on exasperation. Yet, it persuaded Dulles. About this time, the military executive director of the CIA, Colonel Lawrence "Red" White, spoke to Dulles of his worry about the cost of the proposed operation. Couldn't the military pay for the interpretation? Dulles put his glasses on his forehead and replied, "Red, you don't think that after I've taken all those photos, I am going to let somebody else interpret them."[51]

Of course, all was not smooth between the impulsive and determined Land and the rough-edged Johnson, who was stretching design to its limits to develop a plane to bring Ike his postcards from Russia. Land and Johnson fought over the Q-bay. Many years later, Johnson's assistant Ben Rich recalled that "Kelly and Dr. Land argued constantly about each other's needs to dominate the relatively small space inside those bays. Kelly needed room for batteries; Land needed all the room he could get for his bulky folding cameras. Kelly's temper flashed at Land: 'Let me remind you, unless we can fly this thing, you've got nothing to take pictures of.' In the end, they compromised."[52]

The tension around the project had been rising on another front. The Air Force had no liking for the trend toward the CIA's operating its own spy plane. Land and his panel soon learned of this. On 19 October, they sent Allen Donovan as an ambassador to argue their case with Donald Putt, the Air Force deputy chief of staff for development, now a lieutenant general. Donovan came away from the meeting convinced that he had not converted Putt to his point of view.[53]

On 7 November, a B-29 bomber equipped as a reconnaissance plane made another of LeMay's provocative probing flights, this time from Japan over a large airbase in Soviet Asia. It was shot down over the sea. Ten of the eleven crewmen bailed out safely, but the eleventh, caught in his parachute lines, drowned.[54] On 9 November, the day before his twenty-fifth wedding anniversary, Land flew with Killian to Burbank to see a mock-up of the CL-282.[55]

The Air Force continued to work in opposition to the project. Major John Seaberg of Wright-Patterson, who had given the green light to the X-16 and the high-altitude RB-57, persuaded General Putt to call a meeting at the Pentagon on Thursday, 18 November, to discuss the CL-282. Land got wind of this and summoned his panel to Washington on short notice, not only to counter Air Force maneuvers but also to resolve doubts about whether even Kelly Johnson's CL-282 could survive over Russia.

With Land's approval, Jim Baker asked Donovan to join the panel just before the Pentagon meeting with Seaberg. Donovan approached the Old Executive Office Building on Pennsylvania Avenue in a cold November rain. A four-door Ford sedan was at the curb with its engine idling. The driver, committee member John Tukey, called out to Donovan to get in the back seat. Already crowded inside were Land, Baker, Purcell, and James Fisk, deputy director of the Killian TCP study. So that no one would overhear, Tukey drove them around Washington while Donovan answered lingering doubts. With six people inside, the windows fogged up. Land told Donovan that some panel members wondered why another plane, besides the X-16 and the RB-57, was needed. Donovan repeated his list of three requirements for success: a single engine, a sailplane wing, and less stringent structural load requirements. In two hours of conversation, Donovan convinced the doubters that only Kelly Johnson's plane had a chance.

Trevor Gardner and General Putt presided over the meeting at the Pentagon. Land and Fisk attended. Seaberg, briefed in advance about the CL-282, acknowledged that if it, too, used the J-57 engine, it would be competitive with the other two planes. That afternoon, responding to an urgent call from Gardner, Johnson flew in from California.

The next day, Friday, 19 November, Johnson went through hours of grilling from Gardner and five of the six members of the Land committee: Land, Baker, Purcell, Latham, and Kennedy. This session, Johnson remembered afterward, was his most thorough examination since college. It was clear that the CL-282 could fly with the J-57. That clinched it. Johnson went to lunch with Allen Dulles and Air Force Secretary Talbott, one of whom said, "Let's stop talking about it and build the damn plane."[56]

∞

Already, Land and his colleagues had been talking in secrecy with Eisenhower, who strongly expressed his need for frank advice on technical problems. The president referred to them later as "one of the few groups I encountered while in Washington who seemed to be there to help the country and not help themselves." Land recalled almost thirty years later that the president exclaimed, "Oh, I'm so grateful to you fellows who are out of town! You can't think in Washington. You go away and think and then you tell me what you've been thinking. There's no way to think if you live here."[57]

As the U-2 project and the Killian report developed, Eisenhower considered some material so highly sensitive that he had asked Land and Killian to brief him off the record, apparently more than once. Richard Bissell recalled that their "recommendation that the United States should build a reconnaissance aircraft capable of flying at very high altitudes and that the plane should engage in overflights of the USSR was regarded as so sensitive that it was omitted entirely from the committee's final report."[58] This was when they told him about the short-term possibility of a plane with long, narrow, gently tapered wings that would carry it above sixty-five thousand feet, beyond the reach of Russia's existing surface-to-air missiles. Johnson had promised that it would fly eight months after the go-ahead. He even thought, wrongly, it turned out, that the plane would fly higher than Soviet radars could reach.[59]

Eisenhower wanted to be sure that the camera-carrying plane would perform as advertised—a question on which Land had spent months—and was concerned about something even more important. No doubt, the plane would be shot down some day, which would cause a terrible row. Would the pictures, the "take," in intelligence jargon, have been worth the inevitable trouble? Land told him, "If we are successful, it can be the greatest intelligence coup in history." If there were a lot of Bison bombers, the plane would find them.[60]

Michael Beschloss, in *Mayday: Eisenhower, Khrushchev, and the U-2 Affair*, says that "Land and Killian thought that even if the take was marginal, the flights might cause the Kremlin to shift precious rubles from offensive to defensive weapons. They might also demonstrate the futility of Moscow's obsessive secrecy; maybe then the Russians would sign disarmament agreements with adequate inspections."[61] They apparently did not make the argument that overflights might substitute for inspections. Indeed, surveillance continued for decades without inspections on the ground.

Eisenhower approved the idea of having the CIA run the project, because he did not want any armed service being judge and jury, too. That is, the President did not want any service to make up shopping lists for weapons from intelligence that the service collected and interpreted itself. He did not want the Air Force controlling the project that Land had put together, which was first called Aquatone and later Idealist, or aerial reconnaissance in general.[62]

Just a few days after the confrontations in the Pentagon, on 24

November 1954, Killian, Land, Purcell, and Dulles went to see Eisenhower for an off-the-record session. It was the morning before Thanksgiving, apparently just before a meeting of the National Security Council. Eisenhower surprised his visitors by telling them to get going on the project immediately. Dulles immediately called his special assistant, Richard Bissell, and told him to attend a meeting that afternoon, where Bissell was put in charge. Trevor Gardner called Kelly Johnson to start work, and Johnson said he would clear out a hangar that afternoon.[63]

Early in August 1955, at a secret airstrip on the other side of a mountain from the Nevada site for testing atomic bombs, the U-2 took its first flight. About eleven months later, U-2s began flying over Russia.

∞

The collaboration between Land and the others working on the U-2 was remembered warmly. Bissell described the collaboration with admiration:

> [I] greatly enjoyed talking about science and technology. I had particular respect for Kelly Johnson, W. O. Baker [of Bell Telephone Laboratories], and Edwin Land, who were precise in their words and willing to quantify their confidence that something would work or would fail. The intellectual qualities of people like these created a stimulating work environment. In the middle of the program, my staff and I went to visit Din Land at his house in Boston. Art Lundahl recalls "sparks flying and scintillating, cutting-edge ideas" coming from all sides. Was there anywhere else, he wonders, where "this mixture of science and friendship and understanding" could have been experienced "in such a nice fashion."[64]

Killian and his TCP turned in their report officially on 14 February 1955 and, with careful staging, presented it to the National Security Council a month later.[65] It spelled out a timetable for hurrying along to intercontinental missiles, with shorter-range missiles being developed even sooner as insurance. With warheads slimming down, a major concern of the Killian panel was the vulnerability of the bombers, which were then the first line of defense. These needed to be dispersed to more bases, and better protected there.

The report was "one of the most influential in the history of American nuclear policy," according to President Kennedy's national security adviser, McGeorge Bundy: "The TCP report decisively accelerated the development of missiles; it led to an important new departure in the collection of intelligence;

it gave notice of the need to develop early-warning systems not only against bombers but against ballistic missiles; it gave Eisenhower an enduring respect for the value of independent technical advice." In Bundy's view, Eisenhower gave the green light, before the end of 1955, to the intercontinental Atlas and Titan and the intermediate-range Thor and Jupiter, because he saw them as insurance against surprise attack.[66]

Killian kept his eye on the big picture. Although there were some inventions and pulling-together of inventions during the TCP's work, Killian recalled later, the main emphases were different. "We were looking for the big jumps. . . . [W]e were . . . looking at the strategical needs of the country. We had a great effort to appraise the threat at that time and then try to match our technological programming to that threat. And one of the basic aspects of this study and report was a forecasting of the Russian threat as it was likely to develop over the next five years."[67]

One aspect of the report gave Killian special pride: "It re-established a new confidence, a confidence between the scientific community and the government which had been badly impaired by the Oppenheimer case." One reason was that the panel members were very circumspect. There were no leaks. The result was that Eisenhower's relations with scientists became warmer. Killian recalled this cordial relationship:

> The President apparently felt that the study had been helpful to him, and he began then a series of actions that led him to turn to the scientific community for help and advice. He proved from then on out extraordinarily cordial to those people whom he knew in the scientific community, which included Rabi, whom he had known at Columbia, Fisk, and myself. And to widen his contacts within the scientific community beyond Lewis Strauss who had more or less been his chief science advisor, acting in concert with the little group who had been so close to him in the AEC program, Ernest Lawrence and Edward Teller, the Latter brothers and so on.[68]

One of the report's most-remembered passages came from Land:

> We must find ways to increase the number of hard facts upon which our intelligence estimates are based, to provide better strategic warning, to minimize surprise in the kind of attack, and to reduce the danger of gross overestimation or gross underestimation of the threat. To this end, we recommend

> adoption of a vigorous program for the extensive use, in many intelligence procedures, of the most advanced knowledge in science and technology.[69]

Land seldom spoke publicly of his work for Eisenhower. The simplest explanation for his secretiveness is that he wanted to stay in the game, despite changes in civilian and military leaders. To remain credible with them, he never joined the public movements for disarmament that so many of the World War II scientists led.

He loved secrets and identified with spies. He clung to secrecy in the world of patents, which he saw as equalizers with the giant firms, into which he refused to be absorbed. Secrecy also went along with tight control of his time and his accessibility and thus was an essential protection of his autonomy. In other words, he enjoyed the freedom to make particular choices on his timetable and not others'. Almost certainly, he never wished to choose sides publicly between the advocates of unlimited defense efforts and those of restraint in building ultimate weapons. To be sure, the pictures showed only a limited Russian effort in long-range bombers and above-ground, liquid-fueled rockets. Using the same photographs, however, the SAC could make its list of targets ever more specific and ever longer. Another reason for silence, which Eisenhower evidently appreciated, was the need not to spur Russia to countermeasures, such as camouflage or even anti-satellite weapons. In a volatile world, unnecessary insults to Russia should be avoided. The secrecy was eroded significantly only in the 1980s and 1990s, as the Soviet Union careened toward collapse.

This long blackout may have an additional, subtler explanation. Overhead photos helped put the brakes on the arms race in the 1950s, helped keep them on ever after, and made mutual deterrence of the two superpowers cheaper if not more certain. Definite information shortened America's military shopping lists. Thus the development of sure means to detect physical capabilities was a mighty check on the U. S. Air Force. The Air Force fiercely resisted any restraint on building its weapons for what might be a single day of combat and closely studied the possibility of striking first rather than second. In a sense, the Air Force had lost an argument, and the shrewdest policy for the long run may have been to keep from rubbing the generals' noses in this fact publicly. Admittedly, the pictures showed targets, which constituted an argument for more or better weapons to strike them. They may even, in the view of the defense scientist and historian Herbert York, have heightened pressure for a preemptive first strike by making it very difficult to hide anything major.[70]

The American pictures, however, compensated for an uneven flow of detailed intelligence from within Russia. They showed that there were real limits to what the other side, the potential enemy, could do with its resources, no matter how much these resources were concentrated on military strength. Soon after the U-2 photographs began accumulating, it was clear that the Russian long-range bomber fleet was much smaller than the Air Force and the intelligence agencies had projected. The thirty M-4 bombers lined up on Engels airfield near Leningrad were all, or nearly all, that the Russians built.[71] Russia's hints to the contrary were a bluff, and America didn't fall for it. The U-2 photographs of the liquid-fueled, aboveground, intercontinental missiles of the sort that launched *Sputnik I* in 1957 showed no fleet, but rather a mere handful.[72]

The Russians, like the Americans, appreciated that a true land-based missile strike force, able to respond in half an hour to warnings of an attack, would have to use the solid fuels developed for submarine missiles and be based underground in "hardened" concrete silos. That meant waiting a few years to develop missiles like the U.S. Minuteman.

Land's role in Eisenhower's drama of restraint runs counter to the dominant notions of the nuclear age. Most commentators see an inability to stuff the genie back in the bottle, or failed attempts at international control and restraint. The main picture is of a mad momentum, with two superpowers racing far beyond the numbers of weapons needed to deter each other—or anyone else—from nuclear war. Idealistic people thought of themselves as beating vainly on the gates of a process moving toward inevitable destruction, conducted by the sort of people who get and wield power and are inevitably corrupted by it.

Counsels of restraint were heard by the powerful within the government as well as by a frightened public, and actual and even tightening restraint occurred. The usual comment on the nuclear age, which may or may not have ended, resounds with the idea of unrestrained piling up of weapons. There was little confidence among those outside the circle of secrecy that the faith in reason, held by the scientists who opened the way to the nuclear age, greatly influenced what happened. By helping open up a powerful new channel of intelligence, one that revealed the true size of the Soviet effort in strategic weapons, Land gave a powerful example of rational inquiry imposing restraint on supposedly uncontrollable emotional tendencies to make war, and to make war as destructively and absolutely as possible. He helped achieve a restraint by knowing.

16
The Shock of *Sputnik*

> We [must] begin a rebirth of building, using the mind, enjoying the scientific adventure. Otherwise Russian scientific culture will leave us behind as a decadent race. The country no longer feels the thrill of the scientific life. How can we set off on a lot of enormous adventures, under the President, in order to stimulate science?
>
> —Edwin H. Land to President Eisenhower, 15 October 1957

The Russian launching of *Sputnik I* on 4 October 1957 set off a chain of ideas, aspirations, and achievements reaching into the mid-1990s. *Sputnik* precipitated immediate decisions about future American efforts in space. The scientific revolution in World War II and thereafter entered a new phase, and Land was caught up in it. Suddenly, it seemed that the scientific experience would become a major part of the lives of Americans—freed by technology from mere subsistence. Land had expressed such hopes in his talk at MIT a few months earlier. A few days after *Sputnik*, he had the opportunity to express them directly to President Eisenhower.

It was a dramatic time. All over the United States, amateur astronomers used rows of small telescopes, originally set up to track an expected American satellite, to track *Sputnik*. Fearful and aroused, the American public, politicians, military men, and journalists were crying out for expanded efforts in defense, space exploration, and education. The result was a paradoxical mixture of decisions about space that were simultaneously military and civilian, public and secret. Emotions ruled, including the romance of space, which proved enduring. Military and civilian aspects of space were woven tightly together. In the same week of February 1958 that Land dined at the White House, he found himself working both on the rationale and organization of a civilian, nonsecret program of space exploration under what became the National Aeronautics and Space Administration (NASA), and on the deeply secret decisions about how to manage a stumbling effort toward reconnaissance satellites.[1] These satellites would supplement and surpass the vital intelligence from the still-secret U-2 spy planes.

Sputnik I propelled the American public into realizations that three and a half years earlier had confronted the president and the scientists, including Land, when they considered the risks of nuclear surprise attack and determined how to ward them off. As Eisenhower and his advisers saw in the first months of 1954, the public could see in late 1957 that the two sides in the Cold War, armed with intercontinental rockets, were moving technologically toward a deadly confrontation. The issue was deterrence. Did the United States have enough strength to extinguish any Russian thought of an attack?

After the amazing feat of *Sputnik*, a defensive Eisenhower began to seem like the old man that John Kennedy alluded to in 1960, when the senator called for getting "this country moving again." The public had little reassurance to balance its dismay. People knew that the United States had started missile programs, long-range and intermediate-range, land-based and sea-launched. But they did not know what Eisenhower knew: that the American moves, including the types and numbers of missiles ordered, were based on solid information. Not knowing this, the public, politicians, and not a few members of what Eisenhower called in 1961 the "military-industrial complex" demanded more missiles. Eisenhower's appeals for a sense of proportion sounded like excuses for inaction or delay. A large price in public nervousness was paid.

Eisenhower considered telling the public about the U-2, but with the same caution he showed in reviewing the plans for every U-2 flight, he hung back.[2] The president's decision was rooted in his experience of high command in World War II. This studious man had seen, over and over again, the importance of keeping secret, as long as possible, the means used to get the information.[3] Besides, the Soviet Union could not be pushed too hard. Eisenhower reminded his officials that flying over enemy territory was a warlike act and could call for a belligerent response.[4] The Soviet leaders, unable to shoot down the U-2s, had kept their embarrassment secret. From the beginning of his first term as president, Eisenhower sought the means to restrain the arms race and, in his second term, pushed even harder for a decisive meeting with eastern leaders. He wanted to minimize provocations.

Secrecy had another merit, one that Land came to appreciate almost too well. In emergencies, the best way to reach a rapid and effective solution is to bring together small groups of very able people, untrammeled by accountants and politicians and the usual ponderous interactions between government and industry. This was what made the U-2 and its successors, the supersonic Blackbird intelligence airplane and the *Corona* spy satellite, possible. All three efforts were directed by the economist and operations man Richard M. Bissell, Jr., of the CIA, and all three involved Land in figuring out the leanest possible structures and shortest possible pathways to technical success.[5] This experience surely influenced Land's management of both the SX-70 and the Polavision systems introduced in the 1970s.

∞

Beyond the foreboding about war, *Sputnik* intensified peaceful aspirations. Leaders of East and West, spurred by images like Oppenheimer's "two scorpions in a bottle," already were meeting in search of ways to control the escalating arms race. Similarly, scientists from East and West, driven by their own deep knowledge of the new weapons and what they could do, began exchanging information at Atoms for Peace conferences in Geneva in 1955 and 1958. *Sputnik* was part of the scientists' worldwide program of exploration of the earth, the International Geophysical Year (IGY).[6]

Now, the Russians had gained in prestige while the United States, so soon after its overwhelming victory in World War II, saw itself taken down a peg. With memories of the Korean War still fresh, many people already perceived that the time of decisive victories was in the past. The issues between America and Russia were so enormous, and so dangerous, that the two superpowers could challenge each other only indirectly. Too much was at stake ever to stage a "main event" in the center ring.

The shock of *Sputnik* resonated even more loudly than did the immense, largely secret feats of Igor Kurchatov and colleagues such as Andrei Sakharov in matching, within ten years, the Western development of the atomic bomb and its terrifying successor, the hydrogen bomb.[7] Now, led by Sergei Korolyov, the Soviets were in space before the Americans. Frustration, confusion, and hesitation dominated the Cold War. *Sputnik I* was as energizing in its own way as the Japanese attack on Pearl Harbor. Russia had demonstrated a potential leadership in science and technology that might reinforce a drive toward peaceful dominance of the world. In the 1940s, the direct response to Pearl Harbor was pre-dominantly military. In 1957, the challenge was seen from the beginning as equally military and civilian. The technical arena was rocketry, either to strike an enemy thousands of miles away, or to go into space for science, commerce, and adventure. The American response was mighty. The nation pushed into space with a boldness and breadth perhaps unexpected of a pragmatic, consumerist society. In the next forty years, the exploration of space became commonplace, while Land's part in the simultaneously military and civilian drive remained largely unknown.

Although spy satellites were the feature of space work that Eisenhower considered most urgent,[8] they carried cameras that could also be used for the economic study of crops and forests. Satellites that could follow the movement of cloud masses for military planning were equally useful as the beginning of the now-constant warning of destructive storms. Satellites able to link military commanders with distant armies and fleets were equally useful for linking merchant and passenger ships with the shore and with each other. They could transmit business data across continents and oceans, and they could create the possibility of simultaneous worldwide viewing of an event like the first walk by astronauts on the moon. Navigation satellites grew in numbers and accuracy as they were launched over decades. The result was enhanced accuracy of missiles launched from submarines cruising in trackless oceans. Other adaptations evolved eventually for peaceful scientific research, yachting, and hiking. The principal new spy satellite system of the 1970s turned charge-coupled imaging devices toward the earth below, from which they could count virtually every quantum of light reaching them. The technology was adapted to turn outward in the Hubble Space Telescope of the 1980s. The Hubble made some of the most accurate and deeply penetrating observations of the light from the stars and galaxies of the universe. It kept track of the weather on Jupiter and other large planets.

The dual uses of space technology, civilian as well as military, could hardly have developed any faster or more closely together than they did. A few months after *Sputnik*, the Americans discovered, with their first satellites, the belts of particles trapped in the Earth's magnetic field. A failed candidate for a military spy satellite, using television cameras whose signals were radioed to earth, began taking pictures of cloud patterns on 1 April 1960. This peaceful opening of nearly continuous weather monitoring occurred more than four months before an alternative design of the spy satellite *Corona* succeeded for the first time in surveying swaths of the Soviet Union. *Corona* used cameras whose film was returned to Earth in capsules ejected back from space. It covered more territory in a single day's multiorbit flight than had been covered in all the four years of clandestine flights by the U-2 spy plane.[9]

By 1969, when astronauts first went to the moon and back, flights by increasingly capable Russian and American spy satellites occurred so frequently that coverage of each nation's territory by the other was virtually constant.[10] The coverage was indeed so constant that each nation could count on observations by the other to figure in policy decisions. As early as the Cuban missile crisis of 1962, while American U-2s counted Russian missiles in Cuba, Russian spy satellites could photograph American military aircraft jamming the airfields of Florida, ready for the assault that President Kennedy never had to order.[11] Knowing fostered restraint: the Russians withdrew their intermediate-range missiles (IRBMs) from Cuba. The peaceful contest in space, the most dramatic feature of the age of nuclear restraint, thus reached its apogee a decade before the Strategic Arms Limitation Treaty, itself enforced by satellite surveillance, signaled an uneasy truce in the Cold War.

∞

To meet the complex emergency of 1957, Eisenhower again turned to the scientists who had helped him in 1954. While resisting fiercely the attempts to force the ordering of more first-generation ICBMs, he named a presidential science adviser, James Killian, assisted by a powerful, renamed President's Science Advisory Committee, which included Land. The president ordered steps to strengthen scientific and intelligence efforts in the Defense Department. Land helped accelerate the drive to develop a working reconnaissance satellite. A committee that included Land devised a public charter for civilian efforts in space, along with a structure for a civilian space agency. That agency's activities, by their very public nature, would help cloak the military efforts in space that Eisenhower considered far more important. The president lent support to dramatic "big science" projects like the two-mile linear accelerator at Stanford University, and he appeared more than once at conferences of scientists. As Land had eloquently urged, Eisenhower backed the spending of additional money for scientific work in universities and for building up the quality of science teaching in grade and high schools. The increased support for science led soon to revolutions in electronics and biotechnology.

On 15 October 1957, Eisenhower called in the members of the Scientific Advisory Committee of the Office of Defense Mobilization. The urgency resembled that of 1954, but the questions were new: Was the United States behind the Soviet Union scientifically? Could civilian and military science and its funding be organized better? The administration already had approved plans for squadrons of intermediate-range missiles based abroad and for intercontinental Atlas and Titan missiles in the United States, but the systems were still being tested. On 1 October, the Soviet Union announced that it had exploded a large hydrogen bomb at high altitude. Shock waves were measured in Japan. Eisenhower, fighting a national tendency toward hysteria, sought repeatedly to reassure the American public.

Eisenhower's meeting lasted about an hour, from just before 11 A.M. to just before noon, but it dealt with many matters of broad policy. As was customary, Eisenhower's aide Andrew Goodpaster was there to take notes. The excitement he felt is evident in the ruled, yellow sheets deposited in the archives of the Eisenhower Library in Abilene, Kansas.[12]

Although Eisenhower knew that he was in a crisis, he had trouble understanding the furor about *Sputnik*: "I can't understand why the American people have got so worked up about this thing. It's certainly not going to drop on their heads." The first order of business was organization, a subject for action by the president in view of the public furor. He asked how to coordinate scientists' government service, with emphasis on defense, to avoid duplication and waste. While scientists should be free of restrictions in their research, Eisenhower thought, the government needed to be sure that the money was used for research.

The physicist I. I. Rabi, chairman of the committee, said that management of research in government was the committee's central problem. Lots of gripes could be heard. If the subject were gone into thoroughly, all branches of government would be affected profoundly. After Eisenhower praised the work of committees led by W. O. Baker and H. Rowan Gaither as "magnificent," Rabi pushed for a massive examination of U.S. science organization. He saw "something very rotten in the set-up as now arranged." Eisenhower's aide Robert Cutler suggested that Rabi draft a "frame of reference," a blueprint describing what America was doing then and what the government, universities, and industry should do. The president acknowledged that the Defense Department was not organized ideally. "We are looking for the best practical plan for our free democratic government to get as much as we can for our dollar."

The president then asked a more general question. Did the scientists feel that "American science is being outdistanced?" There was a consensus, Rabi replied, that "generally we are in some sense ahead, but in their set-up, in their momentum, the quality of their scientific organization, [the Soviets] have the capability to pass us quickly unless we take stock and change national attitudes and organization."

Land characteristically saw this as the moment to speak up and carry the discussion to another plane. He said that the country recognized that it needed much from science. Science needed the president. The Russians, in their structure, "are seeking to live the life of science and its application. They are pioneering as we did years ago. Science is becoming to them a way of life." The Russians were "teaching their young people to enjoy science." The United States had paused to enjoy the fruits of its economic development. Land urged that "we begin a rebirth of building, using the mind, enjoying the scientific adventure. Otherwise Russian scientific culture will leave us behind as a decadent race. The country no longer feels the thrill of the scientific life. How can we set off on a lot of enormous adventures, under the President, in order to stimulate science?" As he did so often in his life, Land thought of leaping beyond mere reaction.

In a moment of crisis, the scientists were reaching for a decisive change in the status of science in America. They sensed that an embattled Eisenhower was listening to them again. As the historian Robert Divine wrote, the scientists implied that it was "up to Eisenhower to use the shock of *Sputnik* to stress the importance of science to American life, to rekindle the spirit of scientific inquiry, to single out scientists for special attention, and to give science the very highest national priority." Land was urging the president to use the outcry over *Sputnik* to speak out, to "inspire the country—setting our youth particularly on a whole variety of adventures." Young people should feel toward science a spirit, an attitude similar to the excitement about various kinds of athletics in the president's youth.[13] This point was a shrewd hit, because Eisenhower had played football at West Point and then, as a young officer between the wars, coached numerous teams at Army bases.[14] If America were to give science the appropriate emphasis, Land said, it could surpass Russia's scientific community. But at present, America was "not a scientific community enjoying its spirit and morale." Scientists, despite the magnificent technology in the United States, felt alone. It wasn't a matter of money; it was the spiritual component. "The U.S. must be made into a scientific country if it will survive."

Eisenhower did not let this pass unchallenged. Did all Russians feel as Land described? Perhaps it was only the elite. The president acknowledged that he could reinforce a new spirit, but how could he coordinate the effort? What was the government doing? What could it do to help?

What was the governmental role in this scientific endeavor? A presidential speech would not be enough. "We must know where we want to go and how the government must help."

Science was involved in most matters of policy coming to the president, Rabi said, but the president lacked someone near him "who keeps him advised constantly" about science, as there was in economics, health, and defense. Eisenhower asked if it should be a section or an individual. Killian spoke up. The president should have "something comparable to the Council of Economic Advisors." Eisenhower observed that "Congress is jealous of changes," but a mechanism to meet this need might be worked out. If he named a special assistant, how should that person be trained, and in what? Rabi advised Eisenhower to try someone he liked part-time for a while. Killian said that the scientific committee in the room could back up such an adviser. Eisenhower began designing the job. He needed an official who "would keep a record of decisions made" in the president's office in the scientific area. But no one should forget Eisenhower's determination to give priority to weapons of deterrence. There was a "psychological necessity" for maintaining the priority of efforts to develop intermediate-range and intercontinental missiles and hence for not "delaying for less important things."

As the meeting continued, Killian listed things that needed doing "right now," including a speech and the reform of science in the Defense Department. Eisenhower must "publicize the sense of urgency and mission." The people must know that as things were going, "Russia will surpass us." In countering Russia, the nation should look first at research and development in the Defense Department, where a "wonderful chance" for change existed under the new secretary of defense, Neil McElroy. It was a matter more of leadership than of money. Eisenhower immediately ordered that the scientists meet with McElroy, and an aide went out to arrange the meeting for 1:30 P.M.. The president deplored the military focus on installations scattered among the three services and worried about duplication of effort.

Jerome Wiesner of MIT then started a brief, sharp dialogue with Eisenhower. Wiesner had served on the von Neumann committee that had urged all-out development of intercontinental missiles in 1954. The fear of lagging behind Russia should not go so far, he said, as to upset the "pretty good organization" now. Except for the rival intermediate-range missile programs, Thor in the Air Force and Jupiter in the Army, there was no duplication. He called the ballistic missile program "excellent." To be sure, America had started late. Eisenhower interjected that this tardiness would cause "political difficulties." After World War II, the president said, the Americans had gone "aerodynamic," while the Russians had gone "ballistic." It was not mismanagement but a late start on missiles. Wiesner observed, "The people are scared." Eisenhower rejoined, "We can destroy Russia today," to which Wiesner shot back, "But it's ten years from now we are worried about."

Other significant recommendations were put forth. Because Russia had achieved such rapid and massive progress in nuclear weapons and energy, Rabi said, America must cooperate more with Britain and Japan, to "bring the resources of the free world together." Eisenhower picked up the ball at once. He said that a scientific committee was needed in the North Atlantic Treaty Organization (NATO), and for that, the law on the sharing of atomic secrets would have to be revised. Eisenhower called for a press conference the following week on "how to get the scientists into action. Our type of thinking in the U.S. is not scientific enough." Killian spoke of needs involving education as well as science. Land suggested that the president go to meetings of the National Academy of Sciences or of the American Physical Society.[15]

This one-hour meeting proved historic. It led directly to the creation of a presidential science adviser backed up by the new President's Science Advisory Committee (PSAC), and to the strengthening of science in the Defense Department. As Killian looked back later, he was struck by the force of the meeting. To keep American scientific preeminence, the president needed a science adviser. Land had said that the president could do more than anyone else to kindle among young people an essential enthusiasm for science as a joyous, creative activity, "setting our youth on a variety of scientific adventures."[16]

The scientists' conversation, including Land's, affected Eisenhower profoundly:

> In the weeks to come, he would refer to this discussion again and again. Though he felt confident about America's satellite and missile programs, he had become aware of the danger of falling behind the Soviet Union in science and technology through complacency and the human tendency to sit back and enjoy the fruits of material abundance. He was determined to do everything he could to follow Land's advice to elevate the role of science in education, government, and American society at large. Above all, he would try to turn what he called "the current wave of near-hysteria" over Sputnik into an opportunity for constructive change.[17]

Robert Cutler wrote up an urgent summary of the conversation, which he probably gave to Rabi before the scientists went over to the Pentagon for their 1:30 P.M. conversation with Defense Secretary McElroy. Item 1 of the memorandum instructed Rabi to draft a "frame of reference" by early November, spelling out how to coordinate scientific effort better with the Defense Department and other agencies, reviewing what had been done since World War II, retaining as much current organization as possible, and proposing a presidential science adviser backed up by a committee like the Council of Economic Advisors.

Cutler's item 2 addressed Land's proposal: "Presumably, later and as a separate undertaking, there would be developed Dr. Land's proposal of finding some way spiritually to awaken the U.S. to the need of becoming a more scientific community, in order to prevent the Soviet people from pushing their interest in the life of science beyond U.S. scientific endeavors to the serious detriment of the U.S."[18]

In response to Rabi's recommendation, the president wanted Goodpaster to look into cutting down on executive branch security rules that hampered exchanges with allied nations. Cutler should talk to Lewis Strauss, chairman of the Atomic Energy Commission, about a survey of atomic energy laws that might block collaborations like participation in NATO scientific committees. The president would look into Land's idea of attending meetings of scientists. Killian would prepare notes for the ceremony, a few weeks hence, when the atomic energy award named for the late Enrico Fermi would be presented to the Danish physicist Niels Bohr.[19]

At the Defense Department that afternoon, Land repeated what he told Eisenhower: that to have a healthy, productive science, the country must be receptive to it. "We can't isolate our scientists into a few colleges to combat Russia. We must cultivate a way of life." As for science in the Defense Department, he spoke of the need for "a substantive urgency leading to change and solution."[20]

∞

In an atmosphere of urgency, the moves toward naming Killian as science adviser followed swiftly. Eisenhower's chief of staff, Sherman Adams, summoned Killian to meet in his office on 23 October 1957 with Goodpaster, Cutler, and Eisenhower's special assistant for national security, Gordon Gray. Killian had a "carefully prepared" memorandum with him. To get ready for writing it, Killian called together several of his TCP co-workers and others in 1954 to meet in Lloyd Berkner's office in New York. Besides

Land and Berkner, the group included Mervin J. Kelly, president of Bell Labs; Jim Fisk, who would succeed Kelly; Rabi; and Detlev Bronk. They provided their "collective wisdom" to Killian. On 24 October, at the end of a breakfast meeting with Eisenhower, Killian was offered the post of presidential science adviser.[21] The same day, the Air Force's Thor intermediate-range missile was launched on its first full-range flight.[22]

Also that day, the President's Board of Consultants on Foreign Intelligence Activities, of which Land was a member and Killian the chairman, presented its semiannual review. Although the efforts to develop both a supersonic successor to the U-2 and reconnaissance satellites were under way, there seemed to be little prospect that either would be operational before mid-1959. The board urged development of an interim system.[23] On 28 October, Eisenhower demanded a report on the advanced aircraft and the spy satellites from Secretary McElroy and Central Intelligence Director Dulles.[24] With Killian and Land on both the President's Science Advisory Committee and the board of consultants on intelligence, they were virtually in control of the development of U.S. technical means for gathering intelligence, especially in the CIA and the National Security Agency, which monitored communications throughout the world. In an interview in 1983, Goodpaster said that Eisenhower "respected Killian's ability as a 'presiding officer' who could draw people together and get constructive solutions to problems."[25]

Even with the ear of the president, advisers like Land were sailing in choppy waters, as they had in 1954. Despite the emphasis on America's standing in space and the need to defend the adequacy of America's strategic response, the scientists lost no time in broadening their work on nuclear restraint. A major preoccupation that surfaced right after *Sputnik* was suspending nuclear tests. For this, the scientists were ready to engage in immediate combat, even in Eisenhower's presence, with Oppenheimer's nemesis, Lewis Strauss. Rabi wanted an immediate test ban, with provisions for inspection stations in America and the Soviet Union, to deprive the Russians of chances to match a secret American edge in nuclear weapons technology. Strauss rejoined that the Russians would simply steal "all our secrets," as with the atomic and hydrogen bombs, and called his own judgment more mature than Rabi's. The president's aide Cutler related Niels Bohr's view that the Russians had developed their weapons on their own "but had checked their line of development against the data they obtained from us." Eisenhower liked the idea of a nuclear test ban to "freeze" an American advantage. Looking back, however, he said that any delay in developing the hydrogen bomb, pending negotiations with Russia, which Rabi and Oppenheimer had suggested in 1949, "could have been fatal to us." Eisenhower learned of the deep antagonism between people like Rabi and fierce H-bomb proponents like Edward Teller. Eisenhower personally recorded some of the heated exchanges. In the calmly skeptical tone he maintained throughout, Eisenhower observed that "it will be very interesting to observe how soon the Russians are able to make the transition from the initial tests to a true operational capability."[26]

On 6 November, the day before his speech to the nation, Eisenhower tackled a more positive part of the agenda that Land and the other scientists had presented to him on 15 October: strengthening science education. He met with Marion Folsom, secretary of health, education, and welfare, and the assistant secretary, Elliot Richardson, and told them that he opposed a school construction program. In the present public mood, "something new" was needed. Echoing Rabi's and Land's remarks, he said, "Our greatest danger today is failure to educate scientists for the future."[27] Over the next two months, "something new" was defined as a proposal for twenty thousand scholarships a year for four years, federal matching grants for training mathematics and science teachers, money to equip science labs in schools, and money to increase foreign-language training. Such ideas soon were embodied in what was called the National Defense Education Act, the source of substantial additional emphasis on science in American schools in the years ahead.[28]

Land's interest in science education continued for many years. In the 1960s and later, he sponsored experiments in allowing students to pursue science topics by using a mixture of prerecorded materials without interacting with a teacher in the room. In 1968, he and his wife donated $12.5 million anonymously to Harvard to build the Science Center for undergraduates.[29]

Both he and Killian looked beyond science in schools and the training of scientists. In 1966, they collaborated on the Carnegie Corporation study that proposed federal support of noncommercial television. The study was a landmark in the history of Public Television in the United States. Like Killian, Land took pains to say that the recommendations did not denigrate commercial broadcasting. The networks had made and would make great contributions while striving for audiences of twenty million or more. Appealing to mass taste, however, prevented the networks from experimenting the way that public television could with "ways of bringing interest to all aspects of thought, of the ways that children think." In a mass-audience approach, "the kind of sparkle a child shows . . . doesn't come through." American society was changing so rapidly, Land argued in a

Senate hearing, that historic principles of behavior and morality were being lost because there was no language for translating these principles into current terms: "The search for the ways to tell young people what we know as we grow older—the permanent, wonderful things about life—will be one of the great functions of this noncommercial system. We are losing this generation. We all know that. We need a way to get them back."[30]

∞

In the months after *Sputnik*, the nonmilitary side of space continued to demand attention. Proposals for a civilian space agency were proliferating in a Congress controlled by Democrats. On 4 February 1958, Eisenhower announced that Killian was forming a special panel of PSAC to decide on programs and ways of managing them. Purcell of Harvard was chairman. The other members would be Land; Herbert York, the new Defense Director of Research and Engineering; and General James Doolittle, chairman of the agency called the National Advisory Committee on Aeronautics (NACA), which, in the event, would form the nucleus of the new space agency.[31]

The Purcell panel decided not to make a formal report, but instead to work with the *Fortune* magazine writer Francis Bello to write a pamphlet aimed at lay people and titled "An Introduction to Outer Space." Bello was already interested in Land's color vision research. Land, Purcell, and Bello worked on the document in Cambridge. Eisenhower was so pleased with it that he used it kick off a press conference announcing his plans for what was established that year as NASA. On 26 March, Eisenhower wrote in a foreword to the pamphlet, "This is not science fiction. This is a sober, realistic presentation prepared by leading scientists. I have found this statement so informative and interesting that I wish to share it with all the people of America and indeed with all the people of the earth."

The statement identified four major forces pushing America to send probes into space: the "compelling urge to explore," the need to make sure that "space is not used to endanger our security," the need to reinforce national prestige and confidence in American strength, and the opportunity to "add to our knowledge of and understanding of the earth, the solar system, and the universe."

Purcell, Land, and Bello described what keeps a satellite in orbit—where the satellite actually falls continually but so high up it never hits the surface. They explained how much rocket force is needed to send a rocket into orbit or for small scientific packages or craft carrying human pilots to achieve "escape velocity" to reach the moon. While foreseeing several militarily effective uses of space, they said that space was a poor place to store weapons for use in a crisis.

They turned to more credible opportunities. Much would be learned from instrument craft that would not need to come back to earth. Data from Mars, 50 to 100 million miles away, could be radioed back with less powerful transmitters than those of most commercial radio stations. "The cost of transporting men and material through space will be extremely high, but the cost and difficulty of sending information through space will be comparatively low." In the ensuing forty years, automated spacecraft would radio back pictures and much other information from the moon and the inner planets, Venus, Mars, and Mercury; the big outer planets, Jupiter, Saturn, Uranus, and Neptune, and many of their moons; and comets and asteroids—indeed from much of the solar system. As the astronomer Carl Sagan said, the people alive since 1960 were the first generation to see more than vague details of worlds other than our own.

There would be many types of scientific satellites. They could measure the domains of particles and fields in space, which flowed out from the sun and in from beyond the solar system. Satellites could carry an atomic clock in space that would test Einstein's general theory of relativity. They could study the heat flowing to Earth from the sun and the weather that the solar heat drives. They could look deep into space to study the waves—x-rays, ultraviolet, radio— emanated by the universe that are blocked by the earth's atmosphere. With satellites, scientists could detect more clearly the light waves in the visible spectrum that "are smeared by the same turbulence of the atmosphere that makes the stars twinkle."

The authors then turned to the moon: "What scientists would most like to learn from a close-up study of the moon is something of its origin and history. Was it originally molten? Does it now have a molten core, similar to the earth's? And just what is the nature of the lunar surface? The answer to these and many other questions should shed light, directly or indirectly, on the origin and history of the earth and the surrounding solar system."

In July 1969, when scientists opened the first box of rocks and soil brought back from the moon in the Lunar Receiving Laboratory at Houston, they found igneous, low-density rocks. It was the first direct proof that the moon, early in its history, had melted completely through and collected its heaviest materials deep in its interior.

Land, Purcell, and Bello acknowledged that many uses of space were both military and civilian. Satellites in orbit could "serve as high-flying radio relay stations" to send television signals or military messages between continents. Telescopic cameras in space, depending on their size and complexity, would perform much more detailed reconnaissance, radioing data down to Earth, than could a human eye looking down from two hundred miles in orbit. No mention was made of returning film from space.

As in the 1954 Killian study, the authors divided the future into slices. These were called Early, Later, Still Later, and Much Later Still. In the early phase, space-faring would include physics, the sciences of the earth, animals demonstrating the physiology of space, meteorology, experimental communications, and minimal contact with the moon. Later would come extensive communications, astronomy, biology, scientific investigation of the moon, minimal contact with planets, and human flight in orbit. Still later, automated craft would explore the moon and planets, and humans would explore the moon and return. In the distant future, humans would go to the planets. The opportunities in space, however, did "not diminish the importance of science on earth. . . . It would not be in the national interest to exploit space science at the cost of weakening our efforts in other scientific endeavors." The whole business was risky: Because rocketry and other space technology were being pushed to the limit, "failures of equipment and uncertainties of schedule are to be expected." This made it "wise to be cautious and modest in our predictions and pronouncements about future space activities—and quietly bold in our execution."

It was a charter and a prescient forecast. Killian was so proud of this product of PSAC that he reprinted it in his memoirs.[32] A decade later, in the late 1960s, Land, Purcell, and Purcell's son, Dennis, a photographer and software expert, collaborated in developing a tiny camera on a stick that *Apollo 11* astronaut Neil Armstrong used to take stereo close-ups of the strangely reflective lunar soil. Land had enough influence and persuasiveness to shoehorn this project into one of the most massive engineering endeavors in history.[33]

∞

In 1968, Land and other scientists received the National Medal of Science from President Lyndon Johnson in the East Room of the White House. Afterward, Vice President Hubert Humphrey was the host of a luncheon at the State Department. Attending the luncheon were not only the winners but also the heads of the leading federal science agencies and members of the science press. Land was chosen to give the winners' thanks. He told the audience that the only thing the nation could not afford was undue frugality

Figure 12. Meroë Morse, 1944 graduate of Smith College, joins Land's laboratory for twenty-five years' work on black-and-white films.

Figure 13. Succeeding by failing. Fading of early black-and-white pictures forces crash redesign of the film. Curling is a constant challenge.

Figure 14. 26 December 1955. Black-and-white research leader Morse grabs a smoke while holding a camera and test film.

Figure 15. 26 December 1955. Morse also serves as counselor and diplomat.

Figure 16. Mid-1950s. Test photo captures Land, in loafers, on a sunny porch. Relaxing or working?

Figure 17. For Polaroid 1956 annual report, top officers pose. From left: J. Harold Booth, William J. McCune, Robert C. Casselman, Land, David W. Skinner, Julius Silver, Carlton P. Fuller, Donald L. Brown.

Figure 18. 1957 or 1958. President's Science Advisory Committee. Land at upper left, between Detlev Bronk and I. I. Rabi. Sixth from left at rear, James R. Killian. Rear, third from right, Jerome B. Wiesner. Foreground, left, Edward M. Purcell. At front, Hans Bethe.

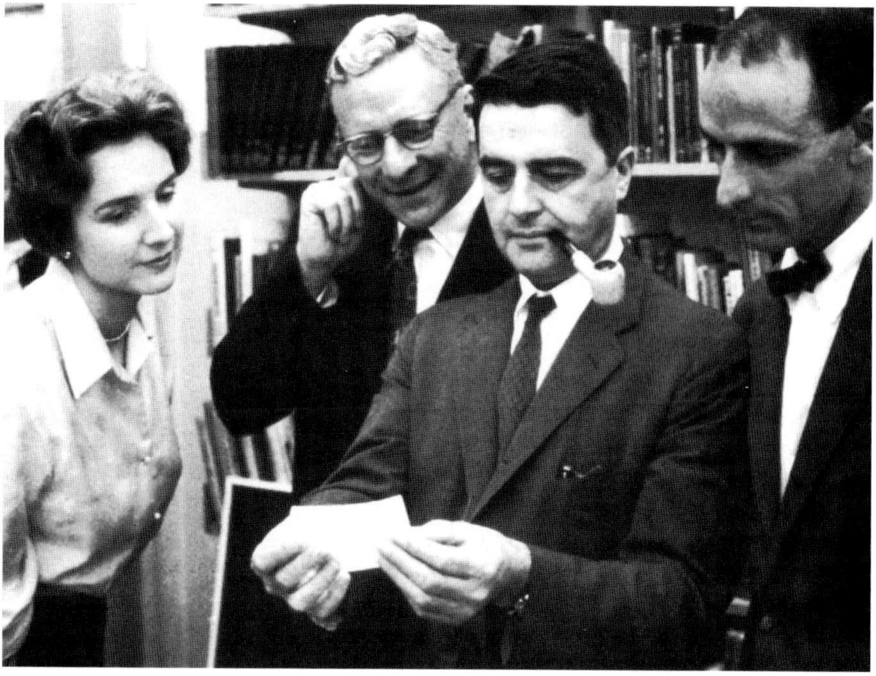

Figure 19. Studying a test print. From left, Morse, Skinner, Land, McCune.

Figure 20. 13 February 1968. For secret and non-secret work, Land receives National Medal of Science from President Lyndon Johnson in White House.

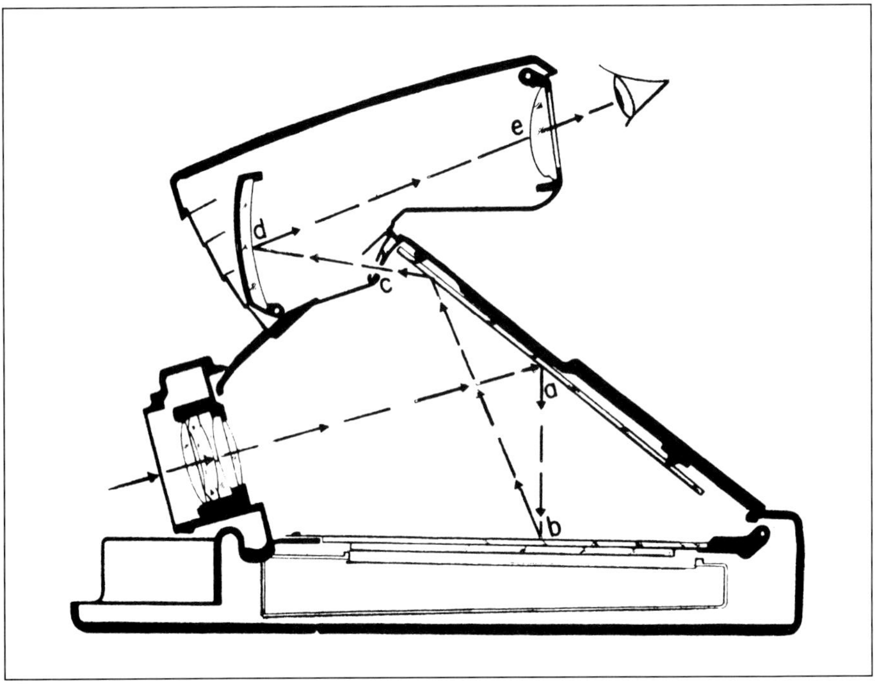

Figure 21. Light path of SX-70. For viewing, no heavy pentaprism but a succession of lenses and mirrors to the eyepiece, with film hidden at bottom.

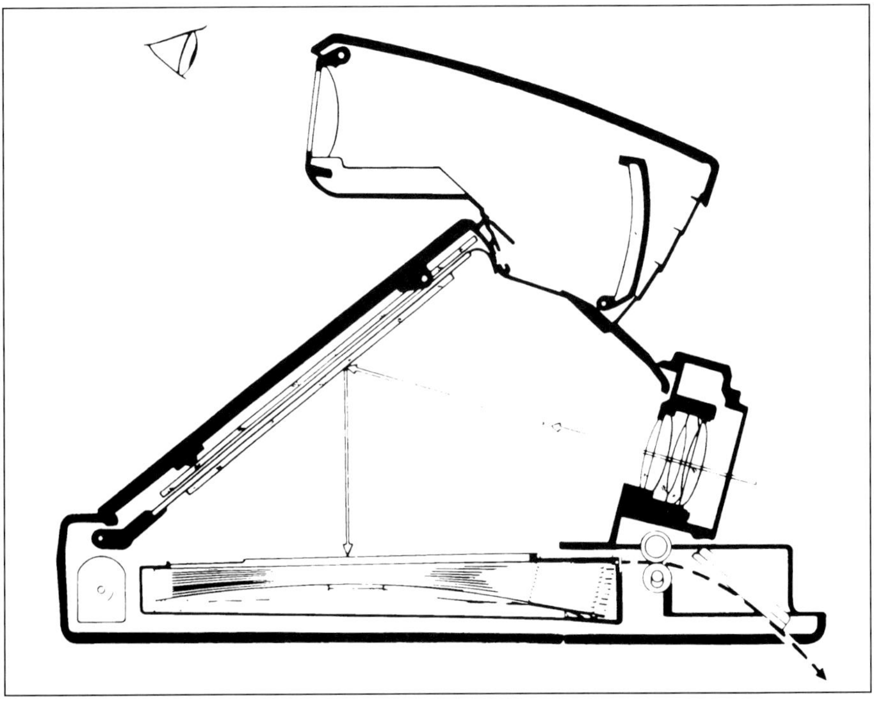

Figure 22. For taking photographs, light from SX-70 lens bounces off a mirror and down to topmost of ten film units in cassette.

Figure 23. Autumn 1972. For *Life* cover, Land photographs children at playground with SX-70 camera, his greatest project. Co Rentmeester, *Life* Magazine, © Times, Inc.

Figure 24. 26 April 1977. Standing next to Polavision player, Land holds up Polavision camera for the press. At right, McCune, promoted to Polaroid president, 1975.

Figure 25. 6 February 1977. Land is inducted into National Inventors Hall of Fame.

in investing in education. Science, he said, was where people could work separately and yet add to each other's work. It was the one place where people could be greater than they thought they could be. He was grateful for the "well done" from the nation, although he had to acknowledge that no government could have prevented any of the winners from working on the structure of nature. "All of us are highly emotional. The emotion is curiosity."[34]

17
Spy Satellites

> Occasionally, our panel meetings would run until midnight, and even then we would look forward to spending 30 minutes after the meeting with Din in his lab, looking at his "Mondrian" or other striking aspects of his current research. I recall that one session ended at daybreak, but that was unusual, even for Din Land.
>
> —Richard L. Garwin, 9 November 1991

One reason that the United States fell behind the Russians in launching a civilian science satellite was President Eisenhower's insistence on the highest priority for military rocket programs, which Killian's committee had endorsed in 1954. The rockets were intended not just for retaliation against an attack but also for putting spy satellites in orbit. For Eisenhower, strategic surveillance was the principal justification for the fabulous expense of going into space. The civilian Vanguard project for the International Geophysical Year would be separate, and public. Military missiles were not to be slowed. Although military components would not be used in Vanguard, the science project did have its indirect military uses. It might distract attention from the highly secret spy satellites. Furthermore, America's first peaceful venture into space not only would be nonthreatening but would establish that space was a domain beyond national boundaries. Spy satellites, when they were ready, thus would be less provocative than spy planes flying just a dozen miles up in the atmosphere. Since U-2 flights began in July 1956, the Soviet Union tracked the flights closely and tried to shoot the planes down. Now, it appeared, the Soviet

Union had done the worried American officials the enormous favor of resolving, at a stroke, the issue of sovereignty over space. There was none.[1]

On 8 October 1957, Eisenhower agreed to consider using an Army rocket as a backup launcher for peaceful space flights, but he made it clear that there would be no abrupt change in course. The last thing he wanted was to reinforce the public perception of a space race with Russia.[2] At a press conference the next day, he said that the United States would not interfere with the top priority of its military missile programs, on which it was spending five billion dollars a year: "Now that isn't any weak, pusillanimous effort; that is a lot of money." As for nonmilitary programs, the nation would stick to its schedule. They had "never been conducted as a race with other nations." While congratulating the Russians on their achievement, he asserted, "The value of that satellite is still problematical." In his view, it would be a long time before satellites could be used for reconnaissance of the earth.[3] Saying that, the president revealed his own emphatic focus on spy satellites as the central reason for going into space.

The Russians had "gained a great psychological advantage throughout the world," but that was no reason "for just trying to grow hysterical about it." Did *Sputnik* affect America's security? he was asked. He replied, "So far as the satellite itself is concerned, that does not raise my apprehensions one iota." Admittedly, *Sputnik* proved that the Russians could send warheads thousands of miles, but it did not prove that those warheads could survive the intense heating of re-entry into the atmosphere.[4] That comment revealed another deep preoccupation of American missile developers. Only recently had test flights with the Army's Jupiter rocket shown that a nose cone that shed part of a plastic skin, in the so-called ablative process, could reenter the atmosphere with its warhead intact. In a televised speech on 7 November, Eisenhower displayed a nose cone recovered from a Jupiter test.[5]

Air Force thinking about reconnaissance from satellites, to be launched by the intercontinental missiles of the future, began in earnest in 1951. At a conference that he organized, Colonel Bernard A. Schriever, later a full general and leader of Air Force missile development, set forth the specifications of a successful spy satellite. It must get daytime views of the whole Soviet Union in a matter of weeks, capturing images good enough to identify harbors, airfields, oil storage dumps, and large residential and industrial areas. Two weeks later, Schriever's idea was tested by scanning a standard photographic mosaic of the Los Angeles area with a television camera and then relaying the image through a television transmitter on nearby Mount Wilson and back to a studio where the mosaic was photographed from the screen. Air Force photo interpreters thought that if the satellite produced images this good, the minimum requirements would be met.[6]

The next month, the Air Force's RAND Corporation issued two more studies: satellites would be useful for both reconnaissance and weather observations. The reconnaissance report rejected the idea of bringing the film back from space, which turned out to be the winning concept for the 1960s. It also rejected scanning photographic images on board for relay back to earth, another technique that was tried although it proved disappointing. The equipment would weigh too much, the study held. The third alternative, television pictures from space, was preferred. Amrom Katz at Wright-Patterson in Dayton and the Boston University group were both skeptical about spy satellites. But late in 1951, tests from thirty thousand feet above Dayton produced images on which one could pick out key streets and bridges. Thereafter, Katz, who later moved to RAND, was a believer.[7]

The studies by Projects Charles and Beacon Hill and by James Baker's special committee all focused forward on spy satellites. The pressure increased after the Killian Technological Capabilities Panel report, which contained Land's call for all-out efforts at overhead reconnaissance of Russia. This report led to Eisenhower's appointment of the intelligence supervision committee headed by Killian and including Land. The Defense Department reponse became more vigorous: a secret spy satellite project, called WS-117L, began in March 1955. Rather slowly, the project was developing photoreconnaissance and detection of the infrared heat rays given off by Soviet rocket launches.[8]

After *Sputnik*, word about spy satellites began to trickle out. Probably through leaks by the Air Force, publicity was given to the Air Force's favorite plan, transmitting satellite pictures to the ground by radio. News reports speculated about satellites carrying television, photographic cameras, and infrared or radar sensors. By August 1957, the Air Force had chosen the method of taking pictures in space, scanning them into electronic form, and radioing them to Earth, using equipment from Kodak, CBS Laboratories, and Philco. An RCA scheme to use television cameras was dropped because it would produce far less detail of features on the ground, and the Army took over the RCA scheme as a possible means of surveying battlefields. This use of television eventually became the civilian effort called Tiros, in which satellites went up to photograph cloud movements from space.[9]

Perfecting spy satellites would take time. Could the researchers design a way station between the subsonic U-2 and satellites? Attention focused on supersonic spy planes. Around this time, Land became head of a small committee to pull together and review designs for the 2,000-mile-an-hour aircraft, the Blackbird or A-12, which not only was to fly much faster and higher, but was to be less radar-detectable than the U-2. Lockheed and the Convair division of General Dynamics were recruited to start designing the plane. Richard Bissell of the CIA knew that the project would cost many times as much as the thirty million dollars spent on the first U-2s and would need very credible review to attract the necessary funds. Accordingly, Land and two aerodynamics experts met on six occasions between the fall of 1957 and 1959, usually in Land's office in Cambridge, to oversee the design of the Blackbird and its systems. Attending the sessions were designers from Lockheed and Convair, the assistant secretaries of the Air Force and Navy, and one or two of their technical advisers. The result was to cut down sharply on red tape and feuds, although the planes actually did not fly until after spy satellites proved themselves.[10]

On 23 October 1957, Eisenhower told Bissell to hold off on U-2 flights in the "tense international circumstances." By the moratorium and through continued secrecy, he intended to preserve the U-2's value as long as possible. It had already bolstered confidence that the Soviet Union was neither contemplating a surprise attack nor engaging in crash development of ICBMs. Given the public outcry, it was tempting to tell the public about the U-2. On 7 November, Secretary of State Dulles suggested that the president reveal that "the United States has the capability of photographing the Soviet Union from a very high altitude without interference." It might calm the American public, Eisenhower acknowledged, but why blow the program's cover after only sixteen months and annoy the Russians in the bargain?[11] He was renouncing a crushing answer to his critics, while keeping open the path to future reconnaissance that would help him hold down the arms race.

∞

On the very afternoon of the scientists' 15 October meeting with Eisenhower, efforts began to strengthen science in the Defense Department. These led to appointment of a Defense Director of Research and Engineering, Herbert York, and creation of the Advanced Research Projects Agency, which still existed in the 1990s. In the conversation ordered by the president, the scientists delivered the message of change to an uneasy Secretary Neil McElroy and Deputy Secretary Donald Quarles. Eisenhower's military aide Goodpaster went along to the Pentagon and kept notes while another aide, Robert Cutler, spelled out the points from the morning meeting with the president. Soon, Killian got to the main point, that military science must change fast: "Now we have a wonderful chance to change the trend." The Scientific Advisory Committee, soon to become the PSAC, "has been troubled about frustrations" in the Defense Department for basic research and research and development.

McElroy cited the high scientific qualifications of his deputy, Quarles. Rabi insisted that it had been hard after World War II to convince the Defense Department of the need for science and research. "DoD is the great scientific consumer. Above all, DoD needs more basic research." The Defense Department had "been wrong" to tie research to specific military missions, narrowing things down too much. It should spend more on basic research than the two hundred million dollars in the previous year.

Land chimed in, "We should be sure the good contributors are supported, continuously. This is a minuscule amount to the total." Rabi said that the military needed contact with scientists and refreshment from them. At this point in the scientists' tirade, Quarles spoke up: Would Congress appropriate the money? He answered his own question: "Not yet, unless Sputnik has converted our people. We must not get apart from the realities." McElroy, more conciliatory than Quarles, said that the climate in the Defense Department was now responsive to change. The CIA science director, Herbert Scoville, remarked that unless America reversed the present trends, the Russians "will, in a few years, have a capability to knock us out."[12]

∞

Studies on spy satellites continued. Little more than a month after *Sputnik*, on 12 November, RAND Corporation sent the Air Force more favorable discussions of bringing back film from space. It would work and could be ready sooner than originally thought. Following up a preliminary study the year before, Merton Davis and Amrom Katz of RAND wrote of "a family of recoverable satellites" that would be launched on a Thor first stage and a Vanguard second stage. Retro-rockets on the satellite would bring down a film capsule from orbit, using a nose cone covered with the newly perfected coating to get through the heat of reentry, and parachutes for an ocean landing. A second report, "An Earlier Reconnaissance Satellite System," argued that the capsule-return idea would give the United States efficient systems earlier than the favored radio-relay idea. Thorny issues of capsule return were also on Land's mind. Jerome Wiesner recalled that one day, Schriever, on a trip back east, came to see him at MIT about the problem. Wiesner telephoned Land and asked if they could come over to Land's laboratory. He assented at once, and a conversation of several hours followed. Land concentrated, as Wiesner remembered, "and by the end of the afternoon, we had a recoverable satellite!"[13]

The three-hundred-pound satellite for film recovery would be stabilized by spinning around its axis. A camera with a focal length of 12 inches would scan about three hundred miles across the line of flight, covering about eighteen thousand square miles in each frame, and distinguishing features on the ground larger than sixty feet across. On a succession of sixteen orbits around the earth in twenty-four hours, the camera would expose a total of five hundred feet of five-inch-wide film, covering four million square miles of the Soviet Union, or half its area. The system could be ready in a year. A later system, also using a Thor launcher, could use cameras carrying much more film with a 36-inch focal length camera and could distinguish features twenty feet across. An ICBM could put up a camera with still more film and a camera with 120 inches of focal length.[14] It was an optimistic picture —too optimistic.

On 25 November 1957, the day that Eisenhower suffered a mild stoke, the Pentagon quadrupled the budget for its WS-117L spy satellite program to $48 million. Then the budget tripled again. By early January 1958, it was arranged that $150 million would be available in the fiscal year starting the following 1 July. To test the recoverable-capsule idea, an Agena second stage would be stacked on top of a Thor, instead of waiting for an Atlas rocket that would allow a larger payload.[15] Again, the better would not be allowed to delay the good. Two top Air Force generals, Chief of Staff Thomas D. White and Bernard Schriever, now head of missile development, told a Senate subcommittee that the work on satellite reconnaissance had leaped forward since *Sputnik*. White talked of television "and other means" to get the pictures down to Earth. Schriever said that work toward recoverable capsules of film could lead to Thor-borne packages going into orbit by the summer of 1958, and a working picture-recovery satellite system by the spring of 1959. The actual date proved to be August 1960.

A third Air Force general, Lieutenant General Clarence Irvine, chief of materiel, sounded a note of great significance for the future. He acknowledged, in answer to a question, that the Russians, too, would build spy satellites, and then each side would know what the other was doing. "I think this would be very helpful. This is the first step toward peace."[16]

∞

On 22 January, with U-2s still flying and their supersonic successors under development, the National Security Council approved Action

Memorandum 1846, giving operational reconnaissance satellites the highest technical intelligence priority.[17] But how could the drive for spy satellites go as fast as possible? There was a precedent: the highly streamlined and ultrasecret U-2 project, run by the CIA. Richard Bissell recalled in his memoirs, published posthumously, how the WS-117L fell into place: "In early 1958, President Eisenhower, prompted by Edwin Land and other members of the Intelligence Panel of the Killian committee, decided that the satellite part of the WS-117L project should be turned over to the CIA–air force operation responsible for managing the U-2. Eisenhower's decision was as unexpected to me as the U-2 decision had been in November 1954. I became head of the joint project, which was also working on the A-12 [supersonic successor to the U-2]. It operated under very tight security."[18]

This maneuver was accomplished by a very public "cancellation" of the recoverable-satellite photoreconnaissance project on 7 February 1958, the date that the new defense science organization, the Advanced Research Projects Agency (ARPA), was created. The project was restarted immediately, under cover, with Bissell in charge and Land's small PSAC intelligence panel keeping an eye on it. Serving with Land for many years on the intelligence panel was his admired friend from Harvard, Edward Purcell. Many years later Purcell recalled that as early as the 1954 Killian surprise attack study, Land "knew more secrets than the rest of us did." Land was "very effective, not merely on the intelligence panel . . . not so much for his technical advice but for his ability to convey in a personal way the relative importance of the things we were talking about. And his boldness, which, of course, was part of his business career: talking about what you really could do if you wanted to. 'Why don't you try that instead of horsing around?' He was very important because, in the first place, he communicated very well with Eisenhower."

Also important, Purcell said, was Land's relationship with Henry Yutzy, Kodak's leading man on high-resolution emulsions. Yutzy was crucial in the struggle to balance the light sensitivity of the emulsion of the film with the resolution of features on the ground, a struggle that continued throughout the U-2 and satellite projects. "He was a very good friend of Din. They were mutual admirers." So whenever questions came up about how to improve the film overall, Land would call up Yutzy. The issues boiled down, Purcell said, to how many binary digits, or "bits" of picture information, could be recorded on a pound of film.

Land's method of working was not formal at all, Purcell recalled. The panel usually talked about technical problems in Land's office at Osborn Street. "It was really conversation. He knew how to communicate, you know."[19]

Bissell recalled that he first heard of *Corona* and his own intended role in running it "in an odd and informal way" from Land. They were already working together on the successor to the U-2, which was nicknamed Oxcart (presumably because of a speed the exact opposite of the plane's). Bissell was called into Allen Dulles's office and, in Land's presence, found that *Corona* had been added to his other assignments. Bissell's instructions were vague: *Corona* was to be split off from WS-117L and be managed like the U-2 and without funds from the Air Force. Many contractors and people were upset when they were suddenly cut off from the project. Only a few who had been working on recoverable capsules were cleared to be briefed on the new project. Bissell expected that the Air Force would contribute the Thor rockets already reserved for *Corona*, but he was wrong. The CIA had to ask for extra funds to buy its own Thors. The project was not announced publicly until the following December, when rocket launchings were about to be started and could not be concealed completely from the press. The cover story was that the launchings were for a scientific program called Discoverer.[20]

The first technical problem that Bissell and his deputy, Major General O. J. Ritland of the Air Force, confronted was whether to keep on with the concept of spin-stabilizing the *Corona* satellites. They had doubts about this idea whereby small rockets would spin the satellite up like a rifle bullet, with the camera lenses pointing through windows in the side of the satellite capsule. The images would be laid down on the film transversely, as Bissell recalled, so as to produce "a series of photographs covering the full extent of the camera's coverage on the ground." In the Davies-Katz RAND Corporation concept, a photoelectric cell operating as a light meter would point out in the same direction as the camera, measuring changing light levels as the horizon appeared beneath the blackness of space and disappeared. When terrain came into view, the photocell would send a pulse of electricity to a clutch that would start the camera motor turning briefly, and when the terrain vanished again, a second signal from the photocell would stop the camera. The satellite would take a series of panoramic scans of the earth below. Lockheed had started building such a craft, but it was never finished.

Many years later, Bissell described an alternative to this photocell idea: "The alternative to this system was to stabilize the capsule with jets and to use a camera that would move with the capsule, taking pictures in a way very similar to the procedure used with the cameras in the U-2 and other reconnaissance aircraft. Eventually we decided that the latter was the way to go, and we replaced Fairchild's spin-stabilized system with a much more convenient camera from Itek."

Ritland and Bissell had become convinced that they would get better pictures from a satellite stabilized in all the three axes of pitch, roll, and yaw by internal flywheels spinning like gyroscopes. The satellite would be kept stationary with respect to the horizon. A benefit of the spin-stabilized craft was that it could use cameras of the sort that Land's colleague Baker had worked on. Baker's cameras had been proven over the years, not only in the U-2 but in the earlier abortive program to send camera-equipped balloons across the Soviet Union.[21] As in the U-2 program, which also had been taken over from the Air Force, the concepts favored originally by the Air Force were set aside.

∞

On 4 February 1958, Killian, George Kistiakowsky, and Herbert York spelled out for Eisenhower the scientists' views of the competing missile projects. The Air Force's Thor was ahead of the Army's Jupiter and had been tested more thoroughly. One could question having two intermediate-range missiles. Solid-fuel rockets such as the Navy's Polaris would not be ready for several years. Titan, with liquid fuels that could be stored on board for long periods, looked like the best booster for space missions. Purchases of Atlas rockets, whose liquid fuel took hours to load, should be stopped after eighty missiles.[22] A little over a month later, on 10 March, Killian and Kistiakowsky met Eisenhower again to urge him to back a "well-conceived basic research effort for the development of solid propellants" and improvements in Titan and to review the proposals for second-generation missiles.[23] That evening, Land attended a dinner that the Eisenhowers gave at the White House for military and scientific officials.[24]

At the beginning of 1959, George Kistiakowsky succeeded Killian as presidential science adviser. Kistiakowsky's view of Land as a national science policy adviser was not always sunny. On the evening of Friday, 30 October 1959, for instance, Kistiakowsky met Land and the chairmen of other PSAC panels. The meeting started "rather badly," according to Kistiakowsky, with a "considerable waste of time." The villain was Din Land, who "launched into a long discourse as to the need for general improvement in the way government does R & D, which has very little connection with our immediate problem." Evidently Land was not the only loquacious panel chairman. In a discussion of strategic weapons and other topics, Kistiakowsky recorded acidly, it was so difficult to stick to the subject that he demanded more self-restraint for the next day's nine-to-five meeting.[25]

Test launches of the *Corona* system began, little more than a year after the project was started, with maximum urgency and secrecy. For more than a year, the launches went very badly. Flight after flight failed, and often the causes of the failures were hard to decipher. There were problems with the rockets, the cameras, and the capsules designed to return the cameras' precious film to the Pacific flotilla of "Flying Boxcar" recovery planes. After each failure, several "fixes" were tried, often with the sometimes-justified fear that the improvements would introduce new causes of failure.[26]

The project called for intense collaboration among many contractors. Lockheed Missiles and Space Division, for example, built the orbiting craft and its Agena rocket. Douglas Aircraft modified its Thor missiles for carrying the *Corona* satellites aloft from California into polar orbit. General Electric built the return capsule with its gold shield against radiation that would spoil the film, and its heat-shedding nose cone. Kodak provided both the film and its later processing, and Itek built the cameras.[27]

By the weekend before Thanksgiving 1959, the project was going so badly that the Itek project manager, Walter Levison, drove to Land's weekend home in Peterborough, New Hampshire, to confess failure. For Levison, it was the blackest moment of his life. He told Land, the head of the small outside committee superintending Corona, that he should carry word of Corona's failure to President Eisenhower. The project would have to "stand down." Levison felt frustrated and humiliated. Land, however, took another tack, calling for redoubled effort over three months to rescue the project.

When Levison was interviewed in 1996, he recalled working around the clock, often sleeping overnight at the Itek workshop in Needham, Massachusetts, which had once been a milk-processing plant. Levison and his chief engineer, Frank Madden, could not tell their families why they had to be absent so many nights and weekends. Nor could they tell their suppliers, who received extremely exacting demands, what the materials were for. They and their co-workers had made a camera that could withstand the rough forces of the launch. Thanks to the spacecraft's controls, the camera could aim steadily at the Soviet Union every ninety minutes as the craft whizzed southward from the North Pole. To get the best possible detail, the camera's two-foot-long lens casing, cast in aluminum, was machined to achieve tolerances of one-thousandth of an inch.

Despite the success with the camera, unpleasant things happened to the film. After a few minutes in the deep cold of space, the innovative acetate film from Kodak grew brittle and cracked, like autumn leaves. After the film had been exposed to a scene below by the Corona's scanning panoramic camera, it became very cold as it traveled to a take-up roll in the recovery capsule. To smooth the film's movements and cut down on the chance of cracks, the Itek crew devised a new gear system. But since the film was still acetate, it still cracked. Eastman had to learn how to coat its emulsion on polyester instead of acetate. There were electrical problems, so-called coronal discharges, that streaked the film. The Itek crew traced the problem to opposite electrical charges on the film and rubber rollers. Struggling for a solution, they added carbon to the rubber to make the rollers slightly conductive, and they used rabbit fur to rub off some of the charge on the film. When that failed, they tried boiling the rollers.

While the Itek engineers picked apart and rebuilt most of their system, the other *Corona* contractors did likewise.[28] Success, however, was still nine desperate months away.

∞

While *Corona* continued to lurch, Kistiakowsky and others became convinced that the long-term arrangements for defining both the missions and the design of American spy satellites must be clarified. The Air Force bitterly resented the CIA's leadership of the *Corona* project and kept trying to grab the steering wheel, as the Strategic Air Command had done with the U-2 project. Meanwhile, the Air Force's own continuing effort to develop spy satellites that radioed pictures from space was not going well.

The project was called Samos after the Greek island of that name. Like the *Corona* project, the Samos program drew heavily on Kodak's technology and expertise. Each program used a very strong polyester film base, which Kodak called Estar. In *Corona*, the film was designed to be brought back to Earth and developed there for analysis. In Samos, the film was to be processed into a readable image on board the satellite, then scanned electronically into binary digits for radio transmission to the ground. In each case, a major concern was to have the precious film show the maximum of detail, especially when the frames were enlarged, "blown up."

In the Samos program, since the film was needed only briefly before scanning, a special system could be used. Kodak called it Bi-Mat. It involved seventy-millimeter rolls of negative, coated on Estar, and corresponding rolls of a second sheet of film that would act like a positive when brought briefly into contact with the negative. Resistance to breaking was not the only reason to use Estar, Land explained in 1981. "You want great precision of dimensions in reconnaissance because the tiny images are going to be magnified enormously and measured." As had happened in Land's sepia process of the 1940s, the second sheet pulled the undeveloped silver halide away from the negative. But in the Bi-Mat process, the purpose, the technique, and the steps were all different. The sheet of interest was the negative, not the positive. As Land testified in 1981 at the Polaroid–Kodak patent trial, "the detail of the terrain below can be better seen in the negative than in the positive." This was because the negative was "primitive"; it had undergone one less step of processing and thus inherently retained more information. The image nevertheless had to be made with "just the right amount of silver to give a beautiful negative when it was peeled off . . . in as short a time as a minute, and then it could be used for electronic retransmission back to the bases."

The method also had its uses for military reconnaissance on the earth. People conducting military reconnaissance wanted both the negative and the positive, at least for a week or ten days. The positive was more delicate and, once peeled off, needed a second sheet as a protector. In the course of his defense work, Land heard about Bi-Mat and appreciated its apparent similarity to his own sepia system. In the 1981 patent trial, he testified about his reaction to Bi-Mat: "I took care not to learn more. And I did not learn more. . . . As soon as I learned of this particular activity, I turned my attention away from it at once." To be a defense adviser, Land explained, "it was important to go to extremes in avoiding any real conflict of interest or implied conflict of interest."[29]

∞

To the scientists, alternatives to the capsule-return scheme looked increasingly dubious. On 5 February 1960, the day after the ninth *Corona* failure, Kistiakowsky told Eisenhower's assistant for national security, Gordon Gray, that the Samos system for instantaneous electronic film readout would not be effective for many years; the best hope still was *Corona*.[30]

The battle for photoreconnaissance continued on many fronts. Also on 5 February, at a meeting of the National Security Council, Kistiakowsky fought a proposal by Joseph Charyk, assistant secretary of the Air Force, for a system for shooting down satellites. He opposed any demonstration of such a system, saying it could "prejudice the use of our reconnaissance satellites." Eisenhower agreed, Kistiakowsky recorded in his diary, but "rather unemphatically . . . [I]t didn't sound like a directive."[31]

In the winter and spring of 1960, military publicity offensives pressed for large additional appropriations for the heat-sensing Midas and the radiophoto Samos satellites. On 19 February, the day after a *Wall Street Journal* article on Midas, *Corona's* tenth launch failed. Seven days after that, the first Midas failed to reach orbit.[32]

Early in April, amid further publicity about Midas and how it would cooperate with the three huge radars of the Ballistic Missile Early Warning System, a U-2 flight found evidence of Russian missile deployment at a northerly site called Plesetsk. Another flight was scheduled for about a month later to check this out. This turned out to be Gary Powers's disastrous flight, which Soviet missiles from the ground cut short at Sverdlovsk, well short of Plesetsk.[33]

On 12 April, Kistiakowsky heard from Bruce Billings, deputy for intelligence to Herbert York, the science chief at the Defense Department, about a plethora of scientific and engineering proposals springing up, creating "proliferation and near chaos." It was hard to shoot down expensive proposals for new systems that would achieve little. Kistiakowsky invited Billings to tell his story to PSAC in May.[34] On 15 April, the eleventh Corona flight put a camera-carrying satellite in orbit and its capsule was ejected for reentry as planned. Unfortunately, the capsule could not be detected as it came down.[35] In an interview twenty-four years later, Richard Bissell recalled the sequence of failures as "a most heartbreaking business." Failure analysis, with spotty data and no testimony from test pilots, was largely a matter of inference.[36]

After Powers was shot down, even before Powers went on trial as a spy before the Soviets, Eisenhower suspended U-2 flights over Russia. Spy satellites were, if possible, even more urgent than before. They needed to work and very soon. Intelligence in general must be improved. On 6 May, Eisenhower's intelligence advisers met with officials such as CIA chief Dulles, Defense Secretary Thomas Gates, and Budget Director Maurice Stans. They agreed to scrutinize U.S. intelligence efforts, in a massive review that lasted until the end of the year. Both Stans and Gates had urged the review, which was headed by CIA Inspector General Lyman D. Kirkpatrick.[37]

Rumors and anxiety about spy satellites spread through the government. On 23 May, Dulles, having heard about the PSAC briefing on military intelligence chaos, called to probe Kistiakowsky's intentions. Reluctant to tip his hand, Kistiakowsky riposted with the idea of a luncheon that would include Defense Secretary Gates "and vaguely suggested a high-powered technical committee . . . to look into the developmental projects, because they are not moving ahead as well as they should."[38] Dulles was clearly worried about his own lack of legal authority over setting military requirements for collecting intelligence.

Three days later, Kistiakowsky started to brief the president and his assistants Gray and Goodpaster on the unsatisfactory progress of Corona and Samos. Eisenhower cut him short. He decided "in the firmest possible terms that a corrective action was necessary." An ad hoc group should look into such issues as "military requirements," which often were so demanding that they delayed projects seriously. The panel should be directly under Kistiakowsky, who would work with Charyk of the Air Force and John H. Rubel, deputy research director in the Defense Department, and not under Defense Secretary Gates. The president instructed Goodpaster, "Tell the Defense Department that I won't approve any money for the projects until I have the information." He was exasperated with the continued feuding over reconnaissance from space. After some dickering with Goodpaster, who didn't like the job's being given to the scientists, a formal directive for the study went to Gates on 10 June. In practice, however, the review was conducted, under Kistiakowsky's supervision, by Killian and Land. They quickly found that the problem was not hardware but management.[39]

Kistiakowsky summarized the situation:

> [T]he recovery of photographic film retrojected from the satellite was suffering from mysterious failures in orbit and from losses of the photographic packages over the Pacific . . . The more advanced Samos project actually was a large collection of efforts, each responding to some particular military requirements, over which no effective controls had been exercised so that some plans were totally unrealistic. The multiple layers of military hierarchy involved caused delays by sudden changes in specifications and other difficulties. It was the situation that our panel was trying to change; the Air Force, aware of our intentions, was coming up with its own plans to clean up some aspects of the situation. Our efforts coalesced, and we could recommend a clear administrative arrangement, bypassing various military echelons and enabling the individual in charge of development projects to report directly to the new National Reconnaissance Office within the Office of the Secretary of the Air Force. The cleanup of the technical proliferation was somewhat less complete.[40]

Land and Killian were moving swiftly to conclusions that many in the military were sure to dislike. Yet, the recommendations would not work without sustained military cooperation. Amid the flood of rumors and discontent, the drafting had to be careful and the rehearsals frequent. On 1 August, Kistiakowsky attended a morning meeting in Killian's office at MIT and came away thinking that "the group is moving ahead well and is coming up with a good recommendation, but the report they are preparing has to be tightened."[41] On the next two days, he received telephone calls reflecting a rumor that control of Samos was going to be given to the CIA. Kistiakowsky denied this, saying that the focus would be on an authoritative organization "of a national character."[42]

After more than a year of heartbreaking failures, Corona was approaching success. The thirteenth flight, without a camera, resulted in successful recovery of the satellite in the Pacific Ocean on 11 August 1960. Just a week later, the fourteenth flight carried a camera into orbit for twenty-four hours. It began the tradition of photographing an air base in the northeast corner of Siberia called Mys-Schmidta, only four hundred miles west of Nome, Alaska, and took pictures of the rocket base at Plesetsk and its associated new rail lines that Gary Powers never reached. The Corona film capsule returned from space on 19 August and was recovered by a Flying Boxcar airplane over the Pacific.[43]

The twenty-pound roll of film, containing three thousand feet of pictures, went swiftly back to Kodak to be developed and then to Washington for the photointerpreters to study. They assembled in the auditorium of the Photographic Interpretation Center, as they had after the U-2 flights. A curtain covered the map of the Soviet Union that had been used to display the squiggles representing the track after each U-2 flight. The center's director, Arthur Lundahl, announced that there was "something new and great we've got here." His deputy opened the curtain. The map showed six or seven stripes coming down from the North Pole across the Soviet Union, representing the more than one million square miles covered by the fourteenth flight of Corona. Cheering, the photointerpreters could look forward to poring over the pictures immediately.[44]

The memorandum on the future organization of spy satellite development was almost ready for presentation to President Eisenhower and the National Security Council. On 22 August, Kistiakowsky met Land, Charyk of the Air Force, and several others, including Carl Overhage, the former Kodak official who now directed MIT's Lincoln Laboratory, and Bissell. Kistiakowsky thought the presentation was "in good shape."[45]

The previous Thursday, the day that the fourteenth Corona went into orbit, Kistiakowsky had not been so satisfied. On "vacation" in Cambridge, he attended an all-day meeting in Land's office. He recalled in his diary that "the whole briefing paper was still in such a lousy shape that I spoke rather harshly." Land, Overhage, and Kistiakowsky's assistant Hi Watters worked all weekend to improve the paper and take it to Washington.[46] It contained the design of what became, on 25 August, the National Reconnaissance Office, with Charyk of the Air Force as its first director.

On Wednesday, 24 August, Kistiakowsky went to Charyk's office in the Pentagon for a rehearsal. He found that Killian wanted to introduce the presentation, although that would normally be the role of Kistiakowsky, Killian's successor as science adviser. "I realized," Kistiakowsky wrote, "that there was some tension between [Killian] and Land as to who was to make the presentation and decided to be gracious and not lay any claims of my own." They then went to the office of the secretary of defense, where they met Gates and his deputy, James Douglas, for another rehearsal. Gates said that the proposed management of spy satellites should be as simple as possible, without review boards. Kistiakowsky disagreed: "I am not very happy about that, but at least we are getting our point that there should be little interference from various military echelons."[47]

At 8:15 the following day, Kistiakowsky, Killian, and Land joined Allen Dulles and National Security Assistant Gray to show Eisenhower the pictures from Corona's first flight and to mention certain spy satellite projects that would be omitted from the briefing of the whole National Security Council. The meeting began with Land's unreeling a duplicate spool of Corona pictures across the carpet of the Oval Office. Land's comment was, "Here's your pictures, Mr. President."[48]

Less than four months after the loss of the U-2, overhead intelligence of the Soviet Union was back in business. Corona flights, to the number of 145, continued until 1972.[49]

∞

At 8:30 A.M. on 25 August 1960, the National Security Council met for an hour to approve the arrangements for the National Reconnaissance Office (NRO), the new agency that Killian and Land recommended for designing and purchasing spy satellites. The NRO remained virtually unknown until the controversy of the 1990s over its expensive building in Virginia and its hidden accumulation of two billion dollars of unspent money. Little leaked out over the years about the bitter controversies between the Air Force and the CIA over designs for strategic and tactical picture-taking, or the growing struggle with Congress over the huge cost of capturing electronic transmissions from space, and taking images at visual, infrared, and radar wavelengths.

At one point in the 25 August discussion, Land "brought the house down," in Kistiakowsky's phrase, when Budget Director Stans was called out of the room briefly. Land said that the government's principal money man was leaving "while it was still cheap."[50]

A key point was that the director of the NRO would report directly to the secretary of the Air Force. Eisenhower said that this was the way to do it, but would defer to the Defense Department. Kistiakowsky reported that Secretary of Defense Gates "said flatly that this is how it will be." Bissell recalled that Eisenhower wanted to be "damn sure" that the arrangement would not lead to Air Force control. The Air Force wanted to put the spy satellites under the control of the Strategic Air Command. Eisenhower was determined that the Air Force not control the analysis of the "take," the precious images that not only identified targets but also monitored the evolution of Soviet military capability. The Air Force could not be both judge and jury.

Approving all of Land's and Killian's recommendations, Eisenhower only regretted that they hadn't been made two years earlier, "so that he would be the guy to see the lovely pictures we would be making. As it is, it will probably be Dick [Nixon] and not him, and he [Eisenhower] won't even have the clearances necessary to see them." In the event, it was John F. Kennedy who defeated Nixon in the 1960 presidential election. When Kennedy saw the photos, he realized that they completely destroyed the "missile gap" on which he had campaigned.

After this triumph, Kistiakowsky found a bit more trouble.

> I discovered later that the recommendations were randomly scattered through the text of the briefing paper, rather than pulled together at the end. After a little difficulty with Killian and Land, who wanted me to rewrite the recommendations even more strongly than Land had stated them, I pulled them together and wrote them in the form in which they were presented. Took a little time to convince Jimmy Lay [James L. Lay, Jr., executive secretary of the National Security Council] that all of these recommendations had really been made, but I guess I managed it. A lesson never to trust anybody to write a formal report without checking it myself. I certainly thought that between Killian, Land, and Watters they would know better than to leave the paper in such a casual form.[51]

Land's responsibilities for spy satellites stretched many years into the future, at least until President Nixon abolished the President's Science Advisory Committee, in part because some of its members opposed policies of his. One of the members of the small, supervisory panel, the Land Panel, was Richard Garwin of IBM, who worked with Land for more than ten years. The panel reported to the president's science adviser, and through him to the secretary of defense and the director of Central Intelligence. The panel's guiding principle, Garwin recalled, was "to maintain technical oversight and openness even in this very secret world, to identify and remedy problems while they could still be fixed, and even to take advantage of unforeseen opportunties." Most problems were resolved by the contractors who built the spy-plane and spy-satellite equipment, "but a visit by the Land Panel helped to ensure that technical management had properly prepared."

Typically, to review programs and proposals and to look at some of the latest reconnaissance images, the Land Panel met in Room 206-208 of the Old Executive Office Building, the high-ceilinged, ornate, nineteenth-century structure across from the West Wing of the White House. According to Garwin, "Din Land kept us on track and inspired us. Our job was not primarily to invent solutions, because there were usually plenty of those to exhaust the budget and the development resources. Rather our job was, as quickly and surely as possible to separate the wheat from the chaff, and to encourage (even selectively breed) the wheat." An example of the panel's success was its evaluation of the Air Force proposal in the 1960s to get its own manned spaceflight program by sending up a Manned Orbiting Laboratory (MOL) for overhead reconnaissance. The panel told President Johnson's science adviser, Donald Hornig, that the job could be done better and cheaper without people aboard. Eventually the MOL program was canceled. If MOL had gone forward, Garwin reflected, the nation would have had a much harder time designing, building, launching, and operating the "highly capable" unmanned satellites of later years.[52]

In a memorial talk in 1991, Garwin said that Land was obviously addicted "to thought and to work," but also brought "qualities of insight and fun." At panel meetings several times a year, the job was "to understand the capabilities of existing systems and the options for improvement . . . [to] evaluate and choose." Sometimes the Land Panel detected "obvious technical mergers to be made." Occasionally, it supplied "a key missing element." Garwin fondly remembered the enthusiastic, congenial meetings with Land:

> When we met at Polaroid, we could look forward to . . . sandwiches brought in from Elsie's [a long-popular establishment near Harvard Square]; my favorite was cream cheese and caviar. Somewhat later, we would meet in the magnificent boardroom at Polaroid, and would be provided dinner by Din's cook [executive

> chef Caroline Pearl, who heard Garwin's talk]. Occasionally, our panel meetings would run until midnight, and even then we would look forward to spending 30 minutes after the meeting with Din in his lab, looking at his "Mondrian" [a feature of the color vision research he began in the 1950s] or other striking aspects of his current research. I recall that one session ended at daybreak, but that was unusual, even for Din Land.[53]

One of the most important reports of the Land Panel in July 1971 most probably concerned the program that resulted in the Keyhole 11 satellites, a kind of Hubble Space Telescope pointed at the earth, which went into service in 1977. Land reportedly advocated the Keyhole 11 directly to President Nixon. The versatile and very expensive spy satellites recorded their images on charge-coupled devices and radioed them to earth via special communications satellites looping high above Russia. They were equipped with enough fuel to adjust their altitude and orientation many times over a lifetime of years. Up into the 1990s, it was U.S. custom to keep two of them aloft at a time. Garwin recalled that the report was so important and controversial that each of the seven panel members had to submit a "formal position." Land assigned Garwin the task of writing a succession of drafts of the report and getting approval from each member, often by telephone from points as far off as Hawaii. Special couriers delivered the drafts to panel members, who were required to read the report without keeping a copy.[54]

18

Demonstrating a "New Medium"

> I've now taken up that little SX-70 camera for fun and become very interested in it. I'm feeling wildly with it. . . . I'm very excited about that little gadget which I thought was just a toy at first. [I was using it] to extend my vision and let that open up new stylistic paths that I haven't been down yet. That's one of the peculiar things about it that I unexpectedly discovered. A practiced photographer has an entirely new extension in that camera. You photograph things that you wouldn't think of photographing before. I don't even yet know why, but I find I am quite rejuvenated by it. . . . It's the first time, I think, that you can put a machine in an artist's hands and have him rely entirely on his vision and his taste and his mind.
>
> —Walker Evans, 1973[1]

On a rainy Friday, 17 March 1972, Land gave a demonstration in his office of the biggest project he had ever carried out, a system of camera and film that he called "a new medium." The visitors found the occasion so much fun that it lasted five hours.[2] All that most people knew was that there was some magic about the huge project, for Land had given it the code name Aladdin, after the boy who rubbed his lamp to release an all-competent djinn. Later, Land abandoned the name, because he feared that captious people might think it stood for "A la Din."[3] Instead, the camera and its film were given the old code name of the 1940s, SX-70, to symbolize the completion of a program toward "absolute one-step photography." The project that first produced sepia was one of a numbered series of "special experiments" during World War II.

This vast SX-70 project of the 1960s and 1970s was Land's greatest technological triumph. It brought together the most varied array of technical talents that Land had ever assembled. In terms of money and the jobs that would have been jeopardized by failure, SX-70 involved the largest risks he had ever run. It plunged Land into hostile relations with longtime colleagues whom he regarded as pessimists interfering with the realization of a dream.

The name of Aladdin, an optimistic character for whom things turn out extraordinarily well, underscored Land's restlessness, inexhaustible energy, and capacity to focus on particular goals. Land was not one to waste his powers on mere follow-up or on topics, however compelling, that showed signs of turning into dead ends. Once a problem was solved as far as he was concerned, it could be turned over to others whose attention he had enlisted. The energy was particularly crucial when a problem turned out to be both vital and not solved, as with the manufacture and exploitation of polarizers over twenty years or with instant photography. Bringing scientific insights and technological inventions into reality, he could immerse himself in a problem so that boredom or existential despair did not exist.

Land intended Aladdin to terminate a succession of shortfalls and compromises and make photography more truly intuitive and impulsive by taking away manipulative barriers. To many amateur and professional photographers, who reveled in the variety and complexity of their equipment, Aladdin was no more welcome than earlier one-step systems. For the mass of photographers, however, instant photography *was* welcome. Time after time, they reached for the minimum of fuss that Aladdin represented.

Through successive phases of simplification, Land hoped to entice laboratory colleagues and engineers to share the promise of the invention and, ultimately, to attract customers. Land was determined to raise this enterprise to a higher plane. He kept insisting that on-the-spot availability of a print would give new artistic freedom to the mass of photographers. An artist by impulse, he demanded that SX-70, like its predecessors, be absolutely new, unexpected, surprisingly useful, emotionally pleasing, and life-changing. Otherwise it would not be worth all the heartbreaking years of trouble to develop it. Like many pioneers in science and engineering over the last several hundred years, Land wanted to do new things, which he hoped to turn into both beautiful and useful experiences. Impatient, even reckless, Land knew that the whole enterprise rested on successful demonstrations.

The 1972 demonstration took place in his inner office. A thick, blond wood door was designed to prevent eavesdropping when a red phone for government calls rang. The carpets were dark red. The wall of windows admitted light, but the windows were covered by filters and gauzy curtains that hid any view of the public housing project across Main Street and muffled the sound of traffic. The books lining other walls gave the sense of a nest sheltered from the outside, despite the scattering of black telephones on tables, shelves, and even the floor. Land always seemed to know who would call him on which phone, and when. The spare spaces in his office that showed up in the photographs taken for *Business Week* nearly twenty years earlier had filled in.

To break the ice, Land, wearing a tweed suit, showed off his new copy of the miniaturized, two-volume Oxford English Dictionary in a box with its own magnifying glass. He expressed surprise at how well he could make out the tiny type without the magnifier. He wondered out loud what the new camera he would demonstrate should be called and suggested the Latin word "*Nunc*," meaning now. During the conversation, Land darted back and forth through a door at the opposite corner from the entrance, leading into an anteroom—more phones in there—and beyond to his lab. There, the organic chemist Stanley M. Bloom and the photographer Inge Reethoff, who did not join the group in Land's library, were preparing film and cameras for the group to use. As he checked how they were coming along, Land joked with the visitors about the carpet, remarking how well it wore, and saying mysteriously that it had cost the company a hundred million dollars. He thought the company should never have departed from linoleum tiles.

There was a search for props. Land remarked that certain children who first had come into the lab when inside their pregnant mothers seemed to know where various objects were and gravitated toward them. One object, brought from a closet near Land's bathroom, was a green frog with a silly red tongue. Its legs could be moved by pressing an air button. Because of its sound, the frog's name was Jibbet. A second prop was a paper tiger from Japan, with a lashing tail and a theatrical, mock-ferocious expression. One tiltable lounger chair, behind the L-shaped array of Land's table and desk, was covered by a multicolored woven blanket. A newer green lounger was placed in the angle of two walls of books, next to a reading lamp. Land sat in it and noticed a hole in one of his socks. He said that this was the sort of thing that happened when his wife was away in Arizona.

Asked about the price that would be charged for the new camera, Land quipped, "It depends on how quickly you want your two hundred million dollars back." He remarked on a favorite theme, that Polaroid's total sales usually about equaled the profits of Eastman Kodak. In years when the ratio was smaller, Land said, he wrote to Kodak's executives to chide them:

"You're slipping." He praised Kodak as "a tremendous company" where people were paid well and did everything well in a "vast number of hermetically sealed subcultures"—and who drank a good deal nightly at the country club.

After several darting trips offstage, Land emerged from the back room with his declaration of independence from Kodak, the uncompromising fulfillment of a program of development nearly thirty years long. The camera was a gleaming packet of metal and leather, with a kind of bump on top, which fit easily into a suitcoat pocket. It was thin, somewhat like a flask or a cigar case, but a little bigger. With such a modest appearance, the camera's stage entrance in the book-lined office was exciting but also strangely muted. The bump that projected from the middle of the hinged back was a sort of clamshell-shaped housing for the viewfinder. This focusing system, as his guests soon found out, did double duty as the means of unfolding the camera to its operating position.

The first step was to practice opening and closing the camera with the aid of the clamshell housing. The lightweight folding structure resembled a cricket. Land told the visitors to place the cameras flat on their extended left hands, and practice holding onto the camera with the right thumb and forefinger only, retracting the other three fingers of the right hand. The right thumb should be placed just behind the right side of the camera's business end. This was the front portion containing the lens, the electronic controls, the shutter, the light-sensing electric eye, rotating wheels to adjust the focus, another tiny wheel for extra-light or extra-dark conditions, and a red button to take a picture. For the most part, users could leave the lighten–darken control at "normal." The index finger of the right hand was used for adjusting the focus wheel.

Under Land's guidance, the visitors practiced approaching objects closer and closer. This was the whole idea. The novice SX-70 photographers looked through a circular eyepiece, which the user did not have to bring right up to the eye, into a ground-glass scene much like the one in conventional single-lens reflex (SLR) cameras. The view came through the lens of the camera, not a separate viewfinder. The shutter was open, and a pivoting mirror within the camera was arranged so that light was reflected upward to the photographer's eye. Closer and closer to the object, the visitors focused and refocused. Finally, they could get no closer. The camera was ten inches away from the target, a teacup, and it was in focus. Land wanted to train millions of photographers to get closer to their subjects.

The visitors did not know the details then, but their view of the teacup was transmitted along an unusually compact and lightweight optical path. Its development had taken years, the ingenuity of designers like James Baker and William T. Plummer, and many hundreds of hours of computer time. The four glass elements of the lens did not project several inches in front of the camera body, as in a typical SLR, but fit comfortably within. The maximum opening of the lens was f/8, that is, one-eighth of its 117-millimeter focal length (the distance between the lens and the film). Of the four lens elements, only the front element traveled back and forth, a total of one-quarter of an inch, to achieve the range of focus between infinity and ten inches.

The means of getting light from the lens to the photographer's eye also was different in SX-70. In the usual SLR, light reflected from the scene through the lens bounced off a pivoting mirror and through a bulky crystal called the pentaprism—which at that time often weighed more than a pound—to be reversed and aimed up to the eyepiece on the upper back of the camera.

The SX-70 camera divided the tasks of the pentaprism among a series of thin glass and plastic mirrors and lenses that weighed as little as possible. Light from the lens first struck the lower part of a trapezoid-shaped mirror fixed to the back of the open camera, at an angle of just thirty-seven degrees to the plane of the film. Protecting the film from light was a pivoting assembly, to whose top was fixed a thin, rectangular, molded plastic mirror, called a Fresnel after the nineteenth-century French physicist who first imagined such a structure. The most dramatic use of the Fresnel was in lighthouses, to focus a beam through several faces of a rotating lantern. Here, it bundled the light from the scene for the photographer.

Earlier Polaroid cameras had used Fresnels, but less dramatically. The SX-70 Fresnel's surface was divided into concentric rings like the glass of a lighthouse. Each molded ring had its own slope, growing steeper toward the outer edge of the bull's-eye, and each ring had a roughened surface analogous to the SLR's ground glass. The beam from this tailored surface shot upward, back to a trapezoidal top extension of the fixed mirror and bounced again, through a pair of tiny metal slits and a tiny lens, out of the camera. The light then spread onto a molded mirror with a nonspherical surface, which aimed the beam to a second nonspherical lens, the photographer's eyepiece. When the camera was opened and pulled erect, both the mirror and the eyepiece had been pulled upright to their working positions under the clamshell-like housing that the photographer had gripped between his thumb and forefinger.

Land opened up a rectangular film box, entirely lined inside with a light-tight foil supplied by DuPont, and drew out a black plastic pack of ten picture units, a little more than three inches on a side. To install the film, he opened the front of the camera by pressing a little blue lever on the right side. The mouth of the film chamber dropped open to reveal two tiny rollers. As he pushed the little pack firmly into the camera, breaking the seal of a tiny slit of a door in the pack, he swung the camera's gaping film door closed, a motor whirred, and a protective cardboard "dark slide" slipped from within the camera. This he put into the now-empty film box. Eventually, that dark slide would carry simple start-up instructions for using the camera, which Land hoped would be "interesting enough" to read.

From another pocket, Land took a Polaroid-designed array of ten flashbulbs in a single assembly, which was being manufactured by GE in its huge new factory. A simple prong at the bottom connected with the camera's controls. To make a good connection, he pressed the array in tightly. The flashbulbs were lined up in a row, five on one side, five on the other, like a superelaborate set of insect antennae attached to the camera. Land said that the camera's transistorized controls were equipped to search the array of ten flashbulbs to find out which ones had fired and which ones were "fresh" and ready to pop. Not until later did Land reveal that the electric power for the camera came from a square, waferlike battery hidden in the bottom of each film pack.

Standing a few feet away from his subject, his face hidden by the camera, Land pointed the camera and focused. Then, his right forefinger dropped down from the focusing wheel to the red button. He pushed it and held his finger there. The motor whirred again, and there was a very bright flash. The picture emerged mysteriously, just as the dark slide had, from the inconspicuous slit in the bottom of the camera. To take the picture, the pivoting mirror within had snapped up against the back interior wall to reveal another mirror, which beamed the light admitted by the shutter down to the topmost film unit. In a fraction of a second, the shutter of Land's camera, which had been open for viewing and focusing, closed swiftly, opened again very briefly, and closed again. It was like a dancer who flashes onto the stage, whirls briefly, and is gone again. About a second later, the film unit that pushed out from between the tiny rollers within was hard and dry, like an oversized playing card.

When Land pushed the shutter button, he had set off an intricately interlocked series of mechanical and electronic operations lasting a second and a half. Scores of camera parts performed a ballet as complex as would occur just afterward in the film. To economize and smooth the flow of one ampere of power from the battery, precise coordination was demanded of electronic switches, power transistors, solenoids, a "walking beam," shutter blades of different weights, the motor, a double train of gears, a cam and a ram, a host of springs, a tiny light-blocking flap on the tip of the pivoting mirror/Fresnel assembly, and the light-sensing electric eye.

A vital feature in the sequence was an electronic delay of forty milliseconds. The delay was called "Y," because engineers at Texas Instruments and Fairchild Camera and Instrument, designing the circuits, had asked "why" the delay was needed, and Polaroid engineers were not yet free to tell them. The delay allowed just enough time for the pivoting mirror/Fresnel assembly to settle firmly against the back of the camera, revealing the second very thin glass mirror for beaming the light down to the film to expose a picture. The output of the Y circuit also sent a signal to allow the shutter to open, the electric eye to start recording light reflected from the subject, and the flash circuit to operate.

With the exposure complete, a patented flexible metal "pick, " whose rear tip bore a tiny projection like that of a crochet hook, pulled the film forward to the spread rollers. The pick was designed so that the notched tip would hold onto the back of the topmost film unit, and only the topmost. It touched the film through a narrow, short slot in the back of the black plastic film cartridge. Gear wheels brought the pick forward a short, carefully measured distance, just enough to pull the film unit into the "bite" of the processing rollers. The pick was latched forward as the spread rollers caught the front edge of the film and began pulling it through. The pod broke at its rear edges; reagent began spreading between positive and negative, in a thin wedge as close to rectangular as the film designers could manage. The gear wheels began cranking the mirror down. The electronics were reset for the next picture.

The film pushed out of the camera. After a run of nine hundred milliseconds, the motor stopped. The mirror was down, and the mirror carrier was latched. The pick was released to return to the rear. The electronics were reset and the shutter opened for the next picture.

After the film came out of the camera, the furious activity within the camera had given way to dead calm. The scene of turbulence shifted to the film, with top and bottom faces made of DuPont Chronar plastic, an improved version of Mylar. The bottom was opaque, the top clear, and they were never pulled apart. The clear top was used not only for exposing the film but also for viewing the resulting image. The final bounce of light off the interior mirror reversed the image from the lens so that the image would be right side up.

Now the photographers confronted SX-70's chemical curtain.Within the wide white borders of the card, visible through the transparent Chronar, was a mysterious, blank, near-square of turquoise, which masked several minutes' worth of controlled chemical violence within. The turquoise, Land said, represented to the eyes the combined color of particles of titanium dioxide pigment and special "opacifying" dyes, whose use he had invented and demonstrated with a simple, pH-sensitive indicator dye. Stanley Bloom had led the team, including Myron Simon, that created the commercial opacifying dyes. Along with reactive chemicals, the components of the curtain had been pressed out of the tiny reservoirs hidden on the back side of the film. The classical Polaroid pod of reagent had been miniaturized. In a layer less than three-thousandths of an inch thick, the pigment and dyes absorbed or bounced the light on a myriad of lateral pathways and directly back to the outside. Further light could not reach the negative, especially in the crucial first seconds of photographic development.

In the now-protected negative, highly alkaline potassium hydroxide was causing "all hell to break loose" in an environment that had been stable since the film had left the factory. Small, mobile auxiliary developers, analogous to those of Polacolor, raced to reach exposed light-sensitive grains of silver halide in three gelatin emulsion layers, corresponding in sensitivity to the three primary colors, blue, green, and red. These chemical messengers donated electrons to exposed grains and developed the silver into its metallic form in seconds. Meanwhile, the alkaline conditions were releasing a new generation of Howard Rogers's large, slow molecules of dye—yellow, magenta, and cyan—linked to developer. Packed into microscopically thin layers, these molecules traveled to the light-sensitive grains of adjacent layers, which were hardly thicker than the grains. Indeed, the whole structure was far thinner than that of Polacolor film and hence used much less silver and gelatin. Classically, the dye developers that found an exposed grain were immobilized, so that dyes would not migrate from the negative where light had struck the grains. The remaining dye developers kept on traveling a tiny further distance, through the chemical curtain, to the patented SX-70 version of the mordant trapping layer. There, the positive color image formed.

Meanwhile, the chemical curtain, which had fallen when the viscous processing fluid had been spread by the rollers, began lifting. With photographic development already complete, the processing chemicals were eating their way into the positive, into a transparent layer of acid polymers. This was a new version of the layers that Land had invented in his crash program of late 1962. As more and more alkaline molecules reacted with the trapped acid molecules, the acid polymer layer was releasing a total of a couple of drops of water. The water diffused throughout the layers of the film and brought down the alkalinity, from a maximum pH value of 14 toward the neutral value of 7. Early in the decline of alkalinity, the opacifying dyes at the surface of the reagent had lost much of their color and revealed the bright white of the titanium dioxide pigment. This formed an increasingly reflective background for the image. Yet the alkalinity remained high enough to complete the image.

∞

Like magic, the lineaments of Land's picture began to emerge through the fading turquoise haze. As seconds passed, the formerly transparent positive began to fill in. The image was emerging. After a minute or so, something quite like a standard color print was available. But events continued subtly for some minutes more. The final result was deep and brilliant. Visitors tried a picture of the green toy frog being chased by the yellow papier-mâché tiger from Japan. One visitor tried a picture of the photographer Marie Cosindas, and Land said that he was stealing his idea. Wearing a dark sweater, Cosindas sat in the green lounger chair next to the tulips. As a notable portrait photographer, she suggested how she should place her hands on her folded arms.

Taking one of the cameras, Cosindas tried several shots of Land. In some, the expression was grim. "That'll scare Kodak," she said. Then she said she felt overwhelmed: the mechanized camera was "out of control." She had difficulty seeing through the viewfinder in low light. She was using flash. More than once, the flashbulb did not fire, so that the camera paused for a time exposure and then, with a whir of the motor, spit out the film unit. The pictures would have succeeded, except that she moved the camera in puzzlement, but she soon got the hang of it.

During and after a sandwich lunch, Land took successions of photos of his visitors, bang, bang, bang, only 1.5 seconds between exposures. Each time, the next picture shoved the earlier one out of the slot and onto the floor. The relatively thick Mylar on both faces of the film, transparent on one side and opaque on the other, protected the emerging images from harm. In contrast to Polacolor, all moisture was imprisoned within the integral film unit. At first, some pictures did not seem highly satisfactory, but later, when the full depth of color had emerged, Land and his guests usually liked the pictures better. Cosindas complained that some of her portraits of Land were too much like snapshots.

Land did a little work on a problem that already bothered him. When the pictures were arrayed against a prepared cardboard frame, the glare from the plastic covers made viewing difficult. He had discovered that they needed to be held at an angle, rather than left flat on the table. For comparisons, Land spread out a number of photographs, showing the pattern of hair on top of a child's head, the depth of color on petals of flowers, the liveliness of a cloud of smoke from a Cambridge chimney. The smoke (probably in violation of some ordinance) boiled up as if it were alive. It was tangible smoke. Looking at the mélange of SX-70 color pictures on the table, Land said that such sessions always resulted in the same profusion.[4]

∞

The technological impresario had shown off the multi-hundred-million-dollar expression of his relentless insistence on the near impossible. Restating Polaroid's fundamental technologies, the new system catapulted Polaroid from heavy dependence on outside manufacturers, to a bid for autonomy, and perhaps dominance, in amateur color photography. In the small confines of Polaroid Corporation, Aladdin/SX-70 was as big a venture as the System 360 development within International Business Machines Corporation in the early 1960s. Requiring so many manufacturing steps and picture-making operations to work together smoothly, the project had some of the complexity of a rocket program. Land's revolutionizing of his own revolution was both visionary and practical. Showing it in public for the first time a month after the demonstration in his office, he said that "photography will never be the same again after today." He seemed to sense that in modern, science-based industry, which he had helped shape, the interval between revolutions in basic technology was decreasing, and that this law applied to Polaroid.

From the beginning, Polaroid cameras were novelties, often given as gifts. The usual pattern was for their owners to use them intensely at first, but eventually less often, and then retire the camera to the shelf. All during the 1960s, increasingly simple cameras exploited very high speed black- and-white films and the new color film. Marketing Vice President Stanford Calderwood and his fellow marketers had wrestled with this problem of "decay" in use. They, and probably Land as well, were haunted by the fear of reaching a plateau. To keep going upward, it was necessary to change the conversation.

To meet this challenge, Land was prepared to push people harder than before. He was ready to run the risk of widening divisions between the technical and marketing sides of Polaroid and between research, engineering, and production. By illness and death, he had lost two people, Meroë Morse and David Skinner, who had served him superbly as buffers. SX-70 overstretched more than once the company's own manufacturing abilities and its ability to supervise outsiders making components. Brushing aside discouragement, Land banished the ultimate leader of manufacturing, Bill McCune, from the project. Marketing the complicated system would be tricky: one component could delay others and try the patience of Polaroid's patient customers. Not only was the company's value in the stock market at risk, but Land severely tried the confidence of his board of directors. They were already worrying about who would succeed him. Land's vision ran counter to many people's view of instant photography, indeed of all amateur photography, as snapshooting under the influence of sentiment.

Behind all this lay the pressures of phenomenal success. The color photography business, instant and conventional, had exploded since 1963, and Polaroid's relationship to its patron Kodak had changed profoundly. The little company was no longer a joke; it was a rival. Polaroid's amateur color business had multiplied faster than expected, even as Kodak had hugely expanded its own color amateur business through its Instamatic camera line, introduced just months after Polacolor in 1963. The tens of millions of Instamatics that poured from Kodak's factories used snap-in cartridges that were far easier for customers to handle than spools that had to be threaded every time they changed rolls of film. Kodak was simultaneously expanding its own color amateur business and supplying larger and larger amounts of negative to Polaroid. One-step photography in color was becoming a significant fraction of amateur picture-taking.[5]

The mutual dependency grew more irksome in proportion to its scale. For Kodak, continuing to supply negative to Polaroid meant increased investment to serve a single customer—which could always decide to meet its own needs for the technology it had developed. What would happen to Kodak's investment then? Kodak wanted an economic use for its instant negative production if Polaroid decided to make its own, and so it extracted from Polaroid a license to enter the peel-apart business. As for Polaroid, it was never certain when Kodak would agree to alter the process to accommodate Polaroid's improvements or to enlarge total production. Kodak had proved reluctant to introduce improvements.[6]

Thus, a not-so-little Polaroid was driven in the direction typically followed by large companies with a commanding position in their fields. That is, it was driven toward direct control of more stages in making and selling its products. Such "vertical integration" consists of steps toward autarchy, back toward raw and intermediate materials, forward to a range of goods sold directly to the public. These steps require that a company train or recruit people who know how to do the new work. This process can be very costly, in terms of money and even customer satisfaction, if product deliveries lag and quality wavers. For Polaroid the first and biggest of these steps was the major decision to make its own color negative and, by extension, many of the dyes and other chemicals for that negative. The process required a scale and a discipline mastered by few companies in the world.

∞

The logic that emerged over the years applied equally to Kodak. As Polaroid seized control of its technological destiny, Kodak was driven, inexorably it seems, into instant photography. The uneasy situation that arose was displayed in the agreement of 1969, under which Kodak would continue manufacturing negative for Polaroid in return for a license to enter the peel-apart instant film business in 1975. This would give Kodak insurance, a market for film it made even if Polaroid became its own supplier. The agreement, however, made an assumption: that the design of the instant film and cameras that used it would change only gradually. For Polaroid, the likely entry of Kodak into Polaroid's exclusive business raised the stakes. The little company might get squashed by the elephant. For this reason, Polaroid must leap higher than mere autarchy in negative production. Land and his people were prepared for the struggle and were more nimble than Kodak. Nearing sixty, Land still thought like a scrappy newcomer. It was a conquistador's throw, like Cortez's burning his ships at Vera Cruz.

An important arena of combat was psychological warfare in advance of the main event, the introduction of the SX-70. Land waged this war aggressively. But Land did not just maneuver. He actually plunged into a new generation of instant photography based on non-peel-apart film. What he and Polaroid came up with was so attractive that Kodak had to scrap its first plans and enter the exigent integral-film business that Land had pioneered.

A force in this evolution was Land's growing impatience. His dream of an ultimate one-step photography still seemed a long way off. The existing process seemed clumsy, and the amount of material to discard was beginning to offend a growing sensitivity about degrading the environment. Land couldn't count on too many years to achieve his goal. With Kodak looming as a threat, Land accelerated the migration into the new territory of Aladdin. He was willing to risk premature obsolescence of the increasingly popular lines of peel-apart color film and cameras that used it.

In the late 1960s, it would have been as uncharacteristic as ever for Land to enter this new world with an evolutionary system. The entirely new Aladdin film required an entirely new camera. Impulsive photography would be restated radically. The camera must be convenient and go many more places than it did before, and hence must be lighter, smaller, and easier to operate. Yet it must deliver pictures no smaller than before and with more brilliant, longer-lasting colors. To achieve a focal length of 117 millimeters in a very compact camera, Land was forced by the laws of optics to develop a camera that would open, and so special structures such as a rubbery, folding "boot," which looked like a bellows, had to be invented and made. The new lens and viewing system should have the simplicity of SLR cameras for naturalness of viewing. Customers should not to have to worry about batteries to power the shutter, the motor, and the flash, and so there must be the invisible flat battery in each film pack. To control the complicated sequence of events in the 1.5 seconds for taking a picture, the camera needed an intricate shutter and unprecedented electronics. To introduce his revolution, Land wanted a fancy-looking camera with the appearance of gleaming metal, the lightness of plastic, and the luxurious touch of top-grain leather panels.[7]

Everywhere Land turned he faced requirements. As in so many systems of our age of technology, complexity was harnessed to achieve simplicity for the user. Suddenly, Polaroid was metamorphosing from a high-technology design shop into a major manufacturing company. As in complex military projects—a school in which Land was an A student—things had to happen in the arbitrary certainty that they would all be ready on time, at the same time. In a merciless triangle of time and money and specifications, it became painfully obvious that Polaroid, as space engineers had learned, could not have all three. At least one of the three must yield.[8] Such tradeoffs are probably easier when the customer is a military service with an open checkbook. A technological toy shop, on the other hand, must get its money from the stock and bond markets, banks, or its own savings. It is innovating in full view of, and with the collaboration of, a public composed of millions of customers.

Was Land impossibly bold, as many Polaroid managers and board members were beginning to fear? Or was he merely submitting to the requirements of a world in which rapid technological advance is inevitable and where nice, sensible companies fade or rust? Land seemed to accept—joyfully, one expects—that one must continue to innovate, even as younger, smaller, and more nimble enterprises spring up to innovate even faster. There seems little doubt that Land embraced this challenge eagerly. The immense gamble of SX-70 was very much his doing.

The scope of the gamble was typified by the vast structure built to coat negative, which, in 1972, was reaching completion on a new site in

New Bedford, Massachusetts. At New Bedford, the water would be ultra-clean, and the air ultra–pure. A five-foot-wide strip of black Mylar plastic would be unrolled to rush through a succession of black chambers, collecting a stack of light-sensitive emulsions containing new dyes from Waltham, timing layers, and other coatings whose unvarying thickness was measured in millionths of a meter. Then, after drying, the film would roll onto another drum for storage.[9] Assuming ten pictures per square foot, to make enough for a billion pictures a year, the plant would have to coat 100 million usable square feet, that is, 23,000 acres, or 36 square miles, of the black plastic base in a year. The annual 20 million linear feet of film, coated at the rate of more than 38,000 feet in each of 522 shifts, assuming operations of 2 shifts a day on five days a week, would stretch almost 3,800 miles. The New Bedford plant obeyed the laws of speed, precision, consistency, and cheapness that were and are demanded more and more in many industries around the world.

The daring of the New Bedford plant stunned the company's directors, who had been a little disappointed that the SX-70 camera wouldn't easily fit into a pocket. When the vast film factory was nearly ready for production, the board members visited, donning white suits and proceeding through an air shower into a clean room, feeling slightly silly. Land told them that the negative coating machine alone cost forty million dollars. It was after he congratulated the plant manager, I. MacAllister "Mac" Booth, that Land made his statement, "Let me know if it works." Director Carl Kaysen recalled more than twenty years later that next to the 1977 remark about the bottom line being in heaven, this was his favorite Land saying. He asked an interviewer, "Can you imagine any other executive of a corporation saying that in front of a board of directors after spending that much money?"

In SX-70, according to Kaysen, "almost every component made demands that were hard to fulfill." As a deputy national security adviser in the Kennedy White House, he had confronted many problems with military purchases. "Looking back, I got the impression that it was almost like building a new fighter [plane]. Every piece in it pushed the others."[10]

∞

Polaroid had learned much in the previous decade about how to build the automated machinery to assemble rectangles of film into packs that were easy to put in and take out of cameras. Now, the company would have to stretch this experience to make the new integral films. Costing one hundred million dollars together, the New Bedford plant, the film assembly plant in Waltham, and the special chemical plant also in Waltham were paid for out of the rapidly accumulating profits of black-and-white and the first color business. Such major spending was justified as a preparation for a future in which many more people than before would be buying and using sophisticated, but deceptively simple, Polaroid cameras. The company would step away from twenty years of using outside camera assembly by such companies as U.S. Time and Bell and Howell. Those two firms had assembled not only the original sepia and black-and-white cameras, but also the new generation of electronically controlled cameras introduced shortly after color film went on the market at the beginning of 1963. Now Polaroid would assemble its own cameras from a rich array of components invented by Polaroid and made by some of America's best manufacturers.

Step by painful step, the procrustean bed of specifications set limits to the design of the folding, motorized, electronically controlled camera with unusually compact optics. With an array of hundreds of transistors, the automatic camera's controls leaped much farther into the electronic age than did any previous camera. Evolving dramatically after their invention in the late 1940s, the transistors had shrunk so much that by the early 1960s, scores of them fit into flat structures called integrated circuits. By 1970, these circuits, continually more elaborate, began to penetrate from defense systems and big computers into consumer products. Companies like Intel, selling memory chips and microprocessors built up on wafers of silicon, had come into existence to make controls and calculators. The personal computer was just a few years away. With such controls, the integral film units could leave the camera in 1.5 seconds and the image could materialize, in the photographer's hand, on a table, or, on a cold day on the ski slopes, in the photographer's jacket pocket. All this went far beyond laboratory magic. To make this startling new camera, Polaroid had purchased an estate in Norwood, Massachusetts, in the late 1960s, and had erected vast factories on it.

19 Collaborators

> What we've done is the inverse of what companies do over the life of a project. Years are passing. [The normal tendency] is to leave out. As we complete the project, it's gotten more complicated. We've made it more sophisticated because we could. . . . The most elegant form [of the system] is the one that's coming out. That is really unusual in technological advances generally. Not a hell of a lot was left out of this.
>
> —Stanley M. Bloom, 21 July 1972[1]

On the rocky way to the 1972 demonstration of SX-70, many problems emerged for the "boss" and his band of innovators. For example, the photos from the new, intuitive process had an old problem: curling. The solution embroiled Land with skeptical co-workers. SX-70 film units were subject to curling even though they had stiff, thick plastic covers and just popped out of the camera into daylight. The plastic front and rear faces of the cardlike units were durable, but they needed to be flexible. Unless they were made of the right material, they might curl, because the chemicals within could act on them at different rates. To avoid this, should the plastic on each face be the same compostion and thickness?

While they wrestled with film structure, Land and his Skunk Works comrades simultaneously confronted the manifold demands of stabilization: keeping the film stable on the shelf before the film was used and stable again once the image had achieved its intended brilliance. But the SX-70 problem was new: the researchers were choosing not to separate the parts of the film but to keep them together forever. Curling thus had to be solved in a way that was compatible with stabilization.

Maintaining stability while avoiding curling brought Land briefly up against the chemical prejudices of his co-workers, who felt deeply that a processed picture should dry out as soon as possible. Hence, one or both of the plastic "supports" of the film should readily transmit water vapor from within. Well-known plastics like cellulose acetate exhaled, and at first, pictures protected by acetate lay pleasingly flat on the laboratory tables. Later, however, they began to curl dramatically. Even if both pieces of the acetate had exactly the same composition and thickness, the chemicals within operated on each piece differently enough to bend one more than the other, like the two metal pieces of a bimetal thermostat.

The workers turned from acetate to a relatively new polyester plastic called Mylar. This plastic was stiff and strong, which was helpful in manufacturing, and turned out to resist curling for years. The two sheets did not curl, even when they were not exactly the same thickness. Not only did the Mylar sheets have "enormous strength and flatness," Land said, but the chemicals appeared to act on the inner edges of each Mylar sheet in precisely the same manner. So far so good. But the polyester let out water vapor from inside very, very slowly. With Mylar, the interior would be moist not just for hours, but for days and weeks, typically two weeks. How could stabilization be achieved in so moist an environment? "It was generally thought," Land said, "that a stable picture would be obtained only if drying was achieved in [a] relatively short time period."

Although Land and his colleagues agreed that they "wanted . . . bona fide symmetry in mechanical properties, so that the two sheets stayed exactly alike," his colleagues objected to a process that "might take ages to dry out, like weeks, and that might lead to an unstable system in which the dyes wander, things might fade, and so on." They were convinced that "a picture could not be left wet." It was "offensive intuitively to most people with chemical backgrounds." Land had to persuade his chemists not only that the patented new acid polymer layer worked efficiently, but that the mechanical benefit of the water-impermeable layers "far outweighed any imagined hazard due to the continued presence of water for the 10 or 15 days, as the case might be."

Observers found the "boss's" need to persuade colleagues incredible. In the *Polaroid v. Kodak* patent-infringement trial in 1981, Kodak's lawyer didn't believe Land's account. His name was on the patent, the "symmetrical supports" patent, wasn't it? Land rejoined that invention in a complex project is social: "Each time a new step or a new invention is incorporated in a program, that program ceases . . . to [be] the particular intellectual property of the person who created the invention and becomes the intellectual property and social property of the whole group working on it." The group felt it had been bold enough in decreeing that a still-developing picture should be brought out into millions of times as much light as it received during exposure. It had taken on "enough of a burden of daring."[2]

Most of the lingering moisture came from the SX-70 acid polymer's elaborately timed work of lowering the alkalinity in the integral film unit. An earlier acid polymer had done analogous work with Polacolor film. In the new integral film unit, which used far less of practically everything than Polacolor film, the acid polymer not only held the acid in place but also held onto the highly alkaline potassium hydroxide once it had finished its dual job of developing the picture and moving dyes over to the image layer. In the new film, the acid polymers also served as the timer for the chemical curtain. "The layers in the positive sheet," Land said, "determine the time and provide the mechanism for making the light-protective opacity vanish."

The symmetrical-supports patent was just one of those at issue in the *Polaroid v. Kodak* case of 1976–85. Another patent covered the two faces of the same impermeable plastic. A stabilization patent applied to both peel-apart and integral films. Polaroid had found that the acid polymer would still work if placed under the negative, rather than in the positive. Indeed, in later SX-70 films, putting the acid polymer on the negative side proved even more efficient. The patents were upheld in 1985.

∞

As Land and his co-workers had found many times, the journey to the preferred solution revealed many alternate ways of doing things. Some of these were hedges against failure or changed circumstances, but others could lay traps for industrial competitors. One of the most remarkable and attractive of the traps was Howard Rogers's completely different design for the film. Rogers invented it on New Year's Day 1968 and disclosed it to patent attorney Stanley Mervis the next day. Five months later, attorney Robert Ford filed the final application for what became U.S. Patent 3,594,165.

It was natural for a Land associate to consider doing the opposite of something, especially when there were obstacles looming. Rogers knew the mainstream specifications for what became SX-70, but his inventive mind kept asking: What if there were roadblocks? The integral SX-70 film would be processed outside a camera as small as mechanics and optics and physics and chemistry would allow. The film required some form of chemical curtain. Mainstream thinking in the lab had turned toward viewing the picture through the same clear plastic through which it had been exposed a moment before, despite the extra complexity in camera design. To avoid reversing the final image, as in a mirror, the camera needed a mirror to give the same left-right arrangement as in the scene. Rogers's ideas were included in the mainstream plan for SX-70. The film would use Rogers's "positive dye developer" concept from Polacolor. In this the dyes would go over to the positive only where exposure had not occurred. A "negative dye developer" would do the opposite, migrating only where exposure had occurred.

Land, committed to his design, already had won his board's approval for big spending on machinery to make the mainstream film. But, as Rogers knew, a crucial building block was still missing from the structure. The indicator dyes, the crucial component of the chemical curtain, had not yet been perfected by Stanley Bloom, who had the whole weight of the project on his shoulders. Close to the anxieties, Rogers knew that as so often before, ideas might not pan out. Bloom's goal was a fancy trick: the opacifying dyes would be colored at the start of processing but become transparent a short while later. The mirror would make the camera bulkier and less convenient. That New Year's Day, Rogers found himself "reviewing what I had been doing," when the thought hit him: Why not solve both problems by making the film work the opposite way? It was the sort of thought that a researcher might have on a holiday. He made a sketch.[3]

Patent attorney Mervis recalled that Rogers's concept called for using the same positive dye developer. Rogers recognized also that reversal emulsions and negative dye developer, later used in Kodak's instant system of 1976, could be used. The clauses of Polaroid's patent covered both types of dye developer as well as other image-forming chemistries.[4]

Rogers's alternate film would free Polaroid from waiting for Stanley Bloom's opacifying dyes. Instead, a layer of reflective white pigment would be built into the film from the start, between the light-sensitive layers and the thin layer where the dye image would appear. Whites would be white as soon as the picture came out of the camera. Rogers thought that would be "more pleasing."

The picture would be exposed on the side opposite from the face through which people would view it. The processing fluid would not spread through the middle of the structure, but between the negative and a spreader sheet. Its activating chemicals would work on the negative first instead of eating into both negative and positive simultaneously. In the fluid would be enough carbon black to shield the negative from further exposure though the film's bottom face.

It was simple and attractive, but the other way had a big head of steam behind it. As Rogers said matter-of-factly in 1981, "There was insufficient incentive to change those plans." Rogers patented his alternative and made some images with his positive dye developer, but the invention went on the shelf with a lot of other Polaroid patents for doing things another way. Kodak, on the other hand, as it struggled in the 1970s for a workable integral film, saw the technical sweetness of Rogers's rejected approach and went for it. The negative dye developer system was a crucial element of Kodak's PR-10 film, introduced in 1976.[5] In the 1985 decision in the *Polaroid–Kodak* patent case, Rogers's rejected concept was ruled valid and infringed.

∞

In the ballet of SX-70, stray light was a constant problem. The chemical curtain protected the front edge of the film unit after it passed through the rollers—but not the trailing edge. To darken the camera's interior further, the camera designers put the tiny slot for the motor-driven pick at the back of the film cassette, instead of at the front. The light-leakage problem was still not solved. Traces of light that were beginning to bombard the front of the film could bounce horizontally within the film to the still-unprotected portion, by a process called light-piping. The whole rear area could receive an unwanted overdose of light, fogging it, in photographic terminology. During that vulnerable fraction of a second, extra protection was required. Mechanical engineers Richard Wareham and Richard Paglia patented a special folding shield structure in the front of the camera, beneath the shutter. This shield bent the film slightly downward and thus lengthened the path for any light straying within the film. Light-piping was reduced.

The solution brought a new problem. The engineers were trying to make the goo push back inside the film, between the positive and the negative, in a wave as square as possible—not like the "tongue" of a piece of pizza dough being rolled out. Would the bending interfere with the square wave? It turned out that the bending was actually helpful. It narrowed the channel for the goo, assuring that a precisely metered amount would spread over the whole three-by-three-inch picture area, with only a tiny amount left over. This feature was also patented.[6]

In its intense exploration of alternatives, the Aladdin/SX-70 project bore some resemblance to the hell-for-leather American missile projects of the 1950s. In those, rival approaches—liquid fuel or solid fuel, intermediate-

or long-range, inertially guided or radio guided—were tried in hopes that at least one would prove viable. But SX-70 also had elements of the "one true way" approach, things that just had to work, like Bloom's opacifiers. Technological modesty, however, was not absent. Certain grandiose notions about the camera were considered early, but were laid aside in favor of slightly less demanding approaches to the goal. These simpler approaches, in turn, gained unexpectedly in sophistication. This was not without precedent. In the Apollo moon project of the 1960s, the single spaceship conceived at the beginning of the enterprise was broken into several pieces, each with a specific mission for a particular stage of the lunar journey. Apollo came to resemble a multi-stage assault on a mountain, usually with more than one way to get back down and with a minimum of weight carried to higher altitudes.[7]

The camera body was the prime example of technological moderation in Aladdin. At first, Wareham and the other mechanical engineers focused on a non-folding prototype even smaller than the final version, with special means of throwing light from the lens onto the film. This had to be abandoned, and the camera was allowed to fold. Either way, the camera was designed in the faith that a way would be found to draw the chemical curtain.

∞

In 1968, Land was certain enough that camera production would start soon to hire Cliff Duncan, an engineer from the space program, to oversee the preparations for manufacturing. Duncan knew that he was entering a bear pit. The project was secret, not only outside the company but within. A small group of engineering personnel was sequestered from the rest of the company, he recalled, "to learn the process of completing the design and building a model." Wareham reported to Duncan, whose office was next door.

On 31 May 1969, just two months before Meroë Morse died, Duncan took a photo of Land as he photographed Morse using an early model, called Prototype 2. This prototype evolved quickly. Some eighteen production engineers, led by Pat Finelli, were brought in, and their tinkering was so extensive that they made a motorized, folding Prototype 3, using integral film, in the latter half of 1969. According to Duncan, a big problem was how to grab the film unit and bring it to the processing rollers. At first, the pick that did this was in the front and it often malfunctioned. The front-mounted pick either failed to catch even one unit or caught more than one and bunched them up in the rollers. With the camera and film being designed simultaneously, Duncan said, things were happening on both sides, and coordination became "very complicated." They were missing deadlines.

Nevertheless, in the summer of 1969, well before settling on a final design, Polaroid was already negotiating with Ray-O-Vac to build batteries, Corning to build lenses, and GE to build a special flash unit. Duncan was worried and wrote Land a personal letter, urging "very strongly that we needed to do something." Land responded characteristically, by forming a new, smaller Skunk Works that included Dick Wareham, Irving Erlichman, Al Bellows, Richard Chen, Laurie Mills, and the astronomer and lens designer James Baker, who worked part-time. They constituted a few more people than one taxicab could hold, but they met in the small room where Land had put together the design of the U-2 spy plane cameras. The "U-2 Room" was near Land's laboratory, "so he could be in and out of the office," Duncan recalled. "He spent more time in our room than he did in the office." Late in the year, Land invented a new transport system, using a pick that grabbed the film unit at the rear. The model embodying the rear-pick system was called U-2. Its motor was toward the front. For loading the film, it had a door that dropped down, instead of a flap used earlier. The next camera, designed by Land and Wareham, was called the U-3. This was operated by a crank instead of a motor. Meanwhile, Land was pulling together the design for an SLR viewfinder.

The U-4 combined the features of the earlier models. Still, it lacked a train of gears to connect the motor in the back to the rollers in the front. Duncan, in fact, was skeptical about a gear train, because of the inevitable small "play" of meshing teeth from one wheel to the next. Instead, the group tried a variety of belts and cables and chains. When they built the U-42, with a gear train, in August 1970, they were on their way to a final design.[8]

The project was bold, even a little crazy. With earnings built up all through the 1960s, Polaroid could afford it. Despite the financial cushion Land was still betting the company. The integral-film gamble threatened the comfortable peel-apart world that had built up so rapidly in the 1960s. Land was not content with other people's ideas about what the company should do or when. He was aggressively determined to take the initiative, in apparent violation of Andrew Carnegie's dictum (which Carnegie often ignored) "Pioneering don't pay!"[9] Land listened to his own drummer. He was like Grant in the Civil War, exploding to timid subordinates, "I am heartily tired of hearing what Lee is going to do. . . . Go back to your command, and try to think what we are going to do ourselves."[10] Land, the inventor-orchestrator insisted on the elaborate adventure of SX-70, introducing a whole series of innovations at once.

∞

Land's teams worked under the pressure of innovations from Kodak. A few days after the 17 March 1972 demonstration, Land displayed the cheapest of Kodak's pocket Instamatics introduced just days earlier. He estimated that the camera cost $3 to make, and gave Kodak $15 of profit before it went to dealers at $18 to be sold at a list price of $28.[11]

In March 1972, Bloom was not yet ready to demonstrate the chemical curtain. He and many others continued to be closeted with their intense, last-minute work. But leading coordinators of camera development were far enough along to come over from their lab on the ninth floor of 565 Technology Square for a demonstration in Land's outer office.[12] Dick Chen was technical assistant to Land, a calm and bright Chinese-born engineer who had joined Polaroid in 1958. He had worked on a Polaroid document copier for much of the 1960s until it was quietly abandoned. Dick Wareham had joined Polaroid in 1951. Both had trained at MIT, Chen as a graduate student, Wareham as an undergraduate before World War II interrupted his studies. Both routinely came to Land's lab.

In the crisis of SX-70, Land employed Chen, whose heavily accented English was hard to follow, to smooth ruffled feathers while relentlessly insisting on bringing everything together on schedule. Chen stood for the idea that the system would come into being, and that all the necessary energy and acquiescence would be found. He was quiet and determined. Although Wareham was equally determined, he was a bright button and a mile-a-minute lecturer. His flashy smile and little lunette glasses gave him a note of creative eccentricity. He had a lifelong enthusiasm for toy trains.

The present camera, Wareham said, had emerged from preceding designs by competition. How, he and his colleagues asked, would a new system overcome the strengths of existing lines? New models had to be so much better that they were worth the trouble. Hints of opportunity came, he said, from the add-on kits offered with existing cameras, particularly those for close-ups and portraits. Because Land was determined to bring amateur picture-takers much closer to their subjects than they were used to, the compact camera needed the remarkably compact, four-element lens from James Baker, which was exceptionally good at close-ups.

For another demonstration in Land's outer office a few days later, Wareham brought props of the sort he loved.[13] Chen extracted the props from a rubber-lined, green bookbag popular in those days with Harvard students, and gleefully described them as "goodies." They were pieces of the camera, and a special cutaway toy fabricated from a partially broken camera that no longer closed completely. One side of the "boot," or bellows, was cut away, so that one could see the mirror/Fresnel assembly pop up after the red button was pushed and then crank downward gracefully while the picture-taking cycle ended.

The train of gear wheels of varying sizes and tooth shapes, plastic and multicolored, a dozen or more, some outside the others, ran along one side of the camera from the thumb-size motor in the back to the tiny rollers in front. One roller was of highly polished metal; the other had a less smooth, rubbery surface. The metal pick, with its carefully calculated slight bends and its tip resembling a crochet hook, was visible. Its work of pulling film units forward, one at a time, had the indispensable help of the absolutely straight plastic side wall of the film pack, and the precisely calculated little notch in the pack's rear wall. Wareham said, "There would be hell to pay if the pick got skewed." The gear wheel that was attached to the pick, he noted, turned about two-thirds as fast as the rollers. The force of the pick should be exerted just a bit beyond the instant when the rollers began grabbing the front edge of the film. With this redundancy of forces on the film, the rollers grabbed the film securely.

Wareham handed over a flat body section with a metallic exterior. The material was strangely lightweight. Delightedly, he asked, "How so?" The material consisted of layers of metal of foil-thickness mounted on a base of glass-filled plastic. Molded with a fairly elaborate inner structure for hooking up with other subassemblies, the plastic had been dipped in a succession of metal baths, where it was electroplated with copper, then nickel, then chromium. Together, the metal layers were about seven-thousandths of an inch thick. By themselves, the three metal layers would have flapped in the breeze.

The bellows-like boot was another Wareham favorite. It was made of a polymer called EDPM, chosen to stand up well to air pollutants like ozone. It was eight to ten thousandths of an inch thick, and it had to fold the same way for the thousands of times the camera might be taken out of a pocket for a picture and then refolded. Another camera fragment showed the shutter housing in the front, with its outer cover removed. A maze of wiring wound around the lens, the electric eye, and the shutter. When the red operating button pushed together two crooked, coppery fingers, an electric circuit closed, so that power could flow to the motor.[14] A few days later, Richard Kee and John Burgarella, leaders in design of SX-70's electronics, explained their system of circuits and switches.[15] The astronomer and optical engineer

William T. Plummer reviewed the complex history of the optical system he had done so much to perfect, including the crossed slits and tiny lens at the top of the camera, the aspheric viewing mirror, and the aspheric eyepiece.[16]

∞

The view of SX-70 according to Wareham was not narrow. He went beyond the keenly felt delights of a toy shop and brought electronics together with optics and mechanics. He told a tale of the tortured optical geometry of light traveling through the camera for viewing scenes and taking pictures; the sharing of tasks and a modest power supply between a motor, gear wheels, springs, and rollers; the points in the sequence of motor and shutter operation where electronic switches were needed; and the materials of the camera's fixed and folding structures.

In his design of elements in the SX-70, Wareham was compressing years of conversations among engineers, and between the engineers and Land.[17] Years later, Wareham remembered those conversations: "He could help in such ways that what seemed impossible wasn't. If you got discouraged, he'd push, as with the batteries, or the film. . . . He made you feel you could do almost anything. He wouldn't let you deviate from what he wanted to have happen. Something got uncorked." To doubters, Land's "killer" retort always was, "Have you tried it?" It was irresistible. Many times, Wareham recalled, Land would "sell me the shirt off my own back, and, when I got outside, I would ask myself, 'Did I agree to *that*?' " Land's suggestions were not casual: "Anything he suggested was not off-hand. It was well thought out. . . . He wasn't really asking people to jump seven feet in the air and stay there. . . . [Land pursued] pretty well-defined goals and came as close as possible, sometimes right on the nose. . . . You knew he wouldn't come to you with some frivolous idea. If he came to you, you gave it all you had." As they worked through the ways something wouldn't work, "there was a good group of guys who caught the same disease. Nobody would let the other guy fall down."

The process was by no means parliamentary. Land always worked with one or two people, or small groups. "There was no big gigantic meeting with everyone putting in their two cents. That was almost forbidden. He wanted total control." Chen's role, as Wareham recalled it, was to do "a lot of smoothing over of Land's life in the lab. . . . He would spend until [midnight] and then go home with him. [On SX-70] Chen was not used as the smart engineer he was." This time, Land needed him for a wide array of psychological services, down to the level of taking a Land laboratory associate out to lunch to hear complaints and mollify.[18]

Confident that the new SX-70 film could be produced, Land insisted, from the middle 1960s, on a camera that was less unwieldy than those Polaroid had been making. Perhaps the unwieldiness explained the premature retirement of so many Polaroid cameras. The camera certainly needed to be smaller and simpler to use. Land carved a block of wood the size he wanted, covered the outside with tan vinyl, and stuck a small lens into one end of the block.[19] He didn't want the camera to open or unfold. But the picture had to be big enough for customers to enjoy it, probably at least three by three inches (Polaroid learned painfully in the 1990s that a smaller picture was rejected by customers). To achieve a sufficient focal length for that size picture in a small, nonfolding camera, light would have to bounce back and forth along a series of mirrors between the lens and the film. But the twisty mirror of this design, Wareham recalled, "really was a false start. It proved not the way to go." Making an inevitable change into a great concession, Land told Wareham: "You're allowed one engineering failure and you've just had it."[20]

To start afresh, Wareham made his move to the ninth floor about 1968, just at the convergence of such film concepts as the opacifier, the correct amount of developer, and the right size of trap to catch any overflow and the opacifier. For Wareham, this meant "alienating myself from everyone." A year or so later, it was evident he would need more people, all of whom worked for Milton Dietz, an engineer reporting to William McCune, vice president for engineering. "It required a big bomb to transfer people. Land came over and said, 'We're gonna have to transfer some people.' " Dietz's engineers didn't get a precise answer when they asked, "To do what?" But they moved. Land forbade McCune and another leading engineer, Otto Wolff, to visit the ninth floor. It was after this managerial earthquake that work went forward toward a folding camera with just one mirror for taking a picture, a camera with what Wareham said in 1973 was "the funny shape we have now."[21]

∞

A fresh problem threatened the new course toward a folding camera: viewing. The very compact Baker lens had "extraordinary range," but how could photographers also use light from the lens itself to look at the scene before taking a picture, and thus not need a cumbersome "telescope"? "Our early attempts were odd outgrowths, like telescopes," Wareham recalled. "We failed miserably. Eventually we thought we would have to give up the folding body, and we even designed some rigid models that looked like the SX-70 when it's open. We worked into 1970. Finally, Land said, 'Forget it.

Keep your heads down on the camera. I'll invent the viewfinder.' That was a good deal, so we grabbed it."[22]

Land's midwinter promise implied huge new pressure on Plummer and Baker in the optical department. They began at once on experiments with models of the grooved, light-bundling Fresnel plastic mirror. These were encouraging, but as things stood, the photographer would have to "press hard against the camera to see into it." Cardboard and wax models of solutions were built nightly, while Baker and Plummer spent nearly two weeks in Land's office talking the models over. Land showed them a conventional SLR camera and remarked that for the photographer, the image "comes magically out of the clouds. It doesn't require explanation, and a child can do the adjustment." Without changing the camera's basic design, Land demanded the same optical immediacy, and at distances of as little as less than a foot.

As Plummer and Baker worked feverishly, they knew that Wareham and "some hundreds of camera designers [were] waiting for their new direction on the product." With little time to spare, a blizzard of options boiled down to "a bead-like hemisphere near the peak of the camera," bouncing light off a concave mirror above the camera "to display the relayed image at a comfortable viewing distance." The concave mirror put the eye in the right place, and the view appeared.

With viewfinder problem solved, astronomer Plummer could take his family to North Carolina to watch the solar eclipse of Saturday, 7 March 1970. The same day, Land summoned his key program people to tell them of the new viewfinder. He let them out briefly for a glimpse of the eclipse, which was only partial in Boston.

For the next few months, the optical department learned how to make and test the components of the innovative viewing system, by increasingly rapid and automated methods. Then Land asked them to start over, because of unusual demands on the photographer, including an awkward angle for viewing. Redesign began at once, with Land praising "our collective courage in starting over." The flat mirror inside the camera was lengthened so it could bounce the light twice. New components were designed and built in cardboard, and the camera designers figured out how to support and precisely place them every time the camera was opened.

Over the years ahead, optical systems kept evolving, and Plummer found himself appointed in 1971 by Land to defend the optics in the face of the design improvements that inevitably came during manufacture. Plummer would be guardian of the camera's "photographic integrity." As each design reached its limits of performance, Land would tell Plummer and his colleagues that "the current design was twice as good as he had last seen it (though half what he was looking for)."[23] He was asking again and again for courage.

Plummer's guardianship was just one sign of how the many parts of the system affected each other. There were so many hard choices, so many trade-offs. The pathway for light to view the scene and to take a picture affected the placement of mirrors for viewing—and for picture-taking. The weight and placement of the mirrors affected the timing of the motor and shutter. To operate smoothly, the tiny motor needed help from the springs and gear wheels. The demand for power from the flat battery was likewise orchestrated, so that the firing of the flash, the openings and closings of the shutter, and the turning of the film-processing rollers did not occur at the same instant.

The petty details added up to a forceful example of how the complex technologies that people live by in the late twentieth century are born. The drama, false starts, byways, and apparent dead ends in Wareham's story were a refreshing departure from the sanitized account of programs that look inevitable only in retrospect. It was a sprightly, optimistic, slightly ironic trip up Dante's mountain of purgatory, the realm of striving. The metal pick, Wareham said with a twinkle, was "the heart of the whole system. If that fails, we're in deep trouble." A particular latch was designed to go forward four times, but only to catch a movable mirror assembly on the fourth time. If it caught at the wrong point, he observed, "We all get fired." When discussing whether to achieve a particular control step mechanically or electronically, he said wryly, "Lucky we're not building a flashlight. It would never work."

Such interactions between optics, electronics, and mechanics were complex. Should a task be assigned to a moving part or to a tiny electronic device in which "only the electrons move"? Wareham's observation was, "We're one happy, small family: we fight most of the time." In Land's world, the specifications were impossible yet had to be satisfied. Dominant as always was Land's insistence that just because a person wants a thing does not mean that it is forbidden by a law of nature. It was fun, Wareham thought. "What's a sunglass company doing with pictures in a minute? Always the wrong people invent the right thing."[24]

∞

Stanley Bloom was busy up to and beyond the moment in April 1972 that SX-70 was demonstrated to the public. His development of the indicator dyes for Land's invention of the chemical curtain was perhaps the second greatest invention made by a Land associate after Howard Rogers' invention of the dye developer. Land enlisted talent like a Toscanini, with concentration and pressure. It was the pressure, in the words of Land's early admirer Percy Bridgman of Harvard, to "do your damnedest." As they worked feverishly in 1972, living a creatively unhappy life in Land's "back lab" on the ground floor of 2 Osborn Street, Bloom and others could be seen eating their sandwich lunches standing up.[25]

Land described the importance of Bloom's work: "From the point of view of systems planning, the assumption that we could solve this problem was probably our most adventurous step. We designed the camera as if we had solved the problem, and carried the camera all the way through engineering while doing the basic research on the chemical task of bringing the picture directly into the light."[26] In 1974, Bloom spoke of "a miraculously complex material." To develop it, in forms that could be mass-produced, "We all had to share the burden of knowing that we had the company's trust when we had not yet completed the company's assigned task." For a scientist assisting so relentlessly optimistic a man as Land, Bloom's demeanor was quiet, even morose. There were slight overtones of weariness. When he presented his work in Boston 1974, there was a burst of song from the neighboring conference room. Bloom said, "That lady has a lot more spirit in the morning than I do," and his audience, many of whom had worked with Land, laughed sympathetically.[27]

Born in 1931, Bloom received a bachelor's degree in chemistry from MIT. He went on to study at Harvard with Robert Woodward, receiving his Ph.D. in 1957, when Land and Woodward got their honorary degrees together. After postdoctoral work in the biochemistry department of Columbia University and at Harvard Medical School and teaching chemistry for two years at Smith College—the source of more than one of Land's laboratory colleagues—Bloom came to Polaroid in 1960. Promotions were fast and steady: research associate in 1965, manager of organic research in 1968, assistant vice president in 1973, vice president and associate director of research (a position also held by Howard Rogers) in 1975, and senior vice president in 1977.[28]

Designing the opacifying dyes for the chemical curtain was agonizing: "You never start with nothing. We knew that some materials color in alkali [the medium in which development takes place]. The clues were in the scientific literature—we had to build on them. But one thing wasn't in the literature: we had to find a material that would totally switch itself off. It's easy to find a substance that will colorize in acid, but we wanted it to have color in a high alkali content, then turn transparent when the alkalinity dropped just a little."[29]

Polaroid patent attorney Stanley Mervis succinctly stated the objective many years later: "This is the key: colored to colorless with just a very small drop in pH from 14."[30] The first demonstration of the concept was in 1968. The first substantial quantity of the opacifying dyes was manufactured in April 1972, the very month of the public demonstration at Needham. It had been twenty-nine months since the first demonstration of the idea's workability in the lab. The pressure was immense. Throughout, Bloom and twenty to thirty colleagues were nagged by the imperative to make "not grams of these materials but tons of these materials . . . at a reasonable price."[31]

The opacifiers seemed even more daunting than the new, highly stable SX-70 dyes, which Martin Idelson and others had begun developing in 1960. The yellow dye was particularly troublesome. The dyes had to meet specifications about sequencing and pacing, on time scales that ranged from months down to a fraction of a second. They had to be brilliant and stable. They had to stay quietly in their special layers and not interact with the special dyes used in adjacent layers to sensitize silver halide grains to particular bands of lightwaves. When they were supposed to move, after a picture was taken and ejected from the camera, the dyes had to migrate—at the desired rates—either into the light-sensitive layers to be trapped where light had fallen, or keep on going to the positive image layer. They also had to stop moving at the right instant.

Amid the chemical violence of processing an SX-70 picture, the dyes had to be unchanging, far more resistant to fading than any dyes that Polaroid had used before.[32] But the system of dyes in the chemical curtain involved special structures that first masked development and then allowed the customer to begin enjoying the picture. The image dyes were supposed to stay around forever, but the opacifying dyes were to stay around just as long as they were wanted, and then go away.[33] This change would happen when the chemical environment became somewhat less alkaline, but not so much less as to stop the ultra-stable image dyes' being "subtracted" out of the negative and finding their way into the mordant trapping layer to make a print.

For dyes that would resist the fading action of sunlight, Polaroid's chemists went to structures with metal atoms, such as chromium or copper, at their centers. Howard Rogers called some of the early experiments "pretty horrible." Because the new dyes tended to move more slowly than their predecessors, it would take longer than before for Polaroid color pictures to reach completion.[34] The "instant" was in danger of getting rather long.

The opacifiers, derivatives of the phenolphthalein used in some laxatives, were an invention on demand, or, as Land called it, "forced evolution." There was no room in the new camera for a dark chamber. The image would have to come together outside the camera. The required temporary filter had to be at least twice as opaque as a filter for viewing a solar eclipse. Sheldon Buckler, the director of chemical research, to whom Bloom reported, said, "The way the camera was defined, something like that had to exist. But the problem was not just that it didn't yet exist, but that we didn't know the phenomenon that would give it the foundation to come into existence," and so, "[t]here were some doubts." For Buckler, it was "the toughest job I've been involved with in my life."[35]

Spurred by Land, the search for the materials of the chemical curtain had begun in 1967. By 1968, eighteen laboratory chemists were at work, looking first for any way to do it, and then for a practical way. Dozens of schemes and scores of compounds were tried and abandoned. Before Bloom and his colleagues were finished, he recalled, they felt that they knew "more about phthalein dyes than anyone else in the world." On 4 November 1969, about fifty Polaroid scientists crowded into a lab for the demonstration of a tiny amount of the winning system. An exposed film unit was re-exposed to the rays of two Sun Guns, delivering as much light as at the peak of Mount Everest. The image began to clear. People cheered and slapped each other's backs. The scientists who brought the first bottle of opacifier to Land's office received in return a cake inscribed: "From darkness there shall come light."[36]

The phthalein dyes that Bloom and his team were seeking needed to be stable for a year on the shelf and, alone or in combination, black, totally opaque, at the maximum alkalinity of pH 14. In an environment as alkaline as pH 14, Bloom said, most materials will simply decompose. The high pH was established within a fraction of a second after the goo from the pods was spread between positive and negative. In the crucial first seconds, when auxiliary dyes were reaching exposed silver-halide grains in the negative, the opacifying dyes cooperated with the titanium dioxide pigment in cutting down the flow of light from outside to less than one-millionth of what it had been only a fraction of a second before, when the picture was taken. The absorptive opacifying dyes contributed all but one tenth of the light-blocking. The light-blocking exceeded expectations, being one hundred times lower than in filters for viewing solar eclipses. After that, the game changed. Just one notch lower on the logarithmic scale, pH 13, the opacifying dyes were to change their structures just enough to be "half colored."

As in so many of the complex systems of SX-70, it was better to share the load on the opacifiers. Instead of one opacifying dye, two were used, so that a single dye no longer had to block light at all visible wavelengths from 360 to 700 nanometers (billionths of a meter). The dyes' partner, the titanium dioxide pigment, amounted to half the one-gram weight of the processing fluid. The two dyes made up a substantial fraction of the rest of the goo. Among other components were the potassium hydroxide for creating the mobile, alkaline environment, a cellulose polymer for making the goo viscous so that it would spread evenly, and a bit of water.[37]

There was another problem: avoiding the leakage of air between positive and negative when film units were made. Bloom and several others worked on it with Frederick Binda, who was a veteran of the earliest work on pods. Excluding air would not only aid the spread of the reactive chemicals, but also cut out a layer-boundary that would have increased the amount of light-piping into the negative. The binding could not be too permanent, however. The reactive fluid must push through. The answer was a tiny amount of polymer in water, which produced a so-called positive-negative polymeric laminate, or PNPL. Land and others originally doubted that this last-minute crash effort would work. "The skeptics were really in the majority down to the wire," Bloom said. But then, one week, people in Land's lab said, "This is the week we start PNPL-ing." Under intense pressure, they "solved some problems that came up literally in 24 hours."[38]

∞

Even after the film designers felt that they had finished, there was one more thing that Land and Bloom worked on: the finished print was too shiny. Land said of the glare, "It's impairing my vision. I can't appreciate the beauty of the photo." Besides, when some pictures were taken, the glare scattered light in such a way that ghost-like images appeared in the prints. So useful in many ways, Mylar plastic was very refractive, that is, light-bending. The cure was an extremely thin anti-reflection coating on top of the film unit, like that applied to photographic lenses. The laboratory of chemist Charles Chiklis was asked urgently for an anti-reflection coating, without being told the reason. He took a sample of a fluoropolymer across the street to Land's laboratory.

Soon after, Chiklis was summoned across the street again: "Come over and see the beautiful results." Land's associates had spin-coated a layer of the fluoropolymer on top of a finished SX-70 picture. Chiklis's "elation lasted only two minutes." Land told him: "That's very good, Charley. Figure out a composition allowing coating at high speed, adhering tenaciously to the [transparent] polyester base, with a thickness no greater than a quarter wave and density 15 milligrams per square foot, with resistance to abrasion, fingerprints, and martinis." Land meant mass production of a layer no more than a quarter of a wavelength of light, that is, no more than 125 nanometers. It took Chiklis and his colleagues six months of feverish work, starting in August 1972, to find the right combination of a low-index coating, including a "magic bullet" component patented in Chiklis's name. Chemistry was Chiklis's part of the enterprise. He didn't "know one end of a [coating machine] from another." Bob Stephens developed the technology of coating.

"Bob Stephens and I worked around the clock for six months," Chiklis recalled in 1978, his eyes glowing. "It really was my first experience working with Dr. Land. I was walking four feet off the ground. No such thing as working too long. My wife was caught up." Six years later, the pressure was still on. Every time a new refinement of the film came forward—some announced, some not—there was a new challenge about anti-reflection coatings, usually involving unwanted interactions with other coatings.

Many film people resisted the idea of antireflection coating from the start, Chiklis said. "Very few thought it would be practical. They thought it would only cut the yield" of finished film. But the coating—one-third of a micron thick, a bit more than Land had specified—was a success. Coated by the mile, the anti-reflection film was announced to the public in 1974, almost a year after it entered production. The result was "a great deal of pride and confidence . . . If they can coat an anti-reflection coating they can coat anything." By the time he made that statement, Chiklis had risen to the rank of assistant manager of polymer research and was managing Polaroid's pilot coating facility. What he treasured most was his chance to work closely with "the more inventive people at Polaroid."[39]

In July 1972, looking back on the development of the SX-70 film, Bloom said with satisfaction, "Not a hell of a lot was left out of this."[40]

∞

Meanwhile engineers had to build both a pilot plant for coating the negative with nine or more microscopically thin layers and the full-scale plant in New Bedford. Early in 1974, *Fortune* described the challenges facing Land:

> However the venture turns out commercially, the mere production of the SX-70 must already be counted as one of the most remarkable accomplishments in industrial history. The project involved a series of scientific discoveries, inventions, and technological innovations in fields as disparate as chemistry, optics, and electronics. Failure to solve any one of

> a dozen major problems would have doomed the SX-70. Still Land remembers the most exciting moments as those when people perceived the way things might be done, rather than the later times when they actually were done. The difference in pleasure, he explains with a smile, is like that between "conceiving a child and having to bring the damn kid up."

To many of the people whom Land drafted from around the company to work in secret compartments on his dream system, the whole thing looked pretty difficult. Wareham said of the specifications, "In retrospect it looks easy. But then it was like trying to run a car without gasoline."[41]

With immense aims and only bright hopes of accomplishing them, Land was sure that the project had to be protected from skeptics. The chief of these was William McCune, who had begun as a quality-control engineer at Polaroid in 1939 and had worked with Land ever since the heat-seeking Navy missile project during World War II. He knew of Land's dislike of skeptics: "One thing about Land—when he is doing something wild and risky, he is careful to insulate himself from anyone who's critical. It's very easy in the early stages to have a dream exploded." In 1977, he put it this way:

> He's a person of very strong convictions. He has to be, to do the things he does. He has to be able to override all kinds of objections and obvious reasons why things are not going to work . . . in order to start out with the bold, imaginative concepts he does, and push them through. I think it's been invariably very big in the history of the company . . . The idea of making a picture come out of the camera into the sunlight and having it develop in the sunlight was absolutely crazy . . . He's very persistent, and he's protective of his persistence. If somebody wants to come around, wants to tell him why it won't work—if he perceives that simply as discouragement of himself—he will throw him out.

Land would stop paying attention, stop talking about the project with the doubter, or only talk "with people who are going to support him."[42]

McCune's responsibilities called for a lot of skepticism. His principal task over the decades was to get Land's systems produced, within and outside Polaroid. He became the chief engineering officer in an enterprise dominated by a man whose primary self-identification was as a scientist.

The trim, athletic McCune was a man of many hobbies, including hiking, biking, skiing, silversmithing, and rebuilding and repairing high-performance automobiles. Like many "execs" in this world, McCune saw himself and projected himself as a balance to Land's dangerous optimism. Not long after the crises of SX-70, he succeeded Land as head of the company.[43]

Land's transfer of engineers from Dietz's group into Wareham's was said to have occurred during one of McCune's vacations at his chalet in Switzerland. The day he got back and convened his camera group, he discovered that some engineers had been transferred to the SX-70 project on the ninth floor. The next day, Land's secretary, Natalie Fultz, called, and put Land on the line. From now on, Land told Polaroid's chief engineer, Land would be in sole charge of SX-70. McCune did not know which surprised or angered him more, sudden removal from his strongest field, camera design, or the uncharacteristic direct order. All of a sudden, some of his best engineers, including Dick Wareham, were not to speak with him. McCune was off the case—but not forever. In 1972, he was called back in to tackle an array of crises with suppliers.[44]

Despite these events, McCune found it possible a few years later to praise Land. "He is very flexible in being prepared to explore any alternative that will get him to his goal." Land did not fix on a single way to the exclusion of better ways. To be sure, said McCune, this was often frustrating to co-workers, who would catch his enthusiasm, plunge into the task, and become convinced that it would work, only to find Land charging off in another direction from which he thought something could be learned. McCune saw a value in Land's impatient refusal to wait for better materials when those available in the lab might answer a question right away. He was "very creative in inventing ways of gaining knowledge in a hurry. He's never contented to wait a week to get the results from testing, or a day. He's right away inventing how the hell you can do it, so you can have the results—now—or in the next hour." The "iterative process" of experiments to decide which road to travel went on "very rapidly like a computer rather than like sitting down with longhand and a pen, pencil, paper."[45] As an engineer preoccupied with quality, cost, and efficiency, McCune appreciated the intellectual efficiency that accompanied Land's intellectual prodigality.

Land was an artist, McCune thought, in bringing people together to work on one or another technical approach. "If he hadn't been an inventor, he would have been a marvelous playwright, because he has a great sense of drama, and a great sense of staging things for gaining the effective command of his audience and taking them where he wants to go."[46]

20

Selling SX-70

> You learn that—far from growing older in the way the world would like you to grow old—you find yourself under better control. You find that you are sustained by the various friends. You find friends and colleagues who themselves grow younger with the passing years. What is extraordinary about Polaroid, unique I think, is that it is the only company that seems to have this capacity for self-regeneration.
>
> —Edwin H. Land, 2 May 1972.

Having created SX-70, Land had to ignite the minds of customers, and not just those eager to adopt ideas early. Despite the risks of over-promising and pratfalls and delays, demonstrations had to convince photo dealers and amateur photographers alike. The vast hurried development of the cricket-like camera and playing-card film aimed to bring the products of science and engineering into everyday life, in a kind of rehearsal for the almost daily innovations of the wired-up 1990s.

The SX-70 of 1972, with its sophistication in the service of simplicity, had both similarities with and differences from its computer-age analog, the Macintosh, which was introduced spectacularly in 1984 as "the computer for the rest of us." The Mac's outward face, including its little smile and its "welcome to Macintosh," symbolized for well over a decade an intuitive and convenient approach for mass users, an ambiance similar to the one that Land had sought for SX-70. The original Apple Macintosh went on the market almost ludicrously underpowered to achieve its goals. Nonetheless Steven Jobs—an intense admirer of Land—and others put across the idea of the Macintosh, with the help of a successful campaign for "free ink," masterminded by the publicist Regis McKenna, that was more elaborate than Land's feats of publicity. As with Polaroid instant photography, there was a sense of having customers innovate along with the Macintosh.

The SX-70 innovations were in place from the start, but it would be a challenge to make enough cameras and film while the public was still enthusiastic. With demonic energy, Land drove to publicize SX-70 almost in opposition to the Polaroid marketing department. As he had for forty years, he not only made demonstrations and gave speeches, but he cooperated once more in a carefully paced series of "exclusives" given to selected outlets and selected journalists. He limited direct quotation and continued to prevent any focus on his family. As he did to the end of his active career, he gave as much focused energy to planning publicity as he did to the architecture of the new photographic system.

Land gradually divulged details of his "new medium," emphasizing several themes. He said that Polaroid was determined to escape from dependence on Kodak and intended to rival Kodak in serving amateur color photographers. At annual spring shareholders' meetings for most of the 1960s and 1970s, he had portrayed Polaroid as a fountain of magic for customers (and shareholders). Now, with increased simplicity, tens of millions of consumers could take more and better pictures.

Land began his campaign of anticiptions and surprises in the spring of 1970, just after the camera's design became final. He foresaw an expanded type of photography that would "go beyond amusement and record-making to become a continuous partner of most human beings. . . . a new eye, and a second memory."[1] Just a few days later, *The Wall Street Journal* wrote of a "spectacular research and marketing battle" building up between Polaroid and Kodak. In only seven years, 1963 through 1969, Polaroid's sales had risen 4-fold, and its profit 6-fold, while sales at the much bigger Kodak rose just 2-fold, and its profits 2.5-fold. Land's view was, "We've always been way ahead of everyone in this field, and with all due modesty we believe we will stay ahead." With just a touch of disbelief and disapproval, the paper gave this capsule portrait of Land and his company:

> Still handsome at 60, with a thick shock of black hair, Mr. Land prowls his camera-cluttered office during an interview, pondering answers to questions. He can be affable or intensely shy. He is indifferent to business details. Until he hired an assistant recently, he often didn't bother to answer letters from top

> executives at other companies. Polaroid has only the loosest kind of chain of command; one [unidentified] executive vice president, for instance, has hot lines direct to sales managers, allowing him to bypass the sales vice president.[2]

Aladdin was just part of the buildup. Land underlined at the 1970 shareholders' meeting that he was not just pursuing a whole new system of still photography, but implied that instant movies were a real alternative if his path to SX-70 were to be blocked.[3]

∞

The next move, in November 1970, was an article in *Fortune*, always a favored vehicle for his viewpoint.[4] Land had gone out of his way to impress its author, journalist Philip Siekman, and spoke freely of his attitude and plans. As Land and Siekman drove around in a rented limousine, to the great new factories, the journalist asked, "It's all so wonderful. You wouldn't, perhaps, be bluffing?"[5] Siekman was dazzled. He wrote of a coming Polaroid–Kodak war for the amateur color-photography market. Siekman had asked for an interview, and, typically, Polaroid told him it was difficult to see Land. "Then, one morning, they called me in NYC and said he could have lunch, today. I flew up expecting lunch with the man, and, maybe, a tour of facilities with a minion. Lunch went through dinner; subjects ranged from the perception of shadow to Victorian novels. We were both taken with *The French Lieutenant's Woman*. Conversation went through the next day, with himself as tour leader. For a long time after, I would get the occasional call from him asking my opinion about something that was on his mind."[6]

In Siekman's account, Polaroid had pulled nearly even with Kodak in U.S. sales of cameras and film. Although Kodak's Instamatic camera was "a success on the order of foot-powered Singer sewing machines and Hoover vacuum cleaners," the company had remained in a "pacific duopoly" with Polaroid. "Kodak could not find a way around Polaroid's high, broad patent wall. Polaroid could not make a camera that was foolproof enough, portable enough, or cheap enough to compete on even terms with Kodak's easy-loading Instamatics." Of Kodak's work on an instant system, Land said that he doubted that Kodak could close Polaroid's twenty-two-year lead. "They don't know what they're getting into."[7] Those who thought Kodak could catch up were "underestimating the power of our imagination."

Kodak liked the "tail-end ride at little risk" from manufacturing ever-larger quantities of negative for Polaroid, but Polaroid's ability to sell millions of cameras was puzzling. Siekman wrote that "the Land camera was—and still is—everything a camera for a mass market should not be. It is too big, too expensive, and too difficult to use. A quick sequence of photographs is impossible. A Land camera user leaves a trail of refuse. Additional prints and enlargements are difficult to obtain. The film seems expensive. And despite elegant innovations that delight the technically minded, it forgives few errors."

Siekman disclosed that the new camera prototypes, "as thick as a cigar case," were very easy to use, and made pictures of unprecedented brilliance and color. Although the camera would sell at more than $150, Land claimed that it would be "more than anybody ever dreamed of having in a mass market." Land seemed to be "gambling that the system will be so different that the public will look on it as a totally new product." Selling it "will take a major shift in attitude toward photography—which, of course, is what Land has in mind." The intended target of this message, Kodak, had a very different outlook from Land's:

> Withdrawn, reflective, dog-restless away from a laboratory where he can patiently, joyously unravel some piece of the skein of knowledge, Land will at times dismiss marketing as what you need "when you don't have an idea." Intently in search of innovation and invention, he professes to believe that the right product will sell itself or, as he says with a smile that acknowledges and thus averts an approach to pretension: "Virtue and a good product are invincible." . . . Because Polaroid views itself as a successful innovator, it is willing to gamble heavily on still more invention. Because Kodak views itself as a giant marketeer with many products and many responsibilities, it leashes its technical confidence with caution and prudence.

Siekman asked a sixty-one-year-old Land to list the qualities of his successor. Land described "such a paragon of talent, intelligence, and virtue" that he burst out laughing. In an oblique reference to his grooming of Stanley Bloom, he said, "We're making him down in the laboratory."[8] Land himself had been worked and reworked in the laboratory. Perhaps his successor would be. The hope was not realized.

∞

Land the innovator knew that he was putting strains on his own company. He wrote shareholders in March 1971 that those who develop new processes in the laboratory think very differently from those who create the new factories, as do "the men who organize ideas and the men who organize men." The new system was not emerging in the neat progression of idea, early research, pilot phase, manufacturing development, and then manufacturing. In a rapidly changing world, the old rule of the chemical industry—nine years from test tube to tank car—would be "disastrous," because science and markets would change, and the interaction between technical subcultures would be lost. "Clearly, then, massive modern programs require nearly complete overlap in time of all phases of the activity from research through development, through manufacturing-development, through manufacturing." The subcultures must work together. "A significant new product in contemporary corporate life emerges on all these fronts at once and then quite suddenly is complete."[9] While enunciating his new model of innovation, he could hear the rumbling of a volcano of discontent in his own company.

A month later, Kodak also beat the drum, telling shareholders that "active development" of its own instant photography systems had begun, and that it hoped to market film for Polaroid cameras within a year and sell an alternative instant photography system by 1975.[10]

Land's next move was to pull his new camera out of his pocket at a shareholders' meeting, although he did not open it, he said, because "the patent department won't let me." The audience applauded enthusiastically. He added, "Aladdin in his most intoxicated moments would never have dreamed of asking his [djinn] for it. . . . It's utterly new in concept and appearance, utilizing an utterly revolutionary flash system, an utterly revolutionary viewing system, utterly revolutionary electronics, and utterly revolutionary film structure." He said that the camera he held was a working model, and that "an awful lot of it" would be ready in twelve months. Perhaps thinking of Kodak, Land said, "It will be like an invincible steamroller coming down the next block."[11]

∞

The wizard of Osborn Street had brought forth new magic that deserved attention, but he did not want to sound too revolutionary. In March 1972, Land reminded shareholders that for twenty-five years, Polaroid had followed "a single direction, a camera and film system that will be with us most of the time, a system that will be a partner in perception, enabling us to see the objects in the world around us more vividly than we can see them without it, a system to be an aid to memory and a tool for exploration." Others, Land said, just regarded instant pictures "as a quick kind of ordinary photography" and did not share the idea of "a new medium" as different from other photography as television differed from radio. The new photography would leave the past and "change the interaction of people with the world around them." There must be "nothing for the photographer to do except to compose and to select the instant at which he wants to go from viewing to having."[12]

Soon after Land's letter, *Business Week* put Land's picture on the cover and gave more details, including the difficulties in making the components of Aladdin.[13] An unnamed executive compared the costly technological cliffhanger to Project Apollo. "The scenario has all the makings of a great industrial triumph or a colossal bust." The article mentioned "computer-crammed" factories that had been built in eastern Massachusetts at a cost of two hundred million dollars, not only for Aladdin, but also for the lower-priority Sesame instant-movie project (chapter 22). The cost of the negative-coating factory at New Bedford alone was sixty million dollars. There, "heavy scrappage costs" plagued the preproduction runs. "Anxious months remain before the pieces fit," the article said, and asked three questions: Is the camera ready for production? Can mass production be achieved in time for the 1972 Christmas season? Will people buy vast numbers of them, especially in the face of coming competition from Kodak? The answers turned out to be no, no—and yes.

As earlier, the effort to sell a product up front led to some focus on Land himself. Land was "redesigning" his company, but who would carry on Land's role as Polaroid's chief innovator? Traditionally Polaroid had been a "strange blend of informality, paternalism, secretiveness, and experimentation." A Harvard Business School professor told the magazine, "Look, Land is creative, and he has the well-grounded suspicion that good, careful, systematic planning can kill a creative company." An unnamed former Polaroid officer said, "Don't kid yourself, Polaroid is a one-man company. It is 80 percent Land's inventiveness and creative ability."

Bringing film and camera manufacturing inside Polaroid was "high technological drama," Land said. The motivations went beyond the search for higher profit margins: "These cameras and film are technologically unique, involving new science at each point of manufacture." He rejected an assertion by a Kodak official that there was no large market for cameras costing one hundred dollars or more, the probable price of Aladdin. "There will be as many of these as there are telephones." Yes, the camera was much larger than a new pocket camera from Kodak, but "we're trying to get $600 worth of camera to market in the $100 range."[14]

Land did not take this high tone with the press alone, but also when, in the presence of Polaroid's directors, he told the New Bedford plant's managers brashly, "Let me know if it works."[15]

∞

The publicity culminated in the Polaroid shareholders' meeting in Needham, Massachusetts, on 25 April 1972.[16] Only nine years after instant-color amateur photography was introduced, Land was entirely restating the field.

Over the previous weekend, the preparations and rehearsals had been elaborate, chaotic, and wearing. In true Landian style, many things were ready only at the last minute. Thriving as usual on the pressure, Land was exuberant. While waiting around for the next thing to happen, he experimented with standing on the floor with both feet together and launching himself up onto the edge of the platform where he would perform a few days hence. Amazingly, he landed there securely, and not just once. Some others could also do this, but others, despite Land's encouragement, could not.

For the rehearsal, it was vital to have enough cameras, flashbulbs, and film in working order. Land's audience would include many, not necessarily sympathetic, analysts from Wall Street brokerage firms, and photo dealers from around the country, who often complained that Polaroid favored mass-market discounters. Many employees and shareholders would be there, along with reporters. The skeptics must be convinced that the new system worked, that it could be made in quantity relatively soon, and that the public would buy and use it.

On a cool, overcast afternoon, thousands of people filed slowly into the huge rectangular solid of the film warehouse in Needham, not far from the famous Route 128. To taped music playing over many loudspeakers, they entered a huge chamber, recently cleared, whose walls were covered entirely in black velvet. Once in their seats, the audience could see a group of octagonal platforms that could be spotlighted or kept in darkness. One of these was for Land. The others were stages where groups of Land's laboratory associates would show off a wide variety of uses of the new camera and film, such as a birthday party or a laboratory microscope. The audience was not allowed to handle the cameras or, indeed, to take any pictures. Elaborate security arrangements had required them to check their cameras at the door. Around each octagon were wooden handrails with a channel inside them. After each picture was taken and had begun "emerging," a Land associate would punch a hole in its base and slip it into the handrail slot, fastening it from the side away from the audience with a stout metal pin. Invented at the last minute, the anti-theft system did not prevent alert representatives of Kodak from scooping up some of the punched-out "dots" for chemical analysis.

At 2 P.M., Land, wearing a portable microphone and transmitter, mounted the steps to his spotlighted octagon and introduced the slate of directors for election. While the ballots were counted, he left center stage. Twenty minutes later, he returned to the octagon, sat down in his spare, modernistic chair, picked up a large meerschaum pipe from the little white Eero Saarinen table next to him, and lit it. Then he pulled the camera out of his pocket. "There's the camera!" he said, jovially. "A record success for concise presentation of a new product." He hadn't been bluffing with the *Fortune* reporter. "It's real, a joy to handle, an exciting package of perhaps 300 transistors wrapped in top-grain leather." The leather's name in the catalog was "Sinful." He put in a film pack, the motor whirred, and the protective film cover came out. As the audience applauded, Land said, "and you are ready to take a picture."

He had momentary trouble. A strip of tape on the back side of the GE flash array, designed to conceal that there were five more bulbs on the back, blocked the camera from completely unfolding to its working position. He switched at once to a sequence of lantern slides to show how the camera worked while handing the camera to Bill McCune, standing in the darkness nearby, to fix it. McCune removed the flash unit, fully opened the camera, pushed the red button to eject one picture, reinstalled the flash unit, and handed it back up to Land.

As the slides were shown one by one, Land said, "You can spill martinis, drop it in the bathtub, put it in your pocket, stack it, give it away." Slides showed color deepening in a test shot, which Land said, "emerges more, and emerges more, and emerges more." The audience applauded. "Nobody in the world has seen this. First time it has been outside the lab. . . . Touch the button, you have the picture." The audience applauded again. He added, "This is a better lesson than you are going to get from your dealer."

He called off the names of demonstrators on the stages: Stanley Bloom, Jeanne Benton, and Linda Melnick on one; Inge Reethoff photographing flowers and fruit on a second; Nick Hadzekeriakides, Barbara Winsor, and Nan Chequer on a third; Mary McCann using the camera with a laboratory microscope and Vivian Walworth with a stereo microscope; Jay Scarpetti and Caroline Pearl photographing such objects as a Persian snuff container borrowed from the Boston store Shreve, Crump, and Low;

Barbara Theobald with a rock garden and live ducklings; a group of men playing poker; and the photographer Marie Cosindas: "See how magnificently she has made the transition!"

The audience was invited to circulate among the octagons. As the audience returned to their seats, Land said the system was "intellectually complicated, operationally simple," and added, with energy, "Can't do it anywhere else than America!" Asked about cost, Land deftly sidestepped the question: "We really do think we have everything. My fantasy is that it'll be as widely used as the telephone." To that end, Polaroid might use surplus income to retool to bring the camera's price down, or perhaps "something might happen technologically," but until it did, Polaroid "would concentrate on getting better at making it." Given the manufacturing problems already emerging, this was a masterpiece of understatement. In one brief answer, Land referred to the hope that the initial Aladdin camera's life on the market would be extended by automation and cost-cutting, and admitted that it was still difficult and costly to make. He added, "After watching you today, we can't make enough." At that moment, most of the working models of the camera were right there in the vast, dark theater.

From the shadows, marketing vice president Peter Wensberg warned Land about the large numbers of previous-model cameras and film in the pipeline. Income from them would be needed to carry the new system through its costly introduction. It was a life-and-death commercial issue. Not skipping a beat, Land responded, "We won't commit to production until we know how rapidly we can scale up." Of the many production problems, Land said with typical jauntiness, "It's a neat position to be in. We like the problem." He added, "We're not making it so well that we can say we're sure we'll make the [unspecified] date . . . A richer answer is that the camera is made of many components and they are going well."

When would the first commercial appear? Land retorted: "I did the first one today. You'll do the next." How much film will camera owners use? "A picture a day without decay. Our experience is absolutely horrible. You can't pick up this camera without running through the pack." He added, "We're not putting film into inventory yet, but we could make what you see today continuously. By sometime late in the year, we would have built up a good inventory." Asked whether he still dreamed of an even smaller camera, he replied that Polaroid had "taken a trunkload of miracles and made it into something. It's just like the husband and the wife forgiving each other the last ten pounds." Additional applications would be for later. "We are pioneering the print field with such expansion that we don't know how to make enough."

The lower-priority options included transparencies, instant movies, and peel-apart film using Aladdin chemicals. "We'll never catch up with ourselves. We'll never have to worry about somebody catching up with us."

Virtually everyone in the cave at Needham was seeing the fruits of Aladdin for the first time. Thousands of employees had been kept in the dark for years, and now Land was committing them to a revolution. Land had to win over the people who would make the new film, assemble the cameras, and sell them. Consequently, early in May, Land went back the Needham warehouse three times to repeat his demonstration for huge groups of employees. He told them that in a company that reinvented itself continually, small groups of pioneers would frequently pull apart, away from the skeptics, insist on the impossible, and build the future. But he had carried SX-70 as far as he could without their help. Land's tone turned valedictory as he mentioned a five-year-old who had just wished him luck:

> Young people are so full of natural faith in life. And then their bodies grow old around them. The world, the literature, the church, all teach us, all teach that you have to grow old, that you have to give up your dreams and ideals. And somehow all that teaching reaches you and then you project back on yourself, and on your friends, the idea, "Oh, yes, we must give up. We must grow older. We must become less than we were." I've had the good fortune, sustained by all of you, to be able to see that that simply need not be true . . . You learn that—far from growing older in the way the world would like you to grow old—you find yourself under better control. You find that you are sustained by the various friends. You find friends and colleagues who themselves grow younger with the passing years. What is extraordinary about Polaroid, unique I think, is that it is the only *company* that seems to have this capacity for self-regeneration.

In recent years, Land said, he feared that the growth of the company, the very growth he had foreseen as a problem in the 1940s, was going to cause Polaroid to lose its way. Through many years of work on Aladdin, he had stuck to one principle: "we would not compromise in this camera with having everything that we thought a camera and film should have."[17]

Holding up an Aladdin picture for another group of employees, Land said it "places before you a thing that is more of the thing than the thing was originally." Of the system, he said, "You couldn't know what it was going to be like before we had done it, because there was nothing like it before." In the new viewfinder, "You see what you're going to get. As you use it, you'll forget you're using it at all." In the new system, if you wanted copies, you could have them right away by taking pictures in rapid succession. The employees applauded. They laughed when he put a picture into a pitcher of water, noting that the film unit was dry, hard, waterproof, and martini-proof.

He would not be swerved from his goal by skeptics. Land implied that he enjoyed the idea of fighting them. "We didn't allow the world to project on this the world's idea of how this ought to be limited." Would there be multiple models of the new camera? an employee asked, perhaps aware of designs for cheaper, nonfolding versions. Land rejoined that the aim was to "concentrate on this one model" and teach people to enjoy it, while steadily dropping the price.

Like shareholders, the employees toured the octagons. When they returned to their seats, a huge dolly laden with a roll of negative from New Bedford—enough for half a million pictures—was rolled around the floor to what Land called "appropriate music," that is, the theme song from the musical *Hello, Dolly!* Land boasted, "Polaroid's the only country that's better than Japan."[18]

∞

A few days later, just after his sixty-third birthday, he took his case to photographic professionals. For his report in San Francisco at the annual conference of the Society of Photographic Scientists and Engineers, a small crew from Polaroid had worked much of the night to set up an octagon in the hotel ballroom. Land had spent part of the day going around the city with noted photographer Alfred Eisenstaedt to demonstrate the camera. Ansel Adams escorted Mrs. Land into the ballroom. Asked if she had been present twenty-five years before at the Hotel Pennsylvania, when her husband had unveiled the first instant photography system, she said that she had missed it because she had a cold. How did she feel now about her husband's work? She replied, with a trace of weariness, "Just wonderful, just wonderful, just like it always was."

The system his audience would see, Land told them, was the realization of specifications he had set out thirty years before in answer to his daughter's question in Santa Fe. He drew laughter when he referred to "those few details that took from 1943 to 1973." He said that Ansel Adams, "who criticizes with love and a very heavy hand," had said of Polaroid's previous cameras, "That's fine, but why don't you make it so that you can see the image on a ground glass?" Land would reply, "But that's impossible, Ansel. How can you have a folding camera with a ground glass and such a big image?" Land told his audience, "Well, this one does."

As the cover sheet of a fresh film pack pushed out of the camera, and he relished the mystery of where the power for the motor came from, Land said, "There's no scientist I know who wouldn't rather be a charlatan. And when circumstances allow you to be both, why it's great fun!" Taking five flash pictures in less than ten seconds, about ten inches away from his meerschaum pipe, Land said, "So now we have achieved our 1943 dream. We've looked at the image in the reflex viewer. We've touched the button five times, and we have five dry pictures." The scientists and engineers applauded. He wanted them to respect the results: "While those are snapshots, they're hand-held, not [taken on] a tripod, they're just things as you go along. I think you will sense in them a new meaning for casual photography that makes it not casual, that gives each user a feeling of personal identification with the world around them in the way that photography has always hoped to do, and which it may have done perhaps for many of the people in this room, but which it has not done for the great mass of people who just move on snapping."

As he got into details, Land remarked ruefully, "Now comes the sad moment of truth in which, regretfully, I have to tell you something of how this is done. Not that I don't enjoy sharing the science, but I always regret going from the simplicity of the end product to something of the intricacies behind it." Of the four-element lens designed by James Baker, Land told them that "it is impossible to design, impossible to make the elements, impossible to center and locate them, impossible to put them together—and it's all going very well." He showed them slides of the light working its way via a succession of mirrors and lenses up through the camera to create a right-side-up, non-reversed image of the scene for the eye of the photographer just behind the eyepiece. The whole camera, he said, weighed "not much more than the prism in the ordinary through-the-lens reflex."

He showed a list of dozens of electronically controlled operations in the 1.3 seconds after the shutter button was pushed: "So all that has happened." The audience applauded. After describing the film's thin layers and metallized dyes, he turned to the chemical curtain. He showed them page after page of compounds in the patent for the opacifying dyes. His audience exclaimed and then laughed when he said, "So if you really want to do this kind of thing, you have to be serious about it!"

His Aladdin colleagues, most of whom were in the room, were astonished that "so many things are working which so few years ago seemed just unthinkably difficult, although rational."

Land mentioned the nontrivial problem of how much processing fluid would spill over beyond the picture area after the tiny rollers spread it between the positive and negative. The solution was "dictatorial. The thing that really made this [film] pack possible was that the Chairman of the Board, President, Director of Research, head of that particular laboratory, and director of this particular project said, 'We're gonna make [the trap to catch excess fluid] no bigger than this and we're gonna contain all the liquids, and anyone who doesn't believe it isn't here anymore.' And some of 'em aren't." The audience laughed.

The many companies cooperating on what became SX-70, Land said, had come together in the manner of World War II: "The bulbs are ready. The glass is ready. The new molding is ready. The rubber is ready. The new integrated circuit is ready. We ourselves, of course, had the tremendous undertaking of building a whole new—the largest installation, factory, in New England, I think—to make our new negative, which is a new kind of negative with all-new dyes. All the reagents in this are new and synthesized for the first time."

The competitive efforts of photographic companies reminded him of William James's "moral equivalent of war." Photography "has been just such a wonderful, inspiring undertaking, giving us such a feeling of what we can do in the United States if you pick the right purpose and go for it together."[19]

∞

The first reactions were all that he could have hoped for. Major news organizations vied for pictures and detailed descriptions of the new system and for exclusive interviews with Land. Finally, the choice went to the weekly news magazine *Time*, which put Land on the cover on 26 June 1972. In a space usually devoted to faces, his face was hidden behind an SX-70 camera that he was focusing. Officials at Kodak said that the magazine had used a crowbar to force Land's cooperation. The article heralded a new era of "pocket photography," a phrase that could apply equally well to Kodak or Polaroid. Kodak was told that the article would feature Kodak. When Land was told of that threat, he "gave in."

With one in five Americans, more than forty million, taking pictures, the article said that photography was being transformed "from mere hobby to a natural, even essential way of looking at the world and capturing life as it is." Cameras could soon be used very widely as "a kind of visual notepad." The "box of magic from Polaroid" was "the most startling and certainly the costliest" of the new cameras. Leaders of the photographic industry did not all agree that it was a new medium, but they were "unanimous that it is a stunning technological achievement."

"Land's unabashed cultivation of the nonexpert photographer" drew scorn from the curator of photography at the Museum of Modern Art: "Land could invent new cameras every hour and still would not increase the awareness of photography as a creative medium, because his cameras are designed for the amateur." The design chief of Nikon disagreed. The immense success of Kodak's first Instamatic after 1963 had created many American photographers who graduated to "our more advanced cameras." Growth of snapshooting created new opportunities at the top end of the business. The magazine gave Land the last word: "Every picture we take—one that is taken with care—should make our lives that much bigger. Photography is an illustration of the use of technology not to estrange but to reveal and unite people."[20]

∞

With expectations so high, there was increased danger of disappointment at any hitch. Indeed, delays in scaling up the manufacture of both cameras and film did add to costs. In April 1972, the company's treasurer had forecast to the press "a very difficult year for earnings."[21] In July, the company reported that second-quarter sales had fallen 14 percent from a year earlier, and profits had sunk 62 percent. For the first half, although sales had risen slightly, profits were off 45 percent from 1971.[22] In the third quarter, earnings were off 35 percent.[23] Perhaps the public had tired of earlier models, or as Wensberg feared, they were holding off for the new system.

Timing remained a problem. The company hedged on whether the new system could be introduced nationally by Christmas. This was the goal, an announcement read, "but experience will tell us how long it will take to build up sufficient inventories for a national introduction of the system."[24] This foreshadowed the first big disappointment. On the Friday before Labor Day, traditionally a very quiet moment on the stock exchanges, the company said that national introduction was off until the following year, although a "limited regional" introduction was possible before then. Polaroid's stock fell $6.75 a share to $113.75.[25]

Polaroid retreated to the pattern of its very first camera introduction in 1948—starting in one regional market and adding others gradually. The chosen venue, south Florida, was even more local than when

Polacolor hit the market in 1963. The limited regional introduction occurred 26 October 1972 in the Fontainebleau Hotel in Miami Beach. The hotel's exquisitely out-of-date, modern-baroque immensity exactly suited the first sales of SX-70 to photo dealers. Land was not there. The photo dealers received small quantities of camera and film and saw the new television commercials starring the British actor Laurence Olivier. A special movie by the designer Charles Eames of Venice, California, was narrated by the MIT physics professor Philip Morrison.[26]

Demonstrations for reporters in New York on 20 October, including a disclosure of prices, were rocky. Donald Dery, the Polaroid spokesman, made the first presentation at *The Wall Street Journal*. After taking half a dozen pictures in succession, Dery explained that the list prices would be $180 for the camera, $6.90 for a pack of ten pictures, and $2.77 for a "bar" of ten flash bulbs (implying a list price of 96 cents for each flash snapshot). There would be a two-stage scheme of bonuses to dealers for each camera and film pack sold, which could reach $10 per camera and 10 cents per film pack. He told the reporters that the information was "embargoed," that is, to be held for release, until the photo dealers' meeting six days later. Already annoyed by the exclusive story in *Time* three months earlier, the *Wall Street Journal* reporters protested, but Dery insisted. He went off to his interview uptown at *Newsweek*. Soon, the *Journal* reporters found out about Dery's call at *Newsweek*, the already-filmed commercials, the Eames movie, a planned seven-page spread in the 27 October issue of *Life*, and a twelve-page special advertising section in the Florida regional edition of *Life* on 13 November. Their irritation got back to Peter Wensberg at Polaroid that day. Not necessarily distressed about all the attention, Wensberg telephoned to say that if *The Journal* thought the information was so important, it could publish it right away.

The paper responded with what amounted to a Bronx cheer the following Monday, 23 October. Untypically, *The Journal* reporters indicated open resentment of public-relations maneuvering, what came to be called "spin" in the 1990s. Polaroid's attempt to keep back details a few more days, they wrote, was "the final move of a well-planned effort over the past few years to create an aura of breathless anticipation around the camera. It seems to have worked remarkably well. Because of Polaroid's program of gradual disclosure, the SX-70 has become probably the most highly publicized camera ever made." An unnamed Wall Street analyst said that Land "has become a real showman. He knows the public is fascinated by his wonderful toy, and he's playing it for all it's worth."

The reporters speculated that the delays resulted from a lack of production know-how. So much of Polaroid's manufacturing had been delegated to other companies, such as Kodak. The camera had never been test-marketed. Two large-volume photo dealers thought it wouldn't sell, whereas two others said it would. One skeptic believed that Polaroid had "outpriced itself." A second dealer declared he would buy only three cameras for each of his fifty stores. An optimist said, "It will be a sellout. We'll never have enough in stock." Another said, "If it's as good as they say it is, it will sell—believe me, it will sell."[27]

21
Crisis

> The test of an invention is the power of an inventor to push it through in the face of the staunch—not opposition, but indifference—in society.
>
> —Edwin H. Land, April 1975

Timing and corporate image were not the only problems with SX-70. There was a fundamental difficulty: focusing the camera. A tense struggle over focusing raged within the company through the high-wire months of 1972 and afterward. Company officers, directors, and customers alike had trouble focusing, particularly in low-light conditions calling for flash. They wanted a traditional cue that the scene was in focus, such as the matching up of the halves of a split circle in the center of the visual field. Land hated it. It violated the spontaneity he was seeking. He felt that a focusing aid spoiled the utter naturalness and sweep of seeing the whole scene that would emerge in the picture. Despite Land's fury, critics within the company insisted that the split-circle focusing aid was essential.

Presenting the details of SX-70 to a professional group, in New York on 15 November 1972, he acknowledged the troubles with focusing. The problem was the worst in faint light requiring a flash exposure. Instead of a split circle, Land was determined "to teach thousands of people to live in the viewfinder." It was vital to see "the whole beauty of the picture, with nothing to break it up, with no rings or prisms in the middle—no little microprisms." He thought people were using the system well in southern Florida. So he had been right to be "a little bit stubborn." He said, "This new art form is indeed coming into being. We have every faith in it and we don't intend to compromise." Proud of his new system and determined to sell it as hard as possible, Land dreamed of "a new technological aesthetic." He still saw an analogy with artists painting while observing scenes or people. An artist "teaches the painting. The painting teaches him. That's why you give up everything to be an artist." SX-70 would be "a transducer between what's inside you to what's outside."[1]

As Peter Wensberg put it, "Reason did not triumph over elegance for another six months," that is, until the summer of 1973, when limited national introduction was near. Then the split circle forced its way into new cameras and was offered to current owners.[2]

∞

On 17 November 1972, Polaroid received an unexpected bit of good news from Rochester. A brief announcement over the Dow-Jones wire chattered into the lobby of Polaroid's headquarters. Kodak would abandon its plans to make peel-apart film for Polaroid cameras. SX-70 had convinced Kodak that it too must leap into integral film. The announcement said that peel-apart systems constituted "a secondary and more limited marketing opportunity." Investment money was tight, and Kodak had to keep expanding the production of Pocket Instamatic cameras and film. There wasn't enough money left over for both integral and peel-apart instant film. As one reporter put it, Kodak was executing an "about face."[3] Land's boldness had at least partially redefined the challenges of his much bigger rival.

A nearly four-year-old crash effort in Rochester had just changed course. Polaroid had told Kodak about the radically new film in April 1968, and in October of that year, Land had shown Henry Yutzy of Kodak, his frequent collaborator on military reconnaissance projects, an Aladdin picture masked to conceal its structure. Soon after, Kodak told Polaroid it planned to terminate the 1957 agreement for supplying negative. It launched a project, called PL-976, to put an instant system on the market in 1976. Deciding in midstream to accelerate, Kodak had then tried for an introduction in 1974 and renamed the project PL-974. In 1970, the focus had become clearer and the effort directed at two goals. Project P-129 aimed at a peel-apart color film for Polaroid cameras, under a new license agreement with Polaroid. But Project P-130 sought "a Kodak film for a Kodak camera," as Federal Judge Rya Zobel described it in 1985.

It was the P-129 peel-apart project that Kodak dropped in 1972, after spending ninety-four million dollars, according to trial testimony years later. Kodak memoranda at the time, according to Judge Zobel, "recognized that any product created by P-129 would be obsolete even if it appeared on schedule." Efforts on the non-peel-apart P-130 redoubled. At the peak, between late 1973 and late 1975, between 1,300 and 1,400 people worked on it, exploring alternate technologies, pushing for inventions where they were needed, and running into numerous obstacles.

Kodak's first camera in this pursuit was called the Lanyard. In this design, picks would advance a picture by grabbing it from the front. The photographer ejected the picture from the camera by pulling a lanyard. After Kodak representatives saw Land's demonstration of SX-70 in April 1972, the Lanyard was abandoned as too big. With the film, researchers came up with two dye-release chemistries by late 1971, but struggled for a year to get sufficient film speed. They struggled, as Polaroid had, with problems of shrouding the negative during processing, keeping the dyes stable, and making a workable layer for taking up the dyes. At the beginning of 1973, Kodak officials were nervous about the future of their instant project: Polaroid had reset the standard they must meet. Even a "me-too" product, not equal to Polaroid's, would take two and a half years. Confronting Polaroid's wall of patents, Kodak's Development Committee suggested in September 1973 that "development should not be constrained by what an individual feels is patent infringement." Polaroid made much of this memorandum during the patent case that eventually drove Kodak from the field.[4]

According to Albert Sieg, the Kodak project leader, chemists in Rochester, France, and England directed their ideas toward an integral film operating so differently from Polaroid's that it would not infringe any patents. Engineers drove toward smaller, simpler, cheaper, and more reliable cameras operated either by a crank in the basic model or a motor in the higher-priced model. When the cameras and film went on the market in 1976, Sieg considered the film's chemistry "the first really fundamental technology since Kodacolor Aero reversal film in 1942." This had been turned into a commercial film in 1946 and a consumer film in 1955. The effort was a crash program like SX-70, Sieg said. "We developed cameras, films, packs, and facilities all simultaneously, rather than sequentially." Perhaps the most novel challenge was machinery for assembling the integral film units by the mile.[5] Kodak's investment, later estimated at two hundred million dollars, supported sales of 16.5 million instant cameras and hundreds of millions of film packs over Kodak's nine years in the market.[6]

The technological first cousin from Kodak severely affected Polaroid.[7] Although Kodak's cameras were clunky and hard to make, the marketing might of the yellow-box company was behind them. Making little if any money, Kodak seized one-third of the instant-photography market. Polaroid lost large profits that it had expected, about $450 million over the next ten years, during which the Japanese photo giant Fuji also entered the one-step market. The lost profits amounted to perhaps $1.30 per share per year, and so dividends were smaller, share prices were held down, and Polaroid had less money to spend on innovation.

∞

Early in December 1972, Otis Bradley, the research chief of Spencer Trask and Company, a man identified as favoring growth stocks, listed Polaroid as one of twelve companies with a potential for annual increases in earnings of 15 percent over the long term. The other companies were AMP, Burroughs, Digital Equipment, Hewlett-Packard, International Business Machines, Motorola, Perkin-Elmer, Raychem, Sony, Texas Instruments, and Xerox.[8] Many of them had bumpy rides ahead.

The SX-70's limited regional introduction began well. Just before Christmas 1972, SX-70 cameras were reportedly very scarce in Florida, having become "clearly a prestige gift for Christmas." Most stores had long waiting lists.[9]

∞

By the time the SX-70 camera went on sale, Land's great technological gamble had been physically embodied on an imperial scale. The provinces—and problems—of the new manufacturing empire were numerous. For the optics, hundreds of thousands of viewing mirrors were coming out of molds and ovens.[10] Under the direction of Richard Brooks, the specialty chemical plant east of Route 128 in Waltham was sending sensitizing dyes to New Bedford.[11] The leader of the giant negative-coating plant was Mac Booth, who succeeded Bill McCune as chairman of the company in the 1980s. As Booth showed visitors around, he candidly discussed yields that were far too low.[12] Visitors to the final-assembly machinery for the film at the Reservoir site west of 128 could see the almost incredible industrial difficulty of bringing the different components of the film units together in the dark and assembling them into packs at the rate of hundreds of thousands a day.[13] The cramped work stations of the shutter-assembly plant behind the multiple, mirrored windows of a former Ford assembly plant on Memorial Drive in Cambridge made clear the highly manual and very costly nature of the process as it then stood.[14] The vast new camera-assembly plant at Norwood was developing a bad case of indigestion at what appeared to be an overdesigned final-testing machine.[15]

The workings of the cavernous New Bedford negative plant were complex and continued to give problems. A special article in *Business Week* late in 1973, after the national introduction of SX-70, noted that a great deal happened after the batches of emulsions and other materials were made up and sent to the vast coating rooms. "As the layers of chemicals are applied, the continuously running film must be alternately dried, warmed, and cooled; steps that call for extremely precise computer control of temperature and humidity along the way." The plant had relied heavily on minicomputers to make what Booth called "a terribly finicky product." Even more of the processes, he was convinced, should be turned over to digital control, so that plant managers could learn swiftly "how many gallons of goop we use, how many square feet of negative we use, and what are the costs involved." Production had to be tightened so that yields and profits would increase.[16]

The crises in manufacturing, both inside and outside Polaroid, challenged Land's hopes to bring down costs, so that the fancy folding camera would have a long run before cheaper models took over. Land wanted the complex introductory camera to be a feature-laden, elegant Tin Lizzy of impulsive photography. In the war on costs, Land loyalists turned urgent attention toward the problem of automation. Even before the end of 1972, quick decisions were needed on how many workers would be hired, and at what pace. On the ninth floor of 565 Technology Square, Wareham led a committee on automation, when the costs of most of the camera's components were way out of line with its introductory price. A lot of automation would be needed quickly. By this quiet effort, Land exerted pressure on the main-line engineering army under McCune, who was already back on the case and doing fireman's work on supply contracts. People whose careers McCune had fostered would do most of the work in routinizing the making of SX-70, but Land didn't expect much initiative from them. Whether all this creative tension was necessary is debatable.

The automation committee was in close and uneasy communication with McCune, usually through an assistant. As the physical, industrial, and commercial realities began to come together, Wareham's committee went through a graduate course in the system, process by process, inventor by inventor, factory by factory. Also at issue was Polaroid's dedication to the individual and collective fulfillment of its employees, or "members." Fostering initiative, flexibility, and loyalty was easier when the number of employees was small and focused on higher-end skills. But employment had tripled in the previous decade, and one model of how to build a lot of SX-70 cameras quickly was to hire hordes of manufacturing workers and fire them as soon as possible. This was new territory for Polaroid. Hitherto, big-scale manufacturing, including that of the cameras, had been left to companies that could tell an assembly-line hand, "You made a mistake? I'll show you one more time. If you do it again, you're fired." Wareham's usually twinkly eyes grew steely as he recalled this practice. Why not automate up front? Why relegate SX-70 to the role of gold-plated ancestor of a succession of boxy little mass-market snapshot cameras?

The cost figures on the blackboards in early October were shocking. How soon could they come down, who would do it, and at what human cost? Suppliers were wrestling with the challenging frontier roles that Land had assigned them. They weren't meeting even current costs and quotas and deadlines. Several were becoming convinced they never would meet Polaroid's goals for quantities and prices in 1973 and later. By late 1972, Irving Erlichman of the ninth floor, who already had designed nonopening versions of SX-70 during the earlier troubles with the viewing system, had come up with a scheme for automating shutter assembly. By then, too, Land had visited each station of the shutter process, just as he had the electronic controls line at Fairchild in California.[17]

Late in the summer of 1972, Land and his wife came back from their usual Southwest vacation with Ansel and Virginia Adams. They had taken many lovely images, but these images carried a disquieting message. Many pictures of the sweeping, arid high country were on the blue side, as if they had emerged on a cold ski slope. The reason was gas leaking from the hidden battery.[18] It was an early warning of problems in Appleton, Wisconsin, part of a long train of disappointment. Polaroid had felt that it had signed with the best when it enlisted the Philadelphia maker of Ray-O-Vac batteries for a wide range of consumer products. There were bigger problems than the gas leak. The specially built new factory in Appleton could not make good enough batteries fast enough to meet the demand aroused by the lyrical publicity. The battery shelf life of only a few months reverberated through film orders to camera orders, making them fitful and jerking costs upward at the factories. The negative-coating factory could not "run full," as it was designed to do, which would cut profits.

A few years later, Sheldon Buckler (later vice chairman of the company) recalled that Ray-O-Vac "had grave difficulties in meeting specifications, quantities, and costs." Polaroid had little hope that Ray-O-Vac could improve. In December 1972, in "a crisis environment," Polaroid made "crucial changes" in the design of batteries and battery-making machines and, "at a mad pace," began building its own factory. In October 1973, the first "live" Polabeam battery was produced. Six months later, the battery machine went into "production mode" in a rented building. In October 1974, with Polaroid's second machine nearing completion, Ray-O-Vac's Appleton factory shut down and Polaroid was making all its batteries. According to Buckler, they were "instantly better." In March 1978, Polaroid opened a new battery plant at its Reservoir site in Waltham.[19]

Although the process was nerve-wracking, the directors approved bringing battery manufacture inside. According to longtime Polaroid board member Carl Kaysen, the decision made sense. Once the engineers learned how to seal the batteries properly, the batteries unexpectedly developed more power than predicted and lasted longer. Batteries rolled off the lines like a river, and Land devoted some effort to finding other markets in flashlights, toys, and so forth, so that the factory could "run full" and achieve its inherent economies. These efforts were halfhearted and met with little success.[20]

∞

When innovations are demanded across a wide front, there will be trouble at multiple points. The historian Thomas Parke Hughes uses the military analogy of "reverse salients," as in World War I. SX-70 was no exception. Challenges multiplied like Job's troubles. Among the immense headaches was the four-element glass lens, made at a special Corning Glass factory in Kentucky that eventually closed. In February 1975, announcing the end of its contract with Polaroid, Corning was scathing. Sales of SX-70 were so disappointing that Corning didn't "have a large enough order to justify continuing production" past midyear. A spokesman said, "This is just a story of a product that didn't do too well in the marketplace."[21] A supplier in Japan was found. The slap at Polaroid had special sting because Land had persuaded Corning's chairman, Amory Houghton, to take on the lens. In 1972, a white papier-mâché lobster in a special glass case, a gift from Houghton, stood prominently in Land's outer office.[22]

Another crisis arose over the camera's electronic controls, made by Texas Instruments and Fairchild Semiconductor. At the November 1972 conference in New York, Land had described the difficulties in making the electronic controls: "I would say both companies [Texas Instruments and Fairchild] have been challenged, to say the least." As usual, he put a good face on it with a flourish: "They just didn't realize how good they were until they had to use their full competence." These difficulties matched those in the laboratory. "I really think that we simply never could have done it if it hadn't been for the continuous inspiration of the pictures themselves."[23]

Early in 1974, Fairchild dropped out altogether and Texas Instruments re-formed a team to find a whole new design to crack the barriers of cost and reliability. When the two companies had begun making control units for SX-70, the cost was thirty dollars at Fairchild and forty at Texas Instruments. Now Texas Instruments could quote six dollars a module and hope for profits as volume increased. According to an electronic-industry trade paper, "Fairchild, on the other hand, did not see anything worth fighting for at the $6 level."[24]

The fitful pace of camera orders aggravated the problem of gradually reducing the prices on such components. Expected cost savings were delayed. This was dangerous, given the intense advance publicity. Customer demand was high, but the cameras and film were not always available. Golden moments passed. In early 1973, a few other warm-weather states—good sites for numerous successful pictures—were added. But the national introduction in September 1973 was nine months late. Even then, numbers were still limited and cameras were strictly allocated among dealers. Demand, and the potential for embarrassment, remained high.

The reaction on Wall Street was more than nervous; it was drastic. During Polaroid's hundredfold expansion from 1950 to 1970, the company had stood out as the wonder stock of a scientific age. Many factors stimulated Wall Street's romance with Polaroid, according to former Polaroid executive Stanford Calderwood, who migrated to the investment business in the 1970s. In an analysis presented to an investment class at Harvard Business School in 1976, Calderwood mentioned four stimulants: "An unprecedented invention, unprecedented patent protection, unprecedented marketing, and an unprecedented evangelist." There was a fifth factor: "Not-so unprecedented laziness among the analysts."[25] In 1974, analysts at a dozen Wall Street firms had projected earnings per share between $2.25 and $3.60, but the actual figure was 86 cents.

Polaroid shares had been very important in the post-Depression, post-World War II history of Wall Street. In 1996, as *The Wall Street Journal* looked back at hundred years of the Dow-Jones stock index, Polaroid was mentioned as one of the special attracting factors of two decades, the 1950s and 1960s, when millions of Americans packed away their post-1929 dread and re-entered the world of equity investments. Polaroid even survived the fearsome collapse of stock values after 1969. It was one of the "nifty fifty" investments that were expected to outperform other companies in the era of high technology. Once Polaroid stumbled over multiple hurdles of its "forced evolution," however, panicky investors dumped the stock. In a year, its value dropped 90 percent from a peak of nearly $149 a share to $14 by mid-1974, 26 percent below a "book value" of the company's assets of more than $19.

The earlier euphoria had some basis in sales and profits. In 1953, the year Polaroid introduced its first camera costing less than $100, sales totaled $25 million. Eight years later, sales had quadrupled. For the next dozen years, Polaroid's sales continued to rise dramatically, sevenfold in 1962 through 1974, compared to a fourfold increase for Kodak. According to Calderwood, the increase in sales had averaged more than 30 percent a year from 1962 through 1969, but, in the next four years, a little above 15 percent. While after-tax earnings per share of stock had increased steadily at Kodak, they had zoomed upward at Polaroid, from 32 cents in 1962, the year before color film went on the market, to $1.81 in 1967, and held this high level for four more years. But then they bumped down to $1.30 in 1972, $1.58 in 1973, and 86 cents in 1974. The price of Polaroid stock exceeded $140 a share in 1969, 1972, and 1973. Throughout the thirteen years 1962 through 1974, Polaroid's stock was valued about twice as high, compared to earnings, as Kodak's. In 1972, the Wall Street price/earnings ratio for Polaroid was 93.5, and even in 1974 it was still 47.7.

It was a hot stock. In 1973, Calderwood noted, the average daily trading in Polaroid shares was almost $6.6 million, a high value for a company valued at $2.3 billion at the end of the year. Even IBM, valued at $35 billion, or seventeen times the market capitalization of Polaroid, had a daily volume of only $15 million, a bit more than twice that of Polaroid, a volatile stock. The price of a share varied sharply between $77 and $127 in 1967, between $87 and $133 in 1968, between $102 and $145 in 1969; and, dizzily, between $51 and $130 in 1970. In 1974, however, a year of deepening recession, the variation—almost all downward—was far worse. At the beginning of the year, midway in the dramatic 90 percent plunge, the price was $88, but in a few months it sank to $14. On a single day, 29 May 1974, the price fell from $56.125 to $43.25 a share. The next day, Polaroid was the most actively traded issue on the New York Stock Exchange—317,000 shares or nearly 1 percent of the total of Polaroid shares oustanding.[26] By March 1976, just before Calderwood's analysis, the price had recovered to $40.125, or twenty-one times earnings. The effect on the value of the 4.9 million shares held by Land, his wife, and their Rowland Foundation was startling. It fell from $700 million at the peak, to less than $70 million, before recovering to $196 million early in 1976.

Many large-capitalization "blue chips" also suffered in the severe bear market. Eastman Kodak went down 65 percent from its high in 1973 to its low in 1974, erasing $15 billion in market value. IBM fell 59 percent in the same period and lost almost $32 billion in market value. There were sharp losses, also, in the valuations of Xerox, Coca Cola, Disney, and Texas Instruments.[27]

∞

Analysts, having been bitten, turned negative. They surveyed camera dealers on the eve of Kodak's 1976 entry into instant photography and found them high on Kodak and lukewarm about Polaroid. The analysts acknowledged Polaroid's very modern plants and its hard-won ability to make film profitably. But Polaroid violated several canons of business: it wasn't getting an adequate return on capital and did no strategic planning or systematic cost control. The visions of stock analysts, brokers, and investors, both individual and institutional, had been blasted.

Land himself did not understand this frenzy very well. His father had preferred real estate to stocks, and Land himself had lost a ten-thousand-dollar nest egg in the collapse of 1929.[28] He was very proud of his complete refusal in the 1960s to join in the orgy of "conglomerating" widely different businesses, which was done in the name of balancing among various profit cycles. Conglomeration aimed at better overall returns than came from knowing your own business and renewing it constantly.

The analysts also were taking revenge for what they saw as Polaroid's "arrogant refusal to take them into [its] confidence until it was too late."[29] But their reaction was excessive. While the stock was plummeting, the company's sales were rising. Customers bought all the SX-70 cameras the company could supply, and the new revenues more than offset declines in sales of earlier models and their films. To be sure, customers used their SX-70 cameras far less often than in Land's ebullient forecast of a "picture a day without decay." Usage fell so far short that the company official designated to talk to stock analysts officially described the film stream as "disappointing."

The 1974 decline in earnings to a level not seen since the early 1950s was not just a blip. It went on for a couple of years. As the company, valued at $4.5 billion in the market, shrank to a valuation of $450 million, and as Land, his wife, and their charities lost a maximum of $600 million before recovering $125 million of it, other investors may have lost billions, depending on when they bought and sold. Calderwood wryly called it "a four billion, four hundred forty million, nine hundred thirty-three thousand, six hundred twenty-seven dollar and fifty cent misinterpretation."[30] The reverberations lasted for decades. In noninflated terms, the Polaroid stock price in the 1990s was not far from its low of the mid-1970s. One analyst took delight in saying in 1991, just after Land's death, that he had always regarded Land as "an arrogant son of a bitch."[31]

∞

During the years of trial, Land kept teaching about SX-70 and trying to sell it. In 1973, each copy of the annual report for the previous year held in its cover a real SX-70 picture of a red rose, one of hundreds taken by Inge Reethoff and a few colleagues over several days with a handful of cameras in the laboratory, using seven hundred dollars' worth of long-stem roses. At the 1973 annual meeting soon after this report, Land called the SX-70 camera "a hand-held factory," more reliable and sturdy than any professional camera. "We believe in the professionalization of the amateur." He organized a shareholders' school for using the camera—with particular emphasis on focusing—conducted at hundreds of round tables, each with a ring of brightly colored tulips flown over from Holland and kept in cold storage until just before the meeting.[32]

At the 1974 shareholders' meeting, Land and his colleagues hooked up an SX-70 to an elaborate array of television monitors, to show the entire audience what the photographer Ed Judice, who had come up onto an octagon in the middle of the crowd, was seeing in his viewfinder (now equipped with a split circle). Judice was focusing on a girl in an orange dress with a violin, a man in a cap lighting and smoking a pipe, and some playful children. Land commented, "There is only one right place for each side" of the picture, and quoted the poet Baudelaire, "Every artist has a critic inside." The audience could see, Land said, that "you cannot separate the composition from the life of the moment. It is all one thing, to be decided in a split second while you're living through it."

Then he leaped ahead to show off a way to take instant color negatives with an SX-70 camera equipped with a special long snout. He counted off the time for the color negative to complete itself, "One chimpanzee, two chimpanzees." Then, "you could put it right in your enlarger and make the print." After longtime employee George Trumbour brought up the millionth SX-70 camera, Land answered questions. He said that if one could make a color negative with SX-70, one could make a black-and-white one as well and "answer an ancient demand."[33]

A few days later, the May 1974 issue of *Consumer Reports* carried an evaluation of SX-70. While the film was easier to use and neater than peel-apart and yielded better colors than Polacolor, the camera was ungainly:

"The total feel was clumsy and unnatural." Focusing was difficult, the exposure system was not omniscient, the camera needed to be carried inside a coat in cold weather, the battery was not always reliable, there was a risk of wasting a shot after taking five flash pictures, and the pictures took ten minutes to complete themselves. Consumers should recall, the magazine said, that Polaroid often introduced "less expensive versions of its photographic innovations." Perhaps the customer should wait.[34]

In July, Polaroid leaders met with analysts to explain why profits in the previous three months had fallen to a quarter of their level a year before. They intended to be reassuring, but phone calls from the analysts there led to so many "sell" orders that trading had to be halted temporarily. Wensberg said that six hundred thousand SX-70 cameras were in owners' hands at the end of March. Since the camera had gone on the market nationally the previous fall, McCune said, six hundred engineering changes had been made in it to cut costs and improve quality. The company, he said, had begun supplying some of its own batteries in April and was now meeting half the demand. Some of the most recently produced batteries had shelf lives of twelve to fourteen months. "We didn't intend" to enter battery manufacture, McCune said. "We've been backed into it."[35]

The problems remained serious. Of the two million SX-70 cameras sold to dealers by the fall of 1974, *Business Week* reported in November, "half still rest on dealers' shelves." Although Wensberg said that the new Model 2 SX-70 camera made money even at its introductory price of ninety-two dollars, an unnamed former Polaroid executive called the introduction "dangerous price cutting." Of the film, Mac Booth of New Bedford said gloomily, "What we need now is volume. We have all that capacity staring us in the face." Land said, "This was no Boy Scout outing, but an expedition over the Pole."[36] For the whole year, the company's sales rose almost 10 percent, but its profits sank 45 percent.[37]

∞

In 1975, under pressure from the board of directors, Land yielded the presidency to Bill McCune, while retaining the titles of chairman and chief executive officer. At the shareholders' meeting that year, with tears in his eyes, he addressed McCune, "You're at bat now." But he stuck to his guns. True inventions should make a society "a little different." He added, "An invention that is quickly accepted will turn out to be a rather trivial alteration of something that has already existed." Above all, a significant invention "must be startling, unexpected. It must come to a world that is not prepared for it." Probably thinking of Wall Street's attitudes, Land said, "The test of an invention is the power of an inventor to push it through in the face of the staunch—not opposition, but indifference—in society."

For the first time in years, Land did not show off a new invention. Instead, he exhibited five huge enlargements of SX-70 photos of the Charles River basin and the Boston skyline, stretching across a twenty-three-foot stage. The display, however, had not been prepared without the usual crisis. He told an interviewer, "Do you know when we first saw it? At two o'clock that day." He meant twelve hours before the meeting. The demonstration called for a special film coating. Land recalled saying, "Let's make a production coat." The production people were incredulous. "They called back and said, 'He's not serious!'" Land said. "I didn't know I was serious, but they knew from long experience that I was, so they made it. This was a typical, natural, healthy, relaxful Polaroid undertaking."

Land kept the focus on SX-70, even though the negative for the display also provided experience for black-and-white negatives and color still transparencies. "We wanted to show people what we already had done," Land said. "I felt it my duty to say, 'You've got the biggest thing that has ever been in photography, and I'm going to hold you right there for a moment. . . . Don't worry about the new things: if there is anything we are good at it is generating those.'"[38] He was even upbeat about the troubles with the battery. Land told Subrata Chakravarty of *Forbes* that they had been good for the company. "Without the troubles, we would have been spoiled and we would have been growing too fast. It was a happy accident, a cloud with a very silver lining. But it was a cloud with a kick like a mule!" He remained certain "that this camera and what it does will be a necessity to everyone once they learn how to use it."[39]

A year later, just as Kodak plunged into instant photography, Land found a new way to send a hopeful message. He highlighted the quality of Polacolor 2, a new peel-apart color film that used the SX-70 dyes. It could be used for portraits twenty by twenty-four inches. At the Boston Museum of Fine Arts, with a camera the size of a room, paintings could be duplicated at full size. He had been skeptical, but when he saw the quality of big images taken through James Baker's special lens, "I jumped on the bandwagon fast." He exulted in full-size pictures that did not lose any information, as was inevitable with smaller reproductions. To applause, he unveiled a full-size replica of one of Renoir's paintings of a young couple dancing at Bougival: "That stood in my office a week. Normally a copy irritates with time. This grows. You're really forlorn when it's taken away from you."

Perhaps thinking of Clarence Kennedy's efforts fifty years earlier to photograph Italian sculpture for art instruction, Land forecast a wide market for the new technique. "In all the small towns, there'll be a museum." This scale was never reached, but twenty years later, Land's associate John McCann continued Polaroid's modest business in museum replicas. Soon after, McCann led an ambitious project of making a full-size replica of Raphael's "Transfiguration" in the Vatican.

Land spoke of the laboratory co-workers who convinced him: "We don't have the guts to stop what others do. . . . We forgive each other. Last year's enemy is this year's friend." He turned to his audience of stockholders and exclaimed, "What a wonderful company it is to treat shareholders not just as investors but people who care about taking pictures!"[40]

∞

SX-70 was a huge gamble that eventually paid off, but bloodily and later than expected, damaging Land's credibility with his fellow managers, with investors, and even with those members of the board of directors who had known him longest. With investors hurt and the status of a glamour investment gone, the company could no longer recruit fresh capital from the stock market, as it had done thrice to create war chests for the next great technical adventure. Still, despite the cultural divisions between marketing and the technical side, despite the sense of rivalry between those loyal to Land and those loyal to McCune, Polaroid got the hang of its revolution, without collapsing. As reliability and output increased, sales rose. Polaroid had continued to crack one seemingly impossible technical problem after another and again turned the results into manufacturable chemicals and devices. Furthermore, the gamble had been financed with the company's own cash.

The technologies that were developed with such risk at the top of the line proved remarkably adaptable—and quickly adaptable—to exploitation at lower prices, even if this happened somewhat differently from Land's hopes. After lower-priced models of the folding SX-70 camera paved the way, a much cheaper, nonopening camera, called Pronto!, which "burned" the same type of film, went on the market just before Kodak's long-delayed entry into instant photography in 1976. Only a year later, Polaroid swept into the bargain basement with OneStep, which also burned integral film and sold in the millions. McCune would recall years later, with pardonable pride, that the profits from OneStep saved the company from the terrible costs of the complete commercial failure of instant movies.

The SX-70 film chemistry proved fundamental. In the mid-1990s, it still was used in the hundreds of millions of color pictures taken by motorized, electronically controlled Sun, Spectra, and Captiva cameras around the world. It was a particular favorite in such third-world markets as Russia, India, and China, which lacked the infrastructure of film-processing labs that were so important to the vast numbers of noninstant cameras in well-off countries.

Land's display of the museum replicas underscored a second profitable reverberation. The SX-70 film chemistry had been adapted to the perennially profitable peel-apart business for amateurs and for technical applications like microscopy. Indeed, many years later, an employee argued that Polaroid should simply have stuck to its still-substantial and still-profitable peel-apart business and foregone the integral-film revolution. Perhaps, in this view, Land's psychological warfare had crazed Kodak twice, pulling it into a business in which it could not win and waving it off from some very easy profits that would not have been subject to legal challenge.[41]

As Land saw it, Polaroid's business situation did not call for conservatism. Instead, the small company had to get out front of its looming giant competitor. Numerical analysts from America's many business schools, if asked, might have dismissed SX-70 as a hopelessly risky business. But Land bid defiance to such analysis. One day in October 1977, he and Irwin Miller, chairman of Cummins Engine of Columbus, Indiana, walked into a reunion seminar at the Harvard Business School. Land told his audience of more-than-usually successful businessmen that it was their type of thinking that closed the laboratories at 4:30 on Friday afternoons.[42] He remembered well his horror of just such an experience at the central laboratories of General Electric more than forty years earlier.

In retrospect, the technologies of SX-70 appeared to be essential to the survival of Land's enterprise. The SX-70 culture showed continued vitality. Sonar and infrared devices for automatic focusing were introduced, and picture-taking become even more spontaneous. The Sun, or 600, series of cameras, brought out in 1981, carried built-in strobes that permitted flash whenever it was needed, not only indoors but also in the shadows that photographers frequently encounter on the bright summer days of weddings, graduations, and vacations. The hidden battery, by then made reliably by Polaroid, was thickened to the size of a Saltine cracker and delivered the needed extra juice. The patented SX-70 technologies were like an endowment.

The mainstream judgment, however, was that Polaroid and Land lost their way in the late 1970s. A decade later, a newspaper account spoke of "an icon to American ingenuity" falling behind when its market matured and "its visionary founder lost his vision." The company had "lost its creative spark." Like many big companies, it "didn't have an encore." Although Polaroid held a monopoly of instant photography, assuring it of "a solid, albeit unexciting future," instant photography had "lost its magic."[43]

The company was vulnerable to the takeover raid launched against it by an organization called Shamrock Holdings in 1988, even though it fought the raiders off. Polaroid rejected the bid, secured approval of its employee stock-ownership plan from a court in Delaware, and, with the help of a "white knight" investor group, began buying back stock, forcing Shamrock to withdraw its three-billion-dollar buyout offer.[44]

∞

Before and after he took over the day-to-day control of the company, McCune's private judgment of Land's performance on SX-70 was caustic, although he praised Land for creating the company's special environment and attracting a wide variety of talent. He referred to himself and Land as brothers who fought a lot. Just after Land's death in 1991, he realized that the company's rapid growth had become a major problem by 1972. With the modest but innovative system of 1948, he recalled, "there were enough people in the United States to buy all we could make." But twenty-five years later, Polaroid was a big company, with a lot to lose by making successful products obsolete.[45]

Late in 1991, McCune added that SX-70 was Land's and Polaroid's "greatest technical achievement but the beginning of a whole series of financial disasters." Both Land and he were at fault.

> He chafed in the 1960s at uncompromising attitudes on product design. He wanted to realize the dream of 1944, where you aimed the camera, pushed the button, and out came a finished picture. . . . [Land] was really determined. Some of us pushed him into compromises. He set up the ninth floor of 565 Technology Square to keep us out. He didn't like us imposing inhibitions on him. The result was that he achieved the camera and the film but they were full of technical flaws. The battery didn't work. The film didn't work. The camera didn't work. The first 300,000 came back for repairs and alterations. Then he asked me back to rescue the thing.[46]

Kodak's entry into instant photography was soon followed by a cruel irony. Instant photography flowered briefly and then stagnated. It was circumscribed by such developments as the increasing popularity of hand-held video cameras, the great increase in speed and convenience of processing noninstant films (at lower cost), and the spread of both increasingly sophisticated and cheaper thirty-five-millimeter cameras. Two iron laws of the age of technology are that a new technology can become more convenient and pleasing than an established one, and that an old technology can snap back, becoming again more convenient and pleasing than its rivals.

22

Instant Movies

> There's a rule they don't teach you at Harvard Business School. It is: If anything is worth doing, it's worth doing to excess.
>
> —Edwin H. Land, 26 April 1977

The crises and partial loss of control left Land undiscouraged. For years, amid all his other projects, he had been sneaking off to what he called a secret nightclub, where he searched for a way to make instant motion pictures. The day-to-day boss of this nightclub for nearly twenty years of near anonymity was the brash and ebullient Lucretia Weed. In her field, she had a level of responsibility similar to Meroë Morse's in black-and-white. A big woman with flashing eyes and a strong sense of humor, expressed often in a staccato laugh, Weed was not afraid to argue with her intermittently available boss and scorned the obsequiousness of other scientist-inventors working closely with Land.[1] In the long struggle to perfect instant movies, Weed, Land, and their collaborators found themselves doing some of the cleverest, most impossible things ever done at Polaroid. The spirit of the enterprise was expressed in the project's name, Sesame, after the magical invocation that Ali Baba used to open the treasure cave of the forty thieves.

Land thought of "this delightful field," the dark companion to Aladdin that led to SX-70, in fairy-tale terms. A year before he introduced the first—and so far the only—instant movies, he reminded readers of a British scientist's reference to the scientist as "a conjurer manqué": "When in due course you come to know how these records—which you will be making of your children at play, your friend's golf swing, your machines in motion—how these records are transformed to finished records in color, then you will understand the conjuring motivation of the inventive scientist. For such is magic."[2]

The mystique of this for Land was deepened by plunging back into the history of color and color photography. The experiments of Maxwell and Ducos du Hauron focused on two methods of photographing color: adding up the primary colors, red, green, and blue, or combining their subtractive, or complementary, colors, cyan, magenta, and yellow. The version of color movies that Eastman had shown to Edison in 1928 was an additive process but did not prove commercial. There was no real success until the Kodachrome subtractive reversal film of 1935, which could be used for stills or movies.

The 1928 Kodak process had used colored stripes. Land thought that his version of stripes could be used as filters in making—and then projecting—color movies. In search of a film that not only would be self-contained but even make the negative virtually disappear within it, he went back over his work in the 1940s with black-and-white film, in which the exposed silver was trapped in the negative and the unexposed silver migrated a few micrometers to form a positive print.[3] The project that Weed led under Land's impulse was vast and astounded and exasperated the many people who eventually were drawn into its toils. Peter Wensberg, writing in 1987, was at his most acid and entertaining in describing the drive to make instant movies and sell them to millions of people: "[A]s in the past, the final product contained elements dictated by what he could do and what nature would not let him do."[4]

∞

The eight-millimeter movie film emerging from Weed's laboratory was, in analogy with SX-70, self-contained. For picture-taking, processing, and projection, it was installed permanently in a cassette, a little smaller than the ubiquitous videotapes of the 1980s and 1990s. Within, one side of the film bore an ultrafine screen of stripes of the three primary colors, filtering light as the picture was taken and imparting color when the image was projected. As movies were taken, the cassette film advanced, frame by frame, in the lightweight camera, and light penetrated a short distance to a black-and-white negative layer of uniform-size grains of light-sensitive silver halide. The layer was hardly thicker than the grains it held. Bleachable "anti-halation" dyes, coated on the film in a mixture with a "stabilizer precursor," minimized the scattering of light from the far side of the negative layer. The full tape consisted of three thousand frames, or about thirty-eight feet corresponding to 160 seconds of viewing.

Once the cassette had been exposed, the photographer simply popped it into a player where the film was rewound at once. The rewinding simultaneously developed and dried the film in about ninety seconds. As the rewinding began, the cover of a tiny reservoir of the honey-colored processing fluid was torn back, and the chemicals were spread in an extremely thin layer on the moving film. Within seconds the developer went to work on exposed grains in the negative and, an instant later, on grains of unexposed silver halide that had moved a short way over to the image layer. Chemicals lying within the film, and others spread with the fluid, such as a silver halide solvent, worked together to complete the image and then stabilize it. The special developer, tetramethyl reductic acid, had to be extremely rapid in its action, and yet be stopped completely after the silver image was finished. The silver complexes gathering thickly in the image layer were reduced into silver, forming a mirrorlike surface. The "covering power" of this layer was ten times greater than that of the silver left behind in the negative. In practical effect, the negative had vanished.

Mechanical instructions for starting and stopping the automated player were built into the film, by perforations. Once the machine had rewound and processed the film, similar built-in instructions told the machine to reverse again and automatically project the images onto the viewing screen in the front. Light from the player's lamp passed into the side of the cassette, through each frame, toward a tiny plastic prism, which bent the light ninety degrees and sent it out of the cassette again through the bottom, past a rotating shutter, through a lens, and onto a tilted, trapezoidal mirror to aim it at the back of the viewing screen.[5]

∞

Sesame was later marketed as Polavision. In Land's world, where revolutions had to be revolutionized, Sesame had been the default pathway if Aladdin (SX-70) ran into too many roadblocks. With the success of SX-70, Land felt that he could now focus on what had been a sideline.

Of course, for Land, roadblocks were made to be pushed aside. There had been many with Aladdin, but there were more with Sesame. Even in 1972, at the height of Land's drive to complete SX-70 and rally the whole company to make and sell it, people at Polaroid whispered about the other project, and whispered contemptuously. They thought that the moment for such a project, if it had ever existed, had passed. In the future lay video recorders, ever smaller, lighter, cheaper, and more ubiquitous—just as Land hoped his cigar-case SX-70 camera would be.

Land would have none of the doubts. For thirty years, he and the company had succeeded in bringing out innovations, often imperfect, to an enthusiastic reaction from the public, which granted the time needed for ironing out the kinks. As for video recording, he denounced it as technically wasteful and physically clumsy, inherently lacking in the exquisitely powerful recording and amplifying that only film could achieve. He pushed toward instant movies with a greater stubbornness and recklessness than he had ever shown before in a life filled with risk taking. He was not just looking for a clever technology that would round out instant photography, even if it could only serve niche markets like sales training. Sesame was intended for the mass consumer. With the most elegantly simple system he had ever worked on, impulsive photography would be carried further than ever. Living, instant images would affect the lives of millions and change their perceptions of the world.

∞

In February 1977, a few months before he demonstrated the Polavision system in the most extravagant of all his public presentations, Land was inducted into the National Inventors' Hall of Fame. As in so many previous ceremonies, his companion was Vladimir Zworykin, inventor of the television tube. Posthumously inaugurated with them were George Eastman for the invention of photographic roll film, Lee DeForest for the invention of the audion amplifier, and Charles Steinmetz for his inventions in the transmission of alternating current.

The inauguration took place at the Crystal Plaza headquarters of the U.S. Patent and Trademark Office near Washington. Land received his five hundredth U.S. patent—for a type of flat battery with extra power for automatic light sources—with a handwritten note on it from C. Marshall Dawn, then commissioner of patents. It was a social event. A photo of Land and Zworykin appeared the next day on the front page of the Style section of *The Washington Post*.[6] As usual, explorers, like Lewis and Clark, were on Land's mind: "However much we become a country of scientists, we will always remain, first of all, that same group of adventuresome transcontinental explorers pushing our way in from wherever it is more comfortable into some more inviting, unknown, and dangerous region."[7]

∞

Polaroid's business looked brisk just then, despite the challenge from Kodak. Shortly before the inventors' ceremony, *Fortune* had reported, with slight exaggeration, that Polaroid had sold 6.8 million instant cameras in 1976 and that Kodak had sold 1 million. Kodak was spending heavily to carve out a share of the market. According to a San Francisco investment analyst, who also ran a photo dealership, it cost Kodak $45 to make each of its EK6 instant cameras and a further $11 to promote sales, and yet Kodak was charging dealers $46, for a loss of $10 per camera. In contrast, Polaroid's Pronto! camera cost $20 to make and $9 to promote. At the same dealer price of $46, Polaroid was making $17 on every Pronto! camera.[8]

That same February 1977, Bill McCune, whatever his private forebodings about Polavision, had much good news to impart at a luncheon in the Plaza Hotel in New York for reporters and Wall Street analysts, thirty years after Land's first public demonstration of instant photography. In 1976, Polaroid's sales had risen 16 percent to $950 million, and after-tax profit had risen even more, by 27 percent, to just under $80 million. Both figures were records, as were the figures for cash on hand, the value of shareholders' equity, and the numbers of cameras (6 million) and film packs (165 million) that had been sold in 1976. SX-70 sales had jumped 50 percent, while sales of the peel-apart Colorpack system had held up. Industrial sales were up 25 percent.

The company's line of cameras would lengthen, McCune said, from four models to eleven, including a cheaper version of the folding SX-70. The list price of the popular nonfolding Pronto! camera, introduced a year earlier, was being cut $7 to $59. In the first year of Pronto! 2.25 million had been sold, including a range-finder model introduced in the fall. Improved SX-70 film, with the antireflection coating devised by Charles Chiklis went on sale nationwide in September 1976. The flat batteries installed in each SX-70 film pack had undergone basic changes in design, and the company was testing a new SX-70 film that not only had a longer shelf life than its predecessors, but formed its images more rapidly and in more brilliant colors.[9]

At the Plaza Hotel, there were heavy hints that Polaroid would show its instant-movie system in April. Wensberg, in introducing McCune, had said that many new products would be introduced over the next three hundred days. "You may have guessed we saved one of the more interesting surprises for the annual meeting." A few days later, *The Wall Street Journal* reported that the new movie system—now that Eastman Kodak had ended Polaroid's monopoly of instant photography—would do much to restore Polaroid's "image of uniqueness." Instant movies, the newspaper said, might revive the sagging home movie business. Bell and Howell, a major maker of home movie equipment, estimated that 716,000 systems had been sold in 1976, or 13 percent fewer than the 825,000 in 1975.[10] For the moment, the paper left aside the implication that Polaroid might be entering a shrinking market.

For many years, Bell and Howell had been a trusted manufacturer of Polaroid cameras. The two companies planned to work together again on the equipment for instant movies. In the summer of 1974, however, Bell and Howell backed out after many arguments (McCune called them "misunderstandings on both sides") over costs and delivery schedules. Soon, the two companies sued each other over ownership of tools designed and built for the joint program.[11] McCune likened the breakup to a divorce. So Polaroid turned to a manufacturer in Vienna, Elektrizitäts-und Metallwaren, or Eumig, a subsidiary of the Bulova watch concern, and signed contracts in 1975.

Many people at Polaroid were nervous. Wensberg professed admiration for the technical tour de force involved: "In true Landian style, it solved a problem in totally unconventional terms." But Land wouldn't take advice. "As usual, he did not seek technical or marketing guidance. The system, as it evolved from a concept, to a laboratory prototype, to an exposure and development system, to a viewing device, was almost entirely his."

The project called for manufacturing on a big scale. Otto Wolff and others bent their ingenuity to create the "Land Line" in Norwood, Massachusetts, with clean rooms, computer controls, laser knives, and a system for moving the film "like an iridescent snake" at high speed "on jets and cushions of air." To Wensberg, it was "one of the most technologically imaginative factories ever built." The Land Line was "proprietary, revolutionary, secret, and extremely expensive." Too expensive. Polaroid planners confronted the awesome fact that "no reasonable combination of unit price or production quantity could begin to bite into the investment." They were putting a film on the market knowing that it would lose money, no matter how popular it proved to be. "From the beginning, the instant transparency was characterized as a monumental product. The need for massive manufacturing capability was never questioned by its designers."[12] In 1982, the monthly *Physics Today* said bluntly: "Instead of coming to grips with Polavision's inherent marketing disadvantages, Polaroid chose to ignore them. Its strategy was simply to distribute this new product as broadly as it had the SX-70 camera five years earlier."[13] Yet, for Wensberg, there were reasons for caution. For one thing, transparencies, even instant ones, needed a projector connected by wire to a plug in the wall. "Spontaneity and immediacy . . . vanished." Eastman Kodak had a commanding position in the market. Kodachrome accounted for 90 percent of the transparency sales in the United States. But the market for transparencies in feature movies, industrial and commercial slides, and amateur photography had reached a plateau, and the market for home movies was declining. After forty years, transparencies had won only a fraction of the market for prints, conventional and instant.

Polaroid was forced into movies, Wensberg thought, because the early Sesame film was unsuitable for stills. In movies, the eye would integrate the many frames "into the illusion of connected motion." Even later versions of the film, while suitable for outdoor daylight, needed a very bright, uncomfortable light for use indoors. The additive transparency film was of such low sensitivity to light, so slow, that still pictures were often blurred by camera motion. Slides made with the Polavision technology could be projected onto large screens. Even used in movies, however, the film was thick and dense, required a bright light, and could only be projected a short distance, onto beaded screens that required people to view them head-on. In Wensberg's view, instant transparencies had been driven into a box.[14]

The Polaroid marketing people were obviously worried in general about the future growth of instant photography, concerned that innovations would cut into profits, and convinced that Polaroid would have to be more dealer-friendly in future. In a 1977 talk in Chicago, Wensberg was not shy about mentioning the fundamental disagreement between marketers, who thought their efforts indispensable to any product, and innovators like Land, who was convinced that the features of innovations sold themselves.[15]

The conflict was not temporary or limited to one industry. On New Year's Eve 1996, *The Wall Street Journal* featured Amar Bose, a mathematically trained developer of high-fidelity speakers who owned more than half the stock in a company whose sales exceeded seven hundred million dollars annually. In a sentence that Land could have spoken, Bose said, "Marketing people's perfect product is something that has one more knob and is one dollar cheaper."[16]

To Land, the drive to Polavision was simple: "The role of industry is to sense a deep human need, then bring science and technology to bear on that need." He wasn't taking the safe road, he explained: "Any market already existing is inherently boring and dull." He admitted that "my view of business and the ordinary business world's view of business are quite antithetical."[17] By the time in 1981 Land said this, it had become clear that his own board of directors had joined the ordinary business world, at least in its judgment of him.

In 1977, Land was less worried than Wensberg. The sophisticated simplicity of the Polavision system was one of his cleverest achievements. McCune, despite his skepticism about its commercial possibilities, said a year later that it was "a technical achievement perhaps as great as the original invention."[18] To Land, it was impossible that such ingenuity would go unrewarded. As early as 1975, however, he acknowledged publicly that instant movies aroused "a large amount of support and a large amount of disagreement" about their potential. He continued to assert that the field would be as large as instant still photography. "They are pictures moving; they are pictures alive." He preferred them to the still-photographer's cries of, "All right! Hold it! That's it!"[19]

∞

Land may have been an "old man in a hurry," rushing Weed's team to get the system out before popular image-capturing passed it by. But in the past, he had coolly killed off projects in which Polaroid could not make a first-class, original, commercial contribution. A salient example was his cancellation of a document copier project in the late 1960s, after years of work at a cost of millions of dollars. Helping to energize Land, surely, was the partly self-imposed bitterness left over from SX-70. After banishing the skeptics, he had to invite them aboard again to sort out a tangle of supplier contracts. And he had yielded the Polaroid presidency as part of a public settlement of the succession.

Of the success of SX-70, Richard Weeks, manager of optical projects for SX-70, recalled in 1994, "He had just gambled Polaroid Corporation's very existence on SX-70 and won the bet. . . . The revolutionary new self-contained film had delayed Kodak's entrance into the instant photography market for years." Having triumphed over "a phalanx of doubters," why should he believe them now? "Had he listened to these timid naysayers in the past, there would be no sheet polarizer, no Polaroid Corporation, no instant photography, no SX-70!"[20] Wensberg wrote that Land, "becoming ever more self-isolated in his company, felt himself a prophet without honor, a general whose captains lagged behind."[21]

As the principal custodian of the field that he had started, Land clearly felt the need to maintain enthusiasm about mass amateur photography. Professionals scorned mere snapshots. Many in his own company seemed to lack the passion needed to sustain the experience of instant photography. Perhaps they didn't care much for mass photography for itself, but only for the profits it brought. As so many times before, he believed that he had to buttress sales by fighting to impose vision and a sense of large purpose. As in any business, there was a danger that the trustees of the business would gradually forget what it was about.

He refused to entertain the idea of instant movies as a niche market. Land gave only peripheral attention to small bread-and-butter applications in business and science, except for microscopy. Instant film, often in "backs" attached to a bewildering array of "conventional" cameras, created instant identification-card photos, recorded bent fenders and other property damage for insurance agents, helped photographers set up portraits and catalog shots, and captured images from electron microscopes and the evanescent traces of oscilloscopes. In 1971, in an earth laboratory, instant film built up a 360-degree panorama of the lunar surface sent back from the *Apollo 15* astronauts' little dust buggy. Studying the array of Polaroid stills, scientists at Mission Control could advise David Scott and James Irwin where to go next for their samples of the moon.[22]

To make "pictures alive" a success, as Land acknowledged in 1975, would require a lot of educating, of creating "an awareness," a process he apparently distinguished from marketing. Inventions had to be startling, but the public also had to be convinced to buy and use the utterly new thing. "It is the public's role to resist. All of us have a miscellany of ideas, most of which are not consequential. It is the duty of the inventor to build a new gestalt, and to quietly substitute that gestalt for the old one in the framework of society." After the inventor succeeds, "no one can understand why it wasn't always there." He spoke of an "extensive teaching program to prepare society for the magnitude of our invention."[23] His comments were a wild mixture of practical vision and exaggeration.

∞

The teaching program began on 26 April 1977. Under cool, gray skies like those of 1972, Land drove up in a Cadillac Seville to the same vast film warehouse where he had introduced SX-70 in a magician's cave of black velvet. Now he was ready to go on stage and make the sales talk of his life, about a system that would carry his field into moving images. He would describe the years of work by scores of people, led by Weed. He was a little grayer, a little slower than he had been five years earlier, but, sensing even more opposition than before, he was even more aggressive.

He did the unveiling twice, first in a pressroom crowded with the largest group of reporters and photographers ever to attend a Polaroid annual meeting, and then before some 3,500 shareholders. Bill McCune's brief demonstration of the simple, boxy SX-70 derivative called OneStep was muted but significant. OneStep's sales were phenomenal from the start. Land began jovially: he had never met an elephant personally, but the project he was about to discuss was a super-elephant, with a nine-year gestation—or was it longer? "The conception of this goes back to the beginning of our interest [in photography]."

For the press, he held up with one hand a simple, flat camera. He put a film cassette into the camera and said, "It is never opened. Nothing ever leaves it. Nothing from outside is brought into it." He took the cassette out and popped it into a slot in the top of a player that resembled a television set. He did not run the player but said, "No switches, no knobs. Just push it and sit down [to watch]" two minutes and forty seconds of film. Once all the film in a cassette had run, the cassette popped out, Land said, so that you could put it on a library shelf. The instant-movie film "goes from the camera where it sees you to the player where you see it." The design, Land said, enters "into the current American modality of television."

A reporter asked about the price range of one hundred to one thousand dollars that had been mentioned in New York in February. "That's accurate," was all Land cared to say. The next question was: When will the new system be equipped with sound? "We've built the factory to put in the magnetic stripe. We're entirely displeased with the sound on all the home systems we've heard. We won't put out sound until we have the last word in electronics."[24] Jerome Wiesner of MIT, who conversed with Land at intervals, had warned him that a system without sound wouldn't sell.[25]

Land met his larger audience shortly after 2 P.M. Lights went down, and then the unexpectedly large concourse of people caught sight of Land striding down the center aisle. They had crowded in to see the latest embodiment of his willful inventiveness. Applause grew as he came near the stage to open the meeting. He began with thanks to his board of directors, from whom he had asked, and would again ask, much forbearance. Land's associate John McCann set up a row of instant-movie viewers. Land mounted the stairs at the right side of the stage. He turned to his audience and said, solemnly, "Today, we are joined together to see the first public demonstration of a new science, a new art, and a new industry."

In a P. T. Barnum touch, circus tunes on tape, one very lively and the next more gentle, came from the loudspeakers. Of course, they both had been played on a calliope. Commanding attention on the stage, a nearly blind, long-haired, apple-cheeked dancer named Carmen paused a moment with her cane in front of a painting of the Massachusetts State House on Beacon Hill. Her two-piece white sailor suit and shoes were set off with red shoelaces, a round Chaplinesque red hat with a turned-up brim, a red scarf, and red stockings. As Carmen began to dance, Land photographed her with a Polavision camera, equipped with a bright light that drew its power from a cord. One reporter wrote of his gesture in picking up the camera as "a conjurer's flourish." Just below the stage, several Polaroid employees also took Polavision pictures. A surrounding ring of press photographers clicked away, recording the dancer and her principal photographer.

At 2:42 P.M., five film cassettes were popped in the five players that McCann had set up. Land's went into the player at the left. About a minute and a half later, motion pictures of Carmen's dance appeared soundlessly on the five screens. Land shook hands with Carmen. Showing lantern slides that illustrated the system's features, Land said, "This is a new mechanism for awakening ourselves to each other." He repeated to his large audience that the film never left the cassette, and that perforations in the film governed the sequence of actions in the player. Rewinding at four hundred feet per minute for processing, it immediately projected the three thousand frames of eight-millimeter film. It wasn't television, building up its image dot by dot, line by line with a beam of electrons. Instead, it was a series of photographs of the entire scene, using the amplification power of a solid-state device called film.

The lights came up. A swarm of Polaroid ushers guided the entire crowd in groups of twenty to a brightly lighted "midway" of scenes with painted backdrops.[26] The ushers had rehearsed the operation many times. Their majordomo recalled that getting the ushers used to moving so many people without confusion was like the Normandy invasion.[27] In each little brightly lighted setting, the audience groups encountered a gaudily costumed young dancer, clown, mime, or juggler—not necessarily employed as such in real life. In a frenetic environment, each member of the group of twenty took a few seconds of film and handed the camera to the next person. When the group had shot its entire two minutes and forty seconds, it moved a short distance to benches clustered in front of a Polavision player. There were twenty clusters, blissfully calm in Wensberg's memory, where the groups could see their own movie projected. More than thirty-five hundred people, most of them untrained in taking movies, ran through the process in forty-five minutes. To Wensberg, however, "The sudden recognition of an inevitable idea was missing."[28]

As the demonstrations drew to a close, Land spoke to a newspaper reporter in the aisle of the auditorium and conveyed the intensity behind his sales pitch, "We're trying to be an inventive community that the country needs a lot of. Help us."[29]

Shortly afterward, the audience had all returned to their seats. Land stood on the stage, surrounded by the mugging crew of mimes, clowns, jugglers, and dancers. It was a scene of humorous exuberance and exaggeration. "We think of photography as the intersection of science and art," Land said. "Here's a rule they don't teach at the Harvard Business School: If anything is worth doing, it is worth doing to excess."

It was time for questions. From the dark to the brightly lit speaker came the most famous question of Land's life: "What about the bottom line?" The question stung. It touched directly on an inherent conflict for the day's chief performer. Land said Polaroid's mission was "to build, in industry, domains that haven't existed before. That helps the economy and brings beauty, but makes it profitable, too. I beseech you to put an end to the phony nonsense of industrial structure. It turns off young people. 'The only thing that matters is the bottom line?' What a presumptuous thing to say. The bottom line's in heaven. The real business of business is building things."

More questions. Could the film be projected on regular projectors? Yes, but Land did not encourage it because of the amount of projector light absorbed in the Polavision film. What electrical power did the camera need? Four AA batteries. What about the auxiliary light? A power cord was needed, but the bulb never got very hot; you could carry it in your pocket. What was the film speed? The film used that day had a speed on the ASA scale of 40. What about editing? You could use the player as an editor by pressing a button to stop projection at the exact frame you wanted. It was "much nicer than an ordinary editor." Could there be larger reels with this system? Land said that larger reels had been designed, but recalled "much misery in past generations watching other people's over-long reels." About the sales challenge, he added, prophetically, "You can't separate this from education."

What about sound? If you don't offer it now, why put on a magnetic stripe from the beginning? Land answered, "Because we don't want [sound] to be that far away. There's a mechanical usefulness to have a thin stripe like that, anyhow. We don't want to re-tool our factories." Asked when he would offer sound, Land replied, "We've done the basic work by having the stripe on." He repeated, with emphasis, what he had told the reporters in the pressroom: "We've been quite dissatisfied with what has been said to be good sound on eight millimeter. We don't want to freeze on a sound system that would be behind the visual."

A photographer asked Land whether the reagent, the processing chemicals spread in an ultrathin layer as the film rewound, evaporated. He indicated evaporation by raising his hand, palm upward. Land replied at once, thinking of the air that the hand had moved, "You just raised a thousand times as much reagent as we used."

The point of the new system was to get away from home movies made over a month or two that then had to be mailed in, processed, and returned. "Whatever charmed you that day will be visible in a few minutes or a few hours when you come home. It will be part of your diary."

∞

Land and his fellow elves of Sesame knew that the lack of sound was a serious defect. Standard home movies and camcorders alike had it. But it was nearly an intractable problem. Because the film cassette was never opened when the movies were taken, processed, and projected, there was "no apparent access for a recording head." Besides, such a recording head would require the tiniest of distances between it and the film for "quality" sound reproduction. The thick polyester base was stiff, however, and could not easily conform to the exact shape of a tiny recording head. Worsening the challenge, the Sesame film moved smoothly as it was projected. For high-quality sound, it would be better if the film paused as each frame moved through the film gate, as in a movie theater. A spinning polygonal prism did this at the movie house, but with fast film taken at a high f-number. The Sesame lens was projecting much slower film, with only 0.97 of the focal length.

Looking everywhere for expedients, the Seasame team brought in William Plummer, the inventor of the improbable series of plastic lenses and mirrors of the seemingly imposible viewing system of SX-70. Plummer's first thought was for the entire projection lens to swing back and forth. But the lens weighed more than a hundred grams (more than three ounces) and would undergo more than forty times the force of gravity as it reversed after each "masking interval" between frames. When the mechanism was tried in the shop, it was noisy.

Plummer "timidly suggested a standard audio cassette" driven in synchrony with the film. "That one was dismissed out of hand as too easy, and not suffiently elegant." Plummer regarded this work as typical of his collaboration with Land, who "made sure that he understood the consequences of each key decision." He told Plummer that "the product-development process was much like trying to reach the roof of a house." Numerous ladders lean against the eaves, but most lack a few rungs. The researcher is tempted to reject ladders with rungs missing near the bottom. Land pointed out, however, that some lack rungs near the top.

Eventually, the Polaroid engineers hit on the trick of rolling a distinct magnetic sound tape with the film tape, and pulling them apart a tiny distance for part of their journey from one spool of the cassette to the other.

When the system was demonstrated at a shareholders' meeting, the sound was of "unprecedented fidelity," Plummer recalled. But by then, Polaroid's instant movies had died in the marketplace.[30]

∞

Some of the press attention to Polavision focused on it as a technical triumph, completing the course of instant photography from sepia to black-and-white to color, to integral film, and finally to moving pictures. But other reactions from the press and investment analysts focused unsympathetically on the "show biz" presentation of Polavision. Land had begun using the annual meeting as a thespian vehicle in 1953, but his magic seemed to be fading. An unnamed former Polaroid employee told *The Wall Street Journal* that Land "likes the idea of the big production. He looks forward to it, thinks about it, plans it, and his employees do what he says to make his idea come true. It is his one show of the year, and he turns showman on his terms and on his turf."[31]

An analyst said that the annual meeting "is an event meant to create wonder and amazement, and to intimidate people from getting into the nitty gritty." To another analyst, Theodore James, Jr., of San Francisco, Polaroid annual meetings were "a self-congratulatory message for management . . . a presentation of their version of reality and a reflection of their philosophy that management should be trusted and holders have no damn business asking questions." To Wall Street analyst Brenda Lee Landry, who had attended for nine straight years, it was "the best show on or off Broadway every year." She added that Land gave "an Academy Award performance."[32]

Fortune, long an ally of Land, carried a brief item about his defiance of the old saw that necessity was the mother of invention: "We are not satisfied with filling known needs." It accused him of verbal sleight-of-hand, trying to dazzle the company's shareholders by saying Polavision "is not home movies. It's a brand new medium." Video discs from MCA-Philips and Telefunken, and video tapes from Sony were on the way, the magazine noted. To be sure, Polavision equipment then cost only six hundred dollars, a third of the price of Sony's videotape machine. But Polaroid's eight-dollar cassette ran less than three minutes. Sony's seventeen-dollar tape ran for two hours, and Polavision would lack sound "for perhaps a year." In that context, the magazine quoted Land's comment that "the bottom line is in heaven."[33]

In a witty opinion piece, Neil Ulman, then Boston bureau chief of *The Wall Street Journal*, asked, "Who needs it?" He made fun of Land's talk of science, art, and living images that create "a new mechanism for relating ourselves to life and each other." He recalled surreptitious viewing of movies in Saudi Arabia, where such exhibitions were strictly forbidden in accordance with Muhammad's denunciation of painted images. At Needham, Ulman found himself in some agreement with the Prophet's stricture. "What benefits, scientific, artistic, or industrial, will Polavision bring? Or is it just a colossal monument, over nine years in the making, the object of lawsuit and countersuit, and the subject of heart-fluttering stock market rumor, all to the insatiable demand of the American consumer for a new gadget?" He grumbled at Polaroid's view that people liked to look at pictures, not to take them. "There is evidently a big market for instant gratification." Ulman was scornful of instant movies: "Perhaps if life can just be stopped on film and played back instantly we shall improve our chances of grasping it more surely, living it a second time around, extracting its meaning to the full." Indicting all photography, he wrote of Muhammad's suspicion that "contemplation of images is more likely to detract from rather than to enhance the relationship of self to reality, life, or the deity." Ulman asked, "Who will give souls to all these images?"[34]

Little more than a week after the extravaganza in Needham, Land carried the case for Polavision to his professional colleagues. His forum for more than an hour after dinner was a carpeted ballroom of the Sheraton-Universal Hotel that looked down on the movie studios of Burbank, near Hollywood. He wistfully told the annual meeting of the Society of Photographic Scientists and Engineers, "Even though this marathon race has been in the running for about 25 years, the end seems sudden."

Carmen danced again, while Land and two officers of the society acted as cameramen. He claimed that the officers would "become better cinematographers than they were. They can see their own work." Land added, "Looks better than it did last week." The film being demonstrated that night had been manufactured with a color screen of 1,500 triplets of stripes per inch instead of the 1,000 in the film exhibited in Needham only nine days before. The slide tray tipped over, scattering the slides over the floor. While these were reassembled, Land ad-libbed about Polavision's history: "The important thing is not the invention, or even the science, but the perception of what will be a human contribution. Fortunately for our organization, people don't see it as a need until we do it." He added, "In this happy field, nobody bothered us at all."

Even alone, the task looked dubious. "Television and color photography are ideologically interchangeable. If you make stripes [as filters for taking the pictures and projecting them], how can you make them fine enough? If the emulsion is sensitive, how can you give it a high enough film speed? What do you do with the negative? Peel it off [as in the original one-step processes] or cover it with a white pigment [as in SX-70]? If you have a transparency, you have to peel the negative off or make it just not be there. Both are quite impossible, so that's why I wanted you to see it [demonstrated] first." Compared to the pleasure of "taking movies of the baby being particularly charming that night, all those difficulties are," and he paused, "fascinating."

Reviewing the history of color photography, Land said that Berthon's invention of light-focusing cylindrical stripes for color movies occurred in 1909, "very recently, the year I was born. Now I know why I'm here. He passed the message." Eastman Kodak, he said genially, had been rushed into commercializing its Kodachrome color film in the 1930s by the development of rival systems called Autochrome and Dufaycolor. Kodak put out Kodachrome in three weeks. According to Land, this crash effort was "the first time our good-natured friends up there [in Rochester] worked nights, Sundays, weekends. Let that be a warning to any enterprising youngster."[35]

Land, Weed, and their colleagues had adapted Berthon's idea for so-called lenticules by using them as the way to inscribe the colored stripes. The lenticules focused light on sensitive material, on the opposite side of the film, that could be dyed afterward. But then the lenticules were dissolved away "at full factory speeds," that is, eighty feet a minute, on the Land Line. Tests had begun with 500 triplets of colored lines per inch, then 750, then 1,000, and now, just before this demonstration, 1,500.

For Polaroid, this "crash effort" had been business as usual. For the occasion, Weed entered the limelight in a long evening dress that seemed out of character with her workaday, no-nonsense style. The keeper of the flame through many shifts in Land's attention could put aside for the moment her constant struggles for access to the boss. One or two reactions and decisions from Land had made a good month.[36] Land paid tribute to her at the end of his talk.

23

Too Late

> There are many people who worked with him who did very well before they had contact with Din, and many of them did well after Din left or they left, but who did *great* when they worked with Din.
>
> —Kenneth Olsen, 9 November 1991

When limited marketing of Polavision began in California late in 1977, the reaction was tepid. Polavision "is going well with some dealers, and there are some problems with some dealers handling it," McCune said early in 1978. Polavision sold better at specialty and department stores, where salespeople "will spend some time to understand it and demonstrate it."[1]

The next month, the new system attracted praise and criticism—in the same magazine, *Popular Photography*. Technology reporter Don Leavitt thought operational simplicity would support amateurs' impulsiveness: "Little ones and big ones as well as everyone in between can make fun flicks and serious flicks and never once have to give technique a second thought."[2] His colleague Leendert Drukker was decidedly less impressed: "How good is it? In comparison to super 8, its quality just isn't in the same league." Next to his commentary was a devastating pair of reproductions of movie frames of a woman model. The Polavision frame was grainy, and its colors heavily skewed toward blue. It compared extremely poorly with Super 8. Occasional blots were apparently caused by faulty processing. The slow film "couldn't seem to cope with dark areas even of front-lighted subjects." Drukker wrote, "For the present, the question is: Will Polavision's amazing ability to yield instant results suffice to overcome its limitations?"[3] Later the same month,

Photo Weekly reported unenthusiastic reactions from California dealers, who said it was "not a good buy for the consumer."[4]

As Polavision was readied for national marketing in the spring of 1978, amid the drumfire of lukewarm or hostile judgments, the broader field of instant photography was flourishing as it never had before—and never would again. A survey of stores showed that Polaroid, in the face of Kodak's growing onslaught, held onto two-thirds of the instant market in 1977. Wall Street smiled. Polaroid stock was selling at more than three times its low several years earlier, although far below its peak.[5]

During the golden glow of mainstream instant photography, Polavision went unmentioned at the April 1978 annual meeting. Instead, publicity focused on a new version of the SX-70 camera using a sonar ranging device, automatically adjusting the lens for more accurate focusing. The introductory list price of $250 was only 7 percent above that of the standard SX-70 model. Emitting tiny inaudible "chirps," and bouncing them off the center of the picture, the device could measure the "time of flight" of the echoes and thus measure distance. The Polaroid electronics pioneer Conrad Biber had worked on it for ten years.[6]

Not until the following year did a kind of saturation set in, and both Polaroid's and Kodak's sales of cameras and film began falling. Visions of huge profits in the future began fading. New technologies—and old ones—were asserting themselves. Video cameras were becoming smaller and cheaper, marching toward the hand-size models of the 1980s that went everywhere and took the impulsive pictures to freeze the happy memories. Conventional thirty-five-millimeter cameras became smaller, simpler, and cheaper, and the public bought them. The price of conventional color prints, the rock on which Kodak's business rested, held steady at about half that of instant pictures. This gave rise to the institution of two prints of every negative, one to keep and one to give away. And the customer could have them very soon after the pictures were taken. Processing laboratories, working with an immense number of outlets, began giving back prints in as little as an hour.

There is little evidence that Land had such a readjustment of the amateur photographic business in mind when he unveiled the big-scale museum replicas in 1976 and his instant movie system in 1977. But over and over in his career, he showed an innovator's sense that the conversation keeps changing. With clouds of apathy hovering over Polavision, Land concluded that he should take over its marketing. His new approach was door-to-door selling, used for encyclopedias and vacuum cleaners. While the skeptical directors looked on, Land started marketing negotiations with Electro-Lux, but they came to nothing.[7]

As the challenge of Polavision intensified, Land's work on color vision claimed more of his attention. The call of basic research was getting louder. Retirement grew more attractive. In June 1978, the sixty-nine-year-old Land began discussing it with his lifelong business adviser and lawyer, Julius Silver, and started conversations about his plans for a scientific lab in which to work after leaving Polaroid. He named the lab project Blandings after a popular book and movie of the 1940s, *Mr. Blandings Builds His Dream House*. There would be no mortgage on the dream house.[8]

Such a freestanding laboratory needed to be open to the scientific world and its criticism and would need bold leadership after Land relinquished it. Thinking of the future, he discussed a deal with MIT, but the arrangement fell apart over the issue of when control would pass to the university. To Jerome Wiesner, MIT's president at the time, it seemed as if Land absolutely could not contemplate his own mortality.[9] Meanwhile, Land instructed Joseph Haley, one of his attorneys, to start negotiating with the Carter family of Carter Ink for the property on the Charles River where the Rowland Institute was built just a few years later. He began discussions with architect Hugh Stubbins, who thought the lab might cost $8.5 million to build.

Early in 1979, negotiations for buying the Carter property were near conclusion. Stubbins gave Land a revised cost estimate of more than $13 million. Land telephoned Silver, who was on vacation in Puerto Rico. For many years, Silver had handled Land's finances. It was obvious that he must fly back immediately to Cambridge to complete arrangements for the new lab. Land made the fundamental decision that it would be a nonprofit institution. To finance the building without debt, Land and his wife sold three hundred thousand shares of Polaroid stock that they had donated to their Rowland Foundation. At a price of about $52.50 per share, the sale yielded more than $15 million. In a public statement, Land looked forward to giving more time to basic research.[10] The signal was clear: Land's exit was prepared.

∞

The new lab was not Land's only philanthropic building project in Cambridge. He also was committing millions to build a new "house" for the American Academy of Arts and Sciences, of which he had been president in 1951–54. The effort satisfied some of his hopes, and disappointed others.

Chartered in 1780, the American Academy was the oldest continuing honorary organization of scientists and other scholars in the United States, and it needed a permanent home.

Land was chairman of a small building committee. He felt that the new house should be near the center of the Boston area, on "neutral" ground, that is, not too close to Harvard or MIT. The first possibility was on the grounds of the Science Museum on the Charles Basin, directed by Bradford Washburn. The idea was to put the elite academy on grounds visited daily by huge numbers of schoolchildren, and thereby draw the academy more into a public exposition of science.[11] Land pledged $8.5 million for the project, the largest grant yet made by the Land family's Rowland Foundation. An architectural firm drew plans, at Land's expense, and the project was announced personally by Massachusetts Governor Michael Dukakis, on 8 July 1976. Press comment was glowing.[12] But one member of the Metropolitan District Commission, owner of the Science Museum property, had not been consulted and fiercely objected to an elitist institution on the site.[13]

The academy would have to go elsewhere. But where? The answer turned out to be a wooded site called Norton's Woods, near Harvard University and owned by it since 1948. For the different site, new architects were appointed, Kallmann, McKinnell and Wood, who were best known for the massive Boston City Hall. The design by Gerhard Kallmann and his colleagues was very different from that of the Science Museum site. Set in the woods, with many windows looking out at the trees, the red brick building looked less like an institution than a private house, with great sloping copper roofs resembling those of a Japanese temple. A central atrium allowed members and visitors to move easily from one room to another, or to gather for receptions and musicales.

Land continued as chairman of the building committee. The other members were the MIT physicist Victor Weisskopf, then serving as the academy's president, and the historian Thomas Boylston Adams. Land knew something about architecture; he had enjoyed working with architects on some of Polaroid's buildings in the Boston suburbs.

His role with the academy was different from the one he played in his two other great building projects in Cambridge. With the Science Center at Harvard, he had maintained his donor's anonymity and taken no part in the design by Jose Luis Sert. Land was far more active with the Rowland Institute on the Charles, which went up at almost the same time as the academy's house. Centered like the academy on a skylighted atrium, the

Rowland was closer to a personal statement. There, he and a personally chosen group of scientists would carry out their experiments, unencumbered by teaching or the search for grants.

By contrast, the academy was for others, a building for socializing and relaxing as well as conferring. It was designed as much for unplanned conversations in a corner as for formal meetings. In 1991, Kallmann gave his view of Land's role:

> [He] was by no means a willful or autocratic patron who would seek to have the architects carry out his wishes or wish to design through them. A personal architectural statement was the last thing he had in mind. The Academy would evidently not be Hadrian's villa, Burlington's Chiswick House, or Jefferson's Monticello. He gave the impression, rather, of being the servant of ideas which he considered to be essential to the Academy process. The communications we received from our patrons were hardly ever prescriptive. Suggestive would be a better word, leaving to the architects the realm which had to be their own responsibility.

The architects and their patrons, Kallmann said, did not aim at "a fashionable, post-Modernist historicism." They wanted neither a stately mansion on the hill nor "a cubist, abstractional early Modernism." They sought a mixture of "the classical villa and rustic shelter, the ideal and the pragmatic, the sublime and the robust."

One day, after visiting the vast New York headquarters of the Ford Foundation, of which he had been a trustee, Land told the architects that he was looking for something quite different. "He did not want the Academy's building to be so beautiful as to suggest that all the world's problems had been solved." The building should have rough edges and avoid perfect symmetry. It should be, Land said, "a house of beautiful ideas . . . a large, comfortable house which would be a refuge from the unstructured intensity of the surrounding world."

The academy's logo showed a stylized labyrinth of the sort devised by Daedalus, the original artificer of Greek legend. So the architects devised "a pattern of informal, interlocking chambers for the seclusion and intimacy of gathering." Besides two dining rooms, there were a library, a study, a garden room at one corner, a small conference room, and, at another corner, a medium-size conference room.

For the largest of the meeting rooms, the architects thought of Greek amphitheaters carved into hillsides. When the foundation walls had been laid out, Land came for a visit. He smiled in recognition. "Ah, Delphi." The half circle of the amphitheater was placed inside a rectangular room. This allowed balconies, which interested Land. Although the room was suitable for performances and meetings of up to three hundred people, it also was equipped for much smaller groups. At Land's insistence, the upholstered benches had retractable armrests for more comfort.[14]

When ground was broken for the building on 2 April 1979, Land focused on the academy's job of promoting informal communication between specialists. To add to knowledge, individuals had to "limit themselves by excluding many other areas." To make sure that ideas moved from one field to another, the academy must provide "intimacy, informality, and friendliness because the transfer usually is not a conscious process. Models for physics may come from music, for chemistry from physics, for art from cosmology."[15]

In the mid-1980s, the room held a day-long conference celebrating the hundredth anniversary of the birth of Niels Bohr. The focus was Bohr's mind, and the audience was intent on what I. I. Rabi and the biographer Abraham Pais had to say. At one point in the proceedings, Land's name was mentioned. Simultaneously many in the audience had the same thought: Is Land here? They turned in unison to look at one of the balconies. Land was there.[16]

∞

In September 1978, Land lost a potential successor as leader of Polaroid's research. Stanley M. Bloom, age forty-seven, died of a heart attack in his cabin aboard the Rhine river steamer that the company had rented for its staff to attend Fotokina, the biennial photography exhibition in Cologne. Bloom had been a central character of the SX-70 adventure, inventing the chemical curtain. For Polavision, he had invented the silver-halide developing agent. He was coinventor of the anti-reflection coating of the SX-70 film, and of the image-stabilization system for Polavision.

An eighteen-year veteran at Polaroid and already a senior vice president, Bloom was tragically young to die. He left a wife and young daughter and son. His name was on more than sixty patents. Land and Howard Rogers had been his collaborators on the anti-reflection coating. On image stabilization for Sesame, Land and Leonard Farney of the black-and-white laboratory had been his partners. At the time of his death, he was working with Sheldon Buckler, head of chemical research, and Gordon Kinsman on improvements to the SX-70 battery. He was also collaborating with Rogers on a new type of dye-release chemistry that eventually was used in the Spectra system of the mid-1980s.

Less than two months after his death, Alan Borror, a colleague, said that Bloom was an inspiring person to work with. "He knew when to let an individual go ahead on his own and take a risk. If others go astray, he would pull them back in. So he managed it well."[17]

Land was bereft. "We gather here to carry on a great man's purposes," he said in a eulogy four days after Bloom died. "Stan had so little time to describe his purposes in words: his active thoughts and thoughtful actions comprised a continuous, unabashed, passionate statement of the wonder of science, the wonder of its application, the wonder of beautiful objects, the wonder of family, and the wonder of the Jeffersonian aspects of America." Bloom "was quite free from those infantile inhibitions against applying beautiful science . . . He saw humanity in the sequence: great dreams, great learning, great using . . . Photography . . . offered him what he most needed, an extended continuum from science to beauty."[18]

∞

Polavision represented great dreams and great learning, but not enough people found it great to use. It was the greatest failure in Land's stewardship of his enterprise, and the proximate cause of his departure from the company he had created. Polaroid had placed big orders, not only for film cassettes, but also for the handheld cameras and the television-like players from the Austrian manufacturer Eumig, after an earlier manufacturing deal with Bell and Howell fell through.

As national marketing began in March 1978 and a five-million-dollar advertising campaign followed the next month, Polaroid had ordered 25,000 sets, had shipped 12,000, and was forecasting 1978 sales of 75,000. Silver, a board member since 1937, was outraged when told that Polaroid's first orders from Eumig had been for 50,000 sets, not a more conservative 5,000.[19]

Sales lagged from the beginning. A court decision recounted that late in October 1978, after some six months of national marketing, Eumig, which earlier had been told to increase production, was told to cut back by 20,000 sets. In mid-November, when monthly sales of Polavision sets were estimated at 15,000 units, Eumig was told to "take out another 90,000 sets and halt production." Eumig replied that it had complied, although it was prepared "to ensure a quick new start-up of production on a reduced scale."[19] A few years later, Eumig went bankrupt.[20]

A special boutique to sell the Polavision system at Bloomingdale's in New York—an often-fruitful means of selling new experiences—was closed. Marvin Traub, head of the store, told Howard Johnson of MIT, a former president of Federated Department Stores and at that time a Federated board member, to inform "the Doctor" that the system wasn't selling.[21] Sales of the boxy little OneStep and the film for it were sorely needed to offset the Polavision losses.

Polavision was a bomb. One estimate is that only 60,000 out of 200,000 sets produced were sold. As Land had been warned, Polavision was too late and without sound, in Richard Weeks's phrase, "a marginal product launched into a rapidly changing marketplace."[22] The images running on the viewer's ground-glass screen were of rather poor quality unless viewed straight on. The tape was very short compared to video cassettes, which had sound and could be edited and reused. It was the SX-70 focusing crisis all over again. Land "overestimated the intrinsic skill level of the majority of Polaroid's customers," Weeks wrote in 1994. Polaroid's most loyal constituency, American mothers, counted on an acceptable snapshot every time. Polavision required more expertise. The film speed was too low, and the processor/viewer was heavy and cumbersome.

Market research, always anathema to Land, might have identified niche markets, but Land wasn't interested. He swung for the fences and struck out. To be sure, he was allowed to strike out. His associates in Polaroid had a hard time talking to him after the crises of SX-70. Some of them felt that the problem was even simpler: Polaroid had simply become too big to turn nimbly on a dime during the normal agonies of innovation. Perhaps the principal officers and board members ended up allowing the old man enough rope—hundreds of millions of dollars worth of it—to hang himself.

At any rate, there came a time in July 1979 when the company announced "a careful review to determine the best basic approach to the overall Polavision program, which continues to represent a substantial call upon cash and earnings."[23] The handwriting was on the wall. Observers of the photographic industry, quoted in the press, turned savage. One said, "It isn't a good product and it isn't selling." Another said, "Polavision is a trade-off of rotten quality for instant pictures." One reporter wrote that "while many engineers and other observers are impressed with Polavision's highly complex technology, this reporter could find no independent defenders of Polavision as a commercial product, not even among those who sell it."

The audit committee of the Polaroid board of directors heard a firm opinion from Polaroid's accountants, Peat, Marwick and Mitchell. The company's accounts could not be certified unless it made a substantial write-off—an acceptance of the loss of a specific sum—of the apparently unsalable Polavision cameras and players. Land fought this with passion. He was furious at the accountants' phrase that the Polavision inventory lacked "utility." This word, he said, was totally inappropriate. The inventions of the film and camera were truly significant, but the marketing invention had not occurred. The assertion that "the marvelous result of scientific research embedded in Polavision had no utility [was] accounting jargon, a cruel misuse of language."[24]

With the board, he turned, as so often before, to a demonstration. Into a directors' meeting, he brought a cumbersome videotaping apparatus, with a bulky camera attached to a portable power supply. The idea was to show the contrast with the simplicity and convenience of Polavision. Director Carl Kaysen was present along with Killian; Henry Necarsulmer, a general partner of Kuhn, Loeb and Company, and chairman of the audit committee; and Richard D. Hill, chairman of the board of First Boston Corporation.[25] This awkward meeting stayed in the minds of the directors. When Bill McCune recalled it in conversation during a 1991 conference in memory of Land, board member Kenneth Olsen looked pained.[26]

Land lost the argument, and in September 1979 Polaroid announced a sixty-eight-million-dollar write-off. The figure included nineteen million dollars for canceling orders for cameras and players that Eumig had not yet built.[27] A few months earlier, Polaroid began laying off one thousand production workers in response to dwindling camera sales.[28] The long contraction of Polaroid had begun.

Land was so furious at Bill McCune, his successor as president, that he campaigned with board members for McCune's removal. Instead, the company's directors reached a contrary decision. They determined that Land, who had been working hard on an improved version of SX-70 film, called Time Zero, should step down as the company's chief executive officer after forty-three years.[29] The board members must have concluded this with some trepidation. After all, Land and his family owned about a seventh of the company's shares, even after the stock sale to pay for the new lab. The history of business, including high-technology business, is dotted with founder-owners who do not submit calmly to losing fundamental arguments with their colleagues, especially over such an issue as the succession. In their old age, both William S. Paley of Columbia Broadcasting System (CBS) and R. W. Woodruff of Coca Cola overthrew their designated successors.

Land had already set in motion the moving sidewalk that he would step onto in case the situation seemed unrewarding at Polaroid. At the Rowland Institute for Science, he would campaign for scientific acceptance of his insights into color vision. After all, the primary reason he wanted a company was as a base for his own research. And Polaroid was his creation. Why act as a blinded Samson pulling down the temple?

∞

Silver was foremost among the board members demanding that Land give up the presidency in 1975 and the post of chief executive officer in 1980. Working with Silver were James Killian, Land's great ally on Cold War problems and Public Television, and a board member since 1959; and Carl Kaysen, a political economist appointed in 1968 when he was Director of the Institute for Advanced Study at Princeton. After Kaysen had approached Land about joining the board of the institute, Land riposted by asking him to serve on the Polaroid board. It was Kaysen's first corporate board membership. He joined the audit committee right away and served successively on the nominations, compensation, and human relations committees.

Kaysen recalled that the big decisions in the late 1960s, to build the big negative factory and raise one hundred million dollars on the stock market to help pay for it, followed serious discussions about a merger between Polaroid and Bell and Howell. Polaroid was on the point of changing from a curious assembly of research and development and marketing, leaving manufacturing to others. Now, Polaroid would suddenly become a big manufacturing concern. But many executives still reported to Land, an arrangement the board considered chaotic. Land enjoyed setting the officers off against each other. He spoke admiringly of the unconventional management methods of President Franklin D. Roosevelt, who regularly gave two or more people overlapping responsibilities. The board was not impressed. It was convinced that management of the rapidly growing company's operations must be strengthened.

Merger would have brought Peter Peterson, then president of Bell and Howell, to Polaroid as chief operating officer. But Peterson, who later became a prophet of doom about American savings in the 1990s, wasn't interested. The board felt more vulnerable than ever to arbitrary decisions by Eastman Kodak, both chief competitor and supplier of color negative.

Silver, a half-time officer of the company, was very close to Land, in Kaysen's estimation. The day before most board meetings, he would come up from New York to Cambridge to talk privately with Land. Silver served on the audit committee and talked frequently with its chairman, Necarsulmer. Jim Killian and Silver were far more influential than Kaysen in forcing McCune's appointment as president at the beginning of 1975. This appointment was the end of a long struggle over the succession. Five years earlier, Stanford Calderwood, the head of Polaroid's marketing, had left when his hopes of promotion were dashed. As McCune moved up, another marketing executive, Thomas Wyman, left Polaroid to become head of the food company Green Giant. He later headed CBS and went into teaching and finance. The board was certain that a non-technical man could not be made the potential successor as head of a high-technology company. As Kaysen remembered the situation, "Wyman wanted answers and Land gave him riddles. He [Wyman] not only did not have technical training, but he had *no* feeling for it."

Inadequate salary was an obstacle to creating a number-two position. Land had to accept higher pay, so that the salary of the number two would be adequate, but it took two years of discussion. Kaysen never heard Silver say directly to Land that he needed a manager. But many years later he was "morally certain" that such a conversation took place. The crucial board discussion on succession was an exchange between Land and board members, after perhaps forty-five minutes of badgering. Kaysen thought later that it was the Boston banker Dick Hill who asked the conventional question: Who takes over if you are run down by a truck? Instantly, Land answered, "That's simple. Bill McCune. He's the only one."

As soon as McCune was in charge, Kaysen recalled, Land felt cut off. He regarded the OneStep as "a piece of schlock." Still, he pushed ahead with Polavision, which McCune estimated cost the company between $500 million and $600 million over four years, $200 million of it in the final year. It was the first time in Kaysen's memory that Land showed "a kind of stubborn insistence on his way and was clearly wrong. He had a way, up to then, of absorbing what others had to say." Although Land "was very resistant to the idea that most people can't focus," he had given in on the split-circle focus for SX-70, after a year of complaining by people like Killian. But Land was "a great teacher and a terrible student."[30]

Silver and Killian, admirers and supporters for decades, were the chief instruments in arranging for Land's surrender of management roles. Kaysen recalled no threat by Land to sell shares and put the company "in play" for a takeover. How did Killian and Silver finally persuade Land to go quietly? Kaysen replied, "It was Land's own vanity. 'Oh, you don't want me? The hell with it.' "[31]

∞

Although the directors had come to think that Land had begun harming his company, they continued to admire him. Among them was Ken Olsen, elected a Polaroid director in 1974. Olsen, the young worker on the seminal Whirlwind computer project and the entrepreneur-founder of Digital Equipment Corporation (DEC), was himself expelled from his own company in the 1990s.

Before the expulsion from DEC, he said in 1991, "I'm very thankful to have had the chances to be with Din." For Olsen, Land "had many of the characteristics of Edison. Edison was, of course, a great inventor. He also was a leader. He led that team that worked with him. He had that family spirit, that enthusiasm, worked them hard. He also was a showman. He realized that an idea that no one knew about was, in effect, not an idea at all." Land's leadership was based not only on his personality but also on "his broad interest in things."

Land was so enthusiastic, Olsen said, that "he would, I think, take credit for things others did. Not in a dishonest way at all, you know, just with enthusiasm. But he was smart in giving responsibility to people. He'd jump in with all four feet when people . . . weren't getting anywhere. . . . There are things to be learned from Din." Olsen said that Land could get others to do their best work. "There are many people who worked with him who did very well before they had contact with Din, and many of them did well after Din left or they left, but who did *great* when they worked with Din."

In contrast to the so-called experts who labored to predict the products of the future, Land invented them. "Din read a lot, learned a lot, but wasn't limited by the literature." He knew where he was headed. "There's an old saying that . . . the person who knows where he wants to go has a big advantage over anybody else. It's particularly true in a team trying to develop new products. . . . The fact that he wasn't always right does not mean that that approach is wrong." The problem with "all of us" in American business, Olsen said, was that "we are lacking that spirit of Din. In effect we kind of outlawed it. . . . There aren't many things done of significance without someone with a passion, and Din is a great example of it."

As head of a public company, Olsen said, Land had "the public breathing down his neck and always [had] to stand up there succeeding or failing every day. . . . He was always in the risk of being in trouble with the public. I think he relished it, and *missed* it when it was gone."

Olsen thought that the instant movies were "one of the most wonderful products Din made. . . . Gee, I thought it was beautiful." He did not blame Land for failing to foresee the flowering of videotape. "Now I have been close to the tape business and recording business. So I never worried about video tape, because I knew too much about it." Videotape, Olsen had been certain "would never be useful for what it is today." Olsen recalled telling Land that physics would make the Polavision system impossible. Land replied, "Look, let me show you," and he convinced Olsen. "I thoroughly enjoyed having him prove my physics was wrong, or that he could beat the physics."

When Land took the directors to Faneuil Hall marketplace in Boston and gave each of them a Polavision camera to shoot movies, Olsen recalled, "I did great. You know, I never touched a movie camera before. . . . The film was beautiful. Wonderful process. As a technician, I could still just admire it. I still have mine. Don't use it. Just admire it. It failed from a business point of view. It was going to fail no matter how well it was done—because video was going to take over." Land's mistake was the scale of commitment to Polavision, Olsen said. His failure was to "make it too big, too big a failure."

When Olsen lectured about the joy and comfort of double-entry bookkeeping, Land didn't understand him. Land's ideas of organization were naive, Olsen said. They were "all dependent upon him being there forever. He may not actually have believed it, but he acted like he believed it." Olsen chuckled and said he found the same formula attractive. Land represented a generation of scientists that Olsen encountered as a young researcher in the late 1940s. These older-generation scientists "blew their own glass, did their own machining, made their own parts. They knew everything and were independent," and created radar and the atom bomb "and all the wonderful electronics." These self-reliant old-timers came up against the fearful challenges of World War II and said, "You know, this war's not going too well. What problem should we solve for 'em?" To Olsen, this was a naive attitude, "but it's a *beautiful* attitude, see?"[32]

∞

On 22 April 1980, the moment came for a public farewell. Land was defiant. The occasion was not seamless with the past. After decades of annual meetings designed to prepare employees and investors alike for the next new thing, the form of the gathering had changed. Rousing product introductions in a darkened film warehouse in Needham gave way to talks on the brightly lit stage of Symphony Hall in Boston.[33]

The much-trodden wooden stage was almost bare. Land later

reflected that industry lacked a Shakespeare.[34] There was a lectern, a Harvard chair, and an MIT chair. On the walls were full-size Polaroid replicas of works in the Boston Museum of Fine Arts, including Childe Hassam's *Boston Common at Twilight*. These were reminders of Land's constant linking of the technology of the amateur snapshot with high art. Toward the end of the meeting, his colleagues on the board of directors presented him with a pair of bull mastiff puppies, to replace two other bull mastiffs that Land had loved and called Per and Se. McCune remarked that "every boy ought to have a dog, in fact, two dogs." They were brought out on the stage, and Land picked one of them up and held it, smiling. At his wife's insistence, the puppies were given away soon afterward. In later years, he would receive photos of them from their new owners.

In the tension of the moment, the Harvard chair was absentmindedly occupied by McCune (a 1937 graduate of MIT), the newly designated successor as CEO. In the MIT chair sat Land. To be sure, many years before, Killian had named Land a visiting institute professor at MIT, and Land gave the MIT commencement address in 1960. But Land had dropped out of Harvard twice, received an honorary Harvard degree, given the Phi Beta Kappa oration there, and long served on the visiting committee for the Harvard physics department. There were some potted palms and space to the right for the Empire Brass Quintet. The jaunty tunes they played could not suppress the tension.

It was time for Land to defend his view of a company and how he ran it, and to define more largely where he thought wealth really came from. He said there were three kinds of equity. First there were the numbers from the balance sheet, and next what he called the inventory of "structured accomplishments." But most important, there was intellectual capital, his kind of capital. The intellectual capital, he said, was formed of "the large generalizations, the deep insights into a physical, chemical, optical, and psychophysical theory, insights which arise in us both as a result of what we have *done*, and as a consequence of our thoughtful analysis of where we might go *next*. It is this intellectual capital that shapes our large plans for the future and makes practical most of our immediate research."

Intellectual capital did not come from dumb luck or trying everything, Land said, despite many people's false evocation of Edison's invention factory down in New Jersey a century earlier. Many people who had worked with Land intently in the laboratory for days and months and years sat in the audience as he spoke. For them and the rest of his audience, Land attacked widely held ideas about empiricism: "There's a tremendous popular fallacy which holds that significant research can be carried out by trying things. Actually it is easy to show that in general no significant problem can be solved empirically, except for accidents so rare as to be statistically unimportant. One of my jests is to say that we work empirically—we use bull's eye empiricism: we try everything, but we try the right thing first!"

Of structured accomplishments, Land recalled fifty years of inspiration, insight, and problem-solving: "techniques for making polarizers, putting curves in sunglasses, making the emulsions in multiple strata with accuracy, syntheses of dyes, knowledge of how to attach development groups to dyes, knowledge of the role developer groups play with relationship to the exposed silver, gelatin, and mordant in the image-forming sheet, constitution of the reagent spread between the negative and the positive."

Land looked out at the audience: "Each of us knows literally thousands of these relationships, and together we know millions. . . . Most important of all, many of us know not only what we know ourselves but also who in our group is likely to know each domain in the rest of it." As an illustration, he pointed to the full-size Polacolor replica of Renoir's *Dance at Bougival*, made by a camera the size of a room, with a lens designed by James Baker. "We have reproduced every microscopic detail down to a twentieth of a millimeter in a way that cannot be reproduced except by making the full-sized unit picture we have here."

He said that he mentioned the replicas of artwork because he believed that "the full human use, full use in the human, of the mathematical, the aesthetic, the technical, the productive, is what is required to lay the basis of contemporary industry." He said, as he had many times before over several decades, that Polaroid "can itself be a company that will rejuvenate the United States into being a joyous, dynamic, consistently surprising activity."

The year before, Land had triumphantly demonstrated Time Zero, a version of the integral SX-70 film in which the pictures emerged very rapidly, indeed more rapidly than in later versions. In the mid-1990s, a photograph of him smiling broadly as he held aloft a Time Zero print at the 1979 introduction was prominently displayed in the lobby of a Polaroid building in Cambridge, just across from the desk from where guards checked visitors and employees of a very different kind of company. The new film, he said, took "a year or two" to bring to the market. This would have been impossible "without the decades of background. . . . Without the remembered thousands of experiments, it would have been impossible to do Time Zero within any of our lifetimes." Such accomplishments led to the only kind of diversification he approved of, that is, products for new markets developing out of what had to be perfected for Polaroid's photographic market: dyes, batteries, non-reflecting coats, sonar distance-measurement for camera focusing.

Without growth in intellectual capital or the array of "structured accomplishments," Land said, the growth of balance-sheet equity would be bound to tail off. He warned against the idea that the rate of equity growth is necessarily slower when a company gets large. He then read off a series of numbers, the value of shareholders' equity, in five-year jumps, from Polaroid's incorporation in 1937. The first number was $500,000. The final one, not counting fresh capital recruited on Wall Street or dividends paid out—totals that were roughly equal—was $763 million. This increase in wealth of about 1,500-fold in forty-three years "was created out of enthusiasm, intelligence, scientific inquiry, engineering skill, and management organization." He raised his finger and pointed directly at the ceiling far above. With ironic emphasis he said that given the trend of the past forty-three years, the only trend acceptable for his successors would have to be straight up.[35]

Land sensed that it was time to get off the stage. In 1982 and 1985, he and his wife sold all their four million remaining shares in the company.

24

Polaroid v. Kodak

> You will not get from this witness any admission that you can simply take one thing away or add one thing and that it has no significance . . . You have to look at the whole thing together.
>
> —Judge Rya Zobel, 1981

In the fall of 1981, in Judge Rya Zobel's federal courtroom in Boston, Land performed for the last time on behalf of the company he had created and would soon leave. Land was defending the novelty and originality of SX-70 patents against Eastman Kodak, once his patron, then his collaborator, and finally his commercial rival. He and Polaroid contended that Kodak got into instant pictures in 1976 only by infringing patents. Kodak denied infringing any of the patents, denounced several patents as a re-treading of old inventions by Land and others, and said that Polaroid could not expect to be the sole innovator in its field forever.

By this time, Land held more U.S. patents than any other inventor except Thomas Edison. The total eventually reached 535. Land and Howard Rogers were the principal inventors of several of the patented products. These included the stiff, water-resistant outer sheets of SX-70 film and the means of stabilizing conditions within, "to keep the visible image the way it was formed," as Land put it. Stabilization was a crucial issue: were Polaroid's systems for sepia, black-and-white, peel-apart color, and integral color conceptually similar? After Judge Zobel asked, "But the general idea is the same isn't it?" Land admitted to a "common denominator of purpose." The timing, the reactions, and the chemistry of each, however, required fundamentally different concepts, according to "a program peculiar to that system." Each type of stabilizing, he said, "is going to involve a program peculiar to that system." He insisted that the concepts were "as different one from the other as the buzz of the bee is from the sting."[1]

Also in dispute were Land's patent for the film-advancing pick and a patent by Dick Wareham, in partnership with Richard Paglia, for bending and shielding the film on its way out of the camera.

Land's direct testimony was a three-day tutorial on the evolution of instant photography. Ten days of cross-examination tested his command of detail, and his temper. Answering hundreds of questions, he seized opportunities for sharp retorts. Kodak's lawyer, Francis Carr, asked, "Would it be fair to say, Dr. Land, that in 1947, you had to make do with the best materials available to you at that time?" Land replied, "I suppose that would be true of everything, always." On the eighth day of trial, Land said, "Why don't you state the question cleanly and I'll answer it cleanly?"[2] When Judge Zobel told him he would have to shout into one microphone, which didn't work, or speak closely to the other, Land joshed about a basic term of patent law: "It shows what happens to a field when it is left to people skilled in the art."[3]

Carr asked him about filing patents during the development of one-step photography: "As you came upon a useful thought, was it your practice to get a patent application on file? I'm talking about the early days now." Land retorted with a basic principle of patenting: "You can't file a patent on a thought. It has to be an operating mechanism."[4]

There was an exchange about the phrase "simple to handle," which came up in questions about the sepia film of the late 1940s. Land said, "I'd have to say we've never found . . . any system that's simple to handle. They all turn out to be an undertaking which yields to planning." What did the word "handle" mean? "We know of the infinite number of chemical complexities, impermanences, difficulties that are a consequence [of] having together, in the first place, problems which were not solved for decades afterwards."

Judge Zobel thought Land had a point. She told Kodak's lawyer that Land "just explained at some length that the term 'simple to handle' can have any number of different meanings. It may be simple for the person who takes the photograph but it may be very difficult to handle for the chemist."[5]

As the days of trial rolled by—they eventually totaled seventy-five—the exchanges were tart. Day after day, Carr hammered away at the originality of the SX-70 inventions, contending that they had been anticipated by "prior art" and so were invalid. He led Land through a maze of patent columns, lines, claims, charts, and examiners' rulings, searching meticulously for an opportunity to get the witness to admit that his previous inventions, sometimes twenty years earlier, were substantially those of SX-70.

∞

The emotion in the case was high because two schools of invention were pitted against each other. Kodak's army of devoted soldiers followed Mees's banner of deciphering the photographic process, marching toward such applications as practical color films for the masses. It was a perfect example of the research collective's taking over from the individual inventor, which worried many people at the end of the Depression because it was such a major factor in twentieth-century innovation. The behemoth with hundreds of researchers confronted a small band of experienced but still-nimble inventors. These stood for the continuing, inextinguishable importance of people who go their own way and come up with insights, devices, and systems that big organizations never thought of, or ignored, because the apparent market was too small to be worth the big company's attention.

Carr's tactics irritated Land. On the ninth day of trial, Land accused Carr of "asking me to be a psychological witness and say: What is the motivating system that makes you make that choice?"[6] On the tenth day, he objected to "the freight train of suppositions the witness is supposed to carry."[7] As Carr asked about his handwriting on some exhibits on the thirteenth day, he observed, "Sometimes I forget, Mr. Carr, which is the defendant."[8]

On the ninth day, Land asked Judge Zobel, "Your honor, is a witness really required to imagine what he would have done in a strained situation?" Zobel replied, "You are doing all right, Dr. Land." Shortly afterward, she told Carr, "You will not get from this witness any admission that you can simply take one thing away or add one thing and that it has no significance . . . You have to look at the whole thing together."[9]

Land did not like Carr's method of picking apart features of complex systems, Polaroid's or Kodak's. On the eighth day of trial, Carr showed him a piece of Kodak instant film, from which the developer pod had been cut away, to ask a question about its structure. Land rejoined that Carr was dividing "a unitary structure of which the essential concept and commercial significance is having a unitary structure . . . and arbitrarily separating them . . . What you are cutting in half and trimming off is the structure of a whole field of achievement." A moment later, Land said, "From this body you have taken the head and left the foot."[10]

Land appealed to Zobel: "The witness is in a strange position. He is expected to be decently responsive. If opposing counsel is trying to obscure where he is going, the witness doesn't know how to be decently responsive." Judge Zobel disagreed: "Dr. Land, I don't believe Mr. Carr is trying to obscure. . . . He is trying to get information from you, and you will have to just do the best you can."[11] She didn't want him to be long-winded. Frequently, as Land began a complicated answer, she admonished him to say either yes or no, or to say he couldn't answer. Despite this injunction, Land answered one question, "I'm afraid the answer would have to be, 'somewhat.' I am not being evasive." And Zobel replied, perhaps wearily, "I know."[12] At one point on the eleventh day of trial, she said, "Let him state the question, Dr. Land, before you suggest another one."[13]

On the seventh day of trial, after struggling to get Land to agree with his description of a chart, Carr told Judge Zobel, "I don't think I could ever get Dr. Land to agree to [what is so]." Land shot back, "I think that's an unfair remark. When you give partial statements that could greatly damage our cause, and when I try to give full statements which support what we have done, I think it's just not right to say: 'I couldn't get the witness to agree with my partial statement.' If you'll make full and accurate statements . . . " It seemed as if his entire career as an inventor was on trial. Judge Zobel brought him up short. "It's true. You don't agree with his partial statement when you regard it as a partial statement." She was telling Land that he had said what he had said, and Carr that he had his answer.[14]

Carr tried to find an inconsistency. A particular dye in Rogers's color experiments was mentioned as being purple or dark brown in an alkaline environment, and yellow in an acidic one. He was focusing on a patent covering the original sepia process, which, Carr contended, anticipated a feature of one of the SX-70 patents. It covered an arrangement for making the environment more acid, less alkaline. Land denied that the SX-70 patent was anticipated. The early feature, he said, was an ultrathin layer, "a stratum of minuscule thickness," of a plastic called CAHP, which was "a common plastic in those days, used about as much as a French cook uses butter." The amount of plastic used was far from enough to increase the sepia film's acidity. "There is no significant role of acidification in this."

But Carr persisted. Rogers' dye was yellow when the negative was peeled apart from the positive. Didn't that mean the dye was in acid conditions? No, Land replied. Remarkably, perhaps uniquely, "when the dye enters the nylon and becomes associated with it in ways we don't understand, then even in that alkaline environment in which it was made, the dye is yellow." The color resulted from the dye's bonding within the nylon. The effect helped Rogers get started on color, "and we gave [it] up rather reluctantly because of its beauty as a chemical-optical phenomenon." Continuing his cross-examination, Carr said, "I want to understand your testimony." Land shot back, "And I want you to."[15]

On occasion, Carr's probing led Land to make general comments on discoveries and commercialization. Land told Carr, "An inventor likes to think that he had an insight. . . . It is customary in writing patents to characterize the discovery as unexpected when, in my opinion, it is usually the insight that is unexpected."[16] When Carr asked whether Land was referring to a commercial development or something on which he would continue development work, Land rejoined, "Those aren't self-evident alternatives."[17]

He told Carr, "As you so well know, the research of science is nothing but failures. You fail and fail and fail, and when you succeed you stop. So the record of science is experiments that didn't work and that are then the basis of one that does work." Work on the matched plastic sheets of the integral film unit of SX-70 showed that "[W]henever you do something new and think it is based on a new principle, you check it in two ways: One by . . . taking other examples that seem to you to involve the same principles; and the other, if you are a good laboratory worker, I guess, is to try the opposite of what you believe and see if [the principle] is there when you do the opposite of what you believe."[18]

∞

Carr's questions before Judge Zobel led into the events that drove Kodak and Polaroid apart—and into their lawsuit. At a meeting in November 1968, Land showed two Kodak executives samples of the new, "integral" color film that eventually was marketed as SX-70.

He was acting in the light of collaboration from the 1930s through the 1960s, which had built "a very healthy relationship—not a sentimental one but a very healthy relationship."[19]

The visitors from Kodak took samples back to Rochester, but, soon after, the pictures were returned. The emissaries had shown them to a colleague. Land was told, perhaps by Bill McCune, that this colleague, whom Land did not name on the witness stand, "took a quick look and then turned away and said, 'I don't want to see these.' "[20] The implication was that Kodak had already decided to go its own way into instant photography.

∞

After years of intense preparation and exhausting pretrial depositions, the trial itself probably provided Land an interesting distraction, although his attention was turning increasingly to the independent scientific laboratory that he was building on the Charles River basin. As soon as he had handed over the reins, his life at Polaroid had become more contentious. Although he remained chairman of the board, he felt left out. He was losing arguments over diversification and was complaining about it in public.[21]

Judge Zobel was an attentive, shrewd audience of one. Named to the federal bench only two years earlier, she was hearing the case without a jury. Inevitably, to brief her on the issues involved in some nine patent disputes, Land and other witnesses gave her much background on photography in general and on instant photography in particular. The seventy-two-year-old Land went over topics like photographic development and stabilization within the special environment of instant films. His own and opposing lawyers pounced on almost every sentence. But Land was agile. He cast himself first as a teacher and then as an expert old man concentrating on the essentials, including the technical details, of his inventions.

As senior instructor of the judge in the history and principles of the field he had created and led, Land provided an intellectual structure for the scientific and technological issues in the trial, and for the judge's decision. But the questions were an obstacle course traversed by a quartet: Land, the witness; his lawyer; Kodak's lawyer; and the judge. Sometimes Land asked to have the question explained to him. Sometimes the judge needed the explanation, or by rephrasing the question, provided it. Sometimes the lawyer for one side objected to the other's question. There were many pauses. Land would have to look up particular columns and lines in the patents and then ask to have the question repeated. In his answers, he insisted that narrow questions left out the complexities, the need to have many materials behave in concert, the many alternate ways to accomplish something.

He was particularly caustic about the large Kodak charts put up on easels where the lawyers, the judge, and the witness could see them. These he repeatedly denounced as inaccurate, incomplete, or hard to read. At one point in the cross-examination, Land said in mock exasperation, "I object to being a witness." The judge responded jokingly that Land was putting his lawyer out of a job.[22]

∞

The historian of technology Elting Morison once wondered whether Land would ever concern himself with something important, rising above the triviality of devising toys for the masses.[23] On one level Land probably agreed with Morison. In 1982, he told a writer that photography was what he did for a living.[24] As discussed chapter 14, he presumably felt he would touch greatness most surely in the field of color vision, a fundamental question of science, in which the brain studied the brain, applying consciousness to study perception. He also exhibited a technological greatness in patent trials of 1954 as well as 1981, when he conveyed an effortless command of every corner of the forests of minutiae in physics and chemistry that was needed to survive in as technologically demanding a field as photography. Undaunted by the detail, he found a good path through, in the courtroom as he had in the laboratory.

For decades Kodak could feel, justly, that it was preeminent in photography, most particularly in the chemistry of film. Next to this Spanish galleon, Polaroid was a trim little frigate. Its band of upstart inventors, led ferociously by Land, opened up fields that appeared too complex or too limited for a big company to enter commercially. Yet, for a time, Polaroid's command of its special type of impulsive photography had created an experience that mass consumers enjoyed about as much as Kodak's color prints.

The growing rivalry had given increasing force to Polaroid's worry that Kodak would never improve its processes for making Polaroid film. Kodak could see more and more clearly where Polaroid was headed, and judged that its own entry into instant photography was inevitable. When Kodak told Polaroid that it wished to end its contract for supplying Polacolor negative, Polaroid asked for renewal. Kodak had agreed, but only with a license from Polaroid to begin making and selling its own peel-apart instant film in 1975.

Although the issues were fundamental, the trial also carried overtones of a grudge fight. Did Kodak just want to see Land's cards after watching his dust all those years? Did Land just want to hold onto his field forever? In her ruling of 1985, Judge Zobel agreed with Kodak that "instant photography is not the perpetual domain of Polaroid."[25] But Land replied, with some justice, that while instant photography was everything to Polaroid, it was just another field to Kodak.[26]

∞

Land explained Polaroid's motivations most clearly at the 1976 shareholders' meeting, just hours after the company brought suit—and just six days after Kodak had introduced its new line of instant cameras and film. With emotion, Land told the shareholders, "The only thing that is keeping us alive is our brilliance. The only way to protect our brilliance is patents . . . This is our very soul we're involved in . . . our whole life. For them it's just another field." He quoted Byron's lines that for a man, love is "a thing apart" but for a woman love is "her whole existence." He added to loud applause, "We intend to stay in our own lot and protect that lot."

A shareholder who also owned Kodak stock asked why Polaroid was suing "those who allowed you to exist in the first place." Wouldn't Polaroid "come out better in continuing to cooperate?" Land replied that patents are assigned by the government to people "who work hard and make real inventions." A right is granted for a limited time and then reverts to the public. "That's supposed to be a stimulus to invention." Many of Polaroid's patents had run out. Others in photography were now using inventions that had been protected. He said that the inventors involved in the patents in the suit numbered about ten, compared to a thousand at Kodak. Kodak had stopped technical interchanges but received "I don't know how many tens of millions" for making the negative without needing a single salesman. Polaroid had paid "the bills instantly and took all the risks." In such a situation, it "wasn't right for us to go on forever." A tacit understanding built up that "we would go our own way in our own way."[27]

The lawsuit, which eventually led to successes for both Polaroid and Kodak, went on alongside intense competition in the marketplace. Each company improved its cameras and films and sought out business and technical customers. The companies had been driven into suspicion and conflict by the nature of what they could invent, and by the astonishing scale of the mass experience with color pictures. As technological cycles grew shorter, the two companies could see the penalties for failure more and more clearly, and that they were on technological treadmills driven by consumer enthusiasm in "conversation" with inventiveness.

Land reveled in the problem of competing with his former patron. He was both thrilled and disappointed that Kodak's system of 1976 was so pedestrian. At the 1976 shareholders' meeting, he said, "We have been in a considerable state of euphoria for the last week. Our concern had been that new products might incorporate or depend on the same brilliant ideas." The audience was so still one could hear a pin drop. Kodak had shown no brilliance. "Everything that was done used techniques extremely familiar to us. . . . It has turned out that it took all their genius to make it possible to play the game with us at all."[28]

Instead of developing something genuinely new, the research army in Rochester accepted that SX-70's features defined the market, and just muscled into it at the very moment when Polaroid could hope to reap the reward of its continued boldness. Land was convinced that he had fulfilled the inventor's duty to come up with devices, systems, and processes that were truly novel and not obvious. Kodak's challenge was not just economic; it was professional.

As rivalry intensified during the late 1970s, the potential for a settlement of the suit receded. Kodak could have been licensed, as before, to use Polaroid's SX-70 inventions. But the competitive world was changing. In the 1970s and 1980s, the chief beneficiaries of such licenses might not have been either Kodak or Polaroid, but Fuji of Japan.[29] Polaroid might have gained anyway by licensing other companies to enlarge the field, as IBM did with personal computers and Apple Computer did not. The overall market might have been enlarged, and Kodak and Polaroid and Fuji might have innovated faster. The boom in instant photography might have continued instead of leveling off, as managers concentrated on pushing integral instant photography to a maximum of customers, most particularly by cutting the cost of film. The continued presence of Kodak in the market after 1985 might have maintained the vitality of a field that had gone stagnant.

Kodak, however, wished to recover its large investment in integral instant film and motorized cameras, to remain in an important amateur market, and to prove the originality of its system. By showing that any injury Kodak may have caused was not knowing and willful, the damages would be minimized if Polaroid won. On its side, Polaroid sought to defend its ony market, avoid licensing, and win big damages.

Kodak's confidence in going to trial on the Polaroid patent suit before Judge Zobel without a jury was strengthened by its victory in the late 1970s in a private anti-trust suit in New York. A jury verdict against Kodak was ringingly reversed by a U.S. Appeals Court that upheld the right of companies that took the risks of innovation to enjoy the fruits of being first.[30] After all, although the judge might be a liberal, in this case it was Polaroid that was the monopolist. The theory did not work. Judge Zobel ruled in September 1985 that Kodak had infringed seven valid Polaroid patents, and a month later she issued an injunction against further sales of Kodak instant cameras and film, refusing to stay the injunction during appeals. Higher courts affirmed her refusal of a stay and her decision.[31]

Even though she agreed with Kodak that Polaroid could not claim instant photography as its "perpetual domain," she pointed out two significant facts. One was Kodak's decision to follow Polaroid into the integral, non-peel-apart field after Polaroid demonstrated it. Another was an internal Kodak memorandum of 1973. This was "by no means decisive on the question of infringement of any particular patent" but it recorded the

Kodak Development Committee's suggestion that progress on the Kodak instant system "should not be constrained by what an individual feels is potential patent infringement."[32]

Judge Zobel struck down Kodak's general contentions that unpublished internal work at Polaroid was "prior art" anticipating the patented inventions, and that Polaroid had not furnished sufficient information to the U.S. Patent Office. She did hold that Polaroid had failed to establish the role of any particular patent in the success of SX-70.

She rejected Kodak's main assertion that SX-70 inventions were anticipated by prior inventions, many of them Polaroid's own, and thus constituted restatements designed to extend old patents. She upheld several of Land's patents for SX-70, including the use of stiff and water-resistant polyester for both outside sheets of the film to resist curling, the placement of the acid polymer layer in the negative (as in the Time Zero film introduced late in the 1970s), and the pick for advancing one unit of SX-70 film at a time into the bite of the processing rollers. Also upheld was the Wareham and Paglia patent for shielding film units from unwanted extra light by bending them downward as they left the rollers. As noted earlier, this step also improved the efficiency of spreading reagent between the positive and negative.

∞

The injunction required Kodak to stop making or selling its PR-10 instant film and its EK6 instant camera as of 9 January 1986. In asking for delay pending appeal, Kodak cited possible negative impacts on both workers and customers. If forced to stop before the appeal were decided, Kodak said, it couldn't afford to reenter the field. Zobel replied tartly, "I am not unmindful of the hardship an injunction will cause—particularly to Kodak customers and employees. It is worth noting, however, that the harm Kodak will suffer simply mirrors the success it has enjoyed in the field of instant photography."

She wrestled with a fundamental conflict between two government policies. One aimed at protecting consumers from inconvenience and employees from unemployment. The other was designed to protect the rights of inventors. The second policy imperative went beyond collecting damages later. Infringement of patents, once found, must be halted promptly. She ruled:

> Since the Court of Appeals for the Federal Circuit decided Smith International in 1983, district courts have held uniformly that once a patent is judged valid and infringed, its holder is

> entitled to injunctive relief. They have found money damages deficient against encroachments on rights of exclusivity, and they have judged the public interest better served by a broad policy favoring creativity than by a narrow protecting of specific customers. Kodak's attempts to elude this clear trend in recent patent law are unavailing.[33]

Kodak was driven back out of instant photography and ultimately was forced to pay damages worth even more than the highest value that Wall Street had ever placed on the Land family's stock. Eastman Kodak paid damages of more than $900 million in 1991, almost ten years after the trial and just after Land's death. The payment was made six years after the injunction issued by Judge Zobel had ended Kodak's venture into instant photography. The amount was fixed in a separate trial on damages, held in 1989. It was the largest infringement award and the largest actually paid in the history of patenting.[34]

∞

The damage trial, also seventy-five days long, focused on whether Kodak's infringement had been willful. To induce Judge Zobel to recuse herself from the case, Kodak cited a potential conflict of interest: the paradoxical fact that her husband had just inherited Kodak stock from his mother. Perhaps she would have been harsher on the issue of willfulness. Getting her off the case was a victory for Kodak. After U.S. District Judge A. David Mazzone ruled that Kodak had not infringed the patents willfully and made an award smaller than Wall Street expected, the price of Polaroid stock fell sharply.[35]

Kodak both lost big and won big. In the first round, higher courts had refused to stay Judge Zobel's injunction and had upheld her conclusions. Kodak had to write off nearly $500 million on now-useless production equipment and inventory and other costs of leaving a line of business. Kodak was saddled with payments to some three million owners of cameras left with no film for them. To add insult to injury, there was a legal tussle over the form of payment, which was not resolved for two and a half years. The second round went much better. The 1991 settlement with Polaroid for more than $900 million, in compensation for profits lost and interest on them, could have been much larger. Polaroid, alleging willfulness, had asked triple damages. Land's company estimated losses far greater than the $500 million in profits it had lost over nine years. Kodak's potential liability was $10 billion or more. By substituting a new judge and persuading him that the evidence was insufficient, Kodak limited its liability to a tenth or less of what it might have had to pay.

Although Polaroid, and Wall Streeters who had speculated on a huge award, were disappointed, the actual sum paid was highly useful to Polaroid. The company had taken on about $1 billion in debt to fight off a takeover attempt in 1988 (which may have been a speculation on a large award from Kodak), including $300 million in preferred stock paying substantial dividends each year. Polaroid used part of the Kodak money to buy out the preferred.[36]

∞

The importance of the *Polaroid v. Kodak* case in the history of the patent system went well beyond the size of the ultimate award, or the unusual spectacle of a dominant company being forced by a much smaller one to quit a significant field. The essence of Polaroid's success was its defense of the novelty and originality of innovations in SX-70, which it managed to differentiate from prior inventions by itself and others. The inventions in the suit clearly covered a wide enough range to drive Kodak from the market if infringement could be proven. Equally clearly, Polaroid drew on decades of experience with instant photography. But the SX-70 inventions met the requirements of a new system. Unlike prior systems, the SX-70 film unit kept its negative and positive together always, on the shelf before use, during the active moments of processing and building up the color image, and then during years of storage and display. The new film unit needed to be driven reliably from the camera after exposure, to make way for another picture at once. The film needed a robust outer structure to protect the image within and to resist the curling that bedeviled photography for decades. The problem of stabilizing conditions within the film, to preserve the image after it took shape, was more demanding than when the negative was peeled apart and discarded as it had been for twenty-five years.

The exact materials, arrangement, and thickness of the various active layers differed from earlier film types. In addition, while developing SX-70, Polaroid's inventors found, as they often had before, alternate methods of reaching particular goals, which also should be patented, and were. Together, the inventions built a wall that Kodak could not go around. Kodak had to use elements of the Polaroid system to make its own integral-film system work. Polaroid's ability to prove that Kodak used Polaroid elements was a success in the system of protecting inventors through patents and assuring them of the profits to plow back into more innovation. A very large company, indeed the dominant enterprise in world photography for most of the past century, was not allowed to appropriate the inventions of a much smaller firm.

∞

By the time the trial ended in 1982, sales of instant cameras and film had fallen to a fraction of their boom levels in 1977 and 1978. The stagnation continued as the parties waited three and a half years for Judge Zobel's ruling, and Land went off to the Rowland Institute. When Kodak was ordered to leave the field, it probably was ready to do so. Once Kodak was gone, Polaroid had the sole responsibility of kindling and rekindling enthusiasm for the photography it had begun and dominated. Polaroid was lord of a desert island.

These uncomfortable trends had not escaped the attention of Polaroid, which eagerly and expensively sought new fields. All through the 1980s, while introducing new generations of instant cameras to maintain film sales and expanding more and more into foreign markets, Polaroid spent about $100 million a year, about 5 percent of sales, on research and development. About half of that, some $500 million over a decade, went for work on electronic means to capture, store, manipulate, transmit, display, and copy images on screens and films alike. The company developed advanced means of scanning images into electronic systems and reading them out. But it never could, either by itself or in partnership with other companies, turn these technologies into sizable and profitable businesses, either for specialized or mass customers. Polaroid stumbled again and again. An impressive medical image system for handling X-rays, magnetic resonance images, and computerized automated tomography was delayed years after it had been shown at a shareholders' meeting and eventually was sold off.

As these struggles continued, wave after wave of the people Edwin Land had inspired left the company and were largely replaced by people who lacked the passion without which nothing is achieved. As the company's focus shifted from science and technology to marketing, uncertainty did not abate.[37] Meanwhile, Kodak stumbled with many acquisitions outside photography, and then, after firing its chairman in the 1990s, pulled in a leader of the electronics industry who proceeded, by selling off the acquisitions and slashing debt, to refocus on imaging with indifferent success. Its stock price fell more than 25 percent from July to December 1997.[38]

Meanwhile, the battleground of imaging was shifting to a new domain: images displayed on computer screens. The pleasure and usefulness of such images helped drive the demand for ever more miniaturized, ever faster electronic chips increasingly adept at storing and processing electronic information. Chip companies began to plunge into basic research of the sort Land had espoused, and to see themselves as more than the makers of components. By alliances and acquisitions, they plunged deeper and deeper into the world of images. Most prominent among the unexpected new forces in imaging was Intel, the principal developer of the microprocessor, which had become by the mid-1990s arguably the most important industrial enterprise in the world.[39]

By 1997, Intel was plowing back $5 billion into research and capital equipment, selling $20 billion worth of microchips, and clearing $5 billion in profits. Intel could no longer simply adapt the basic research of others, but had to do fundamental inquiries of its own. The company's chairman, Andrew S. Grove, said, "We can't rely on others to do our research and development for us." Intel's president added, in a Landian tone, "Now we're at the head of the class, and there's nothing left to copy." Intel had become committed to starting at least two of its "wafer fab" chip factories each year, at a cost of $2 billion apiece. The factories were giant gambles, each costing almost as much as Polaroid's total annual sales. As Land had said in 1977, the business of business was making things—and seeing if people would buy them. When the fabs opened, there had to be uses for what they could make. Increasingly, those uses involved capturing, manipulating, and transmitting images, sopping up the swelling capacities of chips.[40] The millions of transistors in each microprocessor had submicroscopic dimensions reminiscent of Land's polarizer microcrystals of sixty years before. In another bow to Land's first love, optics, the transistors were etched onto silicon with the aid of an advanced form of photolithography.

The day of electronic still photography dawned, and despite vast investment, Polaroid's part was small. The pictures were captured by devices that looked like compact cameras, made by a host of manufacturers, and were displayed as they were taken, on a liquid crystal screen on the back. The picture-taker who liked the image could store it and then, through a little cable, project it on a computer screen or on the same television screen used for displaying videotapes. There the photographer and a small group could enjoy the images together. With the help of the microchips and ever-wider data highways, the possibility of video E-mail became actual. Now hundreds of companies, including the giant Intel, had mounted the treadmill of innovation in images. There lay the innovator's passion and dread that Land had felt.

25

Prospero's Island

> Eventually, Dr. Land, one of those brilliant troublemakers, was asked to leave his own company—which is one of the dumbest things I've ever heard of. So Land, at 75, went off to spend the remainder of his life doing pure science, trying to crack the code of color vision. The man is a national treasure. I don't understand why people like that can't be held up as models. This is the most incredible thing to be—not an astronaut, not a football player—but this.
>
> —Steven P. Jobs, 1985[1]

On 26 July 1982, Land told Polaroid's board of directors that he would resign formally the next day as both chairman of the board and a director. That evening the directors dined at his new, red brick Rowland Institute on the Charles. Construction of the laboratory, designed by the architect Hugh Stubbins, had been completed the previous fall. As always, Land made a mystery of the name Rowland, the same name he and his wife had given to their charitable foundation. The best guess seems to be a combination of Robert Wood's initials, Land's name, and the name of Henry Rowland, Wood's teacher.

As the guests drove over for the dinner, the building had the outward aspect of a fortress. When their cars rolled into the driveway off the boulevard that would one day be named for Land, a large, steel-mesh gate rolled up. On the right a solid metal door rose to let the cars into the parking garage. Once the guests had parked, the garage door opened automatically to let them into the covered part of the drive. The guard at a desk within, able to see the driveway through a window, buzzed them in.

The visitors walked a few paces past the guard's desk to an elevator. One floor up, the elevator doors opened to reveal an interior as open as the exterior seemed closed, a two-story skylighted atrium, with tile floors on either side of the long rectangle, and in the center a Japanese-style garden of rocks and plants. The wide balcony above allowed scientists to stroll between their laboratories while looking down on the garden. Just to the right of the elevator lay Land's own brightly lit suite of a lab and three offices with white walls, surroundings very different from the red-carpeted "Mole's hole" of offices and laboratories at Osborn Street that he had left moments before.[2]

The Rowland Institute embodied the founder's ideas as few structures do. "I've never seen architecture do what that building does," Land said later. "It's generous, carpeted with brick." The idea of an indoor garden, he said, had started with the Boston palazzo of Isabella Stewart Gardner, which was later converted into a museum. A delighted Land spoke of the Japanese garden as "experimental," suggesting "moss gardens in the forest."[3] It was the first thing he saw when he stepped out of his lab. Some months later, as the monthly *Architectural Record* prepared a cover article, Land remarked that he hoped the story would convey a sense of "exclusivity," but that of a "monastery, not a fortress or Xanadu."[4]

In a small kitchen, Land opened two bottles of a rare wine that Julius Silver had contributed to the evening's special dinner, which had been arranged before he told the directors of his plans to leave. As he showed a visitor the ground floor library, the small auditorium for forty people, and the two floors of elaborately equipped laboratories, two Polaroid directors, Frank Jones and Carl Kaysen, both of MIT, were already sipping drinks in the glassed-in third-floor terrace, next to the rooftop greenhouse. The morning after the dinner, Land went ahead with his resignation and it was announced.

∞

In the next few days, as Land prepared responses for assistants to give to press inquiries, he emphasized that Rowland Institute scientists typically worked on some aspect of the interaction of light with matter.

Jeffrey Hoch, finishing a doctoral degree at Harvard, was using high-magnetic-field nuclear magnetic resonance spectroscopy to examine the dynamics of chemical processes, such as the movement of proteins. Robert Savoy, trained at MIT in applied mathematics and psychology, was focusing on the human brain's responses to visual stimuli. Craig Shaefer, who had studied with Woodward at Harvard, was working out new computer methods of modeling chemical reactions. James Foley, who received his Ph.D. from the

University of Wisconsin and had been a research fellow at Polaroid, was synthesizing dye molecules to study energy transfer within and between molecules. The work was aimed at dyes that would be sensitive to laser light and therefore relevant for skin cancer therapy. Another MIT Ph.D., Joel Parks, was using the Rowland Institute's laser to probe chemical reactions when surfaces were bombarded by molecules. Michael Burns, in charge of computer systems, would later turn to collaborations with Jean-Marc Fournier and Jene Golovchenko of Harvard on using lasers to trap what they called "optical matter." Stewart Wilson continued the studies of learning that he had begun with Land's encouragement two decades before. George Flynn of Columbia University was spending three months of a sabbatical as a visiting scientist. The molecular biologist Francis Crick of the Salk Institute, who had turned his attention from the genetic code embodied in DNA to the brain, had been by for a visit and had written a sprightly letter with several admonitions.

Of his own role, Land said, "I don't mind conducting the orchestra if I can play the violin." He had given up his group at Polaroid, whose work might have proven useful in computers, communication, and television, "because everywhere they turned, they ran up against an industrial wall."[5] The Rowland Institute would consist of a small group of equals. The question of succession was left to an unknowable future.

At Polaroid, other key people left in 1982. Several leading executives took advantage of a generous severance offer, and others also resigned. Observers, including one Wall Street analyst, were dismayed. "They lost their most aggressive people. The people who left knew they could get jobs elsewhere." Another analyst said, "I sensed a lack of faith." A university lecturer on industrial relations put it this way: "Even the best people at Polaroid can't be sure today that they'll do well in the long run. . . . Polaroid just doesn't offer the sky anymore."[6]

Land's departure interested many reporters. Although they requested interviews, he granted few. They were less interested in what he would be doing at his new lab than in the end of his association with the company. The reporters usually had to make do with what others said. In one account, Michael Porter of Harvard Business School criticized Land's failure to emphasize marketing, but added, "He'll be remembered as one of the great technical and creative visionaries in American business in the last 30 or 40 years. Here's a guy who had a vision about what technology could do in the photo industry and converted that vision into reality."[7]

To a less friendly Wall Street analyst, Land's departure was "one more encouraging sign that the new management has decided to make money.

While he was at the company, no one was sure whether it was run for a profit or as a non-profit institute."[8] There were other views. Emphasizing the breadth of his interests, an editorial in *The Boston Globe* commented, "Land has, in fact, always been an overachiever."[9] Robert Lenzner, a Globe reporter, wrote that Land was now free to pursue his scientific ideals, having put "prying security analysts, litigious shareholders, management squabbles, and muckraking journalists" behind him.[10] Not quite.

Nicholas Wade, a science reporter serving on the editorial board of *The New York Times*, wrote an editorial, "The Colossus of the Camera," on 5 August. According to Wade, Land violated the rule that no one could excel at both invention and management. "Working continually to renew the remarkable organization he brought into being, Mr. Land attained creativity without chaos. He may be one of a kind, but his approach deserves more imitators."[11]

Also on 5 August, Land showed the Rowland Institute to Deborah Shapley of *Nature*, the English scientific weekly. He particularly wanted her to admire the circular staircase of poplar that rose from the first floor to the atrium. He bounded up the steps two at a time, just as he often had at Osborn Street. The building, he told Shapley, was designed to be "comfortable, inspiring if possible" for "a small number of scientists, each dedicated to his own work yet supportive of the work of others in the group." Introducing the physical organic chemist Jim Foley, who had been next door analyzing a spectrum, he said that Foley "could work on any problem, always excited about what he's done." Praising Foley and the others, Land remarked, "Working with a genius is like being around a fine bottle of wine."

The idea of Rowland research was "creativity without confusion." Each research group should have "as few [people] as possible." Teamwork frequently meant "an administrator who doesn't do much and then says he did it," but real basic research involved doing "what you refused to do until the parents leave the room." The mixed tenses showed that childhood incidents had a present resonance.

Referring to Jeff Hoch, who was working with magnetic resonance spectroscopy, Land said, "We're one big team. Each has his own pet project." Land invoked his own classic concept of suns and satellites: "Each of us is a sun in our own project. I would be the sun on the nature of the visual process. I'd be a satellite with his subject. . . . We understand each other's minds. . . . I don't want anybody in the building who doesn't have exquisite intellectual taste. They gotta know what counts." Money for each project was likely to be modest. "I'm not sure there's any way to be creative except on a shoestring." He admitted, "We have a nice shoe for the shoestring."

The work differed from what he did at Polaroid, where the focus had been products, not putting "profit for shareholders" first. Land disbelieved the usual theory. "I don't think business is run to make money." Admittedly, many a company did not go even as far as introducing valuable new products, let alone increasing "the technological and scientific understanding of fields in which it is making its products." Companies could not make a significant invention unless they were "ready to make a whole series of inventions. . . . The chain of inventions is itself an invention."

Market research would not help. "You have to cultivate people with creative insights. . . . Markets are what you look back to. A market is something that has been created." With his exit, Polaroid would lose its "insulation" from "the judgmental process of the everyday marketing world." There would be a confrontation between two values. The first was "the long-term imaginative program of sensing an unmet human need and bringing it by way of science to fulfillment." The second was "responding to the chorus of external contemporary voices." Shapley asked what would the Polaroid camera be like in the year 2000? "I hope the Polaroid people will guess what I'd like."

The Rowland Institute was "an experiment to see what will happen if competent, intelligent—maybe very bright—people pursue the substance of science itself for its own sake." It was not for profit, but "an unabashed and unashamed exploration of how the human mind works when it occupies itself with science." The work was "not for advancement. There's no place to advance to."[12]

∞

Continuing the work on color vision was his major assignment. He sought to bring his insights to the maximum number of scientists who might use them. He also sought to publicize the work of the Rowland Institute, not to attract grants for the scientists, a process he wanted to avoid, but to discharge the duty of a tax-exempt activity to report its work to the public.

For several years, Land already had hit the trail to get his ideas across, in lectures at Sandia Laboratory and Los Alamos in New Mexico, the Fermi accelerator lab in Illinois, the palace at Versailles, and the California Institute of Technology in Pasadena. For a Caltech poster, Land was photographed looking out of the huge, round window in a rectangular tower at the top of the new Rowland building. Over the next few years, Land continued traveling across the United States and went repeatedly to Europe, speaking at scientific meetings small and large. In Minneapolis in

1982, he spoke at the seventy-fifth anniversary of the Science Museum of Minnesota and at the vast congress of the Society for Neurobiology.

At the Minneapolis museum, he encountered the science writer Jeremy Bernstein, one of the many writers who tried to persuade him to give interviews for newspaper or magazine profiles, to collaborate on his memoirs, or to cooperate on a book about him. For five years, the writer had sought through intermediaries to arrange a profile for *The New Yorker*. Receiving the same award for public exposition of science as Land, Bernstein met Land for the first and only time. Resolved not to bring up the profile, Bernstein was impressed by Land's seeming "straightforwardness." Land pulled out his pocket diary with Bernstein's address and phone number, to show that the interview request was much on his mind.

Bernstein ebulliently told Land that writing about him would furnish an opportunity to learn about the history of photography. He didn't tell Land that he had never owned a camera. Land responded by looking at Bernstein "oddly," and saying, "Photography. . . . photography. . . . That is something I do for a living. My real interest is in color vision."

Bernstein "did not have the slightest idea of what to make of this remarkable statement." He did not know then of Land's near-total separation from Polaroid. "My first, naive thought was to compare his situation with those taxi drivers, bartenders, and elevator operators one encounters in New York who say that what they really do is act, sing, or conduct research in cosmology." Bernstein never heard from Land again.[13]

In April 1983, Land's old colleague Elkan Blout arranged for him to lecture at the National Academy of Sciences in Washington. The next month, Land addressed a meeting organized by the Harvard physics department.

Introducing Land to the Society for Neurobiology in Boston in November 1983, the Nobel prize physiologist David H. Hubel said that Land's finding that "spectral content does not determine the color [was] very counter-intuitive. It took Land to see what a robust, what a powerful, phenomenon color vision can be." In the audience were Land's wife, his two daughters, and their husbands. Despite the buildup and the distinguished audience, Mrs. Land said afterward that her husband's presentation had been ineffective.[14]

Later presentations went better. In April 1984, he flew with his equipment across the Atlantic to Bad Homburg, and again in June for a meeting in Stockholm, arranged by his colleague Semir Zeki of University College, London. Describing it afterward, Land was exuberant: the Stockholm meeting was "a turning point in the history of color vision," because "it was the first time in history anyone ever predicted a color." He said that the audience burst into applause, and that each of the following papers referred to his.[15] After a speech in July 1984 at an international congress in Bristol, England, he carried out a demonstration for British Broadcasting Corporation (BBC) television.[16] The next month, he spoke at a workshop on the "systems approach to color vision" in Amsterdam. In December Land's work was featured in *The Economist* under the title "The Conundrum of Colour."[17]

He didn't convince everybody. Psychologist John Mollon, in the BBC broadcast "Colourful Notions," in January 1985, said that although Land and the scientific establishment were "coming together," Land's ideas "seem so improbable to the majority of scientists working on colour vision that they've simply ignored them." In the BBC magazine *The Listener*, Mollon wrote that Land had been anticipated in the 1790s by the French mathematician Gaspard Monge. The "popular idea" that Land had overthrown previous concepts of color vision was "thoroughly mistaken."[18]

A few days later, the Rowland Institute put out a press release about the work by visiting scientist David Ingle showing that goldfish, although they lacked the elaborate cerebral cortex of humans, still obeyed the rules of Land's retinex theory. The work was published in *Science*, which displayed on its cover a color photograph of the goldfish going for a particular square of color on a Mondrian display at one end of the rectangular fish tank. There was some popular attention. A report in *The Boston Globe* was widely reprinted, and National Public Radio carried an interview with Land in which he repeated that "between the skin and the soul there's a layer of magnificent mechanisms. . . . We should take ourselves seriously."[19]

On two successive nights in April 1985, Land lectured in the auditorium of the building he had donated to the American Academy of Arts and Sciences. Jovially tweaking his critics, he said jokingly that his topic was "Red, white, and green: a report on the sociology of seeing color," and spoke of "a thirty-year search for a few simple laws, valid for a few simplistic situations in the laboratory." He inveighed against explaining effects away. "Don't explain away the wonder. Cherish the wonder and seek the cause."[20]

Three weeks later, his sale of all the remaining Polaroid shares held by him, his wife, and their Rowland Foundation drew far more coverage than the scientific work. It generated an additional $26 million for the Rowland Institute's endowment.

∞

In February 1987, coached by Edward Purcell, Land gave a talk to the small Cambridge scientific club they both belonged to. This was a warm-up for his final lecture-demonstration in March, at MIT. Land was giving a "twilight view" of color vision: "It is hard for us to know how we use it, since it works so powerfully, directly, quickly, innocently." He added, "For the first time in twenty-five years in this field, I feel myself truly satisfied. . . . We don't see light, we see *with* light."[21]

Present at the MIT demonstration was an Italian observer, Giuseppe Piatelli-Palmarini, who wrote an account in Italy's leading daily, *Corriere della Sera*: "How subtle, sometimes, can be the frontier between a masterly lecture and a true and proper 'show.'" One of Land's classical demonstrations, using two slide projectors, showed "the most home-like of scenes: an overflowing fruit bowl, a bottle of Chianti, glass pickle jars, all laid out on one of those checkered table cloths of a trattoria." Again, Land demonstrated that "the colors of the objects were NOT determined by the wavelengths of the objects reflected to the eye. . . . Diverse wavelengths can be seen as the same color and . . . the same wavelength can be seen as diverse colors (as the Chianti teaches)."

Was the effect due to contrast? No, said Land. Were psychologists and anthropologists right in saying that our perception of color "signifies seeing what one expects to see?" Again the answer was no. Zeki had found "single neurons which see one color or another solely according to the retinex scale and not according to wavelength." Land's answer to the puzzle of color vision, Piatelli-Palmarini wrote, was "nothing less than a complex ratio among two luminous intensities, that of the point we observe and that of a nearby surrounding region which is neither too large nor too small."

Land said that the special thirty-thousand-dollar meter for calculating these ratios, which were called designators, was "the only artificial object in the entire history of man that functions really like an eye, that sees what we see, as we see it." The Italian observer thought that in the future, humanity would be hearing less about atomic nuclei or macromolecules or far-off galaxies and more about exactly "how we exist."[22]

∞

Over these years, Land centered his work in his laboratory, which was equipped for experiments in optics and chemistry. Usually the doors of the small offices on the street side were left open to admit more light. A door at the left communicated with neighboring labs. Gradually the walls were covered by floor-to-ceiling calendars, displaying a whole year's engagements at a time—everything from doctors' appointments and haircuts to distinguished visitors and lecture dates. Eventually, one calendar had to be taped to the door opening toward the garden. There were tables for books being consulted and for displaying the results of experiments, many conducted by Bruce Young and Craig Easson. Near the calendars were tables for setting out letters and folders relating to possible engagements. In the center was a small, round card table with a few chairs for having lunch with colleagues and visitors. On a filing cabinet nearby was a ship's clock that had been given to him. Draping an armchair was the blanket of many-colored squares knitted for him long before by a lab associate. To use the telephone, often on its loudspeaker setting, he would go into the small office of his longtime laboratory colleague Sara Hollis "Holly" Perry and sit in an armchair by her desk, where she often took notes.

For full-dress experiments on color vision, Land would go down to an enormous, black room on the first floor, which was equipped with projectors, photometers, and Mondrian displays. On the second floor, he also had an office for transacting business not directly related to his research, such as the difficult conversations with Polaroid officials about his intention to sell all his remaining shares. The office had huge windows looking out onto a terrace and beyond to Beacon Hill in Boston. The views were best at sunset. The carpets and chairs that his wife had chosen were in the subdued grays, browns, and blues of the Southwest, where the Lands had spent some of their best times. The Ansel Adams moonrise print hung just above the white brick fireplace.

In his laboratory, the atmosphere was less hectic than it had been during the crises at Osborn Street. The sandwiches were ordered in as before, but he and his companions ate in a leisurely fashion, sitting down, at the little card table. Land enjoyed excursions for lunch, such as to a crowded Chinese restaurant in Central Square, Cambridge. Even though his diet restricted him from too much protein, he always could nibble from other people's plates. Up to the age of seventy-eight, he occasionally drove associates home from the laboratory. To the relief of his passengers, the second of the compact Cadillac Cimarrons he drove was more high-powered than the first, so that Land could more readily pull out of driveways into a stream of traffic. Later he switched to a Buick.

The lab was enlivened by an ebullient, long-haired, gray and black dog, a Keeshond, who was given the name Designator, or Desi for short. Mostly friendly and fond of games, racing, and jumping, Desi went out for walks along the Charles with Bruce Young. Land was very attached to Desi.[23]

∞

Although Land clearly wanted to spend his remaining energies in science, his decision to leave Polaroid had economic consequences for the company and the Rowland Institute. Even after the sale of 300,000 shares in 1979 and a further 1.5 million in 1981 to build and endow the Rowland Institute, the Land family still held a large share of the company's stock, which they could sell. The company's directors and managers knew that shares could fall into the hands of takeover specialists of the sort who did move in on Polaroid in the late 1980s. There was an immediate divergence of interest. As a non-profit research center, the Rowland Institute needed a stable income that grew at least as fast as inflation. It was not in the institute's interest to hold the stock of a stagnant company. Even if the Lands donated stock to the institute, as they did several times, the most prudent step for managing the laboratory's endowment would be an immediate sale.

The day after the public announcement of Land's departure in 1982, the company's directors and managers began working urgently to buy back shares from the conglomerate called Gulf and Western Industries, headed by the buccaneering Charles Bluhdorn. Some of the conglomerate's shares may have been among those sold by the Lands or the Rowland Institute. As is required of any purchaser of more than 5 percent of a publicly traded company, in December 1981 Gulf and Western notified the Securities Exchange Commission that it had bought 2.2 million shares of Polaroid at an average price of twenty dollars. In the following months, G & W cut its new holding by 300,000 shares.

Polaroid had more than enough money to buy back the rest: cash and marketable securities of $327 million as of 27 July 1982. On 15 August, the company bought 1,896,300 shares, almost 6 percent of the shares outstanding, from Gulf and Western at a price of $24.75 a share. The total cost was $46.9 million, less than a sixth of the company's reserves. To Polaroid it looked like a bargain, even though the price was more than 7 percent above the market, because the company's book value was $29 a share. To Bluhdorn, it looked like a good deal, because he was earning a profit of almost 24 percent on a stock he had held for less than nine months.[24]

In 1985, the Lands donated a further 1 million shares to the Rowland Institute. The 2.56 million shares remaining to them, the Rowland Foundation, and the Rowland Institute were sold for about $72 million. The company leadership was not happy about the size or timing of this sale and hinted to Land that he should wait for the stock price to rise, as it did.

A factor in this thinking was that Polaroid shareholders would be voting on 14 May on several measures designed to hinder hostile takeover attempts.

But in a statement issued to national wire services moments after the stock was registered for sale, Land noted that he and his wife were getting older: "We are both over 75 years of age and it seems wise and prudent to use our resources for maximum good and effectiveness. Like most men of my age who are in good health, I seek to make application of my enthusiasm and accumulated experience—in my case to science, to education, and to sustaining those historic values which have counted for us." Although he had hundreds of companions at Polaroid and remembered them with affection, "my wife and I feel that the time has now come for a final separation from the company we shall never forget."[25]

The divergence of interest surfaced significantly again in June 1987. To save costs of further litigation, Land and the Rowland Institute settled, for six hundred thousand dollars, a suit brought by Irving A. Backman and other shareholders in 1979. They had sued after the first sale of Rowland Foundation shares on 11 January 1979. The sale was made to build and equip the institute. Backman claimed that Land and Polaroid held back information about the costs of Polavision that led, over a few days, to more than a 25 percent drop in Polaroid share prices. The decline began on 23 February, the day that Polaroid announced record profits in the fourth quarter of 1978 and a 28 percent increase in profits for the entire year. The company, Wall Street analysts said at the time, had not given them a strong enough warning the previous fall about the continuing drain from Polavision. Land's settlement eight years later called for up to two hundred thousand dollars in plaintiffs' legal fees and payments of up to seven dollars a share solely to the people who bought the stock on the day that Rowland sold it.

The settlement was arranged just before the suit went to trial in the court of U.S. District Judge John McNaught. Polaroid was also a defendant, but did not settle. A six-person jury found Polaroid liable, saying that holders of 3.9 million shares (more than 10 percent of the total) should be paid $9.75 a share. After the verdict, Backman said, "The failure to disclose information is just as abusive as falsifying information. It shows the arrogance of corporate power." Of Land, he said, "Just because someone has tremendous achievements to his credit doesn't mean he's above the law. It's not quite cricket."[26]

Polaroid took the case up to the U.S. Circuit Court. A three-judge panel heard the case, and Polaroid lost partially and appealed the ruling to the full court. On 2 August 1990, in an opinion written by Senior Judge Bailey Aldrich, the final ruling was, "Plaintiffs have no case." According to Aldrich, Judge McNaught "unhappily failed to see that plaintiffs' case was dead on arrival."[27]

Soon after the suit was settled, the company tried and failed to get Land to appear at an elaborate celebration of its fiftieth anniversary or to grant several retrospective interviews. The divorce was final, however. Refusing all the interview suggestions, he limited himself to a written message, to be read by Mac Booth, the chief executive officer. He wrote of "the relationship we had at Polaroid: the combination of freedom and tight friendly association, the independence of thought and the dependence of multiple partnerships, the relaxed integrity and the intensity of a single clear purpose." Land added, "This message which Polaroid has sent out as far away as Japan has in fifty years saved industry from the depredation of the financial world while freeing it for the support of the financial world."[28]

That year, Peter Wensberg's account of his years at Polaroid was published. In a telephone interview about the book, Land said, "I regard my scientific papers as my essential biography. I pour my whole life into the scientific project I'm investigating. I leave behind me the things I've done in the past to do the work in the present."[29]

∞

Eventually, illnesses closed in. For a time, painful sciatica confined him to an electrically powered scooter to ride the length of the atrium from his laboratory to his office. Kidney troubles, which had involved a war with doctors over many years about his diet, led finally to cancer, removal of one kidney, and the need for frequent dialysis. He was afflicted with shingles and was tortured by the sneezing induced by the pepper-containing lotion he needed. He became largely housebound. On rare occasions, he could be taken out for a drive, with a nurse. Late in 1988, he underwent heart-bypass surgery.

Soon after the surgery, he celebrated his eightieth birthday in the archive room at the Rowland Institute. This room had been furnished gradually. Before it was furnished, prints by Ansel Adams and Clarence Kennedy leaned against the walls, and Land delighted in pointing out how their methods were opposite, Adams using high contrast and Kennedy low. Later, a very long saloon bar that Land had acquired stretched across the room. Behind it were the books from his library at Osborn Street. For the party on Sunday, 7 May 1989, a blustery, cool, clear day, round tables were set up for a festive light lunch from Michela Larson's restaurant in the Carter Ink building across the street. Land's wife, daughters, and sons-in-law attended, as did Ed Purcell. There wasn't room enough for the spouses of Rowland Institute scientists. Because the mélange of medications he was taking induced bouts of hallucinations, Land almost missed the occasion. He arrived nonetheless, cheerily conversed with the guests, and gave a short speech wishing future success to the laboratory family and its experiment in doing science.[30]

∞

Back in June 1986, at the Rowland Institute, a Western Union Mailgram from London told Land: "I have the honour to inform you of your election today as a foreign member of the Royal Society. Burgen, Secretary, R.S."[31] His contributions to science, including his work on color vision, were being recognized signally. Normally he would have traveled to London to sign the members' book, but illness prevented him. Instead, on 9 January 1991, Semir Zeki brought a page of the book across the Atlantic to Land's home at 163 Brattle Street. The page held the signature of the great French physicist Paul Langevin. To officially induct Land and Ed Purcell into the Royal Society, the electron microscopist Hugh Huxley came with Zeki. Looking on were Terre Land and Natalie Fultz, longtime assistant to both Land and his wife.

A year later, Purcell recalled that for the occasion, Land was in a wheelchair, "quite weak. I didn't talk to him except to take his hand. It was important that Zeki have all the time he needed."[32] Land's face showed that he "knew that the time was up," Zeki felt. But Land was not worried. "There was serenity there. There was kindness. There was the knowledge, I believe, that he had lived a full life, that he had enriched many people by contact with them, and that he had achieved a great deal."

Zeki reflected later that "the romantic dream does not belong to romantic youth, and should not be shelved after one passes those years. Because the man who has forfeited the dream is a man who has forfeited, really, the quest to find new things and to contribute in an important way to his society and to his culture."[33]

On 1 March 1991, Edwin Land died.[34] He was buried in Mount Auburn Cemetery in Cambridge.

Bibliography

ABBREVIATIONS

Archives

AC Author's collection.
AN Author's notes.
AT Author's transcript.
DDEL Dwight David Eisenhower Library, Abilene, Kansas.
HUA Harvard University Archives.
LC Library of Congress.
MITA MIT Archives.
MMF Meroë Morse Files, Polaroid Archives (PA).
OSANSA Office of the Special Assistant for National Security Affairs, DDEL.
OSAST Office of the Special Assistant for Science and Technology, DDEL.
PA Polaroid Archives, Cambridge, Massachusetts.
PDC Patent Department Collection, 1929–1935, PA.
PL Polarized Lights folder, PA.
PLC Patent lawyer's chronology, Marks case 1954, PA.
TCP Technological Capabilities Panel (1954–55), DDEL.
VB Vannevar Bush papers, EHL folder, Library of Congress (LC).

Newspapers

American *The New York American.*
BG *The Boston Globe.*
BH *Boston Herald.*
CSM *The Christian Science Monitor.*
Hartford Times *The Hartford Times*, Hartford, Conn.
NYHT *New York Herald Tribune.*
NYT *The New York Times.*
NYWT *New York World Telegram.*
ST *Sunday Times* (London).
WP *The Washington Post.*
WSJ *The Wall Street Journal.*

Periodicals

BJP *British Journal of Photography.*
BW *Business Week.*
C & EN *Chemical and Engineering News*, American Chemical Society.
IES *Transactions of the Illuminating Engineering Society.*

JACS *Journal of the American Chemical Society.*
JOSA *Journal of the Optical Society of America.*
JPOS *Journal of the Patent Office Society.*
LD *Literary Digest.*
MP *Modern Photography.*
OPN *Optics and Photonics News*, Optical Society of America.
PJ *The Photographic Journal.*
PS *Popular Science.*
PSA *The Journal of the Photographic Society of America.*
PSE *Photographic Science and Engineering.*
SAE *The Society of Automotive Engineers Journal* (Transactions).
SMPTE *Journal of the Society of Motion Picture and Television Engineers.*
T & C *Technology and Culture*, Society for the History of Technology, University of Chicago Press.

SOURCES

Books and Journal Articles

Ambrose 1981. Stephen E. Ambrose with Richard H. Immerman. *Ike's Spies: Eisenhower and the Espionage Establishment.* Garden City, NY: Doubleday, 1981.

Ambrose 1983. Stephen E. Ambrose. *Eisenhower,* Vol. 1, *Soldier, General of the Army, President-Elect.* New York: Simon and Schuster, 1983.

Ambrose, 1985. Stephen E. Ambrose. *Eisenhower,* Vol. 2, *The President.* New York: Simon and Schuster, Touchstone, 1985.

Baldwin 1980. Ralph B. Baldwin. *The Deadly Fuze: The Secret Weapon of World War II.* San Rafael, Calif.: Presidio Press, 1980.

Baxter 1946. James Phinney Baxter. *Scientists Against Time.* Boston: Little, Brown, 1946.

Beard 1976. Edmund Beard. *Developing the ICBM: A Study in Bureaucratic Politics.* New York: Columbia University Press, 1976.

Bergson 1911. Henri Bergson. *Creative Evolution.* Translated by Arthur Mitchell, New York: Henry Holt, 1911.

Beschloss 1986. Michael R. Beschloss. *Mayday: Eisenhower, Khrushchev, and the U-2 Affair.* New York: Harper and Row, 1986.

Bissell 1996. Richard M. Bissell. Jr., with Jonathan E. Lewis and Frances Y. Pudlo, *Reflections of a Cold Warrior: From Yalta to the Bay of Pigs.* New Haven: Yale University Press, 1996.

Boring 1950. Edwin G. Boring. *A History of Experimental Psychology.* 2nd ed. New York: Appleton-Century-Crofts, 1950.

Brayer 1996. Elizabeth Brayer. *George Eastman: A Biography.* Baltimore: Johns Hopkins University Press, 1996.

Brown 1960. Donald Brown. Address at Award Dinner, New Jersey Patent Law Association, Robert Treat Hotel, Newark, New Jersey, 11 May 1960. Published in *JPOS,* 42, No. 7, July 1960, PA.

Brugioni 1991. Dino A. Brugioni. *Eyeball to Eyeball: The Inside Story of the Cuban Missile Crisis.* New York: Random House, 1991.

Bundy 1988. McGeorge Bundy. *Danger and Survival: Choices About the Bomb in the First Fifty Years.* New York: Random House, 1988.

Burrows 1986. William E. Burrows. *Deep Black.* New York: Random House 1986. Reprint, New York: Berkley Books, 1988.

Bush, 1945. Vannevar Bush. *Science: The Endless Frontier.* 1945. Reprint, Washington, D.C.: National Science Foundation, 1960.

Bush, 1949. Vannevar Bush. *Modern Arms and Free Men.* New York: Simon and Schuster, 1949.

Bush 1970. Vannevar Bush, *Pieces of the Action.* New York: William Morrow, 1970.

Butters and Lintner 1944. J. Keither Butters and John Lintner. "Effect of Federal Taxes on Growing Enterprises, Study Number 2, Polaroid Corporation." Graduate School of Business Administration, Harvard University, 7 October 1944.

Carnegie 1967. Carnegie Commission on Educational Television. *Public Television: A Program for Action.* New York: Bantam, 1967.

Chernow 1990. Ron Chernow. *The House of Morgan: An American Banking Dynasty and the Rise of Modern Finance.* New York: Simon and Schuster, Touchstone, 1991.

Chernow 1993. Ron Chernow. *The Warburgs: The Twentieth Century Odyssey of a Remarkable Jewish Family.* New York: Random House, 1993.

Cline 1976. Ray Cline. *Secrets, Spies, and Scholars.* New York: Acropolis Books, 1976.

Derry and Williams 1961. T. K. Derry and Trevor I. Williams. *A Short History of Technology from the Earliest Times to A.D. 1900.* New York: Oxford University Press, 1961.

Dickson 1964. John Dickson. *Instant Pictures.* Pelham Books, 1964.

Divine 1978. Robert A. Divine. *Blowing on the Wind: The Nuclear Test Ban Debate.* New York: Oxford University Press, 1978.

Divine 1993. Robert A. Divine. *The Sputnik Challenge,* New York: Oxford University Press, 1993.

EB 1911. *Encyclopaedia Britannica,* Eleventh edition.

France 1912. Anatole France, *Les Dieux Ont Soif.* Paris: GF Flammarion paperback, 1989.

Friedman 1968. Joseph Solomon Friedman. Ph.D., *History of Color Photography.* 2nd ed. London: Focal Press, 1968.

Frisch 1967. Karl von Frisch. *The Dance Language and Orientation of Bees.* Translated by Leigh E. Chadwick, Cambridge, Mass: Harvard University Press, 1967. Second printing 1993.

Gilbert 1996. George Gilbert. *The Illustrated Worldwide Who's Who of Jews in Photography.* Riverdale, N.Y.: George Gilbert, 1996. I am indebted to Vivian K. Walworth for calling Gilbert's book to my attention.

Gorney 1972. Roderic Gorney, M.D. *The Human Agenda,* New York: Bantam Books, 1972

Greenstein, 1982. Fred I. Greenstein. *The Hidden-Hand Presidency: Eisenhower as Leader.* Baltimore: Johns Hopkins University Press, 1994 paperback.

Grove 1996. Andrew S. Grove. *Only the Paranoid Survive: How to Exploit the Crisis Points That Challenge Every Company and Career.* New York: Doubleday, Currency, 1996.

Harvard Alumni Directory, 1995.

Holloway 1994. David Holloway. *Stalin and the Bomb: The Soviet Union and Atomic Energy.* New Haven: Yale University Press, 1994.

Hounshell and Smith 1988. David A. Hounshell and John Kenly Smith, Jr. *Science and Corporate Strategy: DuPont R & D, 1902–1980.* New York: Cambridge University Press, 1988.

James 1977. Thomas Howard James, ed. *The Theory of the Photographic Process.* 4th ed. New York: Macmillan, 1977.

Jenkins 1975. Reese V. Jenkins. *Images and Enterprise: Technology and the American Photographic Industry, 1839 to 1925.* Baltimore: Johns Hopkins University Press, Studies in the History of Technology, 1987 paperback.

Jewkes et al. 1960. John Jewkes, David Sawers, and Richard Stillerman. *The Sources of Invention.* London: Macmillan, 1960.

Johnson 1985. Clarence L. Johnson with Maggie Smith. *Kelly: More Than My Share of It All.* Washington, D.C.: Smithsonian Institution Press, 1985.

Jones 1978. Reginald Victor Jones. *Most Secret War.* New York: Coward, McCann & Geoghegan, 1978 (originally published 1978 by Hamish Hamilton). Reprint, Coronet Books, Hodder and Stoughton, 1990.

Kevles 1987. Daniel J. Kevles. *The Physicists: The History of a Scientific Community in Modern America.* Cambridge, Mass.: Harvard University Press, 1987 paperback.

Killian 1977. James R. Killian, Jr. *Sputnik, Scientists, and Eisenhower: A Memoir of the First Assistant to the President for Science and Technology.* Cambridge, Mass.: MIT Press 1977.

Kistiakowsky 1976. George B. Kistiakowsky. *A Scientist at the White House.* Introduction by Charles S. Maier. Cambridge, Mass.: Harvard University Press, 1976.

Klass 1971. Philip J. Klass. *Secret Sentries in Space.* New York: Random House, 1971.

Lang 1959. Daniel Lang. *From Hiroshima to the Moon: Chronicles of Life in the Atomic Age.* New York: Simon and Schuster, 1959.

Lewis 1991. Thomas S.W. Lewis. *Empire of the Air: The Men Who Made Radio.* Reprint, Harper Perennial 1993.

Lipton 1982. Lenny Lipton. *Foundations of the Stereoscopic Cinema: A Study in Depth.* New York: Van Nostrand Reinhold, 1982.

Major 1971. John Major. *The Oppenheimer Hearing.* New York: Stein and Day, 1971; Scarborough paperback, 1983.

Manchester 1945. Harland Manchester. "The Magic Crystal," A chapter about Polaroid Corporation and Polaroid products in *New World of Machines.* New York: Random House. Reprinted by Polaroid Corporation, 1945.

McCann 1993a. Mary McCann, ed. *Edwin H. Land's Essays,* Volume 1, *Polarizers and Instant Photography.* Springfield, VA: The Society for Imaging Science and Technology, 1993.

McCann 1993b. Mary McCann, ed. *Edwin H. Land's Essays,* Volume 2, *Science, Education, and Industry.* Springfield, VA: The Society for Imaging Science and Technology, 1993.

McCann 1993c. McCann, ed. *Edwin H. Land's Essays,* Volume 3, *Color Vision.* Springfield, VA: The Society for Imaging Science and Technology, 1993.

McDonald 1995. Robert A. McDonald, "Corona: Success for Space Reconnaissance, A Look into the Cold War and a Revolution for Intelligence." *Photographic Engineering and Remote Sensing* 61, no. 6 (June 1995): 689–720 (Appendix I: "Mission Summary").

McDougall 1986. Walter A. McDougall . . . *The Heavens and the Earth: A Political History of the Space Age.* New York: Basic Books, 1986, paperback.

McGraw-Hill 1966. *Modern Men of Science.* New York: McGraw-Hill, 1966.

McHugh 1980. Jeanne McHugh. *Alexander Holley and the Makers of Steel.* Baltimore: Johns Hopkins University Press, Studies in the History of Technology, 1980.

McPherson 1988. James McPherson. *Battle Cry of Freedom: the Civil War Era.* New York: Oxford University Press, 1988.

Misa 1995. Thomas J. Misa. *A Nation of Steel: The Making of Modern America, 1865–1925.* Baltimore: Johns Hopkins University Press, Studes in the History of Technology, 1995.

Morison 1974. Elting E. Morison. *From Know-how to Nowhere: The Development of American Technology.* New York: Basic Books, 1974.

Murray and Cox 1989. Charles Murray and Catherine Bly Cox. *Apollo: The Race to the Moon.* New York: Simon and Schuster, 1989.

Neblette 1977. Edwin H. Land, Howard G. Rogers, and Vivian K. Walworth. "One-Step Photography." In *Neblette's Handbook of Photography and Reprography: Materials, Processes and Systems,* 7th ed. Edited by John M. Sturge. Chapter 12, pp. 256–330. New York: Van Nostrand Reinhold, 1977 (reprinted in McCann 1993a, pp. 205–263).

Neblette 1989. Vivian K. Walworth and Stanley H. Mervis. "Instant Photography and Related Reprographic Processes." In *Imaging Processes and Materials, Neblette's Eighth Edition.* Edited by John Sturge, Vivian Walworth, and Allan Shepp. Chapter 6, pp. 181–225. 1989.

Newhall 1964. Beaumont Newhall. *The History of Photography.* New York: Museum of Modern Art, 1964.

Olshaker 1978. Mark Olshaker. *The Instant Image.* New York: Stein and Day, 1978. Republished as *The Polaroid Story.* Stein and Day, Scarborough, 1980.

Ostroff 1987. Eugene Ostroff, ed. *Pioneers of Photography: Their Achievements in Science and Technology.* Springfield, VA: The Society for Imaging Science and Technology, 1987.

Pocock 1989. Chris Pocock. *Dragon Lady: The History of the U-2 Spy Plane.* Motor Books, 1989.

Powers 1979. Thomas Powers. *The Man Who Kept the Secrets: Richard Helms and the CIA.*New York: Alfred A. Knopf, 1979.

Prados 1986. John Prados. *The Soviet Estimate.* Princeton University Press, 1986.

PY 1973. John Paul Porter et al., eds. *Photography Year 1973.* New York: Time-Life Books, 1973.

Reeves 1993. Richard Reeves. *President Kennedy: Profile of Power.* New York: Simon and Schuster, 1993.

Rhodes 1995. Richard Rhodes. *Dark Sun: The Making of the Hydrogen Bomb.* New York: Simon and Schuster, 1995. Sloan Technology Series.

Rich 1994. Ben R. Rich and Leo Janos. *Skunk Works: A Personal Memoir of My Years at Lockheed.* Boston: Little, Brown, 1994.

Richelson 1987. Jeffrey T. Richelson. *American Espionage and the Soviet Target.* New York: William Morrow, 1987.

Richelson 1990. Jeffrey T. Richelson. *America's Secret Eyes in Space: The U.S. Keyhole Spy Satellite Program.* New York: Harper and Row, Ballinger, 1990.

Rigden 1987. John S. Rigden. *Rabi: Scientist and Citizen.* New York: Basic Books, 1987.

Ruffner 1995. Kevin C. Rufner, ed. *Corona: America's First Satellite Program.* Washington, D.C.: CIA Cold War Records, History Staff, Center for the Study of Intelligence, Central Intelligence Agency, 1995.

Schaffel 1991. Kenneth Schaffel. *The Emerging Shield: The Air Force and the Evolution of Continental Air Defense, 1945–1960.* Washington, D.C.: Office of Air Force History, 1991. I am indebted to Robert Buderi for lending me this book.

Sherwood 1948. Robert E. Sherwood. *Roosevelt and Hopkins: An Intimate History.* New York: Harper and Brothers, 1948.

Shurcliff 1962. William A. Shurcliff. *Polarized Light: Production and Use.* Cambridge, Mass.: Harvard University Press, 1962.

Sloan 1963. Alfred P. Sloan, Jr. *My Years With General Motors.* New York: Doubleday, Currency, 1990 paperback.

Spengler 1928. Oswald Spengler. *The Decline of the West.* Vol. 2,: *Perspectives of World History.* Translated by Charles Francis Atkinson. New York: Alfred A. Knopf, 1928.

Stares 1985. Paul B. Stares. *The Militarization of Space: U.S. Policy, 1945–1984.* Ithaca, N.Y.: Cornell University Press, 1985.

Strauss 1962. Lewis L. Strauss. *Men and Decisions.* Garden City, N.Y.: Doubleday, 1962.

Wall 1970. Joseph Frazier Wall. *Andrew Carnegie.* New York: Oxford University Press, 1970.

Wensberg 1987. Peter C. Wensberg. *Land's Polaroid: A Company and the Man Who Invented It.* Boston: Houghton Mifflin, Peter Davison, 1987.

Wilson et al. 1986. Richard Guy Wilson, Dianne H. Pilgram, and Dickran Tashjian. *The Machine Age in America, 1918–1941.* New York: The Brooklyn Museum in association with Harry N. Abrams, 1986.

Wood 1911. Robert W. Wood. *Physical Optics.* 2nd ed. New York: Macmillan, 1914.

Wurtman 1989. Richard Saul Wurtman. *Polaroid Access: Fifty Years.* Access Press, 1989.

York 1989. Herbert York. *The Advisors: Oppenheimer, Teller, and the Superbomb.* Stanford, Calif: Stanford University Press, 1989.

Zachary 1997. G. Paschal Zachary. *Endless Frontier: Vannevar Bush, Engineer of the American Century.* New York: Free Press, 1997.

Unpublished Sources

Aldrich 1990. Bailey Aldrich, senior judge. "Opinion en banc," 910 F. 2d, pp. 10–24. 2 August 1990, United States Court of Appeals for the First Circuit, appeals 89–1171 and 89–1172, from the United States District Court, Massachusetts; typescript in AC.

Annual Report. Polaroid Corporation annual reports. AC.

Baker 1953. James G. Baker, panel chairman. "Report of the Intelligence Systems Panel to Dr. Theodore von Kármán, Chairman of the Scientific Advisory Board." Presented 21 October 1953, Colorado Springs, Transmitted to EHL, 4 November 1953. MMF.

Beacon Hill 1952. Draft Final Report, Beacon Hill study, Project Lincoln, 30 April 1952, BH 111, revision of BH-90. MMF.

Bloom 1974. Stanley M. Bloom. lecture, annual conference, Society of Photographic Scientists and Engineers. Boston, May 1974, from author's tape. AT

Brandeis 1983. Panel Discussion sponsored by Alfred P. Sloan Foundation, Brandeis University, 16 December 1983. Moderator, Jack S. Goldstein. Participants: Richard Garwin, Edwin H. Land, Edward M. Purcell, I.I. Rabi, and Jerrold R. Zacharias. Transcript, 58 pp. AC.

Bush Papers (VB). Vannevar Bush Papers. EHL folder. LC.

BW interview 1981. Transcript, EHL interview 9 January 1981 by Robert W. Lougee, 32 pp., used for cover article, "Polaroid: Turning away from Land's one-product strategy," *Business Week*, 2 March 1981, pages 108–112.

Calderwood 1976. Stanford Calderwood. Lecture, Charles Ellis course on investment, Harvard Business School, 18 March 1976. AC.

Carnegie Corporation. Archives, New York Public Library, extract copies in PA.
Cohen 1994. Saul Cohen, interview by author, 23 June 1994, AN.
Cresson Medal. Franklin Institute Report 3017, 14 April 1937. AC.
Donohue 1967. Charles M. Donohue, Chemical Engineering Department. "Chronology of Developments of the Polaroid Corporation." Second Edition, 1 January 1967. 29 pp., gift of Bill Page, AC.
Fuller 1943. Carlton P. Fuller. "Corporate History of Polaroid." Typescript, 8 pp. PA.
Garwin 1991. Richard Garwin, "Science and Public Policy." Lecture at "Light and Life: A Symposium in Honor of Edwin Land," American Academy of Arts and Sciences, 9 November 1991. Typescript, AC.
HBS case. Harvard Business School case EA-F 396, 1971. AC.
Hubel 1991. David Hubel. "How Monkeys See Color." Taped lecture at "Light and Life: A Symposium in Honor of Edwin Land," American Academy of Arts and Sciences, 9 November 1991. Typescript, 21 pp. AN, AT.
Idelson 1974. E.M. Idelson. Lecture at annual conference, Society of Photographic Scientists and Engineers, Boston, May 1974. Typewritten transcript from author's tape.
Kallmann 1991. Gerhard Kallmann. "Land as Patron of the Academy Bulding." Address at "Light and Life: A Symposium in Honor of Edwin Land," American Academy of Arts and Sciences, Cambridge, Massachusetts, 9 November 1991. Taperecording. AN, AT.
Killian 1969-70. James Killian. Oral history interviews with Stephen White, Columbia University. On deposit at DDEL, opened 1985.
Land 1942. EHL address to Polaroid Corporation employees, University Theatre, Cambridge, Massachusetts, 23 December 1942. Typescript, 16 pp. PA.
Land 1945. EHL statement, Senate Military Affairs Committees at the Joint Hearings on Science Bills. Typescript, 8 pp. PA; reprinted in McCann 1993b, pp. 7–9.
Land 1946. EHL address to Polaroid Corporation employees, 24 December 1946.Typescript, 35 pp., PA.
Land 1948. EHL address to Photographic Society of America, Cincinnati, Ohio, 5 November 1948. Typescript, 11 pp. Elkan Blout files, EHL, PA.
Land 1951. EHL address, "Optics." Twentieth anniversary celebration, American Institute of Physics, 23–27 October 1951. Typed transcript, 26 pp. PA.
Land 1954. EHL memoranda for Marks case, 6 June 1954. Typescript. PA.
Land 1957. EHL, *Generation of Greatness.* Ninth Arthur D. Little lecture, Massachusetts Institute of Technology. Pamphlet from transcript of tape supplied by Land, Land to James Killian, 23 September 1957. Reprinted in McCann, 1993b., pp. 11–16.
Land 1958. EHL address to Polaroid Corporation employees, 25 June 1958. Typed transcript, 40 pp. PA.
Land 1959. "Condensation of Dr. Land's remarks in Various Departments," 21 December 1959. Typed transcript, 14 pp. PA.
Land 1960. EHL address to Polaroid Corporation employees, Symphony Hall, Boston, 5 February 1960. Typed transcript, 37 pp. PA.
Land 1963. EHL address to Junior Science Symposium, Kresge Auditorium, Massachusetts Institute of Technology, 18 April 1963. Typescript, PA.
Land 1966. EHL, William James Lecture No. 1, Harvard University, 24 October 1966. Typescript, 21 pp.; Harvard University press release, 24 October 1966, listing further lectures scheduled 7 and 21 November and 5 December. PA.
Land 1972a. EHL address to Polaroid shareholders, Needham, Massachusetts, 25 April 1972, AN.
Land 1972b. EHL invited lecture annual convention, Society of Photographic Scientists and Engineers, San Francisco, May 1972. AN, AT.
Land 1972c. EHL address to New York Technical Section, Society of Photographic Scientists and Engineers, Barbizon Plaza Hotel, New York, 15 November 1972. Partial transcript, AC.
Land 1973. EHL remarks, annual Polaroid shareholders' meeting, Needham, Massachusetts, 24 April 1973. AN.
Land 1974. EHL remarks, annual Polaroid shareholders' meeting, Needham, Massachusetts, 23 April 1974. AN.
Land 1975. EHL public lecture, American Association for the Advancement of Science, Imperial Ballroom, Americana Hotel, New York, 8:30 p.m., Tuesday 28 January 1975, AT, AN; AAAS press release, 4 pp. AC.
Land 1976a. EHL address to Polaroid shareholders, Needham, Massachusetts, 27 April 1976. AN.
Land 1976b. EHL, "The Six Eyes of Man," First W.H. Carothers lecture, DuPont Country Club, Wilmington, Delaware, Wednesday, 19 May 1976. Typed transcript, 29 pp. PA.
Land 1977a. EHL address to Polaroid shareholders, Needham, Massachusetts, 26 April 1977. AN.
Land 1977b. EHL invited lecture, annual conference, Society of Photographic Scientists and Engineers, Sheraton-Universal Hotel, Los Angeles, 5 May 1977. AN.
Land 1978. EHL Franklin Institute Medal Day address. Typed transcript, 9 pp., with covering note from Bowen C. Dees, President, Franklin Institute.
Land 1980. EHL address to Polaroid shareholders, Symphony Hall, Boston, 22 April 1980. AT, AN.
Land 1981. EHL address to Polaroid shareholders, Symphony Hall, Boston, 21 April 1981. AN.
Land 1982. EHL address to Polaroid shareholders, Wellesley College, 4 May 1982. Typed transcript, AC.

Land 1985. Robert F. Zalisk interview of EHL, for National Public Radio broadcast 12 February 1985. Transcript provided by Zalisk. AC.

Lyman papers. Theodore Lyman papers, HUA.

Markey 1986. 789 F. 2d 1556-1574. Opinion by Chief Judge Howard T. Markey, United States Court of Appeals for the Federal Circuit, 25 April 1985. Typescript, 43 pp. AC.

Marks case deposition. Transcript of testimony by EHL, in *Alvin M. Marks et al. v. Polaroid Corporation*, Civil Action 53-168-S, U.S. District Court, Massachusetts. PA.

Marks case exhibit. *Alvin M. Marks et al. v. Polaroid Corporation*, 1954. PA.

Marks case memo. EHL memorandum of 6 June 1954, after depositions and before court testimony in Marks case, 15 pp. PA.

Marks case PLC. Patent Lawyer's Chronology, *Alvin M. Marks et al. v. Polaroid Corporation*, 1954. PA.

Marks trial transcript. *Alvin M. Marks et al. v. Polaroid Corporation* before Sweeney, Ch. J, 9 June 1954. PA; Decision in *Marks v. Polaroid Corp.*, 129 F Supp. 243, U.S. District Court, Massachusetts, 1955.

McCune 1977. William J. McCune, interview by author, 13 April 1977. Typed transcript. AN.

McCune 1991. William J. McCune, interview by author, 23 October 1991. AN.

Mindell 1996. David P. Mindell. " 'Datum for Its Own Annihilation': Feedback, Control, and Computing, 1916–1945." Ph.D. diss., MIT, 1996. (Forthcoming, Johns Hopkins University Press.)

Olsen 1991. Kenneth Olsen. "Entrepreneurial Spirit of Edwin H. Land." Taped lecture at "Light and Life: A Symposium in Honor of Edwin Land." American Academy of Arts and Sciences, Cambridge, Massachusetts, 9 November 1991. AT, AN.

Polacolor 1963. Transcript, "Report before Society of Photographic Scientists and Engineers, Atlantic City, New Jersey, 1 May 1963, by Dr. Edwin H. Land, Howard G. Rogers, Dr. Elkan Blout, Dr. Milton Green, Dr. Myron S. Simon, Dr. George Bird." Dr. Richard S. Corley also spoke. PA.

Project Charles 1951. "Problems of Air Defense." Declassified Final Report of Project Charles under Contract No. DA-36-039sc-5450, 1 August 1951. 3 vols. Reproduced by Armed Services Technical Information Agency, Dayton, Ohio. The author is indebted to Robert Buderi for lending this document.

Purcell 1992. Interview, Edward Mills Purcell, 5 Wright Street, Cambridge, Massachusetts, 15 January 1992. AN, AT.

Quinine. Papers on synthesis of Quinine 1942–45, Marks case box. PA.

Rogers 1972. Howard G. Rogers, interview by author, 21 February 1972. AN.

Rogers 1989. Transcripts, oral history interviews with Howard Gardner Rogers by Bill Sugar, Part 1, 8 March 1989, and Part 2, 22 March 1989, PA.

Rogers 1990. Transcripts, oral history interviews with Howard Rogers by Bettye Pruitt, The Winthrop Group, 4 and 9 October 1990. PA.

Rogers 1991. Transcript, interview with Howard Rogers for film shown 7 September 1991 at Polaroid Corporation tribute to EHL, Hynes Auditorium, Boston. PA.

Rogers 1994. Seidman, Jeff, "The Amazing Land Scientist: Fifteen Years of Research Gave Birth to Instant Color Film," *Photo>Electronic Imaging*, vol. 37, no. 8, 1994.

Trial 1981. *Polaroid Corporation v. Eastman Kodak Company*, CA 76-1634-Z. Transcript. AC.

TCP 1955. "Report, Technological Capabilities Panel, James R. Killian, Jr., Chairman, submitted to the National Security Council, 14 February 1955." Office of the Staff Secretary, Subject series, Box 16, DDEL.

West 1951. Cutler D. West. "History of Polaroid Corporation." 28 September 1951. Typescript, 80 pp. PA.

Wheelwright transcript. Taped interviews of George Wheelwright III by Otto Wolff, late 1970s. Transcript, 134 pp. PA.

Whitman, Ann. File, Diary Series, DDEL.

Zeki 1991. Semir Zeki. Taped lecture at "Light and Life: A Symposium in Honor of Edwin Land," American Academy of Arts and Sciences, 9 November 1991, 5 pp. AT.

Zobel 1985. Rya Zobel, District Judge, Decision and Judgment in Civil Action 76-1634-Z, *Polaroid Corporation v. Eastman Kodak Company*, 13 September and 11 October 1985, 641 F. Supp. 828-878. Typescript, 122 pp. AC.

Authors' Interviews, all AN

James Baker; Conrad Biber; Stanley Bloom; Alan Borror; Richard Brooks; Sheldon Buckler; John Burgarella; Michael Burns; Richard Chen; Charles Chiklis; Louis Cincotta; Saul Cohen; Robert C. Duncan; Irving Erlichman; James Foley; Nicholas Hedzekeriakides; Jeffrey Hoch; Martin Idelson; Howard W. Johnson; Carl Kaysen; Richard Kee; Peter Kliem; Edwin H. Land; John J. McCann; Mary McCann; William J. McCune; Stanley H. Mervis; Charles Mikulka; Joel Parks; William T. Plummer; Edward M. Purcell; Howard G. Rogers; Louis Rosenblum; Robert Savoy; Craig Shaefer; Vivian K. Walworth; Richard Wareham; Bradford Washburn; James D. Watson; Lucretia Weed; Richard Weeks; Peter Wensburg; Jerome B. Wiesner; John Wolbarst; Herbert York

EDWIN LAND: A SELECTED CHRONOLOGY IN THE PRESS

1930s

"In the Light of Polaroid," *Fortune*. September 1938.

1940s

"Trade Is Defended in Labor Surplus," with photo of EHL and W.D. Coolidge, captioned, "Two of the Inventors Honored Last Night," *NYT*, Wednesday, 28 February 1940.

"New Secret Film Records Two Photos." AP, Cambridge, Massachusetts, *NYT*, 6 November 1940.

William L. Laurence. Cambridge, Massachusetts, "Synthetic Quinine Produced, Ending Century Search," *NYT*, Thursday 4 May 1944, pp. 1, 10.

William L. Laurence. "One-Step Camera Is Demonstrated," *NYT*, Saturday 22 February 1947.

1950s

"Marketing a Camera Revolution," *BW*, 12 June 1954 (cover). PA.

"Ladies' Day at Polaroid," *Forbes*, 1 July 1954, pp. 24–25. PA.

Francis Bello. "The Magic That Made Polaroid." *Fortune*, April 1959, pp. 157–158.

Francis Bello. "An Astonishing New Theory of Color." *Fortune*, May 1959, p. 195.

Harold M. Schmeck, Jr. "Theory of Color Disputes Newton." *NYT*, 4 May 1959, p. 31.

1960s

"Businessman-Scientist in Focus: Edwin Herbert Land," *Time*, 17 March 1961. PA.

"Unique Company Hits a Photographic Bonanza: Now It's 60-Second Pictures in Color." *Life*, 25 January 1963, pp. 74–75.

"Late Hours, Lovely Girls Help in the Search." *Life*, 25 January 1963, pp. 76–77.

"5,000 Tries for the Key Chemicals." *Life*, 25 January 1963, pp. 78–79.

Alix Kerr. "What It Took: Intuition, Goo." *Life*, 25 January 1963, pp. 80, 83–85.

Gene Maeroff. "Polaroid's E.H. Land Is Named '66 Winner of Michelson Award." *The Plain Dealer*, Cleveland, Ohio, 12 October 1966.

1970s

Philip Siekman. "Kodak and Polaroid: An End to Peaceful Coexistence," *Fortune*, November 1970, pp. 85–86.

"Kodak and Polaroid Are Moving Closer to Battle for the Instant Market." *WSJ*, 28 April 1971, p. 40.

"Dr. Land redesigns his camera company," *BW*, 15 April 1972 (cover), pp. 70–73.

Philip Taubman. "The Most Basic Form of Creativity." EHL interview. *Time*, 26 June 1972, p. 84.

Sean Callahan. "If you are able to state a problem, it can be solved." *Life*, 27 October 1972, p. 48.

Robert Reinhold. "Land Achieves His Dream with New Polaroid SX-70." *NYT*, 30 October 1972, pp. 47–48.

Dan Cordtz. "How Polaroid Bet Its Future on SX-70." *Fortune*, January 1974, pp. 82–87, 142, 144, 146–147.

Richard Kostelanetz. "A Wide-Angle View and Closeup Portrait of Edwin Land and His Polaroid Cameras." *Lithopinion*, Spring 1974, pp. 48–49, 51–57.

Subrata Chakravarty. "An Interview with Dr. Edwin Land: 'People want more from life than an eight-hour day with a martini at the end.'" *Forbes*, 1 June 1975, pp. 48–50.

Peter Pringle. "Mr. Land's Self-Portrait." *ST*, 2 May 1976.

Robert Lenzner. "Land: The man behind the camera: The founder of Polaroid is exacting and charming, a scientist and an entrepreneur, a recluse and a showman. Who is the real Edwin Land?" *BG*, Sunday 17 October 1976.

Diane Winston. "Camp Days Live Again at Nostalgic Reunion: Men of Mooween Gather Every Year to Recall Summers Past." *NYT*, 28 November 1979, pp. C10–11.

1980s

"Polaroid: Turning away from Land's one-product strategy." *BW*, 2 March 1981, pages 108–112.

Michael Jacobs. "The physicist as entrepreneur." *Physics Today* 35, no. 1 (January 1982): cover, pp. 34-40.

Robert Lenzner. "The Promised Land," *BG*, 3 August 1982, pp. 1, 43.

Deborah Shapley. "New Sights for Land." *Nature* 298, no. 5876 (19 August 1982): 701.

Gina Kolata. "Color Vision Cells Found in Visual Cortex," *Science* 218 (29 October 1982): 457–458.

Robert Kanigel. "An intricate edifice: Exploring the architecture of the visual cortex." *Harvard Magazine*, November–December 1984, pp. 41–49.

Matt Ridley. "The Conundrum of Colour." *Economist*, 22 December 1984, p. 81.

Jeremy Bernstein. "I Am a Camera." *The New York Review of Books* 35, no. 6, (14 April 1988): 23.

1990s

Eric Pace. "Edwin H. Land Is Dead at 81; Invented the Instant Camera." *NYT*, 2 March 1991, pp. 1, 29.

Jane Poss. "Edwin Land dead at 81: Polaroid chief left image on industry." *BG*, 2 March 1991, pp. 1, 8.

Richard Weeks, ed., "Special Issue: Edwin Land." *OPN*, vol. 5, no. 10, October 1994.

Notes

OVERTURE

1. "Innovation in America," panel discussion at reintroduction of *Technology Review* magazine, MIT, 23 April 1998. Comments by John Seely Brown, Robert Metcalfe, William Helman, James L. Vincent, and Michael Dertouzos, AN.
2. Land 1980, p. 9.
3. Sean Callahan, "If you are able to state a problem, it can be solved," interview, *Life*, 27 October 1972, p. 48; Robert Reinhold, Cambridge, Massachusetts, "Land Achieves His Dream With New Polaroid SX-70," *NYT*, 30 October 1972, pp. 47–48.
4. Sloan 1963, pp. 252–263.
5. Land 1942, p. 5.

CHAPTER 1, NOONTIME

1. Land 1957. Reprinted in McCann 1993b, pp. 11–16.
2. Charles M. Vest, *Report of the President, MIT, for the Academic Year 1995–96*. Massachusetts Institute of Technology. Vest added, "Certainly his influence can be attributed to the power of his intellect and his dreams, but perhaps it also had something to do with the times, the dawn of the 1960s, when the country was ready to dream of greatness and to take bold action, and did so in many domains—in science and technology, in education, in civil rights."
3. Land 1960, p. 7.
4. Nari Malani to J. R. Killian, 23 August 1957, Arthur D. Little lecture. Copy to Land, 6 September 1957, AC [Arthur Compton] 4 collection, MITA.
5. Frisch 1967, p. 37.
6. McCann, 1993b, p. 39.
7. Box 137, AC 4 collection, Arthur D. Little lecture, MITA.
8. James B. Fisk to Killian, 26 April 1957. Box 137, AC 4 collection, Arthur D. Little lecture, MITA.
9. Land to Killian, 25 May 1957. Box 132, AC 4 collection, Edwin H. Land, MITA.
10. Land 1963.
11. Killian, Box 137, AC 4 collection, Arthur D. Little lecture, MITA.

CHAPTER 2, SELF-TAUGHT BOYHOOD

1. EHL to author, personal communication, 1980s.
2. Gilbert 1996, pp. 197–98.
3. *Bridgeport Post*, 26 March 1948, PA.
4. Polaroid Corporation release, "Edwin H. Land: Biographical Information," February 1947, *NYT* file and PA.

5. *Bridgeport Post*, 26 March 1948; *Bridgeport Sunday Herald Magazine*, 22 March 1959, PA.
6. "H.M. Land Dies; Iron Dealer; Son Invented Polaroid Camera." *New London Day*, 2 April 1965, AC, PA.
7. David Hubel, introduction of EHL public lecture, Society of Neuroscience, Assembly Hall, Hynes Auditorium, Boston, 6 November 1983, AN folder 6 November 1983.
8. "Polaroid's Big Gamble on Small Cameras," *Time*, 26 June 1972, p. 82.
9. Saul Cohen interview by author, 6 January 1993, AN.
10. Saul Cohen interview by author, 23 June 1994, AN.
11. *New London Day*, 2 April 1965.
12. EHL speech at Ralph Lowell Award dinner, Sheraton Boston Hotel, 8 December 1982, AN; *Boston Globe*, 9 December 1982, p. 59 (photo of Land with two Boy Scouts), AC.
13. Stanley Mervis, Polaroid patent attorney. Personal communication, September 1997.
14. Chernow 1993, pp. 90–91, 314, 183, 603–4.
15. Saul Cohen interview by author, 23 June 1994.
16. Robert Lenzner, "Land: The man behind the camera: The founder of Polaroid is exacting and charming, a scientist and an entrepreneur, a recluse and a showman. Who is the real Edwin Land?" *BG*, Sunday 17 October 1976, p. B7.
17. McCann 1993b, p. 47; W. B. Herapath, "On the optical properties of a newly discovered salt of quinine which crystalline substance possesses the power of polarizing a ray of light, like tourmaline, and at certain angles of rotation of depolarizing it, like selenite," *Philosophical Magazine*, 3: 161 [quoted in Shurcliff 1962, reference H-23].
18. France 1912.
19. Bergson 1911, p. 329.
20. EHL, telephone conversation with author, 23 March 1984.
21. McCann 1993c, p. 151; "Our 'Polar Partnership' with the World Around Us," *Harvard Magazine*, 80 (1978): 23. Derived from Phi Beta Kappa oration, 14 June 1977.
22. EHL, "Pointillism and Laser Scintillation: A Posthumous Lecture by R. W. Wood," Rowland-Wood Symposium, Johns Hopkins University, Baltimore, 21 November 1975. Typewritten transcript quoted in McCann 1993c, p. 119. *EB* 1911, 21, p. 938. Sir David Brewster, *The Stereoscope: Its history, theory, and construction*, 1856. Reprint, New York: Morgan and Morgan, 1971, quoted in Lipton 1982 bibliography.
23. McCann 1993c, p. 119.
24. Wood 1911, p. 288.
25. EHL, *The Sciences*, 1978, "Basic Books: Some Notable Scientists Recall the Book That Most Influenced Their Scientific Lives."
26. EHL, "Theory and Application of Synthetic Polarizing Sheets," *Bulletin of the American Academy of Arts and Sciences*, 2, no. 1, October 1948, summarizing talk of 12 May 1948, quoted in McCann, 1993a, p. 83.
27. Philip Taubman, "The Most Basic Form of Creativity," *Time*, 26 June 1972, p. 84.
28. Gorney 1972, p. xix.
29. Diane Winston, "Camp Days Live Again at Nostalgic Reunion: Men of Mooween Gather Every Year to Recall Summers Past," *NYT*, 28 November 1979, pp. C10–11; *Jewish Register*, 28 February 1947, p. 12, PA.
30. Brandeis 1983, p. 43.
31. Donald Brown, undated memorandum, Patent Department Collection, PA.

CHAPTER 3, "FIRST HAPPIEST MOMENT": POLARIZER

1. Spengler 1928, p. 501.
2. EHL, "Polaroid and the Headlight Problem," lecture given on 5 November 1936, *Journal of the Franklin Institute* 224, no. 3 (September 1937): 269–81., quoted in McCann 1993a, p. 7.
3. EHL, "Polarized Light," talk given during New York Philharmonic Symphony broadcast, 25 March 1945, unpublished manuscript quoted in McCann 1993a, p. 32.
4. McCann 1993a, p. 8.
5. Morison 1974, pp. 130–34, 137–39, 143.
6. EHL interview with author, 31 August 1971.
7. Land 1963, p. 11.
8. Exhibited at May 1993 conference of Society for Imaging Science, Cambridge, Mass.
9. Associated Press, Boston, "Award Made to E. H. Land by Academy; inventor, husband of Hartford woman, gets Rumford Gold Medal," *The Hartford Courant*, 26 March 1948, PA.
10. Spengler 1928, p. 505.
11. EHL, conversation in author's presence, 15 November 1972, at meeting of New York technical section, Society of Photographic Scientists and Engineers.
12. Land 1976a, p. 2; *BW* interview, p. 5.
13. Land 1976b, p. 2.

14. *EB* 1911, 10, p. 174.
15. *EB* 1911, 17, pp. 389–90.
16. McGraw-Hill 1966, reprint; Jewkes et al. 1960, pp. 381–83.
17. Marks trial deposition, p. 287.
18. Ibid.
19. Brayer 1996, pp. 500–501; Ostroff 1987, pp. 219–48; McCann 1993a, pp. 277–78.
20. Ostroff 1987, p. 231; McCann 1993a, pp. 277–78.
21. Manchester 1945; Brown 1960, pp. 442–43.
22. Manchester 1945; McCann 1993a, p. 8.
23. Jewkes et al. 1960, p. 382; "Polarisationsfilter: Ein Neues Hilfsmittel der Photographie," *Wissen und Fortschritt* 10, no. 12 (December 1936): 1100–1104, PA.
24. Land 1954.
25. Ibid.; McCann 1993a, p. 8.
26. Land 1942, p. 5.
27. Brown 1960.
28. Pringle, Peter, "Mr. Land's Self-Portrait," *ST*, Business News, 2 May 1976; Land 1942, p. 4.
29. Pringle; EHL interview with author, 31 August 1971, AN.
30. Marks case memo, pp. 6–9.
31. Ibid.
32. Land 1954.
33. EHL, "Some Aspects of the Development of Sheet Polarizers, *JOSA* 41, no. 12 (December 1951): 956–63, quoted in McCann 1993a, p. 100.
34. *BW* interview, p. 32, PA.
35. Land 1976b.
36. Hounshell and Smith 1988, pp. 221–74.
37. Brown 1960, p. 443.
38. Marks case deposition, pp. 294–97.
39. Marks case memo, p. 12.
40. Warfield and Wallace to C. E. K. Mees, 14 August 1929, PA.
41. Land 1954; Marks trial transcript, pp. 552–54, PA.
42. EHL calendar for 1954, MMF.
43. EHL to William W. Fraser, 14 August 1929, Marks case exhibit.
44. EHL interview by author, 31 August 1971.
45. EHL conversation with author, "Black Monday," 19 October 1987.
46. EHL to Irving Weber, 6 June 1930, Marks case exhibit.
47. Weber to EHL, 21 June 1930, Marks case exhibit.
48. Marks trial transcript, 9 June 1954, pp. 554–55, PA.
49. Wheelwright transcript, PA.
50. Ibid.
51. *Harvard University Gazette*, 14 May 1955, HUG 4540.2, 020145. Lyman Papers, HUA.
52. Lyman to A. Lawrence Lowell, 16 January 1930. Lyman papers, HUA.
53. Lyman Papers, R. W. Wood file, HUA. Lyman corresponded warmly with Robert Wood for more than twenty years, exchanging both insights and equipment. In Harvard's Widener Library, the copy of the edition that inspired Land in childhood is inscribed with Lyman's name.
54. Wheelwright transcript.
55. "In the Light of Polaroid," *Fortune*, September 1938.
56. Wheelwright transcript.
57. Ibid.; EHL interview with author, 31 August 1971.
58. Herbert B. Nichols, "New Wonders to See," *CSM*, Weekly magazine section, 18 March 1936, pp. 4–5, PA.
59. Harland Manchester, *Scientific American*, April 1947.
60. *Harvard University Gazette*, Saturday, 6 February 1932; Land 1954; West 1951, p. 2, PA.
61. McCann 1993a, p. 101; Marks case deposition, p. 298; Marks trial transcript, p. 557, PA.
62. Wheelwright transcript.

CHAPTER 4, START-UP

1. Warfield and Brown to Edwin H. Land, 13 June 1933, telegram, PA.
2. EHL to Donald Brown, telegram marked 580-002, PA.
3. Chubb's patent was issued 20 July 1937, Sheet Polarizer suit filed 3 September 1937, PL; *Fortune*, September 1938, p. 77.

4. Donald Brown to Julius Silver, 8 May 1934, Marks case, PLC; D. McMaster, Production Department, Eastman Kodak Company, to Brown, PA; McMaster to Silver, 11 August 1933, Marks case, PLC.
5. H. S. Wherrett to Edwin J. Prindle, 21 January 1933, PL.
6. R. A. Smith to Lewis W. Chubb, 12 December 1933, PL; Prindle to Chubb, 13 December 1933, PL.
7. John J. Serrell to Lewis W. Chubb, 26 June 1935, PL.
8. Morris Chubb to Lewis W. Chubb, 8 March 1935, PL.
9. Lewis W. Chubb to Smith, Prindle, and Serrell, 11 March 1935, PL.
10. Smith to Lewis W. Chubb, 13 March 1935, PL.
11. Lewis W. Chubb to Smith and Serrell, 18 April 1935; R. A. Miller of Pittsburgh Plate Glass to Chubb, 15 May 1935; Smith to Chubb, 17 May 1935; Prindle to Smith and Chubb, 20 May 1935. All PL.
12. Lewis W. Chubb to Smith and Serrell, 4 June 1935, PL.
13. Lewis W. Chubb to L.W. Chubb, Jr., in Ithaca, N.Y., telegram 4 June 1935, PL.
14. Prindle telegram to Lewis W. Chubb, 2 July 1935; Chubb to Prindle, 4 July 1935. Both PL.
15. Smith to Prindle and Chubb, 5 July 1935, PL.
16. Lewis W. Chubb to Prindle, Smith, and Serrell, 6 July 1935, PL.
17. Smith to Lewis W. Chubb and Prindle, 24 July 1935, PL.
18. Chubb, 27 October 1935, PL.
19. All the following correspondence was for 1936 and was found in PL. R. A. Smith to Chrysler Corporation, Attention: Patent Department, 31 January; F. A. Lind to Smith, 3 February; Smith to Lewis W. Chubb and Prindle, 5 February; Serrell to Chubb and Prindle, 6 February; Chubb to Polarized Lights, 6 February; Smith to Chubb, 7 February; Smith to G. P. Doll, 12 March; Chubb to Polarized Lights, 16 March 1936; Polarized Lights to Chubb, telegram, 17 March; Smith to Doll, 10 April; Chubb to R. W. Johnson, 23 April; Smith to Doll, 29 April; Doll to Smith, 2 May; Johnson to Chubb, 25 May.
20. Lewis W. Chubb to Smith and Serrell, 3 February 1936; Smith to Doll, 5 February 1936, PL.
21. Chubb to Polarized Lights, 6 February 1936, PL.
22. Prindle to Lewis W. Chubb, 14 February 1936, transmitting Land-Wheelwright proposal submitted by Brown; Serrell to Chubb, 15 February 1936, with draft proposal; Smith to Chubb, 24 February 1936, transmitting draft outline of agreement. All in PL.
23. Smith, memorandum of meeting with Everett, 19 March 1936; Smith to Lewis W. Chubb, Prindle, Mrs. G. S. Chambers, and Frank Short, 20 March 1936; Everett to Smith, 21 March 1936; Smith to Chubb, 24 March 1936; Smith to Everett, 24 March 1936. All in PL
24. Wheelwright transcript, pp. 17–21.
25. Rogers 1990, p. 4.
26. Wheelwright transcript.
27. Rogers 1990, p. 3; Rogers 1989, p. 26.
28. Rogers 1990, p. 5; Wheelwright transcript, pp. 69–71.
29. Wheelwright transcript, pp. 24–25, 29–30.
30. The author was present.
31. Brown to Silver, 28 April 1934, Patent attorneys' Marks case document, PA.
32. Ole M. Hovgaard to EHL, 17 May 1934; EHL to Hovgaard, 25 July 1934; Wheelwright to Silver, 9 August 1934. All in PA.
33. Silver to Fordyce Tuttle, Eastman Kodak Company, 12 July 1934, Marks case, PLC.
34. Silver to EHL, 27 July 1934, Marks case, PDC.
35. Ibid.
36. *NYWT*, 1 March 1940, PA; Manchester 1945; Wensberg 1987, pp. 41–42, 46–47.
37. Wheelwright to George B. Wells, 7 August 1934; Wells to Wheelwright, 8 August 1934; Wheelwright to Silver, 9 August 1934, Marks case.
38. Wells to Wheelwright, 21 August 1934, Marks case PLC; John M. Wells to EHL, 10 October 1934; Wells to Robert Blake, 27 October 1934, PDC.
39. H. R. Moulton to John M. Wells, 10 May 1935, PDC.
40. Land 1942, p. 7.
41. *BW* interview, pp. 7–8.
42. Wheelwright to Tuttle, 31 August 1934, PDC.
43. DuPont Viscoloid to EHL, 23 November 1934, PA.
44. Brown to Silver, 28 April 1934, PA.
45. EHL, "Pointillism and Laser Scintillation: A Posthumous Lecture by R. W. Wood," Rowland-Wood Symposium, Johns Hopkins University, Baltimore, 21 November 1975. Typewritten transcript quoted in McCann 1993c, p. 119.
46. Wheelwright to Tuttle, 31 August 1934, PA.
47. Tuttle to EHL, 14 December 1934, PDC, PA.
48. Tuttle to EHL, 14 December 1934; EHL to Tuttle, 27 December 1934. Both in PA.
49. Tuttle to EHL, 3 January 1935, PA.
50. Land 1942, p. 7.

CHAPTER 5, GOING PUBLIC

1. "Field for One-Way Glass Broadens, Makes Three-Dimensional Movies Possible and Detects Weak Steel," *CSM*, 30 January 1936. PA; "New 'Glass' Cuts Glare of Light; Aid to Movies and Science Seen," *NYT*, 31 January 1936, *NYT* "morgue" (clipping library) and PA; "No-Glare Glass is Shown Here by Inventor, 25; Ends Auto Headlight Peril," *NYHT*, 31 January 1936, PA; Waldemar Kaempffert, "Three-Dimension Movies," *NYT*, 16 February 1936, *NYT* "morgue."
2. *The Hartford Times*, 14 and 16 January 1936, PA; *The Bridgeport Post*, 16 January 1936, editorial, p. 14, PA.
3. Science Service, "Polaroid Ends Headlight Glare, Gives Windows One-Way Vision," *NYWT*, 16 January 1936, p. 7.
4. *NYHT*, "No-Glare Glass Is Shown Here."
5. Ibid.
6. Land-Wheelwright Laboratories, "Auto Engineers See Polaroid Headlights End Glare Problem," and "Engineers See Flaws in Glassware with Polaroid Strain Detector," press releases, 2 June 1936. PA; EHL, "Polaroid," *SAE*, 40 (1937): 19–20, quoted in McCann 1993a, pp. 1–3
7. EHL, "Polaroid and the Headlight Problem," lecture given on 5 November 1936, *Journal of the Franklin Institute*, 224, no. 3 (September 1937), quoted in McCann 1993a, pp. 5–9
8. Cresson Medal citation, AC. Other leading inventors to receive the Cresson Medal were Frederick Siemens (regenerative gas burner, 1885), Otto Mergenthaler (linotype, 1889), Herman Hollerith (punched-card calculator, 1890), Frederick E. Ives (halftone engraving and color photography, 1893), Nikola Tesla (high-frequency alternating currents), Elisha Gray (teleautograph, 1897), Rudolf Diesel (diesel engine, 1901), Frederick W. Taylor and Maunsel White (treating tool steel, 1902), F. J. Sprague (electric streetcar, 1903), Auguste and Louis Lumière (color photography, 1909), Alexander Graham Bell (telephone, 1912), Charles P. Steinmetz (electrical engineering, 1913), Orville Wright (airplane, 1914), Lee De Forest (audion, 1923), Henry Ford (assembly line, 1928), Elmer Sperry (gyroscope, 1929), Juan de la Cierva (Autogiro airplane, 1933), Robert J. van de Graaf (high voltage electrostatic generator, 1936), and Ernest O. Lawrence (cyclotron, 1937). Physicist recipients included W. C. Röntgen (1897), Pierre and Marie Curie (1909), Ernest Rutherford (1910), J. J. Thomson (1910), A. A. Michelson (1910), Lord Rayleigh (1913), Theodore Lyman (1931), Percy W. Bridgman (1932), and Carl D. Anderson (1937). Among later winners were physicist I. I. Rabi (1942), chemist Willard F. Libby (1957), and physicist Donald A. Glaser (1961), all Nobel prize winners; James A. Van Allen (radiation belts around the earth, 1961), the rocket pioneer Wernher von Braun (1962), and Land's own colleague, the lens developer James G. Baker (1962). Information provided 16 June 1994 by Wendy Ellis, Franklin Institute.
9. Herbert B. Nichols, interview by author, Stoddard, N.H., 3 June 1972, AN.
10. Science Service, "Research Parade," in the auditorium of the National Academy of Sciences, Washington, D.C., 22 and 23 November 1936. Typewritten transcript, pp. 19–20, PA.
11. Material provided by Museum of Science, Boston, 11 August 1994; Kaempffert; Fuller 1943, p. 3.
12. Nichols interview, AN.
13. "The New York Museum of Science and Industry Presents Polaroid on Parade," program, PA; and Land-Wheelwright press release, p. 1, PA; Nichols interview, AN; "Death After Dark: Device to Cut Toll; Headlight Glare Dimmed, Three-Dimension Movies Arrive," *LD*, 12 December 1936, pp. 30–31, PA.
14. Herbert B. Nichols, "New Auto Headlights Put Night Drivers 'In the Purple,'" *CSM*, Friday, 11 December 1936, PA.
15. "Death After Dark."
16. Wheelwright transcript, pp. 77, 80.
17. Wheelwright transcript, p. 82; Chernow 1990, p. 400.
18. Chernow 1993, pp. 397–98, 579, 603. P. 716, "As ever, Jimmy was in headlong flight from his Jewish past."
19. Wensberg 1987, pp. 52–53.
20. Wheelwright transcript, pp. 63–65, PA.
21. "In the Light of Polaroid," *Fortune*, September 1938; Butters and Lintner 1944, pp. 34–35; Harvard Business School case EA-F 396, 1971. AC; West 1951, pp. 4–6.
22. Bill of Complaint, United States District Court, District of New Jersey, *Sheet Polarizer, Inc., vs. Polarized Lights, Inc., and Lewis W. Chubb,* 3 September 1937, PA; R. A. Smith to Harry A. English and Lewis W. Chubb, 21 September 1937, PL; Smith to Chubb, 27 September 1937, PL.
23. Smith to Lewis W. Chubb, 7 October 1937, PL.
24. Strauss 1962, pp. 98–100.
25. Ibid., p. 239.
26. Ibid., p. 96.
27. Smith to Lewis W. Chubb, 16 December 1937, PL.
28. Smith to Lewis W. Chubb, 29 December 1937; Smith to Lewis L. Strauss, 31 December 1937, PL.
29. Lewis W. Chubb to Smith, 29 December 1936, PL; Chubb to Polarized Lights, Inc., 3 January 1938, PL.
30. Chubb to Polarized Lights, Inc., 4 January 1938, PL.
31. Smith to Chubb and Frank Short, 5 January 1938, PL.

32. Ibid.
33. Wheelwright transcript, p. 90.
34. Gerald Adams, "The Shirtsleeve Squire of Muir Beach," *California Living*, San Francisco Sunday Examiner and Chronicle, week of 12 June 1966, PA; UPI, "Green Gulch Ranch to Be Willed to Synanon Foundation," Red Bluff, California, *News*, 13 December 1967, PA; Grover Sales, "The Man Who Gave Away the Green Gulch Ranch," *Pacific Sun*, 26 April–2 May 1985, pp. 1, 3, 5–6, PA.
35. Manchester 1945; Wensberg 1987, pp. 56–57; John A. Norling, "Three Dimensional Motion Pictures," *SMPTE*, December 1939, pp. 627–34; "The Stereoscopic Art," *PSA*, December 1951; Lipton 1982, pp. 128–29.
36. Asssociated Press, Boston, "Honor New England Inventors," *NYT*, 19 February 1940, PA; "Boston Banquet to Modern Pioneers a Great Success," *Industry* [published by Associated Industries of Massachusetts], March 1940, pp. 18–26, 30, 37, PA; *Boston Post*, 3 March 1940, p. 25, PA.
37. "Trade Is Defended in Labor Surplus," with photo of EHL and W. D. Coolidge, captioned, "Two of the Inventors Honored Last Night, *NYT*, Wednesday, 28 February 1940," *NYT* "morgue" and PA; Schenectady N.Y. *Gazette*, 28 February 1940; *Los Angeles Evening Herald*, 28 February 1940, PA; *Business Machines*, Thursday, 29 February 1940, PA; Vincent Lyons, "Precocity of Edwin H. Land, Now Only 30 Years Old, Develops Polarized Light for Many Practical Uses," *NYWT*, Friday 1 March 1940; *Business Week*, 2 March 1940, PA; *Technology Review*, April 1940, pp. 245–46, MITA; *Newsweek*, 21 October 1940, PA.
38. Group photo, *The Plain Dealer*, Cleveland and *Buffalo News*, both 29 February 1940, PA; Lewis 1991, pp. 300–28, 329–34, 356–58. I am indebted to John J. McCann for computerized enhancement of the Waldorf Astoria group photograph.
39. "Boston Banquet." *Industry*, p. 18, PA.

CHAPTER 6, HEADLIGHT GLARE

1. Land 1958, p. 28
2. Ibid.
3. *NYT*, 28 February 1940.
4. Julius Silver to J. H. Hunt, 30 September 1931, PDC.
5. Silver to Hunt, 19 March 1932, PDC.
6. EHL memorandum, week of 11 July 1932, Marks case, reference 5, PA.
7. EHL to Silver, 9 October 1932, Exhibit CCC, 1954 Marks trial transcript, p. 558, PDC, PA.
8. Hunt to EHL, 21 Oct 32, PDC; Silver to Hunt, 23 November 1932, PDC.
9. EHL, "The Polarized Headlight System," lecture to Highway Research Board, 27th annual meeting, in *Highway Research Board Bulletin*, no. 11, 1 June 1948, quoted in McCann 1993a, p. 69.
10. EHL, "The Use of Polarized Headlights for Safe Night Driving," *Traffic Quarterly* 2 (October 1949), pp. 330–39, quoted in McCann 1993a, p. 86.
11. EHL, "Polarized Light in the Transportation Industries," Michigan-Life Conference on New Technologies in Transportation, University of Michigan Official Publication, vol. 42, 1940, quoted in McCann 1993a, p. 19; EHL, "Some Aspects of the Development of Sheet Polarizers," *JOSA* 41 (December 1951): 957–63, quoted in McCann 1993a, p. 105. This article was based on an invited lecture at the society's annual meeting in Washington, D.C.
12. McCann 1993a, pp. 80–81.
13. McCann 1993a, p. 20,
14. McCann 1993a, p. 16.
15. Land-Wheelwright Laboratories, press release, White Sulphur Springs, West Virginia, 2 June 1936, p. 3, PA; EHL, "Polarized Light and the Headlight Problem." *Journal of the Franklin Institute* 224, no. 3 (September 1937). Quoted in McCann 1993a, 5–9.
16. *NYT*, 22 November 1936, p. 8E, PA.
17. Roper, Val J., "Discusses Losses Attending Use of Polaroid," *SAE* 40, no. 1 (January 1937): 20–21; Roper and E. A. Howard, "Seeing with Motor Car Headlamps," *IES* 33, no. 5 (May 1938), based on talk at IES 37th annual meeting, White Sulphur Springs, West Virginia, 27–30 September 1937.
18. Val J. Roper, *SAE* 40, no. 1 (January 1937): 20–21.
19. Val J. Roper and K.D. Scott, "Seeing with Polarized Headlamps, *IES* 36 (1941): 1213.
20. "In the Light of Polaroid," *Fortune*, September 1938, p. 118.
21. Harland Manchester, "The Case for Antiglare Headlights: A simple device that makes night-driving safer will remain under wraps until the public demands its use," *'48 Magazine* reprint, PA.
22. Typescript, 11 pp., listing forty-one issued patents and twenty-five applications, PA.
23. Manchester, "The Case for Antiglare Headlights."
24. Herbert B. Nichols, interview by author, Stoddard, N.H., 3 June 1972, AN.
25. Bert Pierce, "Automobiles: Lights; Tests of Polarized Headlamps Indicate the Value in Cutting Down Glare," *NYT*, Sunday 23 November 1947; "Country-wide Survey to Find Role of Glare in Accidents Urged Before Lamp Change," *NYT*, Thursday 4 December 1947.

26. J. H. Hunt, Highway Research Board, Bulletin no. 11, pamphlet, June 1948, pp. 21–29.
27. McCann 1993a, p. 105.
28. EHL, "The Polarized Headlight System," lecture to Highway Research Board, 27th annual meeting, in Highway Research Board Bulletin no. 11, 1 June 1948, quoted in McCann 1993a, pp. 69–81.
29. *BW* Interview, p. 5.
30. Richard, Kostelanetz, "A Wide Angle View and Close-Up Portrait of Edwin Land and His Polaroid Cameras," *Lithopinion*, Spring 1974, p. 55.
31. Shurcliff 1962, p. 132.
32. Kostelanetz, p. 55.

CHAPTER 7, THREE DIMENSIONS

1. Menu, Eightieth Birthday Tea in Honor of Edwin H. Land, 7 May 1989, AC; "Beauty of Ancient Art through Kennedy's Eyes," *BG*, 12 May 1988, p. 91, with photo of detail of sculpture by Desiderio da Settignano.
2. Gloria F. Seaman, "A Report on the Clarence Kennedy Collection," 3 February 1965, foreword, MMF.
3. "Dr. Kennedy Dies; Art Historian, 79; Ex-Professor at Smith Also Photographed Sculptures," *NYT*, 31 July 1972, p. 30, AC.
4. Seaman, p. 1.
5. H. L. Logan, "Modeling with Light," paper presented at 34th annual convention, Illuminating Engineering Society, Spring Lake, New Jersey, 9–11 September 1940, with photographs by Beaumont Newhall, later published in *IES*, PA.
6. Clarence Kennedy to Roberta Fanseler, arts education assistant, Carnegie Corporation, 23 March 1934, PA.
7. Kennedy to Fanseler, 29 January 1935, PA.
8. Wheelwright transcript.
9. Ibid.
10. A. Pope, Carnegie Foundation for the Advancement of Teaching, to Frederick P. Keppel, president, Carnegie Corporation, 20 June 1935, PA.
11. Wilson et al. 1986, p. 334.
12. *NYHT*, 31 January 1936, PA.
13. *Science* Supplement, 83, no. 2143 (24 January 1936); Land-Wheelwright Laboratories, press release, 30 January 1936, pp. 2–3, PA.
14. *CSM*, 30 January 1936, PA.
15. *NYT*, 31 January 1936, PA.
16. *NYHT*, 14 May 1936, PA; Extracts, Land-Wheelwright Laboratories, PA.
17. "Polarisationsfilter: Ein Neues Hilfsmittel der Photographie," *Wissen und Fortschritt* 10, no. 12 (December 1936): 1100–1104, PA.
18. "Polaroid Light-Polarising Material," *Engineering*, 28 August 1936, reprint, 3 pp., PA.
19. *CSM*, 11 December 1936; "Death After Dark: Device to Cut Toll; Headlight Glare Dimmed; Three-Dimension Movies Arrive," *LD*, 12 December 1936, p. 30, PA.
20. Silver to C. L. Ferrand, Warner Brothers Theaters, 29 September 1933, PA.
21. John A. Norling, *PSA*, November–December 1951, January–February 1952, reprint, pp. 11–12.
22. Ibid, pp. 12–13; Norling, "Three Dimensional Motion Pictures," *SMPTE*, December 1939, pp. 627–34.
23. Richard T. Kriebel, "Stereoscopic Photography," *The Complete Photographer* 53 (1943): 3463.
24. "Land, Edwin Herbert," in *Modern Men of Science* (New York: McGraw-Hill, 1966), p. 284; West 1951, p. 23.
25. Stephen A. Benton, "Edwin Land, 3-D, and Holography," *OPN* (5 October 1994): 41; EHL, "The Six Eyes of Man," in *Three-Dimensional Imaging*, SPIE Proceedings, ed. by Stephen A. Benton, vol. 120 (Bellingham, Wash., 1977), pp. 43–50.
26. EHL, "Vectographs: Images in Terms of Vectorial Inequality and the Application in Three-Dimensional Representation," *JOSA* 30, no. 6 (June 1940): 230–38, quoted in McCann 1993a, p.30.
27. *NYT*, 30 June 1940; Associated Press, Rochester, "3-Dimension Pictures Seen on Single Prints: Polarizing Glasses Used in New Invention," *NYHT*, 4 October 1940.
28. Mindell 1996, p. 314 and footnote; Fuller, 1943, p. 5; Wensberg 1987, pp. 74–75; Vivian Walworth, personal communication, September 1997.
29. Lipton 1982, pp. 37–38.
30. EHL, "Polarized Light," talk during broadcast of New York Philharmonic concert, 25 March 1945, typewriten manuscript in PA, quoted in McCann 1993a, p. 32.
31. Lipton 1982, p. 88.
32. Vivian Walworth, personal communication, September 1997.
33. "New Color System for Movies Shown: Polacolor, Process for Printing Film in Hues, Unveiled at Preview Theater," *NYT*, 17 December 1947.
34. Annual Report 1948, pp. 3–4.

35. "Coming and Going," *Film Daily* (New York), 29 May 1952, PA; Lipton 1982, p. 39.
36. "Edwin H. Land," *Current Biography*, November 1953, *NYT* "morgue."
37. "Theatre Problems—Stereo Movies," handwritten, undated memorandum, MMF.
38. EHL, "Stereoscopic Motion Pictures: A Special Report to the Directors," February 1953, pamphlet, 5 pp., PA; quoted in McCann 1993a, pp. 95–98.
39. Alistair Cooke, "Hollywood's Choice: Wide Screen or Three Dimensions," *The Manchester Guardian Weekly*, Thursday 27 August 1953, p. 7.
40. Bosley Crowther, "Images in Space: New Stereoscopic Movies Make a Mild Impression at the Globe," *NYT*, 8 February 1953, PA.
41. Vivian Walworth, personal communication, September 1997.
42. *The New Yorker*, n.d. (1953?), PA.
43. Graham Clarke, "Projectionists are Briefed by the Experts," and "Faults for All to See," *The Ideal Kinema*, supplement to *Kinematograph Weekly*, 16 April 1953, pp. 3–5, PA.
44. L. W. Chubb, D. S. Grey, E. R. Blout, and EHL, "Properties of Polarizers for Filters and Viewers for 3-D Motion Pictures," *SMPTE*, 62: 120–24, lecture at the Society's New York convention, 8 October 1953, quoted in McCann 1993a, p. 110.
45. William A. Shurcliff, "A Brief Autobiography," 15 December 1992, typescript, pp. 92–93.
46. Vivian K. Walworth, personal communication, 1997.

CHAPTER 8, "THE BEST DAMN GOGGLES IN THE WORLD"

1. Land 1942, p. 8; Fuller 1943, pp. 5–6; Wensberg 1987, pp. 68–69.
2. Baxter 1946; Sherwood 1948, pp. 153–56; Kevles 1987, pp. 293–98, based in part on Kevles's interviews with Vannevar Bush.
3. Mindell 1996, p. 314.
4. West 1951, p. 13; Wensberg 1987, pp. 76–77.
5. Rogers 1990, p. 6.
6. Mindell 1996, ch. 8, "Automation's Finest Hour: Radar and System Integration"; Baldwin 1980.
7. Land 1942, p. 2.
8. *Newsweek*, 26 July 1943 (cover), PA; Wensberg 1987, pp. 72–73.
9. Land 1942, p. 10.
10. Wensberg 1987, p. 71.
11. Land 1942, p. 12; West 1951, p. 14.
12. Polaroid ceremony in memory of EHL, Hynes Auditorium, Boston, 7 September 1991.
13. Mary A. McCann and John J. McCann, "Land's Chemical, Physical, and Psychophysical Images," *OPN* 5, no. 10 (October 1994): 34.
14. Land 1942, p. 13.
15. W. Lewis Hyde, "Good Cheap Camera Filters," *OPN* 5, no. 10 (October 1994): 19.
16. Louis Rosenblum, "Quick Turnaround on Night Goggles," *OPN* 5, no. 10 (October 1994): 14–16.
17. Mindell 1996, ch. 8, "Automation's Finest Hour: Radar and System Integration"; Baldwin 1980.
18. Bush 1949, pp. 25–26, 45; Bush 1970, p. 38; Zachary 1997, p. 113; Kevles 1987, pp. 298–301.
19. David S. Grey, "Digging for the Bomb," *OPN* 5, no. 10 (October 1994): 22, 29.
20. Baldwin 1980.
21. Wensberg 1987, p. 79
22. Grey, "Digging for the Bomb," pp. 22, 29.
23. Wensberg 1987, pp. 77–80.
24. Grey, "Digging for the Bomb," pp. 22, 29.
25. William J. McCune, interview by author, 23 October 1991.
26. Hyde, *OPN* 5, no. 10 (October 1994): 11.
27. Robert Lenzner, *BG*, Monday 18 October 1976, p. 32.
28. Wensberg 1987, pp. 88–89.
29. Land 1946, pp. 12–13.

CHAPTER 9, "WHO CAN OBJECT TO SUCH MONOPOLIES?"

1. Bush 1945, p. 109
2. Larry Owens, "Patents, the 'Frontier' of American Invention, and the Monopoly Committee of 1939: Anatomy of a Discourse," in "Patents and Invention," special issue of *T & C*, ed. Carolyn C. Cooper, vol. 32, no. 4 (October 1991): 1092; Bush 1970, pp. 158–59.

3. Stanley H. Mervis, "Edwin Land—Champion of Patents," *OPN* 5, no. 10 (October 1994): 50.
4. Brown 1960, p. 447.
5. Baxter 1946, ch. 20, "Antimalarials," pp. 299–320
6. EHL to Vannevar Bush, 2 September 1942, Quinine.
7. Ibid.; Baxter 1946, p. 311.
8. Baxter 1946, pp. 308–9.
9. Bush 1970, pp. 43–50; Zachary 1997, pp. 129–30; Baxter 1946, p. 314; Paul DeKruif, "Enter Atabrine—Exit Malaria," *Reader's Digest*, December 1942, pp. 58–60; New York *Sun*, 17 December 1942; Charles Morrow Wilson, "Quinine: Reborn in Our Hemisphere," *Harper's*, August 1943, pp. 275–80, Quinine.
10. Robert B. Woodward to EHL, draft plan for total synthesis, 1 September 1942; EHL to Bush, 2 September 1942, Quinine.
11. Bush to EHL, 4 September 1942, Quinine.
12. A. Newton Richards to EHL, 5 September 1942, Quinine.
13. William Mansfield Clark to EHL, 8 September 1942, Quinine.
14. Robert B. Woodward to Clark, 14 September 1942, Quinine.
15. Clark to Woodward, 21 September 1942, Quinine.
16. Clark to Woodward, 28 September 1942, enclosing memorandum by E. K. Marshall, Jr., Quinine.
17. Clark to Woodward, October 1942, Quinine.
18. EHL to Clark, 2 November 1942, Quinine.
19. Clark to EHL, 4 November 1942, Quinine.
20. EHL to Clark, 9 November 1942; Clark to EHL, 12 November 1942, Quinine.
21. Clark to EHL, 14 December 1942, Quinine.
22. Clark to Woodward, 14 December 1942, Quinine.
23. EHL to Clark, 20 December 1942, Quinine.
24. Clark to EHL, 28 December 1942, Quinine.
25. EHL to Clark, 1 February 1943, Quinine.
26. "Happy," *The New Yorker*, 13 May 1944, Quinine.
27. EHL to Clark, 4 April 1944 (draft 3); 8 April 1944 (draft 4); EHL, notes for telephone call to Bush, 10 April 1944, Quinine.
28. EHL, 14 April 1944, memorandum of Bush conversation that day, Quinine.
29. EHL, 1 May 1944, memorandum for further telephone conversation with Bush, with notation on Bush reaction, Quinine.
30. Ibid.
31. Ibid.
32. Bush to EHL, telegram 2 May 1944, Quinine.
33. Bush to EHL, telegram 4 May 1944, Quinine.
34. Bush to EHL, 9 May 1944, Quinine.
35. D. B. Keyes to Harvey N. Davis, Director, Office of Production Research and Development, War Production Board, 11 May 1944, memorandum with list of attendees, Quinine.
36. Robert Burns Woodward and William von Eggers Doering, "The Total Synthesis of Quinine," *JACS* 66, no. 5 (1944): 849.
37. William L. Laurence, Cambridge, Massachusetts, "Synthetic Quinine Produced, Ending Century Search," *NYT*, Thursday, 4 May 1944, pp. 1, 10; "Synthetic Quinine," editorial, *BH*, 5 May 1944; "Quinidine, Heart Drug, Made Along With Synthetic Quinine," *NYHT*, 6 May 1944; *Nation*, 13 May 1944; "Science and Medicine: Conversion of Coal-Tar Derivative Yields Chemically Correct Quinine," *Newsweek*, 15 May 1944, p. 71; "From Coal Tar," *Time*, 15 May 1944. All previous references in Quinine.
38. "Quinine: Two young chemists end a century's search by making drug synthetically from coal tar," with photographs by Fritz Goro, *Life*, 5 June 1944, pp. 85–88, Quinine, PA.
39. Gerard Piel, "Edwin H. Land," *1992 Century Yearbook*, New York: Century Association, pp. 270–73.
40. Wendell Berge, Assistant Attorney General, to EHL, 5 May 1944; Robert G. Deupree to EHL, 5 May 1944; Carlton Fuller to Berge, 8 May 1944; EHL to Berge, 9 May 1944; Fuller to Deupree, 9 May 1944; Berge to EHL, 17 May 1944; EHL to Berge, 27 May 1944; Fuller to EHL, reporting a visit by Soviet representatives, 1 November 1944; Fuller to U.S. Department of State, advising of a request for a license from the Purchasing Commission of the USSR, 19 January 1945, all Quinine.
41. See the following articles by I. F. Stone in the 1944 issues of *PM*. "Will Cartels Restrict Use of New Synthetic Quinine?" Friday, 5 May; "Must U.S. Soldiers Suffer the Shivers-and-Shakes to Protect Profits for the Quinine Monopolists?" and "If We Can Keep Synthetic Quinine From Cartels Millions of Malaria Sufferers May Get Postwar Relief," Sunday, 7 May; "Hush, Synthetic Quinine Still a 'Military Secret'," Monday, 8 May; "Army Finds Quinine Needs Are Not Acute," Wednesday, 10 May; "To an Indignant Lady," Monday, 15 May. See also Carlton Fuller to John P. Lewis, Managing Editor, *PM*; Fuller to EHL, 10 June 1944; I. F. Stone, "Army, Navy Short of Quinine—and Nothing Is Done," *PM*, Friday, 23 June 1944. All in Quinine.

42. Bush 1970, pp. 128–29.
43. Stone, "Army Finds Quinine Needs Are Not Acute."
44. Bush to EHL, 24 August 1944; Walter Lown to Carlton Fuller, memorandum, 27 July 1944; Fred J. Stock to Lown, 1 August 1944; Lown to Stock, 3 August 1944; Fuller to Stock, 7 August 1944, enclosing list of twenty-four companies expressing interest in the Woodward-Doering process; Fuller to Stock, 10 August 1944; Stock to Fuller, 25 August 1944, enclosing draft letter to companies expressing interest; Fuller to Stock, 31 August 1944, with suggested changes; Stock to Fuller, 9 September 1944, enclosing revised letter. All in Quinine.
45. Stone, I. F., "Will Cartels Restrict Use of New Synthetic Quinine?" Quinine.
46. Fuller to EHL, reporting 29 April 1944 meeting with James B. Conant, 1 May 1944; EHL to Conant, 3 May 1944; EHL to President and Fellows of Harvard University, 6 May 1944; Conant to EHL, 23 May 1944. All in Quinine.
47. In 1996, Harold Varmus, Nobel prize winner and the Director of the National Institutes of Health, told an audience at Harvard that the quinine synthesis had improved the treatment of malaria in the Pacific war. Harold E. Varmus, "Science for the Public Good," *Harvard Magazine*, July–August 1996, p. 61. At a garden party after his talk, Varmus met Woodward's widow, Eudoxia. She gently told him "that her husband's ingenious synthesis of quinine did less to save soldiers from the perils of malaria in World War II than did improved production of atabrine (quinacrine)" (Varmus to editor, *Harvard Magazine*, October 1996, p. 11).
48. Bush 1945, p. 91.
49. Bush 1970, pp. 163–68, 198–99; Zachary 1997, pp. 41–45.
50. EHL, "Research by the Business Itself," talk given at Standard Oil Development Company forum, Waldorf Astoria Hotel, New York, 5 October 1944, in "The Future of Industrial Research: Papers and Discussion"; reprinted in "Selected Papers on Industry", Polaroid Corporation, 1983, p. 5; "Patterson Favors One Defense Unit," *NYT*, 6 October 1944; EHL, "Basic Research in the Small Company," lecture to Chemical Institute of Canada, 24 June 1946, quoted in McCann, 1993b, pp. 1-3.
51. Bush 1945, p. 109.
52. Bush 1945, pp. 107–8.
53. Bush 1945, p. 109.
54. Bush 1945, p. 109; McCann 1993b, pp. 9.
55. "Need of Federal Control of Patents Affecting Radar Use Is Stressed," *NYT*, 31 October 1945, noting approval of a national research foundation and opposition of EHL to patent proposals of Senator Harley Kilgore; EHL statement, 30 October 1945, joint hearings on science bills, Senate military affairs committees, quoted in McCann 1993b, p. 8.

CHAPTER 10, SEPIA IN AN INSTANT

1. *BW* interview, p. 9.
2. Francis Bello, "The Magic that Made Polaroid," *Fortune*, April 1959, pp. 157–58; Richard Kostelanetz, "A Wide-Angle View and Closeup Portrait of Edwin Land and his Polaroid Cameras," *Lithopinion*, Spring 1974, p. 53.
3. Brown 1960, p. 449.
4. Land 1972.
5. Peter Pringle, "Mr. Land's Self-Portrait," *ST*, Business News section, 2 May 1976.
6. Sean Callahan, "If you are able to state a problem, it can be solved," *Life*, 27 October 1972, p. 48.
7. *BW* Interview, p. 8.
8. Ibid., p. 21
9. EHL, "One-Step Photography" (based on Royal Photographic Society lecture, 31 May 1949, London), *The Photographic Journal* 90 (January 1950): 7–15, quoted in McCann 1993a, p. 139.
10. Brayer 1996; Jenkins 1975.
11. *BW* interview, pp. 8–9.
12. Ibid., p. 9, p. 11; Trial 1981, pp. 456–58.
13. Land 1982, pp. 30–31.
14. Trial 1981, direct examination, pp. 37, 34–36, 38; cross-examination, pp. 486–90.
15. *EB* 1911, vol. 21, pp. 485–522, "Photography"; Derry and Williams 1961, pp. 554–55, 651–67; Newhall 1964, ch. 1–4; Ostroff 1987, ch. 1, 2.
16. Jenkins, 1975, ch. 1–10; Brayer 1996, ch. 12.
17. Trial 1981, p. 33.
18. Ibid., pp. 50–51.
19. Brown 1960, pp. 449–50.
20. Stanley H. Mervis, "Edwin Land—Champion of Patents," *OPN* 5, no. 10 (October 1994): 51.
21. Eudoxia Muller, laboratory report, 31 December 1943, PA.
22. Maxfield Parrish, Jr., SX-70 daily report, 12 January 1944, PA.
23. Howard G. Rogers, SX-70 daily report, 30 January 1944, PA.

24. Eudoxia Muller, SX-70 daily reports, 31 January 1944, 26 February 1944, PA.
25. Frederick Binda, SX-70 daily report, 19 October 1944, PA.
26. Trial 1981, p. 422.
27. EHL, "The Universe of One Step-Photography," in Ostroff 1987, ch. 22, quoted in McCann 1993a, p. 267. The article was based on Land's lecture in Rochester, New York, June 1986.
28. EHL, "One-Step Photography," from lecture in London, 31 May 1949, quoted in McCann 1993a, p. 139.
29. Ibid., p. 140.
30. EHL, "The Universe of One-Step Photography," in Ostroff 1987, pp. 219–48, quoted in McCann 1993, p. 265.
31. Ibid., pp. 265–67.
32. EHL, "A New One-Step Photographic Process," *JOSA* 37, no. 2 (February 1947): 66–77, quoted in McCann 1993a, p. 123. The article was based on lecture and demonstration to the Optical Society of America, Hotel Pennsylvania, New York, 21 February 1947.
33. EHL, "One-Step Photography," from lecture in London, 31 May 1949, quoted in McCann 1993a, p. 139.
34. Ibid., pp. 139, 142; EHL, "One-Step Photography," in Neblette 1977, quoted in McCann 1993a, pp. 230–42; Trial 1981, direct examination, pp. 2–12 to 2–15, 2–37; Trial 1981, cross-examination, pp. 446, 455, 476–78, 493, 542–44. 547–55.
35. Mary McCann and John J. McCann, "Land's Chemical, Physical, and Psychophysical Images, *OPN* 5, no. 10 (October 1994): 34; Neblette 1977.
36. Trial 1981, p. 58.
37. Jeremy Bernstein, "I Am a Camera," review of Wensberg 1987, *The New York Review of Books* 35, no. 6 (14 April 1988): 23.
38. Trial 1981, p. 103; Cohen 1994.
39. George Ehrenfried, "Working with Edwin Land," *OPN* 5, no. 10 (October 1994): 56.
40. Land 1946.
41. McCann 1993a, p. 287.
42. Vannevar Bush, "As We May Think," *Atlantic Monthly* 176 (July 1945): 103.
43. Bush to EHL, 2 April 1947, VB.
44. EHL, "A New One-Step Photographic Process," *JOSA* 37, no. 2 (February 1947): 66–77, quoted in McCann 1993a, p. 123.
45. "Photo Finished in 50 Seconds, All Work Done in the Camera," *NYHT*, Saturday, 22 February 1947, p. 1, 9, PA.
46. William L. Laurence, "One-Step Camera is Demonstrated," *NYT*, Saturday, 22 February 1947.
47. "Science: Quick Birdie." *Time*, 3 March 1947, pp. 67–68, diagram by R. M. Chapin, Jr.
48. "Bombshell in Photography?" *National Photo Dealer*, March 1947, cover and pp. 68–70, 141 [missing], 146–47, PA.
49. "Photo Finished in 50 Seconds, All Work Done in the Camera," *NYHT*, Saturday, 22 February 1947, p. 1, 9.
50. "A New One-Minute Process," *Minicam Photography*, May 1947, PA.
51. Editorial, "The Camera Does the Rest," *NYT*, Saturday, 22 February 1947, *NYT* "morgue."
52. Rudolph Elie, Jr., "The Roving Photographer: 'Back to the Farm for Me' Says Photo-Finisher At Exhibition of New Jack-in-Box Camera," *BH*, 6 March 1947, PA.
53. "Notes and News," *American Photography*, April 1947, pp. 4, 61.
54. Elie, "The Roving Photographer."

CHAPTER 11, "A WHOLE NEW INDUSTRY"

1. West 1951, pp. 20–21; Francis Bello, "The Magic That Made Polaroid," *Fortune*, April 1959, p. 158, n.
2. Trial 1981, pp. 97–98.
3. Wall 1970; McHugh 1980; Misa 1995.
4. Annual Report, 1948, p. 3; Wensberg 1987, pp. 95–96, 99–101.
5. Annual Report, 1952, p. 4; and 1957, p. 5; Wensberg 1987, p. 2.
6. Donohue 1967, p. 7.
7. Land 1948, passim; McCann 1993a, p. 268; Trial 1981, pp. 520–21.
8. Lloyd E. Varden, "Comments Regarding 'A New One-Step Photographic Process' by Edwin H. Land," *JOSA* 38 (1947): 69–70; Trial 1981, pp. 458–59.
9. Varden, "One-Step Photographic Processes," *PSA*, 13 (September 1947): 551–54.
10. EHL, "Reply to Lloyd E. Varden's Comments Regarding 'A New One-Step Photographic Process,' " *JOSA* 38 (1947): 70.
11. Neblette 1989, p. 225.
12. Charles Mikulka to EHL, 1 August 1950, handwritten letter, Morse Notebook, "1950," MMF.
13. Charles Mikulka interview by author, 1 March 1972, AN.
14. Norwich, Conn. *Bulletin*, Bridgeport Conn. *Post*, Hartford *Courant*, all 26 March 1948, PA; the citation on gold medal for 1945 presented on 12 May 1948: "Rumford Medal for Discoveries in Light or Heat, awarded by the American Academy of Arts and Sciences to Edwin Herbert Land for new applications in polarized light and photography," PA. The J. D. Sykes memo to Polaroid employees of 21 April 1948 repeats the academy list of previous recipients, including Thomas Edison, Albert Michelson, Elihu Thompson, and seven whom Land knew: Robert W. Wood, Percy Bridgman, Irving Langmuir, Karl Compton, Harlow Shapley, Vladimir Zworykin, and C. E. K. Mees. McCann 1993a, pp. 83–84.

15. E. H. Land, E. R. Blout, D. S. Grey, M. S. Flower, H. Husek, R. C. Jones, C. H. Matz, and D. P. Merill, "A Color Translating Ultraviolet Microscope, *Science*, 109, no. 2833 (15 April 1949): 371–74, quoted in McCann 1993a, pp. 111–17, William L. Laurence, "Living Cells Seen in Natural Colors: New Technique of Translating Ultra-Violet Light Revealed at Cancer Center Dinner," *NYT*, 17 April 1948; Current Biography, November 1953, *NYT* "morgue."
16. *Chemical Trade Journal*, London, 29 April 1949; *Science* 109 (27 May 1949): 549; *NYHT*, Paris edition, 2 June 1949; *Nature*, 2 June 1949.
17. Land 1951, p. 17; *Discovery* (London), August 1951, PA.
18. Dreyfus & Co., "A report on Polaroid Corporation," 15 July 1958, PA.
19. This copy of *Minute Man* (vol. 4, no. 1, Spring 1954, 12 pp.) was addressed to Meroë M. Morse, Suite 220, Hotel Hemenway, Westland Avenue, Boston and is deposited in MMF; "Ladies' Day at Polaroid," *Forbes*, 1 July 1954, pp. 24–25, PA.
20. Donohue 1967, pp. 19–20; Annual Report, 1970, p. 17.
21. "Marketing a Camera Revolution," *BW*, 12 June 1954, cover, reprint, PA.
22. Land 1958, p. 1.
23. Land 1960, pp. 13, 16.
24. Land 1958, pp. 3, 4.
25. Land 1960, pp. 35–36.
26. Land 1958, pp. 5–6, 16.
27. Land 1960, p. 17.
28. Land 1959, p. 1–3.
29. Ibid., p. 9.
30. Ibid., p. 6.
31. Land 1960, p. 26.
32. Land 1959, p. 9.
33. "Businessman-Scientist in Focus: Edwin Herbert Land," *Time*, 17 March 1961, p. 88.
34. "Polaroid Reverses Negro Hiring: President Land pleads with 8,000 employees to tell him how Negroes should be assimilated in all departments," *Post-Gazette*, Boston, 3 May 1968, pp. 1–2.
35. "Polaroid Struggle Lands at New York APS Meeting," *Science for the People*, May 1971, cover and pp. 2, 12–17, kindly supplied by Robert Crease, Brookhaven National Laboratory, 20 June 1996; Wensberg 1987, ch. 21, "South Africa," pp. 153–67.
36. EHL letter to "My dear friends," 20 August 1970, handwritten letter, PA.
37. Robert Reinhold, "Land Introduces 2 Camera Models," *NYT*, 28 April 1971, pp. 63, 71.

CHAPTER 12, BLACK AND WHITE: MEROË MORSE

1. McCann 1993a, p. 269.
2. Thomas C. Mendenhall, President, Smith College, Remarks on presentation to Meroë Morse of Smith College Medal, given annually "to those who exemplify in their lives and services to the community the true purpose of liberal arts education," 23 October 1968, MMF.
3. MMF.
4. Meroë Morse to EHL, Hotel Sacher, Vienna, 11 August 1959, MMF.
5. Morse to Adams, 131 24th Avenue, San Francisco, 11 August 1959, MMF.
6. "Singular Images," comments prepared for Ansel Adams exhibit at the Metropolitan Museum of Art, New York, 1974.
7. Robert Hughes, "Master of the Yosemite," *Time*, 3 September 1979, cover and pp. 36–44.
8. Morse to laboratory staff about course, "Expressive Photography," 14 March 1960, MMF; Polaroid Newsletter, 14 March 1960, MMF; Land spoke of Adams: "By having a tremendous person like Ansel Adams around teaching photography, a sense of what's worthwhile in photography and what counts has spread through the company," Land 1960, p. 29; Stanley H. Mervis, personal communication, September 1997.
9. Morse to Ansel Adams, 17 June 1960, MMF.
10. Morse to Gerry Sharpe, 18 August 1960, MMF; Morse to Adams, 14 September 1960, MMF.
11. Jacob Deschin, "Land Prints in Black," *NYT* (April 1950?).
12. Land 1960, p. 3.
13. Deschin, "Land Prints in Black."
14. Morse to EHL, 25 July 1950, Morse notebook, "1950," MMF.
15. Skinner, David W., to "Din," 12 July 1950, Morse notebook, "1950," MMF.
16. Skinner to "Din," 13 July 1950, Morse notebook, "1950," MMF.
17. Skinner to "Din," 10 August 1950, Morse notebook, "1950," MMF.
18. Morse to EHL, 28 July 1950, Morse notebook, "1950," MMF.
19. Skinner to "Din," 13 July 1950, Morse notebook, "1950," MMF.

20. Morse to EHL, 24 July 1950, Morse notebook, "1950," MMF.
21. "Polaroid-Land Process Now Has Black and White: Here is the first exclusive series of photographs on Type 41 made by amateurs working with Dr. E. H. Land," *U.S. Camera* 13, no. 8 (August 1950): 42–43, PA.
22. Morse to EHL, 10 August 1950, Morse notebook, "1950," MMF.
23. Skinner to "Din," 12 July 1950, Morse notebook, "1950," MMF.
24. Skinner to "Din," 13 July 1950, Morse notebook, "1950," MMF.
25. Morse to EHL, 1 August 1950, Morse notebook, "1950," MMF.
26. Trial 1981, p. 59.
27. Francis Bello, "The Magic that Made Polaroid," *Fortune*, April 1959, p. 162.
28. Carlton Fuller to EHL, 14 August 1956, "EHL Personal file," MMF.
29. Jacob Deschin, "Polaroid's 10 Years," *NYT*, 21 July 1957, *NYT* "morgue," Rowland Institute scrapbook.
30. Personal communication.
31. Morse notebook, "1950," MMF; 1955 letters, MMF.
32. *BH*, 30 July 1969.
33. Morse correspondence concerning DuPont, 1952–1959, MMF, Box 22.30, PA; Kodak correspondence beginning 13 January 1947, MMF, Box 22.32.
34. Morse to EHL, 28 March 1955, MMF.
35. Morse to EHL, 30 March 1955, MMF.
36. Morse to EHL, 4 April 1955, MMF.
37. Morse to EHL, 7 April 1955, MMF.
38. Morse to EHL, 8 April 1955, MMF.
39. EHL, "From Imbibition to Exhibition: A Reconstruction of a New Photographic Process," *Journal of the Franklin Institute* 263, no. 2 (February 1957), lecture at Annual Medal Day, 17 October 1956, quoted in McCann 1993a, pp. 153–56.
40. Wendy Ellis, Franklin Institute, letter to author, 21 June 1994. Among other Potts medal winners were: Igor I. Sikorsky (1933), the helicopter pioneer from Bridgeport, who, with Land, received an honorary degree from Colby College in 1955, and won a National Medal of Science in 1968, the same year as Land; the strobe light pioneer Harold Edgerton (1941); Eugene J. Houdry (1948), the major innovator in petroleum cracking; John W. Mauchly and Presper Eckert, Jr. (1949), builders of the first electronic computer, ENIAC, who also were honored as Modern Pioneers with Land in 1966; Jay W. Forrester (1974), a particular admirer of Land's iconoclastic speech at MIT in 1957, for system dynamics; computer architect Seymour R. Cray (1979); and Uno Lamm (1981), the Swedish pioneer of high voltage direct transmission of electricity.
41. Franklin Institute, Seating Arrangement, Annual Medal Day Dinner, Wednesday, October 1956, PA; Morse to Harley, 24 October 1956, Box 22.31, MMF.
42. Howard Rogers eulogy of Meroë Morse, Harvard Memorial Church, 15 August 1960, typescript, PA.
43. Personal communication.
44. Personal communication.
45. Land 1959, pp. 5–6; EHL, "Industry and the Paradox of Ubiquitous Individuations," lecture at Columbia University, 10 December 1964. Quoted in McCann 1993b, pp. 35, 39.
46. Displayed in Land's laboratory, Rowland Institute for Science, Cambridge, Massachusetts.
47. EHL to author, at Land's home, 163 Brattle Street, 13 May 1972.
48. Cedric Adams, "Reporting at Large," *Valley Times*, North Hollywood, Calif., n.d. (1960?), PA.
49. Land 1958, pp. 35–38.
50. Philip Siekman, "Kodak and Polaroid: An End to Peaceful Coexistence," *Fortune*, November 1970, pp. 85–86.
51. "Polaroid Will Offer Black-and-White Film Requiring No Coating," *WSJ*, 11 March 1967, PA.
52. Donald White, "New film, copier debut at Polaroid meeting," *BG*, 24 April 1968.
53. "Polaroid develops new photographic process," *C & EN*, 24 June 1968, p. 15.
54. Mendenhall, 23 October 1968, PA.
55. Society of Photographic Scientists and Engineers, news release, 22 May 1969, PA.
56. Annual Report, 1969, p. 25, AC.
57. Rogers, eulogy.
58. The author used this office for a few weeks in 1972.

CHAPTER 13, COLOR PICTURES: HOWARD ROGERS

1. "Polaroid Color Film to Be Marketed Jan. 28 In Florida; Dealers Put Cost at $4–$5 a Roll," *WSJ*, 17 January 1963, p. 2; Miami, "Florida Photo Dealers Find New Polacolor Is a Mixed Blessing; Stores Getting Advance Orders for Polaroid Film; Stories on Markups Stir Controversies," *WSJ*, 24 January 1963; Timothy Leland, "After 15 Years, $15 Million: Instant Color Film; 'Improbable' Made Reality by Huge Breakthroughs," *BH*, 24 January 1963, p. 50; Bob

Hering, "Color Photos in 60 Seconds," *PS*, February 1963, pp. 61–64, 208–10; Kevin Brown, "Instant Color Photos!" *Popular Mechanics*, February 1963, pp. 100–105, 206–207; John Wolbarst, "Here It Is: Polaroid Color," *Modern Photography*, March 1963, pp. 60-64, 104, 114; Geoffrey Crawley, "Polacolor," *BJP*, 24 May 1963, pp. 27, 30 .

2. Trial 1981, direct examination, p. 69.
3. Charles Mikulka, interview by author, 1 March 1972, AN.
4. Rogers 1990, pp. 17–18.
5. Ibid., p. 7; Trial 1981, p. 3093.
6. Rogers 1991; Polacolor 1963, pp. 4–5.
7. Rogers 1989, part 1, p. 4; Rogers 1990, p. 7.
8. Rogers 1990, pp. 15–16.
9. Rogers 1994, pp. 8–9, 16, 19, 31; Rogers 1989, part 2, pp. 18, 30.
10. Trial 1981, pp. 67–68.
11. "Background Information about Polaroid Land Color Film," 12 pp., PA; Polacolor 1963; Trial 1981, pp. 3145, 3147–48, 3152, 3159–60, 3164–68, 3418–19, 3431, 3466, 3485, 3489; Rogers 1989; Neblette 1977, pp. 319–29, quoted in McCann 1993a, pp. 255–61; Neblette 1989, pp. 195–203.
12. Polacolor 1963, pp. 2–3.
13. Trial 1981, cross-examination, p. 456.
14. Polacolor 1963, p. 4; Trial 1981, pp. 3093–99, 3117–18, 3139.
15. EHL, "The Universe of One-Step Photography," Ostroff 1987, quoted in McCann 1993a, p. 274.
16. Vivian Walworth, personal communication, September 1997; Neblette 1977, p. 319, citing EHL U.S. patents 2,559,643 (1951), 2,661,293 (1953), and 2,647,049 (1953), quoted in McCann 1993a, p. 255; Trial 1981, pp. 80–82, 85, 3131–36.
17. EHL, "The Universe of One-Step Photography," Ostroff 1987, quoted in McCann 1993a, pp. 274–75.
18. Rogers 1989, part 1, pp. 3, 5–6; part 2, pp. 2–3, 4, 5, 22, 23.
19. Rogers 1972.
20. Rogers 1994. p. 14; Rogers 1989, part 1, pp. 9–14; part 2, pp. 9–10.
21. Rogers 1989, part 1, pp. 9–14; Polacolor 1963, pp. 12–13; Neblette 1977, p. 319, citing EHL U.S. patent 2,968,554 (1961), and Howard G. Rogers U.S. patent 3,019,124 (1962), quoted in McCann 1993a, pp. 255–56.
22. Rogers 1989, part 2, pp. 23–24; part 1, p. 16; Trial 1981, direct examination, pp. 85–86; Neblette 1977, pp. 321–22, citing H. G. Rogers U.S. patent 2,983,606, quoted in McCann 1993a, pp. 256–57; S. M. Bloom, M. Green, M. Idelson, and M. S. Simon, "The Dye Developer in the Polaroid Color Process," *The Chemistry of Synthetic Dyes*, ed. K. Venkataraman, 9 (chapter 8): 331–87.
23. Alix Kerr, "What It Took: Intuition, Goo," *Life*, 25 January 1963, p. 83 (with photographs by Fritz Goro).
24. Ibid., pp. 83, 85.
25. Rogers 1989, part 1, pp. 17–18; Neblette 1977, pp. 321–22, citing E. R. Blout and H. G. Rogers U.S. patent 3,255,001 (1966), quoted in McCann 1993a, p. 257.
26. Trial 1981, direct examination, p. 111.
27. Polacolor 1963, p. 15; Rogers 1989, part 1, p. 22.
28. Polacolor 1963, pp. 15–16.
29. Trial 1981, cross-examination, pp. 508, 510.
30. Rogers 1989, part 2, p. 23; Polacolor 1963, p. 44.
31. Annual Report, 1957, pp. 8, 10.
32. Kerr, p. 83; Rogers 1989, part 1, pp. 23–24.
33. Rogers 1989, part 1, p. 24; Annual Report, 1960, p. 7; "Chronicle of Land Photography," 9 pp., PA.
34. Annual Report, 1974, President's Letter, 25 March 1975; Trial 1981, second day, pp. 30, 31, 44–46; 427–30.
35. Rogers 1989, part 1, pp. 21, 26.
36. Rogers 1989, part 1, pp. 26–27, 42–43, and part 2, pp. 10–11.
37. Trial 1981, p. 435.
38. Rogers 1989, part 1, p. 27.
39. Kerr, p. 85; Trial 1981, direct examination, second day, pp. 22–31, 44–46; Trial 1981, cross-examination, pp. 645–46.
40. "Polaroid's Click—Color Photos," *Newsweek*, 28 January 1963, p. 73.
41. Kerr, p. 85.
42. Polacolor 1963, p. 46; Trial 1981, cross-examination, pp. 646, 702–4.
43. Polacolor 1963, p. 46.
44. Ibid., p. 47; Trial 1981, cross-examination, pp. 558–61.
45. Rogers 1972, p. 5.
46. Polacolor 1963, p. 48.
47. Trial 1981, second day, p. 26.
48. Rogers 1994, p. 16. The scientists gathered around the table were Myron Simon, Elkan Blout, Milton Green, Howard C. Haas, Richard S. Corley, and Rogers.
49. Kerr, p. 86.
50. Philip Siekman, *Fortune*, November 1972, p. 83.

51. Land 1973.
52. Rogers 1991.

CHAPTER 14, COLOR VISION

1. Land 1966, pp. 1–8; Land 1985.
2. Boring 1950, pp. 98–104; EHL, "Experiments in Color Vision," *Scientific American* 200 (May 1959): 84–94, 96–99, quoted in McCann 1993c, pp. 19–21; EHL response to readers' letters *Scientific American* (September 1959), quoted in McCann 1993c, pp. 33-34; EHL, "The Retinex," *American Scientist* 52, no. 2 (June 1964): 247–64, quoted in McCann 1993c, p. 53. The last article was based on EHL's William Proctor Prize address, Cleveland, Ohio, 30 December 1963.
3. F. Dow Smith, "The Vision and Color World of Edwin H. Land," *OPN* 5, no. 10 (October 1995): 30.
4. EHL, "The Case of the Sleeping Beauty or a Case Study in Industrial Research," unpublished transcript of lecture, West Point, New York, 19 May 1955, quoted in McCann 1993c, pp. 3–4; Francis Bello, "An Astonishing New Theory of Color," *Fortune*, May 1959, p. 195.
5. Mary A. McCann and John J. McCann, "Land's Chemical, Physical, and Psychological Images," *OPN* 5, no. 10 (October 1994): 36.
6. Bello, "An Astonishing New Theory of Color," p. 195.
7. McCann 1993c, p. iv, Edward M. Purcell, foreword, "A Memory of Colored Light."
8. EHL, "The Case of the Sleeping Beauty," quoted in McCann 1993c, p. 4.
9. Bello, "An Astonishing New Theory of Color," p. 200; EHL, "The Case of the Sleeping Beauty," quoted in McCann 1993c, p. 3.
10. Jeremy Bernstein, "I Am a Camera," review of Wensberg 1987, *The New York Review of Books* 35, no. 6 (14 April 1988): 24; Jeffrey Montgomery, "How We See Color: New Clues from the Brain," *Discover*, December 1988, p. 54.
11. F. Dow Smith, "The Vision and Color World of Edwin H. Land," *OPN* 5, no. 10 (October 1994): 32; McCann 1993c, pp. 53–60; EHL, "The Retinex," in A.V.S. De Reuck, and Julie Knight, eds., Ciba Foundation Symposium, *Color Vision Physiology and Experimental Psychology* (Boston: Little, Brown, 1965), pp. 217–27, quoted in McCann 1993c, pp. 61–65.
12. EHL, "Some Comments on Dr. Judd's Paper, *JOSA* 50, no. 3 (March 1960): 268, quoted in McCann 1993c, p. 35. Land said, "We have not yet found a situation in which lightnesses have not been able to predict color sensations accurately," EHL, "Colour in the Natural Image," *Proceedings of the Royal Institution of Great Britain* 39, no. 162 (1962): 1–15, quoted in McCann 1993c, p. 45.
13. J. D. Watson, conversation with author, November 1978.
14. Land 1975.
15. EHL, "Our 'Polar' Partnership with the World Around Us," *Harvard Magazine* 80 (1978): 22–25, quoted in McCann 1993c, pp. 151-54. Based on EHL's Phi Beta Kappa oration, Harvard University, 14 June 1977.
16. David Hubel, "The Visual Cortex of the Brain," *Scientific American*, November 1963, W. H. Freeman and Company reprint, 10 pp., kindly provided by Carroll Williams, AC; Robert Kanigel, "An intricate edifice: Exploring the architecture of the visual cortex," *Harvard Magazine* (October–November 1984): 41–49.
17. Hubel 1991, p. 8.
18. "Seeing's Not So Simple, Says Hubel," *Harvard University Gazette*, 21 February 1975, p. 2.
19. David Hubel, *Scientific American*, November 1963.
20. Geoffrey Montgomery, "Color Perception: Seeing with the Brain," *Discover*, December 1988, p. 57
21. Land 1985.
22. Bello, "An Astonishing New Theory of Color," p. 205; McCann and McCann, pp. 36–37.
23. Bello, "An Astonishing New Theory of Color," p. 202.
24. Polaroid Corporation news release for 20 November 1957, PA.
25. Harold M. Schmeck, Jr., "Color Simulated by Picture Device: Black-and-White Slides Are Used in Demonstration at Science Session Here," *NYT*, 21 November 1957.
26. Harold M. Schmeck, Jr., "Theory of Color Disputes Newton," *NYT*, 4 May 1959, p. 31.
27. EHL, McCann 1993c, p. 5; F. Dow Smith, p. 31.
28. Program of the Forty-Third Annual Meeting, Optical Society of America, 9–11 October 1958, with EHL paper scheduled for Thursday 9 October, Wayne Room, Statler Hilton Hotel, Detroit, AC.
29. Jean Pearson, "Color Theory Upset: Black and White Films 'Transformed,' " *Detroit Free Press*, 10 October 1958, p. 1.
30. F. Dow Smith, p. 31.
31. B. F. Skinner to EHL, 19 November 1958, MMF.
32. George Wald to EHL, 19 November 1958, MMF.
33. Meroë Morse memorandum, Tuesday, 10 March 1959, MMF.
34. Bello, "The Magic That Made Polaroid," *Fortune*, April 1959, pp. 124–25.

35. Bello, "An Astonishing New Theory of Color," pp. 144, 206.
36. Schmeck, *NYT*, 4 May 1959, p. 31.
37. EHL, "Experiments in Color Vision," *Scientific American* 200 (May 1959): 84–94, 96–99, quoted in McCann 1993c, p. 31.
38. EHL, "Thinking Ahead: Patents and New Enterprises," *Harvard Business Review*, September–October 1959, quoted in McCann 1993b, p. 44. Based on EHL's lecture to Boston Patent Law Association, 2 April 1959.
39. Lawrence K.M. Ting, "Color Television at Polaroid," *OPN* 5, no. 10 (October 1994): 38–40; Dover, Ohio, *Reporter*, from Science Service, 29 April 1967, "What's New in Patents?" PA; Bello, "An Astonishing New Theory of Color," pp. 205–206.
40. Hubel 1991, p. 1.
41. EHL letter to the editor, *Scientific American*, September 1959, quoted in McCann 1993c, pp. 32–34.
42. Deane B. Judd, "Appraisal of Land's Work on Two-Primary Color Projections, *JOSA* 50, no. 3 (March 1960): 263–64, 267.
43. EHL, "Some Comments on Dr. Judd's Paper," *JOSA* 50, no. 3 (March 1960): 268, quoted in McCann 1993c, p. 35.
44. EHL draft of a letter, 6 September 1985, AC.
45. Author's memorandum 8 March 1972 of demonstration by John J. McCann on 7 March 1972, AC; John J. McCann and Jeanne L. Benton, "Interaction of the Long-Wave Cones and the Rods to Produce Color Sensations," *JOSA* 59, no. 1 (January 1969): 103; John J. McCann, *Science*, 16 June 1972 (cover); David J. Ingle, "The Goldfish as a Retinex Animal," *Science* 227, no. 4687 (8 February 1985), cover and pp. 651–54.
46. The following references are talks by EHL and quoted in McCann 1993c, with page numbers in McCann as noted: "Colour in the Natural Image," 28 April 1961, pp. 41–46; "The Retinex Theory of Colour Vision," Friday evening discourse, Royal Institution, London, 2 November 1973, pp. 95–112; "The Retinex," William Proctor Prize address, 30 December 1963, pp. 61–65; "Lightness, Brightness and Reality," Albert A. Michelson Award address, Case Institute of Technology, 11 October 1966, pp. 67–70. See also EHL and John McCann, "Lightness and Retinex Theory," Frederic Ives medal address to Optical Society of America, 13 October 1967, *JOSA* 61, no. 1 (January 1971): 1–11, quoted in McCann 1993c, pp. 71–84; Land 1966; "Land Presents 'Ratio-Making' Theory As Explanation of Color Vision," *Harvard University Gazette* 69, no. 19 (1 February 1974): 2–3.
47. EHL, "Colour in the Natural Image," quoted in McCann 1993c, p. 43.
48. EHL, "Orthogonalism: Frontier for the Gallant," unpublished manuscript of commencement address, Stanford University, 17 June 1962, quoted in McCann 1993b, p. 43.
49. David Hubel, "The Visual Cortex of the Brain," *Scientific American*, November 1963; EHL, "The Retinex," quoted in McCann 1993c, p. 60,
50. EHL, "The Retinex," quoted in McCann 1993c, pp. 64, 65.
51. Land 1966, p. 21.
52. EHL, "Lightness, Brightness and Reality," quoted in McCann 1993c, p. 67.
53. Gene Maeroff, "Polaroid's E. H. Land is Named '66 Winner of Michelson Award," *The Plain Dealer*, Cleveland, Ohio, 12 October 1966.
54. EHL, and reply by Arthur Karp, *Leonardo*, vol. 5, pp. 284–85, quoted in McCann 1993c, pp. 93–94.
55. EHL and Nigel W. Daw, "Colors Seen in a Flash of Light," *Proceedings of the National Academy of Sciences* 48 (June 1962): 1000–1008, quoted in McCann 1993c, p. 50.
56. EHL, "Our 'Polar' Partnership with the World Around Us," quoted in McCann 1993c, p. 154.
57. Land 1978.
58. Land 1985.
59. Hubel 1991, p. 1.
60. *Optics News*, September 1975, p. 51.
61. *Harvard University Gazette*, 21 February 1975, p. 2.
62. Miranda Robertson, "News and Views: The programming of the visual cortex," *Nature* 253 (27 February 1975): 681–83; Robert Kanigel, "An intricate edifice: Exploring the architecture of the visual cortex," *Harvard Magazine*, October–November 1984, p. 46.
63. Semir Zeki, "The representation of colours in the cerebral cortex," *Nature* 284 (1980): 413–14.
64. Zeki 1991.
65. Zeki, "The representation of colours," pp. 412–18.
66. Zeki 1991.
67. Gina Kolata, "Color Vision Cells Found in Visual Cortex," *Science* 218 (29 October 1982): 457–58.
68. EHL, David H. Hubel, Margaret S. Livingstone, S. Hollis Perry, and Michael M. Burns, "Colour-generating interactions across the corpus callosum," *Nature* 303, no. 5918 (16 June 1983): 616–18, quoted in McCann 1993c, pp. 155–58.
69. EHL with David Hubel and Margaret Livingstone, joint session, 21 September 1982, Harvard Medical School, AN.
70. Kolata, pp. 475–78; "Seeing in Colour," *Nature* 300 (19 November 1982): 220.
71. Hubel 1991, pp. 2–3.

CHAPTER 15, U-2 SPY PLANE

1. Beschloss 1986, p. 72; Brig. Gen. George W. Goddard, *Overview: A Lifelong Adventure in Aerial Photography* (New York: Doubleday, 1969), p. 381, quoted in Brugioni 1991; Ambrose 1981, pp. 95, 121, 123–24, 132, 267–68, 270, 275; Ambrose 1983, pp. 145, 286–92; Ambrose 1981, pp. 228–30, cited in Ambrose 1985, pp. 123, 131, and 227–28; Bundy 1988, pp. 245, 252–53, 325–26, 337–40, notes, pp. 669–81; Divine 1993, pp. 17, 19.
2. The President's Appointments, noting meeting with ODM SAC at 9:30, "requested by Dr. Flemming," Ann Whitman Diary Series, March 1954 (Folder 1), DDEL; Beschloss 1986, pp. 74–75; Killian 1977, pp. 66–69; Rich 1994, Chapter 6, "Picture Postcards for Ike," pp. 117–32; Bundy 1988, pp. 325–27.
3. Lang 1959, ch. 23, "Fallout," pp. 363–82. The following references are cited in Divine 1978, pp. 3–5: Lt. H. Gordon Bechanan and 2d Lt. Charles O. Jones, "Unclassified History of Operation Castle, 1952-1954," pp. 122–29; Edward Teller and Albert L. Latter, *Our Nuclear Future*, New York: Criterion Books, 1958, pp. 88-92; *NYT*, 8 July 1954; *Newsweek* 43 (29 March 1954): 20; Lang 1959, pp. 370–72; and Ralph E. Lapp, *The Voyage of the Lucky Dragon* (New York: Harper, 1958), pp. 27–44. The following references are cited in Divine 1978, p.6: *NYT*, 12 March 1954, and "Operation Castle" study. The following references are cited in Divine 1978, p. 7: *NYT* 17 and 18 March 1954, and *Newsweek*, 29 March 1954. The following references are cited in Divine 1993, pp. 22, 215: Beard 1976, pp. 146–56; Simon Ramo, *The Business of Science: Winning and Losing in the High-Tech Age* (New York: Hill and Wang, 1988), pp. 85–87; Dwight Eisenhower, *Waging Peace*, p. 208; Herbert York, *Race to Oblivion*, pp. 83–84; Rhodes 1995, p. 565, citing Paul Lashmar, "Stranger than Strangelove," *Washington Post National Weekly Edition*, 11–17 July 1994, and Curtis LeMay address, National War College, 18 April 1956, Box 93, LeMay papers, LC; Schaffel 1991, p. 181.
4. David Alan Rosenberg, "A Smoking, Radiating Ruin at the End of Two Hours," *International Security* 6, no. 3 (Winter 1981/82): 3–38; Greenstein 1982, pp. 47–48; Holloway 1994, pp. 336–40.
5. Land 1945, p. 2.
6. Project Charles 1951; Schaffel 1991, pp. vii–ix.; David Alan Rosenberg, "The Origins of Overkill: Nuclear Weapons and American Strategy, 1945–1960," *International Security* 7, no. 4 (Spring 1983): 141–42, 156.
7. 25 April 1951, Box 22.11, MMF; Project Charles 1951, appendix, pp. V–1 to V–23.
8. Project Charles 1951, pp. 45–48.
9. Ibid., p. 3.
10. Beacon Hill 1952.
11. Schaffel 1991, pp. 200–201, 311.
12. Ibid., pp. 201–204.
13. Beschloss 1986, p. 76.
14. Bush 1949, p. 130.
15. "Fifty Are in Group," *Cocoa Tribune*, 22 January 1952, PA. Among the others were Maj. Gen. Donald L. Putt, deputy chief of staff, Development; Detlev Bronk, president of Johns Hopkins and later president of the National Academy of Sciences and of Rockefeller University; Hugh L. Dryden, director of the agency that later developed into NASA; and Allen V. Astin, director of the National Bureau of Standards, who, little more than a year later, survived the attempt of Eisenhower's secretary of commerce to fire him.
16. Major 1971, pp. 158–64.
17. Beacon Hill 1952, p. 1; Brugioni 1991, p. 7.
18. Beacon Hill 1952, pp. 4, 6–10, 13.
19. Ibid., pp. 13–15; on Gopher, see Burrows 1986, pp. 75, 349, citing Richelson 1987, ch. 5, and *NYT*, 6 February 1960.
20. Beacon Hill 1952, pp. 17–20, 23.
21. Baker 1953, pp. 1, 3–4.
22. Ibid., pp. 1–2, 4–5.
23. Ibid., p. 5.
24. Brugioni 1991, pp. 21–22.
25. Baker 1953; Beard 1976, p. 153, citing speech of Bernard A. Schriever, 28 October 1971.
26. Ambrose 1985, p. 38.
27. Burrows 1986, p. 68; Bissell 1996, p. 93, citing Richelson 1987, pp. 139–40, Johnson 1985, p. 120, and Bissell interview of Ben Rich, Farmington, Connecticut, 8 July 1992.
28. Pocock 1989.
29. Beard 1976, p. 144; Beschloss 1986, pp. 73–74, citing interviews with Vincent Ford, Richard Bissell, and James R. Killian; Bundy 1988, pp. 326–27.
30. Klass 1971, p. 15; Beard 1976, p. 157, citing interviews with Reuben Mettler, Thomas Lanphier, Ray Soper, and Simon Ramo. The other members of Von Neumann's committee were Louis G. Dunn of the Jet Propulsion Laboratory, Charles C. Lauritsen of Caltech, Allen E. Puckett of Hughes Aircraft, Jerome Wiesner of MIT, and Lawrence A. Hyland of Bendix Aviation.
31. Burrows 1986, p. 69; Beschloss 1986, pp. 78, 79, 432, citing interview with Robert Amory, 21 May 1983; Brugioni 1991, pp. 15–16; Donald Welzenbach, "Din Land: Patriot from Polaroid," *OPN* 5, no. 10 (October 1994): 24.

32. Beschloss 1986, pp. 73–74.
33. Burrows 1986, p. 69.
34. Beard 1976, pp. 160–61, 168, 172–76, 182.
35. Welzenbach, p. 23, citing interview with James Killian, Cambridge, Massachusetts, 2 November 1983; Burrows 1986, p. 67.
36. Welzenbach, p. 23, citing interview with EHL, Cambridge, Massachusetts 14 September 1984.
37. Ibid.
38. Ibid.
39. Ibid., p. 24.
40. Ibid., pp. 24–25.
41. Ibid., p. 25, citing interview with Garrison Norton, Washington, D.C., 23 May 1983.
42. Brugioni 1991, p. 14; Welzenbach, p. 25.
43. Purcell 1992.
44. Brugioni 1991, pp. 14–15, 22; Welzenbach, p. 25.
45. Welzenbach, pp. 25–26.
46. Ibid., p. 24.
47. Pocock 1989, p. 7; Rich 1994, p. 127; Welzenbach, p. 26.
48. TCP 1955.
49. Brugioni 1991, p. 17; Welzenbach, p. 26.
50. Brugioni 1991, pp. 17–18.
51. Rich 1994, p. 126.
52. Welzenbach, p. 26.
53. Beschloss 1986, p. 81.
54. Welzenbach, p. 26.
55. Pocock 1989, 8; Welzenbach, p. 26.
56. McDougall 1986, p. 229; Killian 1977, p. 241; Brandeis 1983, p. 11.
57. Killian 1977, p. 82; Bissell 1996, p. 94.
58. Richelson 1987, pp. 139–40, citing interview with Robert Amory, 9 February 1966; Brugioni 1991, pp. 18–19.
59. Killian 1977, pp. 82–84; Burrows 1986, pp. 67–68, citing interviews with EHL, 27 October 1984, and James Killian, 11 February 1985; Rich 1994, p. 124.
60. Beschloss 1986, pp. 81–83, 433, citing interviews with EHL, 22 February 1983, James Killian, 22 February 1983, and Andrew Goodpaster, 3 January 1983, 15 March and 2 July 1984; Killian 1977, pp. 82–83.
61. Burrows 1986, pp. 68–70.
62. Beschloss 1986, p. 84.
63. Bissell 1996, pp. 101–102, citing Goodpaster, Memorandum of Conference with the President, 24 November 1954, Ann Whitman Diary Series, ACW Diary, November 1954 (Folder 1), Box 3, DDEL, and Arthur Lundahl interview by Jonathan Lewis, Bethesda, Maryland, 23 January 1992; Welzenbach, p. 28.
64. Robert Cutler to James Killian, 18 March 1955, Records 1952–1961, NSC series, Briefing Subseries, Box 17, Technological Capabilities Panel, Folder 1, OSANSA.
65. Bundy 1988, p. 325.
66. Killian 1969–70.
67. Ibid.
68. TCP 1955; Burrows 1986, p. 67.
69. Herbert York, interview by author, 1 August 1995.
70. Rich 1994, "Other Voices: Marty Knutson," p. 148.
71. Ted Greenwood, "Reconnaissance and Arms Control," *Scientific American* 228, no. 2 (February 1973): 2–13.
72. Beschloss 1986, p. 152; Bundy 1988, pp. 350, 381–82; Prados 1986, pp. 117–18, 335; Reeves 1993, p. 228.

CHAPTER 16, THE SHOCK OF SPUTNIK

1. Appointment Card File, 4 February 1958, Dinner given by President and Mrs. Eisenhower for Military and Scientific Officials, DDEL; Killian 1977, p. 122.
2. Beschloss 1986, pp. 148, 156, 442; Prados 1986, pp. 105–106; Divine 1993, pp. 41, 217, citing Andrew Goodpaster, memorandum of conversation with Richard Bissell, 25 October 1957, SS Alpha, Box 14, DDEL; Bissell 1996, p. 135, citing Jeffrey Richelson, "The Keyhole Satellite Program," *Journal of Strategic Studies* 7, no. 2 (1984): 126.
3. Ambrose 1983, pp. 145, 290–92: Beschloss 1986, p. 81.
4. Beschloss 1986, p. 81; Pocock 1989, p. 7; Rich 1994, pp. 123–24; Rhodes 1995, pp. 564–66; Bissell 1996, p. 94.
5. Bissell 1996, p. 100.
6. Lang 1959, pp. 433–36, 439, 446–47.
7. Holloway 1994; Rhodes 1995.

8. Divine 1993, pp. 100–101.
9. Bissell 1996, p. 138; Richelson 1990, p. 43.
10. Klass 1971, p. 160; Richelson 1990, pp. 353–62.
11. Burrows 1986, pp. 126-27.
12. Appointment Card File, Science Advisory Committee meeting, 10:58–11:55 a.m., DDEL; Records 1952–61, Special Assistant Series, Subject Subseries (A67-50, A67-64), Science Advisory Committee, Folder 3, March–October 1957, OSANSA, DDEL; Killian 1977, pp. 15–16.
13. Divine 1993, pages 12–15, 214, citing Charles J. V. Murphy, "The White House Since Sputnik," *Fortune*, January 1958, p. 100; Goodpaster memcon, 16 October 57, Dwight David Eisenhower Diary, Box 27, DDEL; Robert Cutler, handwritten notes of White House Meeting, 15 October 1957, Special Assistant Series, Subject Subseries, Box 7, OSANSA; Cutler to Rabi, 15 October 1957, Box 1, OSAST.
14. Ambrose 1983, pp. 50–51, 56, 58.
15. DDEL.
16. Killian 1977, pp. 15–17.
17. Divine 1993, p. 15, citing Dwight Eisenhower, *Waging Peace* (Garden City, N.Y.: Doubleday, 1965), pp. 211–12.
18. Robert Cutler, handwritten notes of White House Meeting, 15 October 57, Special Assistant Series, Subject Subseries, Box 7, OSANSA; Cutler to Rabi, 15 October 1957, Box 1, OSAST.
19. Cutler to Rabi, 15 October 1957, White House Office, OSANSA, Records 1952-61, Special Assistant Series, Subject Subseries [A67-50, A67-64], Science Advisory Committee, Folder 3, March–October 1957, OSANSA.
20. Andrew Goodpaster, handwritten notes at 1:30 p.m. meeting in Defense Secretary McElroy's office, 15 October 1957, Records 1952–61, Special Assistant Series, Subject Subseries [A67-50, A67-64], Science Advisory Committee, Folder 3, March–October 1957, OSANSA.
21. Killian 1977, pp. 20–30; Divine 1993, p. 48.
22. Klass 1971, p. 27.
23. Kenneth E. Greer, "Corona," Studies in Intelligence, Supplement, 17 (Spring 1973): 1–37, reprinted in Ruffner 1995.
24. Ibid.
25. Donald Welzenbach, "Din Land: Patriot from Polaroid," *OPN* 5, no. 10 (October 1994): 23, citing Andrew Goodpaster interview of 6 July 1983.
26. Ann Whitman File, Dwight David Eisenhower Diary Series, Box 27, October 1957, DDEL.
27. Divine 1993, p. 56, citing Wilton Persons memo, Dwight David Eisenhower Diary Series, Box 28, DDEL.
28. McDougall 1986, pp. 160, 162, 384; Divine 1993, pp. 164–66.
29. "Gift of $12 Million Is Made to Harvard, *NYT*, 15 June 1968, p. 24, citing *BG* report of 14 June 1968: "An informal poll of knowledgeable Harvard sources not directly concerned with the transaction produced the speculation that the donor is inventor Edwin Land, chairman and president of Polaroid Corporation."
30. Carnegie 1967; Jack Gould, "Tax on New TV Sets Urged To Help Educational Video: Carnegie Report Recommends Nonprofit Corporation to Underwrite System; Manufacturers Appear Skeptical," *NYT*, Thursday, 26 January 1967, pp. 1, 27; James Reston, "A Base for a Milestone: Carnegie Report, Like Land-Grant Act of 1862, May Have Great Impact on U.S. Life," *NYT* 26 January 1967, p. 27; "E. B. White Calls TV A Counterpart to Essay," *NYT*, 26 January 1967, p. 27; Jack Gould, "Television: How to Win Back Our Young," *NYT*, 23 April 1967, giving excerpts from EHL's testimony before Senator John O. Pastore, 13 April 1967.
31. Killian 1977, p. 122.
32. Killian 1977, Appendix 4, pp. 288–99.
33. Thomas Gold, "Apollo 11 Observations of a Remarkable Glazing Phenomenon on the Lunar Surface," *Science* 165 (26 September 1969): 1345–49, cites E. Purcell, E. Land, J. Baker, R. Scott, and F. Pearce "for their contributions in outlining and guiding this camera project," to Eastman Kodak Company "for the design and fabrication of this instrument, and chiefly to Mr. N. Armstrong for his successful use of it"; Walter Sullivan, "Moon Deposits Linked to Solar Flare," *NYT*, 26 September 1969; Purcell 1992.
34. EHL, "Extemporaneous remarks on Behalf of the 1967 Recipients of the National Medal of Science," quoted in McCann 1993b, p. 81. The author was present at the White House and the State Department, 13 February 1968, AN.

CHAPTER 17, SPY SATELLITES

1. Klass 1971, p. 81; Ambrose 1985, p. 428; Divine 1993, pp. 6, 11–12, citing Andrew Goodpaster memcon, 9 October 1957, Staff Secretary, Box 6; Cutler memcon of 8 October 1957, NSC Briefing Notes, Box 13, DDEL.
2. Ambrose 1985, p. 429; Divine 1993, p. 7.
3. Divine 1993, pp. 7–12.
4. Ibid., pp. 7–12, 44.
5. Ibid., pp. 45–46.
6. Richelson 1990, p. 5.
7. Ibid., pp. 7–8.

8. Klass 1971, pp. 83–89.
9. Ibid., pp. 86–87; Stares 1985, pp. 30–31; Divine 1993, p. 7, citing Jack Manno, *Among the Heavens* (New York: Dodd, Mead and Co., 1984), pp. 27, 32.
10. Donald Welzenbach, "Din Land: Patriot from Polaroid," *OPN* 5, no. 10 (October 1994): 22–26, 28–29; Bissell 1996, pp. 99-101.
11. Beschloss 1986, pp. 148, 156, 442; Prados 1986, pp. 105–6; Divine 1993, pp. 41, 217, citing Goodpaster memcon of conversation with Richard Bissell, 25 October 1957, SS Alpha, Box 14, DDEL; Bissell 1996, p. 135, citing Jeffrey Richelson, "The Keyhole Satellite Program," *Journal of Strategic Studies* 7, no. 2 (1984): 126.
12. Appointment card file, DDEL; Andrew Goodpaster, handwritten notes of 15 October 1957, and typed memorandum, 16 October 1957, Office of the Staff Secretary, Box 23, folder 2, DDEL; Killian 1977, pp. 15–16; Beschloss 1986, pp. 75–76, 81; Divine 1993, pp. 12–15, 214, citing Goodpaster, memcon, 16 October 1957, Dwight David Eisenhower Diary, Box 27, DDEL; Records 1952–61, Special Assistant Series, Subject Subseries [A67-50, A67-64] Science Advisory Committee, Folder 3, March–October 1957, OSANSA.
13. Jerome Wiesner, personal communication.
14. Burrows 1986, p. 83; Richelson 1990, pp. 20–21, 23.
15. Klass 1971, p. 88.
16. Ibid., pp. 88–89.
17. Burrows 1986, p. 100; Richelson 1990, p. 26; Divine 1993, p. 83.
18. Bissell 1996, p. 135.
19. Purcell 1992.
20. Prados 1986, pp. 105–6; Ruffner 1995, pp. 5–6; Bissell 1996, p. 135.
21. Bissell 1996, p. 136.
22. Prados 1986, pp. 78, 332; Divine 1993, pp. 100–101, 113–15, citing Andrew Goodpaster memcon of 6 February 1958, Staff Secretary, Department of Defense, Box 6, DDEL.
23. Ann Whitman File, Dwight David Eisenhower Diary Series, Box 31, March 1958, Staff Notes, DDEL.
24. Appointment Card File, 4 February 1958, Dinner given by President and Mrs. Eisenhower for Military and Scientific Officials, DDEL.
25. Kistiakowsky 1976, p. 136.
26. Richard Witkin, "Air Force Forms a Satellite Wing," *NYT*, 20 December 1959, p. 28; Klass 1971, pp. 92–95; Stares 1985, p. 45; McDonald, 1995.
27. McDonald, "Corona," p. 693.
28. Seth Shulman, "Code Name: Corona," *Technology Review*, October 1996, pp. 22–24, 26, 28–32.
29. Trial 1981.
30. Kistiakowsky 1976, 245–346
31. Ibid.
32. Klass 1971, p. 95; Joseph Alsop, "Americans and Russians Reach for Spy in the Sky, *Charlotte News*, 12 January 1960, p. 10A; Louis Kraar, "Spy in the Sky: U.S. Prepares to Orbit Satellite to Keep Tabs on Red Missile Firings," *WSJ*, 18 February 1960, p. 1; Richard Witkin, Cape Canaveral, "First Midas Fails in Orbit Attempt," *NYT*, 27 February 1960, p. 8.
33. Klass 1971, p. 50; Beschloss 1986, pp. 242, 341, 359–61; Associated Press, Moscow, *BG*, 30 April 1990.
34. Kistiakowsky 1976, p. 300.
35. Klass 1971, pp. 95–96; Burrows 1986, p. 106, citing interview with Richard Bissell, 23 May 1984; McDonald, 1995.
36. Burrows 1986, p. 106.
37. Richelson 1990, p. 63.
38. Kistiakowsky 1976, p. 333.
39. Ibid., p. 336.
40. Ibid., p. 378.
41. Ibid., p. 380.
42. Ibid., pp. 381–82.
43. Associated Press, Vandenberg Air Force Base, "Sky-Spying Satellite Is Put in Orbit; Jammed with classified gear," *NYHT*, 19 August 1960, p. 1; *Aviation Week*, 22 August 1960, pp. 33–35; Klass 1971, pp. 98–101; McDougall 1986, p. 224; Richelson 1990, p. 41; McDonald 1995, pp. 690–91, 693; Bissell 1996, p. 138.
44. Richelson 1990, pp. 43, 180, citing Lawrence Freedman, *U.S. Intelligence and the Soviet Strategic Threat* (Boulder, Colo: Westview, 1977), p. 73.
45. Kistiakowsky 1976, p. 384.
46. Ibid.
47. Ibid., p. 387.
48. Richelson 1990, citing interviews with Andrew Goodpaster and an unnamed source.
49. McDonald 1995, pp. 715–17.
50. Kistiakowsky 1976, p. 387.
51. Ibid., p. 388.

52. Richard L. Garwin, "Impressions of Edwin H. Land," *OPN* 5, no. 10 (October 1994): 24–25.
53. Garwin 1991.
54. Ibid.

CHAPTER 18, DEMONSTRATING A NEW MEDIUM

1. Walker Evans, "The Thing Itself Is Such a Secret and So Unapproachable," *Yale Alumni Magazine* 37, no. 5 (February 1974): 16.
2. EHL demonstration to author, 17 March 1972; typed notes and memorandum, 20 March 1972, AN.
3. Carl Kaysen, personal communication.
4. EHL demonstration to author, 17 March 1972.
5. Philip Siekman, "Kodak and Polaroid, An End to Peaceful Coexistence," *Fortune*, November 1970, pp. 82–83.
6. Trial 1981, 435–44; Annual Report, 1969; "Kodak and Polaroid Are Moving Closer to Battle for the Instant Market," *WSJ*, 28 April 1971, p. 40.
7. EHL demonstration to author, 17 March 1972.
8. James C. Elms, director, NASA Electronics Research Center, Cambridge, Massachusetts, interview by author, 1968.
9. Author's visit, negative coating plant, New Bedford, Massachusetts, 25 July 1972.
10. Carl Kaysen, interviews by author, 7 March 1994, 24 June 1994.

CHAPTER 19, COLLABORATORS

1. Interview, Stanley M. Bloom, 21 July 1971, p. 5, AN.
2. Trial 1981, pp. 526, 1020–24, 1103–04, 1110, 1301–02.
3. Trial 1981, p. 3149.
4. Stanley Mervis, personal communication, September 1997.
5. Trial 1981, pp. 3278, 3285, 3294.
6. Trial 1981.
7. Murray and Cox 1989, pp. 113–39.
8. Trial 1981.
9. Wall 1970, p. 259.
10. McPherson 1988, p. 726, citing Horace Porter, *Campaigning with Grant* (New York: The Century Co., 1897), pp. 69–70.
11. EHL, interview by author, 22 March 1972, AN; "How Kodak will exploit its new Instamatic," *BW*, 18 March 1972, p. 48.
12. Richard Wareham and Richard Chen, interview by author, 23 March 1972, AN.
13. Richard Wareham and Richard Chen, interview by author, 27 March 1972, AN.
14. Ibid.
15. Richard Kee, interview by author, 10 April 1972; John Burgarella, interviews by author, 27 April and 27 June 1972, AN.
16. William Plummer, interviews by author, 28 and 29 March, 4 April 1972, AN.
17. Wareham, interviews by author, 23 and 27 March 1972, AN.
18. Richard Wareham, interview by author, 15 March 1995, AN.
19. Dan Cordtz, "How Polaroid Bet Its Future on SX-70," *Fortune*, January 1974, p. 144.
20. Ibid.; Wareham, interview by author, 15 March 1995, AN.
21. Wareham, interview by author, 15 March 1972, AN.
22. Ibid.
23. William T. Plummer, "The SX-70 Camera: The Optics," *OPN* 5, no. 10 (October 1994): 45–48.
24. Wareham, interview by author, 3 April 1972, AN.
25. Author's observation, 1972.
26. EHL, "Absolute One-Step Photography," based on EHL invited lecture, 10 May 1972 (Land 1972b), *PSE* 16, no. 4 (July–August 1972), quoted in McCann 1993a, p. 181.
27. Bloom 1974, pp. 5–6.
28. *The Polaroid Newsletter,* 4 October 1978, pp. 1–2.
29. Cordtz, p. 87.
30. Stanley Mervis, personal communication, September 1997.
31. Cordtz, p. 87; Bloom 1974, pp. 8, 17.
32. McCann 1993a, pp. 180, 191, 257–58; Idelson 1974; E. Martin Idelson, interview by author, 9 November 1978, AN; H. G. Rogers, M. Idelson, R. F. W. Ciecuich, and S. M. Bloom, "Light Stability of New Polaroid Color Prints," *The Journal of Photographic Science* 22, no. 3 (May–June 1974): 138–43, based on talk at symposium, "The Conservation of Photographic Records," Color Group, Royal Photographic Society, London, 20 September 1973; S. M. Bloom, M. Green, M. Idelson, and M. S. Simon, "The Dye Developer in the Polaroid Color Process," in *The Chemistry of Synthetic Dyes,* ed. K. Venkataraman, chapter VIII, vol. 9, pp. 371–80.

33. Stanley M. Bloom, interview by author, 21 July 1972, AN; Bloom 1974.
34. Cordtz, p. 87.
35. Ibid.
36. Ibid.
37. Bloom, interview by author, 20 July 1972, AN.
38. Ibid.
39. Charles Chiklis, interview by author, 9 November 1978, AN.
40. Bloom, interview by author, 21 July 1972, AN.
41. Richard Kostelantz, "A Wide-Angle View and Closeup Portrait of Edwin Land and His Polaroid Cameras," *Lithopinion*, Spring 1974, p. 53.
42. Cordtz, pp. 85–87.
43. McCune 1977, p. 12.
44. Wensberg 1987, pp. 205–8.
45. Ibid., p. 152; McCune, 1991.
46. McCune, 1991.

CHAPTER 20, SELLING SX-70

1. EHL, Letter to Polaroid shareholders, 20 March 1970, Annual Report, 1969, p. 4.
2. William M. Carley, "Girding for Battle: Kodak Sets Challenge To Polaroid Monopoly in Instant Photo Field," *WSJ*, 6 April 1970, pp. 1, 24.
3. *The Polaroid Newsletter*, 15 May 1970.
4. Philip Siekman, "Kodak and Polaroid: An End to Peaceful Coexistence," *Fortune*, November 1970, pp. 82–87, 118, 122, 124.
5. Land 1972a.
6. Philip Siekman, personal communication, 6 February 1997, AN.
7. Siekman, "Kodak and Polaroid," p. 83.
8. Ibid., p. 124.
9. EHL, Letter to Polaroid shareholders, 18 March 1971, Annual Report, 1970, pp. 3–4.
10. Gene Smith, "Eastman Shows Low-light Color Film; Instant Pictures Promised in Future," *NYT*, 28 April 1971, p. 63.
11. *The Polaroid Newsletter*, 17 May 1971.
12. EHL, Letter to Polaroid shareholders, 23 March 1972, Annual Report, 1971.
13. "Dr. Land redesigns his camera company," *BW*, 15 April 1972, cover and p. 70.
14. Ibid.
15. Carl Kaysen, interview by author, Cambridge, Massachusetts, 7 March 1994, p. 2, AN.
16. Land 1972a.
17. EHL, address to Polaroid employees, Needham, Massachusetts, 2 May 1972, AT.
18. EHL, address to Polaroid employees, Needham, Massachusetts, 4 May 1972, AN.
19. Land 1972b; Mrs. Edwin Land, conversation with author, 9 May 1972.
20. William Doerner, associate editor, and Philip Taubman, correspondent, "Polaroid's Big Gamble on Small Cameras," *Time*, 26 June 1972, pp. 80–82, 84, 86, 88.
21. "Polaroid Corp. Delays National Sale of SX-70 Until Early Next Year," *WSJ*, 5 September 1972, p. 6.
22. "Polaroid's Profit Sank 62%, Sales 14% in 2d Period," *WSJ*, 19 July 1972, p. 6.
23. David Brand and Liz Roman Gallese, "Polaroid's Image: Company Proves Adept at Ballyhoo in Putting New Camera on Market," *WSJ*, 23 October 1972, p. 1.
24. "Polaroid's Profit Sank 62%."
25. "Polaroid Corp. Delays National Sale."
26. The author was present.
27. Brand and Gallese.

CHAPTER 21, CRISIS

1. Land 1972c; AN.
2. Wensberg 1987, pp. 198–99.
3. David Brand, "Great Yellow Father: Kodak Dominates Field, Rolls Up Huge Profits But Antagonizes Many," *WSJ*, 15 November 1972, p. 1; "Eastman Kodak says it's concentrating on 'in camera processing system' and no longer intends to make film packs for Polaroid," Dow Jones News Service, 3:53 p.m., Friday, 17 November 1972; David Brand, "Kodak Won't Make Polaroid Instant Film, Plans to Sell Rival Film, Camera Instead," *WSJ*, Monday 20 November 1972, p. 6.
4. Zobel 1985, p. 831.
5. AN; Victor K. McElheny, "In the Beginning Was Dr. Land," *NYT*, 18 April 1976, p. 12 F; Victor K. McElheny,

"Eastman Kodak Demonstrates System for Instant Pictures," *NYT*, 21 April 1976, p. 49; Victor K. McElheny, "An Appraisal: Kodak and Polaroid, Color Systems Differ," *NYT*, 23 April 1976, p. 47; "Kodak Finally Unveils Instant Color Camera," *C & EN*, 26 April 1976, p. 4: author's notes of press visit to Eastman Kodak manufacturing of instant cameras and film, 3 August 1976, AN.

6. "Kodak Postpones Refunds to Instant-Camera Owners," *WSJ*, 9 June 1986, p. 8.
7. Victor K. McElheny, "An Appraisal."
8. Dan Dorfman, "Heard on the Street," *WSJ*, 8 December 1972, p. 35.
9. David Brand,"The SX-70 Camera: It's a Lot Easier to Use One Than to Find One to Buy," *WSJ*, 21 December 1972, p. 10.
10. William T. Plummer, interview by author, 4 April 1972; James G. Baker and Richard Weeks, interviews by author, 8 September 1972, AN.
11. Author's visit to Perkin specialty chemicals factory, 21 September 1972; Richard Brooks, interview by author, 21 September 1972, AN.
12. Author's visit to New Bedford negative coating facility, 25 July 1972; I. MacAllister Booth, interview by author, 25 July 1972, AN.
13. Author's visit to Reservoir film assembly factory, building R-2, Waltham, Massachusetts, 27 June 1972; Curt Foster, plant manager, and John Sturgis, chief engineer, interviews by author, 27 June 1972, AN.
14. Victor K. McElheny, "Blue Sky notes," autumn 1972, AN.
15. Ibid.
16. Robert Metz, "Market Place: Plant Visit Lifts Polaroid Stock," *NYT*, 17 February 1973; "Polaroid: Turning out a finicky product," *BW*, 8 December 1973, p. 78.
17. Victor K. McElheny, "Blue Sky notes," autumn 1972, AN.
18. Author's visit to EHL laboratory, inspection of sample SX-70 photographs, AN.
19. Richard Martin, "Polaroid Announces Low-Priced Camera, Details SX-70 Woes to Securities Group," *WSJ*, 22 July 1974, p. 11; Sheldon Buckler, interview by author, Cambridge, Massachusetts, 9 November 1978, AN.
20. Carl Kaysen, interviews by author, 1994.
21. "Corning Glass to Halt Output of Camera Lens for Polaroid's SX-70s," *WSJ*, 18 February 1975, p. 35.
22. Author's observation, 1972.
23. Land 1972c.
24. Land 1972c; "FC & I, Polaroid Ax Most of Deal," *Electronic News*, 14 January 1974, p. 1; "News Analysis: The SX-70 Polarized Pricing," *Electronic News*, 21 January 1974, p. 1; Tekla S. Perry, "The battle for the SX-70: Fairchild and TI crossed swords when Polaroid, in 1970, promised the winner a contract to supply the electronics for millions of truly automatic instant cameras," *IEEE Spectrum*, May 1989, pp. 45–49.
25. Calderwood 1976.
26. Charles J. Elia, "Heard on the Street," *WSJ*, 31 May 1974, p. 31.
27. Calderwood 1976.
28. EHL, conversation with author, October 1987.
29. Wensberg 1987, p. 204.
30. Calderwood 1976.
31. Conversation with author, Polaroid shareholders' meeting, Wellesley, Massachusetts, May 1991.
32. Land 1973.
33. Land 1974.
34. "The SX-70: Polaroid's Gee-Whiz Machine," *Consumer Reports*, May 1974, pp. 380–81.
35. Richard Martin, "Polaroid Announces Low-Priced Camera."
36. "SX-70 Deglamourizes Polaroid," *BW*, 30 November 1974, p. 90.
37. "Polaroid Net Fell 56% in 4th Period and 45% in 1974," *WSJ*, 19 February 1975, p. 7.
38. Subrata Chakravarty, "An Interview with Dr. Edwin Land: 'People want more from life than an eight-hour day with a martini at the end,' " Forbes, 1 June 1975, pp. 48–50.
39. Ibid.
40. Land 1976a.
41. Personal communication.
42. The author was present.
43. Lawrence Ingrassia, "Fading Picture: How Polaroid Went From Highest Flyer to Takeover Target," *WSJ* 12 August 1988, pp. 1, 14.
44. Alex Beam, "Polaroid stock rises as rumors continue," *BG*, 8 March 1988, p. 49; John Wilke, "Are sharks circling Polaroid?" *BG*, 7 June 1988, pp. 43, 59; Lawrence Ingrassia, "Polaroid Plans Defensive Restructuring, Addition of Line of Conventional Film," *WSJ*, 13 July 1988; Robert J. Cole, "Shamrock Seeks to Buy Polaroid," *NYT*, 21 July 1988, pp. D1, D7; William M. Bulkeley and Bryan Burrough, "Shamrock Holdings Bids at Least $2.28 Billion for Polaroid Corp.," *WSJ*, 21 July 1988, pp. 3, 5; David J. Jefferson, "Roy E. Disney Changes Sneers to Cheers," *WSJ*, 21 July 1988, p. 23; John Wilke, "California group offers $2.5 billion for Polaroid," *BG*, 21 July 1988, pp. 1, 84; Jane Fitz Simon, "Disney: The man behind Polaroid offer," *BG*, 21 July 1988, pp. 35, 45; William M. Bulkeley and Bryan Burrough, "Polaroid's Success in Avoiding Takeover May Rest on Its Use of ESOP as a Defense," *WSJ*, 22 July 1988, p. 22;

Robert Lenzner and John C. Yoo, "Worker ire may hurt Polaroid's defense," *BG*, 23 July 1988, pp. 12, 16; Jane Fitz Simon, "Shamrock, Raider or Investor?" *BG*, 2 August 1988, pp. 37, 43; David Stipp, "Polaroid Board Turns Down Shamrock Offer," *WSJ*, 17 August 1988, p. 12; Jane Fitz Simon and Robert Lenzner, "Polaroid rejects Shamrock's offer," *BG*, 17 August 1988, pp. 77, 83; Jane Fitz Simon, "Polaroid targets 1,500 retirements," *BG*, 19 August 1988, pp. 61–62; Jane Fitz Simon, "Trial Date is set over Polaroid ESOP," *BG*, 23 August 1988, p. 28; "Shamrock's Sweetened Offer is Rejected by Firm's Board," *WSJ*, 25 January 1989, p. C24; Robert J. Cole, $1.1 Billion Polaroid Buyback: Anti-Takeover Plan Includes Stake's Sale To Investor Group," *NYT* 31 January 1989, pp. D1, D19; Jane Fitz Simon, "Ruling blocks Shamrock from taking over Polaroid," *BG*, 24 March 1989; Jane Fitz Simon, "Shamrock withdraws Polaroid bid," *BG* 28 March 1989, pp. 57, 62; William M. Bulkeley and Frederick Rose, "Polaroid Gains Peace Accord; Stock falls $4.50; Shamrock Gets $20 Million and Agrees Not to Seek Control in Next 10 years."

45. McCune 1991.
46. Ibid.

CHAPTER 22, INSTANT MOVIES

1. Lucretia Weed, personal communication, July 1997.
2. EHL, letter to shareholders, 24 March 1976, Annual Report, 1975, p. 4.
3. EHL, "An Introduction to Polavision," *Photographic Science and Engineering* 21, no. 5 (September–October 1977): 225–36, quoted in McCann 1993a, pp. 193, 197.
4. Wensberg 1987, p. 223.
5. Land 1977a; Land 1977b; Vivian K. Walworth, interview by author, Los Angeles, 6 May 1977, AN.
6. William Gildea, "Inventing Their Way to the Hall of Fame," *WP*, 7 February 1977, pp. B1, B3. The National Inventors Hall of Fame began inductions in 1973 with just one person, Thomas Edison. In 1975, William Coolidge, Land's fellow Modern Pioneer of 1940, was one of those inducted. Zworykin (1977) was another. Other Modern Pioneers named later were Leo H. Baekeland (1978), Charles F. Kettering and Edwin H. Armstrong (1980), Henry Ford (1982), Wallace H. Carothers (1984), Willis H. Carrier (1985), and Irving Langmuir (1989).
7. McCann 1993b, p. 51.
8. "Businessmen in the News: At the Company That Never Rests," *Fortune*, January 1977, p. 19, citing estimates by Theodore E. James, Jr.
9. William J. McCune, speech at thirtieth anniversary of one-step photography, Grand Ballroom, Plaza Hotel, New York, 17 February 1977, AN; Victor K. McElheny, "Polaroid Increases Earnings in Quarter 29.1% for a Record," *NYT*, 18 February 1977, pp. D1, D11; "Polaroid Profit Rose 29 percent to High in Fourth Period," *WSJ*, 18 February 1977, p. 7.
10. "Polaroid Corp. Hints It'll Unveil System for Instant Movies, but Spokesman Backtracks," *WSJ*, 22 February 1977, p. 21.
11. William J. McCune, interview by author, Cambridge, Massachusetts, 13 April 1977, AN.
12. Wensberg 1987, pp. 218–19, 225–26.
13. Michael Jacobs, "The Physicist as Entrepreneur," *Physics Today* 35, no. 1 (January 1982): 35.
14. Wensberg 1987, pp. 221–22.
15. Polaroid Corporation, press release, Chicago, 28 March 1977, AC.
16. *WSJ*, 31 December 1996, p. A1.
17. *BW* interview, p. 10; *BW*, 2 March 1981, p. 109.
18. Donald Dery, Polaroid Corporation news release on meeting of analysts and journalists, Waldorf-Astoria Hotel, P.R. Newswire, 31 January 1978.
19. Chakravarty, p. 50.
20. Richard Weeks, "An Artist Who Chose Science and Technology for His Medium," *OPN* 5, no. 10 (October 1994): 13.
21. Wensberg 1987, p. 227.
22. Victor K. McElheny, memorandum, "Creating the Latent Image," February 1972, AC.
23. Chakravarty, pp. 48–50.
24. Land 1976a.
25. Jerome Wiesner, personal communication.
26. Land 1977a.
27. Liz Roman Gallese, "Polaroid Holders Get Instant Spectaculars At Annual Meetings; Edwin Land, Star of Sessions, Deserves Oscar, Some Say; Does Magic Bury Queries?" *WSJ*, 25 April 1978, p. 1.
28. Wensberg 1987, p. 228.
29. Land 1977a. The author was the reporter to whom Land spoke.
30. William T. Plummer, "Leaving No Stone Unturned," *OPN* 5, no. 10 (October 1994): 39.
31. Gallese.
32. Ibid.
33. "For Heaven's Sake, Instant Movies," *Fortune*, June 1977, p. 40.
34. Neil Ulman, "Instant Pictures and Graven Images," *WSJ*, 3 June 1977, p. 8.
35. Land 1977b.
36. Wensberg 1987, p. 219.

CHAPTER 23, TOO LATE

1. Neil Ulman, "Polaroid Sees Pre-Tax Profit Growing Despite Competition," Dow Jones News Wire, 21 January 1978.
2. Don Leavitt, "First look: Polavision instant movies: It's not film, it's not tape, but it may be an entirely new medium of personal expression," *Popular Photography*, February 1978, pp. 68–69, 162–63.
3. Leendert Drukker, "How the system checks out: strong on convenience but a long way from Super 8 quality," *Popular Photography*, February 1978, pp. 69, 72, 163.
4. "Yes & No $$ on Polavision," *Photo Weekly*, 27 February 1978.
5. Jeffrey A. Tannenbaum, "Kodak Price Cut Intensifies Battle With Polaroid," *WSJ*, 9 February 1978, p. 3; Arthur M Louis, "Polaroid's OneStep is stopping Kodak cold," *Fortune*, 13 February 1978, pp. 77–78.
6. Conrad Biber, interview by author, Cambridge, Massachusetts, 9 November 1978, AN.
7. AN.
8. AN.
9. Personal communication, Jerome Wiesner.
10. Rowland Institute, press release, 9 January 1979, issued by Donald A. Dery, Polaroid Corporation, AC, and printed in *The Polaroid Newsletter;* "Polaroid Stock Sale Is Planned as Firm's Chief Says He Will Retire in Few Years," *WSJ*, 10 January 1979, p. 12.
11. Bradford Washburn, interviews by author, 14, 15 July 1994, AN.
12. Governor Michael Dukakis, statement about Museum of Science, 8 July 1976, sent by Donald A. Dery, Polaroid Corporation, AC; "New Academy to be on Charles," *BG*, 9 July 1976, pp. 1, 6; "Academy of Arts and Sciences to build $8M Hub headquarters," *Boston Herald-American*, 9 July 1976, p. 3; "A victory for science, the arts," editorial, *Boston Herald-American*, 9 July 1976; "Academy on the Charles," editorial, *BG*, 11 July 1976.
13. Bradford Washburn, interviews by author, 14, 15 July 1994, AN.
14. Kallmann; *Architectural Record*, November 1981, pp. 79–87.
15. Land's dedicatory words were carved into a wood plaque in the academy's house.
16. The author was present.
17. "Dr. Stanley M. Bloom, 1931–1978," *The Polaroid Newsletter*, 4 October 1978, pp. 1–2; Alan Borror, interview by author, Cambridge, Massachusetts, 10 November 1978, AN.
18. "The eulogy at the service for Dr. Bloom," *The Polaroid Newsletter*, 4 October 1978, p. 1.
19. Wensberg 1987, p. 226.
20. Aldrich 1990, p. 15; AN.
21. Howard W. Johnson, personal communication.
22. Richard Weeks, "An Artist Who Chose Science and Technology for His Medium," *OPN* 5, no. 10 (October 1994): 13.
23. Isadore Barmash, "Polaroid's Future Out of Focus," *NYT*, 21 May 1979, p. D1; Dow Jones News Wire, 5 July 1979; "Polaroid to Report Sharply Lower Net for Second Quarter," *WSJ*, 6 July 1979; "Polaroid Updated: Decline in Profit," *BG*, 6 July 1979; Mitchell C. Lynch, "Reeling Product: Instant Movies Falter; Is Polaroid's Chairman Wrong for a Change? Polavision Just Doesn't Sell; Dealers Even Chop Price to Get It Off The Shelves; But Mr. Land Keeps Trying," *WSJ*, 9 August 1979, p. 1.
24. AN.
25. Carl Kaysen, interviews by author, Cambridge, Massachusetts, 7 March 1994, 24 June 1994, AN.
26. Conversation, American Academy of Arts and Sciences, 9 November 1991. The author was present.
27. Robert J. Cole, "Polaroid Writes Off $68 Million," *NYT*, 13 September 1979, p. D1.
28. Associated Press, "Polaroid, Citing Slowing In Market, to Lay Off 800," *NYT*, 16 May 1979, p. D1.
29. AN.
30. Carl Kaysen, interviews by author, Cambridge, Massachusetts, 7 March 1994, 24 June 1994.
31. Meeting to plan EHL memorial symposium, Garden Room, American Academy of Arts and Sciences, 13 March 1991, AN.
32. Olsen 1991.
33. Land 1980.
34. EHL remarks, Polaroid shareholders' meeting, Symphony Hall, Boston, 21 April 1981, AN.
35. Land 1980.

CHAPTER 24, POLAROID V. KODAK

1. Trial 1981, pp. 2–33, 2–24, 581.
2. Ibid., pp. 842–43, 942.
3. Ibid., p. 810.
4. Ibid., p. 460.
5. Ibid., pp. 937, 941.

6. Ibid., p. 948.
7. Ibid., p. 1051.
8. Ibid., p. 1332.
9. Ibid., pp. 950, 961.
10. Ibid., p. 830.
11. Ibid., pp. 833–34.
12. Ibid., pp. 814, 544.
13. Ibid., p. 1063.
14. Ibid., pp. 730–31.
15. Ibid., pp. 745, 751, 752, 753.
16. Ibid., p. 1067.
17. Ibid., p. 1071.
18. Ibid., pp. 851, 1015.
19. Ibid., pp. 1271–73.
20. Ibid., p. 1276.
21. Land 1980, pp. 8–9; "Polaroid: Turning away from Land's one-product strategy," *BW*, 2 March 1981, p. 109.
22. Trial 1981, p. 621.
23. Howard W. Johnson, personal communication.
24. Jeremy Bernstein, "I Am a Camera," review of Wensberg 1987, *New York Review of Books* 35, no. 6 (14 April 1988): 21.
25. Zobel 1985.
26. Land 1976a.
27. Ibid.
28. Ibid.; Victor K. McElheny, "Polaroid Is Suing Kodak, Charges Patent Violation," *NYT*, 28 April 1976, p. 1 n., p. 57; "Polaroid Suit Charges Eastman Kodak's Instant Camera, Film Infringe on Patents," *WSJ*, 28 April 1976, p. 12.
29. Calvert Crary, *Bear Stearns Litigation Review* (monthly newsletter), September 1982.
30. John McQuiston, "U.S. Jury Finds a Kodak Monopoly In Amateur-Photography Business," *NYT*, Sunday 22 January 1978, p. 1; "Kodak Is Found To Have Broken Antitrust Laws," *WSJ*, 23 January 1978, p. 2; "Antitrust: The legal shockwaves of the Berkey decision," *BW*, 6 February 1978, p. 48; Arnold H. Lubasch, "Berkey Is Awarded $112.8 Million in Suit on Kodak Monopoly," *NYT*, 23 March 1978, p. 1; "Damages Against Kodak Of $37.6 Million: Award in Berkey Photo Suit Seen Tripling, Equitable Relief Still to be Decided," *WSJ*, 23 March 1978, p. 5; Arnold H. Lubasch, "Jury Award To Berkey Is Reduced: Kodak to Pay $27.1 Million In Trust Case," *NYT*, Saturday, 17 June 1978, p. 27; "Kodak's Business in Photo Finishing May Lose Edge," *WSJ*, Monday, 19 June 1978, p. 2; "Kodak Ordered to Pay $5.6 Million to Berkey for Legal Expenses," *WSJ*, 3 July 1978, p. 2; "Kodak Told to Pay $87.1 Million Total to Berkey Photo," *WSJ*, 5 July 1978, p. 5.
31. Arnold H. Lubasch., "Kodak Wins Trust Suit Appeal: The $87 Million Award to Berkey Mostly Reversed," *NYT*, 26 June 1979, p. D1; "Berkey Photo's Victory in Kodak Suit Is Reversed: Court Upholds only $990,000 in Damages, Sends Much of Suit Back for Retrial," *WSJ*, 26 June 1979, p. 2; Tom Goldstein, "Business and the Law: Kodak Ruling—The Guidelines," *NYT*, Saturday, 30 June 1979; "Business International—Kodak: Flash Back," *Economist*, 30 June 1979, p. 80; "Justices Reject Berkey Appeal in Kodak Case," *WSJ*, 20 April 1980, p. 4.
32. Markey 1986.
33. Zobel 1985, p. 10.
34. Zobel 1985, "Memorandum of Decision and Order," p. 7.
35. Reuters, "Kodak Settles With Polaroid," *NYT*, 18 July 1991, p. D8; "Kodak to Pay Polaroid $925 Million to Settle Suit," *WSJ*, 16 July 1991, p. C13; Lawrence Edelman, "Kodak pays Polaroid $925 million, *BG*, 16 July 1991, p. 35. Holusha, John, "Kodak Told It Must Pay $909 Million," *NYT*, 13 October 1990, pp. 33–34; Lawrence Ingrassia and James S. Hirsch, "Polaroid's Patent-Case Award, Smaller Than Anticipated, Is a Relief for Kodak," *WSJ*, 15 October 1990, pp. A3, A18; Jane Poss, "Polaroid wins $909m award from Kodak," *BG*, 13 October 1990, pp. 1, 9; Eastman Kodak Company, full-page advertisement, *WSJ*, 15 October 1990, p. A15; Barnaby J. Feder, "Polaroid's Stock Price Falls Sharply," *NYT*, 16 October 1990, p. D4; Lawrence Ingrassia, "Polaroid Falls 22% on Negative News," *WSJ*, 16 October 1990, pp. C1–C2; Jane Poss, "Investors bail out of Polaroid on report of Kodak award," *BG*, 16 October 1990, pp. 53, 55; "Polaroid, Kodak Each Seek Changes in Patent Award," *WSJ*, 29 October 1990, p. B5; "What Will Polaroid Do with All That Moola?" *BW*, 29 October 1990, p. 38; "Polaroid: What the Bears Are Missing," *BW*, 5 November 1990, p. 138; "Polaroid Corp. Award Against Kodak Is Cut," *WSJ*, 14 January 1991, p. A9; Lawrence Edelman, "Polaroid, Kodak both ready to appeal $873m decision," *BG*, 8 February 1991, p. 56.
36. Holusha, *NYT*, 13 October 1990.
37. States News Service, "Polaroid uses some of award to ease debt," *BG*, 31 July 1991, p. 49; Jonathan Glater, "Polaroid may buy back shares from white Knight," *BG*, 7 August 1991, p. 37; "Polaroid Said to Consider Purchasing a Group's Stake," *WSJ*, 7 August 1991, p. B6; Barnaby J. Feder, "Polaroid to Buy Back Fund's Large Holding," *NYT*, 13 September 1991, p. D3; Diane Tracy, "Polaroid Outlines Plans for Utilizing Kodak Settlement," *WSJ*, 13 September 1991, p. B7C; Ronald Rosenberg, "Polaroid buys common and retires preferred; $925 million settlement finally put

to use," *BG*, 13 September 1991, pp. 71–72; Ronald Rosenberg, "Award increases net at Polaroid, profits off," *BG*, 16 October 1991, p. 64.

38. Bloomberg News, Cambridge, Massachusetts, "Polaroid to Revamp and Cut 1,500 Jobs," *NYT*, 17 December 1997, p. 4; "Business Briefs: Polaroid Will Cut Work Force 15% As Part of a Broad Restructuring," *WSJ*, 17 December 1997, p. B4; Ronald Rosenberg, "Polaroid to let go 850 in Bay State," *BG*, 17 December 1997, pp. C1, C6; Claudia H. Deutsch, "Touching Up a Faded Polaroid: Will Push to Revive Sales Restore Luster?" *NYT* 3 January 1998, pp. B1–B2.
39. Claudia H. Deutsch, "Kodak Raises Its Job-Cut Total Sharply, 6,600 Extra Dismissals Are Blow to Rochester," *NYT*, 19 December 1997, pp. C1, C4; Ross Kerber, "Kodak Boosts Layoff Plan, Restructuring Charge," *WSJ*, 19 December 1997, pp. A3, A6; Jeffrey Benkoe, Reuters, "Kodak adds 6,600 job cuts to restructuring plan," *BG*, 19 December 1997, p. C2.
40. See the following from *Time*, 29 December 1997–5 January 1998: "Man of the Year, Intel's Andrew Grove: His Microchips Have Changed the World—and Its Economy," cover; Norman Pearlstein, "The Man and the Magic," p. 8; Walter Isaacson,"Driven by the Passion of Intel's Andrew Grove," pp. 48–51; Joshua Cooper Ramo, "A Survivor's Tale," pp. 54–63, 66, 68, 70, 72; "How the Chip Works," pp. 76–77; "The Ubiquitous Chip," pp. 78–81. See also Dean Takahashi, "Intel Shifts Its Focus to Long-Term, Original Research; Microprocessor Maker Forms Special Team as 'There's Nothing Left to Copy,'" *WSJ*, 26 August 1996, p. B4; Grove 1996; Andy Reinhardt, "Intel: Can Andy Grove keep profits up in an era of cheap PCs?" *BW*, 22 December 1997, cover and pp. 70–74, 76–77.

CHAPTER 25, PROSPERO'S ISLAND

1. Steven Jobs, interview in *Playboy*, February 1985.
2. The author was present: AN, 26 July 1982.
3. AN, 27 July 1982.
4. AN, Rowland Notebook 2, 28 October 1982.
5. AN, 27 July 1982.
6. Kirk Johnson, "Polaroid's Job Cuts Took Key Workers," *NYT*, 19 July 1982.
7. Michael Blumstein, "Era Ends as Land Leaves Polaroid," *NYT*, 28 July 1982, p. D1.
8. Lawrence Dwyer, "Land Steps Down at Polaroid," *Boston Herald-American*, 28 July 1982.
9. "New Frontiers in Land's Laboratory," Editorial, *BG*, 29 July 1982.
10. Robert Lenzner, "The Promised Land," *BG*, 3 August 1982, p. 1.
11. "Colossus of the Camera," editorial, *NYT*, 5 August 1982, p. A18.
12. AN, Rowland Notebook 1, 5 August 1982; Deborah Shapley, "New Sights for Land," *Nature* 298, no. 5876 (1982): 701.
13. Jeremy Bernstein, "I Am a Camera," review of Wensberg 1987, *The New York Review of Books* 35, no. 6 (14 April 1988): 21.
14. AN.
15. "Central and Peripheral Mechanisms of Color Vision," Program, Wenner-Gren Center International Symposium 43, Stockholm, Thursday and Friday, 14 and 15 July 1984, AC; AN, Tuesday, 19 July 1984.
16. EHL, "Continuing Studies in Retinex Theory," plenary lecture at Eighth International Biophysics Congress, Bristol, England, July 1984.
17. Matt Ridley, "The Conundrum of Colour," *Economist*, 22 December 1984, p. 81.
18. John Mollon, BBC Broadcast, "Colourful Notions," 7 January 1985: John Mollon, *The Listener*, BBC magazine, 10 January 1985.
19. David J. Ingle,"The Goldfish as a Retinex Animal," *Science* 227, no. 4687 (8 February 1985): cover illustration and pp. 651–54; Edward Dolnick, *BG*, 1 February 1985. Also carried in Springfield, Ohio, *Evening News-Sun*, "Research challenges color perception concept," 1 February 1985; Elyria, Ohio, *Chronicle-Telegram*, "Study: 'Color in mind of beholder,' " 1 February 1985; Kingsport, Tennessee, *Times-News*, " 'Color constancy' theory backed by new research," 2 February 1985; *Charlotte Observer*, "Theories on Color Clash," 3 February 1985; *Miami Herald*, "Study: Color in mind of beholder," 7 February 1985. EHL interview by Robert F. Zalisk, National Public Radio, 12 February 1982.
20. Rowland Notebook 3, 9 April 1985, AN.
21. Rowland Notebook 4, 18 March 1987, AN. The site was Room 26-100, Massachusetts Institute of Technology.
22. Giuseppe Piatelli-Palmarini, "The Machine of Vision: A New Theory of Colors," *Corriere della Sera*, Milan, 30 March 1987, p. 3.
23. Author's observation.
24. Joan Fitzgerald, "Polaroid Buys Back Stock," *BG*, 14 August 1982; "Polaroid Buys Back 1.9 Million Shares from Gulf and Western," *WSJ*, 16 August 1982.
25. Rowland Institute, press release, 29 April 1985, AC, 30 April 1985; AN, Rowland Notebook, p. 61, 30 April 1985; "Founder to Sell Polaroid Stake," *NYT*, 30 April 1985, p. D5; Dan Baum, Cambridge, Massachusetts, "Polaroid's Founder to Sell Remaining 8.3% Stake in Firm: Edwin Land Says He Wants to Devote His Resources to Education, Research," *WSJ*, 30 April 1985, p. 24; Wendy Fox, "Land Bids Final Farewell to Polaroid, *BG*, 30 April 1985, p. 41.

26. Alex Beam, "In suit in Boston coutroom, Polaroid headache returns," *BG*, 30 June 1987, pp. 61, 66; Rowland Institute statement to Associated Press, *NYT*, *WSJ*, 2 July 1987; Alex Beam, "Jury finds Polaroid liable in insider suit," *BG*, 3 July 1987; Alex Beam, "Jury says Polaroid should pay $80 million," *BG*, 11 July 1987; Joseph Menn, "Court appoves settlement between Polaroid, investors," *BG*, 16 July 1987, p. 51, reporting earlier settlement by Land, Silver, and Rowland Institute.
27. Aldrich 1990.
28. EHL, message for Polaroid's fiftieth anniversary celebration, AC.
29. Alex Beam, "Edwin Land's Place in History," *BG*, 11 August 1987, pp. 25, 27.
30. The author was present.
31. Western Union mailgram, AN.
32. Edward M. Purcell, interview by author, 15 January 1992, AN, AT.
33. Zeki 1991.
34. Eric Pace, "Edwin H. Land Is Dead at 81; Invented the Instant Camera," *NYT*, 2 March 1991, pp. 1, 29; Jane Poss, "Edwin Land dead at 81: Polaroid chief left image on industry," *BG*, 2 March 1991, pp. 1, 8.

Acknowledgments

My biggest debt in a quest of thirty years is to Edwin Land. Although neither he nor his family cooperated with any book-length biographical project, including this one, he knew as early as 1971 of my interest in such a study. Nonetheless, I worked for a year in 1972-1973 on the task of translating the technicalities of his SX-70 system—developed in tiny "Skunk Works" groups—to the vast majority of his Polaroid colleagues. Later, I was assigned by *The New York Times* to cover the introductions of Eastman Kodak's system of instant photography and the Polaroid instant movie system called Polavision. I was present at many public occasions where Land spoke, from a luncheon talk in Washington, D.C., in 1968 to his eightieth birthday party in Cambridge, Massachusetts, in 1989. From 1982 to 1991, I helped with the press relations of the Rowland Institute, which usually meant telling journalists that Land was not available. By granting few interviews, he showed that he did not have the conventional interest in how history would view him. He said that the only biography he wished to leave was his published papers. These were edited by Mary McCann for publication in three invaluable volumes by the Society for Imaging Science in 1993. My last duty in 1991 was to draft the short announcement of his death. While withholding cooperation, Land and his family were always friendly and courteous.

Indispensable time for organizing the prodigious amounts of material from Land's multifaceted life, and beginning to write about it, was guaranteed by a generous grant from the Alfred P. Sloan Foundation, whose foresight in sponsoring the Technology Book Series is a major step in the popular understanding of technology. In connection with the grant, I had numerous valuable opportunities to discuss the project with Ralph Gomory, Elting Morison, John Armstrong, Simon Michael Bessie, Richard Rhodes, Thomas Parke Hughes, Robert K. Merton, Sam Gibbon, Doron Weber, and Arthur L. Singer, Jr. (with whom I have worked so pleasantly for more than 20 years).

I am happy to thank my agent, Jill Kneerim of Palmer and Dodge, Boston, and her colleague, John Taylor Williams, for their belief in this book and their rigorous insistence on a strong proposal. Working with Merloyd Lawrence and her colleagues at Perseus Books has been an inspiring example of detailed but positive scrutiny of each stage of the manuscript.

Two people who encouraged my career as a science writer over many years were the physicist Edward Mills Purcell of Harvard and Walter Sullivan, science editor of *The New York Times*. Concerned that Land's story would not be told, they encouraged me to accept Peter Wensberg's invitation in 1971 to leave *The Boston Globe* to write Polaroid's explanation of SX-70. Purcell also gave a most illuminating interview in 1992. I owe thanks to Anthony Lukas, a colleague on *The Harvard Crimson*, for his encouragement more than twenty years ago. Over three decades, Howard Rogers, Sheldon Buckler, Richard Wareham, John and Mary McCann, Vivian Walworth, Stanley Mervis, William Plummer, Richard Weeks, James Baker, Lucretia Weed, Howard Berg, Bill McCune, Carl Kaysen, and many other Land colleagues generously saw to my education and fostered the project. Many of them reviewed the manuscript.

Archives have been invaluable, particularly the archives of Polaroid Corporation, so devotedly maintained by Nasrin Rohani, which are a treasure-house of the history of innovation in American industry and deserve further examination by scholars. I am indebted to archivists at the Dwight D. Eisenhower Library in Abilene, Kansas; the Library of Congress; the Massachusetts Institute of Technology; Harvard University; and the Franklin Institute for their kind assistance.

For encouragement and opportunities to discuss the manuscript as it developed, I wish to thank my colleagues at MIT, including Philip Khoury, Carl Kaysen, Kenneth Keniston, Merritt Roe Smith, Sherry Turkle, Jack Ruina, David Mindell, and Alan Lightman, as well as successive classes of Knight Science Journalism Fellows.

Many friends and professional colleagues have sustained me over the years, but none more devotedly than my wife, Ruth Sullivan McElheny.

Index

About the Author

Victor McElheny has been covering an age of technology and science for four decades, for newspapers (including *The New York Times* as its technology reporter), magazines (including *Science* as its first overseas correspondent), and television (including the BBC in London and WGBH-TV in Boston). He also was inaugural director of the Banbury Center of Cold Spring Harbor Laboratory. His 30-year quest of the biography of Edwin Land began in the White House on 13 February 1968, when Land received the National Medal of Science. At the Massachusetts Institute of Technology, he founded and for 16 years has run the Knight Science Journalism Fellowships.